ROCKY MOUNTAIN NATURAL HISTORY

Daniel Mathews

Rocky Mountain
Natural History

Grand Teton to Jasper

Including Photography by
Will Kerling, Tom J. Ulrich,
Daniel Mathews, and others

RAVEN EDITIONS
PORTLAND OREGON

Cataloguing in Publication Data (National Library of Canada)

Mathews, Daniel, 1948-
Rocky Mountain natural history, Grand Teton to Jasper / Daniel Mathews.
Includes bibliographical references and index.
ISBN 0-9620782-2-0

1. Rocky Mountains--Description and travel. 2. Natural history--Rocky Mountains. I. Title.
508.78

First printing.
Designed by Daniel Mathews with guidance from John Laursen and Martha Gannett. Typeset in Minion, designed by Robert Slimbach, and in Stone Sans, by Sumner Stone. Cover designed by Martha Gannett. Cover photos by Daniel Mathews. Back cover map by Rankin Holmes at The Ecology Center. Printed in China on acid-free paper.

Eating wild plants and fungi is inherently risky. Individuals vary in their physiological reactions, and may make mistaken identifications regardless of their level of expertise or the accuracy of printed information they read. The publisher and the author cannot accept responsibility for their health. Readers eat wild foods at their own risk.

This book is for

the fourlegged people

the standing people

the crawling people

the swimming people

the sitting people

and the flying people

❧

that people walking

with them may know

and honor them.

Acknowledgements

First I thank Margot, Gabriel, and Sabrina for putting up with me for months while I was, like, totally obsessed, as some of them might say; and for sharing their joy in small discoveries that went into this book.

Dozens of scientists were utterly generous with their time in helping me to make the book as accurate as I could manage. Despite their efforts, I slipped up here and there—I don't know where, but I haven't the slightest doubt that I did—and for that the fault is mine. Of these dozens, I have to single out Walt Fertig, who promptly reviewed a far thicker pile of manuscript than anyone else, and Gene Humphreys and Jim Jackson, who held my hand for hours and hours as I struggled to sort out the arcane controversies and mysteries of geology. Helpful replies and reviews also came from Ted Barkley, Chris Beaumont, Larry Evans, Laurence Frank, Debra Guernsey, Linda Geiser, Trevor Goward, Rick Halstead, Warren B. Hamilton, the two professors emeriti Paul Hammond, Jan Henderson, Grant Hilderbrand, Stephen Johnston, Peter Lesica, Joe Licciardi, Jeff Lockwood, Bruce McCune, Eldridge Moores, Bob Meinke, Ron Neilson, Craig Oberg, Jim O'Connor, Dennis Paulson, Brian Pratt, Bob Pyle, Doug Reynolds, Roger Rosentreter, Steve Sharnoff, Scott Sundberg, Vance Tucker, John Varley, Byron Weber, Ellen Wheat, Tim Wheeler, and Don Winston.

Anyone else, please forgive me if I have left you out. I couldn't cite every contributor of important research without making this book itself look like an academic paper, so, to those of you whose names don't appear, my apologies.

If there is any field which rebuffed my friendly advances as obstinately as did geophysics, it would have to be digital color management. In that, my patient instructor was Craig Collins, who also scanned, and made good design suggestions.

For excellent, meticulous work on production and design, I thank Martha Gannett, Eric Eaton, Jim Ditmer and Associates, Carrie Meach, PhotoCraft, Altitude Publishing, Ltd., Mountain Press Publishing, and the Ecology Center.

Photography Credits

Cover photos by the author, except Canadian front cover photo (Larch Valley, Banff N.P.) by Douglas Leighton; and the author by Laura Ewig Garnier.

Plants (pages 83–114) by the author, except chocolate lily, spotted coralroot, white bog orchid, *Castilleja hispida* (paintbrush), owl's-clover, and miner's candle by Drake Barton; grouseberry, dwarf mistletoe, golden smoke, and pinesap by Paula Brooks; ladies-slipper, prickly pear, prairie crocus, and bitterroot by Fay Benton Schaller; mountain hollyhock and telesonix by Peter Lesica; and steer's head by Will Kerling.

Fungi and lichens (pages 515–521) by the author, except snowbank false morel, destroying angel, honey mushroom, autumn galerina, scorched-earth cup, *Suillus tomentosus*, *S. brevipes*, and hedgehog mushroom by Kit Scates Barnhart; yellow morel by Harley Barnhart, alpine bloodclot lichen, vagrant form rock-posy, rockworm, and pixie-goblets by Stephen Sharnoff and Sylvia Duran Sharnoff; witch's-butter and gemmed puffball by Larry Evans; and black morel (with Calypso orchid) and tree ear by Drake Barton.

Mammals and birds (pages 522–533) by Dennis and Esther Schmidt, except red-backed vole, thirteen-lined ground squirrel, weasel, otter, sora, kestrel, harrier, red-tailed hawk, golden eagle, tree swallow, dipper, western tanager, yellow-rumped warbler, Cassin's finch, rosy finch, mountain chickadee, yellowthroat, and junco by Tom J. Ulrich; jumping mouse, harlequin duck, Vaux's swift, and downy woodpecker by Richard B. Forbes; and bison, shrew, gopher cores, porcupine, ptarmigan and spruce grouse by the author.

Reptiles and amphibians (page 534) by Alan D. St. John, except salamander by Richard B. Forbes with permission from Orcilia Forbes.

Rocks and geology (pages 536–40) by the author.

Butterflies and sphinx moth (pages 542–46) by Will Kerling. Bluets, mountain emerald, and Hudsonian whiteface by Dennis Paulson. Paddle-tailed darner by Netta Smith (page 546). Other moths, and all insect galls and signs (pages 541) by the author.

Illustration Credits

Maps by Rankin Holmes of the Ecology Center, Missoula.

Conifers and Flowering Trees and Shrubs (Chapters 2 and 3) by the U.S.D.A. Forest Service (artists not known); except yew, ponderosa pine, cottonwood, aspen, elderberries, ninebark, bitterbrush, and pyrola by Willis L. Jepson, courtesy of the Jepson Herbarium; and Douglas-fir, whitebark pine, redcedar, Scouler willow, Geyer willow, coyote willow, grayleaf willow, short-fruit willow, mooseberry, buffaloberry, virgin's bower, mock-orange, spiraea, shrubby cinquefoil, devil's club, cascara, hawthorn, Oregon-boxwood, silverberry, Labrador tea, Oregon-grape, shrubby penstemon, wintergreen, yellow heather, crowberry, dryad, and twin-flower by Jeanne R. Janish and rabbitbrush by John H. Rumely, both by permission of University of Washington Press.

Flowering Herbs and Ferns (Chapters 4 and 5) by Jeanne R. Janish, used by permission of University of Washington Press; except thistle head (page 191), daisy, aster, golden-aster, arnica, butterweed, goldenweed, yarrow, dusty maiden, pearly pussytoes, and sagewort by Elizabeth J. Stephen, by kind permission of the Royal B.C. Provincial Museum; spike woodrush, rushes, bottlebrush squirreltail, groundsel, cow-parsnip, poison-hemlock, and water-hemlock by Willis L. Jepson, courtesy of the Jepson Herbarium; coltsfoot, cutleaf coneflower, western coneflower, and hawkweed by John H. Rumely (UW Press); prairie coneflower and mule's-ears by Bellamy Parks Jansen, by permission of Univ. of Nebraska Press; goldenrod by F. Schuyler Mathews (no relation); and meadow-rue by Barbara Stafford Wilson.

Flower parts (pages 157, 191 left and center); leaves (pages 202, 204); cat tracks (p 384), and antlers (p 394) by Kris Elkin.

Mosses and liverworts (Chapter 6) by Patricia Drukker-Brammall, from *Some Common Mosses of British Columbia* and *Field Guide to Liverwort Genera of Pacific North America*, by W. B. Schofield; by the kind permission of Dr. Schofield.

Mammals, Birds, Amphibians, and giardia by the U.S.D.A. Forest Service, except tailed frog by Pat Hansen, and great horned owl, raven, jays, and Clark's nutcracker by Sharon Torvik, all by permission of the Oregon Dept. of Fish and Wildlife.

Spotted frog and Reptiles by Alan D. St. John; used by permission.

Color fishes (page 535) by Joseph R. Tomelleri; used by permission.

Line art fishes (pages 477–91) by Ron Pittard, used by permission of Windsor/ Nature Discovery Publications (1-800-635-4194); except sculpin by Reeve M. Bailey.

Insects (Chapter 13) by Eric Eaton, original work. Bark beetle galleries (pages 504–06) by the USDA Forest Service, from Pettinger and Johnson (1972).

Geology (Chapter 16) cartoons modified from the following authors: subduction zone courtesy of Warren B. Hamilton; terrane map has appeared in many papers, but I think the original may have been by Peter J. Coney, D. L. Jones, and J. W. H. Monger in *Nature* 288 (1980), p 329; Stephen T. Johnston's (2001) terrane wreck from *Earth & Planetary Sci Letters* 193: 259–72; cross-section of Canadian Rockies from R. A. Price (1988) Geol. Assoc of Canada Special Paper No. 6; Lewis Fault cross-section from Constenius (1996) *GSA Bulletin* 108(1):20–39; Wind River Thrust from Smithson et al (1979) *J of Geophys Res* 84(B11):5958–72; Selkirk Fan from Maurice Colpron et al (1998) *GSA Bulletin* 110(8):1060-74; listric normal faults from Jon E. Spencer (1984) *Geology* 12(2): 95-98; deep-seated detachment from Brian Wernicke (1985) *Canadian J of Earth Sci* 22:108-125; Heart Mountain from Wm. G. Pierce (1987) in *GSA Centennial Field Guide—RM Section*.

Raven emblem (title page) by Barbara Stafford Wilson.

Quotation Credits

Sources for most of the direct quotations of a sentence or less in length can be found easily by looking in the pertinent section of Selected References, page 627. Others are provided here.

Page 3: Dennis Demarchi created the ecosystem map for the B.C. Wildlife Branch. He adapted it for the U.S.F.S. in Ruggiero (1994). (Citation on page 634.)

P 43. Average fire frequencies from Johnson and Fryer (1989) and Cooper et al. (1991). (Citations on page 631.)

P 139: "If I smell smoke…" Judith Myers quoted by S. Milius in *Science News*.

P 287. Campbell, Alsie G., and J. F. Franklin. 1979. Riparian vegetation in OR's W. Cascade Mtns. Bull. No. 14, Coniferous Forest Biome. Seattle: U of WA Press.

P 298. Shaw, Charles G. III, and Glen A. Kile, eds. 1991. *Armillaria Root Disease*. USDA Forest Service Agr. Handbook No. 691.

P 312 sidebar. Moira Savonius (1973) *All Color Book of Mushrooms and Fungi*. NY: Octopus Bks; Vincent Marteka (1980) *Mushrooms Wild and Edible*. NY: Norton.

P 318. Goward, Trevor. 1996. Dust to dust. *Nature Canada*. Summer 1996: 44–45.

P 367. Coyote tale retold by Katherine B. Judson (1910) *Myths and Legends of the PNW*. Chicago: McClurg.

P 413. Lew Welch. 1973. *Ring of Bone: Collected Poems 1950-1971*. Bolinas: Grey Fox.

P 440. Song lyrics S. Dunbar, R. Shakespeare, B. Laswell, B. Collins, K. Berger, and Rammelzee, on *Rhythm Killers* (Island); after Cole Porter, "Come On, Baby" (1928).

P 478. "Idiot Joy" by David James Duncan. 2001. *My Story As Told by Water*. San Francisco: Sierra Club. Used by permission.

P 479. "It leaps again.…" David James Duncan. 1995. *River Teeth*. New York: Doubleday. Used by permission.

P 505. Camel metaphor for ecological threshold effects is David Perry's paraphrase in *Forest Ecosystems* (1994) of D. L. Knowlton.

P 567. The phrase on geosynclinal theory is attributed to James Dwight Dana, 1813–1895; the line by Phil England is from *Nature* 381 (1996), p 23–24.

P 608. Belloc, Hilaire. 1897. *More Beasts for Worse Children*. Reissued 1996; NY: Knopf.

Contents

Plant Finder

ROCKY MOUNTAIN NATURAL HISTORY

                    Asleep,
I thought I was at work dishing hors
d'oeuvres and remembering a dream
of sleeping on a tiny island of whitebark pines in a snow-covered lake
named Snow Lake.

                         Like mist
my dream of everyday fell away and I was
in fact
        on the white lake, waking

                    to the real world.

                    ❧

1

Landscape

Rocky Mountain Natural History was written for any and every knapsack that can't hold a library. In one volume it covers most field guide subjects: plants, mammals, birds, invertebrates, fungi, and the land itself. It describes the behavior of living things, and their relations to each other, to habitat, and to people.

The Rockies are a vast, intricate concatenation of subranges. All are parts of the North American Cordillera ("mountain chain" in Spanish), a continent-long swath of mountain ranges and plateaus. The Rockies were deformed and uplifted mostly between 180 million and 50 million years ago, making them younger than the mountains of eastern North America but older than the northwestern ones. But they are far from moribund, having undergone spectacular remodels by both ice and volcanism within the last two million years.

This book covers just a portion of the Rockies, one defined not by geology but by nonhuman inhabitants. I could say it's defined by one species—the whitebark pine. This tree grows from the Wind River Range north to just past Jasper National Park, and west to the Wallowas. (After a break, it reappears in several coastal ranges). That isn't just happenstance; it's the outline of two natural ecoprovinces. A lot of species reach their southern limit either in the Wind Rivers or in the Bitterroots, and a lot reach their northern limit either in the Bitterroots or just north of Jasper. As mapped by Dennis Demarchi, two ecoprovinces—the Northern Rocky Mountain Forest and the Shining Mountains—meet at the Bitterroots. Together, they constitute what I will call "our range," "our region," or simply "here." (See p 15.)

I call the northerly ecoprovince "Shining Mountains" and the southerly one "Middle Rockies." ("Northern Rockies" has been used too many different ways. To some Canadians, it's a region of Canada, north of Jasper; yet many maps have a Northern Rockies in the U.S., and still others extend the term across the border.)

"Here" is also the one region with a decent chance of holding an intact ecosystem in temperate North America, if the natural top of the food chain—large carnivores—can come back, and stay.

If we look for a pattern underlying our ecological unity, we end up looking at climate. Our range includes the parts of the Rockies with the strongest marine influence—most specifically, a precipitation pattern with a midwinter peak and a late-summer low point. Rocky Mountain slopes facing the Great Plains don't have that pattern, but if you consider the Canadian Rockies or the Beartooths as wholes, you will find the winter-wet pattern in at least parts of them. Outside of our range—from the Big Horns south—wet weather sweeps north from the Gulf of Mexico, with a May or June peak and a plateau from August through March. Our mountains are also wetter because they are farther north: a mountain here with the exact same precipitation as one in Colorado has moister soil because the sun, being lower in the sky, doesn't evaporate moisture as quickly.

This book is about mountains, not croplands and rangelands lying below the lowest forests. I can't draw a clear lower limit; after all, sagebrush-dominated communities grow at every elevation short of alpine ice and rock. Still, some species live almost exclusively in croplands or below "lower forest line." This book doesn't cover them.

Geologically, we have pure sedimentary provinces, a volcanic province, a granite province, metamorphic provinces, and a handful of ancient granite-gneiss ranges. They all have at least one big thing in common: ice, past or present.

The Pleistocene Ice Ages

If you love high-relief scenery, count yourself lucky to have been born in an interglacial stage of an ice age. Mountain erosion without ice produces tame, monotonous slope angles and ridge patterns. Glacial erosion produces all the most spectacular mountainscapes.

Repeatedly within the past two million years, about half of North America was covered by two huge ice sheets similar to those blanketing Greenland and Antarctica today. One lay on either side of the Canadian Rockies. The western one (the Cordilleran Ice Sheet) covered parts of Alaska, the Yukon and B.C., and entered the U.S.

briefly at its last maximum, 17,000 years ago. It reached the Columbia River in NE Washington, and the Mission and Swan valleys in Montana. North of those points the Rockies looked much like southeast Alaska's mountains do today—great banded riverlike glaciers with branching tributaries filling the valleys, and marginal peaks protruding as "nunatak" islands. The icefields on top of Jasper and Banff National Parks are small nunatak landscapes.

Big mountain groups held the ice sheets at bay, but internally they were incised by narrower valley glaciers. Farther south, each big mountain group accumulated its own cluster of valley glaciers. At Yellowstone and the Wallowas, these emanated from broad central ice caps. The hundreds of alpine valley glaciers, more than the two ice sheets, gave our region its facelift (including uplift; see p 570.) Picture a thick glacier flowing for at least 1,000 years wherever you see a **U**-shaped valley cross-section today (e.g., color p 90, bottom left.)

By 14,000 years ago all ice was in full rout, the glacial stage over. By 9,000 years ago the alpine glaciers were likely gone from Wyoming and Idaho. But they came back, at least as vestiges of their Ice Age form, thanks to modest cooling in the last 3,000 years.

One effect of the great ice sheets was to lower sea level as much as 300' [90 m] by retaining ice that would otherwise be water in the oceans. This turned a wide area of shallow sea between Siberia and Alaska into habitable land, allowing many new mammals, including humans, to migrate to the New World. When the ice melted, sea level rose in most parts of the world, while in most of Canada it retreated. That's because the sheer weight of ice pressing down on continental crust makes it float lower on the mantle. (See page 570.) When the weight was removed, the depressed crust began to rise, but so slowly that in many places, like around Hudson's Bay, it's still rising.

This "isostatic rebound" shows that ice sheets, and even glaciers, weigh in as heavyweights—they're geology, not weather! Ice sheets easily contain or channel lava flows, or keep a lid on more explosive volcanoes, as they did in Wells Gray Park. Recent studies suggest they even suppress the overall activity rates of earthquakes and volcanoes.

Ice Age Floods

Valleys throughout our region have strange features that result from short-lived ice or silt dams of the Ice Age. Slopes above Missoula have perfect horizontal incisions—wave-cut lakeshore terraces—up to 970 feet [300 m] above the valley. The valley south of Markle Pass, MT, has ripples—of a shape that forms under rapids—as high as 35' and

300' from crest to crest [10 × 90 m]. The Milk River Valley at the Alberta-Montana line has even bigger ones. There's a 65'-tall [20 m] river bar next to the modest-sized Lamar River just north of Yellowstone. The Elk River valley and others in eastern B.C. have towering bluffs of pure white silt—lake floor sediments that piled up dozens of feet thick, only to be 98% removed, perhaps in a matter of weeks.

From a jetliner on a clear day, eastern Washington looks like a sand castle God grew tired of, and threw a five-gallon bucket of water over—enough water to inundate most of those 20,000 square miles [50,000 km²] at once, carving anastomozing channels through the wreckage, "the Channeled Scablands."

There were huge lakes, and deluges, on both sides of the Continental Divide, and similar ones in Central Asia. The biggest North American ones, as far as we know, were the Bretz or Missoula Floods. They raised the level of the Columbia by 400' to 1,000' [122 to 900 m] at different points. The rate of flow was more than all the world's present-day rivers combined. The source was Lake Missoula, an ice-dammed lake in western Montana with about half the volume of modern Lake Michigan. The lake filled several branches of the Clark Fork drainage when that river's route north to the Kootenay and Columbia was blocked, in the Idaho Panhandle, by a south-flowing lobe of the Cordilleran Ice Sheet. The ice dam either floated or burst when the lake rose high enough, draining the lake rapidly. This happened over and over again, between 40 and 100 times at the end of the last Ice Age. It also happened at the ends of earlier glacial stages. The last flood was about 16,000 years ago. There could plausibly have been people watching it. We can get a glimpse of what they might have seen thanks to the occasional small subglacial outburst ("jökulhlaup") from Yoho's Cathedral Glacier.

The interior valleys of B.C. held enormous lakes, some underneath the ice sheet and others in daylight. Evidence of them—such as the deep white silts around Fernie and Kamloops—is all over the map, on a grand scale. Glaciers carved Lake Okanagan's bed down to 2000' [640 m] below sea level, and later dumped at least 20 cubic miles [90 km³] of jumbled sediment into it. The picture is so complex that most questions about where these lakes drained, and whether there were catastrophic releases like the Missoula Floods, remain unresolved. Many south-directed flood channel landforms have been identified, even high on some slopes. John Shaw is working on a case for central B.C., via the Okanagan Valley, as the biggest source for at least one of the "Missoula" floods.

Glaciers and Icefields

Wherever an average year brings more new snow than can melt, snow accumulates and slowly compacts into ice. Eventually, the ice gets so thick and heavy it flows slowly downhill until it reaches an elevation warm enough to melt it as fast as it arrives. This flowing ice is a glacier, a mechanism that balances the snow's "mass budget."

Ideally, the rate of flow is equal to both the excess snow accumulation in the upper part of the glacier and the excess melting in the lower part; this ideal glacier would neither advance nor retreat. Few glaciers are so stable. Instead, the elevation where the glacier terminates in a melting "snout" advances and retreats (drops and rises) in response to climate trends. (Retreating glaciers don't turn around and flow back uphill, of course. They melt away at the bottom faster than their rate of arrival there.) A glacier "stagnates" after shrinking to where it no longer has enough mass and slope to keep flowing.

You can see the difference between advancing and retreating glacier snouts. The latter are thin, even concave, and surrounded by barren bouldery expanses (moraines) from which they retreated. Advancing glaciers ideally have high, bulging fronts. In reality, most in our region terminate in barrens, since they haven't made up the ground they lost 50 to 130 years ago, too recently for much revegetation. Still, a retreating snout typically tapers, and is dirty and rocky with surface debris concentrated over recent decades. It may be hard to tell where the glacier leaves off and the rock rubble begins. An advancing snout, in contrast, may present a clifflike face where ice blocks come crashing down, or a chaotic expanse of towering seracs.

Glacier ice has a consistency utterly unlike a snowbank. Beneath a "firn" of last year's snow, what was once snow is recrystallized into coarse, nubbly granules with hardly any air space. Eventually that granular texture will grade into massive blue ice, though a microscope will still show a texture more granular than, say, frozen lake ice.

Our temperate-zone glaciers are "warm" glaciers at close to 32° [0° C] throughout, in contrast to "cold" arctic glaciers. Warm glaciers, like ice skaters, glide on a film of pressure-melted water. They pour around bedrock outcrops by melting under pressure against the upstream side of the knob and refreezing against the downstream side (repaying the heat debt incurred by the change of state from solid to liquid). They erode rock ferociously, not because either the water layer or the ice itself is abrasive, but because sand, pebbles, and boulders are gripped and ground along over the substrate. It's

---

the rock sediment load that does the grinding in both glacier and river erosion. The difference between the two is like that between a power belt-sander and a sandstorm. The glacier's grit leaves parallel grooves or "striations" across bedrock convexities. Even some high divides are striated where the Cordilleran Ice Sheet swept across.

As flow accelerates in a glacier, the ice stretches, leaving stretch marks in the form of deep cracks or crevasses. Other crevasses open where glaciers bend or compress. Crevasses are often bridged by masses of recent snow which may or may not be solid enough to walk across. Don't cross glaciers unless you're trained and equipped for it.

Glaciers south of Crowsnest Pass are pretty small, except for one string of them in the Wind River Range. Glacier National Park itself (the Montana one) is named not for its negligible present-day glaciers but for the spectacular work of their much larger former selves.

Canada's Glacier National Park is another story altogether. The Columbia Mountains and central Canadian Rockies have countless square-mile-plus [3+ km²] glaciers, and several icefields. Icefields form where the elevation zones that accumulate ice are so broad and nearly flat that glacial ice has inadequate avenues for flowing downhill. It piles up to thousands of feet thick, and flows outward so slowly that few crevasses form. Low spots on an icefield's perimeter extend tongue-shaped glaciers downvalley to where they can melt. From the valleys we look up and see mountaintop ridgelines iced with sheer white cliffs like edges of a giant butcher's block. Only mountain-climbers truly see the Parks' icefields; scenic overflights are prohibited, and the icefield tours by Snocoach ascend a ways up an outlet glacier, far below the icefield itself. (There are scenic flights over icefields in the Purcells, outside of National Parks.)

Rock Flour

A milky white color in streams, and an insane blue-green opacity in lakes, betray water that recently melted from glaciers. Fine rock particles that the glacier pulverized are in suspension, turning streams whitish, rather than muddy brown, because they have been oxygen-deprived in the deep freeze ever since they were ground, keeping them from altering into clay. What they do in lakes is filed under "Magic," since the color strains credulity no matter how hard I try. It works best where all of the particles except the very smallest have had time to settle out. Uniform in size and distribution, they bounce a narrow blue to green spectrum of wavelengths around, and eventually back at us, while all the other wavelengths drown in the depths.

Moraines and Rock Glaciers

You're gazing at a beautiful blue lake on the edge of a valley or plain, at the foot of a defile down the front of a great mountain range. The lake is one in a row of similar lakes. Each of them formed behind a natural dam called a "terminal moraine." (If it has a manmade dam, you're at the wrong lake; go to the next one.)

A terminal moraine is typically an arc-shaped heap of rocks of all sizes, dumped across a valley by a glacier in pause mode, before it started to retreat. If a valley has several "recessional moraines" in series, each records a minor readvance during a long retreat. Farthest downhill, the terminal moraine likely marks a last Ice Age maximum around 23,000 years ago. The youngest one dates from the third Little Ice Age maximum, in the mid-1800s. (No moraine remains from the two previous maxima; the 1800s advance wiped them out.)

Don't picture a bulldozer. Picture a mobile conveyor belt running in place for a while before backing up; then it retreats, continuing to dump its load. So does a glacier, spreading rocks across the valley floor as a "ground moraine," not so much a heap as a bouldery texture all over the valley floor. It may be pocked with pits or—after soil and vegetation develop—tiny lakes. Pits formed where big ice blocks were deposited among rocks, and then melted. Many moraine boulders have one or more flattened and striated sides that were ground against bedrock while this boulder was on the glacier's sole.

A "lateral moraine" looks like a terrace on the valley flank, perhaps continuous with the arc of an end moraine, but parallel to the valley. It too was left behind by a thinning, narrowing glacier. The glacier's edges carry more than their share of rocks because rocks fall from adjacent cliffs. Below a confluence of two glaciers, two of their four edges merge and become a dark stripe of rocks and dirt down the center of the combined glacier. When glaciers melt away, these median stripes fall into place in the form of "medial moraines" running downvalley below the end of a dividing ridge.

A lobe-shaped expanse of boulders whose pattern suggests flow down a steep mountainside may in fact be doing so. A "rock glacier," it probably started out as a talus slope; gradually the interstices caught rain or meltwater that froze and stayed frozen in a permafrost climate. Eventually enough boulders were suspended in ice that the mass began to flow, like a glacier but too lumpy to glide on its sole. Its flow is all internal, limiting its speed. You could call a really, really, really glacial pace a rockglacial pace. A few rock glaciers are vestigial glaciers, almost melted away: the glacier's toe end, where it is concentrating rock debris (building a moraine) may be last to melt, and may spend its twilight years as a rock glacier. Jasper National Park has the most rock glaciers in our area, because it it coldest and driest—dry enough that snow glaciers don't fill all the available niches.

Cirques and Tarns

Having expended a litre of sweat since that morainal lake on the last page, you're now admiring a small subalpine lake tucked in among cliffs of an amphitheater-shaped hanging valley—a tarn, in a cirque.

Glacially carved valley heads can all be called cirques. The word (it means both *circle* and *circus* in French) refers to the half-bowl shape passed down from Greek amphitheaters to European circuses. It's the classic glacial valley **U** shape, rotated into three dimensions and missing one side. Typically the lip of the cirque, just above the dropoff, is eroded down to bedrock, which is striated. The interior floor (near the tarn, if there is one) often collects fine sediment, and may be marshy. In this case you can predict that the tarn is on its way to filling up and becoming a marsh, and perhaps later a meadow. Tarn is a Scandinavian word for a small lake.

Flat-lying limestone strata in the Canadian Rockies are especially prone to forming cirques—squarish, flat-floored ones. Tarns in these face a different doom: their water, seeping into the limestone, may dissolve it and cut an underground outlet that drains the tarn. This reemerges somewhere below as a spring, perhaps even a mid-cliff spring, a waterfall with no visible means of support.

Some upper valleys feature a series of cirque levels, each marking a long pause in the glacier's retreat. (This would be in the upper, steeper section of the valley, well above sections where similar pauses may have left a series of moraines. See previous page.)

Where the glaciers of two adjacent cirques grow until they almost touch, they leave a saw-edged ridge, an "arête" (a-**rett**). Where the heads of cirque glaciers on three or four sides of a mountain erode back to near each other, they carve a "horn," as in Matterhorn. The two Glacier National Parks have lots of horn mountains.

Permafrost and Its Mysterious Children

Alpine areas—or at least those that aren't permanent snow or slabby bedrock—develop curious small-scale landforms. Most result from "permafrost," the frozen condition of soil whose year-round average temperature is below freezing. Above permafrost usually lies a thawed layer, at least in summer; it gets thinner or may freeze up completely in fall and winter. While plants do grow in this thaw zone, the permafrost layer alters conditions by restricting groundwater, plant roots, and mycorrhizae to the thaw zone. With its drainage blocked, the habitable layer may stay sloppy wet all summer.

That doesn't mean permafrost is easy to spot. In fact, we don't generally know where it is without drilling or digging, and not much of that gets done out of curiosity alone. Naturally, permafrost is more pervasive northward. In Alberta it underlies most of the subalpine zone, but it's missing even from some alpine areas in Wyoming. It reaches lower elevations eastward, because westward-deepening snow insulates the soil, helping it retain warmth from the previous summer. While arctic regions have vast continuous permafrost, permafrost in our mountains is discontinuous, or patchy.

Permafrost on a slope leads to "gelifluction," downslope creepage of a partially thawed layer of soil typically 1' to 1½' thick (30–45 cm]. This produces long-lasting characteristic shapes, "gelifluction lobes and terraces," that are easy to recognize.

As water freezes, it expands by about nine percent as it crystallizes around tiny air pockets. When the water is in joints or cracks in rocks, it expands with enough force to split the rocks; this process, "frost riving" (or shattering) is responsible for turning most mountaintop bedrock into loose rocks and boulders. (Studies have begun to show that colder freezing gets more splitting done than mild freezing does—not quite astonishing, but corrective to the longstanding view that riving is proportional to the number of freezes and thaws.) As a saturated soil surface reaches about 90% frozen, the 10% that's still slushy gets extruded up out of the ground like toothpaste, before it, too, freezes. This "cryoturbation" makes life hard for plants, though some, like dryads, specialize in handling it.

When the slivers of freezing water work on already broken rock, they push it around. This "frost heaving" teams up with gravity, with a net result of gradual mass wastage, or downhill earth movement. This is thought to be the main kind of erosion taking place on gently sloping tundra areas; in fact, it may be the main force flattening the "summit flats" in the Wind Rivers and Beartooths. Here and there, small bedrock "tors" crop out, helping you to see how much bedrock has been broken and removed.

Frost heaving at the surface squeezes bigger stones out of place, nudging them to the surface. Flat sedimentary pieces may gradually form a mosaic-like "pavement," but some long thin ones get stood up on end like random tombstones. Once the surface gets relatively stony, a feedback loop sets up: during each freezing cycle, the 32° freezing front extends deeper under each stonier patch; the adjacent sandy patch then pushes its stray rocks toward that stony hollow as if it were "up." The stony parts get stonier. Given enough centuries, they form polygonal nets, or occasionally circles, on slopes of less than 3°. On slopes between 6° and 15°, gravity stretches these alignments into "stone stripes" running upslope-downslope. Steeper than 30° is too steep to pattern. Fairly uniformly fine soil may yield "unsorted stripes" of alternating vegetation and bare soil.

All these phenomena, called "patterned ground," adorn vast arctic landscapes and parts of alpine ones. Until recently, explanations for them were long on intuition and short on hard data. In 2003, two geomorphologists presented a mathematical model that can produce polygons, circles, and stripes by applying simple frost heaving and feedback loops to different combinations of slope, rock texture, and depth-to-permafrost.

Avalanches

Avalanches come exploding down the same mountainslopes year after year. Some spots get an avalanche every 100 or 200 years, others get several a month. Gullies where they recur are "avalanche tracks;" "avalanche basins" are where these run out at the bottom. Both produce distinctive brushy plant communities (without intact tall trees, natch) which are rich resources for many kinds of wildlife.

Watch sand settling in an hourglass to visualize "powder avalanches," the resettling pattern of loose fresh snow on a slope too steep for it to maintain. Less common, but more deadly, is the "slab avalanche." This occurs where layers of snowpack from different weeks of the winter develop slippery internal boundaries, typically where a snow surface stood in the sun for days or weeks, gradually recrystallizing into larger, rounder grains. This surface got buried, then later recrystallized further as water vapor rose through it. (Such sequences are common in our area.) At some point, under a variety of weather conditions, a huge slab of more recent snow up to several feet thick may slip on that recrystallized boundary, and go plummeting downslope, quickly accumulating devastating force.

Skiers, snowshoers, and snowmobilers all set off avalanches readily. Many die as a result each year. Do not venture onto winter snow steeper than a 25° slope without studying avalanche safety first.

The Big Sky Ranges

It takes vertical relief to lend a sense of scale to the sky. That's why Saskatchewan isn't Big Sky Country. Really big landscape features—distinct mountain ranges, scattered, some near, some very far, separated by big "holes," each range visibly brewing up its own kind of weather on a summer afternoon—now *that's* something that can truly expand a sky. No part of our Rockies pulls this trick off as well as the southwestern quadrant of Montana.

No part shows as much diversity of weather patterns or of bedrock material. Montana's and Idaho's highest ranges—the Beartooths (12,799 feet tall, or 3,901 meters) and Idaho's Pioneers* (12,078'/3,681 m) and Lost River Range (12,662'/3,859 m)—bracket the subregion and represent its wet and dry extremes. Perversely, the Beartooths have the most marine climate (most precipitation, with the strongest winter peak) and the Lost River and Lemhi Ranges, closer to the Pacific, are more continental. These towering Idaho ranges and their broad basins qualify as Big Sky country, partly due to their dry climate. Moist winter air flowing from the WSW gets wrung out twice in western Oregon and then again by the Idaho batholith, leaving this subregion our driest overall. The subregion is almost perfectly congruent with a gap in the distribution of ponderosa pine. Limber pine commonly takes its place. The gap may be attributable to climate, but not to drought *per se*.

One or the other of those two pines dominates mature forests on drier low-elevation forest habitats throughout the Middle Rockies, yielding to Douglas-fir upslope. Higher forests mix subalpine fir, Engelmann spruce, whitebark pine, and lodgepole pine. Lodgepole pine can be abundant at almost any elevation. As a community matures, fir or spruce might replace lodgepole pine; but lodgepole tends to invite recurring fires and can thereby perpetuate itself indefinitely.

Some southwest-facing slopes in the Lost Rivers and Lemhis are so dry that they have no timberline at all, just grassland and sagebrush or mountain-mahogany steppe from bottom to tundra. They look like Nevada: high fault-block ranges running NNW-to-SSE, separated by arid sagebrush flats and alluvial fans. They are true

---

*Montana and Idaho each have Pioneer Mtns., and each have Sawtooths. I call them "Idaho Pioneers" etc. when context isn't enough to locate them.

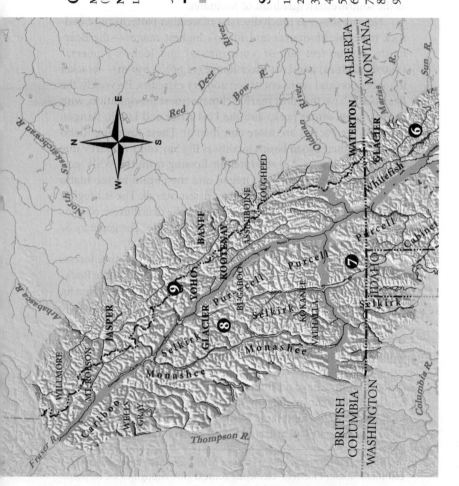

Our Range

Mountain ranges labelled in this font (but only outside of major parks).

NATIONAL PARKS LIKE THIS.

LARGER PROVINCIAL PARKS LIKE THIS.

⌇⌇ Rivers and lakes

┅┅┅ State/provincial boundaries

▬ Subregion boundaries

Subregions

1. Big Sky
2. Yellowstone Volcanic
3. Ancient Wyoming
4. Southern Batholiths
5. Wallowa/Seven Devils
6. Flathead
7. Kootenay
8. Columbia Mountains
9. Canadian Rockies

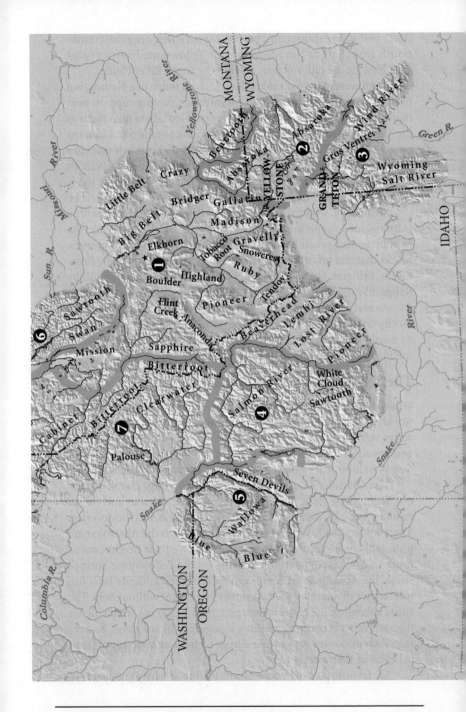

Rocky Mountain ranges and subregions

Basin and Range mountains, part of a system that once ran continuously from here to Nevada, before the Yellowstone Hotspot (page 584) blew up a swath of them, leaving the Snake River Plain.

Southwest Montana ranges don't look so much like Nevada, but most are in fact Basin-and-Range mountains, having risen on normal faults within the last 17 million years. (Geologists map them as the "Rocky Mtns. Basin and Range" province.) Some SW Montana ranges rose much earlier, as part of the fold-and-thrust belt that runs from the Canadian Rockies to the Utah-Wyoming border. (Perhaps much farther.) Not every range is 100% fold-and-thrust or 100% B&R; some, on old faultlines that reactivated, belong to both eras.

Sedimentary rocks intruded by granites predominate, with a scattering of volcanic and metamorphosed material. Exceptions: the Sapphires and possibly the Montana Pioneers are thick granitic blocks that slid off of the Bitterroot batholith (page 599). The Beartooths, Bridgers, Spanish Peaks, Tobacco Root Mountains, and Ruby Range, like the Wind Rivers and Tetons, are made largely of Archean granite and gneiss. The Beartooths—very high but actually not very toothy on top—are a gently sloping dome, deeply cut by glaciers on its northeast flank. The Elkhorns and Adels were carved by erosion mainly out of the bases of andesite stratovolcanoes.

The Yellowstone Volcanic Area

Yellowstone is a unique island in our region. In fact, it's unique in the world, with its plethora of geysers, mudpots, and hot springs. It's an active volcano, with substantial uplift in the last two million years and few signs remaining from all the mountain-building events before 55 million years ago. For more on its geology, see pages 584–89.

The Absaroka Range (ab-**sor**-ka) includes a large chunk of eastern Yellowstone Park. The young Yellowstone volcano and the 50 million-year-old Absarokas are unrelated in origin, but they overlap. Their volcanic soils support similar flora, though the Absarokas are noticeably more fertile. Both presumably owe their height (maximum 12,435 feet, or 3790 m) to being on the Yellowstone hotspot swell: the Absarokas are forms eroded from old andesite tuffs too soft to have maintained their commanding height without help. The entire subregion is a plateau averaging 7500' [2290 m], much higher than any other broad area of gentle topography in our range. As a result, each major Ice Age gave it a huge icefield, at least 4000' [1220 m] thick at Yellowstone Lake.

My favorite part of Yellowstone is the broad valley grasslands of its northeastern quarter. Find a place away from the cars and get a feeling of the pre-settlement West: scan unfenced, unlined expanses looking for bison, pronghorns, elk, two kinds of bears, and now wolves. This American Serengeti isn't perfectly "natural"—fear of humans is abnormally missing now, relative to at least 11,000 years of hunting, and the island of protection may lure large populations into habitats higher than their historic optimal range—but there *were* scenes a lot like it a thousand years ago, at least sometimes. Richly regreening patches among bleached trees killed by the 1988 fires help make it more natural—and more beautiful, at least to my eyes.

Ancient Wyoming

This subregion is our oldest, in bedrock terms. The Tetons and Wind Rivers (Wyoming's highest and most popular ranges) are made mostly of granite, gneiss, and schist more than two billion years old. This is "basement rock." To get to where it is, it rose more than seven vertical miles [11 km] on faults. The Wind River Fault is a "thick-skinned thrust" (page 578): the earth was squeezed until it cracked at about a 30° angle, and this block was pushed up that ramp, eroding all the while. This broad range has broad foothills to hide its glories from vehicle-bound tourists, but viewed from one of its peaks it mixes spires, awesome blocks, and long, long branching tundra "summit flats" almost as high as the highest peak. (That would be Gannett Peak, at 13,804' [4207 m] the highest in our entire range.)

A strand of glaciers near Gannett Peak constitutes about 60% of all glacial area in the U.S. Rockies. (Several authors have perpetuated someone's slip that these glaciers make up the largest batch of ice *in the lower 48 states.* A look at any of Washington's three national parks would quickly disabuse them of such notions. Washington has 75% of the total glacial area in the lower 48.)

Granite of the 13,770-foot [4197 m] Teton Range rose on the northwest end of the Wind River Fault, or a similar fault. But that's ancient history, overshadowed by the young Teton Fault, which has been active for 13 million years and is still as active as ever. A "normal fault," it results from stretching rather than squeezing, and actually drops the rock more than it raises it. That is, it dropped one side (Jackson Hole) 16,000 feet while raising its other side (the Tetons) 7,000 feet. [Dropped 5,000 m, raised 2,100 m.] Erosion of mountains on both sides filled Jackson Hole with sediment, and then a large Ice Age glacier flowed in from the Yellowstone ice cap, hauling off most of the preglacial talus and gouging out lake beds. The faultline runs along the eastern base of the range. Picture it as almost vertical, much steeper than the mountain front. The canyons were continually eating away at the front the entire time the block was rising, and in between the canyons rockfalls and other forms of wasting were at work. Still, for the spectacular steepness of the mountain front we can thank the steepness, speed, and freshness of the fault.

Before the Teton fault parted them, the Tetons were the west end of the Gros Ventre Range. Somewhat younger sedimentary rocks form the surface in the southern Tetons, the Gros Ventres, the east flank of the Winds, and the Hoback, Salt River, and Wyoming Ranges farther south. Check out the Lavender and Red Hills of Gros Ventre Canyon. There was less uplift here than in the Winds, where similar layers eroded off the top, exposing Archean basement at the range crest and west slope. Wyoming's part of the fold-and-thrust belt is the Salt River and Wyoming Ranges—humbler, yet alpine in spots.

The west slopes of the Salt River Range, the Tetons, and the Yellowstone Plateau get the most snow of anywhere south of Montana's Cabinet Range. Prevailing westerlies that hit them haven't crossed serious mountains for hundreds of miles, so they've absorbed moisture and are primed to drop it. The Teton canyons are moist enough for beargrass, oak fern, woodrush, and thickets of fool's-huckleberry. They get some spillover of west-slope snow in winter, and in summer they grow thunderstorms like weeds, while canyon walls enhance shade. Still (this being the south end of our range) evaporation rates make the effective climate drier than places with equal precipitation farther north. Plant communities most resemble those in the rest of the Middle Rockies, with the addition of blue spruce on stream bottoms. Aspen groves fringe the lower timberline areas.

The Wind Rivers are a good notch drier, and lack all the above-mentioned Teton canyon plants. Their eastside limestones favor lodgepole pine; the westside granites favor Douglas-fir. Vegetation within the Wyoming Rockies is often determined less by climate than by bedrock—granite versus limestone versus rhyolite.

Triple Divide Peak at the north end of the Winds drains to the North Pacific, the Gulf of California, and the Gulf of Mexico.

The Southern Batholiths of Idaho

In much of Central Idaho the mountains refuse to line up. They defy individuation and naming as ranges. The entire jumble drained by the Salmon River is known as the Salmon River Mountains, the entire jumble drained by the Clearwater as the Clearwater Mountains. It makes sense to name these mountains after their rivers: the ridges and valleys were determined by stream erosion—by downcutting forces, not by forces of uplift or by differences between rocks. Glaciers were generally scarce and most mountains are essentially ridges, with crests broad enough to carry a gravel road for miles. Broad-topped but craggy: extensive permafrost caused a lot of soil to slough down to the valleys when it thawed shallowly during Ice Age summers, leaving bedrock crags exposed. (More soil washed away during the early 1900s, trampled by eight million sheep hooves each summer. Ketchum was the chief sheep-shipping nexus.) The ridges rarely exceed 10,000' [3,000 m], but their breadth and the height and narrowness of the valleys produce an *average* elevation over 6500' [2000 m] across the batholith, a much larger area of this height than any in Montana. The batholith's chief outdoor-recreation lure is the Salmon River itself.

The rock (mostly granite) and the uplift are fairy uniform across the area known as the Idaho Batholith. Originally a geologic term for a huge mass of granite, "Idaho Batholith" is now essentially a vernacular geographic name, having outlived its usefulness to geologists. First, geologists split it into a younger northern and an older southern batholith, separated by ancient metamorphic rocks. (The northern one falls in a different ecological subregion, on page 22.) Then they found that 30% of the southern "batholith" is actually a few dozen much younger intrusions, some of them, like the Sawtooth batholith, easily identified by pink granite rather than gray. In others, radioactivity long ago turned pink quartz crystals gray.

There is one spectacularly peaked, linear range in the area—the Sawtooths. A fault block range, it reaches 10,751' [3,277 m] and had sizable Ice Age glaciers. It still gets the subregion's heaviest snowpacks today. Redfish Lake, largest in the row of lovely moraine lakes at its feet, is famed for its run of sockeye salmon (now on artificial life support, p 482). The White Cloud Peaks, named for the cirruslike white of their highest granites, are rain-shadowed by the Sawtooths, and had tiny Ice Age glaciers even though, at 11,815' [3601 m], they are the Batholith region's highest peaks.

Some 20% of the subregion (on its eastern side, including parts of the White Clouds) is carved from the bases of stratovolcanoes of the same intense volcanic era as those in the Big Sky ranges, an era that followed close on the heels of the main mountain-building era in the Rockies.

The Wallowa/Seven Devils Terrane

This and the Batholith (above) are the only Middle Rockies subregions with western yew trees, a hint of their slightly milder, moister climate. Wallowa high country fascinates botanists because of its close juxtaposition of limestone, granodiorite, and basalt substrates, each with distinct flora. The limestones, because they are far from other sizable limestone outcrops, have several endemic plants (species found nowhere but there). Hell's Canyon has endemics because it's lower and hotter than anywhere else in our region: 6,000 awesome feet deep [1800 m] and running north-south, it collects hot air on sunny days. It splits this subregion down the middle.

The upper slopes of Hell's Canyon and the Salmon River Canyon display layer upon layer of Columbia River basalt lava, which flooded out from a vast swarm of fissures all over the subregion. The basalt caps the Seven Devils Mountains and about 40% of the Wallowas.

Beneath all the basalt lies a profound anomaly: the Wallowa/Seven Devils is a displaced terrane, a piece of the earth's crust that originated as a volcanic island chain in the Pacific. Amalgamated together with other small terranes comprising the Blue Mountains, it sutured to North America as the oceanic plate it was riding on subducted under the edge of North America. (See page 575.) Limestones and other sediments derive from the islands' offshore slopes. The Wallowa granodiorite rose and solidified during the collision with America, and Columbia basalt flowed much later. Since six million years ago, the Wallowa and Seven Devils mountains rose 6,000' [1800 m] on faults. They are still rising.

Introduction: Shining Mountains subregions

This step north—as long as you stay west of the Continental Divide—leaves behind a few hot-climate species, like mountain-mahogany, but adds several conifers to the forest mix. (That's a departure from a rule of thumb that species diversity decreases poleward.) Subalpine larch enhances timberline scenery, while its cousin, western larch, is a low-elevation monarch. (Both reach a bit farther south, less abundantly.) Western yew is a widely scattered understory tree, and is even the canopy tree of a few valleys. Western white pine also appears, and both of our species of hemlock—one subalpine, one lowland. Western redcedar joins western hemlock in our deepest, lushest, mossiest, quietest forest communities, mainly on stream bottoms.

Flathead Country

Montana's part of the fold-and-thrust mountain belt drains primarily to one fork or another of the Flathead River. Sedimentary rocks of the Belt/Purcell Supergroup supply ninety percent of the backbone; Paleozoic sedimentary rocks in and near the Sawtooths supply the rest. Layers of limestone, dolomite, shale, and sandstone predominate in both, but the Belt is older (Proterozoic), making its rocks a bit more reprocessed, harder, and more interesting to look at than their Paleozoic juniors. Glacier-Waterton International Park owes its topographic salience largely to the fact that its strata are almost horizontal; in the other ranges they tilt, making it easier for rocks to break up and slide down into the rivers, which carry them away.

From the Swan Range westward, bedrock is almost all Belt. The Missions are a mini-Glacier, without the crowds, the roads, the waiting lists for trail permits, or the trail maintenance. Mountains west of them are lower, more heavily roaded, and lightly visited.

Flathead Country's highest peak, 10,466' Mt. Cleveland [3190 m], is just south of the Waterton-Glacier border. Triple Divide Peak, also in Glacier, drains to the Pacific, Hudson's Bay, and the Gulf of Mexico.

The Flathead watershed, west of the Continental Divide, has a distinctly marine climate, somewhat resembling the NW Coast. Glacier-Waterton is the bullseye for wet airflow, which even spills over the divide to produce Alberta's one cranny of rain forest. Other than there, the area east of the divide has the harshest, most continental climate in our region, and the shortest list of conifer species. Chinook winds scour those slopes in winter and spring, and kill a lot of trees. To us, Chinooks may be a relief from fierce cold, warming the air as much as 54° [30° C.] in four hours. But that's no blessing to a tree. The warm dry wind sucks out the needles' moisture, which the tree cannot replace with its roots still frozen. The needles may all die at once, across entire swaths of trees ("red belts") and some of those trees will die. Red belts would seem to favor deciduous trees with no leaves to lose in winter, yet western larch does not grow on the east slope, and broadleaf trees aren't much more prevalent than in the west. Some lower timberlines in central Montana consist of limber pines and Douglas-firs that get increasingly bonsai'd eastward, until they are three-foot bushes you could mistake for juniper. Even though it's completely vulnerable to red belt, scruffy old lodgepole pine is more dominant on the east slope than anywhere, thanks both to its versatile tolerance of harsh conditions and to frequent forest fires.

Kootenay Country

This subregion is our best at growing trees, and at burning them up. Its recipe for conflagration: in winter it is wet and relatively warm, growing lots of vegetation which becomes fuel during the dry summers. In summer it is a lightning corridor. Burned areas that reburn within thirty years may turn into shrubfields and exclude conifers for centuries. Some high slopes in the Clearwater National Forest are still recovering from our region's worst recorded fire season, 1910. More recent burns are widespread, including of course those of 2000 in the Bitterroots. Still, many valleys support verdant old groves.

These mountains embrace several areas geologists call "metamorphic core complexes." I'll leave explaining those for chapter 16, after noting that rich mining districts abound near core complexes. The Coeur d'Alene River and Lake are victims of western mining's all-too-frequent toxicity. We who decline to mine extract something else of value: visual pleasure in cornucopias of beautiful stones.

The northern half of the subregion overlaps "The Kootenays," a vaguely defined area beloved to British Columbians as unspoiled, scenic with huge fjord lakes, and warmer than much of the province.

The subregion's southern end is the large Bitterroot batholith, a mass of 80-million-year-old granitic rocks. It underlies Idaho's Clearwaters, a broad welt of high ridges cut deeply by the gorgeous Selway and Lochsa Rivers and their dendritic lace of tributaries. The Bitterroots at its eastern edge rise higher, to 10,157' [3096 m]. This eastern edge is a core complex, with a history of metamorphism, faulting, and uplift, leaving it a mixture of granitic and metamorphic rocks. Geologist Don Hyndman figured out the formation of the Bitterroot Valley and the Sapphire Range, its opposite side, in terms of a ten-mile-deep block of batholith detaching and sliding down the east slope of the Bitterroots while the core complex rose. This went on in the depths, long before these rocks saw the light of day. He thinks the Washington/Idaho Selkirks (core complex) have the same relationship to the Cabinet Range (sliding block) but the evidence there is scanty. The Cabinets now stand much higher, at 8712' [2655 m] than the dome they would have slid off of. The U.S. Selkirks and a third core-complex range, the Kettles, cover large areas, but are not as high.

The northern two-thirds of this subsection is topographically modest, but has great forested expanses with few people. These offer critical habitat and corridors to megafauna of concern: woodland caribou, wolverines, fishers, lynxes, wolves, and grizzlies.

The Columbia Mountains

The difference between these crystalline peaks and the layer-cake Rockies is hard to miss: these look black, massive, and spiky. Few of them have a gentle side you could build a trail up. Yet this broad wedge of magnificent mountains just west of the slightly higher Rockies seems incurably overshadowed by them. It wasn't always that way. Most geologists see the Columbias as the original core mountains—and for tens of millions of years the highest mountains—in Western Canada. Being the core, they were most subject to collapse. (See page 582).

Neither range had a worldwide reputation until the Canadian National Railway built (largely for reasons of national pride) a transcontinental line before there was a market to pay for it. To create a market to recoup their investment, they promoted tourism and built hotels at Banff, Lake Louise, and elsewhere. Reaching the Selkirks after the Rockies, they found the climate taxing: avalanches kept wiping out their tracks. And crews. Seeing a climate less attractive to tourists, but granitic and metamorphic rocks more alluring to mountaineers, they recruited Swiss alpine guides to be the centerpieces of their Selkirk hotels. They succeeded in kick-starting mountaineering in North America, but the Columbias never came to rival the Rockies in popularity. As of 2003, skiing remains lightly developed, though some skiers have discovered that the snow here (especially where it's driest, overlooking the Rocky Mtn. Trench) is as superior as the rock.

Thanks both to high precipitation and weak summer sunshine, the Columbias' western slopes have the wettest habitats in our range. Many forests here resemble Northwest coastal rain forests. With its heavy fall of wet snow, Glacier N.P. remains Avalanche Central. Crews stay busy every winter shooting off hundreds of artillery rounds at thickening snowfields, to prevent deadly loads from building up.

The subregion naturally divides into four ranges. As its wedge shape narrows northward into the crook of the Columbia River, the Monashees, Selkirks, and Purcells run together, forming a sea of peaks. In the south they are nearly parallel, spectacularly sundered by immensely long, deep fjord lakes. Northward past the Columbia's crook, the wedge continues as a single broad range, the Cariboos. Beyond those, lower mountains continue, but the Shining Mountains Ecoprovince gives way to the black spruces of the boreal forest.

The Columbias are a perplexing swirl in the geologic mosaic that is British Columbia. They mix exotic terranes (erstwhile Pacific islands) with pieces of the continent's offshore shelf. Almost every kind of rock turns up here; gneiss and granite end up salient. As for differences among the four ranges, there are a few simple things I can say: the Cariboos have active young volcanoes. The Monashees have the most granite, and the most really old rocks. The Selkirks (11,592'/3533 m Mt. Sir Sandford) are highest, but the Cariboos (11,500'/3505 m) and Purcells (11,340'/3456 m) come close.

The Canadian Rockies

The Canadian Rockies are starkly linear on an awesome scale.

On the west they are bounded by the Rocky Mountain Trench, the longest, widest, deepest nearly-straight line on any continent. Surprisingly, it's neither a single faultline nor a single river valley. It also misses, by a wide mark, the boundary between ancient North America and a collage of *arriviste* terranes. Within its 1300-mile length [2050 km] it cradles nine different rivers divided by slight rises. Some flow south, some north. In our part of it, the Fraser flows north; the south-flowing Canoe joins the north-flowing Columbia; and the Kootenay flows south away from the Columbia, only to rejoin it 450 miles [730 km] downstream. At times during the last Ice Age, a single huge trunk glacier flowed south through all that, up hill and down dale.

Within the Rockies, nearly all big valleys and ridgelines parallel the Trench. Notches cut across from valley to valley, seemingly at random; glaciers scooped them out, but their locations were predetermined by rivers that were here before the mountains were.

These mountains are chock full of parallel lines when seen in landscape view, as well. Many strata are tipped and folded, but almost always on that same NNW-striking axis, so they're horizontal when viewed from the ENE.

Physiographic subdivisions are, naturally, four narrow strips paralleling the Trench: the Western, Main, and Front Ranges, and the (eastern) Foothills. Most Front Ranges and Foothills are sharply tilted or folded. Strata of limestone and dolomite, being harder than the shales and mudstones, determine where mountains stand tall. Altitudes grade lower from west to east because the compression that caused all this came from the west, so the folds and thrusts are bigger westward. Though somewhat higher, the Western Ranges are also mostly shale, slate, and phyllite in sharply tilted strata.

In contrast, Main Range fault blocks are larger and more horizontal. (See cross-section, page 578–79.) One big section is a single block, the Simpson Thrust. Horizontal strata and an abundance of limestone and quartzite are the Main things that make them higher, and make them, consequently, the Continental Divide. Here's why: when a layer of tough limestone or quartzite ends up steeply tilted, and then a glacier slices off its lower end, the shale layer under it will shear along a bedding plane (what divides two strata) dropping the

Relief, Relatively Speaking

Mt. Robson's horizontal carbonate strata fill the prescription for standing tall. At 12,972', Robson is the highest Canadian Rocky. No, it's more than that, it's the king of local relief, crowned with its own clouds, rising 9741 stupefying feet in 2¼ miles, 10,320' in 7 miles from its park entrance.

Mt. Whitney, CA, the high point in the lower 48 states, is seen by some as a paragon of local relief. It rises 10,550 feet from the Owens Valley, but that's 11¾ miles away. Less than 4000' is gained in any 2¼-mile stretch.

Mt. Sir Donald, BC Selkirks, rises 7810' in 2¼ miles from the Beaver R.

Lake Louise, AB, looks at 5682' of local relief, 3¼ miles away.

Mt. Assiniboine, BC, a glorious exception to the run of blocky peaks in the Main Ranges, rises a mile in 1¼ miles on both east and west sides.

Grand Teton rises 7000' above Lupine Meadows, just over 3 miles away. Its neighbor, Mt. Owen, rises 1 mile in 1 mile from Cascade Canyon. Not even Denali can match a mile in a mile.

Mt. Stimson in Glacier N.P. rises 6222' from its base less than 2 miles away. Local relief over 5000' in 2 miles is common throughout Glacier.

Mt. Cleveland's north wall in Glacier N.P. rises 4626' in 1 kilometer (.6 miles)—a close match for Yosemite Valley's tallest flank, **Half Dome**.

Borah Peak's trail climbs 5250' in 3¼ miles—2¼ miles as the crow flies.

Mt. Shuksan, WA, beats Grand Teton with 7630' in 3 miles; 5000' in 2 miles is common in Washington's North Cascades. Little-known **Pyramid Mtn.** rises 8235' above the bottom of Lake Chelan in 2.9 miles.

Hell's Canyon has 6000' of relief in 2¼ miles, vs. **Grand Canyon's** 5100'.

Long's Peak, CO, rises 3900' in the closest 2¼ miles. About half of that is its awesome vertical face, the Diamond. Colorado has fifty-four 14,000-footers (we have none) but they stand on a high base and are not as steep as the competition on this page. Nearly all are walkups, if not drive-ups.

Mt. St. Elias, standing 18,008' tall on the Yukon/Alaska border, less than 15 miles from a sea inlet, is probably North America's local relief champion. Its south face drops 11,000' in the uppermost 2¼ miles.

whole mass into the valley. Horizontal layers create no such slippery ramps. They keep the Main Ranges high, and also make them blocky, with broad summit surfaces that create icefields by making it hard for ice to find an outlet. The Columbia Icefield straddles the only Triple Divide in North America that waters three oceans—Pacific, Arctic, and Atlantic.

Relief, Relatively Speaking

Mt. Robson's horizontal carbonate strata fill the prescription for standing tall. At 3954 m, Robson is the highest Canadian Rocky. No, it's more than that, it's the king of local relief, crowned with its own clouds, rising 2969 stupefying meters in 3.6 km, 3145 meters in 11 km from its park entrance.

Mt. Whitney, CA, the high point in the lower forty-eight states, is seen by some as a paragon of local relief. It rises 3216 m from the Owens Valley, but that's 19 km away. Less than 1220 m is gained in any 3.6-km stretch.

Mt. Sir Donald, BC Selkirks, rises 2380 m in 3.6 km from the Beaver River.

Lake Louise, AB, looks at 1733 m of local relief, 5.1 km away.

Mt. Assiniboine, BC, a glorious exception to the run of blocky peaks in the Main Ranges, rises 1613 m in 2 km on both east and west sides.

Grand Teton rises 2150 m above Lupine Meadows less than 5 km away. Its neighbor, Mt. Owen, rises a mile in a mile [1613 m] from Cascade Canyon. Not even Denali can match a mile in a mile.

Mt. Stimson in Glacier N.P. rises 1900 m from its base less than 3 km away. Local relief over 1400 m in 3 km is common throughout Glacier.

Mt. Cleveland's north wall in Glacier N.P. rises 4626' in 1 kilometer—a close match for Yosemite Valley's tallest flank, Half Dome.

Borah Peak's trail climbs 1600' in 5.25 km—3.6 km as the crow flies.

Mt. Shuksan, WA, beats Grand Teton with 2325 m in 5 km; 1400 m in 3 km is common in Washington's North Cascades. Little-known **Pyramid Mtn.** rises 2510 m above the bottom of Lake Chelan in 4.7 km.

Hell's Canyon has 1830 m of relief in 3.6 km, vs. **Grand Canyon's** 1550 m.

Long's Peak, CO, rises 1190 m in the closest 3.6 km. About half of that is its awesome vertical face, the Diamond. Colorado has thirty-one 4300-meter peaks (we have none) but they stand on a high base and are not particularly steep. Nearly all are walkups, or even drive-ups.

Mt. St. Elias, standing 5489 m tall on the Yukon/Alaska border less than 25 km from a sea inlet, is probably North America's local relief champion. Its south face drops 3350 m in the uppermost 3.6 km.

2

Weather and Climate

Weather may exert a huge influence on your travels in the Rockies. *Climate* determines the landforms and life forms you will see.

The Air Went Over the Mountain

Hot air rises, right? But the higher you go in the mountains, the colder it is, right? What's going on here?

Mountain weather reflects the instability of air caught between the conflicting forces of nature observed in those two truisms.

The atmosphere is too transparent to get heated very much by sunlight. Instead it's the ground that heats up in the sun every day, and that in turn heats the air in contact with it—the lowest air. As masses of low air heat up, they expand, which is to say they become less dense, or lighter, than the air above them, so they must rise.

As they rise, they become still less dense—not because of heat now, but because of pressure: they moved up to where a shorter column of atmosphere sits on top of them, compressing them less than the taller column did when they were lower. Reducing pressure makes air thinner and colder. The molecules are farther apart; they bounce off of each other less often and slow down, which means they have less energy and are colder. In short, reducing pressure makes a compressible fluid colder. Unlike a lake, whose water—an incompressible fluid with a distinct top boundary—is able to stratify with the warmer water higher, the compressible atmosphere almost always really is colder the higher you get (In theory, dry air cools 5.5° with each

1,000' of altitude, or 1° C. per 100 m. Real-world lapse rates are usually much less, varying with moisture and other factors. And above seven miles/11 km up it gets warmer, for a ways.) The rising hot air and the sinking cold air can't make lasting headway against this law of physics; but that doesn't mean they don't try. Their ongoing struggle to turn things around (forgive the anthropomorphism) produces wind. Their minor, temporary truces are temperature inversions: cold air settles under a layer of warmer air, and the air stills. Inversions are common at night, when the ground is no longer heating up, or in winter. Exceptionally strong daytime heating creates exceptionally strong hot air convection upward and, given enough moisture in the air, thunderstorms. We'll get back to thunderstorms.

Rivers of cold air form on the surface of glaciers, chilled on ice. In general, cold air gravitates to low places. Valley bottoms have cool, moist microclimates due both to cold air drainage and to having far fewer hours of direct sunshine each day. The effect is strongest in east/west-running valleys, weakest in south-draining valleys that are filled with sun at midday. High nonforested peaks and ridges, at the other extreme, receive copious sunlight, and heat up intensely, but their thin air can't hold onto the heat; their net daily rise and fall in temperature are much less than in the lowlands.

The warmest level in mountains is often a midslope "thermal belt" subject to neither cold air drainage nor thin air heat loss. If you want to sleep warmer, you may gain as much as 15° [8° C.] by leaving a stream bottom and camping on a somewhat higher bench.

The air contained in valleys expands in the daytime heat and contracts at night. The resulting "valley winds" and "slope winds" are Gaia's breath on your cheek. A valley wind is a main trunk flow aligned with the valley, whereas the slope wind is a thin sheet of air moving up or down the flanking slopes. Up in the day and down at night is the basic rule for both, but the valley wind, being larger, lags behind the slope wind. In early morning, for example, the upslope wind begins while the night's downvalley wind continues in the valley's center. These winds are strongest in clear summer weather. Occasionally the flow buffets in fierce pulses lasting a few seconds each, just after sunset, when downslope and downvalley winds join forces.

All of these local temperature-related airflows take place in the context of a huge global air convection pattern. I don't have enough space here to explain that one's physics, but it puts our entire range in the belt of prevailing westerlies (actually west-southwesterlies), one of six broad wind belts that circle the world, parallel to the equator. The westerlies actually blow from the WSW, on average.

Mountains' chief effects on prevailing winds are to keep them out of deep crosswise valleys, and to strengthen them across mountaintops and in gaps in the range. Air flow speeds up, just as water does, when constricted in a gorge. The high country is windy.

Mountains Writing Rain

A second key law of physics is that warmer air can hold more water vapor than colder air. Put that law together with the one about rising air chilling, and you get mountains writing clouds and precipitation—"orographic" precipitation, from the Greek for *mountain* and *writing*. Air moving across the land meets mountains, is forced up the mountainslope ramp, inexorably cooling, and at some point commonly getting to where it is too cold to hold the moisture that it held easily when it was crossing the plains. Dry sunny plains, cloudy, snowy or rainy mountains. Wetter west slope, dryer east slope (wherever west winds prevail). As the airflow descends the far slope, the opposite happens, in spades. (See Chinooks, below.)

When water evaporates, it changes to its gaseous state, water

Chinooks

The feet of mountains worldwide are subject to eerie blasts of warm dry wind. Each place has its own name for them. Some Rocky Mountain tribes called them Snow Eaters; now we call them Chinooks. They are common in winter and spring beneath the Rocky Mtn. Front in Alberta and Montana. In a Chinook, a normal orographic effect —westerlies heating up due to rapidly increasing pressure as they descend an east slope— is intensified by high pressure on the east side meeting low pressure on the west. (Precipitation on the west slope prewarms the air it falls from, thanks to another law of physics.) Winds can reach 70 mph [110 kph], and they can stop and restart abruptly, sometimes with brief reincursions of the cold air. Temperatures commonly rise 20° [11° C.] in five minutes, or as much as 60° [33° C.] in a few hours. Snow gets gobbled up fast; sometimes it evaporates as fast as it melts, with no visible runoff.

Many people feel the warmth as a great relief, the wind as a thrill. Others experience aches, malaise, and mental instability. Farmers dread Chinooks as thieves of their hard-earned precipitation. Herbivores throng where Chinooks expose grasses to eat. Trees, especially lodgepole pines, are threatened, life and limb. (See "red belt," page 21.) The Crowsnest Valley has very few lodgepoles; from there to East Glacier, Montana, is the black hole of Chinooks, averaging around thirty a year.

vapor, consisting of individual water molecules pretty evenly and invisibly distributed in the air. When vapor turns back to a liquid, the molecules join in droplets too tiny to see except as large aggregates—clouds, fog, or mist. Cloud droplets, about one millionth of the size of an average raindrop, are too light to fall. Many stay suspended until they warm up and re-evaporate after crossing the mountain crest.

Droplets can collide and coalesce until bulky enough to fall as rain, but that rarely happens over continental interiors. Over our mountains, they freeze first. Most become supercooled droplets—liquid droplets at temperatures well below freezing. They can't

Mountains Writing Clouds

Steady air currents arching just high enough to condense, and then descending, create several distinctive types of stationary clouds:

A cloudcap envelopes a salient peak.

Lenticular clouds—pure white slivers or crescents with the convex side up (their name means lens-shaped) can form either straight above a salient peak, or some distance downwind of it at a little above peak level. Sometimes a few of them stack up over the peak, or line up horizontally downwind of it. In the latter case, picture the airflow over the peak as making a series of waves downwind, just as water in a riffle forms standing waves below a slightly submerged rock.

Rotor clouds are puffy clouds in a row, downwind of a range and parallel to it. They're pretty much the same thing as downwind lenticular clouds but with stronger wind, creating turbulence. Often you can see a rolling-forward motion, as the tops of the puffs ride on faster winds than the bottoms.

A banner cloud is an eddy that hugs a ridge or a salient peak, just below crest level. Air is tumbling over and down, then eddying back up in the wind-protected pocket. The upflowing portion chills and condenses into cloud, the same way upflowing air tends to do anywhere.

Fractocumulus and fractostratus clouds are the little wisps that cling all over a mountainside in moist, fairly turbulent conditions.

A Chinook wall, aligned directly over the range crest, is the lee edge of the huge orographic cloud enveloping the upwind side of the range. It may extend a **waterfall cloud** that pours over a saddle and then vanishes in thin air, like the way Canada's icefields stick our their glacial tongues through low points in the mountain wall

A Chinook arch—a very long stratus formation that cuts off abruptly on a line parallel to the range, may appear over the Plains before a chinook.

crystallize until they find tiny solid particles to crystallize around. Eventually, given continued cooling, a significant number of them do that, and then the supercooled droplets that bump into them can freeze on them, gradually building up enough bulk to fall as snow, sleet, or graupel (unglazed "soft hail"). On descending through the freezing level, they melt into rain, unless of course they find the ground first, while they're still white stuff. In warm dry summer air, the raindrops often complete a full change-of-state cycle, re-evaporating into thin air; these phantom showers ("virga") appear below distant clouds as dark vertical streaks. Showers of graupel are whitish.

If a cloud stays colder than freezing but is not dense enough to precipitate, it will be a cloud of tiny ice crystals. Crystalline clouds are usually filmy, white, with diffuse edges, and they can make a rainbow-colored sun halo or sundogs (a pair of weak "suns," left and right, mounted on the halo). They don't make proper rainbows, which result only from liquid cloud droplets.

So, how exactly do our mountains write the precipitation map? In general, westerlies bring moisture from the Pacific. Each range that the Pacific air mass comes to wrings moisture out of it, and a much drier air mass flows on eastward. The northwest coastal ranges get first whack, and are the wettest places in the U.S. and Canada. But that wrung-out air does steadily pick up new moisture, even from arid steppe land. So as a rule, each range in the Rockies gets precipitation to the degree that the range is 1.) far from, and 2.) higher than the next range to the west. The wettest stretches of the Continental Divide are from Crowsnest Pass to Glacier N.P. (downwind of a slew of broad valleys divided by modest ranges) and the Tetons and southwestern Yellowstone (downwind of the long Snake River Plain).

Occasionally wet weather blows in from the east, especially in winter and in June. Then the east slope is wet, the west side dry, with more precipitation at Banff than Lake Louise, while Golden is sunny.

In summer, the jet stream moves northward, allowing warm moist air masses from the Gulfs of California and Mexico to confront the Pacific air masses. The interplay of air mass movements, orographic temperature gradients, and convection cells of hot air rising off of rocky terrain frying in the midday sun—all channeled by mountain topography—gets wild. Intense small cells may build into thunderstorms, often day after day. (See page 32).

In sum, marine and continental influences interlace in the Middle Rockies. The Shining Mountains are strongly continental east of the Continental Divide, a little less so on the Canadian west slope

---

north of Crowsnest Pass, and otherwise fairly marine, with daily and annual temperature fluctuation ranges less than in the continental areas, but still greater than near the coast. The eastern limit of marine influence is usually mapped as running down the Rocky Mountain Trench, shifting east to the Divide from Crowsnest Pass to Marias Pass, and then hopping progressively westward until it runs down the Idaho Whiteclouds and Pioneers. Nevertheless, way to the east, a snow-heavy swath runs south from the Beartooths and Absarokas to the Tetons and Salt Rivers. As additional remote SNO-TEL sensors get set up in the high mountains, we find that many get a lot of precipitation, with a winter peak. There is still no SNOTEL near the glaciers on the northern Wind River Range, but given that they are by far the biggest ice patch in the U.S. Rockies, I wouldn't be surprised to see winter-heavy precipitation patterns there. Some even turn up as far southeast as Colorado's Front Range, though summer-wet charts certainly outnumber winter-wet ones in Colorado.

Thermals and Cumulus

On a typical summer morning in the West, the sun is strongly heating the ground by midmorning, and the ground is heating the air next to it. This effect is strongest where vegetation is sparsest, due to either aridity or high elevation. Wide areas of sparse vegetation create scattershot patterns of rising warm air masses, or "thermals," more like slow-rising bubbles (picture a lava lamp) than like columns.

All these thermals on a given day in a given area have about the same water vapor content, and for that content level there is a temperature that will force the vapor molecules to coalesce into cloud droplets. The altitude where the thermals reach that temperature becomes the floor for a layer of flat-bottomed puffy white cumulus clouds. Think of each cumulus cloud as the turbulent head on an otherwise invisible thermal. The change of state from gas to liquid releases heat; the warm updraft is reinforcing itself.

As long as the tops of the clouds are crisply defined, like cauliflower, the droplets are liquid, even though they are likely below 32° [0° C.]. If the clouds get taller, their upper parts may crystallize into ice, and the edges will look more diffuse. As an ice crystal collides with supercooled liquid droplets,they freeze around it, and it grows. If it grows as big as a pea, it is a hailstone, but in any case it is more likely to melt into a raindrop, or even to re-evaporate completely before hitting the ground, than to become part of a hailstorm.

Thunder and Lightning

The cloud may keep rising until it hits a stable layer that halts further rising and blows the uppermost ice crystals streakily out in front, forming an "anvil-top." Now it's becoming a thunderstorm. Where hailstones and/or raindrops form a serious mass within the cloud, they drag a lot of air with them—icy air from the top of the storm. This downdraft bursts outward as it hits the ground: you can feel (and often see) the blast of cold air arriving in advance of a downpour.

The southern end of our range tends to get storms earliest, both

Storm Warnings

It takes years of familiarity with the weather of a mountain range to develop a really good eye for weather signs. Whether you have such an eye or not, it is vital to carry into the high country enough insulation, shelter and food to keep you alive if the weather turns bad, and enough navigation aids and skills to get you out again. Always carry warm and waterproof gear for every person. High mountain showers are almost always cold showers; they can be sleet or snow any month of the year. In fair weather, a cloudcap rapidly building on a peak, or a strong buildup of clouds in the distance, can presage a turn. Weather Radios can go backpacking, but to get a signal they have to get a nearly straight broadcast (i.e., no mountains in the way) from a station not too far away. But even without a signal they can transmit a warning: bursts of static may clue you in when nearby clouds are preparing fireworks. Ben Gadd suggests carrying a radio tuned to interstation noise if you're on exposed heights in imperfect weather. (He also warns of a "sucker hole"—a midday hour of misleadingly bright skies.)

Both the chill and the lightning are grave hazards. When we naturalists try to talk you out of your fear of big carnivores, we say your odds of getting eaten are minute compared to your odds of being struck by lightning. Now it's payback time: yes, getting struck by lightning is way too damned likely. You are reasonably safe in a forest, but if you don't have one of those, squat in a dry low spot without a tree, or a few feet out from the base of a cliff. Little caves under cliff overhangs, unfortunately, are not good places to be. Dry moss and grass are good insulators, even snow is better than wet rock. Boot soles are insulators, your hands and the seat of your pants are not. Spread your party out. If anyone develops a blue glow around them, or their hair stands on end, they are building an electrical charge that precedes lightning: drop everything metallic (especially metal-frame packs) and RUN in diverse directions. Give immediate mouth-to-mouth CPR to lightning strike victims, especially those who seem to have stopped breathing. This procedure saves many lives.

in the day (threeish, on average) and in the year (late May having the most). These averages grade later northward, to an August maximum at Jasper—but they're only averages, not assurances.

Afternoon thunderstorms may all dissipate into a clear azure dusk. Under different conditions, thunderstorms that form along a range crest may rush down the canyons in the late afternoon; if their cold air slams into moist warm air at the bottom, it wedges in under the warm air and forces it rapidly upward, creating a new thunderstorm. Several can do this at once, making a "squall line" along the downwind (usually east) foot of the range. A squall line commonly trails a sheet of thin clouds behind it that keep things murky and drizzly for hours. Large-scale weather fronts also create squall lines as well as prolonged, powerful thunderstorms.

Thunderstorms build up electrical charges. Exactly how they do is still pretty mysterious. Positively and negatively charged layers form in the cloud, and locally neutralize each other by means of huge sparks—intra-cloud lightning. Cloud-to-ground lightning is similar; it most often connects positively charged earth to a strong negative layer within a cloud (often above a positive bottom layer). It begins as a descending negative leader which explores more or less randomly, all in a microsecond; when it gets close to a salient point or conductor (a peak or big tree) on the ground, a positive streamer shoots up to meet it. When they connect, one or more "return strokes," often branching, jet up into the cloud at about one-third the speed of light. Those return upstrokes make the big streaks of light.

Air in lightning's narrow path heats instantaneously to 30,000° or so (does anyone really care whether that's Fahrenheit or Celsius?) in an explosive expansion that we experience as a loud noise. When you're quite close, you hear the full sound spectrum, a sharp KER-RACKKKK. Since lower-pitched sounds travel farther than higher-pitched ones, the farther away the lightning is, the deeper it sounds, up to a maximum distance of 15 to 25 miles [24–40 km]. Farther away than that, we hear silence and call it "heat" lightning. Every five seconds the thunder takes to reach you indicates a mile of distance between you and the lightning. [Three seconds indicates a klick.] At twenty seconds or less you should be concerned about it hitting your vicinity very soon.

Aspect

Just as the sun shines hotter at noon than in morning and evening, hotter at the equator than here, and hotter in summer than in winter, it shines hotter on south-facing slopes than on other aspects. East slopes heat best in the morning, west slopes in the afternoon. South slopes have hotter, drier plant community types than north slopes.

Additionally, windward and leeward sides of a ridge have strong snow and rain differences. While the windward side is the wet side as long as you're looking at an entire range, local effects involving individual ridges can be quite the opposite. Rainfall peaks a short way downwind of a ridgecrest before falling off dramatically in the "rain shadow." This could be partly because the clouds release the most rain directly over the ridgeline or even a bit upwind, and then the falling raindrops blow downwind. More important is the way snow blows over the ridgecrest and then immediately settles in the wind lull, often building a cornice that may last, continuously releasing meltwater, well into summer. The lowest slopes on the lee side get the least precipitation, but have the moistest soils, partly because they receive subsurface drainage from the high leeward slopes that get the most rain but have soils too coarse to hold onto it. Over time, cool moist soils are self-reinforcing: they retain more organic content (which holds water) because fire is less frequent and humus decomposition is slower there.

Where WSW winds prevail, the sunlight and precipitation effects combine forces to moisten the northeast sides of ridges.

Microclimates

Any climatic subject you could chart on a regional map is macroclimatic, whereas aspect (above), operates on a smaller "mesoclimatic" scale. Of equal concern to hikers and other creatures is the climate near the ground, the microclimate. A microclimate may be much warmer or cooler than its surroundings for several reasons:

Ground and lakes heat up in the sun, even on cloudy days, and heat the air next to them. High peaks are subject to intense radiation, including heat, thanks to reradiation from clouds, snow or ice. Dark surfaces heat much more than pale ones. Dark, dry humus soil on a high south-facing slope was measured at 175° [79° C.] while the surrounding air was only 86° [30°]. For an alpine lichen, seedling, or crawling invertebrate, 175° summer afternoons may be a fact of life.

Vegetation insulates. The tree canopy, the shrub, herb, and moss layers, and the snowpack are all blankets, keeping everything under them warmer in cold weather, and vice versa. The combination of earth heat retention and snowpack insulation create a winterlong 30–32° [–1 to 0°] environment for rodents that neither hibernate nor migrate seasonally. Deer and elk take "thermal cover" in forests during cold spells; but on summer days the forest is cooler than clearings.

Vegetation and rough topography impede wind. This effect allows cold air collected by sinking (or air heated by warm ground) to stay put longer than they otherwise would.

Ice Over Time

The twentieth century had a warming trend—partly human-nudged Greenhouse effect and partly natural rebound from a cool cycle (the Little Ice Age) which began around 1300 and hit its last low around 1850. Seen in the fullness of time, it was not a very warm century.

The last 14,000 years (the Holocene Epoch) averaged a few degrees warmer, notably during the Medieval Warm Period from 800 to 1250 C.E., and the Hypsithermal (warm) Interval—encompassing the dawn of agriculture and civilization—around 9,000 to 5,000 years ago.

The last 2.4 million years (the Quaternary Period) have been much colder most of the time, cycling between Ice Ages averaging 50,000 years and interglacial stages averaging 18,000, with abrupt hops of many degrees up or down that lasted several centuries.

Earth's history on the whole has been much warmer. The great majority of eras had neither large Polar ice caps nor alpine glaciers at temperate latitudes. Their level of century-scale stability is unknown. Even hundred-thousand-year ice ages would be hard to detect; but

Ancient glaciations of far greater length and intensity punctuate the timeline. One or several "snowball earth" glaciations, each lasting millions of years in the late Proterozoic, surficially froze the entire earth, or perhaps just half of it. Some ancient glaciations may have cycled on and off on a scale of tens of millions of years. We can plausibly interpret those cycles as a youthful biosphere working out a CO_2 equilibrium: plants flourished until they removed too much CO_2, wrecking the greenhouse and icing the earth; volcanos continued to spout CO_2, unabated, until a powerful greenhouse was restored, and so on.

Ice ages have been attributed to an astounding variety of causes. Changes long-lasting enough to bring on a glacial epoch would almost have to trace back to either evolution or plate tectonics. Evolution could have produced bursts of bigger, faster-growing plants, depleting CO_2.

A forest canopy makes the community under it drier or moister at different times. You may notice that rain dripping from a forest canopy starts and ends later than the showers in nearby clearings, and falls as bigger drops. It is measurably less water than in the clearing; some water is absorbed by the canopy and the epiphytic plants on the trunk, re-evaporating eventually without ever reaching the ground. Light drizzle often fails to wet the forest floor at all. On the other hand, when fog sweeps the forest canopy, moisture condenses on foliage, and some drip to the ground as throughfall while a rain gauge in the open receives no precipitation. Since low vegetation can

---

Plate tectonics opened and closed seaways between oceans many times, turning currents on and off; it reconfigured the continents nearer the equator at times, nearer the poles at others; and it produced epochs of greater and lesser mountainousness. Great mountain ranges can reroute global air circulation, or deplete carbon dioxide by accelerating the weathering of rocks (a CO_2-removal mechanism that dwarfs plant photosynthesis). Any scenario could initiate a positive feedback loop via ice and snow reflecting solar radiation back out into space.

As for smaller nudges to make the glacial/interglacial difference, the mainstream hypothesis involves Milankovitch Cycles. The intensity of solar radiation hitting earth varies with at least five aspects of planetary motion (day/night, summer/winter, and three much slower ones). The cycles join forces at calculable intervals, reducing solar heating for long periods. Their compound cycle correlates fairly well with Pleistocene climates, but seems subject to other influences: salinity-based ocean circulation; CO_2 sequestration and release from peat, swamp, forests, etc; methane release from methane hydrates on the sea floor; volcanic dust; extraterrestrial dust from impacts or from belts that the earth may pass through; dust as a feedback loop from glaciation; and the sun's intensity, which varies in at least three cycles.

My guess is that evolution played a central role in the ancient glaciations, and plate tectonics brought on the Quaternary ones, in two steps. First, beginning 40 million years ago the Himalayas rose, depleting CO_2 through rock weathering, thus initiating a long gradual cooling trend. Then 3 or 4 million years ago the Milankovitch Cycle shifted when the redistribution of continents shifted earth's center of gravity slightly, setting the stage for the Quaternary.

At 14,000 years old, the current interglacial is neither warmer nor longer than previous ones of this Ice Age. Nothing in the geologic record leads us to doubt that another glacial stage will come. However, the next re- or deglaciation may be triggered by something new: human-caused excesses of greenhouse gases.

---

catch only a fraction of the the fog that a tall forest can, clearcutting a watershed near a divide can substantially curtail precipitation. Rain, fog throughfall, wind and sun all hit different parts of a tree differently, so that each tree offers several different microclimates.

Snowpack depth is reduced under forest cover. Though most snow that settles in the canopy does reach the forest floor, some of it melts first, and most of it, falling in big clumps, is much compacted on impact. Winter melting is greater in the forest, as the dark canopy absorbs solar radiation and reradiates some heat downward into the insulated forest microclimate. The bright white of snow-covered clearings reflects nearly all of the solar radiation that hits it, and doesn't heat up as much in the cold weather, but in the spring it warms up and melts sooner than snow in the forest. Trees that stand alone hasten snowmelt because, while their insulative value is negligible without a canopy, their heat-absorbing effect is maximized.

The canopy's effects on evaporation are harder to quantify. Gravelly, underdeveloped soil exacerbates understory drought in our mountains. Trees shade the forest floor from the drying sun, but they also suck huge volumes of water up through their roots and transpire it into the air, leaving soils parched. Trees hogging all the water (not the light) is the worst constraint on small plants underneath. Non-green plants deal with this by borrowing water back from the tree roots through fungal lifelines. (See page 188.)

Climate Warnings

The global climate system is unbelievably complex and mysterious, full of triggers, thresholds, and feedback loops. Public discourse gets confused, especially with the fossil fuels industry spending boatloads of cash promoting an illusion that scientists are so divided on global warming that nothing should be done yet. At the same time, scientifically outdated views sometimes crop up on the environmentalist side, as well. If you follow the literature (*Nature, Science*, and climatology journals), here's some of what you've been learning:

Climate fluctuates dramatically over time. (See page 36.)

Higher CO_2 levels and methane levels seem to correlate with warmer climates over geologic time, though it is not clear which is the cause and which the effect; both ways can be explained. These two principal "greenhouse gases," by trapping solar heat in the atmosphere, are responsible for keeping the biosphere warm enough to survive.

CO_2 levels have risen steadily for at least 100 years.

Human activities since the Industrial Revolution have released both CO_2 and methane in large quantities compared with post–Ice Age CO_2 or methane fluxes that we know about. However,

The earth has ways—which we don't understand well—of pumping CO_2 and methane in quantities that dwarf ours. Nor can we predict the effect of the expected increase in atmospheric water vapor. As vapor, it's the most powerful greenhouse gas of all, and heats us, but as low clouds it can reflect heat back into space and cool us. One prominent global-warming skeptic pins his hopes on low clouds.

Global average temperature has trended a bit hotter over 150 years.

It might well have trended hotter anyway, if we assume the Little Ice Age resembled other cycles in the past 10,000 years. Some studies conclude it could not have risen this much without human help. Others find that fluctuations in solar intensity could have produced this much rise all by itself. Many who study climate are puzzled over why the Earth has warmed so *little* over the past century.

Snow and ice trends are poorly known. The Antarctic Peninsula has warmed and lost ice while the vast larger area of central Antarctica has cooled and gained ice. Sea levels have been rising slightly because the sea water is expanding as it warms, not because of ice trends. On the other hand, Ice Age fluctuations did change sea levels by hundreds of feet, and if Antarctica's ice were to melt it would certainly drown the present habitat of hundreds of millions of humans.

Abrupt switching between glacially cold and interglacially mild phases lasting from 1,000 to 100,000 years has been the pattern for 2½ million years. We don't know what triggers these shifts. They are stunningly fast, taking only a decade or two. A changing climate is more likely to "flicker" hot-and-cold, wet-and-drought, than to warm smoothly. Agriculture might plausibly benefit from gradual, predictable warming, but it could not adapt fast enough to feed seven billion people through the course of a flickering climate. (Politicians will be begging climatologists to promise them that this year's 82% crop failure won't happen again next year or the next…)

"Severe" climate phases of a few years or decades were far less apparent during the last 200 years than during the preceding (post–Ice Age) 10,000 years, when they caused several civilizations to collapse and major cities to be abandoned. We've been enjoying a lucky break all our lives, in terms of decade-scale drought and temperature anomalies, and possibly also in terms of "extreme weather events" like hurricanes, heat waves, and cold snaps. All these things are affected by cycles like the El Niño Southern Oscillation. Scientists are only beginning to understand these cycles, which are likely to couple with other climate mechanisms, and come up with big surprises.

Humans carried on, even progressed, during the last Ice Age, but in tiny numbers compared to today's world. Probably there were local and even global human die-offs from time to time.

Nature is resilient over the long run. Ecological communities generally thrived in ice-free areas within a few centuries after abrupt climate shifts—not the same communities as before, of course. One hundred thousand years from now there will be a diverse biosphere; there may not be humans. Nature bats last.

Ecosystem/Climate Feedback

Global-warming optimists like to point to a benign feedback loop: an atmosphere richer in carbon dioxide should accelerate photosynthesis in plants, which should dampen greenhouse changes by consuming carbon dioxide and producing oxygen.

A study trying to spot a trend in tree growth rates in our region does find an overall increase since 1850, strongest in boreal and high-elevation trees, the ones limited by cold weather—suggesting that the cause was warming more than CO_2 itself. Most trees are more limited by water, nitrogen, or other factors than by CO_2, and that limits the benefits of CO_2 enrichment.

But what about the principal that trees can save us by sopping up CO_2? Any effect is short-term unless they can put it somewhere where it will stay for a long time. This is rarely the case.

In any year, plants consume twenty times as much CO_2 as fossil fuels release. They immediately release about half of that CO_2, leaving the other half tied up as biomass. The biomass half will also be released if it burns or decomposes. Carbon tied up in biomass is "sequestered," or in a "sink," in the new language of global carbon politics. Truly long-term sequestration only happens, though, when biogenic carbon gets carried out to the anaerobic bottom of the sea and buried deep in sediment layers—like the shallow Paleozoic seas that produced today's fossil fuels. Coal is the fossil carbon that usually comes to mind, but limestone and dolomite are a much bigger factor.

Northern bogs are among the longest-term CO_2 "sinks" we have today. Their acidity, coldness, and lack of oxygen strongly inhibits bacterial decomposition. Conversely, as they get warmer, bogs and permafrost areas will decompose and release tons of methane and

CO_2, probably worsening the problem far more than they help. Colder forests (i.e., northern or montane ones) are somewhat longer-term sinks than warmer ones, because cool soil temperatures slow down decomposing bacteria and fungi. But that still isn't a long enough term to save us, and will be negated or worse if those forests burn up more often, as predicted, in the warmer world.

Industry-backed voices tell us that cutting "stagnant" old forests and replacing them with "vigorous" 50-year rotations will help "sink" CO_2. They need to do the math. Scientists who did the math came to the opposite conclusion—but either way it's a short-term effect. Every sort of "sinks" approach is not only short-term but fraught with unintended consequences. For example, increasing northern forest cover might warm the earth through the black body effect—dark trees absorbing heat instead of bright snow bouncing it back to space. Increasing vegetation anywhere could tend to calm surface winds, reducing the transfer of mineral dust to the oceans, reducing populations of marine photosynthesizers which are a huge "sink."

Science just doesn't know whether any region can achieve net CO_2 removal by planting trees. The only serious way to way to reduce our effect on the global greenhouse is to drastically reduce emissions, largely by converting from fuels to clean energy sources, and by using far less energy overall. (Hydrogen, by the way, is not a clean energy source, it's just a way of moving and storing energy, so it's only as clean as the actual energy source that produced it.)

On the other hand, forest health in a warming climate may be a good reason for intensified forest management, but only if it's guided with plenty of scientific study, care, and political objectivity. Overly dense tinderbox forests may need to be logged, replanted with a mix of species suited to a range of hotter climates, and then kept thin with prescribed fire and occasional selective cutting. Fire must remain part of the equation, since most western North American ecosystems evolved with fire. Many bird species, for example, require large burnt snags, so logging plans may need to leave some patches uncut, to be torched for burnt snag habitat. At the same time, our high-quality mature forests are already few and far between, and will inexorably shrink further due to fire. Over the short term they need to be maintained (using light undertory fires, but not cutting) as "libraries" of species that may prove useful in a changing world.

Ecosystem health has to be the overriding rule in managing the public lands. That's the most effective way to preserve both a timber resource and a natural ecology in the Rocky Mountains.

The Future Rockies

How will the Rockies change as the globe warms? Most computer models that try to predict climate under increasing greenhouse conditions expect increased precipitation across the whole region, especially in winter—more than enough to compensate for the higher evaporation rates due to heat, and the reduced capacity of an earlier-melting snowpack to store water for the growing season. That would enable conifer forests to expand into many areas that are now dry steppe. A moister climate could even allow some species to expand their range southward; for example, western larch, western hemlock, and redcedar could thrive in northwest Wyoming in a climate hotter and moister than today's. Ranges of ponderosa and whitebark pines are predicted to shrink, and of lodgepole pine to expand.

Predictions of a greener West hold only up to a point: 5° (3° C) of global warming may well green the West up, but if warming continues well beyond that, our region might look more like Arizona—including, like today's Arizona, some green forests at the highest elevations, which then turn into ecological islands; e.g., their small-mammal populations are cut off from most of their conspecifics, so they become prone to inbreeding and local extirpation, and if they survive they become distinct genetic lines.

Increased forested area and density together with heat would almost certainly lead to considerably more fire. Invasive species could benefit from the fires opening up lots of new territory, as well as from human-caused enrichment of both CO_2 and nitrates. We may see great damage from insect infestations and consequent further increases in fire. (Some of our most destructive pests were held in check, in the twentieth century, by average-and-colder winters.) On the other hand, some studies suggest that heat stress and CO_2 enrichment induce our conifers to produce more of the terpenes that help protect them from being eaten.

With or without anthropogenic warming we can expect our glaciers to continue wasting away, especially in the U.S. Rockies, which are on track to lose them altogether around mid-century.

I am concerned that lush subalpine flower meadows may become scarce. Places that have them now could turn to forest, but the places that will have the right temperature and moisture regimes in the future consist largely of rocks and ice today, and would need several centuries for soil to develop before they could support lily swards.

3
Conifers

From Fire Born

Rocky Mountain forests are fire forests. The oldest trees in nearly every forest stand sprouted on ground cleared by fire. Typical forest history analyses find, in Alberta, "that most stands have a less than two percent chance of surviving to 300 years of age"; or, in Idaho, that "fire in these ecosystems is practically a certainty within 400 to 500 years, but natural fire-free intervals are considerably shorter."

Having fire as the main natural disturbance is far from universal among forests. In eastern North America's deciduous forests, for example, trees are felled mainly by wind. Fire is a minor factor there because lightning is typically accompanied by heavy rain, and because there's usually enough summer rainfall to keep forests moist through the hot part of the year. Native Americans used fire to maintain prairies, but these fires rarely took off and burned wild through the forest. But as for wind, any given Eastern spot is likely to see either a hurricane or a tornado at least once every 500 years.

The Rockies, in contrast, have no hurricanes, few tornadoes, and countless lightning strikes in summer, most of them followed by little or no rain. Fires set by Native Americans affected Montana's Rocky Mountain Front, which gets relatively little lightning, but all of the forests west of the Continental Divide probably always had enough lightning fires—with or without additional anthropogenic fires—to account for virtually all of the fire adaptations we see.

In southerly areas where the precipitation peaks in May and June, summers are nevertheless plenty hot and dry for a fierce fire. Northwesterly areas get more precipitation overall, but mainly in winter; you can pretty much count on those forests getting bone-dry by September in at least one summer out of every ten, which is enough. And you can count on a few dry lightning storms. Northern Idaho, the wettest U.S. part of our range, has actually burned the most; not only does it get a lot of lightning, but the greater overall moisture produces denser vegetation, which fuels hotter fires.

In such a fire-ruled ecosystem, one of the most crucial characteristics of nearly every tree species is its fire strategy. This chapter begins with the pines and larches, which have the most remarkable and varied fire strategies, from the fireproof bark of larch and ponderosa monarchs to the uncanny reseeding methods of lodgepole and whitebark pines. Western larch, ponderosa pine, and some whitebark pine communities are adapted to short cycles of frequent, low-intensity fires confined mostly to the understory, or even to the duff layer. Individual trees may survive for three to ten centuries, their lower trunks bearing many scars as a fire history we can read in the tree rings. In contrast, when fire hits communities of lodgepole pine, subalpine fir, and spruces, it tends to climb easily into the low branches, and to kill most or all of the trees—a "stand-replacing" fire. In some areas (such as the Kananaskis spruce-pine forests in the quotation on the previous page) the pattern seems to be forests of trees all the same age. All of them sprouted within a few years after the last fire, and seem destined to be replaced all at once.

By far the most common pattern is a patchy mosaic of stands with varying age structures. This can result from a long history of small patch fires, or from a single big fire that burned patchily, jumping around, replacing some stands, leaving others with intact canopies while burning their herb layers, in others sparing maybe half or a tenth of the trees, and leaving still others untouched. The Yellowstone fires of 1988 produced a perfect example of such a mosaic.

As the plant community redevelops after a fire, we see patterns of some species replacing others. Most pioneer plants either sprout from roots or charred stumps (even after a stand-replacing fire) or grow from seeds adapted to withstand heat or to get transported abundantly. Their seedlings are quick to tap water, nutrients and light. Their shade and transpiration make new microclimates. Their roots, in symbiosis with fungi and bacteria, work over the soil physically and chemically, depleting some nutrients and accumulating others. Many pioneers are fast-growing annuals that donate their entire corpses to the humus fund in the fall; perennials and shrubs contribute leaves. The seeds of more diverse and subtle competitors, trickling in on wind and fur and feces, soon find the environment more congenial than it was at first.

These patterns of change are called "succession." (See sidebar, next page.) In Rocky Mountain fire forests, succession of herb and shrub species in the first years after a fire is clear, but succession of tree species may be obscure. Where the stand-replacing pattern prevails, there is no succession of tree species, i.e., the dominants remain the same indefinitely, through fire after fire. Classical succession theory defined fire and other disturbances as aberrations from succession (which was supposed to be a path toward a "climax" community) but the current view is that more or less constant disturbance on one scale or another is the norm. "Fire guru" Stephen Pyne goes even further: "The norm is the human use of fire everywhere and for every conceivable purpose. Both natural fire and suppression are anomalies because they propose alternatives to anthropogenic fire."

We can divide Rocky Mountain history into four fire regimes: Native American fire management; the Euroamerican settlement era; Smokey Bear; and the Renaissance getting underway today.

Natives set fires for many reasons: to improve visibility for hunting; to foster growth of browse for game; to drive game during a hunt or enemies during war; to maintain huckleberry patches in subalpine areas; to send signals; to clear a defensive line of sight around a village; and so on.

White settlers came up with a few more: miners wanted to see the rocks, stockmen wanted more grass. The settlement era was the most fire-ridden of the four regimes. A possible factor was a natural global warming in the 19th century, ending the Little Ice Age. Most analyses conclude that the region also had a lot of fire 9,000 to 5,000 years ago, when the earth was several degrees warmer than now.

In the 19th Century the conventional wisdom in the West held that fire (especially "light burning" of the herb and shrub layers) was beneficial. By 1900, the newly founded Forest Service challenged that wisdom with a new view developed by European foresters favoring fire suppression as "modern" and "scientific" while mocking traditional burning as "Paiute forestry." Gifford Pinchot, the first head of the Service, saw incineration of marketable wood as a terrible waste which it was his agency's job to prevent; he didn't foresee the myriad unintended consequences of fire suppression. He tried to advance his cause by smearing his chief opponent, the Interior Secretary. President Taft responded by firing Pinchot in January of 1910. That summer, northern Idaho erupted in megaconflagrations. (1910 is still the record year for human deaths in North American forest fires.) The pro-fire faction felt that the fires won the argument for them: the Forest Service couldn't put the fires out. But the Forest Service went after public opinion, spinning the fires as a horrific tragedy which simply must not be allowed to recur, no matter the cost.

Congress joined the fray. Within a year the Interior Secretary resigned, and pro-fire voices went almost unheard for several decades. Anti-fire P.R. was stepped up, culminating in 1942 with the great masterpiece of anti–forest fire propaganda, *Bambi*. The cute

---

Succession vs. Chaos

In the forest you can see a "succession" of gradual changes—different plants increasing or decreasing in number, stature, and health or vigor. Succession used to be described as a linear series with a stable end-state called a climax community; the series would reach climax if it wasn't interrupted by a "disturbance" such as a forest fire, flood, blowdown, landslide, avalanche, or logging. Today, many ecologists avoid the term "climax" (or use oxymorons like "fire climax" and "disease climax") because they see disturbance as the norm, not the aberration. They like the word "stochastic," meaning random. Instead of a linear series we have a chaos of feedback loops and chance events. For example:

Fire-adapted ponderosa pine stands maintain their normal healthy state with the help of frequent low-intensity fires.

Fungal (rot) diseases create canopy gaps by continually killing some dominant trees. Even a hemlock will slow to negligible growth under a closed canopy, and will reach canopy stature only if a gap opens for it to grow into. Most windthrown trees here are victims of rot fungi.

One root rot fungus species lives and expands for well over 1000 years, very slowly killing most trees (some kinds more than others) within its perimeter. The resulting patches have sparser canopies and richer understories and wildlife populations. See page 299.

Mycorrhizal fungi transfer photosynthetic products from big trees that produce them to little seedlings that need them. This subsidy helps determine which seedlings survive long enough to take advantage of a gap and become independent. See page 000.

Plants alter the soil to stabilize their own positions. Though hard to see and poorly studied, the changes are profound. They involve soil texture;

---

fawn gained an ally in 1944: a shovel-wielding bear named Smokey.

At both the beginning and the end of the Smokey Bear period, effectiveness lagged several decades behind consciousness. From 1910 to 1945, U.S. policy was to put out all fires, but the ability to do so suffered from a lack of roads, funds, and technology. Efficacy improved in the 1930s, and more after 1945: with a plethora of parachutes, planes, choppers, funds, and fire retardant, fires were put out pretty quickly. Fire suppression in Canada followed a similar arc.

Here, in sum, is what Smokey's management style led to:

increased density, especially in ponderosa pine communities that would otherwise be thinned by frequent low fires, and in "doghair" (super-dense) lodgepole stands that fire would normally remove;

acidity; beneficial mites and protozoans; beneficial fungi; antagonistic fungi; and "allelopathic" toxic chemicals produced by plants.

Low plants can take over and prevent tree growth indefinitely. In our area, semipermanent brushfields can take over after repeated burns. Even bracken fern can take over and perpetuate itself in a patch; and western yew can take over valley bottoms as long as fire is kept away. Peat moss takes over by altering the water chemistry in saturated soils: many boreal forests tend to be replaced by acidic treeless muskeg except to the extent that tree seedlings germinate on mineral soil raised up on the roots of windthrown trees; killing trees, paradoxically, is the only way to maintain forest there. Chance variables determine these events.

Plants alter climate. Lichen-draped trees can double local precipitation, especially near high ridgelines, by intercepting cloud droplets. Plants increase regional rainfall through transpiration, recycling it back to the clouds. An extreme case is the Amazon rain forest, which is thought to double the rainfall in its entire basin.

Climate is always changing. It can oscillate from year to year (the El Niño/La Niña cycle); it can slide over a 50-year period or flipflop drastically in the space of a decade. Changes can be regional or global, natural or human-caused (pp 36–42).

Browsers, grazers, and their predators alter vegetation. Wilderness cannot remain untouched when the big predators are removed and the browser populations, seeking a new level, become more chaotic.

Feedback loops tend to involve at least three species, often from three kingdoms. Trying to study a relationship between just two species may yield an incomplete or distorted picture. Understanding ecology requires understanding whole systems.

decreased streamflow because thicker forests consume more water;

species shifts—a decrease in fire-adapted pines and larch, an increase in shade-tolerant grand fir, subalpine fir, Douglas-fir, and spruce, and net increases in noxious invasive weeds;

increases in diseases and pests, notably spruce budworm and pine beetles, which prefer denser, slower-growing forests; root and stem rots, which afflict grand fir and Douglas-fir; and dwarf mistletoe, whose slow advance across the land is broken up by each crown fire;

decreases in wildlife diversity;

decreases in soil fertility. At least in the Rockies, more frequent, smaller fires do the best job of recycling nutrients and creating the openings needed by nitrogen-fixing symbiotic plants;

worse fires, and less ability to control them. A run of especially fierce fire years has driven home the fact that fires will get out of control sooner or later, and they're going to be much hotter and harder to contain in denser forests and forests half-killed by disease. For many people looking at fire policy, that's the bottom line: continued fire exclusion is not the no-fire path, it's the path to bigger and worse fires, with likely greater losses of human life and property.

Belief in fire stayed alive in a few iconoclasts, like Adolph Murie and Harold Weaver, and prevailed again in scientific circles by the 1970s. The 1963 Leopold Report was a turning point. But the public, the politicians, and parts of the timber industry are slow to join in. Techniques, funding, and public tolerance for prescribed burning present ongoing challenges, made all the more difficult by anthropogenic change, including invasive species, CO_2 and nitrogen enrichment, and global warming. It will be, at best, many decades before much of the West's forest again approximates its natural fire-adapted structure. And it won't happen unless politicians accept the fact that it often takes more money than it makes: the trees that need to be removed are mostly the small ones, for which there is little market. Just turning loggers loose won't restore fire-adapted forests.

Even forest plans that mix beneficial thinning with prescribed low-intensity fires can restore only ponderosa pine–larch forests. The historical fire regime of our spruce-fir forests is one of occasional stand-replacing fires, and that's what some of our wildlife require.

In western North America, conifers dominate.

A predominance of conifers is the exception in the temperate zone, but the norm in boreal (far northern) forests. Since high elevations have cold climates, montane habitat zones parallel boreal and arctic ones. For that matter, many forests in our region *were* boreal forests during the Ice Ages, leaving conifer seeds much more available than broadleaf tree seeds when the ice retreated. That may have been a major factor, but the explanation is hard to pin down. Certainly present-day coldness cannot account for conifer dominance here. Pacific coastal forests have a mild, benign climate, and conifers dominate at least as much there, probably due in part to that region's wet winters and dry summers. Once summer gets really dry, leaf pores almost close up to conserve water, and that shuts down photosynthesis; dry summers confer an advantage on evergreens, which can accomplish some photosynthesis whenever relatively mild days come along in late fall through early spring. The wet-winter marine influence penetrates much of our region, and where it does so most (BC and northern Idaho), the evergreen advantage is at work.

"Conifer" is a common name for trees and shrubs comprising Phylum Coniferophyta. Many conifers, including all of those in the largest family , the Pines (pages 50–77), bear needlelike leaves and woody "cones." The Yew family (page 78) has needles but bears seeds singly, in juicy, berrylike orbs. The Cypress family (page 79) has cones (except for junipers, with dryish, several-seeded "berries"), and either short sharp needles or, more often, sprays of crowded scalelike leaves. The four other conifer families are not native here.

Several popular terms for plant groups are easily confused. Conifers are "seed plants" (as opposed to spore plants), but they are not "flowering plants" even though a young cone is very much a female flower counterpart, being fertilized by pollen from less conspicuous male "staminate cones" and then producing seeds. Flowering trees and shrubs are "broadleaf" even though a few, like heather, have needle-thin leaves while some conifers, like the bunya-bunya, have rather broad ones. To a forester or a lumberman, conifers are "softwoods"—even those few that are very hard, like yew. "Evergreen" and its opposite, "deciduous," refer to whether the foliage remains alive through more than one growing season. They are not synonymous with conifer and broadleaf, as there are several deciduous conifers, like larch, and a great many broadleaf evergreens.

The needles are bunched differently in these two genera:

Pines bear long evergreen needles in fascicles (bundles) bound together at the base by tiny membranous bracts. The number of needles per bundle is the easiest step in pine i.d.: check several bundles. Five-needle pines (pages 54–59) are loosely termed "white pines" and three-needle pines (page 52) "yellow pines." The East has many two-needled "red pines," but I've never heard our lodgepole called red. Singleleaf pinyon pine, in the SW, has bracted one-needle fascicles.

Larches bear soft deciduous needles, mostly in bunches of 15 to 40 needles from peglike spur twigs about ¼" by ¼" [6 mm].

Lodgepole Pine

Pinus contorta. Needles in twos, 1½–2½" [4–6 cm] long, yellow-green; cones 1½–2" long [4–5 cm], egg-shaped, point of attachment usually quite off-center, scales sharp-tipped; cones abundant, long-persistent on the branch, either closed or open; bark thin (less than 1", or 25 mm), reddish brown to gray, scaly. Almost ubiquitous. Pinaceae. Color p 83.

Lodgepole pines are tricksters on the ecological playing field. They don't bother to compete with our other conifers in size, longevity, shade tolerance, or fire resistance. They excel instead at rapid growth early in life, copiously produced and cleverly designed cones, and tolerance of any kind of soil. Prolific to a fault, they produce both pollen and seeds prodigiously year after year (a rarity among conifers). Their pollen drifts like an amber fog over midsummer's meadows. Lodgepoles release seeds at all times of year; they bear cones at 5 to 20 years of age, younger than other conifers; and their seedlings and saplings grow fastest.

They may get even more competitive as atmospheric carbon dioxide increases. Outdoor experiments with increased CO_2 in North Carolina found that the fastest-growing pine species grew even faster and began producing cones at even younger ages. Lodgepoles hold promise for northward afforestation as climate warms, but they might need to be planted. If the Yukon warms as rapidly as predicted, it would need lodgepoles genetically adapted to southern, not northern, B.C., and they cannot migrate very fast on their own.

Lodgepoles unleash their signature punch after a fire: some of the cones on many lodgepole pines are sealed shut by a resin with a melting point of 113° [41° C.]. The seeds inside, viable for decades, are protected through all but the hottest crown fires by the closed cone. Fire kills the pines but melts the cone-sealing resin; afterward, the cone scales open slowly, shedding seeds on a wide-open field. Lodgepoles produce both "serotinous" cones of this type and non-serotinous cones that open and release seeds as they mature, in proportions varying by region and by age: serotiny is common only after age thirty. Complete nonserotiny is common where poor conditions discourage other trees so well that lodgepole dominance can persist without fire: e.g., parts of the Idaho Batholith where the soil is a coarse granite sand that scarcely retains water.

Breeding like rabbits leads to overpopulation—a "doghair" stand with stems mere inches apart, not only crowding out all other species but severely stunting their own growth. The speed demon slows to a near halt, like the rabbit that lost the race with the tortoise. This looks dismal to foresters and hikers, but isn't so bad in terms of species survival. In nature, these stagnant stands typically persist until fire comes and resets the stage, favoring lodgepole all over again.

Lodgepole pine is the commonest tree in the Rockies from Colorado north. Forests at elevations described as the Spruce/Fir and Douglas-fir Zones are largely dominated in fact by lodgepole pine. It can grow anywhere from lower to upper timberline, but is rarely seen as alpine krummholz. Lodgepole doesn't have a zone named after it because, being intolerant of shade, it is predicted to be replaced in succession by other conifers *if no fire burns the site.*

On the Rocky Mountain Front in Alberta and Montana, where Chinooks blow, lodgepoles are susceptible to "red belt." (Page 21.)

The inner bark layer, or cambium, was an important food for Rocky Mountain tribes. Too thin and dry to eat in winter, it plumps up in May and June when sap flows and pollen flies. Sweet and moist as well as nutritious, it was a treat at that time of year when fresh berries were only a memory and any dried salmon still left was pretty putrid. Though best fresh, cambium could also be dried and stored. Women stripped the bark, using bear shoulderblade, deer ulna, or juniper branch, and then removed the cambium (from either the wood or the bark, depending on season) with a scraper made from another bone or from sheep horn. To avoid killing the tree, they scraped a large patch from just one side. Ponderosa pine, western larch, and western hemlock all provided good cambium, but the abundant lodgepole was most important. As its name records, it was the usual material for teepee and lodge frames.

Ponderosa Pine

Pinus ponderosa (**pie**-nus: Roman word for pine; ponder-**oh**-sa: massive). Also **western yellow pine**. Needles 4–10" [10–25 cm], in bunches of 3 (or of both 3 and 2 in the dwarfed "RM form" in c MT), yellowish green, clustered near branch tips; cones 3–5" × 2–3" [8–13 × 5–8 cm], closed and reddish until late in their second year, scales tipped with stout recurved barbs; young bark very dark brown, soon furrowing, maturing yellowish to light reddish brown and very thick, breaking up into plates and scales shaped like jigsaw puzzle pieces. Dry low elevs. Pinaceae. Color page 83.

Much of ponderosa pines' charm is in the parklike grassy spacing they maintain over the centuries. It evokes the spirit of the cowboy West. It makes you want a horse. That spacing, and the prevalence of the pines and the grass underneath, result from ground fires made frequent by the tree's copious production of long-needled duff. Mature ponderosas are very fire-resistant thanks to high crowns and thick bark; if ignited, the outer bark pops off, landing several feet away. If burnt through in a spot, it plugs the hole with thick resin. But ponderosa saplings are vulnerable. The sapling that stands a good chance of surviving fires to reach fireproof size is the one growing well apart from the two things that could bring fire to it—other saplings, or the thick duff under big ponderosas. Hence the parklike spacing.

As long as the stand is widely spaced, shade tolerance is not an issue, but where fire exclusion and adequate moisture allow, new saplings coming up are mostly Douglas-fir and grand fir, which are less fire-resistant but more shade-tolerant. They are also inferior lumber species in the Rockies, being far more prone to fungal diseases and mistletoe. After years of fire suppression, smaller trees and brush grow into "ladder fuels" that can ignite the tallest pine crowns. At that point light fires become impossible and stand-replacing fires inevitable, without intervention. The forest needs to be thinned a lot, and then maintained with prescribed ground fires.

Stephen Arno and other forest ecologists make a strong case for the ecological benefits of intensively managing nearly all of the West's ponderosa habitat, using both fire and selective commercial logging. It appears impossible to get back the proper parklike structure without intensive management; and increasing production here could spare even-more-irreplaceable tropical forests in the near term, given that we've failed, so far, to curtail demand for wood and paper.

While firs can, in the absence of fire, crowd ponderosas out from much of their range, there is a narrow ponderosas-only belt near lower timberline where no other large tree survives. (Small ones—junipers or mountain-mahogany—may grow there or a bit lower.) The rule of thumb is that ponderosas need 12 inches [30 cm] of annual precipitation, but one stand in central Oregon lives on 8.7" [22.3 cm]—the driest climate supporting forest anywhere in the U.S. West. This stand neatly fills a patch of sandy soil, which permits easier, deeper rooting than the surrounding clayey soil, and absorbs more water. Ecologists have long puzzled over the failure of ponderosa pine to invade the Great Plains, most of which do get the requisite 12".

Our region has a puzzling ponderosa gap between Idaho's Sawtooths and the east foot of the Beartooths, Elkhorns, and Crazies. All those ranges (and others to the east) have ponderosa pine, but within the gap limber pine takes its place at lower timberline. The explanation may involve climate: "undependable springs, or the possibility of frost at any month of the year" are implicated by Eversmann and Carr. Or it may be a relict of conditions that no longer exist.

In mountains immediately downwind of Los Angeles, ponderosa pine is damaged more than other species by ozone pollution (e.g., automobile smog). On the other hand, some models predict it will benefit from the expected increases in CO_2 and temperature within its range, in a way that could counteract the ozone damage. But regional warming scenarios are highly speculative. Time will tell.

Though young ponderosas have made a lot of knotty pine paneling, mature wood is versatile. It's nicely two-toned, with pale yellow to orange-brown heartwood and broad creamy sapwood. Production peaked when there was a lot of old-growth being liquidated.

Commercial pine "nuts" come from piñon and Eurasian stone pines. Other pines' seeds are also delicious and prized by birds and rodents, who bury countless seeds in small caches, intending to come back for them some day but inevitably overlooking some caches, which then germinate. Ponderosa cones have spines to discourage seed eating, or more likely to discriminate among seed-eating species, since pines benefit when animals gather seeds. Animals plant seeds where wind might never carry them, and plant them deeper, in mineral soil often in litter-free spots, sparing seedlings from drought and saplings from ground fire. When you see a clump of pine seedlings within a square half-inch or so, it's a forgotten cache.

Conifers: needles three per bunch

Whitebark Pine

Pinus albicaulis (al-bic-**aw**-lis: white bark). Needles in 5s, 1⅝–3" long [4–7 cm], yellow-green, in tufts at branch tips; cones 1¾–3" [4–8 cm] long, egg-shaped, purplish, dense, long persistent on the tree, rarely if ever opening (except when forced open; see text); cone scales thicken toward tip; staminate cones red; bark thin, scaly, superficially whitish or grayish. Alp/subalpine. Pinaceae. Color p 83.

With their broad crowns and tufted, paler foliage, whitebark pines are easy to tell from the other high-country conifers.

They're easy to tell even in death. If you find yourself in a sub-alpine forest with large, bleached, forked and crooked dead tree trunks towering over young spruces and firs, that was once a fine whitebark pine grove. We're in the midst of a catastrophic decline of whitebark and limber pines throughout most of our region. It seems to be caused by both introduced blister rust disease (page 59) and the ramifications of fire suppression; fire tends to control the pines' worst enemies and competitors. The worst native enemies are dwarf mistletoe and bark beetles. Fire suppression allows overly dense stands of lodgepole pine to stagnate; these attract epidemics of bark beetles, which head upslope looking for other pines after they over-populate their lodgepole resource. They prefer bigger whitebarks, with bark thick enough to protect and nourish their larvae. Most "ghost forests" of whitebark pine were killed by blister rust, but in the area from the Sawtooths to the Bitterroots (which may be too dry for blister rust) bark beetles are the culprits.

While studying whitebark mortality in the Salmon River area, Dana Perkins found some magnificent survivors. The oldest is 1270 years old—placing whitebark pine eleventh on the longest-lived tree species list—and the biggest is 8¾ feet in diameter [2.6 m]. Fires ini-tiated fine stands of large whitebarks in Montana's Mission and Whitefish Ranges, but blister rust killed most of those.

Growth form varies with elevation. In the alpine zone whitebark pine grows as krumm-holz (dense prostrate shrubs). It's a major component of krummholz patches espe-cially in the Wind River, Wyoming, and Salt River Ranges. At its lowest eleva-tions it may grow straight and single-stemmed, resembling lodgepole pine.

Whitebark pines are shade-intolerant and fairly fire-resistant, especially on high sites where they are widely spaced and the undergrowth is low. Fire suppression has tipped the scales in favor of the competition—spruce and fir—and the pine's enemies have piled on, greatly accelerating the decline. Once pines are gone from a stand, even blister rust–tolerant ones won't be able to retake much lost ground until a fire takes out the forest. Pines have failed to return to much of the great 1910 burn in northern Idaho, possibly because blister rust was already making pine nuts scarce in that area.

Normally, whitebark pines reseed into large burns much faster than other trees, because whitebark pine nuts travel on adopted wings. Their own undersized wings remain stuck to the cone scales while the cones remain stuck to the branch. Fat, heavy and wingless, the seeds wouldn't go far in the wind even if the cone did open, but they fly as far as fourteen miles in the beaks of Clark's nutcrackers. Whitebark pine seedlings grow from caches buried and then forgotten by these birds, who prefer to cache seeds in bare or burned areas, enabling whitebarks to broadly recolonize large burns where wind-disseminated trees can only crawl back, generation by generation, from the green periphery.

Nutcrackers cache up to 15 pine nuts together. Several may germinate and grow as a clump. Diana Tomback investigated whether the multistemmed form typical of whitebarks is genetic or a result of clumped seedlings fusing as they grow up. The answer: both, in roughly equal numbers. You can't tell fusers from clones visually.

In another study, she found that patches of whitebark krummholz destroyed by a fire were replanted by nutcrackers within a few years. Krummholz whitebarks don't produce cones (they're too stressed) so there would be no other way for the species to get established on sites where it can't grow erect.

Many characteristics of whitebarks and their Eurasian relatives apparently co-evolved with nutcrackers and *their* relatives, having no obvious adaptive value other than to accommodate these birds. Cones are borne on vertical branches near the top of the tree, making them easy for birds to see and work on. Nutcrackers

---

came to North America from Asia only two million years ago, likely bringing whitebark pine's ancestors with them.

They may even help save the species from blister rust. The fungus kills trees from the top down, eliminating cone and seed production early. In heavily infected stands, nutcrackers are thus forced to find the small percentage of whitebarks with rust-resistant genes. Unfortunately, these desperately hungry nutcrackers will most likely eat a much higher proportion of seeds they collect than normally, but those that they do plant will be selected for resistant genes. We have to hope there are still enough nutcrackers around to take care of the replanting when fires, sooner or later, provide the seedbeds.

Timberlines

"Timberline" is actually a belt encompassing three successive lines:

Tree line is the upper boundary of erect tree growth.

Scrub line is higher; it's the upper boundary of conifer species growing in the low shrubby form called krummholz ("crookedwood").

Forest line separates continuous closed forest growth from the belt of interspersed tree clumps and subalpine meadows. In the Rockies it isn't a very clear concept since, in all but the wettest parts of our range, meadows or steppe enclosed by forest are common at all elevations due to dry exposures, fire history, soil characteristics, etc.

We also have **lower timberlines** below which forest gives way to steppe.

The "alpine zone" is everything above tree line. The "subalpine parkland" is the grove-and-meadow mosaic between forest line and tree line. (The term "subalpine forest" is sometimes applied to the entire belt of spruce/fir forests. There is no really clear or agreed-upon distinction between "montane" and "subalpine forests," so I just think of the broad elevational belt that tends to be forested and to have spruces, subalpine firs, and Douglas-firs as "mid-elevation.")

Each of the lines gets lower northward. Tree line is at roughly 10,000' [3150 m] in the Wind Rivers, 6,000' [1800 m] in Jasper National Park. Heavy snows push forest line down to 5,500' [1650 m] in parts of Glacier National Park—level with many lower timberlines elsewhere in Montana.

Length of the snow-free season is the chief determinant of our upper timberlines. Needles need enough time to grow and then harden to protect themselves against freezing. Once hardened, they can easily take most winter temperatures here.

Needles are also killed by desiccation where they are exposed to

Though long overlooked by forest researchers because of their low commercial value, whitebarks are extraordinarily valuable to wildlife. Grouse find their dense crowns cozy in winter. Red squirrels and both black and grizzly bears eat tons of pine nuts. Bears get them by robbing squirrel middens. Blister rust became widespread in the Yellowstone ecosystem only in the 1990s, but it's already seen as a serious threat to grizzly bear recovery there.

strong warm winds of early spring while the roots are still frozen and unable to replace moisture lost from the needles. They are safe from the wind within snowpack where it reliably persists through winter. Such snow can occur above tree line wherever landforms keep it from blowing away, but is rarely more than three feet deep. That's why we have krummholz. (See page 68.)

Lower timberlines are a function mainly of soil moisture and fire history. Precipitation varies greatly from one range to the next: the Lemhi Range is so dry that lower and upper timberlines are only about 2000' apart in elevation. Timber grows lower on north slopes, where the drying sun is effectively diluted. Airflow patterns within narrow valleys, including temperature inversions, also have strong effects.

Timberline succession moves horizontally—in space—as well as in time. Once a conifer gets established in the open, it's easier for others to get their start right next to it, for two reasons. First, many are adept at "layering," or growing a new stem where branches in contact with earth take root; the parent limb feeds the new shoot intravenously, a big advantage over growing from seed. Second, snow accumulates in a wind-protected pocket on the lee side of existing plants, protecting new starts from desiccation. As a result, trees and krummholz often grow in tight clumps, slowly elongating to leeward. Sometimes the pioneer trees in the center die and nothing but shrubs manage to grow there, leaving a hollow tree clump or "timber atoll."

Timberline is a visible dynamic equilibrium, responding sweepingly to climatic changes—but so slowly that climate may be swinging the other way by the time tree succession gets into gear. Timberline soils and communities today are still recovering from the Ice Age. Nevertheless, charcoal in meadow soil profiles reveals that many meadow areas below tree line have grown trees at least once since the Ice Age; forest is the potential vegetation for most of the subalpine zone.

Limber Pine

Pinus flexilis (flex-il-iss: flexible). Needles in fives, 1½–3" long [4–7 cm], yellow-green, in tufts at branch tips; cones 2–6" long [5–15 cm], egg-shaped, falling from the tree whole and remaining whole while decaying; cones scales thin toward the tip; staminate cones red; young bark thin, scaly, grayish, eventually darkening; ± crooked trees 12–50' tall [4–15 m]. Various dry rocky sites. Pinaceae.

Limber pine closely resembles whitebark pine; the only giveaways are low elevation or, at high ones, much larger cones which do open at maturity, unlike whitebark. South of whitebark's range, limber pine substitutes for it at timberline, playing most ecological roles that whitebark does here, including the mutualistic relationship with Clark's nutcrackers. (See p 446). But that's outside of our range. Here, limber pine often acts like a *lower* timberline surrogate for ponderosa pine, in areas where ponderosa is mysteriously missing. That would be our part of Wyoming, the eastern half of Idaho, southwest Montana, and along the Rocky Mountain Front north of Great Falls, where limber pines grow smaller and smaller and shrubbier and gnarlier eastward—a forest edge feathered out onto the Great Plains. If we look for a pattern to explain the limber/ponderosa difference, we could correlate limber pine with sedimentary bedrock (but only weakly, since it grows on granite in the Winds and on volcanics at Yellowstone) or with harsh climates afflicting the trees with high winter winds, red belt (page 21), and occasional late spring hard frosts.

Limber pine grows where there's just barely enough precipitation for trees, mixing there with juniper, mountain-mahogany, or Douglas-fir, or with prairie only. On the Blackfeet Reservation it was responding to fire exclusion by expanding onto prairie, until blister rust came along. On windswept soil-poor ridges it extends fingers into midmontane and subalpine forests. In Alberta it covers the full range of elevations, sometimes even mixing with whitebark; but BC has ponderosa pine which, as elsewhere, largely excludes limber pine from the foothills. In sum, we might call limber pine an ecological gap-filler, indifferent to temperature to a degree unique among American trees. What its sites have in common is very dry soil and a regional lack of either whitebark or ponderosa pines.

The pine nuts are as big as those of whitebark, and as attractive to bears. While their importance in bear diets hasn't been quantified, one researcher speculates that since limber pine cones grow on low limbs, a grizzly can pick them—an advantage over whitebark cones which they have to dig up from squirrel middens.

Like the Northwest's other five-needle pines, limber pine is dying of white pine blister rust in much of its range. It appears doomed to extinction in Glacier-Waterton Park. Infection is less prevalent southward to the Wind River Range, yet it's hard to say with any confidence that the species will survive anywhere that currently has blister rust. Jasper N.P. looks safe so far, but rust might reach there with a few degrees of global warming. Limber and whitebark pines in Idaho's Sawtooth to Lemhi ranges are escaping, for now, perhaps because that area is too dry for blister rust spores to germinate.

Limber pine communities rarely have enough board feet of wood in them to attract loggers.

Western White Pine

Pinus monticola (mon-**tic**-a-la: mtn. dweller). Needles in fives, 2–4" long [5–10 cm], blue-green with white bloom on inner surfaces only, blunt-tipped; cones 6–10" × 2–4" [15–25 × 5–10 cm], thin-scaled and flimsy for their size, often curved, borne by a short stalk from upper branch tips; young bark greenish gray, maturing to gray with a cinnamon interior, cracking in squares. West of the CD, from the Lochsa R north.

Its Latin name notwithstanding, western white pine grows from low-subalpine forests to coastal bogs. The Idaho State Tree, it once dominated vast forests, and the lumber trade, in northern Idaho. The Idaho Giant, a tree 210' tall and 80" in diameter [64 × 2.05 m], succumbed to bark beetles in 1997. It had resisted the plagues that killed many larger trees by 1955. One was 101" [2.6 m] in diameter.

White pines are sadly diminished today. Most of the ones you see in natural forests today are young, and sick. Commercial success brought them their evil fate: an introduced fungus, white pine blister rust, *Cronartium ribicola*. America's logging industry, after feasting on eastern white pine, *P. strobus*, until that species was depleted, was thrilled to find a bigger white pine species in the Northern Rockies. (The hottest demand, oddly, was for wooden matches in the 1920s, thanks to low content of crackling resins.) Western white pine production peaked then. As the pines were logged, demand for re-planting stock grew so fast that foreign nurseries entered the market. A 1910 shipment of French seedlings to Vancouver brought blister rust, a European disease which was not a big problem in Europe.

Since the rust fungus requires a currant or gooseberry plant as an alternate host, currant extermination programs were carried on for several decades. (See page 134.) They proved futile. Western white pines died off almost as inexorably as American elms and chest-nuts—each a victim of a different European fungus.

Foresters did come up with a better solution, at least for planted forests. They located rust-resistant individuals, bred those in nurs-eries, and saw to it that only resistant stock gets planted any more. Some express confidence that damage to this species "in the future should be minimal." Perhaps resistant strains will be selected natu-rally even in the wilderness, and multiply to some semblance of white pines' former status. But experience with pathogens suggests that blister rust may develop counter-resistance, and natural selec-tion may spread that, too. In nature, species and their enemies co-evolve over many generations; selection eliminates genetic strains that fail to develop mutual survivability. The reason we have so many catastrophic pests (and weeds) in modern times is that trade and travel keep making bad new matchups between pests and hosts. When it comes to living organisms, free trade is a terrible thing.

Western Larch

Larix occidentalis (**lair**-ix: Roman term for larch; ox-i-den-**tay**-lis: western). Needles deciduous, soft, pale green, 1–1¾" [2.5–4.5 cm], 15–30 in "false whorls" on short peglike spurs, exc that needles are single and spirally arranged on this-year's twigs, and often winter-persistent on seedlings; cones 1–1⅜" [2.5–3.5 cm], often persistent, reddish until dry, bristling with pointy bracts longer than the scales; young bark thin and gray, maturing yellowish to cinnamon brown, 3–6" thick [2.5–4 cm], furrowed and flaking in curvy shapes ± like ponderosa pine bark. From Revelstoke, BC and Crowsnest, AB s to OR, wc ID, nw MT. Pinaceae. Color p 83.

A larch is something many people mistakenly think of as a contradiction—a deciduous conifer.* The deciduous needles always set it off visually, even from a distance: intensely chartreuse in spring, then a subtler but still distinctive grassy-green through summer, smashingly yellow for a few weeks in October, and conspicuous by their absence for a five- or six-month winter. You can tell a larch in winter from a maple or cottonwood by its coniferous form (single, straight trunk, and symmetrical branching) and from a dead evergreen by its warty texture (pegs on its twigs). Forests that have western larches commonly have scattered specimens a good two centuries older—and of course much larger—than any of the other trees. They are survivors of the previous forest, which may have been a century or two old when a big fire killed all the others.

Larch ranks among our fastest-growing, longest-living, most fire resistant, most disease resistant, and least shade-tolerant trees—an unusual combination. Since evergreen competitors photosynthesize earlier and later in the year, larch has to make up for lost time with photosynthetic efficiency. This requires full sun and ample groundwater through the dry months. Deciduous needles help larches recover from defoliation by insects—a larch grows a whole new crop of needles every year anyway. It can likewise afford grouse eating its irresistibly tender needles.

Montana's Clearwater/Swan Valley is larch heaven. The champion lives there—over seven feet in diameter, and 162 feet tall [2.21 × 49.4 m]. Floating larch needles carpet the downwind shores of Seeley Lake in winter, and wave action rolls them up into perfect spheres, typically golfball size but ranging up to over a foot [30 cm] in diameter.

Larches should continue to dominate large portions of the Swan Valley. Both the U.S and Canadian Forest Services are beginning to use retention logging to favor larch. They've found larch is the best species to grow there for commercial purposes, as well as to promote tourism: those forests are gorgeous! Favoring larch too much, though, would run the risk of depriving large mammals of the thermal cover (dense, insulating canopy) they need in winter.

---

*Other deciduous conifers are the bald-cypresses, genus *Taxodium*, of southern swamps, and the dawn redwood, *Metasequoia glyptostroboides*. Genus *Metasequoia*, a dominant tree in our region during the Miocene Epoch, was believed to have gone extinct millions of years ago, with the coast redwood its only descendent. Then to the utter astonishment of paleontologists, a few remnant stands turned up in 1946 in remote Chinese mountains.

Favoring larch *without* logging is a problem, since fire is a necessary component of the natural regime that sustains larch forest. The Coram Research Natural Area, near Glacier National Park, was established to preserve fine old-growth larch stands, but without fire, succession will replace its larches with shade tolerant species. Prescribed fire could do the job in some places, but in others the understory trees are already tall enough to act as "fire ladders," so that any fire—natural or prescribed—that ignites them will also torch the larch canopy above. Selective logging of the small trees is the only way to perpetuate old-growth larch forest there, but logging would seem to sacrifice the objective of using the Area to study how nature takes its course. Conversely, nature's way may well be to replace the big larches with a young larch/fir stand; but then for a human lifetime or two we would have no old-growth larch forest to enjoy.

Being our fastest-growing trees, lodgepole pine, black cottonwood, and western larch may be our trees most likely to benefit from global CO_2 enrichment. (See page 40).

Salish and Kootenai people used to draw off larch sap to make a syrup, in the manner of maple syrup.

Subalpine Larch

Larix lyallii (lye-**ah**-lee-eye: after David Lyall, facing page). Also **woolly larch**. Needles deciduous, soft, pale green, 1–1⅜", [2.5–3.5 cm] 30–40 per bunch on short peglike spurs, exc that needles are single and spirally arranged on this-year's twigs, and are ± evergreen on lowest branches of saplings; cones 1½–1¾" [3.5–4.5 cm], bristling with pointy bracts much longer than the scales; this-year's twigs densely, minutely woolly; bark gray, up to 1" [2.5 cm] thick; tree broad-crowned, much-branched and/or multistemmed; rarely a low shrub. Near treeline; from Bitterroots n. Pinaceae. Color p 83.

A paradox: though evergreen conifers generally inhabit colder climates than broadleaf trees, the most cold-loving of all trees are deciduous conifers. Larches are the most northerly and most alpine tree genus: of eleven species, all except western larch reach timberline. Where it is so cold that plants go for months without liquid water at their roots, the winter wind sucks all the moisture (even frozen) out of needles, killing them, nipping any foliage caught showing above the snow; so the outlines of evergreen krummholz show summer hikers the depth and shape of the winter snowpack. But in places we find subalpine larches standing tall above the krummholz, their bare branches relatively safe in winter from both cold desiccation and storm breakage.

Sometimes an early frost "freezes" the needles in place through the winter; they drop when they thaw in spring, and are soon replaced. While the tree's base is still deep in snow, its upper branches leaf out, providing spring's first treat for grouse that survived winter on a diet of tough old fir needles. New larch needles taste like tender young grass, with an initial spicy-resinous burst. Visually, they contrast dramatically with other needles twice a year—bright grass-green in June, yellow in late September (or even August in dry years).

Subalpine larches tolerate greater cold and rawer substrates (e.g., talus and recent glacial moraines) than any other Rocky Mtn. tree, but don't do very well with conifer competition. They keep no low limbs, a habit with one big disadvantage (they can't layer) and one big advantage (ground fires rarely hurt them). They rival whitebark pines in longevity, and far outlive the rest of our timberline trees. The largest specimen—over 6' in diameter and 95' tall [1.8 × 29 m]—is at the southwest extreme of their range, in the Washington Cascades. They cover their greatest expanses in the Purcell Range above Kimberley, B.C., and are calendar photo stars in the Canadian Rockies, but their northward reach stops abruptly just east of Bow Lake. This species-distribution mystery was heightened by the discovery of the remains of a specimen 60 miles farther north, in Jasper N.P.; it lived from about 1000 to 1250 A.D.

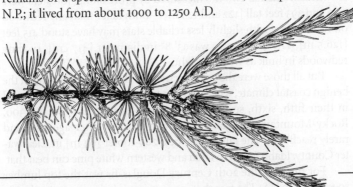

David Lyall was one of the last of the rugged Scots prominent in early exploration of the West. As surgeon-naturalist on the British contingent (Canada being British) of the NW Boundary Survey of 1857–62, he followed a beeline across unknown, precipitous terrain—a heroic task, yet he found energy and enthusiasm for science along the way. He published a *Botany of Northwest America* in 1863. A few years earlier there was a U.S./Mexico Boundary Survey with young Briton **Charles C. Parry** as botanist. He stayed in the west (mainly Colorado) botanizing for decades.

Douglas-Fir

Pseudotsuga menziesii (soo-doe-**tsoo**-ga: false hemlock; men-**zee**-see-eye: after Archibald Menzies, p 67). Needles ½–1½" [1.5–3.5 cm], varying from nearly flat-lying to almost uniformly radiating around the twig, generally with white stomatal stripes on the underside only, blunt-pointed (neither sharp to the touch nor notch-tipped nor broadly rounded); cones 2½–4" × 1½" [4–10 × 3.5 cm], with a paper-thin 3-pointed bract sticking out beneath each woody scale; soft young cones sometimes crimson or yellow briefly in spring; young bark gray, thin, smooth with resin blisters; mature bark dark brown, grooved, with tan and reddish-brown layers visible in cross-section; winter buds ¼" long [6 mm], pointed, not sticky; trunk usually straight. Pinaceae (Pine family). Color p 541.

Common virtually throughout our range, Douglas-fir grows from 55° North, in northern B.C., down to 19° North in central Mexico— the greatest north-south range of any American conifer. It is also the world's tallest species. Conventional thinking ranks it second, behind coast redwood, but that's an artificial truth caused by early logging, which targeted the finest Douglas-fir stands, taking no prisoners and few measurements. Two firs measured by professional foresters were 400 and 393 feet tall [122 and 120 m]—both taller than any redwood on record. One with slightly less reliable stats may have stood 415 feet [126.5 m]. The 400-footer was 13' 8" in diameter [417 cm], rivaling redwoods in bulk as well as height.

But all those were the coastal variety of the species, growing in the benign coastal climate, where firs can keep adding considerable wood in their fifth, sixth, seventh century of life, and may live to 1,300. Rocky-Mountain Douglas-firs grow minimally after age 200, and rarely reach 400. The tallest may be a 209-footer [64 m] in Clearwater County, Idaho. Western larch and western white pine can beat that.

For much of the 20th Century Douglas-fir was the top lumber species in the U.S. The tree that commerce so desires is, again, the big coastal Douglas-fir. The smaller Rocky-Mountain variety is often less valuable than western larch or white pine or ponderosa pine. Worse, in the Rockies it is so prone to attack by bark beetles, tussock moths, spruce budworm, and/or mistletoe that commercial foresters prefer other species in most locales.

By maturity it develops thick, corky bark, and loses its lower limbs, making it quite fire-resistant, exceeded here only by western larch and ponderosa pine. Being more shade-tolerant than those two, Douglas-fir tends to increase through succession in all forests that have it but lack hemlocks, true firs, and spruces. On some severely burned sites, Scouler willows quickly resprout to take over the burned area, and then Douglas-fir is the only tree able to come up in the shade of the willows; its seedlings may grow so close together that they invite another stand-replacing fire, perpetuating a cycle. In the parts of our range that lack ponderosa pine for whatever reason, Douglas-fir, by default, is likely to be the tall tree near lower timberline, often with smaller trees like limber pine, aspen, or mountain-mahogany for company.

Douglas-fir abounds on lower slopes. It may yield in succession to red-cedar or the hemlocks, in the limited areas where they are able to grow. It can generally hold its own against lodgepole pine or grand fir, and may slowly replace ponderosa pine (especially if there are no fires) where they grow together.

After certain hot weather conditions in interior B.C. and northeast Washington, sweet sap sometimes crystallizes all over Douglas-fir needles. This "Douglas-fir sugar," was legendary among area tribes. Native American uses of the tree were generally minor: sap was chewed, thick bark was gathered for fuel, and the trident-bristling cones, either tossed into the fire or gently warmed next to it, fortified people's hopes for a break in the weather. Douglas-fir wood was economically unimportant until white men came with steel tools.

The seedlings are a winter staple for deer and hares, and the seeds are eaten by small birds and rodents. Bears strip the bark to eat its succulent cambium; this wounds the tree, often fatally, by making an opening for invasions of insect larvae or rot fungi.

This tree is named for David Douglas, sometimes thought of as "the Discoverer of Douglas-fir." It is chauvinistic and silly to call any paleface the discoverer of any conspicuous natural feature in the Americas; and even to western science this species was described before Douglas was born, by his compatriot Archibald Menzies, surgeon and botanist on Captain Vancouver's ships in 1791. (Douglas's preparation for his trip included going to Menzies, by then an old man in London, for tutelage in Northwest Coast botany.) The tree didn't escape Lewis & Clark's notice either, in 1805. All that was left for Douglas to do in 1825 was to ship its seeds, and sing its praises, to a waiting England. Douglas called it a pine; later taxonomists tried out "yew-leafed-fir," "spruce," and finally "false-hemlock," while sticking with fir for the common name. In truth it is none of the above. Like our hemlocks and cedars (more misapplied European names) it is in a Pacific Rim genus, having three congeneric species

If I were Pope I would canonize **David Douglas**, giving Northwest backpackers a patron saint. Time and again he set off into the wilderness, usually with native guides or Hudson's Bay Company trappers, but also often alone. He packed a cast-iron kettle, a wool blanket, lots of tea and sugar, tobacco and vermilion dye as trade items, his rifle and ammunition, and pen, ink, and reams of paper for wrapping plants, seeds, and skins—no shelter usually, no dry change of clothes, no waterproofing but oilcloth for the papers and tins for the tea and gunpowder. Often without food in his pack, he might eat duck, venison, woodrat, salmon, or wapato roots; other days he consoled himself with tea, and berries if he was lucky. Once while boiling "partridge" for dinner, he fell asleep exhausted and, waking at dawn to a burnt-through kettle, counted himself clever to boil up a cup of tea in his tinderbox lid.

He approached each Native American as a potential friend, accepting his dependence on them for food, information, or portage while also knowing some of them would rather kill him or steal than barter for his goods. "They think there are good and bad spirits, and that I belong to the latter class, in consequence of drinking boiling water and lighting my tobacco-pipe with my lens and the sun." They probably didn't intend to kill Man of Grass quite as many times as he thought.

Douglas disembarked at the mouth of the Columbia in 1825. By luck, the same ship carried a second Scottish naturalist, **John Scouler**, and they had known each other as schoolboys. Scouler, all of twenty years old, had been hired as the doctor for Fort Vancouver. He made significant botanical finds there and on the Queen Charlotte Islands.

Douglas figured he walked and canoed 6,037 miles [9,737 km] of Washington and Oregon in 1825–26. In 1827 he caught a ride on the Hudson's Bay Express, an annual shipment of furs involving many voyageurs on established routes, with canoes, horses, and outposts waiting for them at several points along the way. The Express crossed the Continental Divide at Athabaska Pass, now on the Hamber/Jasper Park boundary. (The standard route from 1810 to 1850, it has been little visited since then; the railway surveys ignored it.) Douglas named the two peaks flanking the pass for two English botanists, **William J. Hooker** (page 203) and R. Brown. His journal reports climbing Mt. Brown, taking five hours from the pass, but modern climbers doubt any human could have done that. His miscalculation of Mt. Brown's height—17,000' [5,180 m], by far the highest in the Rockies—was accepted and famous for decades. The

in Japan and China and one in a tiny mountainous area of Southern California. Since 1826 it has been planted abroad with great success, especially in New Zealand and Scotland. Douglas and Menzies would be pleased.

---

error started with the map Douglas carried, written by trader David Thompson who calculated Athabaska Pass's elevation from the temperature of boiling water there.

The Express picked up naturalists **Thomas Drummond** and **Sir John Richardson** (p 155) along the Saskatchewan, and ended at Hudson's Bay, where they all caught a ship back to England.

For this entire voyage, the Royal Horticultural Society paid him their going rate, £100 a year plus £66 for expenses. His mission was to ship them seeds or cuttings to grow lucrative exotics in English gardens. He enjoyed minor celebrity in London at first, but soon ran into the proverbial difficulty in keeping his head above water in high society.

He undertook a still more ambitious plan to trek from Northwest Mexico to Sitka, Alaska, catch a ship from there to Kamchatka, and thence hike back to Europe. He did cover central California, the Columbia region again, and BC to north of Prince George—losing all his notes, journals, and instruments in rapids on the upper Fraser—before sailing to Hawaii where, at the age of 34, he came to a gruesome end. Out walking alone with Billy, his faithful Scotty dog, he was gored and trampled in a pit trap for feral bulls. Did he fall, or was he pushed?

Rumors that he was pushed persist to this day.

As a boy in Scotland, Douglas was too rebellious (or hyperactive, in modern jargon) for school. His stonemason father pulled him out at age 11 to apprentice in gardening. As his interest grew, he gleaned a botanical education wherever he could, eventually auditing lectures by Professor Hooker, who then took young Douglas on field trips in the Highlands, was impressed with his fanatical drive and enthusiasm, and sent him off to London and fame. Before sailing for NW America he was briefed by **Archibald Menzies**, the elderly botanist who had been there (and described Douglas-fir) in 1792. Despite his spotty education, Douglas wrote well, sometimes eloquently, in his journals. In contrast with the laconic Drummond—whose response to the Canadian Rockies was just that they "gratified him extremely"—Douglas on Mt. Brown's summit wrote of

...mountains towering above each other, rugged beyond all description; the dazzling reflection from the snow, the heavenly arena of the solid glacier, and the rainbow-like tints of its shattered fragments... the majestic but terrible avalanche hurtling down from the southerly exposed rocks producing a crash, and groans through the distant valleys, only equalled by an earthquake. Such gives us a sense of the stupendous and wondrous works of the Almighty.

Subalpine Fir

Abies lasiocarpa (ay-bih-eez: Roman word for firs; lazy-o-**car**-pa: shaggy fruit). =*A. bifolia** (FNA, CO). Needles ¾–1½" [2–4 cm], bluish green with one broad white stomatal stripe above and two fine stripes beneath, usually curving to densely crowd the upper side of the twig, tips variable; cones purplish gray to black, barrel- to cigar-shaped, 2½–4 × 1¼" [6–10 × 3 cm], borne erect on upper branches, dropping their seeds and scales singly while the core remains on the branch; bark thin, gray, smooth exc on very old bases, without superficial resin blisters, resin in pockets throughout inner bark; upper branches very short, horizontal, lower branches at ground level, long; or shrubby, prostrate. Abundant at timberline, esp eastward; rarely down to low elevs. Pinaceae.

The peculiar narrow spires of subalpine firs stay in my mind's eye as the archetype of a timberline tree. The upper limbs are short because, as in other true firs, they're stiffly horizontal and brittle; if they were long, they wouldn't hold up to subalpine snow and wind.

The long lower limbs escape those stresses by spending the winter buried in the snow. Hugging the ground puts them where they need to be to "layer," or reproduce by sprouting new roots and stems from branches in contact with soil. Subalpine fir is good at layering and at pushing both tree line and scrub line upward. At scrub line it grows in krummholz (prostrate) form, and spreads almost exclusively by layering. Occasionally it produces an asymmetrical, half-dead-looking, little tree with voluminous krummholz "skirts." Such trees were confined for years to the shape of the snowpack; any foliage above the snowpack was killed during winter by a combination of wind desiccation, frost rupturing, and abrasion by driven snow. This is the krummholz way of life. Then, we can suppose, for a few winters there was deeper snow, providing growing room for half a

---

**Flora of North America* splits *A. lasiocarpa*, based more on terpene chemistry than on external characteristics: Rocky Mtn. subalpine fir is *A. bifolia*, and the Cascades and Coast Mtns. have subalpine fir, *A. lasiocarpa*. (Brayshaw, in contrast, lumps both within a transcontinental *A. balsamea*.) In this instance alone I do not use FNA's name, but instead follow most other authorities in retaining *lasiocarpa*. Even the author of FNA's true firs explains his reasoning almost apologetically, saying he decided not to upset the applecart of tradition by lumping balsam fir and Fraser fir (intergradient species of the NE and SE, respectively). Once he had accepted Fraser fir, he felt *A. bifolia* had at least an equal claim to species rank. I'm no expert, but I have trouble with species pairs that have distinct traits only at the poles of their geographic range, and have mingled for millenia in a broad middle range. Dorn (2001) makes a separate argument that if there are two species, then the Rocky Mtn. one is *lasiocarpa*, since Douglas's original type specimen was apparently from the Blue Mtns.

dozen little vertical shoots. The next time a normal-snowfall winter came, one of the shoots managed to survive with some needles on its downwind side—the side relatively protected from desiccation and abrasion. Years later, the little tree is likely still "flagged," its surviving limbs positioned exclusively downwind and above the snow abrasion zone (the first 10", or 25 cm, above protective snow).

Though a little bit of lasting snow may be a conifer's friend up on windswept alpine ridges, deep and long-lasting snow is the main hindrance to tree establishment in subalpine parkland. Conifers need a longer growing season than herbs and shrubs. (See page 56.)

On steep meadows, tree seedlings are often wiped out by snow creep. Some limbs, after being encased in snow the better part of the year, spend the remainder matted with a weird black fungus called snow mold, *Herpotrichia nigra* (meaning "black creeping hair," but much less hairlike than horsehair lichen; both are on color page 520). Luckily, snow mold isn't as deadly as it looks. Other hindrances include soil too sodden, arid, or shallow, or sedge turf too dense.

In Glacier National Park, historical photographs show that subalpine firs have been expanding their clumps, filling in the spaces below treeline, but not pushing treeline upward. This likely reflects fire exclusion, not global warming, and indeed the 1990s in Glacier were no warmer than the late 1930s, when many of these encroaching firs established themselves. Still, an overall rise of treeline over the coming century seems a likely result of global warming.

Since 1957, when the European balsam woolly aphid reached our area, subalpine fir has proven highly susceptible to it, with mortality as high as 80% in a few mid-elevation stands. You can recognize the aphid's victims by their extremely swollen branch tips. Grossly swollen bark ridges—common in parts of Yoho— are caused by a fungal rust disease. In much of the Rockies, subalpine fir and Engelmann spruce are late-successional codominants of subalpine forest, though less abundant than the fire-adapted pioneer, lodgepole pine.

Grand Fir

Abies grandis (**gran**-dis: big). Also **lowland white fir**. Needles ¾–2" [2–5 cm], quite broad and thin, spreading in a flat plane from the twig, notch-tipped to rounded, dark green above, two white stomatal stripes beneath; (needles of top-most branches often neither flat-spreading nor esp dark); cones dense, heavy, ± cylindrical, 2½–4 × 1½" [6–11 × 3.5 cm], greenish, borne erect on upper branches, dropping their seeds and scales singly while the core remains; bark gray to light brown, resin-blistered, becoming ± ridged and flaky with age; branches horizontal. OR, w ID, nw MT, north to Shelter Bay, BC. Pinaceae.

The foliage on a grand fir sapling catches your eye, the tidy flat array of long, broad needles showing off the glossy green color. Flat leaf arrays are primarily an adaptation to deep shady forest, where most rays of light beam from directly overhead. The flat array keeps a maximum amount of leaf surface facing up, to catch them efficiently. Grand firs are only slightly less shade-tolerant than western hemlocks, and require less rainfall, especially on valley bottoms where summer drought is not a problem.

Given a natural regime of frequent low-intensity fires, pines, larches, and Douglas-firs would typically dominate forests where we see grand fir today. Older grand firs may survive low to moderate fires thanks to reasonably thick bark, but the species is rather vulnerable overall because of low branching, shallow roots, and a serious susceptibility to rot diseases, especially after fire wounds its bark. Being so fire-susceptible, grand fir has been the major beneficiary of Smokey's fire-fighting efforts over the past century. This has made it the bad boy among our conifers: most of the notoriously sick, half-dead, and conflagration-prone stands of eastern Oregon and parts of Idaho are overly-dense grand fir stands that filled in where ponderosa pines were logged out.

In the Southwest, grand fir's close relative white fir, *A. concolor*, plays similar roles. Where the two species meet in eastern Oregon and western Idaho they "intergrade," or hybridize in the full range of proportions. Genetic traces of white fir are seen in longer needles, more stomatal bloom in the upper groove, more upward curve from the twig, and less notch at the tip.

Spruces

Picea spp. (**pis**-ia: Roman word, from "pitch," for some conifer). Needles sharp, 4-sided, with stomatal stripes ± equally on all sides, bad-smelling when crushed; they grow from short peglike bases that are conspicuous on the twig after their needles have fallen; cones hang from branches; cone scales thin and close; branchlets hang fringelike from branches, commonly tipped with conelike galls; bark thin, scaly. Pinaceae.

Engelmann spruce, *P. engelmannii* (eng-gell-**mah**-nee-eye: after George Engelmann). =*P. glauca engelmannii* (Brayshaw). Needles ¾–1¼" [2–3 cm], deep blue-green; young twigs minutely fuzzy (through 10× lens); cones 1½–2½" [4–6 cm], scales very thin, flexible, irregularly toothed or wavy along outer edge; crown dense, narrow; or prostrate and shrubby at timberline. A subalpine forest dominant throughout our region.

White spruce, *P. glauca* (**glaw**-ca: pale). Needles ½–¾" [12–20 mm], blue-green with pale grayish waxy coat, most commonly crowding upward and forward from the twig; young twigs hairless; cones 1–1½" [2.5–3 cm], scales stiff, broadly round at tip; bark thin, scaly; crown often rather broad. BC, AB, scattered in n MT, rare in ID.

Colorado blue spruce, *P. pungens* (**pun**-jenz: sharp-pointed). Needles ¾–1¼" [2–3 cm], stiff, very sharp, typically pointing straight out (bottlebrush-like) around the twig, deep blue-green; young twigs hairless; cones 2¼–4" [6–10 cm], scales thin, scales irregularly toothed or wavy along outer edge; bark thin, scaly. Mainly near streams, from Tetons s in WY and extreme e ID.

Spruces are the second most northerly conifer genus (after larches). In the Rockies, Engelmann spruce, subalpine fir, and lodgepole pine dominate the higher forests. Lodgepole is intolerant of shade, and yields to the others in succession, but whether spruce could ever replace fir, or vice versa, has been debated for decades. Spruce has been shown to do a little bit better in the easterly parts of our range where the climate is strictly continental (dry winters with extremes of cold), and it does better on limestone soils. Subalpine fir is more successful where the maritime (winter-wet) influence is felt. East of the Continental Divide, some high areas have no firs, just spruce and pine.

These three species and black spruce (*Picea mariana*, which reaches the extreme north end of our range) hybridize and intergrade in several combinations where their ranges meet. Many, or even most, of the spruces of Idaho and western Montana have

---

characteristics intermediate between white and Engelmann spruce.

Spruces are lovely, with denser, drapier, darker, slightly bluer foliage than our other conifers. (The blueness is too variable to be any help in telling blue spruce from Engelmann. Horticultural blue spruce was bred from some of the bluest *P. pungens* in Colorado.)

Grouse select dense spruce crowns for the warmest, driest roosts. Dense crowns often reach all the way to the ground, and catch fire easily. Engelmann spruces can grow slowly but steadily for three to four hundred years, but rarely achieve that potential because they are so fire-susceptible. Wet locations may protect some of them. They like soils with aerated moisture—streamsides, not marshes.

Many spruce branch tips bear curious conelike appendages— galls, or "houses" for aphid larvae (page 499). Gall tissue is secreted by a plant in response to chemical stimulation, usually by a female insect laying eggs. A spruce aphid's gall envelopes and terminates new growth of the branchlet, but scarcely harms the tree as a whole. The dead needles turn a tan color along with the gall; together they look like a 1–2" [1.2–5 cm] cone with needle-tipped, melted-together "scales" each hooding an opening into a larval chamber. The gall may hang from the branch for years, long after the larvae mature and move on; other insects may colonize it.

Engelmann spruce lumber long went unappreciated, but now has a strong market because it resembles some very white Japanese woods that became scarce. It makes excellent guitar tops if you can find big

Corkscrew Trees

Dead trees in tough high-mountain environments often show sharply spiralled wood grain, once they lose their bark. Two Norwegians recently took on the challenge of explaining this as an adaptation. In their study, northern hemisphere conifers tend to spiral to the right, and southern ones to the left, as you follow a line of wood fiber up. Can you spot exceptions? The pattern is genetic, is strongest in the outermost layers, and is actually reversed in wood from the tree's youth. They also found that northern conifers grow more branches on their south sides (reaching toward the sun); prevailing westerly winds then apply right-handed torque. They propose that evolution has reduced wind breakage by accommodating the torque.

The jury is still out on this hypothesis. Prevailing winds aren't what blows trees down: storm winds are, and these don't have a consistent direction over wide areas. Jan Henderson speculates that spiralling may enable greater height—the best-known competitive arena, for a conifer— via either vertical strength or water conductivity to high treetops.

enough knot-free sections. (Those are easier to find on big, very old, coastal Sitka spruces, which make the wood of choice for piano sounding-boards.) Spruce pitch is chewable, fragrant, and sweetish, but sure sticks to your teeth. To the BC Interior tribes it was more than trailside mouth entertainment, it was a valued trade commodity.

Mountain Hemlock

Tsuga mertensiana (**tsoo**-ga: Japanese word for it; mer-ten-see-**ay**-na: after Karl Mertens, p 152). Also **black hemlock**. Needles ½–¾" [1.2–2 cm], bluish green with white stomatal stripes on both top and bottom, ± ridged, thus ± 3- or 4-sided, radiating from all sides of twig, or upward- and forward-crowding on exposed timberline sites; cones 1–2½" [1.2–6 cm], light (but coarser than spruce cones), often purplish, borne on upper branch tips; bark much furrowed and cracked; mature crown rather broad; also grows as prostrate shrub at highest elevs. Subalpine; BC Columbia Mtns, n ID, extreme nw MT, OR. Pinaceae.

The compact, gnarled shoulders of mountain hemlocks shrug off the heaviest snow loads in the world. At every age, this species' form is brutally determined by snow. The seedlings and saplings are gently buried by the fall snows, then flattened when the snowpack, accumulating weight, begins to creep downslope. Tramping across the subalpine snowpack on a hot June afternoon, you can almost hear the tension underfoot of young trees straining to free themselves and begin their brief growing season. The stress of your foot on the surface may trip an unseen equilibrium, snapping a hemlock top a few feet into the air. After the trees grow big enough to take a vertical stance year round, they may keep a sharp bend at the base ("pistol-butt") as a mark of their seasons of prostration. Even in maturity they may get tilted again, on sites so steep and unstable that even the soil creeps downslope. Their crowns grow ragged from limbs breaking.

Western Hemlock

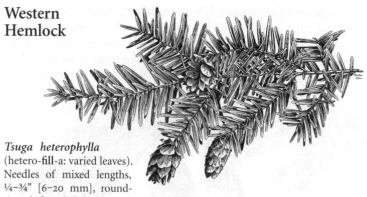

Tsuga heterophylla
(hetero-fill-a: varied leaves).
Needles of mixed lengths,
¼–¾" [6–20 mm], round-
tipped, flat, slightly grooved on top, with white stomatal stripes underneath,
spreading in ± flat sprays; cones ¾–1" long [2–2.5 cm], thin-scaled, pendent from
branch tips; mature bark up to 1' thick, platy, checked (almost as much horizontal
as vertical texture); inner bark streaked dark red/purple; branch tips and treetop
leader drooping. BC, Jasper, n ID, nw MT, WA. Pinaceae.

My image of western hemlock is of a sapling's limbs, their lissome
curves stippled a soft green made incandescent, in the understory
dimness, by a stray swath of sunlight.

Western hemlocks are prolific: notice the profusion of little
hemlock cones on the forest floor, or on the tree, lending it a
purplish cast in the distance. Cones are produced copiously every
year—unlike most other conifers that drastically vary their seed production in order to limit the numbers of seed-eating creatures. Each
year, a mature hemlock drops more than one viable seed per square
inch of ground under it. Only an infinitesimal fraction, of course,
will make it to tree size. More than any other species, western hemlock reproduction is confined to "nurse log" substrates—rotting
logs, snags, rootwads, etc.—especially within the "inland rain forests" of the wet Columbia Mountains.

On the Oregon coast, very young pure hemlock stands produce
organic tissue ("biomass") at the fastest rate yet measured in the
world. Hemlocks achieve their efficiency partly by sheer leafiness—a
six-inch [15 cm] trunk can support over 10,000 square feet [930 m²]
of leaf surface area, almost twice as much as Douglas-fir. While the
greater leaf area catches more light, it also loses more moisture; shade
tolerance seems to be a tradeoff against drought tolerance. (Productivity of NW Coast forests also owes a lot to salmon; see page 481.)

Mature hemlocks, with thin bark and shallow roots, are frequent
victims of fire or wind, and also of heart rot. Nearly all hemlocks that

reach 200 years old in the Rockies are developing heart rot, and will become hollow. *Echinodontium tinctorium*, Indian Paint fungus, is the usual culprit. It produces huge hard conks, once prized and traded throughout the West as the best red face paint. Conks were ground to a powder and mixed with animal fat, though hemlock pitch also sometimes served as a dark base for face paint. Tannin-rich hemlock bark was used to tan skins; to dye and preserve wood (sometimes mashed with salmon eggs for a yellower dye); to shrink spruce

Nurse Logs

The best seedbed for a hemlock is the rotting trunk, stump, or upended rootwad of a fallen tree. Often these "nurse logs" support dozens of seedlings and saplings while the ground in between has none.

Buttresses and prop roots are forms that reveal their origins on nurse logs long after the nursing wood itself disappears. By age ten, a seedling extends fine rootlets down a nurse log's sides to mineral soil. The rootlets grow into sturdy root "stilts" while the nurse log slowly rots out from underneath. At some point the support relationship may reverse, a few chunks of rotting nurse now dangling from tree stilts. Over time, the nurse log disappears and the stilt roots fill in, remaining as buttresses. (Red-cedars, in contrast, get buttresses from their genes.)

A nurse log plainly offers great advantages to a seedling, but what these are has been the subject of a lot of speculation and some research. Here are a few hypotheses:

Water: This writer is convinced that year-round moisture is the key. Well-rotted wood stays sodden all through the summer, not only retaining rainfall but actually manufacturing water as a decomposition by-product. Water is critical in deep forest because the canopy trees consume so much of it, while dim light severely slows growth of a seedling struggling to reach reliable moisture with its root.

Mycorrhizae: Quickly forming a mycorrhizal partnership with a fungus is crucial to conifer seedlings (page 290). But while some mycorrhizal fungi specialize in rotten logs, and link up with nitrogen-fixing bacteria there, at least as many others do that in forest-floor humus.

Moss thickness: In one study in coastal Oregon, soil was covered with a 3" [7 cm] moss mat, too thick for seedlings to root through and reach secure moisture in their first summer. Nurse logs had only a 1" [2.5 cm] moss mat.

Litter: In another study in montane forests, hemlock seedlings were fatally flattened by tree litter coalescing within melting snow. Litter sloughed harmlessly off of the nurse logs.

root baskets for watertightness; to make nets invisible and (some claimed) alluring to fish; and as a styptic to halt bleeding.

Hemlock wood is rather soft, weak and prone to splitting, but resilient and easily worked. In recent years, strips of clear, straight-grained hemlock command high prices for use as mouldings and veneer. But the bulk of the hemlock harvest gets pulped for paper.

Nature Out of Balance?

Scientists increasingly reject the old cliche of "nature always in balance," seeing nature instead as full of chaos, change, and imbalance. Some nonscientists infer that scientists have no stable natural baseline with which to compare human-induced change, or that human-induced change is nothing to worry about because "nature also destroys." Nothing could be more misleading.

It is true that in nature species do travel to new locations and sometimes take over, and other species do go extinct. But these things are happening 100 to 100,000 times faster today, from human causes, than they commonly happen in nature.

Looking at our region, some say that old-fashioned clearcutting followed by slash burning mimics natural disturbance by fire. It does not. Forest fires leave a vital legacy of biomass; traditional clearcuts do not. Logging equipment compacts soil, rips up streambeds, and greatly increases runoff and erosion. Most of the wood in trees killed by fire "lives on" as wildlife snags and nurse logs. Even wood that burns up stays on the site as minerals. Stumps are no match for wildlife snags and nurse logs; on the contrary, they are disease magnets. Clearcuts are good for deer and elk, but lack the diversity of animals and fungi found in burns. Fires themselves are extremely diverse: hot or cool, low or high, spring or fall, huge or small. Compared to that, clearcuts are all alike. Some clearcuts on sunny ridges refuse, decade after decade, and even with multiple replantings, to regrow forests. These were forests well adapted to fire, but they couldn't recover from clearcutting. Alteration of the balance of soil microorganisms is probably the problem.

A second-generation tree plantation may look a bit anemic next to a natural forest. An eighth-generation plantation is more so, after centuries of removing organic material, centuries without nearby old-growth to serve as a genetic lending library. Europe has many eighth-generation and older plantations; even before they started dying from air pollution and acid rain they grew feebly. It's time to lay to rest the hubristic fantasy that western forests will just regrow, as fast as they ever grew naturally, following clearcut after clearcut into the future.

The word "hemlock" traces back to A.D. 700 as the English word for the deadly parsleys notorious for their role in Socrates' execution. The English somehow saw parsley in the lacy foliage of a New England conifer that was new to them; they called it hemlock spruce—later shortened to hemlock.Mountain and western hemlocks seldom grow in the same place. Where they do, they may hybridize naturally.

Exotic species are sometimes carried in by logging and roadbuilding equipment. (And also by recreationists.) Some are serious weeds. Others are deadly pathogens. Our three five-needle pine species are dying out due to an exotic fungal disease brought in the course of timber management. The worst pest of subalpine fir is an exotic aphid.

Equally scary is deforestation that perpetuates itself by changing the climate. For example, new studies suggest that even the Amazon rain forest could permanently turn to shrub-steppe or semidesert if deforestation crosses a certain unknown threshold. Since half the basin's rainfall consists of previous rainfall recycled by plant transpiration, fewer trees will mean less rain. Scanty rain, no rain forest. Closer to home, decreases in precipitation after logging have been measured on ridgetops. Big trees there gain more moisture by intercepting clouds than young trees can, and more than they lose through transpiration.

There are huge differences between anthropogenic instability and natural instability, in which particular places see particular species come and go, while almost always retaining organisms diverse enough to perform each of the whole system's vital functions. We aren't like a forest fire, we're more like an asteroid impact.

By removing fire from the equation for fifty years, we exacerbated tree pathogens and fuel buildup to a point where the inevitable future fires will be far hotter than most historical ones. We probably can't solve this problem without careful, intensive management—a new style of logging, in other words, combined with prescribed burning. In the long run, that path is the least dangerous to human life. It may be politically impossible, though, as long as the public thinks homes in the thick of fire forests are a property right, and blames fires that reach those homes on the government rather than on the homes' builders and owners. Forest homes with wooden roofs, and with brush and tree litter all around, are simply folly, and society does not owe them fire protection.

On the other hand, environmentalists who so mistrust the Forest Service that they would ban all logging on U.S. public lands are cutting off their noses to spite their faces. That way lies conflagration— a path with scant hope of bringing back or of long sustaining any major portion of the West's forest ecosystems.

Western Yew

Taxus brevifolia (**tax**-us: the Greek term; brev-if-**oh**-lia: short leaf). Also **Pacific yew**. Needles ½–¾" [12–20 mm], grass-green on top, paler and concave beneath, spreading flat from the twig, broad and thin, drawing abruptly to a fine point but too soft to feel prickly; new twigs green; male and female organs on separate plants; toxic seeds single within juicy red cup-shaped fruits ¼" diam [6 mm]; bark thin, peeling in large purple-brown scales to reveal red to purplish, smooth inner bark; branches sparse, upper ones angled up, often much longer than the leader; trunk often crooked; sometimes a sprawling shrub. Mainly in moist, valley floor forest, but scattered elsewhere; from Wallowas and Bitterroots north and east to Waterton. Taxaceae (Yew family). Color p 523.

Our yew is an anomaly from almost every point of view. It is a conifer, with evergreen needles—but without cones. Instead it bears its seeds singly (and only on female trees) cupped within succulent red seed coats loosely termed berries, but technically "arils." These are treacherously pleasant-tasting; the seeds of many yew species contain alkaloids capable of inducing cardiac arrest. Attractive but poisonous fruits are few in our area, but smooth bright red berries are good ones to keep your kids away from. (See baneberry, page 265). Birds love yew berries, passing the toxic seeds undigested.

Woodworkers class conifers as "softwoods," by definition, but they know yew is the exception: it is among the hardest of woods. It can be worked with power tools, or carved to make extraordinarily durable and beautiful utensils. The sapwood is cream, the heartwood orange to rose. Yet few have worked it. Loggers used to burn it with the slash, finding it hard to market such small, allegedly scarce trees. But yew often reaches marketable size by hardwood standards.

Native Americans knew better. They made it into spoons, bowls, hair combs, drum frames, fishnet frames, canoe paddles, clam shovels, digging sticks, splitting wedges, war clubs, sea lion clubs, deer trap springs, arrows, and bows. (Yew species were the wood of choice for bows worldwide. The Greek name for yew, *taxos*, spawned both "toxin" and *toxon*, meaning "bow.") Prizing yew for strength, elasticity and hardness, young Swinomish men rubbed a yew's limbs on their own in the belief those qualities would rub off on them. They also sometimes added yew needles to their smoking mixtures, perhaps more for "toxins" than flavor.

The beautiful smooth underbark can be almost cherry red. In 1987, Western science suddenly wanted yew bark. An order was filled for 60,000 pounds [27,000 kg] of bark from which to extract a tiny amount of taxol, soon dubbed the chemotherapy drug sensation of the 1990s. For a few years we feared that the species might be wiped out in its native habitat by free-lance bark strippers. Fortunately, the drug industry soon stopped buying yew bark after finding they could more economically synthesize the drug from cultivated European yew needles. A closely related but potentially more effective and cheaper drug was isolated from a bacterium, so in another decade taxol may be all but forgotten, after serving as an example of life-saving herbal toxins to be discovered growing under our noses.

Yew has completely taken over some valley floors in Idaho and Montana, flying in the face of a common assumption of climax community theory, namely that in succession, taller vegetation tends to shade out and replace shorter. In this case the medium-small tree creates such heavy shade that no saplings but its own can survive. It seems likely, however, that climax yew stands would be extremely rare without human fire-suppression, since even light underburns kill yew. Highly shade-tolerant, yew may suffer when shade is removed, turning orange all over but not necessarily dying. I know one thicket of orange-leaved yew shrubs on a steep, burningly exposed southwest slope, with no sign of ever having enjoyed shade.

Conifers with tiny scalelike leaves

This group is the Cypress family (Cupressaceae). Mature foliage is compressed and scalelike, but many genera have a juvenile phase of sharp, closely packed, spinelike needles up to ¾" long [2 cm]. These differ from other conifer needles in being arranged (like the mature scales) in opposite pairs or in whorls of three. Some junipers may bear juvenile foliage for years, even into maturity on lower branches. Common juniper (included here to keep the family together) grows spinelike leaves exclusively, throughout life.

Western Red-Cedar

Thuja plicata (**thoo**-ya: Greek word for some tree; plic-**ay**-ta: pleated). Leaves tiny, yellowish green, in opposite pairs, tightly encasing the twig, flattened, the twig (incl leaves) being 4–8 times wider than thick; foliage dies after 3–4 years, turning orange-brown but persisting several months before falling; cones ½" [12

---

mm] long, consisting of 3 opposite pairs of seed-bearing scales, plus a narrow sterile pair at tip and 0–2 tiny sterile pairs at base; bark reddish, thin (up to 1", or 25 mm), peeling in fibrous vertical strips; leader drooping; trunk tapered, at maturity ± fluted and buttressed. Moist lowland soils; n ID, nw MT, BC, rare in AB. Cupressaceae (Cypress family).

Cedars are a breed apart, easily recognized by their droopy sprays of foliage and vertical-fibrous bark. The bark is relatively clean, being too acidic to encourage lichens, fungi or moss. Though slow-growing, our cedars resist windthrow, rot and insect attack, and can live more than 1,000 years. Western red-cedars, the family's largest trees, may develop buttressed waistlines 30 to 60 feet [9–18 m] around.

Red-cedar *groves* are a thing apart—quieter; deeper. They occur on moist valley floors (soil moisture 12% through August). Cedars tolerate drier climates than hemlocks, as long as their roots are wet.

For tribes that had it, red-cedar provided invaluable materials. The inner bark, woven after laborious shredding with deer bone, made warm clothing. Unwoven, it was soft enough for cradle lining or menstrual pads; torn in strips and plaited, it became roofing, floor mats, hats, blankets, dishes, or ropes. Buds, twigs, seeds, leaves and bark each had medicinal uses. Cedar charms sanctified or warded off spirits of the recently deceased. Cedar bough switches were skin scrubbers for both routine and ceremonial bathing.

Easy to work with stone tools and fire, cedar made up in durability and aesthetics what it lacked in strength. Cedar heartwood is warm red, weathering to silver-gray; it smells wonderful, resists rot, and splits very straight if it comes from an old, slow-grown tree. Split cedar shakes made superlative roofs in pioneer days.

The Europeans who first named America's scaly-leaved trees "cedars" were either confused or at a severe loss for words. These trees resemble their relatives the cypresses, genus *Cupressus*, and not the true cedars, which have long needles in whorls (like larches, only evergreen) and fat, solid, upright cones (like true firs). The true cedars are three species of *Cedrus*, in the Pine family, native to mountains of Asia and North Africa, and much planted in cities.

Thuja is a Pacific Rim genus, with other species in Northeast Asia. Eastern North America has a *Thuja* they call a "white-cedar," while they call their junipers "red-cedar." Moth-repellent cedar chests are traditionally made from eastern *Juniperus*. False cedars all have pungent smells due to their rot- and insect-repellent chemistry.

Juniper Trees

Juniperus spp. (ju-**nip**-er-us:
the Roman word for it). =*Sabina*
spp. (CO). Mature leaves tiny, scalelike,
yellowish green, tightly encasing the twig, not flattened; leaves on seedlings, saplings, and lowest limbs of
young trees needlelike, ¼" [6 mm], prickly; cones berrylike,
> blue to blue-black, rather dry, resinous, 1–3-seeded, ¼" [6 mm]; many
> plants have only male (inconspicuous) or only female fruits; bark red-
> brown, fibrous, shreddy; dense small conical trees, limbs nearly to
> ground, or sprawling shrubs. Near lower timberline. Cupressaceae.

Rocky Mountain juniper, *J. scopulorum* (scop-you-**lor**-um: broomy).
Leaves opposite, making the stems 4-angled (illustrated at left). Berries
have heavy bluish bloom.

Utah juniper, *J. osteosperma* (os-tee-o-**sperm**-a: bony seed). Leaves
opposite; berries bigger (½", 12 mm), brownish, never blue. Severe
sites, often with limber pine; Lost River and Lemhi Ranges, ID.

Western juniper, *J. occidentalis* (ox-i-den-**tay**-lis: western). Leaves in
whorls of three, each whorl rotated 60° from the next (illustrated at
right). OR, extreme w ID.

Juniper trees, like big sagebrush, are dry-country species with
no defense against fire; their strategy is to grow where fire can't
reach them, i.e., with too little vegetation to spread it. Until this
century, that confined junipers to rocky sites with little soil, but
with fire suppression they have been able to spread. After reaching large size, a juniper tree can survive some low fires because
its own shade and litter create a small grass-free firebreak.

These species achieve their best growth south of here. In the
Sierra Nevada stands a western juniper 12'9" in diameter and 86' tall
[2.46 × 26.2 m], thought to be around 4,000 years old, which puts the
species among the world's top five trees in longevity. A nearly equal
Rocky Mountain juniper grows in Utah's Wasatch Range.

Junipers' insect-repellent and disinfectant aromatics are widely
appreciated. Native Americans boiled juniper leaves to steam sickness out of a house, or to bathe a sick person in juniper leaf tea. Back
east, juniper trees called "red-cedars" (mainly *J. virginianus*) are
made into moth-repellent cedar chests and closets.

Conifers: tiny scalelike leaves

Creeping Juniper

Juniperus horizontalis. =*Sabina horizontalis* (CO). Mature leaves tiny, scale-like but sharp-tipped, waxy green, tightly encasing the twig, opposite (making the stem 4-angled); juvenile leaves needlelike, ¼" [6 mm], prickly; cones berry-like, blue-purple, often with waxy bloom, rather dry, resinous, 1–6-seeded, ¼" diam [6 mm]; plants have only male (inconspicuous) or only female fruits; bark red-brown, fibrous, shreddy; prostrate, mat-forming shrubs. Foothills, esp e of CD. Cupressaceae (Cypress family).

Common Juniper

Juniperus communis (com-**you**-nis: common). Leaves all ¼–¾" [6–20 mm], sharp, closely packed along the twig in whorls of 3, from a ± distinct joint at each leaf base (unlike juvenile *J. occidentalis*, whose 3-whorled needles bend sharply, with no joint, to run down the twig); cones berrylike, blue-black with bloom, round and quite fleshy, ¼–⅜" diam [6–10 mm], 1–3-seeded, resinous but sweet; bark red-brown, thin, shreddy; prostrate, mat-forming shrubs, or in Canada sometimes bushy, up to 3' tall [90 cm]. Wide-spread—steppe to tundra—esp where rocky. Cupressaceae. Color p 83.

One of the world's most widespread conifer species, common juniper is humble, but well suited to cold windswept ridges and slopes where even tall conifer species grow as low creeping krummholz.

Junipers are anomalous among conifers in enclosing their seeds in fleshy, edible "fruits." (Yews cup—but do not enclose—their poisonous seeds in "berries.") Properly speaking, a berry is a fruit and a fruit is a thickened ovary wall, so neither junipers nor yews have true berries; a juniper berry is technically a cone of very few, fleshy, fused scales. It has a sweetish resiny flavor of suspiciously medicinal intensity. Used with restraint, it's a delicious seasoning in teas, stuffings, gin (a word derived from the French *ginevre* for juniper) or your water bottle, if your water has been tasting plasticky. Those with inquisitive palates will try them straight off the bush. Northern Rockies tribes apparently didn't eat many of them, but some said that a few juniper berries would stave off hunger all day, if only because of that resiny persistence on the palate. Birds love them, and disseminate the indigestible seeds.

BEARTOOTH

Engelmann spruce, p 71.

BEARTOOTH

Lodgepole pine, p 50.

BEARTOOTH

Subalpine fir, p 68.

YOHO

Subalpine larch, p 62.

BEARTOOTH

Common juniper, p 82.

BITTERROOT

Subalpine larch and fir, and whitebark pine.

FLATHEAD

Western larch, p 60.

PURCELL

Ponderosa pine, p 52.

Conifers

83

Serviceberry
willow, p 119.

Barclay
willow, p 119.

Quaking aspen, p 115.

Buffaloberry, p 127.

Red-osier dogwood, p 123.

Mock-orange, p 128.

Mountain alder,
p 121, with insect galls.

Bog birch,
p 122.

Blue
virgin's bower, p 127.

Snowberries, p 126. *S. albus, S. oreophilus.*

Red elderberry, p 125.

Blue elderberry, p 125. Black elderberry, p 125.

Red twinberry, p 124. Black twinberry, p 124.

Trees and shrubs: opposite leaves, 5 petals

Subalpine
spiraea, p 131.

Birchleaf
spiraea, p 131.

Shrubby
cinquefoil, p 131.

Sitka mountain-ash, p 130.   Oceanspray, p 133.   Mallow ninebark, p 133.

Shrubs: alternate leaves, 5 petals (Rose family)

Mountain-mahogany, p 145.

Bitterbrush, p 133.

Serviceberry, p 128.

Chokecherry, p 129.

Swamp gooseberry, p 134.

Red gooseberry, p 134.

Wild raspberry, p 131.

Prickly rose, p 132.

Prickly-pear, p 149.

White rhododendron, p 144.

Oregon-grape, p 148.

Snowbrush, p 146.

Labrador tea, p 147.

Poison ivy, p 136.

White dryad, p 154.

Shrubs: various

Kinnickinnick, p 150.

Grouseberry, p 142.

Fool's huckleberry, p 144.

Alpine laurel, p 149.

Pink heather, p 152.

Yellow heather, p 152.

Pipsissewa, p 150.

Low huckleberry, p 143.

White heather, p 152.

Holm's Rocky
Mountain sedge, p 159.

BEARTOOTH

JASPER

VALHALLA

Black alpine sedge ("dams" in foreground), p 160.
Engelmann spruce (one at left), p 71; subalpine fir, p 68.

Cottongrass, p 162.
Water sedge, p 159.

SELKIRK

Mertens' rush (center), p 163.

YELLOWSTONE

Raynolds' sedge, p 161.

Herbs: grasslike: sedges and rush

Cheatgrass, p 167.   Bluebunch wheatgrass, p 165.

Woodrush, p 162.   Alpine timothy, p 165.

Pinegrass, p 166.   Foxtail barley, p 164.

Herbs: grasslike: grasses and woodrush

Glacier lily, p 174.

Fairy-bells, p 172.

Death camas, p 180. Wild chives, p 176.

Yellow bell, p 178. Wood lily, p 178. Bronze bells, p 178.

Bead lily, p 177. Chocolate lily, p 179.

Herbs: showy monocots, 6 stamens (Lily family)

BEARTOOTH WALLOWA SALMON R

Mariposa lilies, p 175: *C. gunnisonii, eurycarpus, elegans*

CRAZY CRAZY SALMON R

Shortstyle onion, p 180.

Death camas, p 180.

Douglas's triteleia, p 177.

MISSION BEAVERHEAD CABINET

Twisted-stalk, p 173. (Corn lily as background.)

Beargrass, p 181.

False Solomon's seal, *M. stellatum*, p 173.

WATERTON

Corn lily, p 182.

GLACIER

False asphodel, p 174.

SAWTOOTH (ID)

Camas, p 179.

BEARTOOTH

False Solomon's-seal,
M. racemosum, p 173.

Herbs: showy monocots, 6 stamens (Lily family)

SWAN

CASCADES

BOULDER

White bog-orchid, p 184.   Striped coralroot, p 187.   Spotted coralroot, p 187.

PIONEER

Yellow lady's-slipper, p 187.   Blue-eyed grass, p 183.

BEAVERHEAD

BRIDGER

Slender bog-orchid, p 184. (Corn lily as background.)   Western iris, p 183.

Hayden's aster,
p 193.

Arctic aster,
p 193.

Showy fleabane,
p 192.

Engelmann's
aster, p 193.

Woolly daisy p 192.

Balsamroot, p 196.

Herbs: daisylike composite flowers (Daisy family)

Mule's-ears,
p 197.

Yarrow,
p 198.

Blanketflower,
p 195.

Arnica, p 194.
Subalpine daisy, p 192.

Parry's
townsendia, p 193.

Goldenrod,
S. multiradiata, p 198.

Butterweed,
Packera. subnuda, p 194.

Butterweed,
P. pseudaurea, p 194.

Dusky butterweed,
p 195.

Herbs: daisylike composite flowers (Daisy family)

Hooker's thistle, p 203.
Bumblebee, p 500.

Pearly everlasting,
p 201.

Elk thistle,
p 203.

Pussytoes,
Antennaria. lanata, p 200.

Pussytoes,
A. umbrinella, p 200.

Alpine
dusty maiden, p 200.

Rocky Mountain
sagewort, p 204.

Western
sagewort, p 204.

Saw-wort,
p 202.

Herbs: thistlelike composite flowers (Daisy family)

Yellow salsify,
p 206.

Orange hawkweed,
p 205.

Orange mountain-
dandelion, p 205.

Stinging nettle,
p 208.

Leafy spurge,
p 207.

Pale mountain-
dandelion, p 205.

Dwarf mistletoe,
p 209.

Arctic willow
(female), p 209.

Arctic willow
(male), p 209.

JASPER   CABINET   BEARTOOTH

Indian paintbrush, p 213: *C. occidentalis, C. hispida, C. pulchella.*

GLACIER

Indian paintbrush hybrid, p 213.

YELLOWSTONE

Dalmatian toadflax, p 212.

GLACIER

Indian paintbrush, *C. rhexifolia:* p 213.

WALLOWA

Primrose monkeyflower, p 212.

GLACIER

Purple monkeyflower, p 212.

Yellow owl's-clover, p 213.

Fuzzy-tongue penstemon, p 214.

Rocky ledge penstemon, p 214.

Cyan penstemon, p 214.

Wyoming kittentails, p 214.

Elephant's head, p 211.

Bracted lousewort (red form), p 211.

Coiled-beak lousewort, p 211.

Oeder's lousewort, p 211.

Herbs: dicots with irregular flowers (Figwort family)

Sweetvetch, p 217.

Silvery lupine, p 218.

Prickly milkvetch, p 217.

Parry's clover, p 219.

Golden banner, p 220.

Sweet-clover, p 220.

Dwarf alpine clover, p 219.

Crazyweed, *O. lagopus*, p 216.

Herbs: dicots with irregular flowers (Pea family)

Steer's head, p 221.

Bee balm, p 216.

Mountain-sorrel, p 216.

Golden smoke, p 220.

Hooked violet, p 222.

Yellow prairie violet, p 222.

Tall larkspur, p 223.

Nuttall's larkspur, p 223.

Monk's-hood, p 221.

Herbs: dicots with irregular flowers

BEARTOOTH

Forget-me-not, p 230.

BRIDGER

Alpine forget-me-not, p 230. Twinpod, p 259.

WIND RIVER

Alpine mertensia, p 229.

WIND RIVER

Parry's primrose, p 226.

GLACIER

Hover fly, p 497.
Lyall's phacelia, p 228.

JASPER

Bellflowers, p 229: *C. lasiocarpa, C. rotundifolia.*

GLACIER

WALLOWA

Flaxflower, p 225.

Silky phacelia, p 228. Alpine sunflower, p 196.

Phlox, p 226.

Rock-jasmine, p 227.

Sky pilot, p 224.

Mist maiden, p 225.

Sky pilot, p 224,
& Alpine sunflower at 12,500' [3800 m].

Jacob's ladder, p 224.

SAWTOOTH (MT)

Spreading dogbane, p 232.

BEARTOOTH

Shooting-star, p 227.

BEARTOOTH

Bluebells, p 229.

TETON

Pinedrops, p 189.

WALLOWA

Waterleaf, p 228.

PIONEER (ID)

Skyrocket, p 226.

SALMON RIVER

Puccoon, p 231.

BOULDER

Miner's candle, p 231.

BEARTOOTH

Bastard toadflax, p 231.

Herbs: dicots: 5 fused petals

Purple saxifrage, p 234.

Redstem saxifrage, p 234.

Alumroot, p 235.

Sibbaldia, p 232.

Yellow saxifrage, p 234.

Blue flax, p 232.

Starwort, p 238.

Mitrewort, p 233.

Geranium, p 236.

Telesonix, p 235.

King's crown, p 236.

Woodland star, p 235.

Lanceleaf stonecrop, p 236.

Queen's crown, p 236.

White catchfly, p 237.

Grass-of-Parnassus, p 233.

Herbs: dicots: 5 separate petals

Western St.-John's-wort, p 240.

Prairie smoke, p 241.

Alpine avens, p 241.

Blueleaf cinquefoil, p 243.

Ivesia, p 243.

Strawberry, p 241.

Silverweed, p 243.

Herbs: dicots: 5 separate petals

Bluebells (blue), p 229.
Colorado blue columbine (white), p 110.

Red columbine, p 110.

Nagoonberry, p 240.

Strawberry bramble, p 241.

Yellow columbine, p 110.

Globemallow, p 247.

Mountain
hollyhock, p 247.

Herbs: dicots: 5 petals, 15+ stamens

American bistort, p 250.

Alpine
spring-beauty, p 247.

Bupleurum, p 253.

Nineleaf
desert-parsley, p 251.

Sandberg's
biscuitroot, p 251.

Tobacco-root, p 249.

Western valerian, p 249.

Poke knotweed, p 250.

River beauty, p 256.

Fireweed (in fall), p 256.

Hairy clematis, p 258.

Monument plant, p 261.

Paintbrush, *C. miniata*, p 213 (red).
Mountain bog gentian, p 262 (blue).

Ragged robin, p 257.

Yellow pond-lily, p 261.

Herbs: dicots: 4, 6, or several petals

Veronica, p 258.

Cushion draba, p 259, with alpine forget-me-not, p 230, cinquefoil, p 243, and moss-campion, p 237.

Wallflower, p 259.

Pinesap, p 190.

Meadow-rue (male), p 258.

Smelowskia, p 258.

Tufted evening-primrose, p 256.

Herbs: dicots: 4, 6, or several petals

Pygmy bitterroot, p 266.

Prairie crocus, p 264.

Bitterroot, p 266.

Cutleaf anemone, p 264.

Towhead baby, p 264.

Sulphur-flower, p 262.

Marshmarigold, p 263, and Globeflower, p 265.

Cushion buckwheat, p 262.

Herbs: dicots: 3, 6, or several petals

4

Flowering Trees and Shrubs

The distinction between trees and shrubs is a loose one. You can call anything a tree that has a single, woody, upright, main stem at least 4" thick or 26' tall at maturity [10 cm or 8 m]. Many species in this chapter grow as either trees or shrubs depending on environment, and every genus here that has a usually-tree species also has at least one usually-shrub species. That rules out dividing the chapter by stature, but it does at least flow from generally larger to smaller genera.

Trees and Tall Shrubs: deciduous, with catkins

Quaking Aspen

Populus tremuloides (trem-you-**loy**-deez: trembling—). 10" diam × 40' [25 cm × 12 m]; leaves 1–2½" [3–6 cm], broadly heart-shaped to round, pointed, bumpy-edged to fine-toothed, on leafstalks 1–2½" [3–6 cm] and flattened sideways; female and male catkins on separate trees; ¼" [3 mm] conical seedpods, in long strings, splitting in two to release tiny seeds; bark greenish white, smooth (at least above the reach of browsers); dark and rough on old trees or where it's been chewed. Salicaceae (Willow family). Color p 84.

Quaking aspen is the widest-ranging American tree, growing from Alaska to New England and down the Rockies and Sierra Madre to Guanajuato. Here it provides most of our fall color—yellow—and countless benefits to wildlife. Almost 200 species of birds and mammals use it, from elk and beaver to grouse and pika.

Aspen leaves quake or flutter in light breezes because their flattened leafstalks (try rolling one between your fingers) flex easily in one direction only, and therefore twist easily. This fluttering suggested the name *tremula* for the Eurasian aspen, and thence *tremuloides* for its American cousin. Quaking in slight wind is probably a useless side effect of a design that excels in high winds, minimizing drag to keep branches from snapping or trees from uprooting. Twisting enables the leaves of a branchlet to all clump together in the wind, combining into a single weathervane.

Aspen leaves often end up decorated by leaf miners (page 513, and color page 541).

Even with bark that offers no defense against fire, aspens are superlatively fire-adapted. When a fire of any serious size sweeps an

---

Aspen, Elk, and Wolves

In most of its range, aspen reproduction from seeds is very rare; it may be a post-fire phenomenon almost exclusively. In much of the range, clonal reproduction from root sprouts hasn't been doing well either; animals eat the suckers up before they reach tree size. Controversy has raged for years, especially at Yellowstone, over whether or not aspen is in a catastrophic decline that begs for human intervention. On the "Too Many Elk!" side, Charles Kay asserts that only overhunting and fire-setting by Native Americans allowed establishment of aspen groves in times past. He checked the inventory lists of all archaeological sites from the last 10,000 years in the Rockies, and found only tiny percentages of elk among discarded meat bones. He contends that elk browsing today endangers an entire aspen community, and damages other plants—cottonwoods, willows, serviceberries, chokecherries, etc.—with cascading negative impacts on beavers and other animals. He advocates active restoration of carnivores (and of bison in Banff and Jasper); use of intentional fires, but only where elk have been reduced; and stringent limits on development. Since elk become habituated to people, and wolves and grizzlies apparently don't, elk have learned to take advantage of development by using lawns and pastures as calving areas.

On the "Leave Nature Alone!" side, Yellowstone's biologists argue that abundant elk certainly don't threaten extinction of aspen, willows, or beaver. (If they consider aspen immortal, they are not alone. Russian botanist Nikolai Lashchinsky told me that the *P. tremula* clones in his study area "never die." Aspen roots there—after 300 years of complete invisibility—sent up abundant suckers when cattle were taken away.) Elk may

---

aspen grove, all the trunks die. But the roots, protected by four or five inches of soil, survive all but the most intense fires, and soon send up "sucker" shoots. This resembles the famous fire strategy of lodgepole pines—die, then immediately reproduce like crazy and shoot up before much competition gets going—but aspens grow even faster, since roots hold many times more energy than seeds can. Apparently fire also triggers germination of seeds buried in the soil; recent burns are the main situation where we ever see aspen seedlings. Almost all aspen trunks originated not from seeds but from root suckers. Entire groves are clones—genetic individuals of just one sex, with one interconnecting root system. Aspen clones can be vast: one in Utah has 47,000 stems, covers 106 acres, and weighs about 6600 tons—arguably the largest living thing (see page 298). A clone's extent is dramatically visible in autumn, since the timing and hue of fall color are identical throughout, while varying from one clone to the next.

reduce most of the aspen to low thickets for long periods, but if so, that's a natural phase which aspens will sooner or later escape, shooting up past browsable height by growing super-fast and/or by loading their tissues with harsh chemicals. In support, their tree ring counts showed that the Park's aspen trunks mostly came up between 1870 and 1895. Though commercial elk hunters ran amuck in the 1870s, there is pretty good evidence of sizable populations by 1883, including signs of browsing in the innermost rings of this aspen cohort, which the saplings survived. They conclude that climate is a key variable in aspen trunk recruitment, as well as in elk numbers, over time, with winterkill during occasional severe winters as the chief limit on elk. They predict at most a 10% decrease in elk due to wolf reintroduction.

Bill Ripple and Eric Larsen propose a new key to aspen survival. Ring-counting a larger range of Yellowstone aspens, they found that new-shoot survival continued, though decreasing, until around 1920—the year when managers trying to restore elk killed 136 wolves, leaving the Park without a wolf pack. They think it is wolves (or wolves and grizzly bears) that allow aspen to grow up, by altering elk behavior. The threat of predation might keep elk from staying put in any one grove long enough to demolish all of its aspen suckers. Or aspen groves might renew themselves—first here, later there—as wolf packs frequent each in turn. One research team has already observed elk and bison mothers in Yellowstone devoting 20% of their time to "vigilance," leaving less time for foraging which, in their calculations, should lead to reduced winter survival even without any kills by wolves. Reintroduction of wolves to Jasper NP in the 1980s was soon followed by a cohort of aspens reaching tree size. We can hope to see this happen in Yellowstone.

Cottonwoods

Populus spp (**pop**-you-lus: Roman for poplar). Female and male catkins on separate trees; round seed pods, in long strings, split three ways to release many tiny seeds with cottony fluff; bark initially smooth, pale gray, breaking into deep furrows toward tree base. Low to mid-elev streamsides. Salicaceae (Willow family).

Black Cottonwood, *P. trichocarpa* (try-co-car-pa: hairy fruit). =*P. balsamifera*. Leaves have a long pointed tip, a broad, round to heart-shaped base; glossy dark green above, light gray beneath, bright yellow in fall, 3–6" [7.5–15 cm] long (longer and ± diamond-shaped on saplings); leaf buds and their fallen scales sticky and honey-scented in spring; leafstalk more than ⅓ as long as leaf blade; vase-shaped trees 30–130' × 6' dbh [9–40 × 2 m]. Our common cottonwood, but rare in and near WY. Illustrated.

Narrowleaf cottonwood, *P. angustifolia* (angus-tif-**oh**-lia: narrow leaf). Leaves slightly darker above than beneath, most often narrowly lanceolate, tapered to the base, 2–4" [5–10 cm] (longer and much broader on saplings); leafstalk longer than a willow's, but shorter than black cottonwood's; leaf buds sticky, mildly fragrant; slender tree, to 70' [21 m]. Common in WY, decreasing n. Not illustrated.

Cottonwoods rarely grow far from water. With their stout crotches 80' up [24 m], or higher, they provide choice nest sites for river-fishing ospreys, bald eagles and herons.

Black cottonwoods are easily our largest broadleaf trees and our fastest-growing trees of any kind, leading to ideas that they are ideal for plantations. Early plantations tried to produce cottonwood lumber, which was an abject failure. A hundred years later, the idea is back, this time to produce either pulp for paper, chips for fiberboard, or biomass (fuel) for power generation. A plantation of "hybrid poplars" is all one clone, with cottonwood genes predominating, and they look eerily uniform in their vast grids, thanks to identical genes and highly mechanized irrigation.

Many recent books combined the black cottonwood, as *P. balsamifera* ssp. *trichocarpa*, with the balsam poplar, a runty tree or tall shrub of eastern and north-central North America. That left me with the awkward dilemma of either calling our statuesque specimens by the common name of their diminutive sibling, or using unrelated-sounding common names for subspecies of the same species. I was relieved to hear that FNA is expected to treat them as two species.

Willows

Salix spp. (**say**-lix: Roman word for them). Male and female catkins on separate plants; males are the fuzzy or fluffy ones called "pussy willows" if they appear before the leaves, but catkins appear at same time as leaves on all the following spp exc *scouleriana* and sometimes *pseudomonticola*; winter buds are capped by a bud scale which they push off in one piece; often thicket-forming shrubs. Streambanks, wet places; a few can grow on open slopes. Salicaceae.

Scouler willow, *S. scouleriana* (scoo-ler-ee-**ay**-na: after John Scouler, p 66). Also **fire willow**. Leaves 2–4" [5–10 cm], broadly obovate with a pointed tip, whitish- or reddish-velvety underneath; flowering early, occasionally before snowmelt; newer stems velvety; bark often skunky-smelling when crushed; shrubs or small trees 3–40' [1–12 m]. Diverse habitats. Illust above and left.

Barclay willow, *S. barclayi* (**bar**-clay-eye: after a Mr. Barclay who collected it at Kodiak Is. in 1858.). Leaves elliptic to obovate, toothed, green at every age, finely hairy even at maturity, at least on midrib; female catkins on short side-branchlets with a few leaves, older stems shiny dark red; mostly 4–12' tall [1–4 m]. Thicket-forming at alp/subalp elevs. Color p 84.

Geyer willow, *S. geyeriana* (guy-er-ee-**ay**-na: after Karl Geyer, p 176). Leaves lanceolate, 6–8× longer than wide, paler beneath but often ± hairy on both sides in midsummer; catkins short, ¼–1" [6–25 mm], on leafy branchlets up to 4" [10 cm] long; smaller stems bluish-waxy-coated; mostly 8–18' [2.5–5.5 m]. US, extreme s BC. Illustrated.

Serviceberry willow, *S. pseudomonticola*. Leaves elliptic to obovate, toothed, reddish and finely hairy when young, maturing smooth and green; mostly 3–12' tall [1–4 m], but can grow as an alpine mat. From c ID and Tetons n. Color p 84.

Rock willow, *S. vestita* (ves-**tie**-ta: with a coat). Leaves oval, heavy, dark green above, with ± deeply incised veins in a net pattern; catkins on 3-leaved side branchlets; 6–48" [15–120 cm]. BC, AB, n ID, n MT. Color p 541.

Coyote willow, *S. exigua* (ex-**ig**-you-a: short). Also **sandbar willow**. Leaves 10× longer than wide, sparsely toothed, same greenish gray on both sides; mostly 5–10' [1.5–3 m]. High, well drained parts of river bars and banks. Illustrated.

Grayleaf willow, *S. glauca* (**glaw**-ca: whitish-coated). Young leaves and branchlets whitish-woolly; older leaves glossy green above, gray beneath, elliptic to oblanceolate, 1–3" [2.5–8 cm]; female catkins ¾–2½" long [2–6 cm]; mostly 2–5' tall [60–150 cm]. Illustrated at right.

Short-fruit willow, *S. brachycarpa* (bracky-**car**-pa: short fruit). Much like grayleaf willow, exc female catkins (the ones like strings of seeds) ¼–¾" [6–20 mm]. Illust at left.

Umpteen species and hybrids of *Salix* line Rocky Mtn. streams and shores. Three are mat-forming alpine subshrubs (page 209) about 2" high [5 cm]. Except for *vestita* with its distinctive foliage, they are notoriously hard to identify; the above descriptions enable a guess, at best.

An anomaly among willows, the Scouler willow can grow in shade or on slopes far from water. It flourishes after severe fires, either invading with wind-carried seeds or resprouting from deep roots. Seeds typically grow into treelike forms, whereas stump sprouts become multistemmed shrubs. It can also grow on gravel bars, but rarely exceeds 4' [120 cm] there.

Willow shoots are choice browse; they're the staple food of moose. The "too many elk in Yellowstone" faction (see p 116) cites a decrease in both willows and aspen. Beaver will browse willows when they have run out of preferred foods, but overall they greatly increase the number of willows as they expand wetlands. Even the cut stems they use in dams often take root and produce new willows.

Many tribes twisted willow bark into twine for fishnets, baskets, and tumplines (forehead straps for loads carried on the back). Poles were cut from willows to frame sweatlodges or to support fishing platforms—which became all the more secure when they took root where implanted in the riverbed. The bark and roots were used in many ways to relieve pain and inflammation, reduce fever, or stop bleeding, including menstruation. European herbalists discovered similar uses, leading to the synthesis in 1875 of a less acidic form, acetylsalicylic acid, a.k.a. aspirin. Paradoxically, aspirin's greatest future value is probably as a blood anticoagulant to help prevent strokes and heart attacks, whereas the related willow bark ingredient, salicin, is an astringent used topically to staunch blood flow.

Alders

Alnus spp. (**al**-nus: the Roman word for them). Leaves 1½–4" [4–10 cm], oval, pointed, toothed or doubly toothed, ± wavy-edged, turn from green to brown late in fall; male and female catkins on the same tree; female catkins woody, like miniature spruce cones, ½–1" long [12–25 mm]; bark ± smooth, gray or reddish. Betulaceae (Birch family).

Mountain alder, *A. incana* (in-**cay**-na: whitish). =includes *A. tenuifolia* (AB). Also **thinleaf** or **river alder**. Leaf undersides whitish; catkins appear in summer, lengthen and open the next spring before leaves appear; female catkins on short stalks. Tall shrubs, often 20–33' [6–10 m]. Bogs, moist forest, and very abundant on streamsides. Illustrated top right, and color p 84.

Green alder, *A. viridis* (**veer**-id-iss: green). =*A. crispa* (AB), *A. sinuata*. Also **slide** or **Sitka alder**. Leaf undersides often sticky, rarely whitish; catkins appear in spring, simultaneous with leaves; female catkin stalks often longer than catkins; sprawling shrubs 5–16' tall [1.5–5 m]. Higher-elev streamsides, seepy slopes, avalanche basins and tracks. Illustrated at right, and below.

Alders host bacteria in nodules on their roots that convert atmospheric nitrogen for plant use, fixing some in the soil and some directly into the plant. Alder leaf litter is plentiful, nitrogen-rich, quick to decompose and give its nitrogen to the soil.

A green alder has the genetic information for growing upright, as a tree, but it also knows how to flex and bow and sprawl where its environment demands. We know best where it's at its worst—the downhill-sprawling "slide alder" of avalanche tracks. What the roaring avalanche finds accommodating, the sweating bushwhacker finds maddeningly intransigent, a tangle of springy, unstable stems always slipping us downslope like flies in the hairy throat of a pitcher-plant. Too often, what we slip onto is a neighboring devil's club. If, like the avalanche, we could stick to downhill travel, we'd have little problem with slide alders.

Almost every tribe that lived near these alders used their inner bark for red and orange dyes—one application being on fishing nets, to make them invisible underwater. Catkin tea was said to improve children's appetites. Alder seeds, buds, and catkins provide critical winter staples for small birds that stay year-round, such as pine siskins and chickadees.

Birches

Betula (bet-you-la: Roman word for them). Female catkins (on same plant as males) erect; their core stems persist after dropping bracts and winged seeds; twigs usually downy; bark has raised horizontal dark streaks ("lenticels"). Betulaceae.

Paper birch, *B.papyrifera* (pap-er-if-er-a: paper-bearing). Leaves pointed-oval, 1½–4" [4–10 cm], with teeth of two sizes, turn yellow in fall; leaf undersides have tiny hair tufts in the forks of veins; bark bronze on young trees, becoming ± chalky white, peeling in papery sheets; tree up to 100' × 3' dbh [30 × 1 m]. Sunny moist slopes, bogs. All the birches hybridize rather freely; BC, AB, n WA, n ID, n MT; ne OR and c ID have hybrids with light brown bark. Illustrated at right, and color p 526.

Water birch, *B. occidentalis* (ox-id-en-**tay**-lis: western). Leaves pointed-oval, 1–2½" [2–6 cm], with teeth of two sizes, turn yellow in fall; young branches covered with tiny wartlike resin dots; bark smooth, dark red to bronze; shrub or tree up to 35' [10 m]. Streambanks and shores. Illustrated at left.

Bog birch, *B. pumila* (pew-mil-a: dwarf). =includes *B. nana*, *B. glandulosa* (USDA, BC). Also **swamp birch, dwarf birch**. Leaves oval to round, ⅜–1¼" [1–3 cm], sawtoothed, net-veined, heavy, leathery, turn orange to russet in fall; young branches covered with tiny wartlike resin dots; bark smooth, dark red; shrub usually 1–6' [30–180 cm]. Willow thickets, bogs, seeps, shores. Illustrated at right, and color p 84.

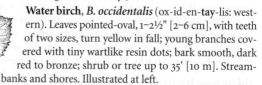

Paper birch bark was made into canoes and beautiful baskets by interior B.C. tribes; the Carrier people even made watertight foldable birchbark canoes. By carefully peeling only the outer layer, they could harvest it without killing the tree. (Don't try it; you haven't been taught how.) Extra-thinly peeled bark made good tinder for starting fires.

Water birch bark was also used for canoes and baskets, when big enough trees were found, but of course it wasn't as beautiful. Its inner bark was used for a brown dye. Some tribes thought birch bark could be brewed into an effective contraceptive and/or abortifacent.

Rocky Mountain Maple

Acer glabrum (**glab**-rum: smooth). Also **Douglas maple**.
Flowers small, green, in small clusters; winged seeds rarely over 1" long, straight-backed, in pairs at ± right angles; leaves opposite, 3- (or 5-) lobed, toothed either sharply or bluntly, red-orange in fall, 2–4½" [10–6 cm], on equally long leaf-stalks; twigs reddish; bark gray to purplish; shrubs or trees up to 40'+ [10 m+]. The champion, near Sandpoint, ID, is 80' tall × 17" dbh [20 × 42 cm]. Ravines, flood-plains, burns, clearcuts, and slopes, below 10,000'. Aceraceae. Color p 541.

Brilliant red blotches that appear on maple leaves in midsummer may be induced by either fungal infection or Eriophyd mites. In either case the mechanism is similar to that of fall color: vessels carrying photosynthetic sugars out of the leaves get blocked, and the trapped sugars are converted into red pigments called anthocyanins. Paradoxically, this maple turns yellow, not red, in fall. In winter its twigs provide vital browse for deer, elk, and sheep.

The wood is hard and strong, but easy to bend and shape after soaking and heating. This made it ideal for many of the most useful implements in a culture with little or no metal. Just for starters, think snowshoe frames, lodge frames, fish net handles, drum hoops, digging sticks, and spoons. One Salish elder called this maple his favorite wood for arrows. Maple bark supplied fiber for tying or weaving.

Red-Osier Dogwood

Cornus sericea (ser-**iss**-ia: silky). =includes *C. stolonifera*. Also **creek dogwood**.
Leaves opposite, 2–5" [5–13 cm], elliptical, pointed, wavy-edged, the veins curving around to merge along the margin, coloring richly but unevenly in fall; 4 white petals, ⅛" [3 mm]; 4 stamens; 4 tiny sepals; flowers in flat-topped clusters; berries dull pale bluish or greenish, ¼" diam [6 mm], single-seeded, un-palatable; new twigs deep red or purplish; shrubs 6–16' [2–5 m]. Wet places. Cornaceae (Dogwood family). Color p 84.

This dogwood's flowers lack the big white bracts we think of as dogwood flowers. You can see a resemblance, though, in the tiny true flowers, as well as the outline, venation, and fall coloring of the leaves. After the leaves fall, rich-red young stems (osiers) remain. "Osier" is an old word from the French, meaning a long new shoot, originally of willow, suitable for wicker. "Dogwood" derives from the Scandinavian *dag*, for "skewer." For the nice salty flavor it infused, the Shuswap and Okanagan also used this species for skewers, and for salmon roasting and drying racks. Dogwood smoke flavor was relished in dried berries, smoked fish, and from pipe bowls as Prince Maximilian noted, presciently, in 1833: "Like all the Indians, he inhaled the smoke, a custom which is, doubtless, the cause of many [lung] diseases. The [mixture] the Indians of this part of the country smoke, is called kini-kenick, and consists of the inner green bark of the red willow, dried, and powdered, and mixed with the tobacco of the traders."

Twinberries

Lonicera spp. (lo-**niss**-er-a: after Adam Lonitzer). Also **bush honeysuckles**. Pairs of flowers—and ¼" [6 mm] berries—on a short stalk from leaf axils; corolla yellow to white, ⅜–¾" [1–2 cm], 5-lobed, tubular, fused over ½ its length; 5 stamens; calyx inconspicuous; leaves smooth above, often hairy beneath; shrubs 2–8' [60–240 cm]. Caprifoliaceae (Honeysuckle family). Color p 85.

Black twinberry, *L. involucrata* (in-vo-lu-**cray**-ta: with involucres). =*Distegia involucrata* (CO). Also **inkberry**, **bearberry**. Flowers hairy, flanked by 2 pairs of heavy, hairy bracts that mature deep carmine red around the glossy black berries; leaves elliptic, pointed, 2–5" [5–13 cm]. Streambanks, seeps. Illustrated.

Red twinberry, *L. utahensis*. Also **Utah honeysuckle**. Flowers without conspicuous bracts, hairy inside but not out; berries red to salmon pink, leaves oblong, rounded at tip, ½–3" [1–8 cm]. Moist, ± wooded slopes.

Coast tribes called black twinberries "crow food," Crow being the only spirit crazy and black enough to relish such bitter black fruit. Interior tribes, calling them "grizzly berries," think bears relish them. "Inkberry" juice was face paint for dolls or dye for graying hair.

Black twinberry plants carry twinning (or oppositeness) to an extreme: opposite leaf axils bear opposite stalks, each bearing a pair of flowers between two pairs of hairy bracts, two of them two-lobed. The bracts typically turn deep magenta and reflex downward over time to better offset the paired, purplish black berries that replace the pale flowers. This display usually hides in a damp thicket.

Elderberries

Sambucus spp. (sam-**bew**-cus: Greek name for them). Also **elders**. Leaves opposite, pinnately compound (rarely twice-compound), 5–12" long [12–30 cm]; leaflets narrowly elliptical, pointed, fine-toothed, ± asymmetrical at base; flowers cream-white, 5-merous, tiny, in dense clusters; berries ¼" [6 mm] round, 3–5-seeded; stems pith-filled; shrubs or shrubby trees 3–20' tall [1–6 m]. Streamsides, thickets, moist forest or clearings. Caprifoliaceae or Adoxaceae. Compare with mountain-ash, page 130, whose leaves are also pointy and pinnately compound, but alternate. Color p 85.

Blue elderberry, *S. mexicana*. =*S. cerulea* (BC, WY, INT, CO), *S nigra* (USDA). Leaflets usually 7, 9, or 11; leaf undersides and twigs whitened; flowers and (later) berries in ± flat-topped clusters without a single central stem; berries blue (blue-black with a waxy bloom). Mainly w of CD.

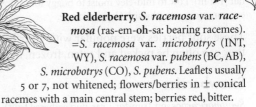

Red elderberry, *S. racemosa* var. *racemosa* (ras-em-**oh**-sa: bearing racemes). =*S. racemosa* var. *microbotrys* (INT, WY), *S. racemosa* var. *pubens* (BC, AB), *S. microbotrys* (CO), *S. pubens*. Leaflets usually 5 or 7, not whitened; flowers/berries in ± conical racemes with a main central stem; berries red, bitter.

Black elderberry, *S. racemosa* var. *melanocarpa* (melon-o-**car**-pa: black fruit). =*S. racemosa* var. *pubens* (BC), *S. melanocarpa*, *S. microbotrys* var. *melanocarpa* (CO). Like red elderberry, but berries black to very dark red; shrubs mostly 3–6' [90–180 cm].

Where they grow together, red elderberry blooms, sets fruit, and ripens a good month ahead of blue elderberry. The blue berries are more popular for jelly, wine, or eating fresh than our red or black ones; legendary elderberry wine comes from an Old-World black elderberry, *S. nigra*. Ugly rumors crop up to the effect that red elderberries are poisonous, but this is normally untrue of the fully ripe fruit. Northwest tribes ate berries of both species, fresh or more often steamed and/or stored until lean times. The Okanagan devised a unique way to refrigerate them. They waited to harvest blue elderberries just before the first snows of winter, then spread the bunches on a thick layer of Ponderosa pine needles and laid another layer of needles on top, to be covered in turn by snow. The berries stayed moist and just above freezing. They were easy to locate, since a bit of

---

berry juice would reach the surface as a pink-tinged blue stain.

Elder bark, leaves, twigs, and roots have been regarded as toxic and/or medicinal. Infusions of them were used to induce perspiration, lactation, or vomiting, or alternatively to reduce swelling, infection, or diarrhea—an odd mix of prescriptions. The soft pith of elder stems was hollowed out to make "pea shooters" for little boys, pipestems for men, whistles to lure elk, and drinking straws for girls during the ritual restrictions of puberty.

Mooseberry

Viburnum edule (vie-**burn**-um: Roman name for it; **ed**-you-lee: edible). Also **moosebrush**, **bush-cranberry**, **squashberry**. Flowers white, in small clusters, ¼" diam, with 5 petals and 5 calyx lobes; berries red-orange, juicy, tart, aromatic, with 1 flat seed; leaves opposite, 1–4" long [2–10 cm] and ± equally wide, sharply toothed, the bigger ones 3-lobed, turning crimson in fall; shrub 3–7' tall [1–2 m]. Low to mid-elev moist to boggy forest; commoner northward. Caprifoliaceae.

These sour berries were popular with all tribes, especially because they can often be picked and eaten, frozen, in midwinter

Snowberries

Symphoricarpos spp. (sim-for-i-**car**-pus: gathered fruit). Also **waxberries**. Flowers pinkish to white, ¼–⅜" [6–10 mm], petals fused at least half their length; berries white, paired or clustered, pulpy, 2-seeded; leaves and twigs opposite, most leaves oval to elliptical, 1–2" long [2–5 cm]; shrubs 1½–4' tall [45–120 cm]. Caprifoliaceae.

S. oreophilus (or-ee-**off**-ill-us: mountain-loving). Flower a tubular bell shape, about twice as long as it is wide; berries ¼–⅜" [6–10 mm]; leaves ± crowded, firm, veiny, slightly rolled under at edges, rarely lobed; robust shrubs spreading by root suckers, often abundant. US and extreme s Canada. Illust. Color p 85.

S. albus (**al**-bus: white). Flower broadly bell-shaped, scarcely longer than wide; berries ½" [12 mm]; leaves thin, often lobed. Color p 85.

I've always thought of this as "popcorn plant," which seems to capture its likeness better than "snow" or "wax," though at the risk of falsely tempting hungry hikers. The lightweight berries, though eaten and disseminated by birds and rodents, are mildly poisonous to humans, causing vomiting, dizziness and mild sedation in children.

Fast-growing non-flowering shoots of *S. albus* have variable leaves, sporting all numbers and sizes of odd-shaped lobes.

Buffaloberry

Shepherdia canadensis (shep-**er**-dia: after John Shepherd). Also **soopolallie, soapberry.** Flowers tiny, yellowish, 4-lobed, the females and males on different plants; berries ¼" [6 mm], yellow to red, bitter, tipped with 4 flat-spreading calyx lobes (illust); leaves opposite, elliptical, ½–2¼" [1–6 cm], green above; undersides have brown scabby dots and a silvery scurfy coating; shrubs 3–10' [1–3 m]. Shrubfields and open forests below timberline. Elaeagnaceae (Oleaster family). Color p 85.

From Montana to the Bering Sea, "Indian ice cream" was made by whisking bitter buffaloberries and water into a rich froth. It's an acquired taste. I guess everyone acquired it. (Except east of the Plains; the plant grows all the way to Newfoundland.) But they were quite happy to add sugar, once it became available.

Buffaloberry seems to be almost indifferent to habitat. The Forest Service report on Montana forest habitats at all elevations divides them into 100 types. Buffaloberry was found in 72, but didn't cover more than 13% of the ground in any one. I'd say it's equally widespread in shrub-dominated communities. Getting nitrogen from symbiotic bacteria on its roots undoubtedly helps.

Virgin's Bowers

Clematis spp. (**clem**-a-tis: a vine cutting). =*Atragene* spp. (CO). Also **clematises.** Four blue to purple petal-like sepals, 1¼–2¼" long [6–10 mm], wrinkly and rather floppy; flowers on 2–6" [5–15 cm] stalks scattered singly along the vine; seeds with long plumey tails, in a dense ball; leaves opposite, compound; low climbing or trailing woody vines, to 8' long [2.5 m]. Open forest. Ranunculaceae (Buttercup family).

Blue virgin's bower, *C. occidentalis.* =*C. verticillaris, C. columbiana* (most books before ±1981). 3 lanceolate leaflets. Color p 84.

Rocky Mountain virgin's bower, *C. columbiana.* =*C. pseudoalpina, C. tenuiloba* (in most books before ±1981). Flowers often ± closed, urn-shaped; 6 or 9 leaflets, often lobed. US.

Like many other members of its family, virgin's-bower contains toxic alkaloids and has been applied externally. As a hair rinse, the Okanagan thought it prevented gray hair, but the Nlaka'pamux treated exzema. The Blackfoot, in contrast, used it as a charm against ghosts, or to heal "ghost bullet" wounds.

Mock-Orange

Philadelphus lewisii (fil-a-**del**-fus: after Ptolemy Philadelphus, King of Egypt; lew-**iss**-ee-eye: after Meriwether Lewis, p 257). =includes *P. trichotheca, P. inodorus* (USDA). Also **syringa**. Flowers 1–2" diam [2–5 cm], fabulously fragrant (rarely in- odorous), in showy clusters; 4 white petals, many yellow-tipped stamens; leaves opposite, oval to lanceolate, with 3 main veins from the base; shrubs 3–10 [1–2 m]'. Rocky slopes, streamsides, cliffs, open woods; sc ID n to Crowsnest. Hydrangeaceae. Color p 86.

As if a mock-orange thicket in the July sun weren't heavenly enough already, you're likely to find it aflutter with swallowtails as well. Ida- hoans made an excellent choice of State Flower, but I'm puzzled that they call it "syringa," the Latin name for garden lilacs (no relation). The fragrance is nothing like lilac, but a lot like orange blossoms which, though also unrelated, at least have four big white petals and many stamens.

Trees and Shrubs: deciduous, 5 petals, 10+ stamens (Rose family)

Serviceberry

Amelanchier alnifolia (am-el-**an**-she-er: archaic French term for it; al-nif-**oh**-lia: alder leaf). Also **saskatoon, shadbush**. Leaves 1–2" [2–5 cm], oval, toothed at tip but not at the base; petals white, ½–1" long [12–25 mm], narrow; the inflorescence of 3–15 flowers is of- ten a jumble of petals; berries ½" [12 mm], several-seeded, red, ripen- ing to purplish black, with bloom; low spreading shrubs to 30' [9 m] trees, though usually less than 10' [3 m]. Sunny slopes. Rosaceae. Color p 87.

Meriwether Lewis said "sarvisberry," as many Easterners still do. The word derives not from "serving" but from *Sorbus*, the European ser- vice tree which is closely related to our mountain-ash (p 130).

The berries are sweet and good, resembling a duller, seedier blue- berry. For Plains tribes they rivalled chokecherries as the commonest berries in pemmican, and for Interior BC nations they were the most highly valued of all berries. Birds, bears, and elk love them and/or the shrub's branches. They love them not wisely but too well, Charles Kay might say. "Serviceberry and chokecherry plants in Yellowstone," he reports, "now average less than 20" [50 cm] tall and produce virtually no berries because they are repeatedly browsed" in stark contrast to plentiful berries in adjacent elk exclosures. (See page 116.)

Chokecherry

Prunus virginiana (**prune**-us: Roman for
plum; vir-gin-ee-**ay**-na: of Virginia).
Leaves 2–4" [5–10 cm], oval, pointed,
fine-toothed; flowers ⅜" [1 cm], white, with
20-30 bright yellow stamens, showy, in dense
racemes 2–6" long [5–15 cm]; cherries oval, ¼" [6
mm], sweetish but astringent, crimson to black;
tall shrubs or small trees up to 30' [9 m]. Thickets
and edges of clearings. Rosaceae. Color p 87.

Chokecherries are named for their powerful pucker-
ing effect. Fortunately, their sweetness preserves better
than their astringency; plains tribes pounded them into
pemmican, settlers boiled them into jelly. Pemmican contained
quantities of pounded chokecherry pits, but we now know that
Prunus pits all contain amygdalin, which breaks down into cyanide,
and have been known to kill small children. (Genus *Prunus* includes
cherries, prunes, and plums.) Nancy Turner speculates that traditional methods of drying may reduce or eliminate the toxins. Chokecherry leaves (without special processing, we assume) are choice
browse for deer and elk, but in large quantities have killed cattle.

Chokecherry is one of several common hosts for tent caterpillars (page 514). These moths have a population outbreak every ten
years or so, consuming billions of leaves down to the midvein and
tenting the remains under cobwebby shelters. This stunts the plants'
growth for the year, but does no lasting damage.

Infusions of chokecherry leaves, twigs, or bark were popular
medicines in times past. Both Anglo- and native Americans prescribed them for diarrhea, intestinal worms, and other stomach ills.
The Okanagan considered them so beneficial to stomachs that they
could prevent postpartum stretch marks. The Blackfoot and others
soothed sore throats and coughs with cherry juice, either fresh or re-
constituted from dried cherries—the original cherry cough syrup.
Meriwether Lewis, camped on the upper Missouri in 1805, cured his
own case of severe stomach cramps with two pints of "a strong black
decoction of an astringent bitter taste," brewed from chokecherry
twigs. He already knew the plant since it grows all the way to the East
Coast (hence *virginianus*). Later, crossing the Bitterroots, the party
held starvation at bay with chokecherries.

Mountain-Ash

Sorbus spp. (**sor**-bus: the Roman term). Leaves pinnately compound, leaflets 7–13, 1¼–2½" [3–6 cm], oblong to elliptical, fine-toothed at the tip but not at the base (compare serviceberry, p 128 and wildroses, p 132), bright yellow and orange in fall; flowers white, fragrant, ½" diam, in dense, flat-topped 1¼–4" [3–10 cm] clusters; berries red to orange, ⅜" diam [1 cm], several-seeded, mealy, bitter; shrubs (rarely small trees) 3–14' [1–4 m]. Moist ± open forest. Rosaceae.

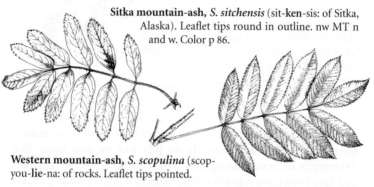

Sitka mountain-ash, *S. sitchensis* (sit-**ken**-sis: of Sitka, Alaska). Leaflet tips round in outline. nw MT n and w. Color p 86.

Western mountain-ash, *S. scopulina* (scop-you-**lie**-na: of rocks. Leaflet tips pointed.

Mountain-ash berries are important forage for birds and subalpine small mammals, especially since they stay on through winter. Judging by reports of birds flying "under the influence," they have enough sugar to ferment on the bush; but if so, it hides behind an acrid taste and a mealy texture. There are few reports of native tribes using them. Wine is sometimes made from the sweeter berries of the European mountain-ash or rowan tree, *S. aucuparia*.

Thimbleberry

Rubus parviflorus (**roo**-bus: Roman word for the genus; par-vif-**lor**-us: small- or few-flowered) =*Rubacer parviflorum* (CO). Leaves 3–8" [8–20 cm], at least as broad as long, palmately 5-lobed (maplelike), fine- toothed, soft and fuzzy; petals white, ½–1" [12–25 mm], nearly round, crinkly; berries red, like thin fine-grained raspberries; stems erect, 4–7' [1–2 m], ± woody but weak, thornless. Moist forest and thickets. Rosaceae.

Fruits of genus *Rubus* are sometimes sorted into raspberries and blackberries, as follows: a raspberry, when picked, is cupshaped, pulling cleanly from its receptacle, or core; a blackberry pulls its receptacle with it. Thimbleberries are raspberries by this definition, but don't taste like a raspberry. Some find them delicious, others insipid, perhaps due to a colorblindness of the tongue. I concede that they're gritty, sometimes dry, acid to the point of cankering, and exasperatingly sparse on the bush, yet I find in a good thimbleberry one of the more exquisite berry flavors on earth.

Wild Raspberry

Rubus idaeus (eye-**dee**-us: of Mt. Ida, on Crete). Leaves 3- (or 5) compound; leaflets elliptical, pointed, toothed, sometimes with a few lobes; flowers white, ¾' [1 cm], in small clusters; berries bright red, juicy, obviously raspberries; thorny canes, 3–6' [90–180 cm], with yellowish, peeling bark, live for two years. Canyon bottoms, forest, or moist talus (incl alpine). Rosaceae. Color p 87.

The American red raspberry is now included in the European species from which horticultural strains were bred.

Spiraeas

Spiraea spp. (spy-**ree**-a: the Roman term). Also **meadow-sweets**. Leaves 1–3" [2–8 cm], oval, toothed on outer half only; flowers pink to white, tiny, fuzzy with 25-50 protruding stamens, in slightly convex-topped heads about 2" [5 cm] across; seed pods tiny, 2- to several-seeded. Rosaceae.

Subalpine spiraea, *S. splendens.* =*S. densiflora* (AB). Flowers pink; leaves downy underneath; shrubs, often prostrate or leaning. Moist meadows, thickets, forest. Color p 86.

Birchleaf spiraea, *S. betulifolia* (bet-you-lif-**oh**-lia: birch leaf). Flowers white to very slightly pink; leaves smooth; usually erect shrub. Open forest. Illustrated. Color p 86.

Shrubby Cinquefoil

Pentaphylloides floribunda (penta-fill-**oy**-deez: cinquefoil-like; flori-**bun**-da: flowers abundant). =*Potentilla fruticosa* (AB). Petals yellow, ½" long [12 mm]; sepals apparently 10 (5 smaller bracts alternate with 5 true sepals); compound leaves of 3, 5, or 7 leaflets, hairy, not toothed; seed pods long-haired; dense, rounded to matted shrubs 6–24" tall [15–60 cm]. Diverse sites, often rocky, but not dry. Rosaceae. Color p 86.

Shrubby cinquefoil or "yellow rose" grows on rocky hills all across the country and in Eurasia, and is cultivated in cities. Under the name *Potentilla fruticosa*, it was until recently the single shrub in a genus of dozens of herbs, the cinquefoils (page 243).

Wildroses

Rosa spp. Leaves pinnately compound; leaflets 5 to 9, oval to elliptical, toothed except at base, 1–2½" [2–6 cm]; flowers pink; fruit orange, turning red or purple, many-seeded, dry and sour; ± thorny shrubs. Moist forests and openings. Rosaceae.

Woods rose, *R. woodsii* (woods-ee-eye: after Joseph Woods). Flowers 1–2" [2–5 cm], in small clusters; thorns usually few; the pair of thorns below axils are heaviest; plants 1–8' [30–240 cm]. Range extends out onto the Plains.

Prickly rose, *R. sayi* (say-eye: after T. Say, p 230). =*R. acicularis sayi* (BC, USDA, AB). Flowers 1½–2½" [4–6 cm]; fruits usually bluish or purplish; plants 1–5', bristling all over with fine straight thorns. Floral emblem of AB; not in OR, rare in ID. Color p 87.

Nootka rose, *R. nutkana* (noot-kay-na: of Nootka, BC). Flowers 2¼–3½" [6–9 cm]; fruits also large, single; thorns mainly in pairs below leaf and branch axils; plants 2–6' [60–180 cm]. All exc AB. Illust at right.

Baldhip rose, *R. gymnocarpa* (jim-no-car-pa: naked fruit). Flowers ¾–1" [2–2.5 cm], single; fruits ⅜" [1 cm], round, unique among these spp in not retaining the 5 sepals; plants 1½–4' [45–100 cm], bristling all over with fine thorns. BC to nw MT to OR.

One wonders if this pale, unassuming five-petalled bloom could ever have carried the mythic and symbolic weight of The Rose that troubadours sang of. Had horticultural wizards been at work multiplying rose petals and colors even before the Middle Ages? Yes, they had. "Hundred-petaled" roses were grown by 400 B.C. Our wild rose's fruit, the rose "hip" or "apple," has lots of vitamin C, and sometimes a breath-freshening flavor after a few frosts have broken it down.

Friedrich (also spelled Frederick) **Pursh**, a German botanist, spent several years in the eastern U.S., where he came into possession—somewhat mysteriously—of the prize set of unpublished plant specimens of the era: those from the Lewis and Clark Expedition. He published them in his *Flora Americae Septentrionale* (1814), the first attempt at a coast-to-coast American flora. Detractors claimed he had no right to publish these specimens, let alone to take many of them to Europe, as he did. To be fair, overacquisitiveness was rife among naturalists of that century, even some great ones, and Pursh at least did a creditable job of naming and describing. He spent twelve years on an intended second magnum opus, a flora of Canada, only to see it totally lost in a fire.

Mallow Ninebark

Physocarpus malvaceus (fie-zo-**car**-pus: bladder
fruit; mal-**vay**-see-us: mallow—). Also **sevenbark**.
Flowers small, white (stamens often pink), in dense
hemispheric heads 1¼–2" diam [3–5 cm]; two pistils per
flower become two 1-seeded seed pods per cluster; leaves
1–3" [2–8 cm], palmately veined and 3- (rarely 5-) lobed,
coarsely toothed; bark peeling, reddish or yellowish brown;
shrubs 3–8' tall [1–2.5 m]. Widely scattered, but locally a shrub
layer dominant under Douglas-fir. Rosaceae. Color p 86.

Ninebark bark shreds and peels in layers—but rarely,
if ever, so many as nine, or even seven.

Ocean-Spray

Holodiscus discolor (ho-lo-**dis**-cus: entire disk; **dis**-color:
variegated). Also **ironwood, arrowwood, creambush,
rock-spiraea**. Leaves 1–2½" [2–6 cm], roughly oval, with coarse teeth
and often fine teeth upon those; flowers tiny, whitish, profuse in 4–7"
[10–18 cm] conical clusters; seeds single in tiny dry pods; clusters of pods
persist in place through winter; shrubs 4–12' [1–4 m]. In sun, often near
streams, up to mid elevs; BC, WA, OR, ID, w MT. Rosaceae. Color p 86.

Blooming with masses of tiny cream-white flowers in parallel sprays,
ocean-spray resembles an ocean wave breaking. "Arrowwood" and
"ironwood" refer to Native American uses for the straight branches
when fire-hardened—arrows, fishing spears, digging sticks for clams
and roots, roasting tongs, drum hoops, and baby's cradle hoops.

Shrubs: deciduous, 5 petals, 5 stamens

Two shrubs with composite flowers are in this group, p 138. Dogbane,
p 232, and baneberry, p 265, sometimes mistaken for shrubs, are not.

Bitterbrush

Purshia tridentata (**pur**-shia: after F. Pursh, opp page;
try-den-**tay**-ta: 3-toothed). Also **antelopebrush**. Calyx
funnel-shaped, fuzzy, 5-lobed, petals yellow, flat-
spreading, ¾" diam [2 cm]; capsules 1-seeded, long-
pointed; leaves aromatic, ¾" long [2 cm], very narrow, 3-pointed and -veined, grayish, white-woolly
underneath, edges rolled under; stiff bushy shrubs 3–6'
[1–2 m] tall, rarely up to 10' [3 m]; leaves sometimes persist through
winter. Steppe, open forest; US, extreme se BC. Rosaceae. Color p 87.

Shrubs: deciduous, 5 petals (Rose family)

Bitterbrush thrives on sites marginal for forest growth, like the lower timberline zone. It enjoys an advantage in being able to fix nitrogen, fertilizing itself and its plant community. Few of our common shrubs fix nitrogen. Of course, plants can't do it themselves: bacteria in nodules on their roots fix the nitrogen. They can fix even more if the same roots also host mycorrhizal partners. (See page 290).

Though bitter to us, it is rated just about tops by all Rocky Mountain browsers. Protein content is a major concern to browsers, and bitterbrush is protein-rich. Years of heavy browsing ('hedging') often give the shrubs a low, mounded form.

Bitterbrush and big sagebrush share the name *tridentata* and the leaf shape it refers to, and also a fuzzy gray leaf surface and many of the same sites. Their flower structures, however, are utterly different, and they are unrelated; the leaves evolved convergently in adapting to similar habitat. (Sagebrush leaves do not roll under at the edges, and are equally woolly on top and bottom; see page 138.)

Currants and Gooseberries

Ribes spp. (**rye**-beez: Arabic word for rhubarb). Sepals 5, united about half their length; 5 petals smaller and less colorful than sepals, attached just inside calyx mouth alternately with the 5 stamens; leaves palmately lobed; weakstemmed shrubs. Grossulariaceae (Currant family). Color p 87.

Swamp gooseberry, *R. lacustre* (la-**cus**-tree: of lakes). Also **black prickly currant**. Flowers saucer-shaped, pinkish, 10–15 in pendent clusters; berries hairy, purplish black; leaves hairless, ½–2½" [1–6 cm]; stems covered with tiny prickles, larger spines whorled around stem nodes; straggly or sprawling shrubs. Forested wet spots, esp mid elevs. Color p 87.

Red gooseberry, *R. montigenum* (mon-**tidge**-en-um: mtn. race). Also **alpine prickly currant**. Flowers saucer-shaped, pinkish, 4–8 in pendent clusters; berries hairy, red-purple; leaves sticky-hairy, ½–1¼" [1–3 cm]; numerous large prickles at stem nodes, no fine prickles; spreading shrubs 8–24" [20–60 cm]. Rocky sites, esp alp/subalpine. Color p 87.

Wax currant, *R. cereum* (**see**-ree-um: wax). Flowers pale yellow, sticky-hairy, tubular, ¾" long [2 cm], ending in short spreading calyx lobes; berries red; leaves grayish, ± round, ½–1¼" diam [1–3 cm], toothed, gummy, musky when crushed; stems lack prickles. Sunny slopes, to timberline; US and dry se BC.

Sticky currant, *R. viscosissimum* (vis-co-**see**-sim-um: stickiest). Flowers greenish or pinkish white, bell-shaped, 3–10 in loose clusters; berries black; leaves, young stems, berries, and flower bases downy and sticky; leaves musky, 1–3½" [2–9 cm], with 3 (or 5) shallow rounded lobes. Forest, aspen groves; Crowsnest s.

Northern black currant, *R. hudsonianum*. Flowers white, 6–15, almost saucer-shaped, in a slender ± erect raceme; berries black, often with waxy bloom; entire plant ± sticky hairy, rank-smelling; leaves 1½–4½" [4–11 cm], with 3–5 pointed lobes. Stream banks, forests, meadows.

Gooseberries have nothing to do with geese; the word is from the French *groseille*, as is the family name, Grossulariaceae. Gooseberry plants differ from currants in having prickles. All Rocky-Mountain *Ribes* fruits are edible and nutritious, and most were eaten both fresh and dried by most tribes. Today's writers recommend them only to the starving or insatiably curious; some say that certain species are worth eating, but don't agree as to which ones. Some currants take your mouth to the movies, running sweet moments tightly sandwiched between sour and bitter episodes; others are only insipidly bitter. Some tribes used large gooseberry thorns as fishhooks, others as needles for tattooing or for removing splinters. Beware, they inflict painful allergic reactions in some people.

Ribes species are prey to white pine blister rust, an introduced fungus that devastates five-needle pines (page 59). The fungus must alternate between *Pinus* and *Ribes* hosts, so Plan A for saving pines was the "War on *Ribes*." Unhappily for *Ribes*, this coincided with Plan A for fighting the Great Depression—to create of millions of subsistence-wage public service jobs. Soon, 13,000 men were on the WPA and CCC payrolls killing shrubs, and when those men went off to fight the Great War, this little war conscripted delinquent teens and POWs. Some 444 million currant and gooseberry plants died in the northern Rockies between 1930 and 1946. In the 1950s the government, now short on manpower, escalated the war with new herbicides.

In the end, *Ribes* won. The Forest Service gave up and went looking for more benign ways to deal with blister rust. Thirteen million gallons of 2-4-D and 2-4-5-T were just a drop in the bucket that would have been needed for the number of shrubs out there. Why didn't the government figure that out sooner? Another pointless ecotragedy brought to you by Hubris Productions.

Granted, currants do have a remarkable ability to germinate and grow from very old buried seeds, whenever the shade is removed—a fire response strategy they share with snowbrush.

Western Poison-Ivy

Toxicodendron rydbergii spp. (toxic-oh-**den**-dron: poison tree; rid-**berg**-ee-eye: after Per Rydberg). =*Rhus radicans* (AB). Leaves compound, leaflets 3 (rarely 5), 2–5" [5–13 cm], narrowly pointed, with a few variable lobes; flowers ¼" diam [6 mm], greenish white; berries white, up to ¼" [6 mm], in dense, erect clusters, single-seeded, ± striped longitudinally; shrub up to 3' tall [1 m]. Fairly dry low-elev clearings, outcrops. Anacardiaceae (Cashew family). Color p 88.

Leaflets in threes almost always.

Some leaflets crimson by late summer, and the rest by fall.

New foliage reddish and glossy in spring.

Translucent white berries (for mnemonic aid, think of blisters) in bunches, present by late summer and persisting in winter.

Unlike nettle stingers—an elaborate and effective defense against browsing—poison-ivy/oak/sumac poison has little survival value to the plant. Call it an accident of biochemistry, or one of the commonest allergies in *Homo sapiens*. Other species are unaffected; they gather the nectar, eat the berries, or browse the leaves with impunity or even enthusiasm. In humans, susceptibility can be acquired but rarely shed. Many people sure of their immunity have tried to show it off, only to get a rude shock a couple of days later. Apparently this never happened to Leo Hitchcock, senior author of *Flora of the Pacific Northwest,* who liked to show off by casually picking specimens with his bare hands on class field trips. Lore has it that immunity can be cultivated by eating tiny leaves over the period of their development in spring. **Don't try it.**

Symptoms, if any, appear 12 to 72 hours after contact. If you itch within minutes of laying eyes on poison-ivy, that's from other irritants, like anxiety. If you wash all exposed parts within ten minutes with soap and hot water (or, in the field, with Tecnu) and quarantine your exposed clothes and pets until you can launder them, your odds of escaping are still excellent. The allergen, urushiol, is in the sap; a light brushup hardly brings any out. A few people, though, are alarmingly sensitive. There have been fatalities from poison-ivy smoke inhalation—drownings in a sea of blister fluid in the lungs. (The toxin is destroyed by complete burning, but smoke may carry unburned particles.)

For most of us, the only defense needed is to know when we are going into areas where poison-oak or ivy grows, and then to know the characteristics, spot the plants without fail, and circumvent them. If you want to take greater precautions, try Ivy-Block, a new patented barrier cream that you spread on your skin.

Devil's Club

Oplopanax horridus (op-lo-**pan**-ux: heavily armed cure-all; **hor**-id-us: horrid). Leaves 6–15" diam [15–38 cm], palmately 7–9-lobed, fine-toothed, all borne ± flat near top of stem; leafstalks and undersides of main veins densely spiny; flowers ¼" [6 mm], whitish, in a single erect spike up to 10" tall [10 cm]; berries bright glossy red, 2–3-seeded, up to ¼" [6 mm]; stems 3–12' tall [1–3.5 m], ½–1½" thick [1–4 cm], punky, crooked, usually unbranched, entirely covered with yellowish tan prickles. Seeps and small creeks, often under cedar, in the wetter ranges; n ID, w MT, wet Columbia Mtns. Araliaceae (Ginseng family).

To a European, the general features of the vegetation are entirely such as he is familiar with…with the exception, that there are two common plants, Panax horridum *and* Dracontium camtschaticum, *[skunk cabbage] which differ so entirely from the surrounding vegetation, as to exert a very considerable influence on the physiognomy. (R. H. Hinds, 1844, The Botany of the Voyage of H.M.S. Sulphur.)*

Devil's club prefers cold, shaded, sopping, "gloomy" spots; a devil's club thicket is Thorniness in the form of knobby, twisted, tangled, untapering stalks rising out of wet black earth. In summer these hide devilishly under an attractive umbrella of huge leaves. Worse, the spines inject a mild irritant. The scarlet berries, eventual centerpiece to the broad table of leaves, aren't recommended either.

Oplopanax is an oxymoron. *Oplo* implies weaponry, while *panax* is a cure, as in *panacea*. Devil's club may seem more weapon than cure; the "cure" half of its name refers to its relative ginseng (genus *Panax*), perhaps the most cross-culturally recognized of all herbal panaceas. Under devil's club thorns lies a thin bark which natives used medicinally, magically, and cosmetically. It was thought to alleviate such diverse ailments as colds, rheumatism, excessive milk, amenorrhea, and body odor (a concern of hunters when near game), and yes, Moerman does list it as a "panacea" in the view of two BC tribes. The Cheyenne and Crow smoked devil's club roots, mixed with tobacco, to cure headaches.

Big Sagebrush

Artemisia tridentata (ar-tem-**ee**-zha: Greek word for worm-woods, honoring either a goddess or a queen; try-den-**tay**-ta: 3-toothed). =*Seriphidium tridentatum* (CO). Composite flower heads drab yellowish, tiny, in loose spikes, blooming late Aug and Sept; leaves spicy-aromatic, grayish-woolly, wedge-shaped, ± shallowly 3-lobed at the tip, average ½" wide [12 mm]; bark shreddy; average 2–6' tall [60–180 cm] on steppe; more often 1½–3' [45–90 cm] in mtns. All elevs exc alpine; US, dry BC valleys, extreme. sw AB. Asteraceae. Color p 541.

Silver sage, *A. cana* (kay-na: gray). =*S. canum* (CO). Leaves narrowly linear, simple, rather limp; 1–2' tall [30–60 cm]; common in Idaho and ne OR.

The prairie is barren and inhospitable looking to the last degree. The twisted, aromatic wormwood covers and extracts the strength from the burnt and arid soil. (John Kirk Townsend in Wyoming, 1834)

Townsend grudgingly conceded it "perfumed the air, and at first was rather agreeable." Euroamerican pioneers reacted to sagebrush with distaste or suspicion. Subsequent overfamiliarity led to feelings ranging from ironic affection to contempt. Sagebrush was long just an economic pest. Cattle won't eat it, so it increased under heavy grazing. Sheepmen sometimes overgrazed elk sedge on purpose, hoping for grasses to take over, and got erosion and sagebrush instead.

More recently we have come to see the sagebrush community as one we need to save. Fire, cheatgrass, and development are converting one to three million acres a year, out of 150 million sagey acres. More shocking still, global warming is projected to render most of the U.S.'s Sagebrush Empire inhospitable to sagebrush by 2090.

Sagebrush's fiefdom is the steppes below lower timberline. The steppe variety is defenseless against fire; it dominates where aridity keeps plants from growing close enough together to carry a fire—or at least did until cheatgrass invaded. (See p 169.) In the mountains we mostly have a smaller variety, *A. tridentata* ssp. *vaseyana*, which does send up stump sprouts after a fire.

Sagebrush is only moderately adapted to dry conditions. It needs about 7" [18 cm] of annual precipitation, which doesn't give it much of an edge on juniper. Fuzzy-surfaced gray leaves help by reflecting light and by stilling the air at the leaf's surface, but don't retain water as effectively as waxy-surfaced leaves,which in turn are less effective than leafless photosynthetic stems (as in cacti and Mormon-tea). Big sage does have a few moisture tricks up its sleeve. It produces two generations of leaves per year: large three-lobed ones grow in spring when moisture is in relatively good supply, and tend to wither and drop in midsummer. Leaves produced in late summer (and persisting into winter) may lack lobes and are much smaller, so they don't allow as much water to transpire. As for roots, sagebrush sends down a few very deep fine ones to get some moisture during the drier seasons, while most of its roots form a wide dense network in the top fifteen inches of soil, the optimum pattern for grabbing water during and after the brief thundershowers typical of the arid West.

Domestic sheep and pronghorns eat some sagebrush, but prefer other foods. Pronghorns in many parts of their range depend on sagebrush browse to get them through the harsher winters. The leaves are nutritious—high in both protein and fat—but fiercely defended by unpalatable volatile terpenoids (the fragrance we all notice). Deer are able to belch the volatiles out after segregating them while cud-chewing. Few animals can do that. When a sagebrush is nibbled on, airborne concentrations of at least one volatile, methyl jasmonate, increase as much as tenfold. Nearby plants—including unrelated neighbors, such as a tobacco species in one experiment—step up their own production of defensive chemicals in response. Some scientists in this field like to call that "communication between plants," while others scoff: "If I smell smoke and run from a burning house, was that communication between the fire and me?"

Riders of the Purple Sage refers, with poetic license, to big sagebrush. The Southwest has a shrub called purple sage, which is in the mint family along with culinary sage. Sagebrush, in contrast, is related to culinary tarragon and absinthe (page 204).

Rabbitbrush

Ericameria spp. (erica-**me**-ria: heath—). =*Chrysothamnus* spp. (in most books pre–1997). Composite flower heads bright yellow, forming massed showy rounded clusters (which may persist, dried and pale, into the next summer); each head taller than wide, consisting of about 5 disk flowers (no rays); leaves linear or threadlike, usually silvery, ± limp; branches numerous, silvery, rather soft; broomy shrubs 1–4' [30–120 cm]. Low to mid-elev grassland-steppe and pine forest. Asteraceae.

Rubber rabbitbrush, *E. nauseosa*. Gray-green overall due to fine felt-like wool on leaves and stems; twigs flexible; n to Kootenay N.P. but not in AB RMs. Color p 544.

Green rabbitbrush, *E. viscidiflora* (vis-id-if-**lor**-us: sticky flowers). Plant dark green overall, with little or no wool; twigs brittle. US.

Rubber rabbitbrush—a stump-sprouter which livestock avoid—tends to increase after fire or overgrazing. Rabbits as well as pronghorns browse it. It exudes a latex which engineers were able to turn into good rubber; desert tribes chewed it to relieve thirst. The Navaho used their variety of *nauseosa* as an emetic or cathartic. Tribes of the northern Rockies used it to cure diarrhea or coughs, making either a tea or a smoke of whole branches.

Buckthorns

Rhamnus spp. (**ram**-nus: Greek word for them) Leaves 2–6" [5–15 cm], oval, with recessed side veins strikingly parallel to each other; flowers tiny, greenish, 4- or 5-lobed, clustered in leaf axils; berries ¼" [6 mm], 3-seeded, red ripening to purple-black, poisonous. Rhamnaceae (Buckthorn family).

Alderleaf buckthorn, *R. alnifolia* (al-nif-**oh**-lia: alder leaf). Leaves pointed, with small rounded teeth, and 5–8 pairs of recessed, parallel pinnate veins young twigs downy; shrub 2-8' tall [60–240 cm]. Mid-elev streamsides with mtn alder; US, and n to Windermere.

Cascara, *R. purshiana* (pur-she-**ay**-na: after F. Pursh, p 132). =*Frangula purshiana* (USDA). Leaves round-tipped, with 10–12 pairs of veins, minutely ± toothed; 4 or 5 white petals; shrub or tree up to 33' [10 m]. Low-elev streamsides, moist forests; n and w ID, wet Columbia Mtns.

Most parts of the buckthorn plant are powerfully laxative. For some decades there was a lucrative trade in cascara bark for this purpose—and many girdled trees died—but "cascara sagrada" is no longer a popular medicine.

Redstem

Ceanothus sanguineus (see-an-**oath**-us: thistle, a puzzling name; san-**gwin**-ius: blood-colored). Also **buckbrush.** Flowers tiny, white, in dense fluffy 2–5" [5–13 cm] clusters; petals, sepals, and stamens 5; seed pods of three 1-seeded cells; leaves 1½–4" [4–10 cm], oval, fine-toothed, sometimes ± sticky above, hairy along the veins beneath, with 2 veins from base nearly as heavy as midvein but not reaching the tip; stems purplish; shrubs 3–10' [1–3 m]. Sunny slopes; w MT, n ID, OR, WA, sc BC. Rhamnaceae.

Though redstem was once called Oregon-tea, any tea made from its leaves would be ersatz ersatz. The reference is to New Jersey–tea, an eastern *Ceanothus* brewed by patriotic colonists wanting to declare their independence from the tea taxed under the Stamp Act. Like its close (but evergreen) cousin, snowbrush, p 146, redstem nourishes both four-legged browsers and nearby plants, since it fixes nitrogen.

Black Hawthorn

Crataegus douglasii (cra-**tee**-gus: strong; da-**glass**-ee-eye: after D. Douglas, p 66). Leaves 1–3" [25–75 mm], obovate to wedge-shaped, fine-toothed all around and also coarse-toothed at the outer end; branches armed with stout ½–1¼" [1–3 cm] thorns; flowers ½" [12 mm], white, in small clusters; 10 pink/white stamens; berries ⅜" [1 cm], purplish-black when ripe, edible but dry and insipid; tall shrubs or small trees up to 18' [5.5 m]. Streamsides up to timberline. Rosaceae.

Elk relish hawthorn leaves, and manage to browse them, however thorny. Rocky Mountain tribes ate the mealy, flat-tasting berries.

Silverberry

Elaeagnus commutata (ee-lee-**ag**-nus: Greek for some willow; com-you-**tay**-ta: bartered). Also **wolf-willow**. Flowers yellow inside, silvery outside, bell-shaped, 4-lobed, 1–3 per leaf axil, strongly sweet-scented, ¼–½" long [6–12 mm], persisting on the tip of the berry; berries silvery, mealy, ⅜" [1 cm]; leaves elliptical, 1–3" [25–75 mm], heavily silver-scurfy on both sides; branches dark red, brown-scurfy when young; shrubs 3–12' [1–3.5 m]. Thicket-forming, low- to mid-elev gravelly soils, either arid or streamside. Elaeagnaceae (Oleaster family).

Silverberry was valued most for its bark, usable in basketry, twine, or whisks for "Indian ice cream" (p 127). The stripy seeds were sometimes used as beads, and sometimes eaten, either with the dry berry or after stripping that off. The genus also includes the Russian olive tree, originally imported as an ornamental but now notoriously invasive of streamsides throughout the arid West.

What two words in the English language each consist of four Es, four As, and four consonants? Hint:

Find them on this page, p 93, and p 283.

Huckleberries/Blueberries

Vaccinium spp. (vac-**sin**-ium: the Roman term). Leaves elliptical; flowers pinkish, small, globular, with 5 (rarely 4) very short, bent-back corolla lobes, and similar calyx lobes on the tip of the berry. Ericaceae (Heath family) or Vacciniaceae. Individual species described on following pages.

This diverse and well distributed genus has always been of intense interest to bears, birds, native people, and hikers. Toward summer's end, some bear scats are little more than barely cemented heaps of huckleberry leaves; soon the "cement" decomposes, and you may wonder how these heaps of dry leaves came to be so neatly molded. The bears lack the patience to pluck the berries singly; who can blame them, with only a month or two left to fatten up for hibernation?

Blueberries are good for us! Their blue pigments are flavonoids that work in our bodies as antioxidants, and perhaps more. Rats fed a rat equivalent of one cup of blueberries a day were able to reverse the effects of aging on memory. That is, the older rats' memories kept improving until they could beat young rats on memory tests.

Northwest tribes used carefully timed fire to maintain extensive berry patches. That legacy dwindled under Smokey's anti-fire administration, but the Forest Service lately rediscovered the beauties of a low blaze; one USFS report assigned twice as high a cash value per acre per year to berries as to the trees likely to replace them on subalpine sites. (Maybe they never should have made Smokey out to be a bear; any self-respecting bear would prefer Native American management to the huckleberry-squelching that goes on in Smokey's name.)

"Huckleberry" vs. "blueberry" is a murky issue. In the East a related genus (*Gaylussacia*) with seedy black berries has first claim to the name huckleberry. Some authors use the old English names "whortleberry" and "bilberry", but I have trouble saying those with a straight face. Another calls them all blueberries, even the "red blueberries." I call cultivated ones blueberries, wild ones huckleberries unless they're low and very blue. Only Easterners will be confused.

Our region has about twelve species of *Vaccinium*. North of Crowsnest Pass, the genus also includes cranberries and lingonberries (page 151), with evergreen leaves and sour red berries.

Grouseberry, *V. scoparium* (sco-**pair**-ium: broom—). Berries bright red, ⅛" diam [3 mm]; leaves ¼–½" [6–12 mm]; plants 4–14" tall [6–12 mm]; twigs green, with angled edges, numerous, broomy. Subalpine, in sun or shade. Color p 89.

Grouseberry is abundant on dry habitats. The fruit is tasty if its ripens, but hard to gather in quantity.

Dwarf blueberry, *V. cespitosum*. Berries light blue with heavy waxy bloom, without conspicuous calyx lobes; flowers much longer than wide; twigs reddish to greenish, angled; leaves slightly toothed, prominently net-veined beneath; plants 2–12" tall. [5–30 mm] Meadow and open forest, all elevs, esp alp/subalpine; often with beargrass.

Some say this charming dwarf of the subalpine heath parkland is the very choicest huckleberry.

Black huckleberry, *V. membranaceum* (mem-bra-**nay**-see-um: thin). =Includes *V. globulare* (BC). Also **thinleaf** or **tall huckleberry**. Berries black to dark red, juicy, delicious; leaves 1–2½" [2–6 cm], thin, pointed, minutely toothed; 2–6' tall [30–120 cm]. Low subalpine. If separated, *V. globulare* differs in more bluish berries, round (not oval) blossoms, and a rounded to obtusely-pointed leaf. Illustrated.

Top huckleberry for combined availability, flavor, and texture, the black huckleberry is the mainstay of the Wild Huckleberry industry. Though it grows and bears fruit most lavishly in burns and other clearings, it also dominates the shrub layer in many montane forests.

Oval-leaf huckleberry, *V. ovalifolium*. =includes *V. alaskaense* (BC). Berries blue with bloom or purplish black without bloom; leaves ¾–2½" [2–6 cm], smooth edged; shrubs 1½–5' [45–150 cm]. Subalpine forests; wet Columbia Mtns, sw AB, nw MT, n ID. Illustrated at left.

Usually a straggly understory shrub, oval-leaf huckleberry is prepared to burst forth after fire or clearcut. Its berries tend to be sparse, seedy, and sour.

Bog blueberry, *V. uliginosum* (you-li-gin-**oh**-sum: wet). =includes *V. occidentale* (WY, CO). Flowers/berries often in clusters of 2–4, from leaf axils; berries blue, with 5 calyx lobes still showing; leaves without teeth. Alp/subalp bogs, shores, pine forests; not in our part of BC. Illustrated at right.

Low huckleberry, *V. myrtillus* (mer-til-us: myrtle). =includes *V. oreophilum*. Berries black or bluish (to reddish in hybrids with grouseberry; twigs green, sharply angled, downy; leaves ½–1¼", fine-toothed; ± broomy shrubs 4–14", resembling (and often associating with) grouseberry. Widespread in subalpine fir and lodgepole forests. Not in OR. Color p 89.

White Rhododendron

Rhododendron albiflorum (roe-doe-**den**-dron: rose tree, a doubly misleading name; al-bif-**lor**-um: white flower). =*Azaleastrum albiflorum* (CO). Flowers white, ¾" diam [2 cm], broadly bell-shaped, petals fused no more than ½ their length, 1–4 in clusters just below the whorl-like leaf clusters at branch tips; leaves elliptical, 2–3½" [5–9 cm], glossy, bumpy, slightly reddish-hairy; capsules 5-celled; bark shredding; leggy shrubs 3–6' [1–2 m]. Subalpine forest and shrubfields; all exc WY. Ericaceae (Heath family). Color p 88.

It's hard to see these blossoms — so modest by garden "rhodie" standards — as rhododendrons. But few who reach timberline by foot would slight their beauty. The plant mixes with dominant fool's-huckleberry and black huckleberry in high forests, but can grow above their elevational limits. The proportion of rhododendron increases with elevation and latitude.

Fool's-Huckleberry

Menziesia ferruginea (men-**zee**-zia: after A. Menzies, opp page; fair-u-**jin**-ia: rust-red). Also **false-azalea**, **rustyleaf**. Flowers ¼" [6 mm], pale rusty orange, jar-shaped, pendent on sticky-hairy pedicels, calyx and corolla shallowly 4-lobed, stamens 8; seed capsules (illust) 4-celled, dry; leaves 1½–2½" [4–6 cm], elliptical, seemingly whorled near branch tips, often hairy, coloring deeply in fall; bark shreddy; leggy shrubs 3–11' [1–3.3 m]. Cold, moist sites in mid elev to subalp forest. Ericaceae. Color p 89.

This plant has no berries to tempt anyone, no matter how foolish, so I'd call it a fool's fool's-huckleberry. True, its summer foliage might be carelessly mistaken for the other tall heath-shrubs, black huckleberry and white rhododendron. It often grows with them (contrasting from them in being much bluer) but in some Montana and Alberta ranges it is a thicket dominant all on its own. It's damned tough to bushwhack through. Sometimes the tall heaths encircle an expanding tree clump (see page 57) or fill in among scattered trees invading subalpine meadowland.

Most Heath family species have five petals and five sepals, but have aberrant 4-merous individuals. This is one species where fours are the norm.

Our broadleaf evergreens, called sclerophylls ("hardened leaves"), have heavy, rigid leaves that can dry out partially in summer without wilting. This reduces transpiration, conserving water. They can also get a bit of photosynthesizing done during warm breaks in late fall and early spring.

A single representative of the cacti also lands in this section, since it stays equally green at all seasons.

Mountain-Mahogany

Cercocarpus ledifolius (sir-co-**car**-pus: tailed fruit; lee-dif-**oh**-lius: leaves like Labrador-tea). Flowers yellowish, 1–3 per leaf axil, ½" diam [12 mm], with numerous stamens their showiest parts; 5-lobed calyx has fine wool; seeds have 2–3" [5–8 cm] feathery tails; leaves aromatic, evergreen, lanceolate to elliptic with downrolled edges, untoothed, ½–1½" [12–38 mm] long, finely woolly at least underneath; branches ± reddish; gnarly-branched shrubs 3–10' [1–3 m] or small trees to 40' [12 m]. Dry rocky slopes at all elevs; US, esp ec ID. Rosaceae. Color p 89.

Mountain-mahogany is so named because its wood is exceptionally heavy and hard. As firewood it is nearly smokeless, hence prized by rustlers and others wishing to escape notice. The plant is most conspicuous around the steppe/forest margin,

Archibald Menzies was the first European scientist in the Northwest south of Alaska. On the strength of a first brief and relatively inconsequential visit to Vancouver Island, in 1787, he was appointed surgeon-naturalist on H.M.S. *Discovery* under Captain George Vancouver. Menzies' journal records the *Discovery*'s 1792 landing at Discovery Bay, Washington, and the naming of many land and water features after officers on the ship (Puget, Whidbey, Baker, Vancouver) and Englishmen the captain admired (Rainier, St. Helens, Hood). The ship's mission allowed Menzies little time for botanizing ashore, and his live collections all died on board, but his plant descriptions and dried specimens that did reach England aroused intense interest in the Northwest, eventually leading to voyages by David Douglas and others. Menzies was an old man by 1824, when young Douglas visited him for a briefing on Northwest American plants.

where it forms pure stands on some slopes in the southernmost part of our range. Browsing mammals love it, as they do most of our nitrogen-fixing shrubs, and often reduce it to a low hedgelike form.

Snowbrush

Ceanothus velutinus (see-an-**oath**-us: thistle, a misleading name; ve-**lu**-tin-us: velvety). Also **tobacco-brush, cinnamon-bush, sticky-laurel.** Tiny white flowers in dense fluffy ± conical 2–5" [5–12 cm] clusters; petals, sepals, and stamens 5; seed pods of 3 separating, 1-seeded cells; leaves 1½–3½" [4–9 cm], oval, fine-toothed, often tightly curling, heavily spicy-aromatic, shiny and sticky above, pale-fuzzy beneath, with 3 ± equally heavy main veins from base nearly to tip, robust shrubs 2–6' [60–180 cm]. Dry, sunny clearings; not in c MT or the AB parks. Rhamnaceae (Buckthorn family). Color p 88.

Snowbrush invades burns, including slash-burned clearcuts. Its seeds are activated by the heat of a fire and the increased soil warmth of a new clearing. The young shoots grow slowly, but can crowd out annuals like fireweed within a few seasons, fertilized by nitrogen-fixing bacteria they host in root nodules. Snowbrush can grow densely enough to prevent conifer establishment. That has been seen as a problem in the Cascades, but in central Idaho Douglas-fir seedlings are said to actually prefer snowbrush cover. Certainly in the long term its nitrogen should aid conifer growth. (Dozens of herbs in the legume family also fix nitrogen, as do six other shrubs common in our region: bitterbrush, redstem, snowberry, mountain-mahogany, and the alders. Snowbrush is the only one whose N legacy has been calculated and found to amount to a large fraction of total usable N in its soil. Partly, that would be because so much of it tends to grow in one place.)

Between fires, snowbrush reproduces mainly by stem sprouts and root suckers. The seeds fall to earth and usually lie dormant—and viable as long as 200 years—waiting to be reawakened by a fire. The reappearance of a full-blown snowbrush community centuries after snowbrush was shaded out of the forest will seem miraculous.

Though not as delicious to browsers as its deciduous kin, redstem (p 140), snowbrush becomes critically important to deer and elk in the winter when other browse plants are leafless.

"Tobacco-brush" refers to the leaves' fragrance in the afternoon sun. Rumors of use in smoking mixtures are few and questionable.

Oregon-Boxwood

Paxistima myrsinites (pa-**kis**-tim-a: thick stigma; mir-sin-**eye**-teez: myrrh-like). Also **mountain-box-wood, myrtle-boxwood, mountain lover**. Flowers ⅛" [3 mm] diam, clustered in leaf axils, dark red petals and whitish stamens and sepals each 4 (but flowers are few and far between, some years); capsules splitting in two; leaves opposite, ½–1¼" [12–30 mm], elliptical, shallowly toothed, glossy, dark above; twigs reddish, 4-angled; dense shrubs 10–40" [3–12 m]. Forested slopes from Waterton s. Celastraceae (Staff-tree family).

Florists use sprays of Oregon-boxwood interchangeably with evergreen blueberry from the NW coast. Opposite evergreen leaves (unique here) distinguish this plant from the heath shrubs. (Actually they aren't perfectly opposite, and botanists who look at them under a microscope declare them alternate; but on casual inspection they pass for opposite.)

Labrador Tea

Ledum spp. (**lee**-dum: Greek name for an unrelated plant). Also **trapper's tea**. Flowers white, ½" diam [12 mm], in showy rounded clusters; 5 petals, 5-10 stamens; leaves ¾–1½" [2–4 cm] oval, thick, evergreen, resinous, paler beneath, the edges ± rolled under; twigs sticky-hairy; shrubs 1½–5' [45–150 cm].Ericaceae (Heath family).

L. glandulosum (glan-dew-lo-sum: with glands). Leaves white or green beneath. Subalpine meadows, bogs, frost pockets in open forest. Illustrated.

L. groenlandicum (green-**lan**-dic-um). Rusty wool under leaves. BC, AB from Kananaskis n. Color p 88.

All across the continent, leaves of this genus were popular as a stimulant tea. Tribes of our region may have learned this use from whites, as suggested by the traditional names trapper's tea and Hudson's Bay tea. The toxic/stimulant alkaloids are much stronger in *L. glandulosum* than in *L. groenlandicum*, which enjoyed far more use as tea. I don't recommend either, but especially not *glandulosum*.

The difference between subshrubs and herbs is one of degree: woody parts are hard to detect in very small plants. For category purposes, we'll take most evergreen leaves as proof of perennial aboveground (shrubby) parts. There are also cases of borderline evergreenness— small species (with deciduous relatives) that adapted to long-lasting snow by keeping leaves in place and green, ready to photosynthesize, through one winter; they wither as they are replaced by new foliage the next summer. Alpine ecologists call such leaves "wintergreen" or "persistent." We'll treat them as herbs; see alpine willows, p 209; penstemons, p 214; violets, p 222; sibbaldia, p 232; sandwort, p 237; partridgefoot, p 243; dwarf raspberries, p 240; kittentails, p 257; wild ginger, p 265; bitterroots, p 266. Also usually perceived as herbs (with dark evergreen leaves borne flat on the ground) are rattlesnake-plantain, p 185, and pyrolas, p 238.

Oregon-Grape

Berberis repens (ber-ber-iss: Arabic word for barberry; ner-**vo**-sa: veiny). - =*Mahonia repens* (USDA, BC, WY, CO), *B. aquifolia* var. *repens*. Also **mahonia**. Flowers yellow, in a terminal group of 3–7" [8–18 cm] spikes amid a cluster of sharp ½–2" [1–5 cm] bud scales; petals/sepals in 5 concentric whorls of 3, outer whorl(s) ± green; berries ⅜" [1 cm], grapelike, purple with a heavy blue bloom; leaves compound, crowded at top of stem, 10–16" long [12–38 mm]; leaflets 11–21, spiny-margined (hollylike), pointed-oval, palmately veined; stems unbranched, 4–18" [10–45 cm]; inner bark yellow. Berberidaceae (Barberry family). Color p 88.

Oregon-grape leaves are evergreen, but a few may burst into crimson at any time of year. The stamens snap inward at the lightest touch to shake their pollen onto a bee.

The berries (not grapes) have an exquisite sourness not balanced by much sweetness. They're juicy, you might try one or two for a little mouth excitement. Native Americans considered them starvation fare, but quickly learned to love them once they obtained sugar. Oregon-grape jelly and wine are traditional since pioneer days.

The roots are another story. Virtually every American *Berberis* was used medicinally, especially for stomach ills and dysmenorrhea. Today, one ingredient (berberine) is a recognized antibiotic. Another was recently found to help overcome bacterial resistance to berberine and other antibiotics—showing promise as a way to combat antibiotic-resistant strains of staphylococcus, which are a serious threat in hospitals. The roots are buried deeply enough to resprout after moderately hot fires.

Shrubby Penstemon

Penstemon fruticosus (**pen**-stem-un: almost a stamen; fru-tic-**oh**-sus: shrubby). Flowers ± lavender, 1–2" long [2–5 cm], all tending to face one way; corolla swollen-tubular, with 5 (2 upper, 3 lower) short rounded flaring lobes; a broad ± hairy sterile stamen rests on the throat; fertile stamens 4, paired; sepals 5; leaves opposite, finely toothed, narrow (exc oval around Wallowas); dense shrub to 12" tall [30 cm]. Rocky places at all elevs. Scrophulariaceae (Figwort family). Similar to rocky ledge penstemon, color p 214, but with woodier stems.

Prickly Pear

Opuntia fragilis (o-**pun**-cha: Roman word for some plant; fra-**jil**-iss: brittle). Flowers showy, pale yellow, 2" diam [5 cm]; many petals, sepals , and stamens; fruits ± fleshy, sweet, red, oval, ¾" long [2 cm]; stems fleshy, in scarcely flattened segments that break apart easily, ½–1¼" [1–3 cm] spines in clusters of 3 to 7; mostly prostrate, mat-forming cactus. Lower-elev grasslands. Cactaceae (Cactus family). Color p 88.

Against the thorns of this plant I found that mockasons are but a slight defence. (John Bradbury, 1811)

Prickly pear flesh is palatable once you get past the spines. The Salish learned to burn off the spines and squeeze out the flesh to eat it, and ranchers learned to use grass fires to burn off the spines so that four-legged browsers would eat it, thus reducing the ranch's cactus infestation. The sweeter "pears," popular in the hot southwest, are usually small, dry, and scarce in our region.

Alpine Laurel

Kalmia microphylla (**kahl**-mia: after Per Kalm; micro-**fill**-a: small leaf). Corolla pink, bowl-shaped, ½" diam [12 mm]; sepals tiny, green; flowers 3–8 in terminal clusters; capsules 5-celled, with long style; leaves opposite, ½–1" long [12–25 mm], narrow, often with rolled-under edges; spreading subshrubs to 6" [15 cm]. Marshy subalpine soils. Ericaceae (Heath family). Color p 89.

Alpine laurel's profuse pink blossoms brighten up high seasonal bogs and soggy alpine slopes right after snowmelt. Look closely: ten little bumps on the odd-shaped buds hold the ten anthers (stamen tips). When the flower opens, the stamens are spring-loaded to throw their pollen on the first insect to alight.

This plant and its relatives are toxic. Laurel is a common name for *Kalmia* of all sizes, though they aren't related to the Laurel tree (*Laurus*) that wreathed champions in ancient Greece. Pioneers also called rhododendrons "mountain laurel."

Pipsissewa

Chimaphila umbellata (kim-**af**-il-a: winter loving; um-bel-**ay**-ta: bearing flowers in umbels). Also **prince's-pine**. Stamens and pink-to-white petals flat-spreading, pistil fat, hublike; flowers ½" diam [12 mm], nodding; leaves 1–3" [2–8 cm], very dark, narrowly elliptical, saw-toothed, ± whorled on lower ½ of stem; 4-12" tall [10–30 cm]. Shady forest. Ericaceae (Heath family) or Pyrolaceae. Color p 89.

Pipsissewa's success under heavy shade suggests dependence on mycorrhizae, which often leads to spotty distribution. Its leaves, "*Foliachimaphilae*," used to sit on apothecary shelves as a remedy for bladderstones. They are harvested still (overharvested in locales) more to flavor the world's most famous soft drink than for herbal remedies.

Kinnickinnick

Arctostaphylos uva-ursi (arc-tos-**taf**-il-os: bear grapes; **oo**-va-**ur**-sigh: grape of bears). =includes *A. adenotricha*. Also **bearberry**. Flowers pinkish white, jar-shaped, with 5 bent-back lobes; berries bright red, ¼" [6 mm], dry and mealy, flat-tasting; leaves ½–1¼" [1–3 cm], round-tipped, widest past midlength; thin gray bark flakes off, revealing smooth red inner bark; prostrate shrubs usually rising 2–6" [5–15 cm]. Rocky sites. A similar plant with bright green deciduous leaves and a juicy berry is red bearberry, *A. rubra*; on alpine rocks from Banff NP north. Ericaceae. Color p 89.

"Kinnickinnick" was an eastern intertribal trading word meaning "smoking herbs." Hudson's Bay Company traders brought the word west and applied it to this plant the natives taught them to smoke, often mixed with tobacco for better flavor. The berries seem to please bears and heather voles, but among native Americans they were starvation fare or adulterants for sweeter berries. This is a valuable pioneer on volcanic or glacial soils, and a fine ground cover in gardens.

Alpine Wintergreen

Gaultheria humifusa (galth-**ee**-ria: after Jean-François Gaultier; hue-mif-**you**-sa: trailing). Flowers white to pinkish, bell-shaped, about ⅛" long [3 mm], from leaf axils; berries smooth, red, up to ¼" [6 mm], delicious; leaves thick, dark green, oval, ± pointed, ½–¾" [1–2 cm]; spreading shrubs 1–6" tall [2–15 cm]. Subalpine forest and meadow edges. A similar plant with fine hair on calyx and berries, mainly in BC and nw MT, is *G. ovatifolia*. Ericaceae.

Aromatic wintergreen oil comes from *Gaultheria* leaves, mainly the eastern checkerberry, giving *Gaultheria* a better claim than *Pyrola* or *Chimaphila* on the common name "wintergreen." Wintergreen gum and candy today get the key oil, methyl salicylate, either synthetically or from black birch twigs. It has long been popular both as a flavoring and as a medicine whose best use is as a topical counter-irritant, i.e., a balm that soothes deep aches by heating up the surface flesh. This versatile volatile is released by many plants when aphids attack them, by tropical orchids to attract bees, and by butterflie males as an anti-aphrodisiac they leave on females, post-coitally, to decrease the female's chance of mating again. The spicy little berries have some of it in them, so don't overdose.

Lingonberry

Vaccinium vitis-idaea (vac-**sin**-ium: the Roman term; **vie**-tis-eye-**dee**-ee: grape of Mt. Ida). Also **mountain cranberry, cowberry**. Flowers pink, small, globular, with 4 very short, ± flaring corolla lobes; berries dark red, shiny, tart, persistent through winter (flavor is improved by frost); leaves ½–¾" [1–2 cm], round-tipped obovate, dark-speckled beneath, edges rolled under; shrub up to 8" [20cm] but more often foming prostrate mats. Gravelly to boggy sites, all elevs; Canada. Ericaceae (Heath family) or Vacciniaceae.

Mountain Heathers

Cassiope and *Phyllodoce* spp. (ca-**sigh**-a-pee and fil-**od**-os-ee: characters in Greek myth). Ericaceae (Heath family). Alp/subalpine. Color p 89.

White heather, *C. mertensiana* (mer-ten-zee-**ay**-na: after Karl H. Mertens, below). Also **moss heather.** Corolla bell-shaped, white; flowers pendent from axils near branch tips; capsules ± erect; leaves ⅛" long [3 mm], densely packed along the stem in 4 ranks, thus square in cross-section; spreading, mat-forming shrubs 2–12" [5–30 cm]. All exc WY. Illust at right.

Four-angled heather, *C. tetragona* (teh-**trag**-a-na: four sided). Like the preceding, but with a pronounced groove down the center of each rank of leaves. All exc WY and OR.

Pink heather, *P. empetriformis* (em-pee-trif-**or**-mis: crowberry shaped). Corolla pink, bell-shaped; flowers 5–15 in apparent terminal clusters, erect in bud, pendent in bloom, then erect again as dry capsules; leaves needlelike, ¼–½" [6–12 mm]; dense matted shrubs 4–10" [10–25 cm] or up to 15" [38 cm]. Illustrated at left.

Yellow heather, *P. glanduliflora* (gland-you-lif-**lor**-a: glandular [sticky] flower). As above, exc corolla cream yellow to off-white, narrow-necked jar-shaped. Illust at right, and p 153.

Heather-dominated communities in the Rockies are on cold, wet sites in the alpine and subalpine zones.

Heinrich Mertens accompanied the Russian Count **Fedor Lütke** on his globe-circling voyage of 1826–1829, when both were in their early thirties. In London in 1829 their tales so impressed David Douglas (page 66) that Douglas became obsessed with completing his second trip to the West by sailing from the Russian colony at Sitka to Siberia. He would then have walked the length of Siberia, collecting plants.

Mertens died the following year. His plant discoveries at Sitka, Southeast Alaska, include a half-dozen species named *mertensiana* (*mertensianus, mertensii*) and as many more named *sitchensis* (*sitchense*) as well as the partridgefoot, *Luetkea,* but not *Mertensia,* the bluebell genus which was named earlier in honor of his father, botany professor **Franz Karl Mertens.**

These often result from deep late-lying snow, such as the drifts that form just to the lee side of a ridge. Along its lower edge, the pink heather may grade into a black alpine sedge bed which had even later-lying snow, perhaps in the hollow of an alpine gelifluction terrace. The same sequence occurs in open subalpine forests where airflow and shade patterns around the trees create snowdrifts. Not surprisingly, these communities get less common southward, and don't occur in Wyoming. *Cassiope* foliage is almost like clubmoss; *Phyllodoce* foliage is more like common juniper or crowberry. Still, heathers plainly resemble each other in their flowers and habitat.

Vast communities known as "heath" took over much of Scotland following deforestation and heavy sheep grazing hundreds of years ago. They are dominated by species of *Cassiope*, *Phyllodoce*, *Erica*, and especially *Calluna*—all called "heather" by the Scots. The "Scottish heather" of gardens is *Calluna vulgaris*.

Crowberry

Empetrum nigrum (em-**pee**-trum: on rock; **nye**-grum: black). Flowers tiny, brownish purple, in leaf axils, ± 3-merous (maximum of 3 stamens, 3 petals, 3 sepals, 3 bracts), stamens twice as long as other parts, or sometimes stamens or pistil lacking; berries blue-black, ⅛–¼" [3–6 mm], juicy, 6–9-seeded; leaves needlelike, crowded, ¼–½" [6–12 mm], with rolled edges; mat-forming prostrate shrubs, erect stems to 6" [15 cm]. Rocky slopes; not in WY. Ericaceae or Empetraceae.

Crowberries stay somewhat sweet and juicy all winter on the plant under the snow blanket, making them a crucial resource for ptarmigan, grouse, bears, and Alaskan Inuit. For my taste, they are minute, scarce, and insipid.

Dryads

Dryas spp. (**dry**-us: a kind of nymph, in myth). Also **mountain-avens**. Petals 8 (rarely 9 or 10), ⅜–½" [10–13 mm]; calyx 8-(10)-lobed; stamens and pistils numerous; as seeds mature, the styles grow long and plumey, and twist together into a point when immature or wet, then opening into a fluffy tuft; leaves evergreen, leathery green above, white-woolly beneath, oblong with scalloped, rolled-under edges, ± prostrate on ground; plants mat-forming, spreading by prostrate woody stems; 1-flowered stalks 1–8" tall [2–20 cm]. Mid-elev gravel bars to alpine tundra, usually on calcareous terrain. Rosaceae (Rose family).

White dryad, *D. octopetala* (oc-ta-**pet**-a-la: 8 petals). Petals white. Illustrated. Color p 88.

Yellow dryad, *D. drummondii* (dra-**mon**-dee-eye: after Thos. Drummond, opposite page). Petals yellow. Canada, n MT, OR, WA. Illustrated.

Mats dominated by dryads form "spotted tundra," a classic component of both arctic and alpine tundras all the way around the northern hemisphere. Dryads pioneer on rocky, unstable soils which are often bare of snow in winter. Their evergreen leaves are ready to photosynthesize, however briefly, whenever the temperature ventures above freezing. Their ground-hugging shape avoids drying winds, and freely rooting prostrate stems hold fast in mobile soil. The roots host nitrogen-fixing bacteria, an invaluable feature of many pioneer species but one found in very few small alpine plants. The parabolic bowl-shaped solar-tracking flowers focus and hold solar heat, speeding the flower's maturation and making a warm spot attractive to pollinators that need to bask in order to get their mornings going in frigid air. *D. octopetala* augments solar heat with internal respirative heat, raising air temperature in the bowl by 27° [15° C], in one study, and a visiting fly's body temperature by 15° [8.3° C].

Dryads, generally considered calciphiles, have been found only on sedimentary bedrock in Montana, but on some edges of their range they grow on igneous substrates—on basalt dikes with some calcium content in the Wyoming Absarokas, for example. It may be less the chemistry of the limestone that they prefer than the higher water content (compared to granitic soils) leading to frost heaving, a problem which few of the competitors' roots can handle.

Soil-movement stress characterizes another habitat typical of dryads (especially the yellow): the upstream ends of gravel bars in mountain rivers. Here it's raging spring floodwaters that sweep over the top of the dryad mat while shifting the gravel particles around its roots. After the water recedes, having taken most of the smaller soil particles with it, the coarse gravel that remains drains quickly, making it the most drought-stricken part of the river bar.

A popular rock-garden plant was bred from European varieties of our white dryad, but our natives don't transplant happily.

Thomas Drummond and **Sir John Richardson** went on **Sir John Franklin**'s second expedition into Arctic Canada. Richardson was also on Franklin's first, returning without his specimens and barely even alive. He was brave enough to try again, but twice was enough: he stayed home from Franklin's tragic third expedition—which ended with everyone slowly starving, freezing, or getting eaten—and lived on as a famed naturalist, knight, and author of a fauna of boreal America.

Young Drummond, meanwhile, separated from the party and spent winter alone in an improvised brush hut in the Alberta foothills, relying on game for food. That was two months without seeing a soul, six months without a conversation in a shared language, and many months with only dormant snow-covered plants to study. The doughty Scot summed up his relations with grizzlies thus: "The best way of getting rid of the bears, when attacked by them, was to rattle my vasculum or specimen-box, when they immediately decamp."

Summing up the Canadian Rockies near Jasper, he was equally imperturbable: "They gratified me extremely."

His daily routine along the Saskatchewan River gives an idea of how hard naturalists worked: "When the boats stopped for breakfast, I immediately went on shore ... proceeding along the banks of the river, and making short excursions into the interior, taking care, however, to join the boats, if possible, at their encampment for the night. After supper, I commenced laying down the day's plants, changed and dried the papers of those collected previously; which occupation generally occupied me till daybreak, when the boats started. I then went on board and slept till the breakfast hour, when I landed and proceeded as before."

He had met David Douglas (page 66) in Scotland. The Hudson's Bay Express reunited them on the Saskatchewan in 1827, and they took the same ship back to England. Douglas, apprehensive about sharing his findings with a competitor, was stunned when Drummond freely shared his own. Their quality impressed him, too.

Before his unexplained death in Cuba in 1835, Drummond spent two years making the first extensive botanical exploration of Texas. He dreamed of settling in Texas and starting a family, if only he could save up enough money for five acres and two cows.

Twinflower

Linnaea borealis (lin-ee-a: after Linnaeus, below; bor-ee-**ay**-lis: northern).
Flowers pink to white, two per stalk, conical, pendent, ½" long [12 mm], 5-lobed, stamens 4; capsules 1-seeded; leaves opposite, very shiny, dark, ¼–1" [6–25 mm]; spicy- or anise-fragrant esp in warm sun; flowering stalks 3–5" [8–12 cm], reddish, with 2–6 leaves on lower half only; from long leafy runners. Moist forest. Caprifoliaceae (Honeysuckle family) or Linnaeaceae (WY, CO).

Linnaeus, who chose the scientific names for thousands of plants, didn't name any for himself, but is said to have asked a colleague to name this one after him. He then wrote, "*Linnaea* was named by the celebrated Gronovius and is a plant of Lapland, lowly, insignificant, flowering but for a brief space, after Linnaeus who resembles it." This charming humility was perhaps devious: though tiny and simple, the twinflower grows throughout the cooler third of the Northern hemisphere, and is widely admired. He liked to hold a sprig of it when posing for portraits.

Carolus Linnaeus is considered the "Father of Systematic Biology" or taxonomy. In his day, naturalists often improvised Latin descriptions many words long for any plant or animal under discussion. Linnaeus made everyone's life easier with his idea that this should be reduced to a two-word ("binomial") name that all scientists would agree upon for each kind ("species") of organism, with the first name ("genus") being a broader category often embracing several species. During his lifetime (1707–78) he published hundreds of species, including most of our genera that occur in Europe and quite a few that don't. He usually took genus names used by classical Greek or Roman natural history authors like Theophrastus and Pliny.

Carl's father coined the name Linnaeus by putting a Latin ending on the Swedish word for linden, a tree growing on the family farm. (Swedish peasants up until then had not had surnames that passed from generation to generation.) Though christened "Carl Linnaeus," Carl wrote his name either fully Swedified, Carl von Linné, or more often fully Latinized, Carolus Linnaeus.

5
Flowering Herbs

Defined as seed plants without woody stems, the flowering herbs include most plants thought of as "wildflowers," as well as grasslike plants. Some wildflowers, even small ones, are shrubs. Distinguishing herbs from shrubs can be tricky. Slightly woody little "subshrubs" are in this chapter unless they have heavy evergreen leaves at least an inch off the ground to prove there's a woody stem there. The latter type includes the heathers and twinflower, pages 152 and 156.

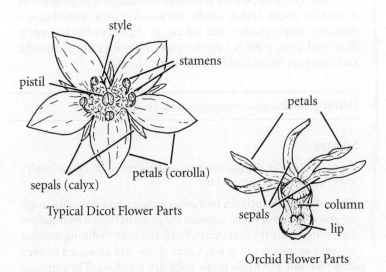

Typical Dicot Flower Parts

style
stamens
pistil
petals (corolla)
sepals (calyx)

Orchid Flower Parts

petals
column
sepals
lip

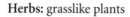

Herbs: grasslike plants

Grasses, sedges and rushes are the three huge families of grasslike plants. To tell them apart, roll a stem between thumb and forefinger:

Sedge stems are triangular in cross-section, with V-shaped leaves in 3 ranks along the 3 edges. ("Sedges have edges.")

Grass stems are round and hollow, with a swollen node at the base of each leaf.

Rush stems are round and pith-filled; their leaves too are often tubular, especially near the tip; the pistils and seedpods are 3-celled.

"Sedges have edges" is clearly true throughout genus *Carex* (most of our sedges) but some sedges (e.g., cottongrass, p 162) have rounded stems that become vaguely triangular near the top.

Positive identification of grasslike plants requires a whole vocabulary of grass parts and a microscope. For this book I chose a modest number of species, out of hundreds growing here, and describe them minimally. If both habitat and description fit what you're looking at, then you have an educated guess of what it is.

Beargrass, p 181, is a lily you might mistake for a sedge when its flowers are absent, as they usually are; its leaves are V-shaped in section, dry, pale, abrasive, and robust, in abundant thick clumps. Blue-eyed-grass, p 183, is a slender iris that blooms early and briefly, and then goes unnoticeable in grassy meadows.

Herbs: grasslike, with triangular stems (sedges)

Sedges

Carex spp. (**cair**-ex: Roman word for sedge). Cyperaceae (Sedge family). Mertens' sedge is illustrated at left.

The sedge family includes bulrushes or tules, and the more tropical genus Cyperus, which includes the papyrus from which ancient Egyptians made the first paper. Here, the overwhelming number of sedge species are in genus *Carex*. Some like saturated or even submerged soil, but many prefer cold, dry meadows. The common denominator of sedge habitats is stress; i.e., they benefit when the grasses they compete with are in any way handicapped, and tend to increase with altitude and latitude. Most require full sun; the two common forest species here are elk sedge and Ross's sedge. Both root-sprout to increase after fire, and are common in all Idaho/Montana forest types except cedar/hemlock. Elk sedge also stands out among sedges in providing forage important to elk and even bears. Water sedge is valuable forage for waterfowl, but most sedges are rarely grazed at all.

When a *Carex* sedge blooms, straw-colored stamens in conspicuous disarray adorn the sides of parts of the flowering spikes. Stamen-bearing units are male flowers; two or three headless threadlike stigmas tip each female flower, and a dark scale covers much of its outer surface. The number of stigmas and the distribution of stamens are used in sedge identification. For an oversized illustration, picture the grass plant we know as corn: the male spikes (tassels) form a terminal cluster atop the plant, while numerous stigmas (silks) show that the lateral spikes (ears) are all female. Those are unisexual spikes. Bisexual spikes, in a clever twist of jargon, are either *androgyn*ous or *gynecandro*us, depending on whether males or females are on top.

Sedges with two stigmas per female floret

Holm's Rocky Mountain sedge, *C. scopulorum* (scop-you-**lor**-um: of rocks). Flower spikes ½–1¼" [1–3 cm, several, the terminal one usually male; female flowers dramatically black (or purplish black) with tan or light green edges; plants 4–16" [10–40 cm]. Wet alp/subalpine meadows; abundant in s MT, WY. Illustrated at left, and color p 90.

Water sedge, *C. aquatilis* (a-qua-til-iss: of water). Spikes up to 2" [5 cm], terminal one male or androgynous, lateral ones female, erect; plants 16–40" [30–100 cm], rhizomatous. In water or wet soil; common. Illust at right, and color p 90.

Dunhead sedge, *C. phaeocephala* (fee-o-sef-a-la: dun head). Flower spikes pale, few, small, closely clustered; spikes with female flowers above males, or sometimes all female; plants 2–12" [5–30 cm]. Abundant in alpine tundra and rock fields. Illustrated at left.

Herbs: grasslike, with triangular stems, 2 stigmas

Sedges with 3 stigmas, usually less than 10" [25 cm] tall

Ross's sedge, *C. rossii* (ross-ee-eye: after John Ross, polar explorer). Flowers fewer than 10 per stem, scarcely ¼" [6 mm] long, framed between 2 bracts that extend well past flowers; often some stems very short, hiding spikes down among the leaves; plants 4–12" [10–30 cm], in clumps. Dry forests. Illustrated at right.

Blackscale sedge, *C. atrosquama* (atrosquay-ma: black scale). =*C. atrata* (WY). Spikes ⅓–¾" [8–20 mm], female flowers purplish black; males on lower part of top spike, plus sometimes a few at base of lateral spikes; lowest spike ± leaning; plants 6–20" [15–50 cm]. Alp/subalpine meadows. Illustrated at left. Similar *C. epapillosa*, with lower spikes drooping, largely replaces it in WY and sw MT.

Blackroot sedge, *C. elynoides* (el-in-**oy**-deez: like *Kobresia* spikesedges). Spike single, slender, cylindrical, tan to dark brown, female flowers fewer than ten, enlarging and spreading out at maturity; leaves wiry, resembling the 2–6" [5–15 cm] stems. WY, e, ID, c and sw MT; extensive dense turf on dry tundra ridges where soil has developed; limestone material preferred.

Curly sedge, *C. rupestris* (roo-**pes**-tris: of rocks). Spikes single, slender, cylindrical, brown to purplish; leaves flat at base, up to ⅛" [3 mm] wide, curly at tip; plants 2–6" [5–15 cm] single or in small tufts, not dense turf. Dry, wind-blasted alpine slopes, esp on limestone; may form cushions scattered across harsh alpine gravels, with white dryad, or may form alpine turf with grasses. Illust bottom right.

Black alpine sedge, *C. nigricans* (nye-grik-anz: blackish). Flower spike single, quite dark, male flowers above females; leaves 4–9 per stalk, ± curling; plants 2–4" [5–10 cm], turf-forming. In small hollows, alp/subalpine; more abundant northward. Illustrated top of next page, and color p 90.

Dense, turfy beds of black alpine sedge underlie the latest-melting patches of snow. Once they dry out, they offer a perfect spot for basking, tumbling, or sleeping. What's good for you is in this instance tolerated by the flora, too, as these sedges are relatively resilient. Not even sedge turf is immune to trampling, though: camp on sedge beds only when away from trails, pick beds unmarked by previous campers, and move on after one or two nights.

To deal with its short growing season, black alpine sedge is a speed demon among grasslike plants, setting seed as soon as 13 days after its release from snow. (Typical nearby plants take 42–56 days.) Even that is rarely quick enough, so it spreads mainly by rhizomes, producing a turfy, rather than clumpy, growth habit.

Sedges with 3 stigmas, usually more than 10" [25 cm] tall

Elk sedge, *C. geyeri* (**guy**-er-eye: after K. A. Geyer, p 327). Spike single, androgynous; female flowers 1–3, large (¼" + three ⅜–⅝" stigmas, or 6 mm + 10–15 mm), set off from the close-packed males; leaves about as tall as the stems; plants 6–20" [15–50 cm], in clumps; a huge fibrous root system hides below its modest stems. Dry forests; Crowsnest to Tetons, and w. Illustrated at right.

Mertens' sedge, *C. mertensii* (mer-**ten**-zee-eye: after Karl Mertens, p 152). Flower spikes dense, cylindrical, ¾–1½" [18–45 mm], several; male flowers (darker) take up the lower half of the terminal spike, and at most the lowest few scales of the other spikes; stem edges sharp, rough; leaves flat, bigger ones all at least a few inches up the stem; plants 1–3' [30–90 cm]. Moist openings up to near timberline; ID, w MT, n to Waterton. With stems arcing gracefully under the weight of its nodding spikelets, it can be the prettiest sedge. Illustrated on p 158.

Raynolds' sedge, *C. raynoldsii* (**ray**-nuld-zee-eye: after Capt. Wm. Raynolds, p 242.). Flower-spikes ½–1¼" [12–30 mm], typically four, the top one male and much more compact than the others; female flowers ± puffy, dramatically black and green; plants 8–28" [20–70 cm]. Meadows, mainly below forest line; from Crowsnest south. Color p 90.

Showy sedge, *C. spectabilis* (spec-**tab**-il-iss: showy). Spikes ⅜–1¼" [1–3 cm], 2–5+, the terminal one male, lowest one spreading, on a long stalk; lateral ones may have a few males at top; blackish scales needle-tipped with 1-mm awns; plants 6–24" [15–60 cm]. Subalpine meadows, mainly in westerly ranges. Illustrated at left.

Short-stalk sedge, *C. podocarpa* (po-doe-**car**-pa: foot fruit). Similar to preceding, but lacks awns, and lower spikes often completely droop. Subalpine meadows; abundant from Glacier north.

Payson's sedge, *C. paysonis* (pay-**so**-niss: after Edwin Payson). Similar to short-stalk sedge, but spikes all ± erect on (ironically) shorter stalks, and leaves all ± basal; plants 6–18" [15–60 cm]. Subalpine meadows, willow thickets; abundant in s MT, WY. Not illustrated.

Cottongrass

Eriophorum (airy-**ah**-fur-um: wool bearing). Also **Alaska-cotton**. Spikelets 2–5, becoming white, cottony tufts ¾–1¾" [2–4 cm] long (in seed); leaves triangular near tips; stems ± round to triangular, 8–36" [20–90 cm]. High bogs. Cyperaceae. Color p 91.

Up in Alaska, the sight of mile after mile of cottongrass blowing in a breeze, is hard to forget. Here, it common in subalpine bogs.

Herbs: grasslike, with round, pith-filled stems

Woodrushes

Luzula spp. (**luz**-you-la: light—). Flowers tiny, dry, green to brown, with 6 tepals and 2 sepal-like bracts; seed capsule has 3 cells with 1 seed each. Juncaceae (Rush family).

L. hitchcockii and *L. parviflora* (hitch-**cock**-ee-eye: after C. L. Hitchcock; par-vif-**lor**-a: small-flowered). *hitchcockii*=sometimes included in European *L. glabrata.* Inflorescence very loose, often arching; leaves grasslike, wide, flat, finely hair-fringed, from sheathing bases without swollen nodes; plants 6–20" [15–50 cm]. Abundant in alp/subalpine forest and meadows; scattered in mid-elev forest. Illustrated at right. Color p 91.

L. spicata, (spic-**ay**-ta: spiked). Inflorescence a single, usually nodding, bristly spike ½–1¼" [12–30 mm] long; plant 2–16" tall [5–40 cm]. Alpine. Illustrated at left.

Like the glacier lily, the subalpine woodrush may melt its own hole to bloom through a few inches of dwindling snowpack. Its ancient name, *gramen luzulae* or "grass of light," observed the grace of an otherwise inconspicuous plant when bearing dewdrops in the morning light. More shade-tolerant than most grasslike plants, the woodrush can indeed grow in the woods, particularly near timberline, but it's more abundant in open meadows and on moraine gravels. The three-celled seed capsule in the rush family contrasts with one-celled, one-seeded fruits of grasses and sedges.

Rushes

Juncus spp. (**junk**-us: Roman word for them).
Flowers of 6 dry green to brown tepals and 2 outer
bracts; seed capsule has 3 cells, each with many
seeds; leaf blades (if any) tubular, resembling the
dark green, tubular, pith-filled stems. Juncaceae.

J. drummondii (dra-**mon**-dee-eye: after Thos. Drummond, p 155). Flowers 1–3, green, seemingly borne on
the side of the stem because a leaf borne just below them appears
to be the stem continuing; capsule blunt; tepals ¼" [6 mm]; stems
6–14" [15–35 cm]; in dense clumps; alp/subalpine. Illust at right.

J. parryi. (**pair**-ee-eye: after Chas. Parry. p 63). Flowers 1–4, narrow,
green, seemingly borne halfway up the stem because the 1–5" [3–12
cm] upper bract looks like more stem; capsule sharp-tipped; tepals ¼"
[6 mm]; stems 4–12" [10–30 cm]. Streambanks to dry meadows, mainly
alp/subalpine; Banff s.

J. arcticus. =*J. balticus* (WY).* Flowers in a seemingly lateral spray; stem
1–4' [30–120 cm], apparently leafless (upper bract looks like a continuation of the stem, and lower leaves are reduced to sheaths) each rising
singly from the rhizome; forms broad patches (not clumps) in marshes
at all elevs.

J. mertensianus (mer-ten-zee-**ay**-nus: after K. H. Mertens, p 152). Flowers dark
brown, tiny (⅛" long), many, in a compact, round terminal cluster; leaves 1–4,
the uppermost one angled off just below the inflorescence; stems 4–12" [10–30
cm]; in dense clumps; alp/subalpine. Illustrated below. Color p 90.

Rushes are tough, reedy, deep green, round-stemmed,
round-leaved plants with chaffy tufts, often nearly
black, for flowers. Most are small. (Big "bulrushes"
or "tules" are not rushes but sedges.) Rushes
commonly grow in wet places, including bogs and
marshes, but in the high country you often see them
in dry meadows and gravels. Since rushes become
utterly unpalatable by maturity, arctic rush can become weedy in heavily grazed meadows.

The Okanogan allegedly used
Mertens' rush in witchcraft. Large
rushes, like arctic rush, were woven
into baskets and sleeping mats.

*Whether to separate *J. arcticus* from
J. balticus is a longstanding issue; FNA
treats *balticus* as strictly Eurasian, at
least for now.

Herbs: grasslike, with round, hollow stems

Grasses

Family Poaceae.*

Bearded grasses (awns 1"/25 mm or longer)

Foxtail barley, *Hordeum jubatum* (hor-dee-um: barley, a misleading name; jew-**bay**-tum: bearded). =*Critesion jubatum* (CO). Spikelets 1-flowered, each functional spikelet tightly flanked by two slenderer sterile ones; awns ½–3" long [12–75 cm], purple to bronze to frosty green; bristly spikes arch in youth. Though native and gorgeous, foxtail barley grows like a weed (i.e., mainly on disturbed ground) and antagonizes cattle and their owners by piercing soft tissue when grazed. Color p 91.

Bottlebrush squirreltail, *Elymus elymoides* (el-im-us: the Greek term; el-im-**oy**-deez: like *Elymus*, an absurd name now that this species is in that genus). -=*Sitanion hystrix*, a beautiful name I am loath to part with. Spikelets of 2–6 florets in a 1½–6" [4–150 cm] spike which looks strikingly brushlike thanks to the many awns, ¾–4" long [2–10 cm]; plants 4–20" [10–50 cm]. Dry rocky soil, pine forest to alpine.

Columbian needlegrass, *Achnatherum nelsonii* (ac-**nath**-er-um: awned scale; nel-**so**-nee-eye: after Aven Nelson). =*Stipa occidentalis, S columbiana, S. nelsonii;* incl *A. occidentale* (BC). 1-floret spikelets held tightly erect against the main stem, in a 2–12" [5–30 cm] spike; awns ¾–2¼" long, twice-bent, spreading at various angles; leaves often inrolled; plants 8–40" [20–100 cm].

Needle-and-thread, *Hesperostipa comata* (hes-per-o-**sty**-pa: western grass; co-**may**-ta: hairy). =*Stipa comata.* Spikelike 3–10" [8–25 cm] panicle bristles with 4–8" [10–20 cm] (!!!) awns which are ± twisted and curled and/or crooked; leaves narrow, rough, inrolled; stems clumped, 12–28" [30–70 cm]. Rocky soil at low to mid-elevs. Corkscrew shape of awn can spin the seed as it falls, helping plant it in the soil; increases with overgrazing.

---

*The grass family was previously known for centuries as Gramineae—simply the Latin word "grasses." See fn, p 191.

Grasses with narrow flower spikes

Bluebunch wheatgrass, *Pseudoroegneria spicata* (soo-doe-reg-**nair**-ia: after another genus; spic-**ay**-ta: spiked). =*Elymus spicatus* (WY), *Agropyron spicatum.* Large (6–8 floret) spikelets form a 3–6" [6–12 cm] ± intermittent spike; bent awns ¼–¾" [1–2 cm] long or (esp in OR, ID) absent; plants 24–40" [60–100 cm], in clumps. Grasslands, all elevs but primarily low. Illust at right, and color p 91.

Blue wildrye, *Elymus glaucus* (**glaw**-cus: bluish pale). 3–5-floret spikelets in a 2–8", often nodding spike; awns vary from 1" to absent; leaves flat, ⅛–½" wide; plants 16–48". All elevs; often in gravelly soils, incl river bars. Illust at left.

Giant wildrye, *Leymus cinerea* (**lay**-mus: anagram of *Elymus*; sin-ee-ria: ash gray) =*Elymus piperi* (AB). Massive 4–10" [10–25 cm] spike with several spikelets at each node; awns short or lacking; leaves and stems robust, often harsh with fine hairs; 3–10' tall [1–3 m], in huge clumps. Plains, ravines, streambanks at low elevs. Eaten as a grain by Shoshoni and others; stout stems used as toy arrows, fire pokers, etc.

Hairy wildrye, *L. innovatus.* (in-o-**vay**-tus: forming offset plants) =*Elymus innovatus* (AB, WY). Spike 4–10" [10–25 cm]; short awns; spikelets finely hairy, often purplish; leaves rough, less than ¼" wide [6 mm]; 1–3' tall [30–90 cm]; can form a clumpy turf. Foothills, lodgepole forest; Glacier n, abundant in AB.

Crested wheatgrass, *Agropyron desertorum* (agro-**pie**-run: wild wheat; dez-er-tor-um: of deserts). =*A. cristatum* (WY). Also **rescuegrass**. Short-awned spikelets in two tidy ranks, forming flattened, erect 1¼–4" [3–10 cm] spikes; leaves flat; 12–40" tall [.3–1 m], in clumps. Asian; planted (and invasive) in sage/grassland. Illust at left.

Blue grama, *Bouteloua gracilis* (bo-tel-**oh**-a: after the Boutelou bros; **grass**-il-iss: slender). =*Chondrosum gracile* (CO). Bristly, often purplish spikelets tightly aligned on one side of stem, in 1–3 sickle-shaped spikes; leaves often hairy, curly; plants 8–18" [20–45 cm]. Dry foothills, mainly e of CD. Illustrated at right.

Alpine timothy, *Phleum alpinum* (**flee**-um: Greek for some grass). =*P. commutatum* (CO). Short-awned, often purplish spikelets form a single dense, neatly cylindrical ½–1¾" [1–4 cm] spike; leaves flat, edges feel raspy; plants 4–20". [10–50 cm] Moist alpine to mid-elev meadows. Color p 91.

Downy oatgrass, *Trisetum spicatum* (try-**see**-tum: 3-awned; spic-**ay**-tum: spiked). Spikelets of 2–3 florets forming a 1–3" [2–7 cm] spike, often purplish; awns ¼" [6 mm], bent outward; plants 4–16" [10–40 cm], often fuzzy all over. Common from alpine ridges to spruce/fir forest. Illustrated at left.

Herbs: grasslike, with round, hollow stems

Pinegrass, *Calamagrostis rubescens* (cal-a-ma-**grah**-stiss: reed grass; roo-**bes**-enz: reddish). Flowering stems abundant in recent burns, otherwise few or absent, the plant spreading mainly by rhizomes; 3–6" [8–15 cm] spikelike panicle of 1-floret spikelets; awns bent at midlength, barely protruding; leaves narrow, flat to inrolled (not creased), rough to touch; plants 16–40" [40–100 cm]. Pine forest, often with elk sedge. Color p 91.

Purple reedgrass, *C. purpurascens* (purpur-**ass**-enz: purplish). Like pinegrass, exc awn only slightly bent; panicle usually purplish; plant 12–30" [30–75 cm]. All elevs; dominates some tundra turfs on calcareous soil in sc ID and sw MT. Illust at right.

Spike fescue, *Leucopoa kingii* (lew-co-**po**-a: white bluegrass; **king**-ee-eye: after Clarence King, p 242) =*Festuca kingii, Hesperochloa kingii*. Florets 3–5 in awnless spikelets; panicle dense, almost spikelike, the branches ± erect ; leaves ⅛–¼" wide [3–6 mm], bluish; stems 1–2' [30–60 cm], in dense clumps with many dry bases from previous years. Dry rocky soil; mid-elev forest to tundra; WY, c ID, s MT. Illustrated at left.

Grasses with ± awnless florets in open panicles

Northern sweetgrass, *Hierochloë odorata* (higher-o-**clo**-ee: sacred grass). =*H. hirta* (USDA, BC, CO). Yellowish 1-floret spikelets in a delicate 2–5" [5–12 cm] panicle; leaves vanilla-scented; stems 12–20" [30–50 cm] with purplish bases. Widely scattered in mtn meadows. All tribes craved this fragrance, using the plant as a sachet, an incense burned ceremonially, a hair rinse, a strand in hair braids, etc. The aromatic ingredient, coumarin, is used by Anglos as a flavoring, and is under study as a powerful antioxidant; but see p 000. Illustrated.

Redtop, *Agrostis stolonifera* or *A. gigantea* (ag-**ros**-tiss: Roman term for some grass; sto-lon-**if**-er-a: with runners). =*A. alba*. Purplish 1-floret spikelets in a delicate 2–10" [5–25 cm] panicle; leaves flat, midvein prominent ; plants 8–40" [20–100 cm]. European; invasive on streamside gravels and moist disturbed areas.

Bluegrass, *Poa* spp. (**po**-a: roman term for some grass). Florets 2 or more in modest awnless spikelets; leaves rarely wider than ⅛" [3 mm], flat or folded most of their length, but near the tip folded and upcurved like a canoe. Ubiquitous; *P. pratensis* (the lawn grass called Kentucky bluegrass though actually from Europe) invades throughout our range, esp under grazing pressure, to which it is highly resistant. Native species also abound, notably *P. alpina* and *P. arctica* in alpine tundra, *P. wheeleri* (a.k.a. *P. nervosa*) (illustrated) abundant in open forest, esp in WY, and *P. secunda* from grasssland-steppe to subalpine.

Grasses with short-awned florets in open panicles

Bluejoint reedgrass, *Calamagrostis canadensis.* Spikelets of 1 floret in a 3–8" [8–20 cm] panicle with branches either flat-spreading or erect; purplish where alpine; each floret encloses one awn among many finer straight hairs; leaves usually flat, droopy, rough; plants 1–4' [30–100 cm]. Dominant grass of wet meadows; floodplains.

Tufted hairgrass, *Deschampsia cespitosa* (desh-**amp**-sia: after J. L. A. Loiseleur-Deslongchamps; see-spit-**oh**-sa: growing in bunches). Also **salt-and-pepper grass.** Panicle 4–10" [10–25 cm]; spikelets pale and/or purplish black (often bicolored); two florets barely stick out between two slightly longer scales (glumes); awns protrude slightly; leaves creased; plants 8–36" [20–90 cm]. Higher meadows and open forest ; abundant on moist, snow-protected alpine sites. Illust at left.

Purple hairgrass, *Vahlodea atropurpurea* (va-**load**-ia: after Martin H. Vahl; at-ro-pur-**pew**-ria: black purple). =*Deschampsia atropurpurea* (WY). Purplish spikelets of 2 florets sandwiched between and nearly hidden by two longer scales (glumes); awns completely hidden, less than ⅛" [3 mm], bent inward; panicle 2–4" [5–10 cm]; leaves flat; plants 6–24" [15–60 cm]. Subalpine.

Idaho fescue, *Festuca idahoensis* (fest-**you**-ca: Roman word for it). Spikelets of 4–7 florets forming a 3–6" spikelike panicle, with short (⅛", or 3 mm) awns; leaves narrow, wiry, dark green; plants 12–32" [30–80 cm]. All elevs, grassland or open forest. Illust at right.

Sheep fescue, *F. saximontana* and *F. brachyphylla* (sax-i-mon-**tay**-na: RM; bracky-**fill**-a: short leaf). Both spp formerly included in the European *F. ovina.* Spikelets of 3–4 florets in a narrow 1–3" [3–8 cm] panicle; awns less than ⅛" [3 mm]; leaves inrolled, in a dense basal tuft; plants 4–16" [10–40 cm]. Alp/subalpine. Illust at left.

Mountain brome, *Bromus carinatus* (bro-mus: Roman term for a grass; karen-**ate**-us: keeled). =*B. marginatus* (US DA), *Ceratochloa carinata* (CO). Robust flattened spikelets of several florets; panicle 4–10" [10–25 cm], branches ± erect; leaves ± flat, soft; stems 1–4' [30–100 cm], usually hairy. Mid-elev meadow and forest. Panicle illustrated at right.

Cheatgrass, *B. tectorum* (tec-**tor**-um: of roofs, once a common habitat in Europe). =*Anisantha tectorum* (CO). Also **downy brome, downy chess.** Delicate-looking 8–26" [20–65 cm] grass in small tufts, finely hairy ± all over; lower panicle branches often droop; awns ½" [12 mm], about as long as the floret; an annual, it comes up in winter or spring, usually dries out by midsummer. European; dry rangeland, disturbed ground. Spikelet illustrated at right. Color p 91.

Herbs: grasslike, with round, hollow stems

Grasses, classically personified as humble, are in reality taking over the world. They are the most successful plant family, if judged by their rate and breadth of genetic diversification in recent geologic time.

Grasses coevolved with grazers. Here, that would be bison, bighorn sheep, many small mammals and, to lesser degrees (counting only the vertebrates) elk, pronghorn, and moose. More recently, the ascendency of grasses was magnified by the rise of agriculture, which focused on grass seeds (grain) and grass-eating mammals (grazers). Millions of cattle and sheep grazed the West before the science of grazing ecology got up and running. This makes it hard for scientists to figure out what the American grasslands were like when only natives grazed. But here's some of what is believed:

Blue grama and buffalo grass, *Buchloe dactyloides,* codominated the shortgrass prairie ecosystem which supported the bison. This was the high, dry, western belt of the Great Plains, butting up against the Rockies on the west and merging eastward into the rainier, lusher tallgrass prairie. Tallgrass produced far more biomass, but these two scruffy, durable shortgrasses were better able to nourish tens of millions of half-ton grazers, thanks to anomalously high protein ratios. Though described above as growing 8 to 18 inches high [20–45 cm], blue grama was more often 1 to 4" [2–10 cm] when subjected to both bison and typical High Plains rainfall. Despite appearances, it thrived under the abuse. The trampling herds were harder on competing grasses than on blue grama, and they repaid grama with lots of nitrogen in the form of urine and manure. Blue grama recycled the nitrogen back into protein, which nourished the bison, and so on.

In general, moderate grazing—even by cattle—stimulates the health and productivity of many grasses. The troubles with cattle include their inclinations to hang around by streams and ponds, damaging soil and vegetation, and to herd up and not move around much until shooed, which leads to patchy overgrazing. Badly overgrazed and compacted soils (a common condition 70 to 120 years ago) are prone to invasion by non-native plants. This is especially true in Intermountain grassland whose grasses—chiefly bluebunch wheatgrass and Idaho fescue—evolved with few bison and with little grazing by other hooved animals. Both the bunchgrasses and the cryptobiotic crusts (page 319) in the soil get broken and damaged by trampling. Many scientists believe that livestock grazing, while potentially benign on sod-forming grasslands, is always harmful to Intermountain bunchgrass communities.

Cheatgrass, a non-native, has taken over an estimated 100 million acres. It expands thanks to a nefarious cycle involving sagebrush and fire. In native sagebrush grasslands, most grasses are perennial bunchgrasses; they grow in tight clumps. With scant rain, clumps and sagebrush alike grow rather widely spaced, their roots reaching out to seize moisture from the nearly bare ground in between. Fires, where they can't jump from clump to shrub to clump, spread spottily, sparing plenty of individuals.

Cheat, on the other hand, is the one annual among the grasses described above. That means that cheat plants are all new each year, growing from seeds. Their tufts grow closer together, being smaller and faster-growing. They build up strong root systems in fall and winter, giving them the jump on bunchgrasses, which grow their roots in spring. By midsummer they set seeds and dry out completely, becoming totally unappealing to grazers but highly attractive to fire. They spread fire so well that Great Basin brushfires now tend to be all-consuming. With plenty of cheat in the basin to provide seeds, the next round of plant cover will have even more cheat, and the next fire will come sooner, before sagebrush has a chance to reestablish. The cheat/fire cycle reduces soil nitrogen, another factor in excluding the pre-existing vegetation. Believe it or not, the Intermountain sagebrush ecosystem is threatened. Most range managers now agree on the need for a massive campaign to restore perennial bunchgrasses and sagebrush. It won't be easy to come up with either the money or the techniques. One bunchgrass known to be easy to establish is crested wheatgrass, but it is itself a non-native invasive weed. Cattle love crested wheat, so vested interests often support planting it but not, say, bluebunch wheatgrass, let alone sagebrush. Westerners traditionally think of sagebrush as all too abundant.

Identification of grasses requires a special vocabulary. Keeping it to a minimum, grasses are flowering plants with simplified, undecorated, single-seeded dry flowers ("florets") each with three stamens and a usually two-styled pistil. (These sexual parts are short-lived and easily overlooked.) The florets are flanked several scales or bracts. Since the bracts are arranged alternately, in two ranks, rather than whorled, they are not sepals or tepals like the six whorled, scale-like tepals of a rush flower. In many species, bracts bear stiff hairs ("awns"); look for awns when you identify grasses. One or more florets and their bracts along a single axis make a "spikelet." Several spikelets attach to the main stalk either directly, making a "spike," or by small stalks (often branched) making a "panicle."

Herbs: grasslike, with round, hollow stems

Cattails

Typha latifolia (**tie**-fa: the Greek term; lat-if-**oh**-lia: broad leaf). Flowers minute, chaffy, in a dense round smooth spike of two distinct portions, the upper (male) thicker when in flower but withering as the lower (female) thickens and turns dark brown in fruit; stalks 3–10' [1–3 m]; leaves half as tall by ¼–¾" [6–20 mm], smooth; from rhizomes in shallow water. Typhaceae (Cattail family).

Cattail marshes are avidly sought out by migrating waterfowl and by hunters thereof. Many tribes wove the stalks (never the leaves) into thick, spongy mats for mattresses, kneeling pads in canoes, packsacks, baskets, rain capes, and temporary roofs in summer. Oddly, only a few of the tribes ate cattails, though the rhizomes and inner, basal stalk portions are pretty good baked, raw, or ground as flour.

Herbs: showy monocots

Monocots and dicots are named after and defined by their respectively single or paired seed leaves, or "cotyledons" (the first green part[s] to sprout from a newly germinated seed). Since those are ephemeral, monocots are often known by two less reliable traits:

parallel-veined leaves; and

3-merous flowers (3 petals and 3 sepals, but often these are nearly identical, so we call them 6 "tepals" in an inner and an outer whorl.)

The monocots on the following pages are distinguished from the grasslike monocots by (most of them) broader leaves and (all of them) moist, generally delicate flower parts evolved for visual attractiveness—in a word, showy. Most fall into the Lily, Iris, and Orchid families according to whether they have 6, 3, or 2 stamens, but the Arum family has its parts (inconspicuously) in fours.

Very few dicots have reliably 3-merous flowers. Only two such genera are in this book, and they don't have parallel leaf veins: wild ginger, p 265; and buckwheats, p 262.

Skunk-Cabbage

Lysichiton americanus (lye-zih-**kite**-on: loose tunic). Flowers green-ish yellow, 4-lobed, 4-stamened, ⅛" [3 mm] diam, many, in a dense spike 2½–5" [6–12 cm], partly enclosed or hooded by a yellow, par-allel-veined "spathe"; leaves all basal, ± net-veined, oval, eventually up to 3' × 1' [90 × 30 cm] or even bigger; from an enlarged fleshy vertical root. Wet ground; all exc WY. Araceae (Calla-lily family).

Many plants evolved sweet fragrances that attract sugar-loving pollinators, like bees. Others, such as the Eastern and European species of *Symplocarpus* (a different "skunk-cabbage") evolved putrid smells that attract pollinators, like some flies and beetles, that feed on, shall we say, decaying or-ganic matter. Our skunk-cabbage lies in between, attracting bees as well as beetles, distinctly skunky to the human nose but not foul, merely rank, like long-faded skunk aroma. It releases differ-ent odors at different temperatures, each odor matched to the kind of pollinator likely to be out and about at that temperature.

The Calla-lily family has a characteristic inflorescence consist-ing of a spadix (a fleshy spike of crowded flowers) and spathe (a large bract enfolding it). These organs have a voluptuous look; Walt Whit-man named a book of suggestive poetry after one genus, *Calamus.*

In the case of our skunk-cabbage, spathe and spadix thrust up from wet ground in early spring. Leaves come later, and keep grow-ing all summer to reach sizes unmatched north of the banana groves; they were widely used as "Indian wax paper" to wrap camas bulbs, berries, and other foods for steam pit baking or for storage. The leaf bases and the roots are marginally edible after prolonged cooking or storage breaks down the intensely irritating, "hot" oxalate crystals.

Elk and bears eat them, with no complaints recorded. Food or not, skunk-cabbage was regarded as strong medicine —for example, to induce labor, either timely or abortive. Later, some white man patented and sold it under the name "Skookum."

Wapato

Sagittaria cuneata (sadge-it-**air**-ia: arrowlike; cue-nee-**ay**-ta: wedge-shaped). Also **narrowleaf arrowhead**. Petals 3, white, spreading, nearly round, ⅜–¾" [1–2 cm]; 3 sepals green, pointed; many stamens; pistils on separate, ball-shaped female flowers, less showy and usually borne lower on the stem; flowers (both

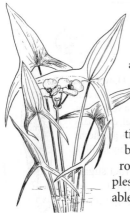

sexes) in whorls of 3; leaf blades from narrowly 3-pointed to roundly arrow-shaped, 1–5" long × 1–3" broad [2–12 × 2–8 cm], on long leafstalks from the base which is usually submerged in water. Alismataceae (Water-plantain family).

In fall the slender **wapato** rhizomes produce egg-sized potatolike tubers, with a flavor a little like roasted chestnuts. Traditionally retrieved from the mud with the toes, by humans, or with the bill, by ducks, wapato roots were widely traded among the first peoples, and by Lewis, Clark, & Co.: "it has an agreeable taste and answers very well in place of bread."

Herbs: showy monocots with 6 stamens (lilies)*

Fairy-Bells

Prosartes spp. (pro-**sar**-teez: for use in crafts?). =included in the European genus *Disporum* (USDA, AB). Flowers ¼–½" [6–12 mm], white, bell-shaped, pendent in pairs (or sometimes 1 or 3) from branchtips; berries yellow to red, egg-shaped, ¼–½" [6–12 mm], ± edible (juicy, sweetish but insipid); leaves 2–5" [5–12 cm], wavy-edged; stems 12–30" [30–75 cm], much branched. Liliaceae.*

P. trachycarpa (tray-key-**car**-pa: rough fruit). Berry finely pebbly, holds 6–12 seeds; leaves smooth, at least above. Forests and aspen groves. Color p 92.

P. hookeri (**hook**-er-eye: after Sir Joseph Hooker, p 203). Berry smooth, holds 4–6 seeds; leaves finely hairy. Forests, from Bitterroots north. Illustrated.

A cure for snow-blindness, according to the Blackfoot, would be to place a fairy-bells seed under each eyelid and hold it there overnight.

---

* Plants in this section are lilies *sensu latu,* or "in the broad sense." They are in a single large Lily family according to some taxonomists (including USDA) but have been separated into several families by others, in accord with molecular studies. *Flora of Wyoming* (2001 3rd Edition) recognizes 12 lily families (in WY alone), outdoing the ten lily families in *Colorado Flora*. FNA published its lilies in late 2002, using the single large family, but hedging its bets by "suggesting" how it would place species in segregated families if it were confident that current molecular data would not continue to be refuted by newer data. Those families are named second, after Liliaceae, in this section. See p 609.

Twisted-Stalk

Streptopus spp. (**strep**-ta-pus: twisted foot). Flowers bell-shaped, one (sometimes two) beneath each leaf axil; berries red, ¼–½" [3–12 mm], juicy, sweetish but insipid; leaves 2–5" [5–12 cm], tapered, elliptical. Liliaceae.

S. amplexifolius (am-plex-if-**oh**-lius: clasping leaf). =*S. fassettii* (CO). Tepals ½" [12 mm], dull white, reflexed from near midlength; style unbranched; flower stalklets sharply kinked; stems 12–40" [30–100 cm], much branched. Moist forest. Illustrated above, and color p 93.

S. lanceolata (lan-see-o-**lay**-ta: narrowleaved). =*S. roseus*. Tepals ⅜" [1 cm], variably streaked rose with white, slightly reflexed at the tip; style 3-branched; flower-bearing stalklets straight to curved; stems 6–14" [15–35 cm], rarely branched, arching. Moist forest in BC.

Twisted-stalk discretely hides its flowers under its leaves —quite a trick, since the the crotch *above* each leaf bears the flower. Look closely to see the flower stalk where, fused to the stem, it runs up it to the next leaf base. (The first leaf can't have a flower under it.) The berries were called "snakeberries" by the Lillouet, "witchberries" by the Haida, and "Grizzly Bar's favorite food" by the Kootenai, who considered them poisonous. Other nations (including their Okanagan neighbors according to one source) ate them with gusto.

False-Solomon's-Seal

Maianthemum spp. Flowers white, fragrant, many, in one terminal inflorescence; berries ¼" [6 mm], round; leaves heavily veined, pointed, oval to narrowly elliptical, 2–7" [5–18 m]; stems arching, unbranched, often zigzagging at leaf nodes; from horizontal rhizomes. Widespread. Liliaceae or Ruscaceae (see fn).

M. stellatum (stel-**ay**-tum: starry). =*Smilacina stellata*. Tepals ¼" [6 mm], flat-spreading; flowers 6–18; berries longitudinally striped, ripening dark red to blackish; stems 8–24" [20–60 cm]. Color p 93.

M. racemosum (ras-em-**oh**-sum: bearing flowers in racemes, a misleading name). =*S. racemosa, M. amplexicaule* (CO). Tepals minute, stamens longer (⅛", or 6 mm); flowers in a ± conical fluffy panicle; berries speckled at first, ripening red; stems 1–3' [30–90 m]. Color p 94.

False clues galore: this genus bears scant resemblance to Solomon's seal (genus *Polygonatum*). *Racemosa* isn't racemose, but s*tellata* is. I find false-Solomon's-seal berries sometimes delicious (not purgative, as some authors report) but often insipid. Both species grow in deep woods but also in clearings and open slopes. Form varies with habitat. In deep shade, *stellata* spreads its leaves flat from a bent-over stem; in sun, it holds its stem upright, grows narrower leaves, angles them upward, and folds them sharply at the midvein.

False-Asphodel

Triantha glutinosa and *T. occidentalis* (try-**anth**-a: 3 flower; gluten-**oh**-sa: sticky). =*Tofieldia glutinosa* (most texts). Also **tofieldia**. Tepals white, ⅛–¼" [3–6 mm], persistent while the 3-styled pistil grows out past them into a fat, reddish, 3-celled capsule; flowers/fruit in a dense cluster atop an 8–20" [20–50 cm], sticky, hairy stem; 1–3 grasslike basal leaves 2–6" [5–15 cm], and sometimes 1–2 smaller stem leaves. Wet places, mainly subalpine; *glutinosa* in Canada, *occidentalis* from s Can southward. Liliaceae or Tofieldiaceae. Color p 94.

Trillium

Trillium ovatum (**tril**-ium: triple; oh-**vay**-tum: oval). Also **wake-robin**. Three petals 1–3" [25–75 mm], white, aging through pink to maroon; 3 sepals shorter, narrower, green; flowers single, on a 1–3" [25–75 mm] stem from the whorl of 3 leaves, 3–7" [8–18 cm], often equally broad, net-veined exc for the 5 or so ± parallel main veins; plants 6–16" [15–40 cm], rhizomatous. (Rarely with 4 or 5 leaves and/or petals and sepals, instead of 3 each.) Low forest, all exc (probably) WY. Liliaceae or Melanthiaceae.

For most flowers that shift color as they age, as trilliums do, the advantage is in using the aging blooms to help make a grander display to attract pollinators from afar, but then showing them whiter blooms that have more viable pollen. Later in the season the trillium switches to a gastronomic insect lure: it packs its seeds in a gummy oil which ants, the usual disseminators, find tasty.

Glacier Lily

Erythronium grandiflorum (air-ith-**roe**-nium: red—, the flower color of some species; gran-dif-**lor**-um: large-flowered). Tepals golden yellow, 1–1½" [25–38 mm], spreading to reflexed either in an arc or from the base; flowers ± nodding, single or sometimes 2–6 on a 6–12" [15–30 cm] stalk; capsule erect, 1" tall [25 mm], 3-celled and -sided; 2 leaves 4–8" [10–20 cm], basal, wavy-edged; from a scallionlike bulb. Abundant around timberline, scattered at lower elevs. Liliaceae. Color p 92.

Glacier lilies can generate enough heat to melt their way up and bloom through the last few inches of snow. (See p 247). Fluttering with illusory fragility in subalpine breezes, they offer themselves as vehicles for those anthropomorphic virtues we love to foist on mountain wildflowers— innocence, bravery, simplicity, perseverance, patient suffering, etc. "They toil not, neither do they spin." They don't taste half bad either. (Bulbs, leaves, and flowers are edible, but not a good idea except when starvation threatens.) The seed pods are food for hooved browsers, and the bulbs are an important "garden vegetable" (p 000) for grizzlies. They survive fires well.

Common names in this attractive genus are legion. One name for the entire genus is "dogtooth-violets"; several European species are violet, but resemble violets in no other way.

Mariposa Lilies

Calochortus spp. (cal-o-**cor**-tus: beautiful grass). Petals creamy white, or sometimes purplish, drying yellowish, ⅝–1½" long [15–38 mm], almost as broad; sepals pointed, much smaller; flowers 1–5; seed pods have persistent 3-branched styles; the only large leaf basal, ± grasslike; stem 4–20" [10–50 cm]; from a small, deeply buried bulb. Liliaceae.

C. apiculatus (ay-pic-you-**lay**-tus: with a small point). Petals have a small dark dot near the base, an abruptly narrowed basal neck, and dense white (and yellow) hair over at least their lower ⅓; seed pods nodding, 3-winged; basal leaf up to ⅝" wide [15 mm]. WA to nw MT and north to Radium. Illust.

C. gunnisonii (gun-ih-**so**-nee-eye: after John Gunnison, p 242). Each petal has a purplish basal spot, a purplish transverse band about ⅓ of the way up and branched- or knobby-tipped hairs in between; sepals also have a purplish basal spot and band; seed pods narrow, erect; leaves narrow, inrolled, several. WY, sc MT. Color p 93.

C. eurycarpus (yer-i-**car**-pus: broad fruit). Petals have a large purple blotch near center, and just a few hairs below that; seed pods erect, with three broad wings; basal leaf up to 1" wide [25 mm]. NE OR, c ID to c MT and w WY. Color p 93.

C. elegans. Long white hairs cover at least the lower ¾ of petals; petals and sepals often have a ± crescent-shaped purple spot; seed pods nodding, with 3 broad wings; leaf flat, much taller than stem. OR, c ID, sw MT. Color p 93.

"Cat's-ears" is the most pictorial of many flattering names given to these sensuous blossoms, all the more admired for being prohibitively hard to cultivate. Most species need bone dry soil before the bulb goes into healthy winter dormancy. Several members of the genus (including sego lily, the Utah state flower) are desert flowers, with lavender to white flowers. There was an era when gardeners and nurseries attempted cultivating them on a grand scale; many species were nearly loved to death in the process. The leading *Calochortus* taxonomist was also a leading collector: he actually boasted of his "record" pace of 4000 bulbs dug per day! Plainly there was nothing like today's awareness of species endangerment.

A Cheyenne warrior about to race a horse would feed her a mariposa lily bulb to help her win.

Wild Onions

Allium spp. (al-ium: the Roman term). Flowers ¼–⅜"
long [6–10 mm], several, on stalklets all from one spot
between pointed, onionskinlike segments of the spathe that
encased the inflorescence in bud; stems often bunching;
from small onions with the trademark aroma. Liliaceae or
Alliaceae.

Nodding onion, *A. cernuum* (sir-new-um: nodding). Inflorescence broad, nodding (often erect in fruit); tepals pink or
white, oval, much shorter than stamens, all ± alike but in separate inner and outer whorls; stem 8–20" [20–50 cm]. In sun, all
elevations. Illustrated.

Karl Andreas Geyer came west with Sir William Drummond
Stewart's 1843 expedition, the first pleasure trip to the Rockies.
The party camped on Persian carpets under crimson canopies.
Geyer left the party at the Big Sandy in Wyoming, carrying on westward,
at first alone but soon with Jesuit missionaries—a giant step downscale:
"the hospitality the Jesuits showed to me was scant and beggarly." From
their Flathead valley mission to the Coeur d'Alene area was "one of the
most terrible journeys I have ever made, especially in the midst of winter,
crossing 76 times streams. Some we had to swim... Owing to the diffi-
culties ... I could not pay proper attention to the vegetation. But this
much I do know, that I saw [a coast redwood]." Inattentive to the vegetation? No kidding. But only that one time.

A diligent and competent botanist, Geyer was, on the other hand,
short on charm and business ethics. He reneged on a contract to deliver
his collections to eminent botanist **Georg Engelmann** in St. Louis (who
would then have described them); overstayed his welcome at the Chem-
okane Mission (the missionary's wife wrote "we are determined to be rid
of him"); and left Chief Factor McLoughlin scrambling to find out whose
credit line Geyer had been charging supplies on.

On his return to Germany after eleven years away, he looked, to his
friends, "at least twenty years older." His several thousand specimens
were offered for sale to wealthy collectors at $10 per hundred. Such sales
provided a major part of a field botanist's paltry income.

Alexander Gordon, another botanist who started out in Stewart's
party, had the temerity to write to Sir William Hooker (p ooo) politely arguing for higher prices for his rarer specimens, but had to settle for the
usual £2 per hundred—only to be thwarted from selling any specimens
at all. He and **Joseph Burke**, a third botanist in the party, failed to make
their deserved marks in botanical history because of shipping damage to
their collections: Burke's rotted while taking fifteen months at sea, and
Gordon's went down with their ship.

Short-styled onion, *A. brevistylum* (brevis-**tie**-lum: short style). Tepals pink, all ± alike, 2× longer than stamens; leaves 3+, flat; stem 8–24" [20–60 cm]. Wet meadows and streambanks at all elevs. Color p 93.

Geyer's onion, *A. geyeri* (**guy**-er-eye: after K. A. Geyer, opposite page). Tepals pink or white, all ± alike, not quite hiding stamens; leaves 3+, channeled; stem 4–20" [10–50 cm]; in our common variety, *tenerum*, flowers are few and sparse, many being replaced by little bulbils, which reproduce clonally. Wet meadows. Illustrated.

Hooker's onion, *A. acuminatum* (a-cue-min-**ay**-tum: pointed). Tepals pointed, purple or pink to (occasionally) white, the outer whorl ± spreading, bell-shaped, inner whorl smaller, narrowly jar-shaped; leaves 2–5, withering before flowers open, much shorter than the 4–12" [10–20 cm] tubular stem. Dry foothills.

Wild chive, *A. schoenoprasum* (skee-no-**pray**-zum: reed leek). Tepals pink or white, all ± alike, longer than stamens; flowers closely clustered, blooming in sequence from center outward; leaves 2, tubular, their bases sheathing the stem for several inches. Gravelly streambanks, wet meadows. Color p 92.

An onion is easy to recognize (and sometimes hard to miss) because it smells like an onion. If it doesn't, don't try a taste test; it might be death camas. If you want it for seasoning, just clip a few leaves. Digging up the puny bulb isn't worth the trouble, and kills the plant. Along with the above common species, we have several rare ones in need of protection.

Douglas's Triteleia

Triteleia grandiflora (try-tel-**eye**-a: 3 ends; grand-if-**lor**-a: big flower). =*Brodiaea douglasii*. Also **gophernuts**. Flowers ½" long [12 mm], sky blue, several, on stalklets all from one spot between narrow bracts; stamens attached at unequal heights on the 6 tepals inner faces; leaves 1 or 2, flat, grasslike. Dry slopes from RM Trench s. Liliaceae or Themidaceae. Color p 93.

Triteleias and the similar brodiaeas resemble onions, taste rather like onions and were a major food resource. For gophers, they still are.

Bead Lily

Clintonia uniflora (clin-**toe**-nia: after DeWitt Clinton; you-nif-**lor**-a: one flower). Also **queen's-cup, bride's-bonnet**. Flowers single, white, ± face-up, broadly bell-shaped to nearly flat-spreading; 6 tepals ¾–1" [20–25 mm]; berry intensely blue, ⅜" diam [1 cm], many-seeded, inedible; two or three leaves 3–6" × 1–2" [7–15 × 2.5–5 cm], heavy, smooth, ± shiny, basal, sheathing the 2–4" [5–1 cm] stalk; from slender rhizomes. Moist woods, all exc WY. Liliaceae. Color p 92.

The beady blue berry is more striking than the formal white blossom. It was used sometimes as a stain, never as a food.

Alp Lily

Lloydia serotina (**loy**-dia: after Edward Lloyd; sir-**ot**-in-a: delayed). Flowers 1 or 2, face-up, conical to saucer-shaped; 6 tepals barely ½" [12 mm], white with dark veins and often a purplish basal tinge; seed pod egg-shaped, ¼" [6 mm]; leaves very narrow, few, sheathing the 2–6" [5–15 cm] stalk; bulb sheathed in dry leaves of previous years. Alpine, esp on limestone-derived soil. Liliaceae. Illust at right.

Tiger Lily

Lilium columbianum (**lil**-ium: Roman word for lily; co-lum-be-**ay**-num: of the Columbia River). Flowers/fruit nodding, several, on long branches from the 2–4' [50–100 cm] stem; tepals orange with small maroon spots, 1½–2½" long [4–6 cm] but so strongly recurved as to make a ± full circle; capsule fleshy, 1½–2" [4–5 cm]; leaves 2–4" [5–10 cm], narrow, in whorls largest near midstalk; from a large, many-cloved bulb. Clearings and thickets up to timberline, mainly w of CD. Liliaceae.

The rather bitter bulbs were eaten by most tribes.

Wood Lily

Lilium philadelphicum (filla-**del**-fic-um: probably after the city). Flower 2–3" long [5–8 cm], erect atop 1–2' [2.5–5 cm] stem, red-orange, purple-spotted near base, bell-shaped, usually single; capsules fleshy, 1" [2.5 cm]; leaves 2–4" [5–10 cm], narrow elliptical, the upper ones in 1 or 2 whorls; from a many-cloved bulb. Clearings, mainly near and e of CD. Liliaceae. Color p 92.

Stave off the temptation to pick or dig up this attention-grabbing flower, and leave it for others to enjoy *au naturel*. Rampant picking has badly reduced its numbers.

Bronze Bells

Stenanthium occidentale (sten-**anth**-ium: narrow flower; ox-i-den-**tay**-lee: western). Flowers several, pendent, narrowly bell-shaped, ⅜" long [1 cm], varying from burgundy red to greenish cream; six tepals all alike; 2–3 leaves basal, up to 1" wide [2.5cm]; stem 8–15" [20–38 cm]. Moist to wet alp/subalp sites, c MT and c ID northward. Liliaceae or Melanthiaceae. Color p 92.

Yellow Bell

Fritillaria pudica (frit-il-**air**-ia: checkered; **pew**-di-ca: modest). Flowers yellow, pendent, narrowly bell-shaped, ⅞" long [22 mm], usually single; six tepals all alike; leaves ± grasslike, two or several; stem succulent, 4–12" [10–30 cm]. Blooms early; grasslands, ponderosa pine woods. Color p 92.

Chocolate Lilies

Fritillaria spp. Also **rice-root lily, mission bells, leopard lily, fritillary**. Tepals inward-curving, brownish purple mottled with yellowish green; flowers pendent, 1–4; capsule 6-winged; leaves 2–5" [5–13 cm], narrow, both whorled and single; stem 5–36" [13–90 cm], from a bulb of a few large garliclike cloves with many tiny ricelike bulblets. Grassy slopes below treeline. Liliaceae.

Fritillaria affinis (**aff**-in-iss: related). =*F. lanceolata*. Tepals ¾–1⅓" [2–3 cm]; capsule ¾" [2 cm]; leaves ⅛–1" wide [3–25 mm]. n ID, se BC.

Fritillaria atropurpurea (at-ro-pur-**pew**-ria: black purple). Tepals ½–¾" [1.2–2 cm]; capsule ½" [1.2 cm]; leaves ⅛–¼" wide [3–7 mm]. c ID, s MT, WY. Illustrated.

These elegant flowers sell themselves short, with camouflage coloring and a smell that draws flies. The bulbs and rice-like bulblets were a major food in the old days; they're bitter and too rare to dig up now. When the Haida were introduced to rice, they named it "fritillary-teeth."

Camas

Camassia quamash (ca-**mass**-ia **qua**-mosh: two versions of a Chinook Dialect term from an originally French word). Tepals blue-violet, ¾–1½" [1–4 cm], narrow, the lowermost one usually noticeably apart from the other five; inflorescence roughly conical; capsule ½–1" [12–25 mm], splitting three ways; leaves narrow, basal/sheathing, shorter than the 8–24" [20–60 mm] stem; from a deepset bulb. Seasonally moist meadows. Liliaceae or Agavaceae. Color p 94.

Camas bulbs were a vegetable food prized by most tribes from western Montana to the coast. Camas cakes were second only to dried salmon in trade volume, especially on the British Columbia Coast where no camas grows. In many tribes, a family would mark out, "own" and maintain a camas patch year-round for generations Their digging sticks and timed fires promoted overall growth of camas and also weeded out death camas when in flower and easy to recognize. That made it safe to dig camas before or after flowering, in accord with local taste regarding when the bulbs are best. (Nevertheless, many people died from eating death camas. Camas bulbs are not recommended to hikers.) Camas culture was true agriculture—something anthropologists used to say neither Plains nor Northwest Coast cultures engaged in. Compared to the many early–Nineteenth Century reports of vast seas of blue, camas prairies have since lost much of their camas through neglect, even where they were never plowed. The Nez Perce War was touched off by white settlers plowing up camas prairies for pastures.

Quamash cuisine according to David Douglas: "A hole is scraped in the ground, in which are placed a number of flat stones on which the fire is placed and kept burning until sufficiently warm, when it is taken away. The cakes, which are formed by cutting or bruising the bricks and then compressing into small bricks, are placed on the stones and covered with leaves, moss, or dry grass, with a layer of earth on the outside, and left until baked or roasted, which generally takes a night. They are moist when newly taken off the stones, and are hung up to dry. Then they are placed on shelves or boxes for winter use. When warm they taste much like a baked pear. It is not improbable that a very palatable beverage might be made from them. Lewis observes that when eaten in a large quantity they occasion bowel complaints… Assuredly they produce flatulence: when in the Indian hut I was almost blown out by strength of wind."

The flatulence is attributable to inulin, an indigestible sugar that takes the place of starch in camas bulbs, Jerusalem artichokes, and a few other vegetables.

Death Camas

Zigadenus spp. (zig-a-**dee**-nus: paired glands). Also **zygadene**. Flowers white, ± saucer-shaped, in a tall raceme, withered tepals persistent; capsules ½–¾" [12–20 mm], splitting, 3-celled, 3-styled; most leaves basal, narrow, sheathing, but often 2 or more along the 8–30" [20–75 cm] stem; bulb 1" [25 mm]. Liliaceae or Melanthiaceae.

Z. elegans (**el**-eg-enz: elegant). =*Anticlea elegans* (CO). Tepals all alike, ⅜" [1 cm], with a heart-shaped greenish spot near the base; leaves, stem often with whitish coating. Subalpine forest to alpine tundra. Color p 92.

Z. venenosus (ven-en-**oh**-sus: poisonous). =*Toxicoscordion venenosum* (CO). Tepals less than ¼" [5 mm], inner ones slightly longer than outer, all with a ± oval greenish spot near base. Abundant among lower-elev grasses. Color p 93.

One of these two species earned the name "death camas." Back during camas digging days, *Z. venenosus* doubtless killed more people in the Rockies than any other plant ever will. Today it maintains its reputation with occasional sheep deaths. No humans are known to have been killed by *Z. elegans*, which is less toxic and prefers elevations where edible camas is uncommon. No one would mistake the small white flowers of death camas for the big blue ones of camas, but mistakes occur when populations of the two are intermixed and both have just come up, or gone to seed or withered.

Beargrass

Xerophyllum tenax (zero-*fill*-um: dry leaf; *ten*-ax: holding fast). Stamens longer than tepals; flowers white, fragrant, saucer-shaped, ½" diam, many; inflorescence at first nippled, bulbous, 3–4" diam [7–10 cm], elongating up to 20" [50 cm], the lowest flowers setting seed before the highest bloom; capsules 3-celled, dry; leaves narrow, tough, dry, V-grooved, with minutely barbed edges; basal leaves largest, 8–30" [20–75 cm], in a large dense clump; stalk to 60" [150 cm], covered with small leaves; from rhizomes. Abundant in both subalp meadows and forests. Liliaceae or Melanthiaceae. Color p 93.

Once you've seen beargrass in bloom you will have no trouble ever recognizing its wonderful flower heads again. But the flowering schedule is erratic. You often see only the bunched leaves. Communities of beargrass may go for years without one bloom—and then hundreds bloom at once. That often happens for several years in a row after a fire that reduces the tree canopy but leaves the soil cool enough for the beargrass roots to survive and resprout. Like the century plant, beargrass clumps grow slowly, accumulating photosynthates for years before venturing a flowering stalk. Having flowered, the clump dies, but its nutrients are siphoned off through the rhizome to a new offset clump.

Spring's tender leaf bases figure in bear diets, hence "beargrass"; but the neatly clipped leaf bases you see here and there are more likely the work of a "brushpicker" gathering foliage for the florist trade.

By summer the leaves are wiry and strong. Native Americans wove them into baskets and hats. David Douglas wrote, "Pursh is correct as to their making watertight baskets of its leaves. Last night my Indian friend Cockqua… brought me three of the hats made on the English fashion, which I ordered when there in July; the fourth, which will have some initials wrought in it, is not finished, but will be sent by the other ship. I think them a good specimen of the ingenuity of the natives and particularly also being made by a little girl, twelve years old… I paid one blanket (value 7 shillings) for them."

Douglas' imaginative biographer, William Norwood, read between the lines of Douglas's journal to argue that Douglas, in his cavalier praise for a little girl's ingenuity, was disguising a romantic entwinement with a nubile "Chinook princess."

Corn Lily

Veratrum spp. (ver-**ay**-trum: true black). Also **false-hellebore**. Flowers saucer-shaped, numerous; styles 3, persistent on the 1"-long 3-celled capsules, but lacking from the (staminate) lower flowers; leaves mostly 5–12" [12–30 cm], coarsely grooved along veins, oval, pointed; stem 3–7' [1–2 m], from a thick black rhizome. Wet meadows, mainly subalpine; forests in BC. Liliaceae or Melanthiaceae.

V. viride (**veer**-id-ee: green). =*V. eschscholtzii* (AB). Flowers pale green, ½–¾" diam [12–20 mm], in a loose panicle with drooping branches. From ID and s MT north. Color p 94.

V. californicum. Flowers dull white, or only slightly greenish, ¾–1½" [2–5 cm], in a dense panicle with ascending branches. From ID and s MT s. Illustrated.

Heavy beds of snow lying on steep meadows tend to creep downslope through the winter, scouring vegetation from the surface. Woody seedlings are frustrated year after year, while herbs with fat storage roots and fast spring growth are favored, perpetuating the meadow. On many wet slopes, blunt corn lily shoots are the first plants to thrust upward as snow recedes. Looking almost Venusian—startlingly clean and perfect—when they first unclasp from the stalk, before long they are often ragged, with help from foraging elk and insects.

Conspicuous browsing does not prove the plant safe to eat: many ewes that ate *V. californicum* have given birth to one-eyed lambs. Scientists traced the problem to an alkaloid they named cyclopamine after the mythical one-eyed monster. Long listed as promoting tumors, cyclopamine now turns out to *kill* some cancer cells very nicely, particularly medulloblastoma, a brain cancer in children that has no approved treatment to date. Better yet, no harm has been apparent in either ewes themselves nor lab mice dosed with cyclopamine. Look for extensive harvesting of corn lilies in the near future. But don't munch on the plant: both roots and young shoots are toxic, and used to be ground up for a crop insecticide (by farmers) or for a sinus-clearing snuff (by several Rocky Mountain tribes.) Every tribe that knew the plant used some part of it— sometimes burned as a fumigant, sometimes worn around the neck as a charm to ward off evil.

Western Iris

Iris missouriensis (eye-ris: rainbow; miz-oo-ree-**en**-sis: of the Missouri River). Flowers pale blue, 2 (rarely up to 4); consisting of 3 spreading sepals , 3 erect petals, and 3 smaller petal-like parts (pistil branches) ± resting on the sepals and hiding the stamens; stem 10–20" [15–50 cm]; leaves grasslike, basal; capsule 3-celled, splitting; from horizontal rhizomes. Moist-in-spring sites, to mid elevs. Iridaceae (Iris family). Color p 95.

Iris was the Greek goddess who flashed across the sky, bearing messages—the rainbow. Some *Iris* species in the West were tough enough to use in cordage, but this one found only medicinal uses—very diverse ones. The Shoshoni, for example, put it on tooth cavities, venereal sores, earaches, burns, and rheumatism.

Blue-Eyed-Grass

Sisyrinchium spp. (sis-er-**ink**-ium: the Greek term, derived obscurely from "pig snouts"). 6 tepals all alike, blue with yellow base, ¼–¾" [6–20 mm]; stamens fused into one 3-anthered column; flowers 1 or a few; leaves grasslike, all ± basal (exc the bracts at base of flower stalks: the longer bract looks like a continuation of the stem above the flowers) shorter than the 6–14" [15–35 cm], 2-edged stem. Dry grassy sites that are briefly moist in spring. Iridaceae. Color p 95.

These delicate perennials complete their active season in wet soil in a few weeks of spring, then wither and die back for the rest of the year, going dormant through the summer. (See p 248.)

Irregular dicots, pages 210-23, have no more than 5 petals. In any case, the orchid's flower structure is a snap to recognize; one petal, lowermost and thrust forward, is always utterly unlike the others and usually much larger. It's called the "lip" and serves as a platform for insect pollinators. Above the lip is a combined stamen/pistil structure called the "column." (Illustrated on page 157.)

Orchid flowers are among the most elaborate insect lures on earth. While the flowers evolved outlandishly, the roots mostly atrophied: a majority of orchid genera are rootless tropical lianas. Our orchids have vestigial root systems that tap into preexisting networks of fungal hyphae.

Bog Orchids

Platanthera spp. (plat-**anth**-er-a: broad anther). =*Limnorchis* spp. (CO), *Habenaria* spp. Also **rein orchids**. Flowers in a tall spike; lip with a long downcurved spur to the rear, two sepals horizontal, the other sepal and two petals erect, hooding the column. Orchidaceae.

White bog orchid, *P. leucostachys* (loo-co-**stay**-kiss: white spike). =*Limnorchis dilatata* (CO). Flowers white, spicy-fragrant, in a dense 4–12" [10–30 cm] spike; stem 8–40" [20–100 cm], with many clasping leaves, lower ones up to 10" × 2" [25 × 5 cm], much smaller upward. Wet ground, often subalpine. Illust.

Round-leaf bog orchid, *P. orbiculata* (or-bic-you-**lay**-ta: circular leaf). Flowers white to greenish or yellowish, in a loose spike; stem 8–24" [20–60 cm], leafless exc for a few tiny bracts; basal leaves typically 2, oval to nearly round, 2–6" [5–15 cm]. Shady forest; ID and nw MT n.

One-leaf bog orchid, *P. obtusata* (ob-too-**say**-ta: blunt leaf). =*Lysiella obtusata* (CO). Flowers yellow-green to almost white, in a loose spike; stem 2–8" [5–20 cm], leafless; single basal leaf blunt elliptic, 1–4" [3–10 cm]. Moist spots in forest.

Slender bog orchid, *P. stricta* (**stric**-ta: drawn tightly together). =*H. saccata*. Flowers green, sometimes purple-tinged, in a loose spike; lip narrow, much longer than the round, ± scrotum-shaped spur; leaves oval to elliptic, sheathing the stem; 8–20" [20–50 cm]. Wet ground. Color p 95.

The distinguishing feature of bog orchids is a narrow nectar-filled pouch or "spur" projecting rearward from the lip. The spur is an element in the grand pattern of orchid evolution, which has allied each variety and species of orchid with one species of insect, or at most a very few. Even in one species, the white bog orchid, spur length may vary radically, presumably to attract moths, butterflies, or bees and flies. This insect is not only powerfully attracted, but also physically unable to extract nectar from two successive blooms without picking up pollen from the first and leaving an adequate dose of it on the stigma of the second. Bog orchids' devices include:

proboscis-entangling hairs to engage the insect for a little while;

adhesive discs that stick to the insect's forehead while instantly triggering the stamen sac to split open;

little stalks that each hold a cluster of pollen to the adhesive disc (now on the insect's head), at first in an erect position that keeps the pollen *away* from the stigma of that same flower, but then (when the insect flies on) drying out and deflating into the right position to push the pollen onto…

the gluey stigma of the next flower of the same species that the insect visits for more nectar.

All this just to minimize waste of pollen in the wrong places.

The inch-long apparent stalk between the flower and the stem is actually the flower's ovary; a 180° twist in it shows that the lip evolved from what was originally the uppermost petal.

Rattlesnake-Plantain

Goodyera oblongifolia (**good**-yer-a: after John Goodyer; oblong-gif-**oh**-lia: oblong leaf). Flowers greenish white, many, in a one-sided spike up to 5" [12 cm]; lip shorter than and hooded by the fused, ¼"-long [6 mm] upper petals, all connected to the stalk by a twisted ovary; leaves 1½–3" [4–8 cm], in a basal rosette, thick, evergreen, very dark glossy green, mottled white along the veins; stem unbranched, 10–16" [25–40 cm]. Dense forest. Orchidaceae.

"The Klallam informant, who is a devout Shaker, said that since she is a Christian she should not think of such matters, but formerly women rubbed this plant on their bodies to make their husbands like them better." —Erna Gunther

The intensity of the snakeskin pattern on the leaves varies, even among side-by-side plants. Sometimes only the midvein is white, but usually there is enough white pattern to tell these leaves from those of

Goals of Evolution?

The idea (expressed above in regard to orchid design) that species evolved certain traits in order to accomplish certain functions is a time-worn misconception about evolution. A few respected scientists uphold subtle versions of this concept, but they are far outnumbered. The consensus view is that huge numbers of new traits turn up randomly, through genetic mutation. A tiny proportion of them just happen to confer some advantage on individuals that happen to get them. Over time, individuals that draw lucky straws (advantageous traits) tend to produce more offspring than others (by surviving longer, by attracting more mates, etc.) and their offspring that inherit the trait also reproduce prolifically, preserving the trait in increasing numbers of descendents, until nearly a whole species carries it. Meanwhile, some other traits appear and persist without any adaptive value whatsoever.

Since that explanation is so unwieldy, I succumb to the charms of the teleological fallacy—an easy-to-grasp figure of speech.

white-veined pyrola (page 238). This is one orchid with enough leaf area to make it nearly independent of its mycorrhizal partners by the time it matures.

Ladies'-Tresses

Spiranthes romanzoffiana (spy-**ranth**-eez: coil flower; roman-zof-ee-**ay**-na: after Count Rumiantzev, below). Flowers ± white, ½" long [13 mm], seemingly tubular, in (usually 3) ranks in a 2–6" [5–15 cm], dense, coiled-looking spike (perhaps suggesting a 4-strand braid); leaves sheathing, mostly basal; stem up to 24" [60 cm]; from swollen roots in wet ground. Wet meadows and streambanks, up to timberline. Orchidaceae. Illustrated.

Twayblades

Listera spp. (**lis**-ter-a: after Martin Lister). Also **big-ears**. Flowers pale greenish, small (about ½", or 13 mm), several, in an open, short-stalked spike; broad lip petal, upper 2 petals slender, resembling the 3 sepals; leaves 2, broad, 1½–2½" [4–6 cm], apparently opposite, clasping the stem at mid-height, tips pointed; stem unbranched, 4–12" [10–30 cm]. Forest shade. Orchidaceae.

L. cordata (cor-**day**-ta: heart-shaped). Lip petal splits into two long pointed lobes, like an inverted Y.

L. borealis (bor-ee-**ay**-lis: northern). Lip petal broad at base, ending in two broad short round lobes.

L. convallarioides (con-va-larry-**oy**-deez: like lily-of-the-valley). Lip petal narrow at base, widening to two broad short round lobes, like a narrow inverted heart.

L. caurina (caw-**rye**-na: of the NW wind). Lip petal has two tiny but long and pointed side-lobes at its base, and almost no notch at all at the tip.

Though diminutive and dull, a twayblade is every inch an orchid, as testified by its glues and mechanisms for sticking pollen onto visiting insects—often mosquitoes. (And who better than an orchid to testify? Those two words derive from *orchis* and *testis*, the Greek and Latin words, respectively, for testes.)

Count Nikolai Rumiantzev (or Romanzoff) financed Captain Kotzebue's Russian exploration of 1815-18. **Johann Friedrich von Eschscholtz** and **Adelbert von Chamisso** were the naturalists. They collected extensively in Alaska and California, but apparently sailed right past BC, Washington and Oregon. Chamisso, a poet from Berlin, was the primary botanist while Eschscholtz, an Estonian doctor, preferred insects.

Lady's-Slippers

Cypripedium spp. (sip-rip-**ee**-dium: Venus' slipper). Also **moccasin flower**, **Venus-slipper**. 1 to 3 flowers; lip 1" [13 mm] long, very bulbous, with purplish veins and a yellow staminate structure at its base; upper sepal and lateral petals brownish purple, about 2" [5 cm] long, slender, often twisted; stem 6–24" [15–60 cm], with several broad, clasping-based, 2–6" [5–15 cm] leaves, a smaller bract beneath each flower. Wet soil in bogs, forests. Orchidaceae or Cypripediaceae (CO). Illustrated (the two are ± identical in black-and-white.)

C. montanum. Lip white. Waterton s.

C. parviflorum (par-vif-**lor**-num: small flower). =*C. calceolus* (CO). Lip yellow. Canada (rare in US). Color p 95.

Calypso Orchid

Calypso bulbosa (ca-**lip**-so: "Hidden," a sea nymph; bulb-**oh**-sa: bulbous). Also **fairy slipper**, **deer's head orchid**. Flower single, pink; lip slipper-shaped, almost white, magenta-spotted above, magenta-streaked beneath; other petals and sepals all much alike, narrow, ¾" [2 cm]; leaf single, basal, growing in fall, withering by early summer; stem 3–7" [75–175 cm], from a small round corm. Moist, mature forest. Orchidaceae. Color p 515.

A close look reveals these little orchids to be just as voluptuously overdesigned as their corsage cousins, which evolved bigger to seduce the oversized tropical cousins of our insects. Get down onto their level to see and smell them, using a handlens if you like, but don't pick them. Their bulblike "corm" is so shallowly planted that it's almost impossible to pick them without ripping the corm's life-lines. A calypso is dependent on its fungal and plant hosts (see page 290); its single leaf withers and is gone early in the growing season. Like other orchids, it produces huge numbers of minute seeds (3,770,000 seeds were found in one tropical orchid's pod) with virtually no built-in food supply, and an abysmal germination rate. They germinate only if particular species of fungi are already growing there and can supply nutrients. The black specks filling vanilla beans and vanilla ice creams are familiar examples of orchid seeds.

Coralroots

Corallorhiza spp. (coral-o-**rye**-za: coral root). Entire plant (exc lip) dull pinkish brown, or rarely pale yellow (albino); flowers ¾–1¼" [2–3 cm] long (half of that being the tubular ovary), 6–30 in a loose spike; leaves reduced to inconspicuous sheaths on the 6–20" [15–50 cm] stem. Forest. Orchidaceae.

Western coralroot, *C. mertensiana* (mer-ten-see-**ay**-na: after Karl Mertens, p 152). Lip redder than plant, often with one or two spots or blotches.

Spotted coralroot, *C. maculata* (mac-you-**lay**-ta: spotted). Lip usually white, with many magenta spots (sometimes also on petals). Color p 95.

Striped coralroot, *C. striata* (stry-**ay**-ta: striped). All petals and sepals brownish- to purplish-striped. Color p 95.

Coralroots usually grow in forest stands with few herbs or shrubs. They blend in with the duff and sticks until a shaft of sunlight hits, suddenly incandescing their eerie, translucent flesh. Their rhizomes do resemble coral—curly, short, knobby, and entirely enveloped in soft fungal tissue. As in other orchid genera, a seed's embryo develops only if penetrated, nourished, and hormonally stimulated by a minute strand ("hypha") from a fungus in the

Non-Green Plants

Some of our most intriguing herbs have no chlorophyll, and obtain all their nutrients from fungi. Non-green plants were long called "saprophytes," defined as obtaining their carbohydrates from dead organic material, but that isn't what they do. Their carbohydrates come from living green plants via living mycorrhizal fungi (page 290) which pass them along to the non-green plants below ground. The saprophyte concept was first debunked in 1882, and its coffin was nailed up between 1960 and 1987, yet it continues to pop up ghoulishly in new books, even books by botanists. Some botanists alter the word's definition just to fit these plants, in conflict with others that apply it to fungi and bacteria that really do live on dead material. Efforts to coin a better term came up with "epiparasites" (indirect parasites) and "mycotrophic achlorophyllous angiosperms," or "mycoheterotrophs" for short. Some scientists call them "cheaters, i.e., parasites of the mutualism that [mimic] the mutualist but do not provide the usual benefits" to the partner. For our purposes, "non-green plants" will do just fine.

The mycorrhizal symbiosis must have evolved because it lets fungi and plants utilize each other's strengths—the fungi's efficient uptake of water, phosphorus, and nitrogen, and the plants' ability to make carbohydrates out of air, water, and sunlight. Some mycorrhizal plants, it seems, gradually contributed less and less to this exchange, and got away with cheating as long as there were other plants supplying the soil. Fungal hormones suppress root hair growth and stimulate the orchid to produce mycorrhizae instead (page 290). In the case of coralroots, no root hairs ever form. The vestigial leaves do not photosynthesize; oddly, the flowers' ovaries do, but not in significant quantities.

Herbs: dicots, non-green

Pinedrops

Pterospora andromedea (tair-**os**-por-a: winged seed; an-drom-ed-**ee**-a: a name from Greek myth). Entire plant gummy/sticky, monochromatically brownish red exc for the amber, 5-lobed, jar-shaped corollas; flowers many, on down-curved stalks; capsules ± pumpkin-shaped; leaves brown, small and sparse on the 12–48" [30–120 cm] stem. Forests. Monotropaceae. Color p 189.

This year's glowing amber stalks of pinedrops, our tallest non-green species, shoot up alongside last year's still-standing dry brown stalks.

---

same fungus. As the cheaters evolved, organs they no longer needed atrophied; they ended up with vestigial leaves, little or no chlorophyll, and no real roots—nothing but a stalk of flowers reproducing, while using the trees above for leaves and the fungi below for roots.

Definitive proof of whether this symbiosis is mutualistic or parasitic has resisted all efforts, so far. Non-green plants do produce chemicals that some researchers call "vitaminlike" because they strongly stimulate growth of both the fungal and green hosts. But that doesn't prove beneficence: parasites like mistletoe commonly stimulate growth in their hosts, but sap the hosts rather than energizing them. Tom Bruns and colleagues saw clues that one monotrope "cheater" they studied was benefitting its truffle partner, while they doubted this was true of two orchids. They saw no evidence of benefit to the fir tree in either case.

Non-green plants often show up during what foresters call the "stem exclusion phase"—the period in the development of a forest when competition among trees (for light and water, especially) is most intense, and consequently few understory plants remain and the weaker individual trees die (i.e., are "excluded.") Logging schemes that use repeated thinning to mimic fire, bypassing the stem exclusion phase on the way to big marketable trees, might miss out on something important: the non-green community might never develop. For example, our most valuable single mushroom, the matsutake, is a cosymbiont of non-green plants.

As the name implies, they may be found under (and mycorrhizally linked to) ponderosa pines, but also under Douglas-fir or, for that matter, all kinds of trees all across the continent. But as their direct fungal partners, in contrast, they apparently accept only one species. These symbiotic fungi are mostly boletes or truffles, and the pine family provides most of the green hosts. All but one non-green species in our area is either an orchid or in family Monotropaceae, which consists of non-greens formerly included in the heath family.*

Indian Pipe

Monotropa uniflora (ma-**not**-ra-pa: flowers turned one way, a meaningless name for a one-flowered plant; you-nif-**lor**-a: one-flowered). Also **ghost-plant**, **corpse-plant**. Entire plant fleshy, white or pink-tinged, drying black; flower single, narrowly bell-shaped, ½–¾" [12–20 mm], mostly 5-merous (occasionally 4–6), pendent, but erect in fruit—a soft round capsule; leaves translucent, small; stems densely clustered, 2–10" [5-25 cm]. Dense forest; not in WY. Monotropaceae or Ericaceaae or Pyrolaceae (CO).*

A strange plant, but a familiar one all across the continent. Mushrooms in the Russula family are the usual cosymbionts here, and Douglas-fir is often at the far end of the pipeline. Don't pick Indian pipes—they'll just turn black and ugly within hours.

Pinesap

Hypopitys monotropa (hye-**pop**-it-iss: under pine). =*Monotropa hypopithys.** Entire plant fleshy, yellow (rarely red) to straw, tinged with pink, drying black; flowers narrowly bell-shaped, ⅜–¾" [1–2 cm], mostly 4-merous (rarely 5), several, initially all downturned in one direction, but erect when fruit matures; seed capsules round, soft; leaves translucent, small; stems clustered, 2–10" [5-25 cm]. Dense forest. Monotropaceae.† Color p 190.

Digging up a pinesap (don't!) would reveal a soft mycorrhizal root-ball only a couple of inches deep. Species of *Boletus* (page 305) are common partners of this species, and a pine or other conifer is almost always hooked up to the same bolete.

---

*Several competing concepts for splitting the Heath family are seen in recent books. Dorn (WY) stands by keeping it all one, and is backed up by a committee of Ericaceae specialists which formed just to settle this issue, and took four years studying the state of knowledge on it.

†Generations of taxonomists have quarreled over these vice-versa binomials. At issue: how closely related is pinesap to Indian pipe? DNA studies now find the two plants far from being each other's closest kin, so they shouldn't be in the same genus. My guess is that pinesap will go back to genus *Hypopitys*.

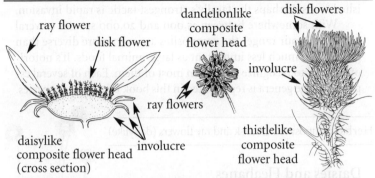

ray flower

disk flower

dandelionlike
composite
flower head

disk flowers

involucre

ray flowers

daisylike
composite flower head
(cross section)

involucre

thistlelike
composite
flower head

Picture a daisy. Seeming petals radiate from a cushiony "disk" in the center. On closer examination, the base of each petal-like "ray" enwraps a small pistil. The ray and pistil together constitute a "ray flower," not a petal; the petal-like length is an entire corolla of petals, fused then split down one side and flattened. The central disk turns out to be lots of little flowers too—"disk flowers"; each has stigmas (usually two) poking out of a minute tube of five fused stamens, within a larger tube which is the (usually five-lobed) corolla. What we saw at first as one flower is a "composite flower head," the characteristic inflorescence of the family Asteraceae, or composites.* "Involucral bracts" surround the head as sepals do the flower in other families. Sepals, if present, take the form of a "pappus"—a brush of hairs, scales or plumes that remain attached and grow as the seed forms, usually to provide mobility via wind or fur.

Some composites, dandelionlike, have only ray flowers and no disk. In these the ray flowers are bisexual, with stamen tubes as well as pistils. Other composites have only disk flowers, and some *appear* to have only disk flowers because their inner and outer flower types are equally unshowy; we will call both rayless kinds "thistlelike."

The tight fit of the stamen tube around the style is a mechanism that prevents self-pollination. As the pistil grows, it plunges all the pollen out of the tube; once its tip has grown free of the tube, it can

---

*This family was long known as the Compositae, until it was ruled that all families must have names formed from the name of a member genus and the suffix *-aceae*. The term "composite" is still heard, especially in the form "D.Y.C." ("damned yellow composite"), an expression voiced by cranky botanists who sometimes punt rather than pursuing tricky identifications within large genera like *Arnica, Hieracium*, or *Erigeron*.

---

split, exposing stigmas on the inner faces of its two branches.

Composite flowers excel at producing copious fat, well nourished seeds. Perhaps the family's strongest tactic is rapid invasion.

With somewhere between 15,000 and 20,000 species (several hundred in our range) the composites are even more diverse than grasses, but much less important as large-animal foods. It's notoriously hard to recognize all or even most of them. Each of several especially large genera is represented in this book by two to six species.

Herbs: composites with disk and ray flowers (daisylike)

Daisies and Fleabanes

Erigeron spp. (er-**idge**-er-un: soon aged). **Daisy** and **flea-bane** ± interchangeable. Rays relatively narrow and numerous; disk yellow; involucre has just one row of equal bracts. Asteraceae.

Cutleaf daisy, *E. compositus* (com-**poz**-it-us: compound). Head single, rays 20–60, white (may be pinkish or bluish); leaves basal, compound with slender leaflets in threes. Sandy or rocky soils, mid-elevs and up. Illustrated.

Showy fleabane, *E. speciosus* (spee-see-**oh**-sus: showy). Heads several; rays 60–150, blue-purple (rarely pink or white), very narrow; leaves all the way up stem, narrow elliptical, edges smooth. Moist sites in sun. Color p 96.

Subalpine daisy, *E. peregrinus* (pair-eg-**rye**-nus: wandering). Heads usually single; rays 30–80, violet (rarely pink or white), ⅜–1" [10–25 mm]; involucre woolly or sticky from top to bottom; leaves basal (few and tiny on alpine plants) and a few small ones on stem. Moist sunny sites, mainly alp/subalpine. Color p 97.

One-flower daisy, *E. simplex.* Head single, rays 50–120, lavender to white; leaves narrowly oblong, mainly basal; stem sticky-hairy; stem, involucre, and often the leaves woolly; 1–8" tall [3–20 cm]. Alp/subalp; US. Canada has similar *E. grandiflorus,* with lots of hairs that are long but not sticky.

Woolly daisy, *E. lanatus.* Head single; rays 30–80, white to pink, ⅜" [1 cm]; leaves narrowly oblong, with two side teeth on some; involucre ± purple, ¼–⅜" [8 mm] tall; plants 1–4" [3–10 cm], long crinkly hairs all over. Alpine. Color p 96.

Golden fleabane, *E. aureus* (aw-**ree**-us: golden). Rays bright yellow, ⅓" [8 mm]; leaves basal on long stalks; plant 2–7" [5–17 cm], finely woolly. Alpine; Canada.

Daisies generally bloom during the spring flowering rush, earlier than most composites, suggesting the Latin name. Insecticidal properties implied by "fleabane" are Medieval superstition, or confusion with *Pyrethrum* daisies. The name "daisy" (originally for the English daisy, *Bellis perennis*) traces back to "day's eye" in Old English.

Asters

Rays 6–60, ¼–¾" [6–20 mm]; disk yellow; involucre has unequal bracts in 3 rows. Asteraceae. Treated until recently as spp. of the (now European) genus *Aster*.

Leafy aster, *Symphyotrichum foliaceum* (sim-fee-ah-trick-um: joined hairs; fo-lee-**ay**-shum: leafy, ref to the bracts) =*A. foliaceus* (BC, AB), *Almutaster foliaceus* (CO). Rays violet to blue; several heads; lowest row of involucral bracts biggest, leaflike; stems 8–24" [20–60 cm]. Moist, ± sunny sites, all elevs. Color p 96.

Engelmann's aster, *Eucephalus engelmannii* (yew-sef-a-lus: true head; engle-**mah**-nee-eye: after George Engelmann). =*Aster engelmannii* (BC, AB). Rays about 12, white or pale pink; involucre reddish; stems 2–5' [60–150 cm], ribbed, mostly unbranched, leafy all the way up. Moist, ± open forest. Color p 97.

Showy aster, *Eurybia conspicua* =*A. conspicuus* (BC, AB). Rays violet to blue; several heads; involucre sticky; leaves sharp-toothed; stems 1–3' [30–90 cm]. Moist, ± sunny sites, up to mid-elevs. Illustrated.

Arctic aster, *E. merita*=*A. sibiricus* (BC, AB). Rays violet; a few heads; involucre purplish; leaves narrow, stiff, toothed or not, fuzzy; stems 4–12" [10–30 cm], not sticky. High elevs. Color p 96.

Hayden's aster, *A. alpigenus* var. *haydenii* (al-**pidge**-en-us: alpine; hay-**den**-ee-eye: after F. V. Hayden. p 242). =*Oreostemma alpigenum* var. *haydenii*. (WY, CO, USDA). Rays purple; head single; stems 1–3, ± sprawling, 2–5" [5–12 cm]; leaves basal, linear, pointed, 2–4" [5–10 cm]. Alp/subalpine; US. Wallowas have bigger var *alpigenus*. Color p 96.

Asters generally bloom later than daisies and have fewer, wider rays.

Hairy Golden-Aster

Heterotheca villosa (hetero-**thee**-ca: varied cups; vil-**oh**-sa: woolly). =*Chrysopsis villosa*. Heads 1" [25 mm] diam, golden yellow; rays 10–25; all green parts coarsely hairy (though variably so); leaves all on stem, ± elliptical; stems 4–20" [10–50 cm], usually branched. Rocky sites at all elevs, esp lower. Asteraceae. Illustrated.

Parry's Townsendia

Townsendia parryi (town-**zen**-dia: after David [*not* John K.] Townsend; **pair**-ee-eye: after Chas. Parry. p 63). Striking 2–3" [5–8 cm] flower heads on 3–8" [8–20 cm] stems; rays lavender to blue; disk yellow; leaves basal (plus a few tiny stem leaves), spoon-shaped, not toothed. Dry meadows and gravels, from low prairie to alpine. Asteraceae (Aster family). Color p 96.

Of the several similar **townsendias**, a few have white rays; many stand barely an inch high, resting their flower directly on the rosette of leaves. The Blackfoot gave their horses townsendia tea as a medicine.

Arnicas

Arnica spp. (**ar**-nic-a: lambskin, referring to leaf texture). Heads entirely yellow, single to few, blooming in early to mid summer; leaves opposite, plus some in non-flowering whorls from the rhizome; stems 4–24" [10–60 cm]. Asteraceae. Color p 97.

A. rydbergii (rid-**berg**-ee-eye: after Per Rydberg). Rays 7–10, ½" [12 mm]; leaves ± smooth-edged, narrow-elliptical, with 3–5 ± parallel main veins; stem 4–12" [10–30 cm]. Alp/subalpine. Illustrated.

A. cordifolia and *A. latifolia* (cor-dif-**oh**-lia: heart leaf; lat-if-**oh**-lia: broad leaf). Rays 8–15, ½–1¼" [12–30 mm]; leaves ± toothed, broadly oval exc for the heart-shaped basal leaves often seen on *cordifolia*. Ubiquitous in open forest and meadows—perhaps the most ubiquitous flower in our range.

Several tribes used arnicas as a plaster for sore or injured muscles or joints; European herbalists made similar use of their *Arnica montana*. *A. cordifolia* readily resprouts from deep roots after a fire.

Butterweeds

Packera spp. (after John G. Packer, who modestly declined to use the name in *Flora of Alberta*). =*Senecio* spp. (AB, INT). Also **groundsels**. Rays 7–14, ½–¾" [12–20 mm]; disk and rays yellow; deep involucre with one row of bracts. Asteraceae.

P. pseudaurea (sue-**dor**-ia: false gold). Several heads; basal leaves fine-toothed broad oval, on long stalks; stem leaves much narrower, few, with long lobes on basal half, teeth on outer half; stem 2–30" [5–75 cm]. Moist places in forest. Color p 97.

P. streptanthifolia (strep-tanth-if-**oh**-lia: leaves like twistflower). Like *pseudaurea*, exc leaves 3-6× longer than wide, the basal ones ± smooth on lower half, toothed on upper half. Illust.

P. cana (**cay**-na: gray). Leaves and stems white-hairy; basal leaves usually entire, stem leaves few and small, often toothed; 5–16" tall [13–40 cm]. Common at prairie and alpine elevs.

P. subnuda (sub-**new**-da: almost hairless). =*S. cymbalarioides* (AB, INT). Leaves and stems scarcely hairy; basal leaves often scalloped, with a ± round blade on a long leafstalk; stem leaves few and small; 2–12" tall [5–30 cm]. Alp-subalpine. Color p 97.

Several species in this genus poison livestock, and several, including *P. pseudaureus*, have been used medicinally.

Groundsels

Senecio spp. (sen-ee-she-oh: old man). Rays few (4–10 or rarely none) sparse and disorderly; disk yellow; involucre a deep cup of bracts all in one row; heads several; stem 1–5' [30–150 cm]. Moist forest and meadows. Asteraceae.

S. triangularis. Rays ¼–½" [6–12 mm], yellow; leaves narrow-triangular, 3–7" [75–175 mm], all on stem. In saturated soil. Illustrated at right.

S. integerrimus (in-te-**jer**-im-us: very smooth-edged). Rays ¼–½" [6–12 mm], yellow to white, or lacking; leaves on long stalks, ± elliptical, mainly basal, smaller upwards.

S. megacephalus (mega-**sef**-a-lus: big head). Rays ½–⅞" [12–22 mm], yellow; leaves 3–7" [75–175 mm], gray-hairy, narrow, rather stiff, mainly near base. Rocky alp/subalp sites; MT, ID, n to Crowsnest.

Dusky Butterweed

Tephroseris lindstroemii (tef-**rah**-sir-iss: ash-colored chicory; lind-**strö**-me-eye: after Axel Lindström). =*Senecio fuscatus* (Int), *S. lindstroemii* (BC). Also **twice-hairy groundsel.** Alpine dwarf with large heads of a distinctive rich saffron orange color; 1 or a few heads; rays 7–12, ½–¾" [12–20 mm]; involucre a deep cup of bracts all in one row; green parts have thick cobwebby hair. Beartooths and Absarokas (disjunct from its boreal range). Asteraceae. Color p 97.

Blanketflower

Gaillardia aristata (gay-**lar**-dia: after Gaillard de Marentonneau; air-iss-**tay**-ta: with bristles). Also **browneyed Susan.** 1–4 large (2–3", or 50–75 mm) heads per stem; rays golden yellow, ending in 3 long lobes; disk at first orange and nearly flat, expanding to a bulbous, bristly red-brown button; stems and leaves hairy. Low-elev grassland, forests. Color p 97. Similar **blackeyed Susan**, *Rudbeckia hirta*, of the lower Great Plains also invades some RM roadsides.

Goldeneye

Heliomeris multiflora (helio-**me**-riss: sun part). =*Viguiera multiflora* (WY). Heads yellow, several, ¾–2" [2–5 cm]; rays 10–14; disk hemispheric, yellowish to brown; leaves mostly opposite, narrow, pointed 1–3" [25–75 mm]; stems 1–4' [30–100 cm]. Steppe, gravel bars, dry clearings; sw MT south.

Goldflower

Tetraneuris acaulis (tetra-**new**-ris: 4 veined; ay-**caw**-lis: stalkless). =*Hymenoxys acaulis* (AB), *Actinea acaulis*. Similar to preceding; solitary yellow heads mainly face up; leaves all basal, without teeth or lobes. All elevs; WY, MT, s AB.

Alpine Sunflower

Hymenoxys grandiflora. (hi-men-**ox**-iss: sharp membranes)=*Rydbergia grandiflora, Tetraneuris grandiflora* (USDA, CO). Also **old-man-of-the-mountains**. Huge yellow heads mainly face east, or toward their sun exposure; disk often 1" [25 mm] or wider, rays 3-toothed; leaves of many narrow lobes, both basal and on stem; plant woolly, 2–12" [5–30 cm]. Alpine rock crevices and meadows, to highest elevs; c MT southward. Asteraceae. Color p 105.

Woolly Sunflower

Eriophyllum lanatum (area-**fill**-um: woolly leaf; lan-**ay**-tum: woolly). Leaves, stems and involucres all thickly white-woolly; rays about 8, ⅓" [9 mm]; heads all yellow, single; leaves on stem, usually linear; stems 5–24" [13–60 cm], many, weak, in thick clumps or sprawling mats. Dry sites at all elevs. Asteraceae.

Little Sunflowers

Helianthella spp. (he-lee-anth-**el**-a: little sunflower). Big (1¾–4", or 45–100 mm) yellow flower heads mainly face south or southeast; leaves ± opposite, long and narrow, without teeth; 1–5' tall [30–150 cm]. Asteraceae.

H. uniflora. Flower head single; leaves have 3 main veins. Clearings, s BC south.

H. quinquenervis. (kwin-kwe-**ner**-vis: 5 veins). Usually 3 flower heads; leaves with 5 main veins, rough. Aspen groves, clearings, e ID and sw MT south.

These plants are often covered with ants that eat nectar secreted around the involucre. While swarming the plant waiting for more nectar to ooze out, the ants chase away flies attempting to lay eggs on the flower, where the fly larvae, later in the season, would eat the sunflower seeds. The plants' reproductive success rate is correlated with the presence of ants, showing that the symbiosis is mutual. Ant/plant mutualisms are well known in the tropics, but unusual here.

The common sunflower, *Helianthus annuus,* a coarser, rougher plant with dark brown flower disks, grows in some mountain valleys.

Balsamroot

Balsamorhiza sagittata (balsam-o-**rye**-za: balsam root; sadge-it-**ay**-ta: arrow-shaped). Heads all yellow, single, 2½–4" diam[6–10 cm]; leaves all basal (exc one or two small bracts on stem), long-stalked, triangular, 12" × 6" [30 × 15 cm]; plant silver-velvety, esp under leaves when young, 10–30" [25–75 cm], in thick clumps. Sunny, often south-facing dry slopes. Asteraceae. Color p 96.

Balsamroots put on spectacular massed displays. They are also a food plant. Deer and elk eat the leaves, and all tribes ate the young shoots, the seeds, and the fat, fragrant, slightly woody taproot. Since the root survives most fires, balsamroot may be very abundant in burns.

Mule's-Ears

Wyethia spp. (wye-**eth**-ia: after Nathaniel Wyeth, p 222). Heads 2½–6" diam [6–15 cm], 1 to several; leaves have thick white veins; basal leaves up to 20" × 6" [50 × 15 cm], tapering, stem leaves similar but 1–4" long [25–100 mm]; plant 10–24" [25–60 cm], in thick clumps. Sunny slopes up to timberline; in US. Asteraceae.

W. helianthoides (he-lee-anth-**oy**-deez: sunflower-like). Heads white to cream; leaves finely hairy. Moist meadows. Illustrated.

W. amplexicaulis (am-plex-ic-**aw**-lis: clasping the stem). Heads bright yellow; leaves dark, heavy, ultraglossy with an aromatic varnish, hairless; stem leaves clasping stem. Color p 97.

Mule's-ears resemble balsamroot, and Native Americans ate them in most of the same ways; for example, roasting, grinding, and eating the seeds as a mush.

Lyall's Goldenweed

Tonestus lyallii (ton-es-tus: anagram of *Stenotus*, a relative; lie-**ah**-lee-eye: after David Lyall, p 63). =*Haplopappus lyallii*. Also **iron plant**. One flower head per stem, yellow; 10–35 rays; involucre has both leafy and membranous bracts; leaves narrow but stalkless, basal and then much smaller up the stem; plant sticky-hairy, 1–6" [5–15 cm]. Alpine. Asteraceae.

There are other alpine goldenweeds, all placed in *Haplopappus* by lumpers but in three different genera by splitters. Three are similar enough to fit the above description except for the word "sticky." The stickiness also distinguishes this plant from golden fleabane, p 192.

Herbs: daisylike composites

Goldenrods

Solidago spp. (so-lid-**ay**-go: healing, based on Medieval beliefs). Heads yellow, numerous, in one terminal cluster; rays 5–18, small. Asteraceae.

S. canadensis. Inflorescence pyramidal, usually with flowers along only one side of each branchlet; stem hairy, at least near top, 1½–6' tall [50–180 cm], very leafy; no basal leaf cluster. Moist meadows and clearings. Illustrated.

S. missouriensis. Inflorescence ± round-topped; stem smooth, 1–3' [30–90 cm], largest leaves in a basal cluster. Moist meadows, prairies, and clearings.

S. multiradiata (multi-ray-dee-**ay**-ta: many-rayed). Rays 10–18; leaf edges have fine teeth and a fringe of hairs; stems minutely hairy, 2–18" [5–45 cm]. Rocky sites, often alp/subalp. Color p 97.

S. simplex var *nana* (**nay**-na: dwarf). =*S. spathulata* var. *nana.* Inflorescence ± round-topped, rays 5–10; leaves basally crowded, tapering to leafstalks; stem smooth, 2–6" [5–15 cm]. Alp/subalpine.

Yarrow

Achillea millefolium (ak-il-ee-a: after Achilles; mil-ef-**oh**-lium: thousand leaf). =*Achillea lanulosa* (CO). Rays 3–5, white (rarely pink), ⅛" [3 mm] long and wide; disk yellow; heads many, in a flat to convex inflorescence; leaves narrow, extremely (though variably) finely dissected, fernlike, aromatic; to 3' [90 cm], or dwarfed (alpine). In sun. Asteraceae. Color p 97.

Achilles, the Greek hero of the Trojan war, was taught by Chiron the Centaur to dress the wounds of battle with yarrow. Native Americans also used yarrow poultices, and drank yarrow tea for myriad ailments. They steamed the homes of sick people with the pungent smell of yarrow leaves—rather like rosemary and sage—or simply inhaled the smell to soothe headaches. In Chinese Confucianism, the yarrow stalk oracle was systematized as the *I Ching.*

Some divide this species several ways on the basis of degrees of leaf dissection, but it seems that transplants will, over a few years, alter their leaf shape to fit their new environment, nearly matching yarrows around them.

Prairie Coneflower

Ratibida columnifera (ra-**tib**-id-a: a mystery name; col-um-**nif**-er-a: column bearing). Also **Mexican hat**. Rays 3–7, yellow (or occasionally purple), drooping, ½–1½" [12–38 mm]; disk cylindrical or conical, much taller than wide, its flowers blooming progressively upward in a visible ring; leaves pinnate; 1–4' tall [30– 120 cm]. Grass-land or steppe of valleys and foothills. Asteraceae.

The brilliant Turkish-born Franco-American-German naturalist Constantine Rafinesque (1783–1840) taught evolution a half-century before Darwin. He authored countless names of both plants and animals—too many for his own good. His later years were sucked into a downward spiral of taxo-nomic splitting, leading to rejection by the scientific community, poverty, bitterness, and alleged mental instability (leading to even worse splitting, etc.… you get the picture). After he died, most of his specimens were thrown out. No clue survived him as to how he came up with *Ratibida*.

Cutleaf Coneflower

Rudbeckia laciniata (rude-**beck**-ia: after Olof Rudbeck, Sr. and Jr.; la-sin-ee-**ay**-ta: cutleaf). =*R. ampla* (CO). Rays 6–16, yellow, somewhat droopy; disk barrel-shaped, yellowish to grayish; leaves compound and lobed, 4–10" [10–25 cm] wide; stem 3–6' [1–2 m]. Asteraceae. Wet places, esp on Great Plains.

Herbs: composites without rays (thistlelike)

Western Coneflower

Rudbeckia occidentalis (ox-i-den-**tay**-lis: western). Disk purplish black, cylindrical to conical, up to 2¼" [30 mm] tall, surrounded by floppy green bracts; leaves alternate, long-pointed oval, often toothed; rank-smelling coarse 2–6' [.6–2 m] plants often in clumps. Clearings. ID, sw MT, WY.

Though native, this black-headed plant is a serious pest on mountain meadows and clearcuts in Idaho, sometimes thriving to the exclusion of either trees or palatable forage. Cattle eat everything else in the meadow to avoid coneflower, enabling it to take over.

Most rayless composites are in the chicory tribe within the aster

---

family. Outside that tribe, this species and a scattering of others (and even local growth forms) stopped producing rays in a shift away from pollinators like bees that are drawn to bright colors. They often have rank smells that attract flies or ants instead.

Dusty Maidens

Chaenactis spp. (kee-**nac**-tiss: gaping rays). Roundish heads of white to creamy pink disk flowers so large you can see they are 5-lobed corollas with protruding 2-branched styles; involucre sticky-hairy; leaves lacy, fern-like. Asteraceae.

C. douglasii (da-**glass**-ee-eye: after David Douglas, p 66). Also **false yarrow**. Stems 4–20" [10–50 cm], almost always branched, bearing several heads. All elevs, esp Ponderosa pine foothills; US & s BC. Illustrated.

C. alpina. Stems 2–4" [5–10 cm], usually unbranched, bearing one head (rarely 2 or 3). Alpine; in US. Color p 98.

Pussytoes

Antennaria spp. (an-ten-**air**-ia: antenna—). Disks dirty white, soft-fuzzy, deep, surrounded by numerous scaly bracts (not ray flowers); heads several, ¼" diam [6 mm]; leaves woolly, mainly basal. Mainly on dry rocky ground, all elevs; tends to increase with overgrazing. Asteraceae.

A. lanata (lan-**ay**-ta: woolly). In clumps, often broad, but without runners; basal leaves 1–4" [2.5–10 cm], linear, ± erect; stems 4–8" [10–20 cm]. Color p 98.

A. rosea (**ro**-zia: rose-colored). =includes *A. microphylla* (WY). Mat-forming, from leafy runners; sepal-like bracts pink to greenish white; leaves less than 1" [25 mm]; stems 3–15" [7–37 cm].

A. media and *A. umbrinella* (um-brin-**el**-a: brown, small). *A. media*=*A. alpina*. Mat-forming, from leafy runners; bracts blackish (sometimes white-tipped on *A. media*); few leaves over 1" [25 mm]; stems 1–6" [2.5–15 cm]. Color p 98.

Alpine forms of many composites, including *umbrinella* and *rosea* pussytoes, usually reproduce asexually, the ovules maturing into seeds without being fertilized by pollen. Any given patch is likely a female clone, with or without interconnecting runners. Such plants adapted to a severe climate in which the blooming season all too often zips by in weather too nasty for small insects (pollinators of minute flowers like these) to be out and about.

Since each clone's flowers look alike over a wide area while differing from other clones, many were named as species. Weeding out unwarranted species names is taking a lot of close taxonomic study.

Pearly Pussytoes

Antennaria anaphaloides (an-af-a-**loy**-deez: like everlasting). =A. *pulcherrima* (CO, BC). Disks white, soft-fuzzy, deep, surrounded by many white bracts (not ray flowers); heads in a cluster up to 2" wide; leaves narrowly elliptic, 1–8" [2.5–20 cm], much larger toward base, woolly, with a few parallel veins; stems 8–20" [20–50 cm]. Dry rocky sites below treeline. Illust.

Pearly Everlasting

Anaphalis margaritacea (an-**af**-a-lis: Greek term for it; margarit-**ay**-sha: pearly). Disks ± yellow, surrounded by tiny papery white bracts; heads ⅜" [1 cm] diam, in a convex cluster; leaves 2–5", linear, woolly (esp underneath), all on the 8–36" [20–90 cm] stem, lowest ones withering. Roadsides, burns, clearcuts; or alpine. Asteraceae. Color p 98.

Instead of ray flowers, everlasting has dry white involucral bracts that persist everlastingly, in the field or in a vase.

Spotted Knapweed

Centaurea stoebe (sen-**tor**-ia: plant of Chiron, the centaur; **stee**-be: Greek word for an unrelated plant). =C. *maculosa* (WY), *C. biebersteinii* (USDA), *Acosta maculosa* (CO). Disk flowers pink-purple, showy, the outermost ones much larger, slender-lobed; involucres narrow-necked, ½" tall[13 mm], with striped, black-tipped bracts; leaves dotted, cut in many slender lobes, coated with wool that rubs off; plants 1–5' [30–150 cm], much branched. Rangeland, roadsides. Asteraceae. Color p 545.

Genus *Centaurea* ranges from garden bachelor's-buttons to several of the West's worst weeds. All are Eurasian. Spotted knapweed ranks as Montana's worst weed, infesting 7.2 million acres [29,000 km²]. It was originally brought here on purpose, as honeybee forage. Diffuse knapweed, *C. diffusa*, has spread as a tumbleweed across 12.2 million acres [40,000 km²] of eastern Oregon and Washington and adjacent Idaho. (The prototypical Plains tumbleweed is Russian thistle, no relation.) Yellow star-thistle, *C. solstitialis*, is prettier perhaps, but meaner, with long involucral spines. Knapweeds produce allelopathic chemicals that poison the soil against competitors. As they replace grasses they increase erosion of soils and sedimentation of creeks. With seeds that stay viable in the soil for years, they are tough to eradicate. Domestic goats can do a good job on them, at least locally. Many invertebrates that eat them in their native lands have been identified, and are being tested in hopes of finding a few that might offer biological control without disastrous ecological blowback.

Trail-Plant

Adenocaulon bicolor (a-den-o-**caw**-lon: gland stem; **by**-color: two color). Also **pathfinder**. Flower heads tiny, white, several, in a very sparse panicle on a 10–32" stalk [10–80 cm]; leaves all on lowest part of stem, triangular, 4–6" [10–15 cm], dark green on top, white-fuzzy underneath. Moist forest; BC, sw AB, nw MT. Asteraceae.

Unlike most of its family, trail-plant is adapted to deep shade. The leaves are large, thin, and flat-lying—easy to recognize by their shape, while the flowers are rarely noticed. (They attract small flies by their smell, not their looks.) The combination of weak leafstalks and high contrast between upper and lower leaf surfaces led to the common name; a good woodsman tracking a large animal through the woods appreciated a conspicuous series of overturned trail-plant leaves. The sticky seeds also "trail" us by adhering to our legs. And then there are the tiny circumlocuitous trails of leaf-miners (p 513) etched across many trail-plant leaves by summer's end.

Coltsfoot

Petasites (pet-a-**sigh**-teez: hat-shaped). Also **butterbur**. Flower heads usually with a few tiny rays, many, in a ± open round cluster; stems 4–24" [10–60 cm], with clasping elliptical leaflike bracts 1–2" long [2–5 cm]; true leaves rise 10–24" [10–60 cm] on stout leafstalks from other points on the rhizome, woolly underneath, ± sawtoothed, up to 12" by 8" wide [30 by 20 cm]. Wet ground. Asteraceae.

P. sagittatus (sadge-it-**ay**-tus: arrow-shaped). Flowers ± white; leaves triangular, with small teeth. Illustrated at right.

P. frigidus. Flowers usually pinkish; leaves deeply lobed. Canada. Illust at left.

Fast-growing coltsfoot shoots appear early in lower forests. The flowers wither before the leaves reach full size in midsummer. Both species have edible parts, and are salty enough that ash prepared from them was valued as table salt.

Saw-Worts

Saussurea (so-**sure**-ee-a: after Horace and Theodore Saussure). Disk flowers dark purple, narrow-tubular, protruding among fluffy white pappus bristles; heads several, crowded; involucre cobwebby; leaves alternate. Asteraceae.

S. americana. 10–40" tall [.25–1 m]; leaves narrowly triangular, neatly sawtoothed. Moist meadows, esp subalpine; ne OR, c ID, nw MT, s BC, s AB. Illust.

S. densa. =*S. nuda* ssp. *densa* (BC, AB). 2–8" tall [5–20 cm]; leaves narrow elliptic, toothed irregularly or ± untoothed. Alpine; n ID, MT Flathead Range, BC, AB. Color p 98.

S. weberi (web-er-ee: after Wm. A. Weber). Much like *S. densa.* Sw MT and WY.

Thistles

Cirsium spp. (sir-shium: swollen veins — an early medicinal usage). Thick-stemmed herbs; leaves have spine-tipped pinnate lobes; these native spp have no spines on leaf faces, and have cobwebby wool on stems. Asteraceae. Color p 98.

Hooker's thistle, *C. hookerianum* (hooker-ee-**ay**-num: after W. J. Hooker, below). Heads creamy white; involucre covered with cobwebby white wool; stem tapering, 1–2½' [2.5–6 cm]. Canada, n ID and nw MT.

Elk thistle, *C. scariosum* (scary-**oh**-sum: like thin paper, ref to inner involucral bracts). =Includes *C. tioganum, C. drummondii,* and *C. foliosum* (USDA, WY). Heads pink-purple to yellowish white, in a massive terminal cluster; stem (if present) extra thick, even near top, 0–6' tall [0–2 m]. Low to mid-elev meadows.

Wavyleaf thistle, *C. undulatum* (un-dew-**lay**-tum: wavy). Heads pink, widely separated at branch tips and axils; each involucral bract has a pale stripe and a long spine; leaves woolly beneath and sometimes above; stem spineless, fairly slender, 1–3' [30–90 cm]. Scattered at lower elevs; Waterton Lakes south.

Thistle taproots and peeled stems are nutritious and tasty, highly rated in both ethnobotanical and survival-skills texts. Even horses may — very carefully — munch the sweet-nectared flowers. The plant responds with profuse branching if its main stem gets munched. In Yellowstone, elk thistle is known as Everts' thistle after Truman Everts, who survived on thistle roots for a month in 1870 after being separated from his party, his horse, gun, tent, etc. Being biennials, elk and Hooker's thistles grow only a broad rosette of leaves the first year. In its second (or sometimes third) year, elk thistle may bear its

---

Sir William Jackson Hooker, a leading British scientist of the nineteenth century, developed Kew Gardens into a great institution filled with plants sent from all over the world during the era of plant hunters. Earlier, while professor of botany in Glasgow, he noticed the astonishing zeal of a teenaged gardener there, and took this David Douglas as his protege on field trips; eventually he sent him off to explore North America. Hooker catalogued and named hundreds of new plants sent back by Douglas, Menzies, Drummond, Gairdner, Tolmie, and others. They include Hooker's onion but not Hooker's fairy-bells (named after his son **Sir Joseph Hooker**, a plant hunter and colleague of Darwin.) Tradition rules out honoring oneself in a scientific name, but common names often honor the namer.

---

flowers either right on the rosette or on a stem, sometimes both ways in the same meadow. Three European species are nasty weeds; one (illustrated top right on p 191), is misnamed "Canada thistle."

Sageworts

Artemisia spp. (ar-tem-**ee**-zhia: the Greek term). Also **wormwoods, mugworts.** Flower heads tiny, pale yellowish, within small cups of fuzzy bracts; leaves often spicy-aromatic. Asteraceae.

Western sagewort, *A. ludoviciana* (lu-doe-vis-ee-**ay**-na: of the Louisiana Purchase area) Leaves silvery-fuzzy on both sides, linear or pinnate-lobed or with just a few irregular, fingerlike lobes (illust at right); 1–4' tall [30–120 cm]. Dry meadows, all elevs.

Tarragon, *A. dracunculus* (dra-**cun**-kew-lus: little dragon, old name for it, from Arabic *tarchon*). =*Oligosporus dracunculus* (CO). Also **dragonwort.** Leaves not silvery, but sometimes long-hairy underneath, with strong or weak tarragon aroma, linear or rarely with a few linear lobes; 1½–5' tall [45–150 cm]. Steppe, dry meadows, low to mid-elevs. Illustrated.

Rocky Mtn. sagewort, *A. scopulorum* (scop-you-**lor**-um: of rocks). Involucres blackish; leaves mostly silky-fuzzy on both sides, predominately basal; 2–12" tall [5–30 cm]. Dry alp/subalpine sites; US. Color p 98.

Michaux's sagewort, *A. michauxiana* (me-show-zee-**ay**-na: after botanist Andre Michaux). Flowers and bracts often purple-tinged; leaves silvery-fuzzy beneath, ± greener above, the biggest ones bi- or tripinnately lobed; 6–16" tall [15–40 cm]. Rocky slopes, mid-elev to alpine.

Arctic sagewort, *A. norvegica* (nor-**vedge**-ic-a: of Norway). =*A. arctica* (USDA, CO). Heads relatively large, to ⅜" diam [1 cm], nodding; bracts black-edged (illustrated); leaves green, scarcely at all fuzzy, bipinnately lobed, basal ones much the largest; 4–20" tall [10–120 cm]. Dry meadows, mid-elev to alpine.

Wormwoods are proverbial "bitter herbs," figuring in several dire biblical prophesies which seemed to come true when the town of Chernobyl ("wormwood" in Ukrainian) became synonymous with disaster. Aromatic wormwoods of Europe include the intoxicating absinthe, the bitter *vermouth* ("wormwood" in German) that flavors aperitif wines, and the culinary herb tarragon, *A. dracunculus*, also native here. The Crow called it "wolf perfume." Shrubs of this genus perfume about three-fourths of the West. You guessed it: they're called sagebrush. (Page 138). Sage aromas led most Western tribes to value the genus above all others for ceremonial and purification purposes. Burned for its smoke, infused in grease or water, or just tied up to waft about, sagewort was variously reported to drive away evil spirits, mosquitoes, weakness, snow blindness, colds, headaches, menstrual irregularity, tuberculosis, underarm odor, eczema, and dandruff. An Asian wormwood terpene, artemisin, is the drug of choice in China for malaria strains that show resistance to chloroquinine, and western drug companies are testing synthetic variants of it.

Herbs: composites without disks (dandelionlike)

Mountain-Dandelions

Agoseris spp. (a-**gah**-ser-iss: goat chicory). Head single; plants milky-juiced; leaves basal, ± linear (rarely with a few widely spaced teeth). Asteraceae.

Pale mountain-dandelion, *A. glauca* (**glaw**-ca: silvery pale). Rays yellow, drying pinkish; highly variable as to leaf shape, stature, and hairiness; 4–32" tall [30–80 cm]. Common, in sun, all elevs. Color p 99.

Orange mountain-dandelion, *A. aurantiaca* (or-an-**tie**-a-ca: orange). Rays red-orange, drying purplish; 6–12" [15–30 cm]. Uncommon, in sun, mid-elevs to alpine. Color p 99.

Agoseris flower heads often close up on hot days. The resemblance to common dandelions (*Taraxacum* spp) is obvious in the flowers and seed-parachutes, but not the leaves, which usually lack teeth. If you happen across a toothed variety of *A glauca*, the teeth are still much smaller than the lobes on the weedy European dandelions—two species which have invaded even remote alpine tundra here. We also have two native alpine dwarf *Taraxacum* species, but they're rare.

Hawkweeds

Hieracium spp. (hi-er-**ay**-shium: hawk—). Flower heads ½–1" diam [12–25 mm]; stems milky-juiced. In sun. Asteraceae.

H. scouleri (**scoo**-ler-eye: after John. Scouler p 66). =includes *H. cynoglossoides* (USDA, WY). Heads several; leaves long, elliptical; involucres, stems, and leaves (at least beneath) covered with long white hairs; 12–40" tall [30–100 cm]. All elevs.

H. gracile (**grass**-il-ee: slender). =*H. triste* (WY, INT), *Chlorocrepis tristis* (CO). Heads yellow, few or single; involucres finely dark-haired; leaves ± basal on long stalks, oval, smooth; stem 2–12" [5–30 cm], fuzzy. High meadows. Illustrated.

H. auranticacum (or-an-**tie**-a-cum: orange). Also **king devil**. Heads burnt orange, clustered; plants 8–28" [20–70 cm], densely hairy. Disturbed soil; European weed. Color p 99.

The milky juice of hawkweeds and mountain-dandelions dries into "Indian bubble-gum," which was chewed for mouth entertainment or cleaning.

Salsify

Tragopogon spp. (trag-a-**po**-gon: billygoat beard). Also **goatsbeard, oyster plant**. Head single, 3–4" [75–40 mm] diam incl the spiky green bracts sticking out way past the ray flowers; in seed, looks like a huge dandelion head, each seed with a parachutelike pappus ½" [12 mm] or wider; stem milky-juiced, swollen below the head; leaves tough, grasslike, clasping the stem; 1–3' tall [30–90 cm]. Roadsides, rangeland; European weeds. Asteraceae.

T. dubius. Flowers yellow. Color p 99.

T. porrifolius (por-if-**oh**-lius: leaves like a certain onion). Flowers purple.

Cultivated *T. porrifolius* is the most delicious root vegetable I ever tasted. I failed to detect oysters, though. Sad to say, rumors of the far more abundant wild *T. dubius* being its equal are, well, dubious. H. D. Harrington reports searching far and wide in the Rockies and finding *dubius* always "small, fibrous, woody, and tough."

Weeds

I became a settler in Iowa twenty-two years ago and have seen great changes.... Mayweed and dog fennel, stinkweed and mullein have taken the place of 'purple flox and the mocassin flower.' (Edwin James, 1859.)

Non-native weeds have profoundly damaged huge portions of the West's open rangeland. They displace both native flora and the native fauna that has evolved in dependence on it. They do enormous economic damage when they invade crops and pastures. In some instances they sharply increase soil erosion (knapweed, p 201) or bring fire to community types that rarely carried fires before the weeds invaded (cheatgrass, p 169). Competition from non-natives is a factor in most species extinctions.

Most problem weeds are not particularly "weedy" or aggressive in their native lands. (Canada thistle in Europe is an exception.) We can generalize loosely that without human help, species rarely travel around the globe very fast, and that as long as they stayed put, fungi, bacteria, and grazers that consume them coevolved with them, maintaining a level of control so that no one plant tended to take over. Accordingly, scientists who seek ways to control a weed look to that plant's native lands to see what eats it there. They choose a few promising pests (usually insects) and set them up in carefully quarantined tests for several years to see

---

Stinging nettle's four tiny sepals are so obscure that getting close enough to see them could inflict pain. Other than that, you should look closely for sepals before turning to this section. Find barely countable sepals or petals on mountain-sorrel, p 221; pussypaws, p 215; skunk-cabbage, p 171; bunchberry, p 177; desert-parsleys, p 251; and baneberry, p 265.

Leafy Spurge

Euphorbia esula (you-**forb**-ia: good fodder, a Roman name for other members of the genus, grotesquely misapplied here; **ess**-you-la: Celtic for "sharp," ref to acrid juice). =*Tithymalus uralensis, T. esula* (CO). Numerous pairs of yellow to green, round or heart-shaped bracts, ⅝" [15 mm], flank 4-lobed, ⅛" [3 mm], conical greenish involucres, each holding one 3-tipped pistil and several stamens; no petals or sepals; linear leaves, 1–3" [25–75 mm], densely clothe the many side branches; stems milky-juiced, 1–3' [30–90 cm]. Rangeland, cropland; Russian weed. Euphorbiaceae. Color p 99.

Spurge, Public Enemy Weed #1 in eastern Montana and Alberta, is allelopathic to other plants and toxic to cattle and people. It can grow back from bits of its roots as deep as 30' down [9 m]; neither herbi-

which ones could be introduced without risk to desirable native plants. But this method is slow, expensive, and far from fool-proof.

The alpine and subalpine zones in our range are relatively free of non-native plants, but even those zones are being devastated by the loss of whitebark and limber pines (p 54) to a fungal disease—an invasive species from another kingdom.

Invasives may sound less apocalyptic, and get less media coverage, than global warming or toxic pollution, but they are one of the biosphere's most daunting problems. Promoters of "free trade" seem unaware that free trade in unprocessed logs and wood chips is a deranged policy, risking introduction of pests or diseases whose potential for economic harm makes any near-term profits look like chump change. As of 2003, there is a terrifying possibility that "sudden oak death," a newly invasive algal disease, could wipe out Douglas-fir and/or the coast redwood.

Since they are by definition opportunistic, weedy plants are likely to take advantage of any openings created by rapid climate change. Since they tend to be heavy nitrogen consumers (whereas natives are more efficient and conservative) the weed problem is expected to worsen with continued global nitrogen deposition—the airborne and waterborne spread of agricultural fertilizers.

cides nor fire nor uprooting are much use against it after its first few years, when the roots are smaller. It shoots its seeds explosively as far as fifteen feet, and they also float, so that streams disperse them. The best hope for controlling leafy spurge probably lies in finding the right insect to bring in to eat it. Nine species (including a fly called *Spurgia esulae*) have already been tested and released; we await results. Sheep browse spurge contentedly, and may be of some help.

Genus *Euphorbia* includes those spiny succulent house plants often mistaken for cacti. It is so large and diverse it serves taxonomic splitters as a poster child, but most authors (outside of Colorado; see page 610) keep it intact not because they like it that way but because they think the paper accurately splitting it has yet to be written.

Nettle

Urtica dioica (**ur**-tic-a: burning; die-**oy**-ca: with male and female flowers on different plants, a name untrue of our nettles). = *U. gracilis* (CO). Flowers 4-merous, tiny, pale green, many, in loose panicles dangling from the leaf axils, the panicles unisexual, with females higher on the plant (our varieties); leaves opposite, sawtoothed, pointed/oval, 2–6" [5–15 cm]; stem and leaves lined with fine stinging bristles; 2–6' tall [60–180 cm] from rhizomes. Moist forest, clearings. Urticaceae (Nettle family). Color p 99.

Nettles are seen mostly as a must to avoid, but older traditions both here and in Europe held them the most estimable of weeds. They're food: the young plants make excellent greens. They're fiber: the mature stems were made into high-quality twine, cloth and paper, substituting for flax in wartime as recently as World War II, and several tribes here made nettle-twine nets for ducks and fish. They're medicine: the sting helped stoical native hunters stay awake through the night, and tasty nettle tea has a worldwide reputation for potency.

Nettle stingers are tiny hypodermic syringes, like bee and ant stingers. Formic acid, the bee-sting toxin, was long but erroneously thought to be the main toxin in nettles, which in fact inject a cocktail of acetylcholine, hydroxytryptamine, and a histamine. Stingers evolved as a defense against browsing, but they don't save nettles from Milbert's tortoiseshell and other caterpillars. One folk remedy holds that if you pull up the nettle that bit you, you can soothe the sting by crushing juice onto it from the nettle root. Thorough steaming or drying renders nettles harmless. If you ever camp in spring near a good bed of nettle shoots a few inches high, cook them up. Wear long sleeves and gloves (or socks) over your hands, lop them with your knife, and steam them limp in half an inch of water. (If cooked only *al dente*, they have enough bristle left to worry your lips and tongue.) Butter, sour cream, feta or bleu cheese, crepes, mmm…

Alpine Willows

Salix spp. (**say**-lix: the Roman term). Female and male catkins on separate plants; prostrate shrubs in cushiony mats to 4" [10 cm] tall. Alp/ subalp. Salicaceae (Willow family).

Arctic willow, *S. arctica.* Catkins 25–60-flowered, ½–2" long [12–50 mm]; leaves ½" (up to 4", or 10 cm, in Canada), point-tipped, green above, grayish beneath. Dwarfed alpine *S. glauca* (p 119) can be indistinguishable from this. Similar Alpine willow, *S. petrophila*, with ± hairless leaves, was included in this species until recently. Color p 99.

Cascade willow, *S. cascadensis* (cas-ca-**den**-sis: of the Cascades). Catkins 15–25-flowered, ⅜–¾" long [1–2 cm]; leaves ¼–½" [6–12 mm], point-tipped, both sides green.Illustrated.

Snow willow, *S. reticulata* (ret-ic-you-**lay**-ta: netted) =*S. nivalis* (USDA). Leaves round-tipped, ⅜–1½" long [1–4 cm], leathery, green above, grayish beneath, conspicuously net-veined.

True willows reduced to carpet stature are common in alpine tundra.

False-Bugbane

Trautvetteria caroliniensis (trout-vet-ee-**ria**: for Ernest Rudolf van Trautvetter; carol-in-ee-**en**-sis: of the Carolinas). Flowers white, in broad rough clusters, consisting mainly of many stamens (up to ¼", or 6 mm), the 3–7 sepals falling off as the flower opens; leaves predominantly basal, 4–10" wide [10–25 cm], deeply 5–7-lobed; 20–36" [50–90 cm]. Moist spruce-fir forest; YS north. Ranunculaceae (Buttercup family).

Dwarf Mistletoe

Arceuthobium spp. (ars-you-**tho**-bium: life on junipers). Tiny (1–4", or 2–10 cm) branching, olive to dull blue-green or orange-green growths on conifer branches; flowers budlike, same color as plant; berries ± bicolored, with bluish-coated base and paler tan outer half; no recognizable leaves. Viscaceae (Mistletoe family). Color p 99.

Occasionally you spot mistletoe on branches near eye level, but what you see more often is "witches' brooms"—big lumps in conifer crowns, consisting of massed unhealthy twiggy branches. Color p541

Herbs: flowers without petals or sepals   *209*

A parasite, dwarf mistletoe extends threadlike roots inside tree limbs, inducing the tree to branch way too much. Mistletoe sucks the tree's energy, stunting its growth and slowly killing it.

Dwarf mistletoe berries explode when ripe, shooting the single seed as far as 40 feet [12 m]. Some 70,000 seeds per year may get shot from one infested conifer. Gummy-coated, they stick if they hit another branch. When rain comes along, the gum dissolves, letting the seed slide down a needle to the twig. The berries are eaten enthusiastically by all of our grouse species and several songbirds, but are destroyed by digestion—unlike the bigger berries of Christmas mistletoes, which are disseminated mainly via bird droppings. Nevertheless, birds do spread dwarf mistletoe seeds that stick to them by chance. Though infrequent, this long-distance mode of spread is important to a plant that otherwise can only crawl from tree to tree.

Several dwarf mistletoe species look much alike, but specialize in one or two species of host tree. They are a serious economic problem in our region. They often spread after selective logging is used in an effort to mimic natural fire regimes. (Actual fires do remove a lot of mistletoe, since brooms are ferociously flammable.) Sometimes the only cure is to log the infected tree species completely out of the stand. But from an ecological point of view, mistletoe (like other conifer pathogens) fosters plant diversity as well as creating ideal nest sites for animals including owls, accipiters, and flying squirrels.

Herbs: dicots, strongly irregular flowers

Irregular flowers are those in which the petals (or the sepals, if they are the showy parts) are not all alike. You might think of them as bilaterally—as opposed to radially—symmetrical, but there are exceptions; some lousewarts are twisted and have no symmetry at all.

Irregular flowers display advanced specialization of form. Each species matches a particular form and size of insect, for pollination. Irregular shapes run in families: you can probably think of the three familiar shapes—orchids, sweetpeas and snapdragons—which represent our three biggest families of irregular flowers, the Orchidaceae (p 183–88), Fabaceae (pp 216–20), and Scrophulariaceae (pp 211–15).

Flowers are not placed here if the irregularity consists only of unequal-sized, but otherwise similar, petals or lobes. For example, veronica, p 258, and kittentails, p 257, each have four small blue to lavender petals. Cow-parsnip, p 255, has five unequal but similar two-lobed white petals, and a flat-topped Parsley-family look.

Louseworts

Pedicularis spp. (ped-ic-you-**lair**-iss: louse—). Corolla fused, with two main lips, the upper ± long-beaked, the lower usually 3-lobed; calyx irregularly 2–5-lobed; capsule also asymmetrical; leaves (exc on sickletop lousewort) fernlike, pinnately compound; flowers many, on an unbranched stem. Scrophulariaceae (Figwort family).

Sickletop lousewort, *P. racemosa* (ras-em-**oh**-sa: bearing racemes). Also **parrotbeak**. Flowers (our variety) white, beak curled strongly sideways, so inflorescence looks pinwheel-like from above; leaves reddish, ± linear, fine-toothed, all on stem; 6–18" [15–45 cm]. Openings near tree line; or alpine.

Elephant's head, *P. groenlandica* (green-**lan**-dic-a: of Greenland, a mistaken name). Flowers purplish pink, in a dense spike, elephantlike (upcurved beak as the trunk, lateral lower lobes as the ears); leaves preponderantly basal; 8–16" [20–40 cm]. Rills and boggy meadows, alp/subalp. Color p 101.

Oeder's lousewort, *P. oederi* (ö-der-eye: after George C. Oeder). =includes *P. flammea*. Flowers few, in a short squarish cluster, yellow, with a tall beakless hood that may be crimson or yellow; leaves mainly basal; 3–7" [8–18 cm]. Alpine gravel; Kananaskis north, and disjunct in the Beartooths. Color p 101. A similar yellow-flowered species from Banff north is *P. capitata*.

Pretty lousewort, *P. pulchella* (pul-**kel**-a: beautiful). Like Oeder's, but with purple flowers. Alpine; WY, sw MT.

Bracted lousewort, *P. bracteosa* (brac-tee-**oh**-sa: with bracts). Flowers yellow, purple, or dark red, scarcely beaked, in a robust cobwebby-haired spike; stem leaves as big as basal ones, aging purplish; 24–36" [60–90 cm]; lush meadows, mid-elevs to lower alpine. Color p 101.

Coiled-beak lousewort, *P. contorta*. Flowers pale yellow (less often pink to purple), in a loose spike; beak semicircular, arching back into lower lip; leaves mostly basal; 8–14" [20–35 cm]. Alp/subalpine turfs. Color p 101.

The louseworts are as curiously irregular and varied a genus of flowers as you could ask for, deserving their curious pictorial names. "Lousewort," however, dates from an ancient superstition that cattle got lousy by browsing louseworts. Each of the flower shapes suits the anatomy of one or more species of bumble bees— pollinators of the hundred or so species of louseworts as well as monkeyflowers, penstemons, and many other family members. The tip of the beak (or "trunk" in one case) positions the stigma to catch pollen from the bee's legs or abdomen.

Monkeyflowers

Mimulus spp. (**mim**-you-lus: mime or clown). Flowers snap-dragonlike: corolla has a long throat, hairy inside, and 2 upper and 3 lower lobes; calyx angularly 5-lobed; stamens 4, paired; leaves opposite; stems in dense clumps on runners or rhizomes. Wet places, mid-elevs to alpine. Scrophulariaceae (Figwort family).

Purple monkeyflower, *M. lewisii* (lew-**iss**-ee-eye: after Meriwether Lewis, p 266). Flowers deep pink to violet; leaves sessile, pointed, 2–3" [5–15 cm]; plants 12–36" [30–90 cm], sticky-hairy. Color p 100.

Yellow monkeyflower, *M. guttatus* (ga-**tay**-tus: spotted). Flowers yellow, throat often red-spotted, 5+ per stem; 4–30" [10–75 cm].

Mountain monkeyflower, *M. tilingii* (til-**ing**-ee-eye: after Heinrich S. T. Tiling). Flowers yellow, ¾–1½" [2–4 cm] (large for a tiny plant), throat ± red-spotted, 1–4 per stem; leaves ⅜–1" [1–2.5 cm]; plants 2–8" [5–20 cm]. Illustrated.

Primrose monkeyflower, *M. primuloides* (prim-you-**loy**-deez: primrose-like). Flowers ¼–⅝" long [6–15 mm], yellow, often red dotted; dwarf, mat-forming or erect, with long straight white hairs. OR, ID. Color p 100.

Yellow monkeyflowers thrive both in and alongside small streams including (at Yellowstone) hot-spring outlets that maintain warm, snowfree banks with green growth year-round.

Both "monkey" and the "mime" in Mimulus are impressions of this fat irregular blossom as a funnyface.

Dalmatian Toadflax

Linaria dalmatica. (lin-**air**-ia: flax—) =*L. genistifolia* ssp. *dalmatica* (BC, CO). Flowers yellow with an orange throat, in long spikes; corolla 5-lobed, 1–1⅝" long [2.5–4 cm] including the long rearward spur; leaves 1–2" [2.5–5 cm], pointed oval, clasping the stems, smooth-edged; 1–3' tall [30–90 cm]. Disturbed ground in valleys; European. Scrophulariaceae. Color p 100.

Though neither visually repulsive nor dangerous to stock, toadflax edges onto most top ten lists of weeds threatening our region.

Similar butter-and-eggs, *L. vulgaris* (with linear leaves that don't clasp the stem) is a garden flower now also seen as a serious weed.

Blue-Eyed Mary

Collinsia parviflora (ca-**lin**-zia: after Zaccheus Collins; par-vif-**lor**-a: small flower). Also **innocence**. Corolla ¼–⅜" [6–10 mm]; blue to violet, the upper two lobes fading to white; lobes 5, the lower central one inconspicuous, creased shut to enclose the stamens and style; calyx 5-lobed, green; flowers in axils of upper, often whorled leaves; lower leaves opposite, ± linear; plants annual, 2–14" [5–35 cm]. Meadows, up to lower alpine. Scrophulariaceae.

Indian Paintbrush

Castilleja spp. (cas-til-**ay**-a: after Domingo Castillejo). Inflorescence most often red, varying to every shade of pink, magenta, orange, yellow, and greenish white; true flowers subtended and largely hidden by brightly colored bracts (lower bracts grading to green at their bases); calyx narrowly 4-lobed, same color as bracts; corolla a thin tube, dull green; leaves (incl the colored floral bracts) often narrowly 3-, 5-, or 7-pronged, elliptical, their main veins appearing parallel; stems usually several, unbranched, from a woody base. Widespread, in sun. Scrophulariaceae. Color p 100.

C. miniata (mini-**ay**-ta: cinnabar-red). Floral bracts scarlet (less often yellow-orange), deeply lobed; 8–30" tall [20–75 cm]. Widespread, foothills to treeline.

C. pallescens (pal-**ess**-enz: turning pale). Floral bracts yellow; they and most leaves usually have 5 slender lobes. WY, MT, e ID. Illustrated.

C. rhexifolia (rex-if-**oh**-lia: leaves like *Rhexia*). Floral bracts usually ± rose-purple, very shallowly lobed. Alp/subalp.

C. hispida (**hiss**-pid-a: bristly). Floral bracts red- to orange-tipped, 3- or 5- lobed; most leaves deeply lobed, with stiff white hairs. Dry forest or grassland up to mid-elevs.

C. sulphurea and *C. occidentalis*. Floral bracts usually pale yellow, scarcely lobed; leaves unlobed or a few with 2 small side lobes. Foothills to lower alpine; all exc OR, w ID.

C. pulchella (pul-**kel**-a: beautiful). Floral bracts streaky pink-purple and yellow; leaves usually have 2 side lobes; foliage soft-hairy; 2–5" tall [5–13 cm]. Alpine; WY, MT, possibly ID.

Indian paintbrush is easily recognized as a genus, but notoriously hard to identify to species. Hybrids (color p 100) abound. Neither color nor hairiness is reliably diagnostic, though within a given area the members of a species match up pretty closely.

Paintbrushes are partially parasitic, especially on grasses and composites. ("Partially" means that they also photosynthesize.) By late summer they often seem to hog all the water, staying green and turgid while their hosts wither.

Yellow Owl's-Clover

Orthocarpus luteus (ortho-**car**-pus: straight fruit; **loo**-tee-us: yellow). Corollas yellow, tubular, the closed upper and lower lips equal in length; flowers in a slender spike; floral bracts and upper leaves 3-lobed, sticky-hairy, lower leaves linear, all on the 4–16" [10–40 cm] stem. In sun, low to mid-elevs. Scrophulariaceae. Color p 101.

Owl's-clover looks a lot like a paintbrush and not much like owls or clover. It differs from paintbrush in being an annual plant, and in having its floral color in its corollas, not its bracts.

Penstemons

Penstemon spp. (**pen**-stem-un: almost a stamen, referring to the sterile one; *Intermountain Flora* came up with this translation, more plausible than the usual "five stamen"). Also **beardtongues**. Corolla swollen-tubular, with 5 (2 upper, 3 lower) short rounded flaring lobes; a broad ± hairy sterile stamen rests on the throat; fertile stamens 4, paired; sepals 5, hardly at all fused; leaves both opposite and basal; from ± woody bases. Rocky places and dry meadows, mostly below tree line. Scrophulariaceae. About 200 *Penstemon* species grow here.

Small-flowered penstemon, *P. procerus* (**pross**-er-us: tall and noble; hmmn. Well at least it's slender). =*P. confertus* ssp. *procerus* (CO). Flowers usually blue/ purple, ¼–½" [6–13 mm], sticky-hairy, in 2–6 whorls; leaves narrowly elliptical, to 3" long [7.5 cm]; stem 4–24" [10–60 cm]. Common, all elevs. Illustrated.

Yellow penstemon, *P. confertus* (con-**fur**-tus: crowded). Flowers pale yellow, white, or pink-tinged, ¼–½" [6–13 mm], in 2–8 whorls; leaves elliptical, to 4" long [10 cm]; stem 8–24" [20–60 cm]. All exc WY.

Whipple's penstemon, *P. whippleanus* (whip-l-**an**-us: after Lt. A. W. Whipple, p 242). Flowers deep purple to almost black (less often cream with fine purple lines), ¾–1⅛" [20–30 mm], in 1–4 whorls; leaves linear to elliptical; stems 8–24" [20–60 cm]. Aspen groves to alpine; WY, sw MT, e ID.

Cyan penstemon, *P. cyaneus* (sigh-**an**-ius: sky blue). Flowers brilliant blue, 1–1⅓" [25–35 mm], in widely separated hairless whorls at leaf axils; rosette of basal leaves much bigger than stem ones; 12–28" tall [30–70 cm]. WY, sw MT, c and e ID.Color p 101.

Alberta penstemon, *P. albertinus* (al-ber-**tie**-nus: of Alberta). Flowers rich royal blue, ½–¾" [13–20 mm], in widely separated sticky-hairy whorls at leaf axils; stem leaves smaller than basal ones, 4–16" tall [20–60 cm]. From c ID n to Crowsnest Pass. Illustrated.

Rocky ledge penstemon, *P. ellipticus*. Flowers lavender, 1–1½" [12–40 mm], in small clusters tending to all face one way; leaves crowded, usually minutely toothed, some ± evergreen; stems ± prostrate. Rock crevices; c ID and Bitterroots n. Color p 101.

Fuzzytongue penstemon, *P. eriantherus* (airy-**an**-ther-us: woolly anthers). Flowers usually lavender with dark guide lines, ⅝–1⅜" [15–35 mm], in 3–6 whorls; throat full of long hairs; leaves ± linear, with a few small teeth; plant finely hairy; stem 8–24" [20–60 cm]. All exc Wallowas, n ID, or extreme w MT. Color p 101.

Woolly Mullein

Verbascum thapsus (ver-**bas**-cum: Roman name for it; **thap**-sus: a Roman site near Tunis). Flowers yellow, in a massive spike atop a 2–7' [60–210 cm] conical, gray-woolly plant; corollas 5-lobed, only slightly irregular; leaves fleshy, basal ones up to 16" × 5" [40 × 13 cm], getting smaller upward along stem; biennial, producing just a basal rosette in its first year. Roadsides, overgrazed range; European. Scrophulariaceae. Color p 544.

Mullein has been in the herbal apothecary since Roman days, and spread in Native American medicinal use about as fast as it invaded. Among several active compounds it contains the insecticide rotenone, leading prudent herbalists today to avoid it. *Voyageurs* called it *tabac du diable*—the devil's tobacco.

Wyoming Kittentails

Besseya wyomingensis (**bess**-ia: after Chas. E. Bessey). Erect flower spikes bristling with purple ⅜–½" [12–13 mm] stamens, 2 per flower, next to the 2 or 3 small greenish calyx lobes; no petals; leaves elliptic, scalloped, both basal and (much smaller) alternate; entire plant has fine gray wool; 4–18" tall [10–45 cm]. Typically with sagebrush and/or on outcrops; foothills to alpine, from Banff s. Scrophulariaceae. Contrast featherleaf kittentails, p 257. Color p 101.

Pussypaws

Calyptridium umbellatum (cal-ip-**trid**-ium: with a cap over the seed—not true of this species; um-bel-**ay**-ta: with flowers in umbels). =*Cistanthe umbellata* (USDA, WY), *Spraguea umbellata*. Flowers rust-pink to white, in fluffy, chaffy heads on prostrate stalks reaching well past the basal rosette of tiny, narrow leaves; sepals 2, round, ⅛–⅜" diam [3–12 mm], sandwiching and nearly hiding the 4 much smaller petals and 3 stamens (illustrated). Alp/subalpine rock crevices, scree, disturbed sandy soil; US, BC. Portulacaceae (Purslane family).*

Giant Hyssop

Agastache urticifolia (a-**gas**-ta-kee: many spikes; ur-tis-if-**oh**-lia: nettle leaf). Also **horsemint**. Corolla purplish pink to white, ½" [12 mm], tubular, shallowly 5-lobed, mostly encased in the 5-pointed calyx; 4 stamens sticking out; flowers in a ± crowded spike; leaves opposite, toothed, heart-shaped to pointed-elliptic; stems square, 1–4' [30–120 cm], often crowded. Moist soil, low to mid elevs. Lamiaceae (Mint family).

---

*Recent DNA analysis finds none of our "Purslane family" members closely related to *Portulaca*. The requisite new family for them has yet to be named.

Self-Heal

Prunella vulgaris (pru-**nel**-a: purple, small; vul-**gair**-iss: common). Also **all-heal**. Corolla blue-purple, ¼–¾" [6–20 mm], 4-lobed; upper lobe hoodlike, lower lobe li-plike, fringed; calyx half as long; stamens 4 (rarely lacking); flowers bloom sequentially upward, in a crowded broad-bracted spike of opposite pairs neatly offset 90°; leaves opposite, elliptical, 1–3" [25–75 mm]; stem squarish, 4–16" tall [10–40 cm], or sprawling. Sporadic up to mid elevs. Lamiaceae (Mint family).

The mint family is loaded with medicinal, poisonous and culinary aromatic herbs, including catnip, pennyroyal, horehound, oregano, sage, savory, thyme, and of course peppermint. Europeans once believed in self-heal as a panacea; in tribal and modern herbal lore it's prescribed to heal sores, wounds, and chapped skin.

Bee Balm

Monarda fistulosa (mo-**nar**-da: after Nicolas Monardes; fist-you-**lo**-sa: hollow). =*M. menthifolia*. Also **wild bergamot, horsemint**. Showy bright pink flowers in a whorl atop a mint-aromatic 1–2' [30–60 cm] plant; corolla 1–1½" [25–40 mm], tubular, hairy, 2-lipped; calyx 5-toothed; style and 2 stamens sticking out; leaves opposite, grayish, toothed, pointed-oval; stems square. Moist soil, low prairie to near tree line; YS and c ID north to Banff. Lamiaceae. Color p 103.

While a bee dives deep into the tube for nectar, the stamens and stigma arch over its back to deposit and pick up pollen.

Antiseptic and sedative powers of the leaves were recognized by Native Americans, European herbalists, and scientists alike. The aromatic oils perfumed Crow tresses, Kootenai sweatlodges, and Cheyenne horses. Chewed leaves anesthetized toothaches and skin irritations. A jug of tea induced sweating and, in combination with a sweatbath, was thought to cure fevers, colds, pneumonia, and most stomach and kidney complaints. This treatment got one of Lewis and Clark's men back on his feet overnight.

Locoweeds

Oxytropis spp. (ox-**it**-ra-pis: sharp keel). Also **crazyweeds**. Flowers pealike, in ± egg-shaped clusters; leaves near-basal, densely silky-hairy, compound (pinnate exc in *O. splendens*); to 12" tall [30 cm]. Fabaceae (Legume family).

O. splendens. Flowers magenta (drying to blue), 12–40; plants heavily silver-hairy; leaflets in whorls of 3–5 around the leafstalk. Low to mid-elevs, mainly e of CD, MT north; common on roadsides.

O. sericea (ser-**iss**-ia: silky). Flowers pale yellow, sometimes pink-tinged, 10–30; upper petal notched; calyx has fine black and white hairs; pod thick-walled, drying rigid; leaflets typically 7.

O. besseyi (**bess**-ee-eye: after Chas. E. Bessey). =*O. nana* ssp *argophylla*. Flowers purple; upper petal sharply notched; calyx with coarse long white hairs; leaflets 11–13. Gravel; WY, s MT, e ID. Color p 102.

O. campestris (cam-**pes**-tris: of fields). Flowers pale yellow (sometimes white), 6–12; upper petal has slight, rounded notch; calyx has fine gray hairs; pod very thin-walled; leaflets 11–25; stalks several, 3–15" [8–38 cm]. Alpine (var *cusickii*, illustrated) and arid meadows.

Locoweeds of this genus and *Astragalus* got their ill repute from several rangeland species that sabotage muscular coordination and vision in cattle that graze them in quantity. Surprisingly, mountain goats graze alpine species; uncoordinated purblind mountain goats would not presumably have survived natural selection to this day.

Prickly Milkvetch

Astragalus kentrophyta var. *tegetarius* (a-**strag**-a-lus: Greek name for some legume; ken-tro-**fie**-ta: spur plant; teh-jet-**air**-ius: roof—). =*A. k. implexus* (CO). Flowers purple, ¼–⅜" [6–10 mm], 2-lipped, nestled into a mat of tiny (¼", or 6 mm) spine-tipped leaflets, 5–9 per pinnate leaf. Tundra, granite outcrops, clay badlands; WY, sw MT, c ID, ne OR. Similar *A. vexilliflexus* has ± clustered flowers, a bit paler, rising higher above the leaves. Color p 102.

Sweetvetch

Hedysarum spp. (hed-**iss**-a-rum: Greek name for some "sweet smelling" plant). Flowers pea-like, ¾" long [2 cm], in a ± one-sided raceme; seedpods 2–6-seeded, flat, strongly narrowed between seeds; leaves pinnately compound; delicate plants 6–24" tall [15–60 cm]. Open mid-elev forest to alpine meadows.

H. sulphurescens (sulphur-**ess**-enz: yellowish). Flowers yellow to cream. Color p 102.

H. boreale (bor-ee-**ay**-lee: subarctic). Flowers purple. Illust.

Roots of yellow sweetvetch provide the bulk of grizzly bear diets in some seasons in the Canadian Rockies. (Grizzlies rely analogously on glacier lilies at Glacier and biscuitroot at Yellowstone.) David Hamer reports that the root digging seasons can last from April to June, before green vegetation is plentiful, and again through the critical fall fattening-up season of years when the buffaloberry crop is poor. Native peoples ate these roots too. Some called them "grizzly bear roots."

Lupines

Lupinus spp. (lu-**pie**-nus: the Roman term). Flowers blue to purple (some of the many other spp and varieties white or yellow), pealike, small (½", or 12 mm), many, in ± conical racemes; calyx 2-lobed; pods hairy; leaves palmately 5–10-compound; leaflets center-folded. Fabaceae (Legume family).

Silvery lupine, *L. argenteus* (ar-**jent**-ius: silver). Back of upper petal hairless or with just a few silky hairs; leaves densely silvery-haired beneath, less so or smooth above; plant bushy, 5–40" [12–100 cm]; alpine form, var. *depressus*, is 5–10" [12–25 cm]. All elevs, abundant; Waterton and s. Color p 102.

Silky lupine, *L. sericeus* (ser-**iss**-ius: silky). Back of upper petal silky-haired; flowers in ± separated whorls; leaves almost all on stem; plant more slender, covered with rusty to whitish silky fuzz, 14–32" [35–80 cm]. Lower elevs.

Dwarf lupine, *L. lepidus* (**lep**-id-us: charming). =*L. lyallii (BC)*, *L. caespitosus* and *L. sellulus* in (USDA). Back of upper petal hairless; leaves mainly basal, often taller than flowers; flower whorls crowded; plant 3–15" [8–38 cm], densely silky-haired on all green parts. All elevs, n to Crowsnest Pass. Illust.

Arctic lupine, *L. arcticus*. =*L. latifolius subalpinus*. Upper petal hairless; leaves mostly on stem, minutely hairy beneath, smooth or modestly silky above; plant 5–12" [12–30 cm]. Wet Columbia Mtns of BC. Illustrated at left.

A bumblebee in search of lupine nectar might be overwhelmed by too many choices, so the lupines help her out: the upper petal has white spots that act as nectar guides. As a blossom ages, the spots turn magenta. Bees learn to skip those blossoms, since their nectar is depleted. Efficiency is increased for the flower as well as the bee, since stale pollen is kept out of circulation.

Like many plants adapted to the alpine environment, the first three species are coated with fine hairs. In the 1980s, Mt. St. Helens provided a test of the benefits of pubescence. Dwarf lupine pioneered all alone on barren areas of ash. Arctic lupine also came back early, but only where mixed with other species. Both clearly benefit from being able to fix nitrogen. Both quickly send taproots to draw water from at least 10" [25 cm] down, and both have leaf adaptations to minimize water loss when it gets hot and dry: arctic lupine draws its leaves up into a cone shape; in so doing it sacrifices much of its ability to photosynthesize on the hottest days. Dwarf lupine relies entirely on its thicker coat of shiny silky hairs that reflect back some of the intense light, and hold some of the drying wind away from the leaf surface. It proved able to photosynthesize at temperatures up to 104° [40° C], while arctic lupine gave up at around 86° [30° C]; botanist Jeff Braatne found this to be the key difference. Dwarf lupine also turns its leaves to face the morning and evening sun, maximizing photosynthesis at cooler times of day, and stays green through winter, making the most of early- and late-season sun. Other studies have shown that both hair and waxy coatings protect by reflecting ultraviolet radiation, which is much stronger at higher elevations, and can damage tissue.

Legume-family plants fertilize forests by putting nitrogen into the soil in a form all plants can use. But silky lupine decreased in abundance, along with the nitrogen fixers snowbrush and bitterbrush, as our forests became denser and shadier due to fire suppression over the past century. They have been scarce for so long that a single fire (or chainsaw thinning event) may not be enough to bring them back in healthy numbers.

We don't know for sure why the Romans named these flowers after wolves. It may indicate an affinity they felt—remember their myth of a she-wolf as the mother, or at least the wetnurse, of Rome. Or they may have decried lupines as killers of sheep; they are toxic, to varying degrees. Sheep have died from grazing silky lupine. ("Lupine" means "of wolves" or "wolflike" in English, too.)

Notice the way a little sphere of dew or rain is held on the center point of each leaf.

Alpine Clovers

Trifolium spp. (try-fo-lium: three leaf). Flowers tubular, 2-lipped, ⅜–⅞" long [10–22 mm]; calyx with 5 long pointed lobes; compound leaves of 3 leaflets; flower clusters rising from a dense mat of leaves. Alpine, in WY and sw MT. Fabaceae

T. parryi (**pair**-ee-eye: after Chas. Parry. p 63). Flowers rose purple, in round clusters; calyx hairless. Color p 102.

T. dasyphyllum (das-if-**ill**-um: shaggy leaf). Flowers rose purple (or upper petals often pale yellow) in round clusters; calyx hairy.

T. haydenii (hay-**den**-ee-eye: after F. V. Hayden, p 242). Flowers magenta and pale yellow, ± drooping; calyx hairless; leaflets ± round. Absarokas, sw MT, ec ID. Illustrated.

T. nanum (**nay**-num: dwarf). Flowers magenta, just 1 to 4 per cluster. Color p 102.

Sweet-Clovers

Melilotus spp. (mel-i-**lo**-tus: honey *Lotus*). Many-stemmed weeds with small (¼", or 6 mm) pea-like flowers in curved one-sided racemes 2–5" long [5–8 cm]; compound leaves of 3 toothed elliptical leaflets; plants 2–7' tall [60–210 cm], sweetly fragrant, esp while drying. Roadsides, disturbed ground; Eurasian. Fabaceae.

M. officinalis (o-fiss-in-**ay**-lis: medicinal). Flowers yellow. Color p 102.

M. albus (**al**-bus: white). Flowers white.

Sweet-clovers are beloved of bees, cows, highway departments, and herbalists. They contain blood anticoagulants related to warfarin, the common rat poison. They get listed as both "preferred forage" and "potentially toxic to stock." Like other noxious invaders, they displace native vegetation.

Golden Smoke

Corydalis aurea (cor-**id**-a-lis: the crested lark; **aw**-ria: gold). Flowers yellow, in compact side clusters; petals 4, upper one with a round-tipped rearward spur; inner two ± hidden; sepals 2, falling off early; stamens 6; seeds black, in slender, curved 1" [25 mm] pods; leaves powdery-coated, pinnately twice to 4× compound, fernlike; sprawling annual or biennial plants, stems to 20" long [50 cm]. Burns, gravel bars, lower forests. A similar but erect plant, with pink flowers, from Glacier north is *C. sempervirens.* Fumariaceae (Fumitory family). Color p 103.

Golden Banners

Thermopsis spp. (ther-**mop**-sis: like lupine). Also **false lupine, golden** or **yellow pea** or **bean, buck bean, buffalo pea** (as the Blackfoot called it because it bloomed as the bison left their winter range.) Flowers bright yellow, pealike, ¾–1" [20–25 mm], in columnar racemes; leaves compound, alternate; 3 leaflets plus 2 smaller "stipules" clasping stem at leaf base. Fabaceae (Pea Family).

T. montana (mon-**tay**-na: montane). Leaflets usually oval, up to 4" long; pea pods straight; 18–40" tall [45–100 cm]. Moist meadows; wc MT, c ID, WY.

T. rhombifolia (rom-bif-**oh**-lia: rhomboid leaf, ref to stipules). Leaflets pointed elliptical, up to 1¾" long [45 mm]; pea pods C-curved; 6–16" tall [15–40 cm]. Dry grassland, mainly e of CD; Banff south. Color p 102.

This toxic color swath tends to increase with heavy grazing.

Steer's Head

Dicentra uniflora (di-**sen**-tra: two spur). Bizarre little pinkish flower resembles a horned skull, ⅝" long [15 mm], with 2 petals fused (the muzzle) and 2 curved back (the horns); 2 sepals; 6 hidden stamens; stalks 1-flowered, 2–4" [5–10 cm]; leaves lacy, compound, on 2–4" stalks attached to flowers belowground. Toxic. Blooms soon after snowmelt; moist gravels, steppe to treeline; OR, ID, nw WY. Fumariaceae. Color p 103.

Mountain-Sorrel

Oxyria digyna (ox-ee-ria: sharp—; **didge**-in-a: two ovaries). Flowers tiny, greenish, of 2 erect and 2 spreading lobes, 2 stigmas and 6 stamens, in rough spikelike panicles; fruit rust red, tiny, 2-winged; leaves kidney-shaped, 1–2" broad [2.5–5 cm], on long basal leafstalks, coloring brilliantly in fall; stalks several, 4–18" [10–45 cm]. Wet alp/subalp rocks and gravels. Polygonaceae (Buckwheat family). Color p 103.

Mountain-sorrel leaves offered a lemony note to salmon roe when boiled and pressed into cakes. Their tart acids include ascorbic (good for you) and oxalic (bad for you). Do snack, but not to excess.

Monkshood

Aconitum columbianum (ac-o-**nigh**-tum: Greek name for it; co-lum-be-**ay**-num: of the Columbia River). Sepals 5, petal-like, blue-purple, the upper one hooding, helmetlike; two true petals small, hidden under hood; flowers ¾–1½" tall [2–4 cm], in an open raceme atop the 1–7' stem [30–210 cm]; leaves 2–5" diam [5–13 cm], palmately deeply incised. Moist sites, US and s BC. Ranunculaceae (Buttercup family) or Helleboraceae. Color p 103.

Most blue irregular flowers are bumble bee-pollinated. Monkshood's odd-shaped flower excludes from its nectary all insects except highly motivated, intelligent bumble bees, whose advantage to the plant is their fidelity; having been once well rewarded with monkshood nectar, they will visit only monkshoods, whose pollen will then not be squandered among a haphazard sequence of flower species. Monkshood is listed as toxic to humans and stock, but biologists found lots of it in elk scats in the the Blue Mountains.

Herbs: irregular dicots

Violets

Viola spp. (vie-**oh**-la: the Roman term). Petals 5, the lowest one largest, bulbous at its rear end, with dark purple guide lines; sepals 5; stamens 5, short; capsules split explosively to propel seeds. Violaceae (Violet family).

V. canadensis. =*V. scopulorum* (CO). Flowers ½" wide [12 mm], several, ± white inside with yellow center, violet on back; leaves heart-shaped, pointed; stems leafy, 4–16" [10–40 cm]. Usually in low to mid-elev woods.

V. adunca (a-**dunk**-a: hooked). =*V. labradorica* (CO). Flowers ½" wide [12 mm], lavender to blue with white center, with an upcurved rearward spur; leaves ± heart-shaped; stems 1–4" [2.5–10 cm] when in flower. Widespread; dwarfed form in wet high meadows. Color p 103.

V. orbiculata (or-bic-you-**lay**-ta: round, ref to leaf). Flowers yellow; leaves scalloped, bluntly heartshaped to nearly round, dark green, persisting through winter; 1–2" stem [2.5–5 cm]. Moist forest. Illustrated at right.

V. sororia (sor-**or**-ia: sister). =*V. nephrophylla* (USDA). Flowers 1" wide [25 mm], lavender to blue; leaves basal, heart-shaped, up to 2¾" wide [7 cm]. Wet places. Illustrated at left.

V. praemorsa (pre-**mor**-sa: an hors d'oeuvre?). =formerly included in *V. nuttallii.* Flowers yellow; leaves blunt-tipped elliptical; 1–5" stem [2.5–13 cm]. Pine forest, alpine wet spots. Color p 103. Similar *V. vallicola*, with leaf blades that widen toward the base, is mainly found in steppe and dry grassland.

Thomas Nuttall probably collected and named more new species from west of the Mississippi than anyone else. He came along at the ideal time: crossing the Rockies was easier and safer for him than for Lewis or Douglas, but there were plenty of conspicuous species still to be described. Following early work on Great Plains flora, he wrote his magnum opus, *The Genera of North American Plants*, in 1818.

In 1834, the visionary settler/entrepreneur **Nathaniel Wyeth** persuaded Nuttall to quit his prestigious chair at Harvard and join an expedition to the Oregon Territory. Nuttall collected all along the way, then sailed to Hawaii, California, and home via Cape Horn. Having exhausted his savings on the expedition, he retired to an inherited estate in his native England.

His enthusiasm inspired praise from every botanist who saw him, and more than a little derision from others.

"When the boat touches the shore, he leaps out, and no sooner is his attention arrested by a plant or flower, than everything else is forgotten. The inquiry is made, ou est le fou*? where is the fool? ... he is gathering roots."* (Henry Marie Brackenridge, *Views of Louisiana*)

V. purpurea (pur-**pew**-ria: purple). Flowers yellow; leaves ± purple-veined, with several blunt lobes; 2–6" stem[5–15 cm]. Scattered, usually on dry soils, all elevs; from s MT south and west.

Many **violets** bloom soon after the retreat of snow, often so early and chilly that pollinators are not yet on the wing. If pollination fails, they respond with a second batch of flowers: greenish, low, inconspicuous, and "cleistogamous" ("closed marriage") or able to pollinate themselves without ever opening, for sure-fire seed production. All violets, including garden pansies, have tasty, nutritious leaves and stems, but poisonous seed and roots.

Larkspurs

Delphinium spp. (del-**fin**-ium: Greek name for them, from "dolphin"). Flowers deep blue to violet, ¾–1¼" diam[2.5–5 cm]; sepals 5, petal-like, spreading, the upper one with a long nectar-bearing spur behind; petals 4, the upper 2 spurred (within the sepal spur), often much paler; leaves 2–5" diam[5–13 cm], narrowly palmately lobed and/or compound. Ranunculaceae (Buttercup family) or Helleboraceae.

D. glaucum (**glaw**-cum: whitish). =includes *D. occidentale* (WY). Many flowers, in a tall raceme, sometimes becoming washed-out in color; upper petals white-edged; stem hollow, 3–7' tall [30–120 cm]. Dry meadows, all elevs. Color p 103.

D. bicolor. 3-12 bright blue-purple flowers; upper petals (not sepals) ± white with blue lines; stem solid, 6–20" [15–50 cm]. Grassland, open woods, up to lower alpine. Illustrated.

D. nuttallianum (nuttle-ee-**ay**-num: after Thos. Nuttall, p 222). Like *bicolor*, exc stamens are exposed under the lower 2 petals, whose tips are split at least ⅛" [3 mm] deep; there's an easier difference in the roots, but I dislike uprooting plants just to i.d. them. Steppe, pine forest, sometimes alpine. Color page 103.

Though lethal only when eaten in quantity, larkspurs have killed more cattle than any other western genus. The seeds have for millennia been ground up to poison lice.

Herbs: regular flowers, 5 petals

These typically have 5 sepals and 5, 10, 15 or more stamens in addition to their 5 petals or corolla lobes (fused petals); the female parts aren't in fives. Also included, on pages 249–55, are flowers with just one set of conspicuous flower parts in fives — either petals or sepals but not both, and not the stamens. These variables tend to reveal family relations. The rose family mostly has 15 or 20 stamens; the

---

phlox family has 5; purslanes have 2 sepals and parsleys have none.

If you have a 5-petaled flower that you can't locate here, try these leads: shrubs include many 5-petaled genera; if they're very low and barely recognizable as subshrubs, they'll be with the shrubs on pages 148–56 if the genus as a whole is evergreen. Irregular dicots, pages 211–223, mostly have 5 corolla lobes, but these lobes are very unlike each other. Composites, p 191, have tight heads of tiny florets which are technically 5-parted, and sometimes visibly so. Gentian and starflower, p 262–23, have 5 petals in many of their blossoms, but usually have 6 or 7 on at least as many others in the vicinity.

Herbs: 5 fused petals, 5 stamens

Jacob's Ladder

Polemonium pulcherrimum (pool-**ker**-im-um: most beautiful). Flowers light blue with yellow center, ½" wide [12 mm], not tightly clustered; corolla lobes spreading, from a short flaring tube; leaves pinnately compound, mostly basal, leaflets at least ¼" [6 mm]. Mainly alp/subalp and 4–10" tall [5–25 cm], though c ID and sw MT have a bigger, coarser mid-elev variety. Polemoniaceae (Phlox family). Color p 105.

Sky Pilot

Polemonium viscosum (pol-em-**oh**-nium: Greek word for it; vis-**co**-sum: sticky). Also **skunkflower**. Flowers bright blue, ⅝–1⅛" [15–28 mm], in a hemispheric cluster; corolla lobes flaring from a narrow tube; leaflets tiny, crowded, appearing whorled; plants 4–14" [10–35 cm], often skunky smelling. Polemoniaceae (Phlox family). Color p 105.

Like most flowers, sky pilots produce a sweet flowery fragrance in their nectaries to attract nectar-feeding insects as pollinators. In many individuals, this is overwhelmed by a skunky aroma on sepals and bracts below the flowers. One researcher thinks the stink serves to repel ants; she smells it only on plants at elevations where ants abound. Unlike pollinating bees and hover flies, nectar-feeding ants slip right past the pollen-bearing stamens on their way to robbing the nectary, and often destroy the pistil in the process. See if you can find both skunky and sweet-smelling sky pilots, and any pattern of either ant presence or elevation separating them.

Skyrocket

Ipomopsis aggregata (ip-a-**mop**-sis: like morning-glory; ag-reg-**ay**-ta: clustered). =*Gilia aggregata*. Also **scarlet gilia**. Corolla scarlet, trumpet-shaped, the slightly flaring tube twice as long (½–1¼", or 12–30 mm) as the slightly recurved, pointed lobes; stamens borne near mouth of tube; leaves much-dissected, lobes linear; stems to 3' [90 cm], many-flowered, or dwarfed (4", or 10 cm) at high elevs. Dry meadows, scree, ledges; US and se BC. Polemoni-aceae (Phlox family). Color page 106.

The long tubular corolla and bright red color are clues that this flower evolved with hummingbirds as pollinators. Most insects cannot see red, but hummers crave it. From the Wind River valley south, many skyrocket flowers are white or light pink, perhaps with red speckles, instead of scarlet. In some populations the same hillside—or even the same plant—switches from red blooms in July to pale ones in August. This happens where hummingbirds migrate through and are gone by August, leaving white-lined sphinx moths (p 546) as the best available pollinators. At night, the moths don't see red flowers very well, and mainly visit white flowers.

The plant lives as a rosette of leaves for two to five years before producing one flowering stem and then dying.

Flaxflower

Linanthus nuttallii (lin-**anth**-us: flax flower; nut-**all**-ee-eye: after Thos. Nut-tall, p 222). =*Leptosiphon nuttallii* (WY), *Linanthastrum nuttallii* (CO). Corolla white, with 5–6 flat-spreading lobes at the end of a hairy straight tube; 3 stig-mas and 5 stamens just emerge from tube opening; leaves seemingly linear, ¾" long [2 cm], in big whorls, but actually these are leaflets of palmately compound leaves; numerous leafy stems, to 12" tall [30 cm], from woody bases. OR, c ID, WY, MT Bitterroots. Polemoniaceae. Color p 105.

Alpine Collomia

Collomia debilis (co-lo-mia: gluey; **deb**-il-iss: weak). Corolla trumpet-shaped, ½–1" [12–25 mm], streaky white to light pink (or brilliant deep pink in w-most WY); stamens sticking out, sometimes blue-tipped; leaves alternate, crowded, ± sticky-hairy, usually oval, to 1" [25 mm]; dense cushions 2–3" deep [5–8 cm]. Unstable high-elev gravels; c ID and Bitterroots south. Polemoniaceae.

Phlox

Phlox spp. (flocks: a Greek flower, meaning "flame").
Corolla white, pink, or pale blue, with 4–6 flat-spreading lobes at the end of a straight tube; 3 stigmas usually just visible in the tube opening; leaves linear,
pointed; numerous leafy stems, from woody
bases. Polemoniaceae.

P. longifolia (lon-jif-oh-lia: long leaf). Corollas
typically light pink; leaves ¾–3" [2–8 cm]; plants
3–16" [8–40 cm], not matted. Sagebrush. Illust.

P. multiflora. Corolla usually white; leaves ½–1¼"
[12–30 mm]; 2–4" tall [5–10 cm]. All elevs, c MT s.

P. pulvinata (pul-vin-ay-ta: cushion-forming). =*P. sibirica* ssp. *pulvinata* (CO).
Corolla white to light blue, ½–⅝" diam [14 mm]; calyx sticky-hairy; leaves ¼–½"
[6–12 mm]; dense mats 1–3" thick [2–8 cm]. Alp/subalp; WY, sw MT. Color p 105.

P. hoodii. Corolla ⅜" diam; calyx and leaf edges cobwebby-haired; leaves ¼" [6
mm], stiff, spinelike; dense mats 1–3" thick [2–8 cm]. Lower elevs; US and AB.

High ridges colonized by phlox fail to retain much soil or snow; both
blow away. Winter subjects plants that lack a snow blanket to ferocious drying winds and to hundreds of freezing/thawing cycles; yet
the plants withstand frost action whose powers of pulverization are
amply displayed on nearby rocks. Though the rocks continually
break up, their particles tend to blow away as they reach soil size, preventing soil from accumulating.

Alpine phlox exemplify the "cushion" form adapted to this extreme environment. The smooth convex surface eases the wind on
over with minimal resistance, and even more so when the plant con-
tours itself in the lee of a large rock or a crevice between rocks. The
tiny, crammed leaves live in a pocket of calm partly of their own
making, and there they trap windblown particles that slowly become
a mound of soil. Cushion plants also tend to have really long taproots (e.g., 8–15', or 2.5–4.5 m). Ridgetops receive their share of snow,
but wind and the coarse rocky substrate allow little of it to stay there.

Parry's Primrose

Primula parryi (**prim**-you-la: small, first, ref to blooming; **pair**-ee-eye: after
Chas. Parry, p 63). Flowers 3–12, brilliant magenta with yellow center, ¾" [2 cm]
diam; corolla lobes shallowly notched at tip, spreading flat from a narrow tube;
stamens within opening; calyx sticky; leaves basal, succulent, bright green, shallowly toothed, erect, up to 12" [30 cm]; plants to 12" [30 cm], sometimes ±
skunky. Moist, wind-sheltered alp/subalpine sites; from c MT and c ID south.
Primulaceae. Color p 104.

Rock-Jasmines

Androsace spp. (an-**drah**-sa-kee: Greek word for some sea plant). Also **fairy candelabras**. Fragrant; corolla white to cream yellow, aging pink, jasmine-fragrant; stamens hidden within tube; calyx cup-shaped, 5-lobed; leaves basal, lanceolate. Primulaceae (Primrose family).

A. septentrionalis (sep-ten-trio-**nay**-lis: northern). Corolla lobes cupped, ⅛" [3 mm] diam, barely longer than the calyx lobes; flowers in an open cluster; plant ± annual, 1–10" tall [3–25 cm]. All elevs; weedy in gardens. Illustrated.

A. chamaejasme (cam-ee-**jaz**-me: dwarf jasmine, ref to fragrance). =*A. lehmanniana*. Corolla lobes spread flat, ¼" [6 mm] diam, surrounding a yellow to orange eye; flowers in a compact rounded cluster; leaves ¼–⅜" long [6–10 mm], in dense mats; plant white-hairy, 1–4" tall [3–10 cm]. Mainly alpine, esp on limestone-derived soil. Color p 105.

Douglasia

Douglasia montana (da-**glass**-ia: after David Douglas, p 66; mon-**tay**-na: montane). Corolla deep pink, ⅜" diam [1 cm], lobes shallowly notched at tip, spreading flat from the narrow tube; stamens barely appearing at opening (in contrast to moss campion, p 113); flowers single on 1–4 tiny stalks per rosette; leaves linear, pointed, ¼" [6 mm], in rosettes aggregating in low mosslike mats. Alpine, esp on limestone; Waterton s. Primulaceae (Primrose Family). Color p 542.

Shooting Stars

Dodecatheon spp. (doh-de-**cayth**-ee-on: twelve gods). Magenta 5-lobed corolla and calyx bent sharply back (e.g., upward), ½–1" long [12–25 mm], fused "collar" portion usually yellow; stamens tightly clasping pistil, or slightly spreading; flowers several, many facing down (i.e., the petals up) but all erect in fruit (a capsule); leaves basal, stalked; stem 2–18" [5–45 cm]. Widely scattered; commonest in alp/subalpine wet places. Primulaceae (Primrose family).

> *D. pulchellum* (pool-**kel**-um: beautiful, small). =*D. pauciflorum, D. radicatum*. Stamens are joined and columnar nearly half their length. Color p 106
>
> *D. conjugens* (**con**-jug-enz: joined). Stamens are joined and columnar less than ¼ of their length.

The kind of flower shape we call "shooting stars" and botanists call "reflexed" is also common in the nightshade family, which includes tomato and potato plants. These flowers are all "buzz pollinated." That means the stamens are designed to spew pollen only in response to furious vibration. Bumble bees visiting the flowers stay in place

---

for a moment, vibrate their wings, and are rewarded with a shower of pollen. For the plant, there is efficiency in attracting faithful bumblebees, which on any given day visit one species of flower over and over again, and thus don't waste the flower's pollen by losing it on another kind of flower—even though the bumble bee is also smart enough to eat all the pollen she can. Some other flowers (pages 211, 218, 221) accomplish the same thing with robust, irregular flower shapes that only a bumble bee can unlock.

Waterleaf

Hydrophyllum capitatum (hydro-fill-um: water leaf; cap-it-**ay**-tum: flowers in heads). Flowers lavender or bluish to white, in spherical heads bristling with stamens; corolla ⅜" [1 cm]; calyx bristly; leaves pinnate, rising above the flower heads; leaflets 5–9, lobed. Sagebrush, aspen groves, moist open forest; Crowsnest s. Hydrophyllaceae (Waterleaf family). Color p 106.

Mist Maiden

Romanzoffia sitchensis (romans-**ah**-fia sit-**ken**-sis: after Count Nicolai Rumiantzef, who funded a scientific expedition to Sitka, Alaska). Flowers white, funnel-shaped with 5 round lobes, ¼–½" [6–12 mm], in loose racemes on leafless 2–10" stalks [5–25 cm]; leaves basal on long stalks, round, ½–1½" wide [12–38 mm], with coarse blunt teeth; resembles a more delicate brook saxifrage (p 107), but has fused petals. Seepy rock ledges, mainly alp/subalpine; n ID and w MT north. Hydrophyllaceae. Color p 105.

Phacelias

Phacelia spp. (fa-**see**-lia: bundle, referring to the dense inflorescence). Flowers crowded, bristling with stamens about twice as long as corollas (up to ⅞", or 22 mm); calyx hairy. Rocky places. Hydrophyllaceae.

Silverleaf phacelia, *P. hastata* (hass-**tay**-ta: halberd-shaped—not true of our varieties' leaves). Also **scorpionweed**. Flowers dirty white to lavender; inflorescence often curled, uncurling as it blooms progressively upward; leaves gray-silky- coated, narrow elliptical, with a few prominent depressed veins; plants up to 24" [60 cm] if erect, but often sprawling. All elevs; Banff s. Illust.

Silky phacelia, *P. sericea* (ser-**iss**-ia: silky). Flowers purple (to blue or white) in a ± tall spike; stamens pale-tipped; leaves; leaves silky-haired, mostly basal, pinnate-lobed almost to midvein, the lobes again divided; subalpine form 4–9" [10–23 cm], densely hairy; mid-elev form 10–36" [25–90 cm] and less hairy. Color p 105.

Lyall's phacelia, *P. lyallii* (lie-**ah**-lee-eye: after David Lyall, p 63). Flowers blue-purple in a short spike; stamens pale-tipped; leaves with coarse, usually sticky hair, dark green (not silvery), coarsely pinnate-lobed, mostly basal, cushion-forming; stem 3–10″ [8–25 cm]. Alpine; MT n to Crowsnest. Color page 104.

Most of our several *Phacelia* species have both alpine (compact) and mid-elevation (leggy) varieties. The silky is most striking, with ornate leaves and a compact, colorful inflorescence. Cutleaf kitten-tails (p 257) is unrelated but remarkably similar.

Bellflowers

Campanula spp. (cam-**pan**-you-la: small bell). Also **Scottish-bluebells, harebells.** Corolla pale blue, bell-shaped; pistil 3-forked. Campanulaceae (Harebell family).

C. uniflora. Flower single, ¼–½″ [6–12 mm]; leaves untoothed; 1–4″ tall [3–10 cm]. Alpine. Illustrated.

C. lasiocarpa (lazy-o-**car**-pa: shaggy fruit). Flower single, ⅝–1¼″ [15–30 mm]; calyx base hairy; leaves fine-toothed; plant 1–6″ [3–15 cm]. Alpine; Banff and n. Color p 104.

C. rotundifolia (rotund-if-**oh**-lia: round leaf). Flowers several, ⅝–1¼″ [15–30 mm]; stem leaves linear; basal leaves ± round on long stalks, often withering before flowers open; 6–30″ [15–75 cm]. Widespread, e.g., dry meadows. Color p 104.

Bluebells

Mertensia spp. (mer-**ten**-zia: after Franz K. Mertens, p 152). Also **lungworts.** Corolla blue, pink-tinged at first, ½–¾″ [13–20 mm] , short-lobed, narrowly bell-shaped and pendent, stem leaves pointed-elliptical, often with bluish bloom; robust plants, 1–5′ [30–150 cm], usually in clumps. Lush subalpine meadows. Boraginaceae (Borage family).

M. campanulata (cam-pan-you-**lay**-ta: bell-shaped). Calyx cup-shaped, short-lobed. Only in southernmost c ID mtns.

M. ciliata (silly-**ay**-ta: fine-haired along edge). Calyx lobes long and narrow; upper leaves sessile; basal leaves, if present, not heart-shaped. OR, WY, sc and e ID, MT s of Helena. Color p 106.

M. paniculata (pa-nic-you-**lay**-ta: flowers in panicles). Calyx lobes long and narrow; upper leaves short-stalked; basal leaves heart-shaped, long-stalked. BC, OR, n and sw ID, MT nw of Missoula.

Alpine Mertensia

Mertensia alpina. Flowers brilliant royal blue, face-up in small clusters; corolla wider than long (not bell-shaped), with flat-spreading lobes on a short tube; leaves narrow elliptical; 2–10″ tall [5–25 cm]. Alpine, locally abundant: the major blue spots on the Beartooth Highway at times; WY, s MT, e ID. Color p 104.

Forget-Me-Not

Myosotis asiatica (my-o-**so**-tiss: mouse ear). =*M. alpestris, M. sylvatica.* Flowers sky blue with yellow center, ¼" diam [6 mm], in clusters; corolla lobes spread flat from a short tube; leaves oblong, hairy, basal ones to 5" long [12 cm], stem ones to 1½" [38 mm]; hairy stems 3–16" [8–40 cm]. Moist mid-elev to alpine soil. Boraginaceae. Color p 104.

Alpine Forget-Me-Not

Eritrichium nanum (er-it-**trick**-ium: woolly hair; **nay**-num: dwarf). =*E. elongatum, E. aretioides* (CO). Flowers sky blue with yellow center, ¼" diam [6 mm]; corolla spreading flat from a short tube; leaves oblong, hairy-tufted, ⅜" [1 cm], crowded in a mat; stems ½–4" [1.2–10 cm]. Alpine; WY, c ID, MT. Boraginaceae. Color p 104.

The intervals of soil are ... covered with a carpet of low but brilliantly flowering alpine plants ... rarely rising more than an inch in height. In many of them, the flower is the most conspicuous and the largest part of the plant, and in all, the colouring is astonishingly brilliant....

May the deep cœrulean tint of the sky, be supposed to have an influence in producing the corresponding colour, so prevalent in the flowers of these plants? (Edwin James on Pike's Peak, 1820)

This dwarf, the official flower of Grand Teton National Park, holds the wildflower record for greatest intensity per millimeter of height.

Edwin James became, in 1820, the first botanist in the alpine zone in Western North America, and the first Euroamerican to ascend a 10,000'+ peak there. His tundra firsts include the alpine bluebells. Major Long, the expedition's commander, named the mountain James' Peak, mistakenly believing that they had already passed Pike's Peak farther north. That northern one became Long's Peak, and poor James ended up without a peak in his name. Captain Zebulon Pike had set off to climb *his* peak in 1806, but turned around some 15 miles short, reporting that "no human being could have ascended to its pinical."

Long's expedition was trumpeted as the Yellowstone Expedition, but budget-cutters in Washington trashed that objective and redirected Long when he reached present-day Omaha. (He travelled that far by steamboat in 1819, just 12 years after Lewis and Clark's return; the West was getting developed fast!) A second botanist, **Thomas Say**, was assigned to cover "Zoology, &c.," including "the diseases, remedies, &c. known amongst the Indians." Say's name remains better known to birders than botanists. Late in the trip a group of soldiers deserted after stealing the saddlebag containing all of Say's notes, which they doubtless jettisoned while searching in the bags for anything "useful."

Puccoon

Lithospermum ruderale (lith-o-**sperm**-um: stone seed; roo-der-**ay**-lee: of waste places). Also **western gromwell**, **stoneseed**, **lemonweed**. Flowers pale yellow, ⅜" diam [1 cm], in leaf axils; corolla lobes spreading flat from a narrow tube; leaves linear, 1–4" [2–10 cm], many, hairy, all on stem; stems several, rough-hairy, 8–28" [20–70 cm]. Dry meadows and open forest to mid-elevs. Boraginaceae. Color p 106.

Use of the roots for red dye or (mixed with grease) face paint was so widespread that settlers called puccoon "Indian paint." The Okanagan dyed fishing lines, believing that puccoon masked human odors. Some women took puccoon to suppress fertility; lab work confirms that puccoon suppresses some reproductive hormones and organs.

Miner's Candle

Cryptantha celosioides (cryp-**tanth**-a: hidden flower; sel-oh-see-**oy**-deez: like cockscomb, a houseplant). =*C. nubigena* (AB), *Oreocarya celosioides*. Flowers white with yellow center, ⅜" diam [1 cm], initially clustered ± spikelike; corolla lobes spreading flat from a narrow tube; calyx and leaves bristly; lower leaves spoon-shaped, trending smaller and linear upward on stem; thick central stem much the largest, 3–20" [8–40 cm]; plant usually biennial. Low-elev dry grasslands, pine forest; OR to c MT, n to Crowsnest. Smaller-flowered *Cryptantha* spp. grow farther n and s. Boraginaceae. Color p 106.

Buckbean

Menyanthes trifoliata (men-**yanth**-eez: monthly flower; try-fo-lee-**ay**-ta: 3-leaved). Corolla white (often purple-tinged), ¼–½" [6–12 mm] long and wide, with hairy-faced flat-spreading lobes on a straight tube; stamens purple-tipped; flowers in a ± erect, columnar raceme; three leaflets elliptical, 2–5" [5–13 cm]; stems and leafstalks usually ± prostrate and submerged; from rhizomes. Bogs and ponds. Menyanthaceae (Buckbean family).

Bastard Toadflax

Comandra umbellata (co-**man**-dra: hairy men, ref to stamens; um-bel-**ay**-ta: flowers in umbels). =*C. pallida*. Calyx lobes white to purplish, narrow, petal-like; lobes still conspicuous on the bluish to brownish ¼" [6 mm] egg-shaped fruits; flowers in a round clusters atop unbranched but clustered 2–14" stems [5–35 cm]; leaves bluish-coated, somewhat fleshy, linear to narrow elliptical, untoothed, alternate, all up and down the stem; partially parasitic on roots. Sandy soil, foothills to timberline. Santalaceae (Sandalwood family). Color p 106.

The oily fruits, especially when green, are tasty—but don't gorge.

Spreading Dogbane

Apocynum androsaemifolium (a-**pos**-in-um: Away, dog!; an-dro-**see**-mif-**oh**-lium: leaves like *Androsaemum*). Flowers pink, fragrant, ¼–⅜" [6–10 mm], bell-shaped with flaring lobes, clustered; leaves opposite, oval, ± glossy above, pale beneath, spreading flat or drooping; stems milky-juiced, smooth, often reddish, much branched (resembling a shrub); seeds cottony-tufted, in paired, slender 3–6" pods [8–15 cm]; plants 1–2' [30–60 cm]. Dry, ± shady sites, up to tree line. Apocynaceae (Dogbane family). Color p 106.

The Salish sewed hides into teepees using Indian-hemp, *A. cannabinum*, the strongest twine available to Rocky Mountain tribes. Dogbane was occasionally substituted for it. To humans and perhaps also to dogs, dogbane is purgative, diuretic, and may cause heart irregularities. It attracts a wide assortment of butterflies and bees.

Herbs: 5 separate petals, 5 stamens

Sibbaldia

Sibbaldia procumbens (sib-**ahl**-dia: after Sir Robert Sibbald; pro-**cum**-benz: prostrate). Petals tiny, yellow, sitting on top of 5 slightly longer green bracts alternating with 5 much larger (up to ¼", or 6 mm) green calyx lobes; leaves 3-compound; leaflets ½–1½" [12–38 mm], 3(–5)-toothed at the tip, white-hairy; leafstalks and flower stems rising 2–4" [5–10 cm] from rhizomes or prostrate stems. Alp/subalpine. Rosaceae (Rose family). Color p 107.

Blue Flax

Linum lewisii (**lye**-num: Roman name for flax; lew-**iss**-ee-eye: after Meriwether Lewis, p 257). =*Adenolinum lewisii* (CO), *L. perenne*. Petals pale blue with yellowish base, ½–¾" [12–20 mm]; sepals ¼" [6 mm]; 5 styles; several flowers on each of the many stem branches; leaves linear, ⅓–1" [9–25 mm], all up and down the 6–30" [15–75 cm] stem; in alpine zone, petals, leaves, and plant are about half the above sizes. Dry meadows or open woods, all elevs. Linaceae (Flax family). Color p 107.

Wild Sarsaparilla

Aralia nudicaulis (a-**ray**-lia: early Quebequois name for it?; nu-di-**caw**-lis: naked stem). Flowers ¼" long [6 mm], greenish white, 5-petalled, in a few open round clusters ± hidden beneath the leaf on a 4–12" [10–30 cm] leafless stalk; berries ¼" [6 mm], dark purple, with 5 tiny styles; compound leaf rises on a 6–20" [15–40 cm] stalk from rhizomes; leaflets usually 15 or 9, oval, fine-toothed. Moist forest; n WA, n ID, nw MT, BC, AB. Araliaceae (Ginseng family).

Sarsaparilla was the great American "tonic" of the 19th

Century. The genuine item came from several Latin American species of *Smilax. Aralia,* though unrelated, provided a similarly root beer-flavored adulterant or surrogate. It had its own reputation, learned from eastern tribes starting in the earliest 1600s, as invigorating, healing, sweat-inducing, and pimple-clearing. There is a little flavor in the berries, more in the roots. The roots survive most fires, and resprout.

Mitreworts

Mitella spp. (my-**tel**-a: mitre—). Also **bishop's caps.** Petals branched, threadlike, sticking out between whitish calyx lobes; flowers 10–20 along a 6–14" [15–35 cm] stalk; leaves ± kidney-shaped, scalloped to toothed, basal, stalked. Moist subalpine forest or meadow. Saxifragaceae (Saxifrage family).

M. breweri (**brew**-er-eye: for Wm. Brewer). Petals ± yellow-green, 5–9-branched; stamens aligned with calyx lobes; calyx saucer-shaped. Banff to nw MT. Illust above.

M. pentandra (pen-**tan**-dra: 5 stamens). Like *breweri,* exc stamens aligned with petals. Color p 107 (right).

M. trifida (**trif**-id-a; 3-forked). Petals white or purplish, with 3 thick branches; calyx bell-shaped. Illustrated at right.

M. stauropetala (stor-o-**pet**-a-la: cross petals). Petals white, with 3 slender branches; calyx bell-shaped. U.S. Color p 107 (left).

M. nuda. Petals ±white, 9-branched; 10 stamens; calyx saucer-shaped. C MT n.

The seed capsule looks like a mitre—a bishop's tall, deeply cleft hat.

Grass-of-Parnassus

Parnassia fimbriata (par-**nas**-ia: of Mt. Parnassus, or mtns in general, poetically; fim-bree-**ay**-ta: fringed). Petals white, ¼–½" [6–12 mm], long-fringed near the base; flower in late summer, single on a 6–16" [15–40 cm] stalk; leaves heart-shaped, basal, long-stalked, plus one small leaf sessile halfway up stem. Wet meadows, streambanks, esp subalpine. Parnassiaceae (or Saxifragaceae). Color p 108.

Herbs: 5 separate petals, 10 stamens

Leatherleaf Saxifrage

Leptarrhena pyrolifolia (lep-ta-**ree**-na: slender anthers; pyro-lif-**oh**-lia: pyrola leaf). Petals white, minute; flowers tightly clustered; seed pods red, paired; stem dark red, 8–18" [10–45 cm]; leaves toothed, rounded-elliptic, thick, crinkly-leathery, shiny bright green, 1–3" [25–75 mm], basal, plus 1–3 small ones clasping stem. Alp/subalpine streambanks, wet gravels; BC, AB, n ID, w MT. Saxifragaceae. Illust.

As a maroon tint massed along rocky streambanks, these seed-heads and stems are sometimes recognizable from hundreds of yards away.

Herbs: 5 separate petals, 5 or 10 stamens   233

Saxifrages

Saxifraga spp. (sac-**sif**-ra-ga: stone break). Delicate single-stemmed, several-flowered herb from a basal rosette or mat of leaves; petals and sepals 5; pistil often enlarges into 2 horned pods while petals are still in place. Mainly alp/subalpine. Saxifragaceae.

Spotted saxifrage, *S. bronchialis* (bronk-ee-**ay**-lis: windpipe, ref to inflorescence branches). =*Ciliaria austromontana* (CO). Petals white, speckled with red or orange; stems have scattered small leaves; basal leaves crowded, sharp, linear, ¼–½" [6–12 mm]. Rock crevices; Tetons north. Illust at right.

Redstem saxifrage, *S. lyallii* (lye-ah-lee-eye: after David Lyall, p 63). =*Micranthes lyallii*. Petals white; sepals and pistil often deep red; stem leafless, often maroon; leaves nearly round, ½–1½" wide [12–38 mm], coarsely toothed on outer half. Wet gravels; BC, AB, w MT, n ID. Color p 107.

Brook saxifrage, *S. odontoloma* (o-don-ta-**lo**-ma: tooth fringe). =*Micranthes odontoloma* (CO), *S. arguta* (older texts). Petals white with yellowish spots near base, nearly round exc for a short neck; stamens broadened, white; leaves ± round, stalked, 1–3" wide [25–75 mm], with large, even teeth, slightly fleshy; stem 6–12" [15–30 cm], leafless, with fine wool near the top. Wet places, esp subalp. Illustrated at left.

Yellow saxifrage, *S. aizoides* (ay-**zoy**-deez: like genus *Aizoon*). Petals yellow, alternating with green sepals; leaves matted, succulent, sharp-tipped, narrowly oblong, ¼" long [6 mm]; 1½–4" tall [4–10 cm]. Wet gravels; Canada, Jasper to Kananaskis. Color p 107.

Purple saxifrage, *S. oppositifolia* (opposite-if-**oh**-lia: opposite leaves). Petals pink to purple; flowers ± bell-shaped, ⅓" [9 mm], emerging singly from a mat of tiny leaves in scale-like opposite pairs; minute hairs along leaf edges; 1–2" high [2.5–5 cm]. Alpine rockfields, favoring limestone substrates. Color p 107.

Bog saxifrage, *S. oregana* (or-eg-**ay**-na: of Oregon). *Micranthes oregana* (CO). Petals pale greenish, inconspicuous or often lacking; leaves fleshy, oblong shallowly toothed, 2–7" [5–18 cm]; stems sticky, thick, fleshy, often reddish, 10–30" tall [25–75 cm]. Marshy meadows; from Crowsnest south. WY and s MT have mainly the petalless type, which USDA treats as *S. subapetala*. Illust at left.

Saxifrages in their native habitat seem to live up to their "rock breaker" moniker, but the name actually derives from the Medieval herbalists' Doctrine of Signatures: a few European species were prescribed for breaking up bladderstones because they have little bulbs that were said to resemble bladderstones.

Tiarella

Tiarella trifoliata (tee-ar-**el**-a: crownlet; try-fo-lee-**ay**-ta: 3-leaved). =includes *T. unifoliata*. Also **sugarscoop, laceflower, foamflower, false mitrewort**. Flowers tiny, white, many, in a sparse raceme on an 8–22" [10–55 cm] stalk; petals threadlike, un-branched, less visible than the stamens; ovary and subse-quent capsule of 2 very unequal sides; leaves mostly basal on short leafstalks, hairy, toothed, from 3-lobed to 3-compound and incised, 2–4" [5–10 cm]. Dense forest. Saxifragaceae.

By midsummer, many tiarella leaves display pale curlicues, tracks of leaf-miner larvae (see p 513). Look closely to see the larva at the front end of the track.

Alumroot

Heuchera cylindrica (**hoy**-ker-a: after J. H. von Heucher). Flowers in a crowded cylindric raceme, cup-shaped, creamy (sometimes pinkish), lacking petals; sta-mens hidden within the 5-lobed calyx; 2 styles emerge as seeds grow; leaves basal, oval with coarse lobes and teeth, on long stalks; stem 6–32" [15–80 cm], leafless. Rock crevices, mainly mid-elevs; Absarokas n to Banff. Saxifragaceae. Color p 107.

Telesonix

Telesonix heucherifomis (tele-**son**-ix: distant claw, ref to long-stalked petals; hoy-ker-if-**or**-mis: like alumroot). =*Boykinia heucheriformis, B. jamesii, T. jamesii*. Petals violet, ¼" [6 mm], ± peeking out between the 5 calyx lobes; leaves kidney-shaped, doubly toothed, stalked, smaller upward; calyx and stem sticky-hairy; stems 1–several, scaly-based, 2–6" [5–15 cm]. Alp/subalpine limestone crevices. US, and disjunct in Canada from Saskatchewan R. north. Saxifragaceae. Color p 108.

Woodland Star

Lithophragma glabrum (lith-o-**frag**-ma: stone breaker; **glab**-rum: smooth, ref to leaves, not stem). Also **starflower, rock star, prairie star**, etc. Petals white, ¼", deeply lobed—shaped ± like a maple leaf; 5-lobed calyx and stems often sticky-hairy; leaves deeply palmate-lobed, the basal ones stalked, and much larger. Sagebrush, aspen groves, rocky slopes, all elevs. Saxifragaceae. Color p 108.

Look for minute maroon bulbs in the upper leaf and branch axils. They can germinate and grow after the stem topples—a way of cloning. Some specimens produce lots of these, and few or no flow-ers. Older floras separated plants with bulbils as *L. bulbifera*. Similar *L. parviflorum* rarely has bulbils, and has fine hair under its leaves.

Geraniums

Geranium spp. (jer-**ay**-nium: crane—). Also **cranesbills**. Flowers 1–1½" diam [25–38 cm], saucer-shaped, few to several; sepals and upper stems sticky-hairy; seed-pods split open explosively; leaves deeply 5-lobed, the lobes again split; basal leaves long-stalked, stem leaves small and stalkless; 1½–3' tall [45–90 cm]. Geraniaceae.

G. viscosissimum (vis-co-**see**-sim-um: stickiest). Petals strong pink with purple veins; sticky hairs white- or yellow-tipped (sometimes not sticky in WY). Mainly in dry meadows, aspen groves, etc. Color p 107.

G. richardsonii (richard-**so**-nee-eye: after Sir John Richardson, p 155). Petals white (sometimes light pink), with purple veins; sticky hairs purple-tipped. Mainly in open forest.

King's Crown

Sedum integrifolium (**see**-dum: the Roman term, derived from "sitting"; in-teg-rif-**oh**-lium: untoothed leaf). =*Rhodiola integrifolia* (USDA), *Tolmachevia integrifolia* (AB, CO), *S. rosea* (INT). Also **roseroot**, **midsummer-men**. Petals deep red, shorter than ¼" [6 mm]; stamens protruding; seed capsules five per flower, deep red; flowers several, crowded, male and female flowers on separate plants; leaves pale green, rubbery; stems 2–8" [5–10 cm], unbranched, in clumps, from rhizomes. Alp/subalpine, often where wet; from Banff s. Crassulaceae (Stonecrop family). Color p 108.

Queen's Crown

Sedum rhodanthum (ro-**danth**-um: red flower). =*Rhodiola rhodantha* (USDA), *Clementsia rhodantha* (CO). Also **rose crown**. Petals pink to white, ¼–⅜" [6–10 mm]; flowers have stamens and pistils; plants 2–14" [5–35 cm], much like king's crown (above) and may grow with it; Weber says you can tell queen's crown by a raised midrib on leaf underside. Mid-elevs to alpine, often where wet; c MT south. Crassulaceae. Color p 108.

Lanceleaf Stonecrop

Sedum lanceolatum (lan-see-o-**lay**-tum: lance—). =*Amerosedum lanceolatum* (CO). Petals yellow, pointed, ¼–⅜" [6–10 mm]; flowers several, in ± compact broad-topped clusters; seedpod 5-celled, starlike; leaves alternate, fleshy, ± tubular, crammed together, often turning red; plants low, 3–8" [8–20 cm], spreading by rhizomes and/or runners. Dry rocky places. Crassulaceae. Color p 108.

Fat succulent leaves, like cactus stems, maximize the ratio of volume to surface area, and hence the ratio of water capacity to water loss through transpiration. Even with leaves for storage tanks, stonecrops grow only while water is available, and store water mainly to subsidize flowering and fruiting. Water-filled leaves might be vulnerable to frost damage, but stonecrops resist freezing and do very well in the alpine zone. You can squeeze liquid water out of stonecrop leaves at temperatures that will freeze it immediately.

Moss-Campion

Silene acaulis (ay-**caw**-lis: stalkless). Also **moss pink, cushion pink, carpet pink**. Petals pink (occasionally to white), separate though they form an apparent tube, bent 90° to spread flat; styles and/or stamens often protruding; styles usually 3; calyx shallowly 5-lobed; leaves linear, pointed, thick, crowded, to ½" [12 mm]; mosslike mats 2" [5 cm] thick. Alpine. Caryophyllaceae (Pink family). Color p 113.

The Pink family is so called not because the petals are pink but because they are pinked, or notched at the tip. Pinked petals do run in the family, but other family traits such as ten stamens and unfused petals are more reliable, and they distinguish moss-campion from phlox and douglasia. (See page 226 on cushion plants.)

White Catchfly

Silene parryi (sigh-**lee**-nee: a Greek elf?; **pair**-ee-eye: after Chas. Parry. p 63). Petals white or lavender-tinged, each deeply 4-lobed, with 2 more small lobes on the throat—a seeming inner whorl of 10 petals; calyx 5-lobed, hairy; leaves narrow, 1–3" [25–75 mm], 2 or 3 pairs opposite, the rest basal; stem 6–15" [15–38 cm]. Alp/subalpine. Caryophyllaceae. Color p 108.

Sandworts

Petals white, ¼–½" [6–12 mm]; sepals ⅛–¼" [3–6 mm], blunt (pointed in some other sandworts); 3 styles; leaves linear, opposite; in tufts or mats. Caryophyllaceae or Alsinaceae.

Arctic sandwort, *Minuartia obtusiloba* (min-oo-**art**-ia: after Juan Minuart; ob-too-si-**lo**-ba: blunt-lobed). =*Lidia obtusiloba* (CO), *Arenaria obtusiloba*. Flower usually single; leaves ¼", dense, on prostrate stems; capsule splits three ways; stem 1–3" [25–75 mm]. Alp/subalpine gravels and crevices.

Thread-leaved sandwort, *Arenaria capillaris* (air-en-**air**-ee-a: sand—; cap-il-**air**-iss: hair-leaved). Several flowers; basal leaves ¾–1¼" [2–3 cm], dense; stem leaves ⅜–¾" [1–2 cm], 4–10; capsule splits six ways; stem 2–6" [5–15 cm]. Rocky sites, esp steppe or alpine. MT north.

Arenaria melanocephala of the seashore doesn't look much like *Arenaria capillaris* of the mountains. The first one is a bird. Rules prevent duplicate genus names only when they're in the same kingdom.

Chickweeds

Cerastium beeringianum (ser-**ast**-ium: horn—; be-ring-ee-**ay**-num: for Graf von Beering). Petals white, each with two round lobes; styles usually 5; calyx 5-lobed; flowers 1–6 per stem; leaves oblong, ¼–1" [6–25 mm], opposite, but most of them crowded in a basal-seeming mat; entire plant sticky-hairy; 4" to (rarely) 10" tall [10–25 cm]. Alp/subalpine.

C. arvense (ar-**ven**-see: of fields) =*C. strictum* CO. Nearly identical; typically leggier and not sticky. All elevs. Caryophyllaceae or Alsinaceae.

Starwort

Stellaria americana (stel-**air**-ia: star—). Also **American chickweed.** Petals white, ¼–⅜" [6–10 mm], deeply notched; sepals pointed; green parts sticky-hairy; leaves opposite, ± oval, stalkless; stems lax, plants low or prostrate. Alpine rocks; MT, Waterton. Caryophyllaceae or Alsinaceae. Color p 107.

Pyrolas

Also **wintergreens, shinleafs.** Usually in moist forest. Pyrolaceae or Ericaceae.

Heart-leaved pyrola, *Pyrola asarifolia* (**peer**-a-la: small pear, ref to leaf shape; a-sair-if-**oh**-lia: wild-ginger leaf). Petals spreading, pink to red, style strongly downturned; flowers 8–25 on a 6–16" [15–40 cm] stalk; leaves evergreen, dark, basal, long-stalked, round to heartshaped, 1–3" [2.5-7.5 cm].

Greenish pyrola, *P. chlorantha* (clor-**anth**-a: green flower). =*P. virens.* Petals spreading, white to greenish or yellowish; style downturned; flowers 2-8; leaves basal, stalked, nearly round, ± fine-toothed, 1–2" [2.5–5 cm], often paler above than beneath; stem 3–8" [8–20 cm]. Esp common in AB.

White-veined pyrola, *P. picta* (**pic**-ta: painted). Petals spreading, pale, greenish to purplish, style downturned; flowers 5-20 on a reddish, 4–12" [10–30 cm] stem; leaves evergreen, basal, egg-shaped, 1–3" [2.5-7.5 cm], dark green, white-mottled along the ± pinnate veins (compare Rattlesnake-plantain, p 185). Illustrated.

Pyrolas are mysterious and interesting at first glance, and all the more so when you know they demonstrate a transition in the evolution of non-green plants, and in human science regarding non-green plants.

(Page 188.) When the West was first botanized, reports came back of totally leafless but healthy specimens otherwise resembling the familiar genus *Pyrola* (It's hard to identify pyrolas to species without benefit of leaves.). These were formally named *P. aphylla*, but later they turned out to be other pyrola species in "degenerate" form. Apparently individual pyrolas may hover at the threshold of non-greenness. As a young forest matures around one of these plants, competition for light and water intensifies; the weaker individuals die and the stronger ones jettison any leaves that aren't in a position to pull their own weight. That applies to trees, shrubs, and subshrubs alike, but for a period (foresters call it the stem exclusion phase) most of the survivors are the taller trees; the forest floor can get pretty bare, and pyrolas, small orchids, and non-green plants—all of which get most or all of their carbohydrates from the tree canopy via mycorrhizae—become conspicuous.To some pyrolas, apparently, it's the *leaf* exclusion phase: they let their leaves atrophy, and fall back on their fungal partners to deliver all the photosynthate. They can regrow leaves another year if a few trees die, bringing back better light conditions. The evolution of non-green plants may well have included a stage just like that, and then taken the next step: loss of the ability to photosynthesize.

Single Delight

Moneses uniflora (mo-**nee**-sees: single delight; you-nif-**lor**-a: one flower). =*P. uniflora*. Also **wood nymph**. Flowers single, ½–1" [12–25 mm], waxy-whitish, fragrant; petals flat-spreading; pistil fat, straight, 5-tipped (like a chess rook); leaves oval, usually toothed, ½–1¼" [12–30 mm], from lower ¼ of 2–6" [5–15 cm] stem; often on rotting wood. Pyrolaceae or Ericaceae (see fn, p 190). Illustrated at right.

Both *Moneses* and *Orthilia* were long included in genus *Pyrola*.

One-sided Pyrola

Orthilia secunda (or-**thill**-ia: straight, small; se-**cun**-da: with flowers all to one side). =*P. secunda*. Flowers greenish white, bell-shaped, with long straight style, 5–15 all facing ± the same way; leaves 1–2½" [25–60 mm], variably egg-shaped, running up the lower half of the 3–7" [8–18 cm] stems from rhizomes. Pyrolaceae or Ericaceae. Illustrated at left.

Herbs: 5 separate petals, 10 stamens

St.-John's-Worts

Hypericum (hi-**per**-ic-um: Greek word for it, meaning "under heath"). Flowers deep yellow, orange in bud; stamens showy, as long as the petals; capsule 3-celled; leaves opposite, oval to oblong, ± clasping-based, with tiny translucent spots ("perforations") visible against light. Clusiaceae (=Hypericaceae).

Common St.-John's-wort, *H. perforatum*. Also **Klamath weed.** Many flowers, in a ± flat-topped cluster; petals often edged with tiny black dots; sepals narrow, 3× to 5× longer than wide— stems 1–3' [30–90 cm]. Roadsides, rangeland; European weed.

Western St.-John's-wort, *H. scouleri* (scoo-ler-eye: after John Scouler, p 66). =*H. formosum*. Few flowers; sepals oval, less than 3× longer than wide— stems 4–24" [30–90 cm]. Wet soil, esp low subalp; Crowsnest south. Illustrated above, and color p 109.

The Old-World St.-John's-wort was gathered as a spell for St. John's Eve, June 23. It's now an abundant roadside weed in the West and its flowers are a popular herbal treatment for depression. There is good evidence that they are effective in mild cases, but not for serious chronic depression. As with other herbals, the dosage and side effects are poorly known. (Rigorous testing, after all, is the chief difference between herbal medicines and prescription drugs, most of which originated as herbal compounds.) St.-John's-wort contains photosensitizing toxins, meaning they leave eyes and sensitive skin prone to severe reactions to bright sunlight. These made Klamath weed a killer weed, inflicting serious losses of sheep and cattle in Oregon and California in the early 1920s and '30s. Between the 1940s and 1960s, biological pest control got one of its first wins, using an introduced beetle to delete Klamath weed from the West's Worst Weeds top ten list. Despite the much-touted success story, in the Okanagan Valley the weed is increasing even with the beetle around.

Dwarf Raspberries

Rubus spp. (**roo**-bus: Roman word for them, based on 'red'). Toothed compound leaves; thornless stems 1–6" [3–15 cm]. Moist forest from Glacier n and w. Rosaceae.

Nagoonberry, *R. arcticus.* =*R. acaulis* (WY), *Cylactis arctica* (CO). Petals pink, spreading flat; fruit red raspberry-like; 3 rounded leaflets; no runners. Meadows or moist forest; also disjunct in nw WY. Color p 110.

Dwarf raspberry, *R. pubescens* (pew-**bess**-enz: downy). Also **dewberry.** Petals white to pinkish, erect, ⅛–¼" [3–6 mm]; sepals bent back; fruit a small, deep red blackberry; 3 (rarely 5) pointed leaflets; trailing stems downy.

Strawberry bramble, *R. pedatus* (ped-**ay**-tus: 5-leafleted). Petals white; fruit of 1–5 glossy red 1-seeded drupelets ¼" long [6 mm]; 5 leaflets; from smooth, ± woody runners. Color p 110.

Though they vary a lot, these berries at their best miniaturize the essence of raspberry flavor as perfectly as wild strawberries do the essence of strawberry.

Wild Strawberries

Fragaria spp. (fra-**gair**-ia: the Roman term). Petals white to pink-ish, nearly circular, ¼–½" [6–12 mm]; sepals apparently 10; stamens 20–25; berry up to ½" long [12 mm]; leaves 3-compound, toothed coarsely and ± evenly, on hairy leafstalks; 3–8" tall [7–20 cm], with long reddish runners. Open forest and aspen groves to sub-alpine basins. Rosaceae.

F. vesca (**ves**-ca: thin). Most leaves minutely hairy on top, ± bulging between veins; seeds on surface of berry. Illustrated.

F. virginiana (vir-gin-ee-**ay**-na: of Virginia). Most leaves smooth and flat on top; seeds imbedded in pits on berry surface. Color p 109.

Close kin of these morsels are served in the most famous restaurants in France. Mountain tribes also used the leaves and roots, mainly as poultices and as antidiarrheal teas.

Prairie Smoke

Geum triflorum (**jee**-um: Roman word for it; try-**flor**-um: three-flowered). =*Erythrocoma triflora* (CO). Also **purple avens**, **old-man's-whiskers**. Flowers usually pendent, in threes, dull reddish, 1" long [25 mm], vase-shaped, scarcely opening; petals yellow to pink, mostly hidden by the 5 reddish sepals and 5 bracts; seeds long-plumed; leaves mostly basal, finely cut (fernlike), hairy; 8–16" tall [20–30 cm]. Prairies, meadows at all elevs. Rosaceae. Color p 109.

Alpine Avens

Geum rossii (**ross**-ee-eye: after Capt. James Ross, explorer of both Poles, who first collected this flower in the High Arctic). =*Acomastylis rossii* (CO). Flowers 1–4, saucer-shaped, ½–1" diam [12–25 mm]; yellow petals fall soon fall off, leaving green (or purple-tinged) flowers of 5 true sepals alternating with 5 narrower bracts; leaves mainly basal, pinnately compound, the larger leaflets again deeply 3–5-lobed; stems rise 2–10" [5–25 cm] from extensive mats of leaves. Tundra from OR, c ID, and MT Bitterroots south. Rosaceae. Color p 109.

Alpine avens dominates great expanses of tundra, especially in south-ern Montana. Its unusually high storage capacity for carbohydrates in its roots helps it survive the occasional extra-poor (or heavily grazed) growing season. It is also one of the first plants to reestablish

Many scientific names around the West honor U.S. Army officers who commanded parties exploring the West in the 1850s and 60s: Capt. **John Gunnison**, killed by native warriors in 1853; Lt. **Robert S. Williamson**, survivor of an attack that killed his commanding officer in 1849; Lt. **Amiel Weeks Whipple**, who explored in 1853-54; Lt. **Joseph Christmas Ives** in 1857; Col. **William F. Raynolds** in 1860; and Capt. **Clarence King** in 1867. While their primary mission was to find the best routes for railroads to connect the East to California's gold, Congress also wanted to know about the Rockies, and sent scientists and even artists on these expeditions.

Geologist John Strong Newberry (who described Newberry Caldera, Oregon) collected the first specimen of Ivesia while under Lt. Ives' command, leading me to suspect the name Ivesia chiefly honors him rather than the usually-cited Yale professor Eli Ives. En route to picking Ivesia, Ives and Newberry ascended the Colorado River through the Grand Canyon, making Newberry the first geologist there, eleven years before John Wesley Powell. I would have wanted to return a favor to Lt. Ives, too!

Clarence King was a geologist, not a soldier at all, yet at the age of 25, apparently on the strength of sheer meteoric charisma, he was commissioned as a captain and given Army funding for a major expedition for which he was invited to write his own orders! Later he became the first head of the U.S. Geologic Survey. His was the first Army expedition to include a photographer (Timothy O'Sullivan), perhaps seeking to correct the melodramatic, romanticized image of the Rockies that easterners were getting from painter Albert Bierstadt. "What has Bierstadt done," King fumed, "but twist and skew and distort and discolor and belittle and be-pretty this whole doggoned country? Why, his mountains are too high and slim; they'd blow over..."

One day a man showed up barefoot asking for work. King hired him as a dishwasher and muleskinner. When the expedition's botanist fell ill, this man, Sereno Watson, took over plant collecting duties; he turned out to be a Yale medical graduate who had blown off a career as a doctor to wander the West. His collections on the King expedition led him back to Harvard and the eminent Asa Gray, who groomed Watson to succeed him at the pinnacle of America's botany establishment. Even there, Watson remained reclusive.

The era of post-Army exploration began with professor **Ferdinand Vandiveer Hayden**, who first saw Yellowstone as Colonel Raynolds's geologist, but returned in 1871 (and many more times over the next fifteen years) with his own purely scientific expeditions, the "Hayden Surveys," funded by the Interior Department.

a claim on barren "gopher blowouts" (page 000). Broad adaptability surely contributes to its abundance: in the Colorado snow depth study (sidebar, next page), it was found growing in every depth category, with greatest frequency smack in the middle.

Ivesia

Ivesia gordonii (ive-zia: see opp page; gor-**doe**-nee-eye: after A. Gordon, p 000). Yellow petals peek from between greenish-yellow sepals; flowers in ball-shaped clusters; leaves basal, 1–4" [2–10 cm], pinnately compound, bottlebrush-shaped, with ⅛–¼" [3–6 mm] segments; leaflets and sepals finely hairy; stem 2–7" [5–18 cm]. Mainly alpine. WY, sw MT, c ID, OR. Color p 109.

Partridgefoot

Luetkea pectinata (**loot**-key-a: after Count Lütke, p 000; pec-tin-**ay**-ta: cockscomb—, ref to leaf shape). Flowers white to cream, ¼" diam [6 mm], in a compact raceme on a± woody 3–6" [8–15 cm] stem; leaves ± persistent, finely dissected into about 9 narrow lobes, mostly basal from runners or rhizomes; carpet-forming. Alp/subalp, Bitterroots north. Rosaceae.

Silverweed

Potentilla anserina (po-ten-**til**-a: small but mighty, ref to medicinal uses; an-ser-**eye**-na: of ducks). =*Argentina anserina* (USDA, CO). Petals yellow, sepals apparently 10; flowers 1" diam [25 mm], single on 1–5" [2–13 cm] leafless stalks from rosettes of pinnate leaves; tiny leaflets alternating with saw-toothed bigger ones; spreads by runners, these and under- (rarely both) sides of leaves densely silver-haired. Gravel bars, wet meadows, disturbed ground, foothills to subalpine. Rosaceae. Color p 109.

The Blackfoot used silverweed runners to tie up leggings and bundles. The long taproots were an important food for many tribes.

Cinquefoils

Potentilla spp. Petals shallowly dished at tip; 5 true sepals alternate with 5 shorter bracts (illust); leaves mainly basal, compound; leaflets 1–1½" [25–38 mm], coarsely toothed to narrow-lobed. ± sunny sites at all elevs. Rosaceae.

Early cinquefoil, *P. concinna* (con-**sin**-a: well crafted). Petals yellow; stem and leaves gray-woolly; basal leaflets 5 or 7; stems sprawling. Illustrated.

Blueleaf cinquefoil, *P. diversifolia* (div-er-sif-**oh**-lia: varied leaf). Petals yellow;

5 or 7 leaflets up to 1½" [4 cm] long, with long teeth, but not near base, smooth or minutely downy. Alp/subalpine, abundant. Color p 109

Slender cinquefoil, *P. gracilis* (grass-il-iss: slender). Petals yellow; 5–9 leaflets at least 1¼' [3 cm] long; with long teeth all the way to base, strongly grayish underneath; 6–18" [15–45 cm] tall. Mid-elev grasslands. Illustrated.

Littleleaf cinquefoil, *P. brevifolia* (brev-if-oh-lia: short leaf). Petals yellow; basal leaves parsleylike, with many tiny lobes, forming a ± dense cushion. Alpine; OR, ID, WY, and extreme s MT.

Tall cinquefoil, *P. arguta* (arg-you-ta: sharp-toothed). =*Drymocallis arguta* (CO). Petals cream white; flowers held tightly together on erect branchlets; leaves pinnately compound; 16–40" tall [40–100 cm].

Sticky cinquefoil, *P. glandulosa* (glan-dew-lo-sa: with sticky hairs). =*Drymocallis glandulosa* (CO). Petals white to yellow; basal leaflets 5–9 (illust); plant sticky, usually hairy, 6–18" tall [15–45 cm].

Cinquefoil species are hard to identify; many are highly variable as to leaf shape, hairiness, and habitat. As a group they can be mistaken for buttercups until you spot the bracts.

Buttercups

Ranunculus spp. (ra-**nun**-cue-lus: froglet). Petals glossy yellow; seeds in a conical head; stem 3–8" [7–20 cm]. Ranunculaceae (Buttercup family).

Sagebrush buttercup, *R. glaberrimus* (gla-**bear**-im-us: smoothest). Leaves not toothed; basal ones elliptical k, larger stem leaves 3-lobed. Sagebrush to (rarely) alpine, from Banff s. Color p 545.

Snow Depth Specialties

Most alpine plants are adapted to specific snow durations and depths. Shifts in vegetation could be a good indicator of climate trends, once we have a database correlating snow with particular species. Skip Walker's research team has measured depth and duration over many winters at an array of alpine sites in Colorado. Their list shares many of our species. Here I adapt it, adding [in brackets] a few species that Walt Fertig suggests from study of the Beartooth Plateau.

0–10 inches optimal winter maximum depth

Dense spikemoss	Moss-campion
Goldflower	Spike woodrush
[Cushion phlox, *P. pulvinata*]	[Sheep fescue]

10–20 inches

Curly sedge	Pixie goblets (lichen)
Arctic sandwort	Map lichen
Alpine clover, *T. dasyphyllum*	Worm lichen

Snow buttercup, *R. eschscholtzii* (ess-**sholt**-zee-eye: after J. F. von Eschscholtz, p 000). Leaves variably 3-lobed to 3-compound. Similar *R. adoneus* (also called snow buttercup, and sometimes treated as a subspecies) has very finely cut leaf lobes less than ⅛" wide [3 mm]. Abundant in wet alp/subalpine meadows. Illustrated.

Plantain-leaf buttercup, *R. alismifolius* (a-liz-mif-oh-lius: water- plantain leaves). Leaves elliptical, smooth or shallowly toothed, never deeply lobed or compound. Wet meadows; OR, ID, far w MT.

Buttercups are called *Ranunculi* ("littlest frogs") for being small and green around the edges of ponds. They are called buttercups for the peculiar waxy (cutinous) sheen of their yellow petals—your first clue for telling buttercups from cinquefoils (above). The surer clue is that buttercups lack the five sepal-like bracts (two, flanking a sepal, are illustrated on page 243).

Snow buttercups are good solar trackers, bending to face the sun as it crosses the sky. Their sensors and bending mechanism are in the upper stem, which will bend with the sun even if the flower has been clipped off. Tracking to focus the sun's heat on the flower's sexual organs dramatically improves the fertility of the pollen. It may also help attract insects that need to bask (see page 154).

Buttercup stem juices are blistering irritants. Mountain tribes used them as arrowhead poisons and also (cautiously, I imagine) as poultices for sore joints, toothaches, etc.

20–40 inches
Rocky Mtn. sagewort
Alpine daisy
Arctic willow

Holm's Rocky Mtn. sedge
Arctic gentian
Alp-lily

40–80 inches
Alpine avens
Marsh-marigold

American bistort

80–120 inches
Tufted hairgrass
Haircap moss, *P. piliferum*
Snow buttercup, *R. adoneus*

Sibbaldia
Yellow Indian paintbrush
Pygmy bitterroot

120–160 inches
Parry's alpine clover

160–220 inches
Parry's primrose
Arctic bluegrass

Drummond's rush

Herbs: 5 petals, 15+ stamens

245

Columbines

Aquilegia spp. (ak-wil-**ee**-jia: Roman word for them, from either "water carry" or "eagle," ref to claw-shaped flower). Flower shape unique: petals form a cup in front, a long spur behind; petal-like spreading sepals; leaves 9-compound with round-lobed leaflets, most basal, stalked. Alp/subalpine moist crevices, meadows; mid-elev openings. Ranunculaceae or Helleboraceae. Color p 110.

Colorado blue columbine, *A. coerulea* (see-**rue**-lia: blue). Flowers large, white (or sepals blue, rarely); spurs 1–2" long [2–5 cm]. WY, sw MT, c ID.

Yellow columbine, *A. flavescens* (fla-**vess**-enz: yellowish). Flowers yellow.

Red columbine, *A. formosa* (for-**mo**-sa: beautiful). Sepals and spurs red, petal cups yellow. OR, BC, ID, Jasper, Beartooths, Absarokas.

Limestone columbine, *A. jonesii* (jones-ee-eye: after Marcus E. Jones). Alpine dwarf 2–5" tall [5–12 cm]; flowers light blue, spurs ⅜" [1 cm]; leaflets thick, grayish, fuzzy, tiny, very crowded in a mosslike cushion. Limestone terrain; Waterton s. Illustrated.

July 5, 1845. The flowers very large and beautyfully white, with varieties shaded a clear light blue—In my opinion It is not only the Queen of Columbines, but the most beautyful of all herbaceous plants—I never felt so much pleasure in finding a plant before.
August 27, 1845. After a short search I found the Columbine I so much desired… The seed vessels were about half emptied by the wind—I collected seeds until it became dark, & commenced again the next morning as soon as it became sufficiently light…

> It takes off a great deal of the pleasure of collecting knowing as I do that Mr. Geyer passed through this country in the seed season. (Joseph Burke; see page 000.)

Oh, the fickle pleasures of a plant hunter!

The shape of columbine flowers is unmistakable; the colors vary. The Colorado state flower is blue and white in Colorado, but most often all white in our range. Yellow columbine may be flushed with pink after messing around with red *A. formosa* where their ranges meet. Being interfertile, columbine species that occur together owe their separate identities to the color preferences of different pollinators. White-lined sphinx moths flying at dusk see white best, and are the pollinator *A. coerulea* evolved for; their tongues are exactly long enough to reach the nectar at the tip of the spur. Where the same species is blue it is hedging its bets, attracting both sphinx moths and bumblebees. Bees have to nip the bulbous spur-tip to get the nectar; they go around to the front door for pollen. Hummingbirds and some bees are most drawn to the red/yellow combination.

Mountain Hollyhock

Iliamna rivularis (ili-**am**-na: a mystery name; riv-you-**lair**-iss: of brooks). Also **streambank globemallow**. Flowers pale pink or lavender, 1½" diam [4 cm], in tall hollyhocklike clusters; leaves palmate-lobed, maple-like, 2–6" [5–15 cm]; robust herbs to 6' tall [180 cm]. Streambanks, ditches, disturbed clearings; Crowsnest south. Malvaceae (Mallow family). Color p 110.

Growing from long-buried seeds, mountain hollyhock occasionally produces spectacular displays a couple of years after a severe fire.

Globemallows

Sphaeralcea spp. (sfee-**ral**-sia: globe mallow). Flowers orange to brick red, 1–1½" diam [25–40 mm], in short spikelike clusters; petals heart-shaped; leaves alternate; plant hairy. Prairie, steppe, ponderosa pine forest. Malvaceae.

S. munroana. Calyx subtended by 3 tiny linear bracts; leaves oval in outline, with teeth and shallow lobes; 8–30" tall [20–75 cm]. ID, OR, sw MT.

S. coccinea (coc-**sin**-ia: scarlet). Calyx without bracts; leaves deeply narrow-lobed, or palmately compound; 4–8" tall [10–20 cm]. WY, MT e of Missoula, Canada s of Crowsnest. Color p 110.

Herbs: 5 petals, 2 sepals

Springbeauties

Claytonia (clay-**toe**-nia: after John Clayton). Petals ¼–½" [6–13 mm], slightly notch-tipped; 5 stamens; 2 sepals; stem leaves 2, opposite, ½–3" [12–75 mm], lanceolate to elliptic. Portulacaceae).

Western springbeauty, *C. lanceolata* (lan-see-o-**lay**-ta: nar- - - rowleaved). Petals white (rarely yellow, in e ID) usually with fine pink stripes; stems 3–6" [8–15 cm], ± succulent, hollow, weak, several-flowered, basal leaves few or none; from a bulbous root. Meadows and forest at all elevs, esp subalpine. Illustrated at right.

Alpine springbeauty, *C. megarhiza* (mega-**rye**-za: big root) Petals pink to white; basal leaves numerous, fleshy, spoon-shaped; stem leaves small, occasionally lacking; stems numerous, ± recumbent, often reddish; from a long taproot. Alpine rocks. Illustrated below, and on color p 111.

Western springbeauty exemplifies a strategy based on timing. It begins growing at its bulb tip in September, when many neighbors are dying back. During winter, insulated to just below freezing by soil and snow, the shoot

---

inches up to the soil surface. Few plants are active at such low temperatures; all are arctic/alpine specialists.

As soon as the snow melts away from the shoot in spring, springbeauty bursts to its full height of three or four inches [10 cm], expending in a few days its disproportionately large reserve of starches. It can even push through the last inch or two of snow by combusting some of the starch to melt itself a hole. It uses its thin-fleshed hollow stem as an internal greenhouse. When stored carbohydrates are burned off during the quick burst of growth, some of the heat produced is retained in the stem, making the internal air temperature warm enough for photosynthesis even when the outside air is not. Waste carbon dioxide from respiration stays inside, available for synthesis into new carbohydrates. It can complete its life cycle in two to four weeks—blooming, setting seed, and photosynthesizing like mad to store up starches for the next spring. Then it withers, existing only underground for late July and August.

Some plants on this schedule—called "spring ephemerals"—live on semiarid land with just a few well-watered weeks following snowmelt. Others, in lush subalpine meadows, use the stepped-up timing to jump the gun on big leafy plants that monopolize the light later in the season. Springbeauty succeeds in both of those situations.

With their concentrated starches, springbeauty bulbs are good survival forage. They taste radishy. Unfortunately, they're depleted when in bloom and hard to locate at other times, so leave them in peace unless starvation impends. They were a major food item for first nations in interior BC, and still are one for marmots and voles.

Miner's-Lettuce

Montia spp. (after Giuseppe Monti). Petals ⅛–½" [3–6 mm], white or pink with pink veins; sepals 2, unequal; stamens 5; stem 2–10" [5–12 cm], ± succulent, several-flowered; spreading by runners. Wet places in forest. Portulacaceae (Purslane family).

M. parvifolia (par-vif-**oh**-lia: small leaf). Leaves basal, and smaller ones alternate. MT, ID, OR, BC, Waterton.

M. chamissoi (sha-**miss**-o-eye: after A. von Chamisso, p 000). =*Crunocallis chamissoi* (CO). Leaves opposite. WY, sc MT, and west. Illustrated.

Forty-niners learned to eat miner's-lettuce to avert scurvy, the vitamin C deficiency disease. Luckily for them, they had larger, tenderer members of the genus to work with.

If there's just one whorl of petals/sepals, they're sepals by definition, no matter how colorful or tender. Technically, then, no flowers have 5 petals and no sepals, but quite a few appear to. Parsley family flowers have a vestigial whorl or fleshy ring barely perceptible below the 5 petals. This ring is a calyx, but its lobes are so reduced ("obsolete") as to be indetectable. In valerian, sepals unfurl only as the flower goes to seed, so they can't be seen on the bloom.

Valerians

Valeriana (va-lee-ree-ay-na: strong—, ref to medicinal potency). Corolla white, 5-lobed; 3 stamens; calyx seemingly lacking; each seed grows a little parachute of plumes; foliage rankly aromatic, esp when drying out or frostbitten in the fall; 1–4' tall [30–120 cm]. Valerianaceae.

Sitka valerian, *V. sitchensis* (sit-ken-sis: of Sitka, AK). Flowers ⅜" [1 cm], tubular, slightly asymmetrical, initially pink; terminal inflorescence rounded, 1–3" wide [2–8 cm]; lower ones smaller, in opposite pairs; leaves opposite, compound; leaflets usually 3 or 5, pointed-oval, vaguely toothed. Subalpine meadows, moist montane forest; all exc WY. Seed, flower, and whole plant illustrated.

Tobacco-root, *V. edulis* (ed-you-lis: edible). Flowers ⅛" [3 mm], flaring, in a tall, narrow, loose panicle; basal leaves 3–16" long [8–40 cm], most of them simple and quite narrow, though a few may be divided into linear leaflets, as are the few pairs of small stem leaves. Open forest, meadows; all exc AB. Color p 111.

Western valerian, *V. occidentalis* (oc-sid-en-tay-lis: western). Flowers ⅛" [3 mm], flaring, in one round-topped head ½–1¼" wide [1–3 cm]; leaves both basal and opposite, untoothed, either simple and pointed-oval or pinnately 3–11-compound. Diverse habitats up to low-subalpine meadows; ID, MT, WY. Color p 111.

Valerian root recently regained its ancient reputation as an herbal tranquilizer and mood elevator. The Blackfoot and Okanogan sometimes spiked smoking mixtures with leaves of Sitka valerian, which today fetches some of the highest prices paid to commercial foragers, leading to local overharvesting. "It is most effective," writes herbalist Michael Moore, "when you have been nervous, stressed, or become an adrenalin basket case, with muscular twitches, shaky hands, palpitations, and indigestion." Thanks, I'll be sure to remember that.

Mountain tribes used tobacco-root roots as poultices on bruises and wounds, and also ate them. Poisonous raw, they became a favorite vegetable after cooking for a day or two. Whites gave them mixed reviews, at best. Captain Frémont found them "rather agreeable," provided he was sufficiently famished, but his cartographer called them "the most horrid food he had ever put in his mouth." Tastes like chewing tobacco, smells like stinking feet.

As snowmelt releases the subalpine meadows, deep red-tinged shoots of Sitka valerian soon shoot up abundantly. The redness disappears as the foliage matures, lingering longest in the budding flowers but disappearing as they mature to white. Most redness in plants comes from anthocyanin ("flower blue"), a complex carbohydrate pigment that may be red, blue, or anywhere in between; it shifts between red and blue like litmus paper, depending mainly on acidity.

Anthocyanin is suspected of several functions in high elevation plants. First, it filters out ultraviolet radiation, which can be at least as hard on plant tissue as on human skin. Ultraviolet is most intense at high altitude, where there is less atmosphere to screen it, and most intense when sunlight peaks, at the summer solstice. In June the high country is still snowbank-chilled, and plant tissues young and tender, so that's where and when anthocyanin is brought out.

Second, while reflecting ultraviolet radiation, it also seems to absorb and concentrate infrared radiation, heating the plant.

Third, anthocyanin is an interim form for carbohydrates on their way up from winter storage. To bloom and fruit early in their short growing season, high-country plants must store huge quantities of carbohydrates in their roots, and then move them up fast after snowmelt, or even before (see springbeauty, page 000). In de-reddening, valerian stuffs itself with preserves from the root cellar.

Bistorts

Polygonum (pa-**lig**-o-num: many "knees" or stem joints). =*Bistorta* spp. (CO). Flowers white, small, chaffy, fetid, in a dense head; 5 unequal calyx lobes; no petals; 8 unequal stamens; stem leaves few, ± linear, sheathing; basal leaves much larger (3–6", or 7–15 cm,on 3–6" leafstalks), elliptical; stem unbranched. All elevs; but esp in alp/subalpine meadows. Polygonaceae (Buckwheat family).

American bistort, *P. bistortoides* (bis-tor-**toy**-deez: like European bistort). Flower spike often ½" [12 mm] or wider, almost as wide as tall; 8–30" tall [20–40 cm]. Color p 111.

Alpine bistort, *P. viviparum* (viv-**ip**-a-rum: giving birth to live young, ref to bulblets in place of flowers). Flower spike narrow, its width averaging about one-third of its height, or ⅓" [9 mm], with tiny pink bulbs in place of flowers in the lower portion. Illustrated.

The flowers stink, probably to draw flies, but bears and elk eat the roots and shoots, respectively, and so did the Blackfoot and Cheyenne.

Poke Knotweed

Polygonum phytolaccifolium (fight-a-lackey-**foe**-lium: leaves like poke). =*Aconogonum phytolaccifolium*. Flowers tiny, white or greenish,in big long-branched panicles; 5 unequal calyx lobes; no petals; 8 unequal stamens; leaves white-veined, heavy, pointed-oval, 2–6" [5–15 cm]; stem has a big brownish sheath next to each leaf base; stems clustered and branched, stout, 2–6' tall [60–180 cm]. Alp/subalpine meadows with a history of overgrazing; OR to w MT. Color p 111.

Biscuitroots

Lomatium spp. (lo-**may**-shum: hem—, ref to seed margins). Also **desert parsleys**. Apiaceae (Parsley family). Flowers tiny, in many ½" [12 mm] balls (like fireworks) on unequal rays from top of stalk; leaves lacy, much compounded. Open, often rocky slopes. Apiaceae (Parsley family).

Cous, *L. cous* (cows: Nez Perce word for it). =includes *L. montanum*. Flowers yellow; each ball-like flower cluster subtended by an involucre of often purplish, ± oval, ⅛–¼" [3–6 mm] bracts; leaves variable; plant 4–14" [10–35 cm]. US. Illustrated.

Sandberg's biscuitroot, *L. sandbergii* (**sand**-berg-ee-eye: after John H. Sandberg). Flowers yellow to orange; leaves ¾–3" long in total [2–8 cm], with 3 branches each twice-pinnate, with tiny ± linear leaflets; plant from almost ground-hugging to 12" tall [30 cm]. Alp/subalpine gravels; n ID and ne MT, n to Crowsnest. Color p 111.

Narrowleaf desert-parsley, *L. triternatum* (try-ter-**nay**-tum: thrice divided in 3). Flowers yellow; leaves at least 3×3 compound, the leaflets threadlike, rather soft, ½–4" long [1–10 cm]; plant 8–16" [20–40 cm]. Low to mid-elev dry meadows. Color p 111.

Chocolate-tips, *L. dissectum* (dis-ec-tum: finely cut). Flowers purple-brown or yellow; leaves at least twice pinnate, the leaflets very slender; stem hollow, often purple, 20–60" [50–150 cm]. Low to mid-elevs, Banff south.

Lomatium, which also includes plants called hog-fennel and desert-parsley, is a large and tricky genus in a large and tricky family. The parsley family includes carrots (called "Queen Anne's lace" when growing wild), parsnips, celery, fennel, and dill.

Though it's often hard to identify species in this family, it's usually easy to pick them as members of the family. Most bear "umbels," umbrella-shaped inflorescences in which many flower-stalks branch from one point subtended by bracts; in most genera (including this one) these stalks in turn bear "umbellets" subtended by "bractlets." Leaves are often filigreelike (twice- or thrice-dissected). The family's robust taproots range in edibility from the many garden vegetables to deadly poison hemlock. Some tribes reportedly ate young chocolate-tips roots, but others poisoned fish and lice with them. Cous roots were the chief vegetable of some Columbia Basin tribes. The risk of deadly mistakes forbids my recommending them, but Yellowstone grizzly bears apparently have no trouble getting the i.d. right: cous provides them a major diet component for a period of early summer.

Yampah

Perideridia montana (per-id-er-**id**-ia: with a coat around it; mon-**tay**-na: montane). =*P. gairdneri* (USDA, CO). Flowers white (rarely pinkish), tiny, in flattish inflorescences 1–3" diam [2–8 cm]; seeds ± spherical in outline, with ribs; leaves on stem, of 3–7 linear leaflets 1–6" long [2–15 cm], often withering by flowering time; stem slender, 1–3' [30–90 cm]. Meadows, open forest; Kananaskis s. Apiaceae.

The mild, sweetish tubers of yampah were so popular that Blackfoot kids would dig them up and snack on them while playing, whereas a shaman would carry them at all times and then fake digging them up, using a special bear claw, as a cure for virtually any ailment. They were also popular with Lewis and Clark's men, and with trappers and traders. The tubers smell like parsnips but look quite different, tapering to both ends and often growing two or three per plant. The distinctive grasslike leaflets make i.d. less risky than with other edible parsleys; the one toxic family member in our region with long linear leaflets, *Cicuta bulbifera*, is distinguished by growing in wet ground and by bearing tiny bulbs in some of its leaf axils.

Snowline Spring-Parsley

Cymopterus nivalis (sigh-**mop**-ter-us: wavy wings, ref to seed capsule; niv-**ay**-lis: of snow) =includes *C. bipinnatus.* Flowers minute, white, in several ball-like clusters; leaves blue-gray-coated, basal, once or twice compound, the leaflets minute, forming a mosslike cushion flanked by dried leafstalks of previous years. Rocky sites, foothills to alpine; from nw MT south.

Fernleaf Lovage

Ligusticum filicinum (lig-**us**-tic-um: the
Roman word for it, "Liguria—"; fil-**iss**-in-
um: ferny). Also **licorice-root**, **loveroot**.
Flowers white (rarely pinkish), tiny, in 1–3
flattish inflorescences 1–4" diam [2–10 cm];
leaves lacy, compound in fine linear leaflets;
stem 20–40" [50–100 cm], from a thick taproot. Meadows, open forest; WY, e ID, sw MT.
Apiaceae.(Parsley family).

Sweet Cicely

Osmorhiza spp. (os-mo-**rye**-za: aro-
matic root). Tiny flowers in a loose broad inflorescence; plant fragrant, delicate, 1–4' [30–120 cm]. Crowsnest south. Apiaceae

O. occidentalis (oc-si-den-**tay**-lis: western). Also **sweetroot**. Flowers yellow; seeds slender, without bristles; leaflets, 3, 9, or more, saw-
toothed; stems often clustered; root has strong sweet licorice fragrance. Open slopes, thickets. Illustrated.

O. berteroi (bare-**tare**-oh-eye: after Carlo Giuseppe Bertero). =*O.
chilensis* (CO, and all writing before about 1995). Flowers greenish
white; seeds slender, with bristles that cling to clothing; leaflets
usually 9, oval, toothed, the larger ones often with a few
lobes; mild licorice fragrance; stem solitary. Forest.

Herbalists tout sweetroot as a fungicide, and the
Salish used to smoke it. I would stay away from any
internal use because of deadly relatives (next page).
Sweet cicely seems able to grow in almost any sort of
forest. The Forest Service paper on Montana forest habitats at all elevations divides them into 100 types. *O. berteroi* was found in the sample plots of 87 out of 100, but
covered barely 1½% of the ground.

Bupleurum

Bupleurum americanum (bew-**plu**-rum: "ox rib," Greek word for some plant).
=*B. triradiatum*. Also **American thorow-wax**. Flowers yellow (or purplish),
tiny, in several small balls on ray stalks from top of stem; each ball, and also the
whole inflorescence, is subtended by a whorl of pointed-elliptical bracts; leaves
simple, untoothed, narrow, up to 6" long by ⅜" wide [15 by 1 cm], progressively
smaller upward; 2–12" tall [5–30 cm]. Tundra, dry meadows, rock outcrops; US,
Waterton. Apiaceae (Parsley family). Color p 111.

Poison Hemlock

Conium maculatum (co-nium: Greek word for it; mac-you-**lay**-tum: spotted).
Flowers white, tiny, in flattish inflorescences 2–3½" diam [5–9 cm]; larger leaves
lacy, compound, commonly 6–12" long [15–30 cm]; leaflets typically pinnate-lobed;
stem purple-splotched, at least near base, 2–8' [60–240 cm]. **Deadly poisonous.**
Roadsides, ditches; European weed. Apiaceae (Parsley family). Illust above right.

Water Hemlock

Cicuta maculata (sick-**you**-ta: Roman word for some poisonous parsley; mac-
you-**lay**-ta: spotted). =*C. douglasii* (CO. Most northern Rockies populations
were determined in 1980 to belong to *C. maculata* of eastern NA, rather than
the very similar *C. douglasii* of the Pacific NW, where they had long been
placed. Both species are common in e BC.). Flowers white (or greenish), tiny,
in flattish inflorescences 2–5" diam; leaves usually thrice-compound; leaflets 5×
longer than wide, 2–5" by ½–3" [5–12 by 1–7 cm], toothed, leaf veins directed at
the notches, not the tips; stem base forms a thick hollow bulb with several horizontal partitions; stem 2–7' [60–210 cm]. **Deadly poisonous.** Streamsides,
marshes, below 8,000' [2450 m]. Apiaceae (Parsley family). Illust above left.

Known in England as cowbane. "Early in the spring, when livestock
that have been confined to a barn are first turned out to pasture, they
may pull up and eat the whole base of the plant. One is enough."
(*Intermountain Flora*). Serving as judge, jury, and executioner, this
hemlock and the one (below) that killed Socrates have made careless
plant foraging a capital offense in the West. Even Native American
children were sometimes poisoned when they used hollow hemlock
stems, mistaken for cow-parsnip, as pea shooters. While there are
strong differences between the hemlocks and their sought-after rel-

atives—cow-parsnip, biscuitroots, and yampah—the gravity of the risk demands absolute focus on plant identification. (And stops me from recommending any wild foods in the parsley family.)

Cow-Parsnip

Heracleum lanatum (hair-a-**clee**-um: the Greek term, after Hercules; lan-**ay**-tum: woolly). =*H. maximum* (USDA, BC), *H. sphondylium* (CO, WY). Flowers white; one to several inflorescences nearly flat, 5–10" diam [12–25 cm], petals near edge of inflorescence much enlarged, 2-lobed; stamens 5; 3 huge leaflets 6–16" wide [15–40 cm], palmately lobed and toothed; stems juicy, aromatic, hollow, 3–10' [1–3 m]. Moist thickets; all elevs. Apiaceae. Illustrated p 254 center.

Cow-parsnips, avidly eaten and widely eradicated by cows, are also browsed by wild herbivores. The fetid flowers draw flies. Native Americans ate the young stems, either raw or cooked but always peeled first to remove a weak toxin which causes skin irritations in reaction to sunlight; they taste milder and sweeter than the rank odor leads you to expect. Poultices and infusions of the leaves and the purgative roots held high repute as medicines.

Angelica

Angelica arguta (an-**jel**-ic-a: angelic, ref to medicinal power; arg-**you**-ta: sharp-toothed). Flowers white (or pinkish), tiny, in flattish inflorescences 3–6" diam [7–15 cm]; leaves usually twice-compound; leaflets scarcely 2× longer than wide, 2–5" × ½–3" [5–12 × 1–7 cm], toothed; stem 2–7' [30–210 cm]. Flowers attract beetles. Moist ground in forest. Apiaceae.

Herbs with 4 petals

Skunk-cabbage, p 171, is a 4-merous monocot. Leafy spurge, p 000, has a tiny 4-lobed involucre but no petals or sepals. Stonecrops, p 236, usually have flower parts in fives here, but occasionally in fours.

Willow-Herb

Epilobium anagallidifolium (ep-il-**oh**-bium: upon pod; ana-gal-id-if-**oh**-lium: with leaves like *Anagallis*). =*E. alpinum*. Flowers deep to pale pink, nearly flat, ¼–½" diam [6–12 mm], usually 2–4 per stem, nodding when in bud; 4 petals, 2-lobed; 4 sepals and 4 stamens borne at the tip of a very slender maroon ovary; the ovary matures into a maroon seedpod that

---

splits into 4 spirally curling thin strips, releasing tiny downy seeds; leaves narrowly elliptical, ¼–1" [6–24 mm], all on stem; stems red, 2–10" [5–25 cm], in sprawling patches from runners. Two taller and straighter relatives with minutely toothed leaves are combined with this one as *E. alpinum* in some texts. Moist alp/subalpine sites. Onagraceae (Evening-primrose family).

Fireweeds

Chamerion spp. (ca-**me**-ree-on: dwarf oleander, in shortened form). = *Epilobium* spp. (BC, AB). Flower/seed structures as in *Epilobium*. Onagraceae.

Fireweed, *C. angustifolium* (ang-gus-tif-**oh**-lium: narrow leaf). =*C. danielsii* (CO). Flowers pink to purple, nearly flat, 1¼–2" diam [3–5 cm], blooming progressively upward in a tall conical raceme; leaves 3–6" × ¾" [8–15 by 2 cm]; plant 3–8' tall [30–240 cm]. Abundant in avalanche tracks and basins, recent burns, clearcuts, etc. Color p 112.

River beauty, *C. latifolium* (lat-if-**oh**-lium: wide leaf). =*C. subdentatum* (CO). Also **dwarf fireweed, red willow-herb.** Flowers deep pink to purple, nearly flat, 1–1½" diam [25–38 mm]; leaves 1–2" × ½–¾" [25–50 by 12–20 mm]; 3–24" tall. River bars (esp e of CD) to alpine talus. Color p 112.

With its copious plumed seeds that fly in the wind, fireweed is a major invader of burns, from Rocky Mountain clearcuts to bombed urban rubble in Europe. If that makes it a "weed," so be it, but it is native, beautiful, nutritious, and a poor long-term competitor, yielding its place to later-successional plants after a few years. Unlike many pioneer herbs, it is a perennial, and seems to require mycorrhizal partners. Lacking them, fireweed seedlings on deep Mt. St. Helens ash in 1981 weakened and died without flowering.

Fireweed does persist indefinitely in the north, beautifying vast areas of Alaska too severe for trees. It was mainly northerly tribes that ate its inner stems as a staple food in spring. (Caution: may prove laxative.)

Tufted Evening-Primrose

Oenothera caespitosa (ee-**noth**-er-a: Greek word for some relative; see-spit-**oh**-sa: in clumps). Also **sand lily, moon-rose, rock-rose,** etc. Petals 1–1½" [25–38 mm], white, turning rose-purple, fragrant, blooming around sunset then withering within 24 hours; flowers up to 5" high [12 cm], reaching that height entirely on the basal tube of the calyx from a base below ground level; calyx lobes narrow, sharply bent back; seedpod woody, 1–2" [2–5 cm], splitting 4 ways; leaves basal, oblanceolate, 4–8" [10–20 cm], raggedly toothed. Gravel roads and dry clay soils, foothills to (rarely) alpine; US (and on plains in AB). Onagraceae (Evening-primrose family). Color p 113.

Sphinx moths come to pollinate this sensuous lady of the night.

Ragged Robin

Clarkia pulchella (clar-kia: after William Clark, below; pool-**kel**-a: most beautiful). Unique flowers of 4 fuchsia petals ± asymmetrically presented, each with 3 squarish lobes on a long slender base; calyx bent back, often all 4 lobes together on one side; 4 fertile + 4 stunted stamens; ovary like a long swollen flower stalk; leaves all on stem, linear, ¾–3" [2–8 mm]; plant annual, several-flowered, 4–24" [10–40 cm]. Sagebrush and ponderosa pine; c ID, w MT, Teton County WY. Onagraceae. Color p 112.

Kittentails

Synthyris spp. (**synth**-er-iss: fused doors). Corolla pale blue to lavender, unequally 4-lobed, ⅜" [1 cm], in small racemes; 2 stamens protrude somewhat; leaves basal, 1–2" [2.5–4 cm]. Scrophulariaceae (Figwort family).

Featherleaf kittentails, *S. pinnatifida* (pin-a-**tif**-id-a: with finely cut leaves). Stems to 8" [20 cm]; leaves finely pinnate-lobed. Alpine; WY, sw MT, c ID. Illustrated.

Mountain kittentails, *S. missuricus* (miz-**oo**-ric-us: of the Missouri R). Stems to 12" [30 cm]; leaves round to kidney-shaped, with coarse blunt teeth. ne OR, c ID.

Meriwether Lewis and **William Clark**'s voyage of 1804–06 is so well known it needs no lengthy description here. Less well known is that biological discovery, not exploratory heroics, was its greatest distinction. After all, Alexander Mackenzie had crashed on through to the Pacific at Bella Coola in 1789, but he and others in the Northwest were interested in little but profiting from furs. Though not scientists by profession, Lewis and Clark were briefed intensively on natural history, taxidermy, cartography, etc, before they set out. And they did their natural history well. Lewis rivalled Douglas and Nuttall in the number of first collections of Western plants credited to him, and far surpassed them in writing down all he could learn from the tribes he met about the plants—often going so far as to try out Native American medicinal treatments on his men.

The medicine Lewis really needed was a good antidepressant. Near the Continental Divide, the apex of his great adventure, he turned 32 and reflected, "I have in all human probability now existed about half the period which I am to remain in this Sublunary world. I have as yet done but little, very little, indeed, to further the hapiness of the human race or to advance the information of the succeeding generation. I view with regret the many hours I have spent in indolence..." Hardly.

His mysterious death just four years later may have been murder, but his friend Thomas Jefferson believed it was suicide.

Veronicas

Veronica spp. (ver-**on**-ic-a: from a Greek term). Also **speedwell**. Corolla blue-violet with yellow center, unequally 4-lobed, nearly flat, ⅜" diam [1 cm]; in a small raceme; leaves opposite; stem 2–12" [5–30 cm]. Scrophulariaceae (Figwort family).

V. wormskjoldii (vormsk-**yol**-dee-eye: after Morten Wormskjold). =*V. nutans* (CO). Style and stamens shorter than petals; leaves lanceolate, ½–1½" [12–38 mm]. All elevs, but mainly alp/subalpine, often where moist; all exc AB.

V. cusickii (cue-**zick**-ee-eye: after William Cusick). Style and stamens longer than petals; leaves lanceolate, ½–1½" [12–38 mm]. Mainly alp/subalpine, often where moist; BC, WA, OR, ID, MT. Color p 113.

V. serpyllifolia (sir-pil-if-**oh**-lia: thyme leaf). =*Veronicastrum serpyllifolium* (CO). Stamens about as long as petals; leaves elliptical to oval, ⅜–1" [10–25 mm]; stem often partly prostrate. Moist sites below treeline; introduced.

Hairy Clematis

Clematis hirsutissima. (**clem**-a-tis: a vine cutting; her-sue-**tea**-sim-a: very hairy). =*Coriflora hirsutissima.* (CO). Also **leatherflower, vaseflower, sugarbowls**. Unique nodding vase-shaped flowers, 1 per stem, consisting of four heavy, recurved petal-like sepals ranging from rich indigo to drab gray-brown; sepals, stems, and leaves all gray-haired; leaves much-dissected, fernlike; 8–20" tall [20–50 cm], in clumps. Dry lowlands; all exc AB. Color p 112. Ranunculaceae (Buttercup family). Color p 112.

Meadowrue

Thalictrum occidentale (tha-**lic**-trum: the Greek term; ox-i-den-**tay**-lee: western). Sepals 4 (or 5), greenish, ¼" [6 mm]; petals lacking; flowers many, in sparse racemes, male (illustrated above) and female (below) on separate plants, the males with numerous stamens of long yellow anthers dangling loosely by purple filaments; females less droopy, with several reddish pistils that mature into a starlike rosette of capsules; leaves twice- or thrice-compound, leaflets ¾–1½" [2–4 cm], round-lobed (similar to columbine); plants 20–40" [50–100 cm]. Open forests to subalpine meadows. Ranunculaceae or Thalictraceae. Color p 113.

I often see male meadowrues associating exclusively with other males, and females with females—an apparent inefficiency which I cannot explain.

Smelowskia

Smelowskia calycina (smel-**ow**-skia: for Timotheus Smelovskii; cay-lis-**eye**-na: with a calyx). Flowers cream white or purple-tinged, ⅜–¾" diam [1–2 cm], several, in roundish clusters; sepals fall off when flower opens; leaves crowded, basal, 1–4" [2–10 cm], pinnately compound or -lobed, gray-fuzzy; low mat or cushion plants. Alpine. Brassicaceae (Mustard family). Color p 113.

Wild Pennycress

Thlaspi montanum (**thlas**-pie: Greek word for some cress; mon-**tay**-num: montane). =*Noccaea montana* (WY, CO), *T. fendleri*. Also **candytuft**. Petals white or pink, ¼" [6 mm], spoon-shaped; 4 wee sepals; flower clusters at first broad-topped, becoming tall and open as first flowers go to seed; basal leaves spoon-shaped, ¾–2" [2–5 cm]; stem leaves much smaller, linear, clasping stem; hairless plants 1–12" tall [2–30 cm], in small clumps. In sun, foothills to alpine; US. Brassicaceae (Mustard family). Illustrated.

Cushion Draba

Draba spp. (**dray**-ba: Greek word for some cress). Flowers yellow, ¼" [6 mm], in small clusters; 6 stamens; seedpods elongated; leaves and stems hairy; few or no stem leaves; basal leaves crowded, paddle-shaped, mostly ¼–½" [6–12 mm]; above the mat of leaves rise a few 2–8" [5–20 cm] stems. Alpine rocks. Brassicaceae. Color p 113.

Easily half a dozen species of draba fit the above description, and others yet are similar but white-flowered, or similar but taller and less matted. Telling them apart requires a lens strong enough to see the branching patterns of the hairs. Even scientific papers often punt.

Twinpod

Physaria didymocarpa (fiz-**air**-ia: bellows—; did-im-o-**car**-pa: twin fruit). Flowers yellow, ½" [12 mm], somewhat flaring, in small clusters, on short ± prostrate stems; seed pods inflated into 2 bulbous lobes, each with 4 seeds; leaves blue-silver with fine hairs, thick, spoon-shaped but often slightly toothed so as to form a distinctive spade shape, in a spiralling rosette. Dry gravels, often alp/subalpine. Brassicaceae (Mustard family). Color p 104.

Wallflowers

Erysimum spp. (er-**iss**-im-um: Greek word for them). Petals round; flowers many, in a round-topped cluster; seedpods very narrow, splitting in 2; leaves 2–5" [5–12 cm], narrow, most in a basal rosette, a few on the stem, sometimes shallowly toothed; plant grayish-hairy. Hot dry grassy spots, mainly low. Brassicaceae.

E. capitatum (cap-it-**ay**-tum: flowers in heads). =*E. asperum* (BC, AB, WY). Also **prairie rocket**. Petals ¼–½" [6–12 mm], brilliant yellow, less often orange; 12–40" tall [30–100 mm]. Crowsnest south. Color p 113.

E. inconspicuum. Petals ⅝–1" [15–25 mm], yellow; 12–40" tall [.3–1 m]. Illust.

Bunchberry

Cornus unalaschkensis (**cor**-nus: horn; oona-lash-**ken**-sis: of Unalaska, AK). =*C. canadensis* (USDA, BC, AB, WY), *Chamaepericlymenum canadense* (CO). Also **ground-dogwood**. True flowers tiny, 4-merous, in a dense head ½–¾" diam [12–20 mm] surrounded by four white bracts, ½–1" [12–25 mm] long, often mistaken for petals; ; berries red-orange, several, 1-seeded, ¼" diam [6 mm]; leaves pointed, oval, 1–3" [2–7 cm], in a whorl of six beneath each inflorescence, and in whorls of four on flowerless stems (technically 4-leafleted basal leaves) nearby; stems 2–8" [5–40 cm], from rhizomes. Moist forest. Cornaceae (Dogwood family).

Why does this flower—a mere six-inch subshrub—look so much like a dogwood flower? Because the dogwood tree is the bunchberry's closest relative.

Northern Bedstraw

Galium boreale (**gay**-lium: milk—, ref to old use for clabbering cheese; bor-ee-**ay**-lee: northern). =*G. septentrionale* (CO). Corolla white, 4-lobed, flat, ¼" diam [6 mm]; true flowers tiny, 4-merous, in a dense head ½–¾" diam [12–20 mm]; 4 stamens out to sides, alternating with lobes; no sepals; flowers many, in a panicle; leaves in whorls of 4, lanceolate, 3-veined, 1–2" long [2–5 cm]; lower axils often bear branchlets with smaller leaves; stems square, 8–32" tall [20–80 cm], from creeping rhizomes. Forest, thickets, meadows, to just above treeline (where dwarfed); often abundant. Rubiaceae (Madder family).

Sweet-Scented Bedstraw

Galium triflorum (try-**flor**-um: three flowered). Corolla white, 4-lobed, flat, up to ¼" diam [6 mm]; sepals lacking; flowers usually in sparse threes branching from leaf axils; leaves in whorls of 5 or 6, narrow-elliptical; stems minutely barbed, four-angled, generally sprawling or clambering, dense. Widespread in forest and thickets. Rubiaceae.

The clinging tangles of weak bedstraw stems are irresistibly easy to uproot by the fistful; they are the plant's way of attaching its seeds to passing animals. Where other plants have barbed fruits for this purpose, bedstraw barbs its entire stem, and breaks off at the roots. It used to get put in straw mattresses to perfume them.

Monument Plant

Frasera speciosa (**fray**-zer-a: after John Fraser; spe-see-**oh**-sa: showy). =*Swertia radiata*. Also **green gentian, elkweed**. Petals pale green, purple-flecked, ½–1" [12–25 mm], oval, spreading almost flat; sepals linear, as long as petals; 4 stamens; flowers whorled in upper leaf axils, forming a massive column; stem leaves lanceolate, in whorls of 3–5; basal leaves oblong, 10–20" [25–50 cm]; flower stalks 2–5' [30–150 cm]; last year's thick broken dry stalks persist through summer. Sagebrush or dry meadows; US from c ID e. Gentianaceae. Color p 112.

The monument plant starts as rosette of few leaves and builds its resources year by year—sometimes over 60 years—until it is strong enough to bloom. Having bloomed once, it dies. Toppling over, it may cover its own seeds, providing shelter that keeps the seedlings moist the next year; in years to come, its own progeny may reuse its nutrients. In this "post-mortem nurture by decomposing parents," monument plant resembles salmon and praying mantids.

Herbs: dicots; 3, 6, or several petals or sepals

Most 3- or 6-petaled flowers are monocots (pp 158–88) with 6 or fewer stamens and a total of 6 petals and sepals; most monocot leaves have conspicuous parallel veins. The dicot plants that follow don't share those characteristics. "Several" means varying (within the 5 to 10 range) from flower to flower. Most *apparently* several-petaled flowers are composites (pp 191–206); their seeming petals are ray flowers.

Yellow Pond-Lily

Nuphar polysepala (**new**-fer: from the Arabic term; poly-**see**-pa-la: many sepals). =*N. lutea* (BC, USDA, CO). Also **wokas**. Four to eight bright yellow, heavy, roundish petal-like sepals 1½–3" long [3–8 cm]; 4 smaller green outer sepals; true petals and stamens numerous, much alike, crowded together around the large parasol-shaped pistil; leaves heavy, waxy, elongated heart-shaped, 6–18" long [15–45 cm], usually floating. Widespread in ponds and slow streams up to about 6' [2 m] deep. Nymphaeaceae (Water-lily family). Color p 112.

Many tribes ate either the spongy rootstocks or the big hard seeds—parched, winnowed, ground up, and boiled into mush—and some still do today. Oddly, Nancy Turner's Okanogan informants said the roots were considered poisonous, while the stems could be used to alleviate toothache. External applications of the mashed roots for pain relief were even more common than food uses.

Recent studies suggest water-lilies are among the closest living relatives of the very first flowering plants that ever evolved.

Gentians

Gentiana spp. (jen-she-**ay**-na: Greek name, honoring King Gentius). Corolla with 4–7 (most often 5) shallow lobes, and fine teeth on the "pleats" between lobes; calyx lobed or not; leaves opposite. Gentianaceae (Gentian family).

Mtn. bog gentian, *G. calycosa* (cay-lic-**oh**-sa: cuplike). =*Pneumonanthe calycosa* (CO). Also **explorer gentian**. Flowers deep indigo blue, single, 1½" tall; leaves blunt oval, ½–1½" [12–38 mm]; stems 3–12" [8–30 cm]. Alp/subalpine wet meadows. Color p 112.

Pleated gentian, *G. affinis* (a-**fie**-nis: related). =*Pneumonanthe affinis* (CO). Flowers blue, 2–3 per stem, 1" tall [25 mm]; leaves lanceolate, pointed; stems 3–12" [8–30 cm]. Diverse sites at all elevs. Plant and inter-petal pleats illustrated at left.

Moss gentian, *G. prostrata.* =*Chondrophylla prostrata* (CO). Flowers blue, wholly or partly pale, single, ½" tall [12 mm], the lobes (most often 4) spreading wide in sun, but quickly closing when shaded; leaves ± oval, clasping, ¼" [6 mm]; stems 1–3" [25–75 mm], often partly prostrate; biennial plant.

Arctic gentian, *G. algida* (al-jid-a: cold). =*Gentianodes algida* (CO). Flowers single, oversized (1½–2" [3–5 cm], ± white with purple streaks; leaves linear, often appearing basal on low plants; 2–8" [5–20 cm] tall. Arctic; WY and s MT. Illustrated at right.

A yellow-flowered European gentian has a long history in herbal medicine, but our species are valued most for their beauty—all the more so in late August and September, when other subalpine flower shows are over. The flowers tend to close up when shaded by clouds, or when chilled, effectively saving pollen from getting splashed away during summer storms.

Buckwheats

Eriogonum spp. (airy-**og**-a-num: woolly joints). Calyx 6-lobed; petals lacking; stamens 9; flowers in round clusters, small, on short stalks coming out of a conical involucre with or without lobes; leaves basal. Rocky dry places, alpine to steppes. Polygonaceae (Buckwheat family). Each species varies as to hairiness, flower color, etc., in this large genus, so i.d. will be tentative at best.

Cushion buckwheat, *E. ovalifolium* (oh-val-if-**oh**-lium: oval leaf). Flowers cream, becoming rose-edged; leaves densely matted, silvery white all over (mainly OR) or ± green on top, often quite round on alpine plants; one flower cluster, including several tiny green involucres close together, per 1½–7" [3–8 cm] stem. Color p 114.

Yellow buckwheat, *E. flavum* (flay-vum: yellow). Flowers bright yellow or orange-tinged; several flower clusters on stalklets that meet at a whorl of leaves; leaf blades 4–6 times longer than wide; leaves usually hairy on both sides, forming wide mats; stems 2–8" [5–20 cm].

Sulphur-flower, *E. umbellatum* (um-bel-**ay**-tum: flowers in umbels). Also **umbrella plant**. Flowers cream or reddish to bright yellow; stalklets of the several flower clusters meet at a whorl of leaves whose stem may meet others at a lower whorl; leaves usually almost smooth on top, fuzzy white beneath; leaf blades 3✕ longer than wide; stems 4–12" [10–30 cm]. In late summer the leaf mats turn into lovely mosaics of red, green, white, and cream. Color p 114.

Matted buckwheat, *E. caespitosum* (see-spit-**oh**-sum: in clumps). Flowers yellow, becoming rose-edged; leaves densely matted, grayish green, fuzzy; one flower cluster, cupped in one green involucre with long bent-back lobes, per 1–3" [25–75 mm] stem. US.

Sorrel

Rumex acetosa ssp. *alpestris* (**roo**-mex: Roman name for it; a-see-**toe**-sa: vinegary). =*Acetosa alpestris*. Flowers brick red, tiny, in 4–8" [10–20 cm] panicles; 6 sepals, but only 3 conspicuous ones; no petals; pistils and stamens on different plants; leaves narrowly arrowhead-shaped, the lower ones to 4" long [10 cm] on longer stalks; one or several unbranched stout stems 10–40" [25–100 cm] tall. Moist sites, to alpine elevs. BC, AB, Glacier, Beartooths, Absarokas. Polygonaceae (Buckwheat family). Illustrated.

Garden sorrel, subspecies *acetosa* from Europe, sometimes escapes. Our native subspecies is just as tasty, but overdosing on the oxalic acid can upset your stomach.

Starflowers

Trientalis spp. (try-en-**tay**-lis: ⅓, implying 4" height?). Flowers white to pink, 1 to few, ½" diam [12 mm]; petals, sepals and stamens each 5–8 (most often 6); leaves pointed-oval; capsule spherical; 3–8" tall [8–20 cm]. Primulaceae (Primrose family).

T. arctica. =*T. europaea arctica* (USDA). Leaves up to 2" [5 cm], smaller downward along the stem. Bogs; BC, AB, n ID.

T. latifolia (lat-if-**oh**-lia: broad leaf) =*T. borealis latifolia* =(USDA). Leaves 1½–4" [4–10 cm], in a single whorl. Moist forests; BC, AB, n ID. Illustrated.

Marshmarigold

Caltha leptosepala (**cal**-tha: goblet; lep-toe-**see**-pa-la: slender sepals). =*Psychrophila leptosepala* (CO); =includes *C. biflora*. Sepals 6–11, white, petal-like, ½–¾" [12–20 mm], often a few of them 2-lobed; petals lacking; stamens and pistils many; flowers usually two, on a forked 3–10" [8–25 cm] stem; leaves basal, kidney-shaped, 2–4" wide [5–10 cm], on 2–3" [5–8 cm] leafstalks, ± fleshy, edges

± scalloped, often curling. Alp/ subalp streamsides, boggy meadows. Ranunculaceae or Helleboraceae. Color p 114.

Pasqueflowers

Anemone (a-**nem**-a-nee: Greek word for it, after Na'man,
a name of Adonis). Also **windflowers**. Sepals 5–9, petal-
like; petals lacking; many stamens and pistils; usually 1
flower per stem exc in *A. multifida*; leaves palmately twice- or
thrice-compound, mainly basal, long-stalked; one whorl
of smaller leaves at midstem. Ranunculaceae.

Prairie crocus, *A. patens* (**pay**-tenz: spreading).
=*Pulsatilla patens* (USDA), *P. ludoviciana* (CO). Sepals blue or purple, ¾–1½" [2–4 cm], flowering early,
before leaves unfurl; stem later grows to 6–16" [15–40
cm]; styles grow to ¾–1½" [2–4 cm], feathery, in a
round head, as seeds mature; plant covered with long
white hairs. All elevs; exc OR. Color p 114.

Towhead baby, *A. occidentalis*. (ox-i-den-**tay**-lis: western).
=*Pulsatilla occidentalis* (USDA, CO). Sepals white, ½–1¼" [1.2–3
cm], appearing early, before leaves unfurl; stem later grows to 1–2'
[30–60 cm]; styles grow to 1–1¾" long [25–45 mm], feathery and
droopy, as seeds mature; plant covered with stiff white hairs; basal leaves fernlike. Subalpine; all exc WY. Illustrated in flower above; in seed on color p 114.

Cutleaf anemone, *A. multifida* (mul-**tiff**-id-a: many cuts) =includes *A. teton-
ensis* (USDA, WY). Sepals 5–6, ⅜" [1 cm], color highly variable: from magenta
inside and out to blue, cream, or pink (most authors emphasize white, with some
tint on outside of petals); flowers after leaves unfurl; styles less than ⅛" [3 mm];
seed heads woolly, round, ⅜" diam [1 cm]; stem ± silky-haired, 5–20" [12–50
cm], often 2–4-branched above leaf whorl. All elevs. Color p 114.

Fellfield anemone, *A. drummondii* (drum-**on**-dee-eye: after Thomas Drummond, p 155) =includes *A. lithophila* (USDA, WY, AB). Sepals 6–9, ⅜" [1 cm], ±
white, often blue outside, flowering after leaves unfurl; styles ⅛" [3 mm]; seed
heads woolly, round, ⅜" [1 cm]; stem ± silky-haired, 4–10" [10–25 cm], not
branched above base. Alp/subalpine.

Rocky Mountain tribes were aware of toxins in these bitter plants.
Some used them to kill fleas; others inhaled their aromas or their
smoke as a remedy for headaches and colds. Crushed leaves were
used to stop nosebleeds or as a poultice for skin problems—which
seems perverse, since they can blister skin.

The most strangely lovely of subalpine "flowers" is actually the
seed head of the towhead baby. It looks like something Dr. Seuss
would have dreamed up. The flower attracts less attention, blooming early when the plant is only 2–6" [5–15 cm] tall and lingering
snow is keeping most hikers away.

Globeflower

Trollius albiflorus (**tro**-lius: trollflower, the German word for it; al-bif-**lor**-us: white flower). =*T. laxus* (USDA). Sepals 5–12, petal-like, white or greenish, often aging yellow; petals lacking; many stamens and pistils; 1 flower per stem; dry seedpods form a tight goblet-shaped head; leaves of 5 or 7 long palmate lobes, irregularly toothed, mainly basal and long-stalked, plus one at midstem; stem hairless, 8–16" [20–40 cm]. Wet soil near melting snow, mid-elevs, and higher. Ranunculaceae or Helleboraceae. Color p 114.

Baneberry

Actaea rubra (ac-**tee**-a: elder, for the similar leaves; **roob**-ra: red). Numerous ¼" [6 mm] white stamens are the showy part of the flower; 5–10 petals (occasionally lacking) white, smaller than the stamens; 3–5 sepals petal-like but falling off as the flower opens; flowers (and berries) in a ± conical raceme; berries ⅜" diam [1 cm], glossy bright red (or occasionally pure white); leaves 9 to 27-compound, leaflets pointed-oval, toothed and lobed, 1–3" [2–8 cm]; stem 16–40" [40–100 cm]. Lower forests. Ranunculaceae or Helleboraceae.

These, our most poisonous native berries, are less than deadly. A handful could render you violently ill, but even a small taste should start you spitting fast enough to save your stomach the trouble.

Goldthread

Coptis occidentalis. (**cop**-tiss: cut—; oc-sid-en-**tay**-lis: western). Petals and sepals similar, each 5–8, greenish white, threadlike, ⅛–⅜" long [3–10 mm]; petals (the shorter ones) with a tiny gland on a broad spot near the base; stamens many; long-stalked basal leaves of 3 leaflets, each toothed and ± lobed, shiny, evergreen; roots bright yellow beneath their bark; stems 4–8" [10–20 cm]. Moist shady forest, from nw MT and n ID north. Ranunculaceae.

Goldthread solutions were long used for mouth sores in both European and native cultures. There do seem to be promising antibiotics present—and a potential threat of overexploitation.

Wild Ginger

Asarum caudatum (**ass**-a-rum: the Greek word for it; caw-**day**-tum: tailed). Calyx brownish purple, with three long-tailed lobes 1–3" [2–8 cm]; petals lacking; 12 stamens ± fused to the pistil; flower single on a prostrate short stalk be-

---

tween paired leafstalks; leaves heart-shaped, 2–5" [5–12 cm], finely hairy, spicy-aromatic, rather firm and often persistent, on hairy 2–8" [5–20 cm] leafstalks. Moist forests. Aristolochiaceae (Birthwort family).

This odd plant we call wild ginger is unrelated to ginger, and even the tangy fragrance isn't really close, yet its stems as a seasoning found favor with cooks of trapping, pioneering, and wild-food stalking eras alike. The earthbound, camouflaged flowers are less fragrant. They attract creeping and crawling pollinators.

Bitterroot

Lewisia rediviva (lew-**iss**-ia: after Meriwether Lewis, p 257; red-i-**vie**-va: revived, ref to Lewis's dried original specimen, which grew when replanted years later in Philadelphia). Flowers pink, apricot, or white, 2–2⅜" diam [5–6 cm], borne very low to ground, one per stem in small clumps; 10–18 petals and 5–9 sepals both showy; leaves basal, linear, initially fleshy but usually withered by time of flowering. Arid gravels, mainly at lower elevs; all exc AB. Portulacaceae (Purslane family—for now; see footnote, page 215). Color p 114.

It's easy to see why this dramatic bloom is Montana's State Flower and was a favorite of Meriwether Lewis. He found it on the banks of "Clark's River," now called the Bitterroot. When he tried eating the roots, though, he found them nauseatingly bitter. The Salish nation prized them above all plant foods, but used several methods to minimize bitterness: digging them in spring when the leaves first appear; digging only from certain locales—especially the lower Bitterroot Valley—known to produce relatively mild roots; discarding the core of the root; or eating them after a year or two in storage. The root is small and the plant sparse (and must have been sparser still where it was heavily picked) so it took a few days to fill a bag. Each year when bitterroot was first dug, Salish and Kootenai bands held one of the year's biggest feast events, the First Roots ceremony.

Pygmy Bitterroot

Lewisia pygmaea. =*Oreobroma pygmaeum* (CO). Petals 6–8, pink to white (sometimes greenish), ¼–¾" [6–10 mm]; two sepals, several stamens; leaves basal, linear, to 3" long [8 cm]; stems mostly 1-flowered, 1–3" [2–8 cm], with a midstem pair of tiny bracts. Rock crevices, alp/subalpine gravels. Color p 114.

6
Ferns, Clubmosses, and Horsetails

The old term "vascular cryptogams" defines this informal group of plants. "Vascular" means having vessels, or veins—tiny tubes for conducting water and the vital materials that water can dissolve. Vessels are tiny, but have conspicuous effects. Without them, a plant can't raise its vital fluids more than a few inches from its moisture supply. Nonvascular cryptogams (mostly mosses and liverworts) are necessarily diminutive, while ferns and horsetails are taller, typically 6" to 60" [15 to 150 cm]. In the Mesozoic era, before seed plants took over, forests of fern and clubmoss "trees" dominated the land. Today's clubmosses are short enough to confuse with mosses, but still have plumbing like their arborescent forebears.

"Cryptogam" ("hidden mating") means that the sexual process in these plants is tiny and brief compared to the showy flowering and fruiting of seed plants, and doesn't produce seeds capable of extended dormancy or travel. The traveling function is left up to an asexual stage in the cryptogam life cycle—a one-celled spore. (Genetically, plant spores are more like pollen than like seeds.)

On ferns, "sori"—clusters appearing as tiny spots, lines, or crescents on the leaf underside—release the dustlike spores. Each sorus may have a tiny membrane shielding it, or rolled-under leaf margins may shield rows of sori. Each frond and its stalk from the rhizome is a leaf; it is pinnately compound, or divided into "pinnae." While a pinna may be again compounded one or more times, pinnae are always the units branching directly from the central stalk.

Western Polypody

Polypodium hesperium (poly-**poe**-dium:
many feet, referring to the blunt rhizome branchlets;
hes-**per**-ium: western). Leaves 3–12" [8–30 cm], green
through winter, dark, smooth; pinnae broadly round-
tipped, often not separated all the way to the stalk;
sori large, ± round, exposed. Moist, shaded rock
surfaces in ID, MT, BC. Polypodiaceae.

These dark, leathery leaves last all winter,
but often fall short of lasting all summer.
New leaves sprout with the fall rains. The
roots taste of licorice, with a moment of
sharp sweetness, then a bitter aftertaste. The
related licorice fern, *P. glycyrrhiza,* enters our
range in the Clearwater valley. Licorice proper,
Glycyrrhiza glabra, is not a fern at all, but shares
some chemistry ("glycyrrhizin," naturally).

Holly Fern

Polystichum lonchitis (pa-**lis**-tic-um:
many rows; lon-**kigh**-tiss: spear—). Leaves
6–24" [15–60 cm], dark, leathery, once-compound, in
clumps; pinnae (illustrated above) asymmetrical at
base, finely toothed, the teeth sharp and curved forward; stalk bases have long scales; sori round (illust lower left). Rock crevices, mid-elevs to
subalpine; mainly w of CD. Dryopteridaceae.*

Sword Fern

Polystichum munitum (mew-
nigh-tum: armed). Leaves
20–60" [50–150 cm], dark, leathery, once-compound, in huge clumps; each pinna asymmetrical at
base, with an upward-pointing coarse tooth; stalks
densely chaffy; sori round. Moist forest in BC, extreme

*Dividing the ferns into families is a work in progress. The
ones given here follow FNA. WY uses different names for the
same groupings; CO splits them much smaller. (See page 610.)

Lace Ferns

Cheilanthes spp. (kye-lanth-eez: margin flower). Also **lip ferns**. Leaves 3–10" [8–25 cm] tall, slender, evergreen, pale, at least twice compound, in clumps; leaflets tiny, reddish-woolly underneath, with margins rolled under, covering the sori. Rocky sites in sun. Pteridaceae.

C. gracillima (gra-**sil**-im-a: slenderest). Stalks have narrow scales, not hairs. On igneous rocks, almost entirely well w of CD. Illustrated.

C. feei (**fay**-eye: after A. L. A. Fée). Stalks have sparse hairs. On calcareous rocks.

Not all ferns are particularly moisture-demanding. The little lace fern and the two that follow are drought-tolerant, living almost exclusively in crevices of cliffs and rockpiles.

Brewer's Cliff-Brake

Pellaea breweri (pel-**ee**-a: dark—; **brew**-er-eye: after Wm. H. Brewer). Leaves 2–8" [5–20 cm] tall, slender, evergreen, only once compound; upper pinnae simple, oblong; lower pinnae deeply, unequally 2-lobed, mitten-shaped, or rarely 3-lobed; margins rolled under, covering the sori; stalks shiny dark brown, easily snapping off at any of several visible articulations near the bottom; leaves usually far outnumbered by snapped-off old stalk bases. Rock crevices; ID, WY, w MT. Pteridaceae.

American Parsley Fern

Cryptogramma acrostichoides (crypto-**gram**-a: hidden lines; across-tic-**oy**-deez: top row—) =*C. crispa*. Also **rock-brake**. Vegetative leaves 3–8" × 2–4" broad [8–20 × 5–10 cm], rather leathery, firm, yellow-green, at least twice compound, in clumps; fertile leaflets on 7–12" [17–30 cm] stalks, slender, tightly rolled (illustrated). Dry rocky sites in sun, all elevs. Pteridaceae.

Parsley fern has spore-bearing leaves very different from its vegetative leaves—often twice as tall, but fewer, and not fine-toothed and parsleylike as the sterile vegetative leaves are.

Ferns: evergreen

Cascades Parsley Fern

Cryptogramma cascadensis. =C. crispa. Leaves thin, withering in fall; otherwise like the preceding. Dry to fairly moist sites in mountains. ID, BC, and extreme w MT. Pteridaceae. Not illustrated.

Fragile Fern

Cystopteris fragilis (sis-**top**-ter-iss: bladder fern, ref to the covering of the sorus; fra-**jil**-iss). Also **bladder fern**. Leaves 5–14" [12–35 cm], twice or thrice compound; strung out along the rhizome rather than truly clumped; stalk slender, somewhat translucent; sori enfolded in a membranous sheath a bit like a wall sconce (illustrated; this is the positive way to tell it from woodsia, below). Widespread and common; often in ± shady rock crevices with some moisture. Dryopteridaceae.

Fragile fern is all over the map. Not only does it grow all across the continent, but in the Rockies it can grow in sun or shade, on limestone or granite, and from foothill sagebrush to alpine talus. The cheat sheet on Rocky Mtn. fern i.d. says: until proven otherwise, it's fragile fern.

Woodsia

Woodsia spp. (after Joseph Woods). Leaves 3–14" tall [8–35 cm], twice compound; stalks reddish brown, scaly; in clumps together with last year's broken bases; sori initially seen with star-like remnants of their membranous cover. Dryopteridaceae.

Oregon woodsia, *W. oregana*. Leaf undersides hairless; sorus illustrated at left.

Rocky Mtn. woodsia, *W. scopulina* (scop-you-**lye**-na: of the Rockies). Leaf undersides covered with white hairs (illustrated, next to sorus). Talus and other rocky sites.

Spiny Wood Fern

Dryopteris expansa (dry-**op**-ter-iss: oak fern; ex-**pan**-sa: broad). =*D. austriaca.* Also **shield fern**. Leaves 8–36" tall [20–90 cm], broadly triangular, thrice compound, in small clumps; sori round-shielded; stalk bases scaly. Moist forest; YS, w MT, n Id, and n. Dryopteridaceae.

Male Fern

Dryopteris filix-mas (fie-lix-**mahss**: male fern). Leaves 15–40" tall [38–100 cm], narrowing at both ends, twice compound; leaflet margins toothed; stalks and leaflet undersides ± covered with chaffy hair-like scales; sori around a kidney-shaped shield. Moist sites at moderate elevations. Dryopteridaceae.

Medieval herbalists named the lady and male ferns, and prescribed their powdered roots and leaf infusions for jaundice, gallstones, sores, hiccups, and worms. Only since 1950 has male fern as a dewormer fallen from medical favor, replaced, in Leo Hitchcock's words, "by synthetic drugs with a greater margin between the therapeutic and the toxic dose." Native peoples used them medicinally, and ate baked rhizomes of these and other ferns.

Male ferns grow northward to near Banff. North of there you may find the fragrant wood fern, *D. fragrans*, with small dark green leaves and a sweet scent.

Oak Fern

Gymnocarpium dryopteris and *G. disjunctum* (gym-no-**car**-pium: naked fruit). Leaves 6–18" tall [15–45 cm], broadly triangular, thrice compound, rising singly from runners; sori exposed; stalks pale, slightly scaly. Moist forest—the herb-layer dominant in some western hemlock or redcedar stands; less often in full sun, where it tends to be yellowish and ± curled up. Dryopteridaceae.

Oak fern appears to have three similar leaves on each stalk. Technically, this is a single leaf with two

---

basal pinnae, left and right, each nearly as big and as dissected as all the remaining pinnae put together.

A 1993 genetic analysis found *G. dryopteris* to be a case of two branches of the family tree rejoining through hybridization. It separated *G. disjunctum* of the PNW as one of the parent species. This has been widely accepted, but Bob Dorn compared the paper to the eleven herbarium specimens it cited from his own state, Wyoming, and concluded that "the determined specimens are mostly exactly opposite to the key characteristics." If others look, and agree, it may soon be another example of a briefly accepted name change.

Western Maidenhair Fern

Adiantum aleuticum (ay-dee-**an**-tum: not wetted; a-**lew**-tic-um: of the Aleutian Islands). Formerly included in *A. pedatum*, which is now restricted to eastern NA. Leaf blades 4–16" [10–40 cm], fan-shaped, broader than long, twice-compound; sori under rolled edges; stalks black, shiny, wiry. Saturated soil or rocks in shade. Pteridaceae.

This is our easiest fern to identify. Its striking shiny black stalks are our only ones that split into two slightly unequal branches, the pinnae spreading fanlike. Infusions of this fern were used to enhance the black sheen of Native American maidens' hair, yet Anglo sources contend it was the masses of fine dark root hairs that suggested the common name.

Lady Ferns

Lady fern, *Athyrium filix-femina* (ath-**ee**-rium: no shield; fie-lix **fem**-in-a: fern-woman). Leaves 16–50" tall [40–125 cm], narrowing at both ends, twice or 3× compound; sori exposed, (initially shielded on one edge); stalk base scaly. Common on forest streambanks, wet ravines. Dryopteridaceae. Illustrated.

Alpine lady fern, *A. alpestre*. =*A. americanum, A. distentifolium*. As above but smaller (8–32" tall) and more finely incised; sori not shielded by a membrane. Locally dominant in patches of wet subalpine talus.

Bracken

Pteridium aquilinum (teh-**rid**-ium: from the Greek term for fern, derived from "feather"; ak-wil-**eye**-num: eagle—). Also **brake fern**. Leaves 24–80" [60–200 cm] tall, ± triangular, twice to thrice compound, undersides fuzzy; sori under rolled edges. Widespread on ± sunny sites. Dennstaedtiaceae (Bracken family).

Bracken has a the widest native distribution of any vascular plant in the world. No fern grows as tall or as fast; bracken has been measured at 16' [40 cm] in western Washington, and clocked at several inches a day. Though rarely much taller than three feet in the Rockies, it is no less aggressive here. It owes its success partly to "allelopathy," or secretion of chemical compounds that are somewhat toxic to other kinds of plants, and partly to vegetative reproduction, sending numerous new shoots up from the rhizomes. In some burns and clearcuts it seems able to hold off conifer reproduction for years.

Young bracken shoots or "fiddleheads" are sometimes eaten. They taste like asparagus with a dash of almond extract and an unnervingly mucuslike interior. Most Northwest tribes ate bracken fiddleheads or rhizomes, or both. Stockmen, however, list bracken as a poisonous plant. It's true: 600 dry pounds [265 kg] of bracken consumed within a six-week period are enough to kill a horse. Cows are less sensitive, their lethal dose around a ton. They don't graze it eagerly, but if their winter hay is weedy with bracken it can slowly do them in. The toxin, thiaminase, is an enzyme that breaks down vitamin B1, and vitamin B1 is the antidote. Thiaminase is equally toxic to humans, i.e., not very toxic; there is no record of a human stuffing down enough bracken to induce vitamin deficiency.

Unfortunately, deadlier flavonoids lurk here. Bracken has been found to damage chromosomes, and a certain rare stomach cancer has a relatively high incidence in Japan and Wales, two far-flung lands where bracken has long been a popular food. Consume bracken fiddleheads rarely, if at all, as mouth entertainment, not a whole salad; and watch out for the vaguely similar unfurling shoots of monk's-hood, a very toxic plant. (Safe fiddleheads grow on the ostrich fern, *Matteucia struthiopteris,* in wet bottomlands in BC.)

Ferns: deciduous   *273*

Rocky-Mountain Spikemoss

Selaginella densa, *S. scopulorum* and *S. standleyi* (sel-adge-in-**el**-a: from a Roman term; scop-you-**lor**-um: of the Rockies; **stand**-lee-eye: after Paul Standley, who collected and wrote the first Flora of GNP). =All are sometimes treated as varieties of *S. densa*. Spore-bearing portions of stems dull green like the sterile portions, but slenderer and neatly four-ranked; spores ± orange; forms small mats or clumps. Rocky sites, all elevs; abundant in alpine sedge turfs, cushion plant mats, etc. Selaginellaceae.

Clubmosses

Lycopodium and *Diphasiastrum* spp. (lye-co-**poe**-dium: wolf foot; di-fay-zee-**ass**-trum: two-sided). All were included in *Lycopodium* until a recent six-way split. Spore-bearing "cones" straw-colored, usually erect. Stiff clubmoss throughout our range, the others from Bitterroots n and w. Lycopodiaceae.

Ground-cedar, *D. complanatum* (com-pla-**nay**-tum: flattened). Cones ⅝–1¼" [15–30 mm], on branched stalks; foliage flattened, cedarlike, leaves of three distinct shapes in the dorsal, ventral, and two lateral ranks (illustrated at right). Sandy woodland soil.

> **Alpine clubmoss**, *D. alpinum*. Cones ⅜–1" [10–25 mm], arising directly without a stalk from the leafy stem; lateral leaves curled, much larger than the dorsal/ventral leaves (illustrated at right). Alp/subalpine.

> **Ground-pine**, *L. dendroideum* (den-**droy**-de-um: treelike). Cones ⅞–2" tall [22–50 mm], on a few of the many branches of the treelike or shrublike 4–10" [10–25 cm] stalk; leaves needlelike, short. Forests or bog edges. Not illustrated.

> **Running clubmoss**, *L. clavatum* (cla-**vay**-tum: club-shaped). Cones ¾–3" tall [2–8 cm], on long, often branched stalks, from leafy runners. Forest. Illustrated at left.

> **Stiff clubmoss**, *L. annotinum* (an-oh-**tie**-num: marked yearly). Cones ⅝–1⅜" [15–35 mm] tall, on ± crowded, mostly unbranched 4–8" [10–20 cm] erect stalks; leaves shiny, rather stiffly spreading, and long: ¼–½" [6–12 mm]. Usually under conifers. Leaf and whorl of leaves illustrated at right.

Spikemosses and clubmosses behave much like mosses, including their seeming ability to resurrect, when wetted, from a dead-looking dried-up state. Their vessels, however (which mosses lack) enable their leaves to be thicker and more evergreen than moss leaves, so their closest relation is to ferns, and their closest semblance might be to heather or juniper: high elevation clubmosses may go unnoticed among heathers. They bear spores at their leaf bases, but not on all their leaves. Most species have visibly distinct, erect fertile portions loosely termed "cones" terminating some of their branchlets. In club-mosses these are more distinct than in spikemosses.

Of all plant and fungal spores, only clubmoss spores entered commerce, partly because they're easiest to collect. The cones were cut off, dried, pounded, rubbed, and finally sifted to collect the spores, used for centuries to dust wounds, pills, condoms, and babies' bottoms (no joke) and as flash powder. Spores are extremely fine, smooth, slippery, nonreactive (except in the noses of allergy victims), water-repellent, and nonclumping. You may have noticed these qualities in pollen, which descended from spores through evolution.

Pollen and spores need to be water-repellent and nonclumping to maximize air travel, their *raison d'etre*, in the rain.

Horsetails and Scouring-Rushes

Equisetum spp. (ek-wis-**ee**-tum: horse tail). Thickets of hollow vertical stems with many sheathed joints; from blackish rhizomes. Equisetaceae.

Common horsetail, *E. arvense* (ar-**ven**-see: of fields). Reddish tan to almost white spore-bearing stems (illustrated left) come up in early spring, soon wither; 1–3' [30–90 cm] green stems of summer (illustrated above right) have jointed, wiry, whorled branches which you might mistake for leaves, and have 8–10 shallow vertical ridges. Widespread; abundant in saturated ground at all elevs; weedy on roadsides.

Wood horsetail, *E. sylvaticum* (sil-**vat**-ic-um: of forests). Our only horsetail with branches sub-branched; sterile stems 12–28" [30–70 cm], green; spore-bearing stems come up whitish and unbranched, later turn ± green and grow a few whorls of branches. Burns, bog edges, saturated mead-ows. ID, BC, AB. Illustrated at right.

Marsh horsetail, *E. palustre* (pa-lus-tree: of marshes). All stems branched and green (but die back in winter), with 6–10 strong vertical ridges; producing blunt-tipped spore-bearing cones in summer. Typically emergent from shallow water; from Bitterroots n. Illustrated at right.

Smooth scouring-rush, *E. laevigatum* (lee-vig-**ay**-tum: smooth). =*Hippochaete laevigata* (CO). Stems annual, unbranched or rarely with a few branches; most sheaths entirely green; stems smooth or weakly ridged; cone tips blunt. Wet ground, all elevs. Illustrated top left

Scouring-rush, *E. hyemale* (hi-em-**ay**-lee: of winter). =*Hippochaete hyemalis* (CO). Stems evergreen, unbranched, ⅛–½" diam × 1–5' tall [3–12 mm × 30–150 cm], with 18–40 fine vertical ridges; most sheaths show a blackish ring; cones sharp-pointed. Wet ground, low to mid-elevs. Two lower left illustrations.

Long ignored for being primitive, common, and monochromatic, horsetails won their hour of media glory for sending the first green shoots up through Mt. St. Helens' debris of May, 1980. They can crack their way up through an inch of asphalt on highway shoulders. No wonder swimmers felt strong after scrubbing themselves with horsetails! And gardeners feel weak after weeding them.

Leaves on *Equisetum* are reduced to sheaths made up of fused whorls of leaves, often straw-colored, growing from nodes at regular intervals along the stem. On horsetails, whorls of slender green branches grow just below the leaf sheaths, from the same nodes, producing a bottlebrush shape. The branches themselves have little nodes and sometimes little branchlets.

Most tribes ate the new fertile shoots and heads of common and giant horsetail eagerly. They were spring's first fresh vegetable—succulent beneath the fibrous skins which were peeled or spat out. (But beware: like bracken, page 273, horsetails cause thiaminase poisoning in cattle.)

Scouring-rushes (and some horsetails) have been picked worldwide for scouring and sanding—polishing arrow shafts, canoes, and fingernails, for example—thanks to silica-hardened gritty bumps on their skins.

7

Mosses and Liverworts

The nonvascular spore-bearing plants have little ability to conduct water and dissolved nutrients from the substrate up into their tissues; in many of them conduction takes place mainly along the outside of their stems, aided by surface tension. They compensate with an ability to pass water through their leaf surfaces almost instantly, both absorbing it and giving it up easily. After a few dry days in the sun, a bed of moss may be grayish, shriveled and brittle, and look quite dead. But let a little dew or drizzle fall on it, or a little water from your bottle, and see how the leaves revive before your very eyes, softening, stretching out and turning bright green. Again, when the temperature drops below freezing they give up their free moisture to crystallize on their surface, rather than inside where it would rupture cells.

Lichens share many of these characteristics with mosses and liverworts (though unrelated to them) and may lead similar lives. All three grow abundantly on trees and rocks, undergoing countless alternations between their dried-out and their moist, photosynthetically active states. When they grow on trees or other plants they are called "epiphytes" ("upon-plants") meaning that they use a living plant to hold them up off the ground, but draw little or no material out of it.

Mosses that grow on the forest floor stake out a seasonal niche as much as a spatial one, living their active season in spring and—where there is no snowpack—winter. Quick recovery from nightly frost is essential. By summer these mosses are shaded out by perennial herbs and deciduous shrubs, and go largely dormant until fall.

The sexual life cycles of spore-bearing plants evolved before those of seed plants, and are more primitive but emphatically not simpler; they're so complex and varied that I won't even attempt to describe them. Many mosses and liverwort species propagate vegetatively from fragments much more often than from spores. Some produce multicelled asexual propagules called "gemmae," just for this purpose. In mosses and seed plants both (see page 200) adaptation to arctic and alpine climates often entails virtually abandoning sexual reproduction in favor of cloning, either vegetative or by unfertilized spore or seed formation.

The "fruits" of mosses are spore capsules, usually borne on slender vertical fruiting stalks. To release spores, most open at the tip after shedding first an outer cap, the "calyptra," and later an inner lid, the "operculum." Most keys to mosses first separate two primitive families (Sphagnaceae and Andreaeaceae) with spore capsules that don't fit that description at all, and then divide the rest into two growth forms based on where on the stem the fruiting stalks attach:

fruiting from the tip of the leafy shoot, and typically **growing upright** in crowded masses or small tufts; or

fruiting from midpoint(s) along the year's new leafy shoot, which is typically **arching, trailing or pendent.**

Season of fruiting varies with species, but can last several months. Positive identification of most mosses requires not only fruiting specimens but also a microscope and a technical key. The following pages offer tentative identifications of a few common species, with or without the help of a 10× or 12× handlens or monocular. A basic handlens is cheap, and the plant forms it will reveal are gorgeous.

Mosses: upright, fruiting at the tip

Haircap Mosses

Polytrichum spp. (pa-**lit**-ric-um: many hairs). Stems wiry, rarely branched, vertical, in dense colonies; leaves ⅜" average, narrow, inrolling when dry; sheathing the stem at their bases; stem and stalk (or sometimes entire plant) rich reddish; capsule single, 4-angled (after dropping the hairy cap), initially cloaked in a densely long-hairy cap. Polytrichaceae.

P. commune (com-**mew**-nee: common). Leaves finely toothed, long and tapering after a broad sheathing base; capsule held horizontal; shoots often branching, robust: 2–8" + 1–3" stalk [5–10 + 2–8 cm].

P. piliferum (pil-**if**-er-um: hair-bearing). Leaves end in
a whitish translucent hair tip; shoots smaller: ¼–1¼" +
¾–1¼" stalk [6–30 mm + 20–30 mm stalk]. Dry rocky soil.
Illustrated at right.

P. juniperinum (jew-nip-er-**eye**-num; resembling juniper).
Leaves ± bluish-coated, ending in a short reddish hair tip (with
10× lens); leafy shoots 1–4" + 1–2½" red fruiting stalk [3–10 + 2–6
cm]. Sunnier sites, incl disturbed soil, at all elevs. Illustrated at left.

Haircap mosses are palpably more substantial
than other true mosses, almost resembling small
evergreen shrubs like heather or juniper. Their
stems contain a bit of woody tissue, and primitive water vessels. They can even store carbohydrates in underground rhizomes, like higher
plants. The leaves, too, are more complex and
thicker than the translucent, one-cell-thick leaves of
most mosses. Several species of haircaps have
translucent leaf margins that, in drying, curl
inward to protect the chlorophyllous cells.
These traits generally adapt the haircaps to sunny
sites, as well as to human use—the tough stems were
plaited for baskets or twine, and the whole plants used
for bedding. Linnaeus reported sleeping well on a
haircap moss mattress on a trip to arctic Scandinavia.

Bearded Moss

Polytrichastrum alpinum (pa-lit-ric-**ast**-rum: somewhat like
Polytrichum). =*Polytrichum alpinum, Pogonatum
alpinum*. Stems wiry, reddish, ¾–4" tall + ¾–2"
stalk [2–10 + 2–5 cm], unbranched or slightly
branched, vertical, in dense colonies; leaves heavy
but fairly soft, narrow, tapering gradually, fine-
toothed their entire length, the bases clasping the
stem; capsule held somewhat leaning, cylindrical
(not angled) underneath a densely hairy cap. On
moist soil in forest or alpine tundra. Polytrichaceae.

To distinguish this from *Polytrichum* species,
which it often grows near, look for the round
(not angular) capsules and, if you have a handlens, the teeth all along the leaf margins, which it
shares only with the more robust *Polytrichum
commune*.

Mosses: upright, fruiting at the tip

False Haircap Moss

Timmia austriaca (**tim**-ia: after Joachim Timm; aus-**try**-a-ca: of Austria). Stems 1–5" [3–12 cm], red to orange, unbranched, ± erect; leaves ¼" long [6 mm], narrow, fine-toothed most of their length, the bases clasping the stem, often orange-tinged at base and/or at tip; spore capsules nodding to inclined, sparse. Usually in shade, on logs, cliff ledges, etc. Timmiaceae.

Since these leaves are just one cell thick (like most mosses, but unlike the haircap family, above) they are rather translucent, and they crumple up against the stem when dry. The spore capsules, if you can find one, do not have hairy hats.

Alpine Schistidium

Schistidium apocarpum (shis-**tid**-ium: split—; ap-o-**car**-pum: fruiting at the top). =*Grimmia apocarpa, G. alpestris.* Tiny cushions in rock crevices, deep green when wet, drying almost black, with a silvery surface sheen from whitish translucent hair tips on the leaves; stems about ½" [12 mm]; spore capsules usually numerous, much less than ⅛" tall [3 mm], rarely protruding above the leaf tips. On high-elev rocks. Grimmiaceae.

Reflective whitish hair tips on moss leaves, like the silvery hairs all over some higher plants, conserve water on sunny sites by reducing heat absorption. An experiment found them to be 35% effective on a similar *Grimmia*; clumps with all their hair tips clipped off lost half again as much moisture in a day as the unclipped controls. Alpine rock surfaces are ferociously hot habitats—they exceed 150° [66° C] on some summer afternoons.

Frayed-Cap Moss

Racomitrium canescens (ray-co-**mit**-rium: ragged hat; cay-**ness**-enz: grayish-white) and *R. elongatum.* Stems 1–3" [2–8 cm], sprawling in large mats but typically erect near the tips, ± flattened because most of the leaves are on two opposite ranks of short branchlets; spore capsules vertical, on ½" [12 mm] stalks that twist counterclockwise when dry; leaves taper to whitish translucent hair tips that give the whole mat an ash-gray color when dry. In sun, on rocks, sand or gravel outwash, etc; often abundant. Grimmiaceae.

Erect-Fruited Iris Moss

Distichium capillaceum (dis-**tick**-ium: two-ranked leaves; cap-ill-**ay**-shum: hair—). Stems ½–3" tall [3–12 cm], rarely branched, densely packed in clumps; leaves slender, tiny, clasping stem, opposite (i.e. the shoot is flat); lower stem covered with fine reddish-brown rhizoids; capsules erect, smooth, on ⅜–¾" [1–2 cm] stalk. Wet rocks, rotten logs, or streambanks at all elevs. Dicranaceae.

Crisping Cushion Moss

Dicranoweisia crispula (die-cray-no-**vie**-sia: a compound of two other genus names; **crisp**-you-la: leaves crisping). Stems ⅜–1" tall [20–25 mm], dense, forming round cushions or flat carpets; leaves ⅛" [3 mm], yellow-green to dark green, or occasionally blackening, needle-thin and tapered, twisted when dry; capsule is nearly straight and erect, yellow-brown; stalk ½–1" [12–25 cm], yellow-brown. On high-elev rocks (esp granite) or trees. Dicranaceae.

Rosette Moss

Rhizomnium punctatum (rye-zoam-**nigh**-um: moss with rhizoids; punk-**tay**-tum: dotted). Stems 1–2" tall [25–50 mm], unbranched, forming loose mats; leaves egg-shaped, narrowing to the base, from bright to milky green, or sometimes reddish, forming a rosette of very large, broad, to ⅜" long × ¼" wide [10 × 6 mm] leaves at the top, smaller and scattered downward; lowest stem covered with red-brown hairs (rhizoids); fruiting rarely seen. Seeps, wet rotting logs. Mniaceae. (The illustration is of a con-gener which is ± identical in macroscopic black and white.)

These are among the largest leaves you'll see on moss. At 12× magnification, held up against light, their cells can be just discerned, and a distinct border of different cells around the edge should be clear. They shrivel drastically when dry.

Red-Haired Screw Moss

Tortula norvegica (**tort**-you-la: twisted, referring to capsule tip; nor-**veh**-ji-ca: of Norway). Stems ½–4" tall [1–10 cm], with few or no branches; leaves oblong with red midvein and red hairlike tip; spore capsule tiny, slender, cone-tipped, on ⅜–¾" [1–2 cm] stalk; the "twisted" or "screw" part, under the cap of the capsule, looks like a narwhal horn under a 12× lens. Alpine. Pottiaceae. Similar *T. ruralis* (illustrated), at all elevs, has white leaf-tip hairs; sometimes grows on dried cow pies.

Peat Mosses

Sphagnum spp. (**sfag**-num: the Greek term). Robust mosses typically in deep spongy mats, the stems crowded, supporting each other; where growing in sun, can be brilliant scarlet (especially *S. capillifolium*) to rich wine-red (*S. warnstorfii*); typical color in shade is pale glaucous green, paler and less yellowish than other mosses; *S. fuscum* is strongly brown-tinged above, straw-colored beneath; leaves tiny, mostly crowded on ¼–¾" [6–20 mm] branches, the branches (these three species) mostly tufted at the top; fruiting stalks short, several per shoot tip, each bearing one ± spherical blackish capsule which releases spores all at once, explosively. Typically floating in slow-moving water; or terrestrial on seeps; all elevs. Sphagnaceae. Color page 519.

Peat mosses are the most primitive mosses, and at the same time the most important mosses both ecologically and economically. Estimates have them covering one percent of the earth's continents—making them one of the most extensive of all dominant plant types. They owe their success to their ability to change their environment to suit themselves and discourage others. Growing in slow-moving cold water, they draw oxygen and nutrients out of the water and replace them with hydrogen ions mainly in the form of uronic acids. The water, if it's too slow to replace itself frequently, is eventually too acidic and too poor in oxygen and nutrients to support the other plants growing there. At this point a whole new set of plants takes over, with peat moss the dominant. The new community is a "mire" or "peat bog" as opposed to a nonacid "marsh" or "fen." (Peat mosses thrive in the acids they themselves create, but they die in the sulphuric acids resulting from acid rain.)

Also suppressed—by cold, lack of oxygen, and certain antibiotics produced by peat mosses—are the bacteria that normally perform decomposition duties underwater. Very little decomposition takes place in a mire. The floating mass of peat moss lives and grows on top, and dies bit by bit just below. The dead layer underneath gets thicker and thicker, since it can't decompose. This can go on indefinitely, the dead peat compacting into a deposit of biomass which can be dug up, dried, and burned. Peat for fuel exceeds garden peat moss as the chief economic use of sphagnum, and the essence of peat smoke is the key to the most interesting malt whiskies.

Different successional pathways from peat moss are possible. The peat moss surface may rise high enough above waterline—

either by floating or by thickening to rest on the bottom—to become a seedbed for dry-land plants including conifers. This is a common pathway by which glacial cirque tarns (small lakes in high basins) are converted to forests. In steep mountain terrain, though, tarns usually have plenty of streamflow to avoid ever turning into mires. They silt up and turn into glorious meadows after a marshy (not boggy) transitional phase.

Sphagnum species specialize. *Sphagnum fuscum* forms hummocks in bogs. You'll often see brown *fuscum* on top of a hummock (the driest part), scarlet *capillifolium* on the sides, and green species in the soggy hollows between hummocks. *S. warnstorfii* grows in fens rather than bogs, typically associating with sedges, which don't tolerate bogs, rather than with other peat mosses. Robust, pale green *S. squarrosum* (illustrated) avoids wetlands; it grows on moist shady forest floor.

To native tribes, peat moss was an irreplaceable material. Its phenomenal water-absorbing capacity made it perfect for diapers, cradle lining, and sanitary napkins. Expectant mothers gathered quantities of peat moss, sometimes lining the entire lodge for a birthing event. Other mosses were used for sponging, padding, and wiping in areas without peat mosses. Most native languages didn't distinguish types of moss other than peat moss, but among peat mosses they knew pink ones made the best diapers, while red ones were to be avoided.

Granite Moss

Andreaea rupestris (ahn-dray-ee-a: after G. R. Andreae; rue-pes-tris: on rocks). Plants brownish black even when wet (unlike schistidium, p 280; check with a few drops of water), in tight tufts usually less than 1" high [25 mm]; leaves minute; capsule hardly raised above the foliage, black, much less than ⅛" [3 mm] tall, opening by four lateral slits rather than at the tip. On rock (especially igneous rock) in full sun. Andreaeaceae.

The sooty pigmentation of this odd moss consists mainly of red anthocyanins on top of green chlorophylls; the former are there to protect the latter from the intense ultraviolet radiation that blasts exposed high-altitude sites.

A primitive family, granite mosses are set well apart from other mosses by their leaf cells and capsule structure.

Yellow Star Moss

Campylium stellatum (cam-**pill**-ium: curved, referring to capsules; stel-**ay**-tum: star-shaped). Stems 1–4" [2.5–10 cm], ± sprawling, irregularly branched, often forming deep mats or tufts; leaves
broad-based and tapering, rather coarse and chaotically spreading, resembling star points, bright green to golden yellow; spore
capsules rarely seen, curved, on 1" [2.5 cm] stalks. A dominant
among mosses on seeps and marshes (not bogs). Amblystegiaceae.

Beaked Moss

Eurhynchium pulchellum (yew-**rink**-ium: true beak;
pool-**kell**-um: adorable). Stems creeping, like
fine yarn, much branched, with rhizoids all
along attaching them to substrate;
leaves minute, broad, tips blunt
under 10× lens; spore capsules
horizontal to inclined, on
¼" [6 mm] vertical stalks
that mature red-brown. In forests, esp on
tree bases and logs. Brachytheciaceae.

Rope Moss

Rhytidiopsis robusta (rye-tiddy-**op**-sis: looks
like genus *Rhytidium*). Also **pipe-cleaner
moss.** Yellow-green to brownish moss in loose
mats, the strands looking thick and ropy due to
close-packed leaves and sparse branch-
ing; stems yellow-green; leaves ¼" [6 mm], irregularly deeply
wrinkled (under lens), tending to curve all to one side
of stem; fruiting stalks 1" [25 mm], red-brown; capsules often sharply crooked downward. Subalpine forest floor, from Bitterroots north. Hylocomiaceae.

Big Shaggy Moss

Rhytidiadelphus triquetrus (rye-tiddy-
a-**del**-fus: wrinkled brother, ref to genus
Rhytidium; try-**kweet**-rus: 3-cor-
nered). Light green moss in coarse
mats; stems red-brown, often partly
upright; leaves triangular, ¼ ×
⅛" [6 × 3 mm], faintly but
neatly pleated (under 12×

lens), sticking out all ways from the stem; fruiting stalks few, 1" [25 mm]; capsule ± bent, maturing in autumn. On humus, logs, rocks, or trees (esp deciduous) from Bitterroots n; abundant in wet BC Mtns. Hylocomiaceae.

Fern Moss

Hylocomium splendens
(hi-lo-**coe**-mium: forest
hair; **splen**-denz: lustrous). Also **stairstep moss**. Glossy
gold to brownish
green moss in a stepwise growth form—each
year's growth, shaped like
a tiny fern with branchlets subbranched, rises from a midpoint
on the previous year's stem,
growing vertically at first and
then arching into a horizontal
position; a stem may show ten

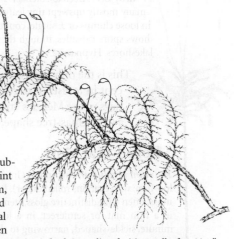

or more such steps, but only the upper 1–3 look very alive; fruiting stalks few, ½–1"
[12–25 mm] tall, red, not twisted; capsules ⅛" [3 mm], horizontal; leaves minute. Forms luxuriant mats on rocks, logs, and
earth. Boreal forests; alpine slopes. Hylocomiaceae.

Big Redstem

Pleurozium schreberi (ploo-**row**-zium: side
branch; **shreb**-er-eye: after J. C. Schreber). Stems
4–6" [10–15 cm], red-brown; shoots ± featherlike but much less even and perfect than
fern moss or knight-s-plume; leaves minute, blunt-tips visible with 10× lens; spore
capsules curved, ± horizontal, on 1–2¼"
[25–55 mm] red-brown stalks; forms goldengreen carpets on relatively dry parts of forest floor,
from Bitterroots n. Hylocomiaceae.

Knight's-Plume

Ptilium crista-castrensis (**till**-ium: feather; **cris**-ta castren-sis: a plumed military crest for wear when in camp).
Stems 1–4" [2.5–10 cm], featherlike because very finely,
closely, evenly branched, and evenly tapering to tip; leaves minute, all
curving with point toward stem base; spore capsules few, inclined to
horizontal, red-brown, on 1–2" [2.5–5 cm] red-brown stalks; forms
golden-green carpets on relatively moist parts of forest floor; throughout our range exc OR and w ID. Hypnaceae. Illustrated at right.

Palm-Tree Moss

Climacium dendroides (cli-**may**-shum: ladder—; den-**droy**-deez: treelike). Stems 1½–3" [38–75 mm] tall, erect, with many mostly upswept tiny leafy branches from the upper half; in loose clumps or ± single, connected by rhizomes; illustration shows spore capsules, though they are rarely seen. Bogs, seeps, lakeshores. Hypnaceae.

This is the only tree-shaped moss in our region, except in forests of northern Idaho and the Kootenays where Menzies' tree moss grows; the latter has a Christmas-tree shape, and often bears capsules.

Rolled-Leaf Moss

Hypnum revolutum (**hip**-num: Greek term for moss; rev-o-**loo**-tum: with margins rolled under). Rather fine golden-green moss, often with distinctive gloss; stems either creeping, in a thin mat, or semierect, in a loose mat; leaves minute, sickle-shaped, narrowing to slender points in long arcs to one side and down; from above (under 10× lens), the shoot looks like a braid; rolled-under leaf margins (illustrated) are distinctive but not highly reliable, and may require a microscope; fruiting stalks rarely seen, ⅜–1" [1–2.5 cm], capsules curved. Rocks or soil, near CD in WY, MT, and Canada. Hypnaceae.

Aspects of Tree Trunks

According to the old saw, mosses grow on the north sides of trees. Actually they grow on the wet sides. These might well be north sides due to shade, all other things being equal—on flat terrain with trees straight as plumb lines, for example. But mountain trees often lean downslope. Their upper sides (e.g., south sides of trees on a north-facing slope) catch the rain and grow most of the moss.

Moist bark also favors lichens, though if mosses and lichens compete head-on, mosses can exclude lichens. The dry side may appear bare, but often it is covered by crust lichens which, being easily shaded out, are at the bottom of the pecking order for good microhabitats.

The very moistest microsites are flaring tree bases and the tops of larger limbs. Both accumulate litter, which breaks down into humus and eventually forms soil, at least in the wettest parts of our range.

Up on the tree trunks and branches, these sorts of differences determine a whole set of zones for different epiphytes.

Curly-Leaf Moss

Hypnum circinale (sir-sin-**ay**-lee: coiled). Very fine, delicate mosses in thin waterfall-like mats most often on conifers; stems reddish; leaves minute, narrowing (under 12× lens) to slender points in long arcs (to nearly complete circles) all to one side of stem, giving the shoot a braided look; fruiting stalks ¼–½" [6–13 mm], not twisted when dry; capsules very short (much less than ⅛", or 3 mm), maturing in winter. Low on conifer trunks in w MT, c and n Id, and Canada. Hypnaceae.

Liverworts

Thallose Liverworts

Order Marchantiales. Bright green, ± leathery flat lobes textured with close regular rows of bubblelike pale bumps; lobes regularly branching in 2-way equal splits; tall (¾–4", or 2–10 cm) fruiting stalks present only briefly, in spring.

Marchantia polymorpha (mar-**shahn**-tia: after Nicolas Marchant; poly-**mor**-fa: many forms). Surface often bearing conspicuous cups holding a few gemmae (vegetative propagules); fruiting stalks umbrellalike, the female ones 9-lobed; on streambanks, burned or disturbed earth; weedy in greenhouses.

Conocephalum conica (co-no-**sef**-a-lum: cone head). No gemmae; surface bumps very large and close-packed; fruiting stalks mushroom-like, the conical head fringed with spherical spore-capsules; aromatic when crushed; widespread on moist earth, esp streambanks. Illustrated.

This type of liverwort bears no obvious resemblance to either leafy liverworts or mosses. It's more likely to be confused with foliose lichens, but the "liverlike" textural pattern distinguishes it from the "lunglike" branching ridges of lungwort or the patternless black speckles on green dog lichens (page 320). Coincidentally, liverwort, lungwort, and dog lichen are all names bestowed by medieval herbalists who looked for images of body parts—God's drug prescriptions—in the plant world. The bumps that give liverworts their alleged liver texture are air chambers, each opening to the outside by a tiny pore. They offer a favorable environment for photosynthesis.

Conocephalum is named for a female "cone head" that rests on the liverwort's surface for several weeks in spring, waiting for liverwort sperms to swim to it through a film of rain or dew or in the splash of a raindrop. When the spores are ripe and weather permits, the head is raised a few inches into the air in the space of a few hours by a stem of special cells that don't grow or multiply; they simply balloon lengthwise upward. This unorthodox manner of growing a stalk offers speed but not durability. You'll be lucky if you ever catch one of these cute but short-lived fruitings.

Rarely do ecologists pinpoint a plant's habitat as boldly as Alsie Campbell describing *Marchantia* streamside habitat: "Occasionally a semiporous barrier will be deposited upon a slightly sloping, nonporous surface across which water seeps all year, such as a small log impeding drainage from an almost flat rock. If there is no disturbance, organic matter and extremely fine inorganic particles build up and form an aqueous muck." Campbell concluded *Marchantia* has "practical" importance in treacherously hiding slick footing.

Leafy Liverworts

Order Jungermanniales. Mosslike growths of branched, flattened ribbonlike strips (about⅛" wide, or 3 mm) of leaves neatly overlapping in 2, 4 or 5 ranks.

Barbilophozia lycopodioides (bar-bil-o-**foe**-zia: bearded tuft-branch; lie-co-po-di-**oy**-deez: like clubmoss). =*Lophozia lycopodioides*. Leaves frilly, more than 1 mm wide, four-lobed, each lobe coming to a tiny point (barely visible under 10× lens); in two ranks; leaves overlap like shingles; stems 1–2½" [2.5–6 cm]long, sparingly branched. Abundant in moist subalpine forest, less common in alp/subalpine meadows. (The illustration is of *B. barbata*, shich looks quite similar.)

Leafy liverworts are easily mistaken for mosses at first glance. The most dramatic difference is in the spore-bearing stalks. Those of mosses are sturdy and conspicuous several months out of the year, but the watery, insubstantial stalks of liverworts are rarely seen, since they last only for a few spring or summer days. The foliage is just as distinctive, at least from close up; contrasted with moss foliage, it reminds me of small plants flattened by winter snows.

8

Fungi

The mushroom is not the fungus—at least not by itself. Neither is a puffball, or a shelf fungus on a tree. Each is a fruiting body (what we might loosely call a fruit) of a fungus organism which is many times larger and longer-lived. As an apple tree produces apples to carry its seeds, the fungus produces mushrooms or other fruiting bodies to disseminate its spores.

A graphic illustration is provided by a "fairy ring"—a circle or partial circle of mushrooms that comes up year after year. These mushrooms are fruits of one continuous fungus body whose perimeter they mark; it expands year by year as the fungus grows within the soil. In some years the mushrooms may fail to appear, but the fungus is still alive and growing; it merely didn't get the moisture or other conditions for fruiting, that year. The largest fairy rings on record are over 600' [180 m] in diameter. Dividing that by the observed rate of growth yields a likely age of five to seven centuries. Still larger rings made by honey mushrooms (page 000) are visible from airplanes over forests: they are circular dents in the tree canopy, consisting of sick and dying trees attacked by the fungus. Some map lichens (page 000) are calculated, extrapolating from diameter, to be 4,000 years old, rivaling the oldest trees. Each of these fungal circles is a genetic individual, but not exactly an individual as we normally understand the term. In any case most mushrooms are not individuals. (But see morels, page 310.) The living, growing body of a fungus is a network of tiny tubes called "hyphae" (singular: "hypha").

Except when they aggregate in bundles or in fruiting bodies, hyphae are too fine to see or handle; they range from 2–10 microns thick.

A fungus is also not a plant; in fact it's more closely related to an animal. (Fungi and animals apparently diverged evolutionarily about 800 million years ago, 200 million years after their joint genetic line diverged from the plants.) Fungal cell walls get their strength from a material called chitin which also makes insect skeletons; they contain no cellulose, the characteristic fiber of the plant kingdom. Also like animals, fungi obtain their carbohydrates from photosynthetic (green) organisms. Animals get them by eating, whereas fungi employ any of four nutritional modes:

Mycorrhizal: connecting to plant roots for exchange of nutrients and water. (See sidebar below.)

Lichenized: enclosing and "farming" algae and cyanobacteria.

Saprophytic: decomposing (i.e., rotting) dead organic matter.

Parasitic: drawing nutrition from living plant or animal matter.

The first two modes, which cover a majority of the multicelled fungi, are "mutualistic" symbioses, meaning that they may benefit both the fungal and the green partners in the relationship. The third and fourth modes do not benefit the plant hosts as individuals, but they

The Fungus/Root Symbiosis

Let's set the record straight: the Web of Life is not a metaphor, it's literal truth, and it's made of fungi. Wags call it the wood-wide web. The word "mycorrhiza," coined in 1885 from Greek words meaning "fungus" and "root," names a special growth that connects fungi with plant roots. Simply put, the job of root hairs in plants is actually performed mostly by fungi in symbiosis with plants. Soon after a plant germinates from seed, its rootlet is likely to meet up with a fungal hypha. Each produces compounds that stimulate and alter the growth of the other, forming a joint fungus/root organ (the mycorrhiza) that immediately goes into use as a nutrient loading dock. Some plants start even earlier: orchid seeds typically require hyphal penetration before germinating.

The hyphae in some types of mycorrhizae grow into a net around the root tip. In others they digest root cell walls, penetrate and inhabit the cells, and eventually are digested back by the cells. In any case the hyphae hormonally suppress the formation of plant root hairs, while at the same time they provide a preestablished network of root hair surrogates vastly finer and more efficient than the plant's own roots. (The math: an absorptive plant root hair is about 1 mm in diameter; a hypha

benefit plant communities immensely. We need rotters to clear away dead material, to recycle nutrients and, on a grander scale, to keep the world from bursting into flame due to a build-up of plant-produced oxygen. Even parasitic fungi, though usually thought of as diseases, may be beneficial if we take a broader view. (See page 299.)

Recent studies find that many fungi are carnivorous on top of the other modes. Fungi previously regarded as saprophytes have been caught supplementing their diets by killing small animals and sucking them dry. They can either splash poison on their prey or set a hyphal loop as a snare, then tighten it to strangle the victim. Prey identified so far include nematodes (simple worms) and springtails (insects). (See sidebar foot of page 293; and page 304.)

The first thing to understand about fungus/plant relations is that they're what what makes the world go around, or at least the terrestrial part of the world. When life first moved from the sea onto the land, it did so by means of partnerships between primitive fungi and algae. The algae evolved into the first plants, and plants coevolved with fungi up to the present day. Mycorrhizae and primitive lichens each count among the very oldest multicelled terrestrial fossils ever found. About 90% of plant species are known to form mycorrhizae, and the remaining 10% are rife with other

---

is about .003 mm; ∴ the hypha can provide about 300 times as much absorptive surface area per mass.)

In addition to water, mycorrhizal fungi can deliver nitrogen and phosphorus that would otherwise be available to plants. Phosphorus is critical on limestone-derived soils in the Rockies, because under alkaline, calcium-rich conditions almost all of the phosphorus atoms form compounds that plants cannot use until fungi break them down. Fungi can also bore right into solid rock, extracting nutrients. At Yellowstone, scientists found a mycorrhizal grass thriving around springs in soil too hot for either the grass or the fungus to survive alone.

The fungus receives carbohydrates in exchange. Most mycorrhizal fungi are totally dependent on their plant partners. Few plants are equally dependent on fungi, since most plants have the genetic information for making root hairs to obtain water and minerals. Planted in a moist, nutritious substrate, a seedling may do just that, while resisting mycorrhizal infection of its roots. But in many tougher or densely competitive situations, nonmycorrhizal seedlings don't survive. On a hot logged-over slope, Douglas-fir seedlings proved more likely to survive if planted right next to heath-family shrubs, because suitable mycorrhizae partner heath shrubs. In a similar study, seedlings survived only if they

---

trans-kingdom mutualisms. Mosses—the broadest plant group not yet known to be heavily mycorrhizal—are colonized by cyanobacteria which fix nitrogen for the mosses, as they do for lichenized fungi. Sedges have relatively few mycorrhizae, but are infested by microscopic internal fungi called endophytes, which protect them from pathogenic microorganisms. (One study found that only a single gene mutation is required to turn a pathogenic microfungus into a beneficial one; such an adaptation could benefit the fungus, which presumably can live longer in a healthy host than a dying one. No wonder fungal endophytes are proving to be extremely common in leaves.) Conifers, the backbone of Western ecosystems, are 100% mycorrhizal *and* generally infested with needle endophytes that help protect them from grazers and pathogens *and* often festooned with lichens that may fix nitrogen.

This small chapter can only hint at the hundreds of kinds of fungi that grow here. Even a multivolume set of books would only hint: one leading mycologist estimates there are 1,500,000 species of fungi in the world, of which 5% have been named. Classification of fungi into families and orders is in a similarly primitive stage of development, so I won't be naming those higher taxa.

---

were inoculated with a teaspoonful [3 ml] of forest soil. The active ingredients in this elixir of life are poorly known, but mites, nematodes, bacteria, and other microorganisms are present in great numbers and variety, and surely share credit with the 100 feet or so of hyphal tubes per teaspoon of soil [10 m per ml]. Timber industry nurseries have learned to inoculate seeds with suitable fungi.

Most plants have many mycorrhizal species as potential partners. Douglas-firs may have two thousand. A tree forms mycorrhizae with several species at a time, and grows best if it has a range available for changing conditions. Each fungus has its own special abilities.

While the typical terms of barter are carbohydrates in return for water and minerals, other exchanges are common. During dry seasons the water flow is likely to reverse, with deep-rooted trees supplying most of the network's water. Small plants can receive carbohydrates from overstory plants via shared fungal partners. Suzanne Simard measured the transfer of carbohydrates to Douglas-fir seedlings from birches above them; this nurture increased when seedlings were made needier by shading them. Tree seedlings, of course, switch from receiving to donating carbohydrates after they grow big enough, but non-green plants are lifelong "welfare cheats." (See page 188.)

Mycorrhizae exude some carbohydrate into the soil, making the soil

Fly Amanita and Panther Amanita

Amanita spp. (am-a-**night**-a: Greek term for some fungus on Mt. Amanus). Cap usually sprinkled with whitish warts; stem white, with skirtlike ring near the top and a bulbous (not quite cuplike) base; gills and spores white.

Fly amanita, *A. muscaria* (mus-**cair**-ia: of flies). Also **fly agaric.** Cap typically yellow in most of our range, but may be bright red (esp in wet nw) tan or white; bulb at stem base tapers upward, with about 4 concentric rings. On soil, mainly in fall. Color p 518.

Panther amanita, *A. pantherina* (panther-eye-na: panther—). Cap typically tan (ranging from brown to nearly white); bulbous base has a single heavy, rolled upper edge which may or may not pull away from stalk. Common under aspen or Douglas-fir; spring, fall or rarely winter. Color p 518.

Fly amanitas, Europe's long-held archetype of malevolently alluring toadstools, are curiously unpredictable hallucinogens. Viking warriors ate them to prepare for battle; it helped them go "berserk"— irrationally fearless. Neurophysiology shows this mushroom's toxins

---

more cohesive, more porous, and better aerated. They also help protect plants from disease. Root rots (parasitic fungi) have a harder time attacking roots mantled in healthy mycorrhizae, which form both a physical and a chemical barrier. Some fungi compete with others by secreting selective toxins; many secrete antibiotics (e.g., penicillin) that suppress bacteria, including some plant pathogens.

Mycorrhizae—together with nitrogen-fixing cyanobacteria, which also pervade many soils—are offering scientists a new picture of the all-important nitrogen cycle. Some mycorrhizal plants meet their nitrogen needs in substrates where it had previously been thought that all the nitrogen was organically bound up, unavailable to plants. Apparently some fungi have a unique ability to break proteins into amino acids and make these available to their plant partners. Others attack and digest live animals—a concentrated nitrogen source available to few plants. John Klironomos measured the transfer of nitrogen to white pine seedlings from soil insects killed and consumed by the pine's mycorrhizal partners; the pines in his experiment were getting as much as 25% of their nitrogen from insect protein. He began the experiment intending to observe and measure these insects—springtails—eating various fungi. He said it was "as shocking as putting a pizza in front of a person and then having the pizza eat the person."

---

inhibiting functions of the amygdala, which include fear and the assessment of pleasant and unpleasant sensations. Siberian tribes and ancient Hindus used amanitas for religious experiences. So do some Westerners, taking "folklore" precautions. I suspect the varied results have less to do with technique than with luck and genetics. A wild-eyed euphoric stranger on a trail once handed a fly amanita cap to two friends of mine, who downed it on the spot. One had an enhanced afternoon while the other, from the other half of the same cap, was in abject misery. Cramps, spasms, sweating, vomiting, lethargy, dry mouth, stupefied sleep, manic behavior, and subsequent amnesia are symptoms often reported, with death very unlikely, though that too has been recorded. I can't recommend this gamble.

The problem of identification within this freely hybridizing genus makes it worse. The panther is considered deadly, even though its toxins seem to be just higher concentrations of those (muscimol, ibotenic acid and a little muscarine) found in the fly amanita—not the liver-destroying cyclopeptides of the following species. Panther and fly overlap in terms of color. In any case, they do look fine. Trailside specimens are a scenic resource **to be left untouched.**

"Toadstool" is an old British word that lumps together all poisonous or unsavory mushrooms. There is no "way to tell a mushroom from a toadstool." You always have to identify the particular species.

Panther amanitas have little to do with panthers (leopards) aside than being tannish and spotted, but fly amanitas have centuries of experience poisoning flies. They were traditionally left around the house broken up in saucers of sugared milk—children beware! Dried amanitas are said to hold a fatal attraction for dogs and cats.

Death Cap and Destroying Angel

Amanita spp. Flesh, gills, and stem white; stem cylindrical or slightly smaller upward, slender, with a tattered skirtlike ring (sometimes missing) and a ± bulbous base in a thin white cup (requires careful excavation to see; the cap often barely emerges from ground, and may have dirty surface); spores white. Becomes fetid with age. **Do not taste.**

Destroying Angel, *Amanita ocreata* * (oc-ree-ay-ta: sheathed). Cap white. In spring. Color p 518.

Death Cap, *A. phalloides* (fal-oy-deez: phallus-like). Cap light yellow-green to

---

*PNW specimens previously identified as *A. verna, virosa,* and *bisporigera* belong to *A. ocreata*; the other 3 spp. have not been confirmed here. The name "destroying angel" includes all pure white spp. with cyclopeptide toxins.

tan, rarely almost white. Late summer and fall. European; found so far in NA mostly near cultivated filberts, chestnuts, and oaks, but may spread.

Lovely but monstrously poisonous, the **death cap** and **destroying angel** are our most dangerous fungi, and they seem to be on the increase, especially in the suburbs. It's worth knowing their characteristics even though they're rare.

All amanitas have white spores and more or less white gills. Most have a definite ring around the stem, the remnant of a "partial veil" that extended from the edges of the cap, sealing off the immature spores to keep them moist. Most emerge from a "universal veil," an additional moisture barrier that wraps the entire young mushroom, from under its base to all over its cap. As a young "button," each amanita fruiting-body in its universal veil is egg- to pear-shaped, resembling a puffball but with the outline of cap and gills visible in cross-section. Remnants of this veil *usually* persist as a cup or lip around the base of the stem, and/or on top of the cap in the form of warts, crumbs or broad patches. But absence of these remnants doesn't disprove any amanita, since the stem easily breaks off above the cup, and the cap crumbs can wash off.

All white-spored, white-gilled mushrooms should be carefully examined for ring and cup. Genus *Amanita* contains good edibles, some of them popular in Europe, but the chance of misidentifying a deadly one leads American guides to caution against all amanitas. (By the same reasoning, this book doesn't recommend any stemmed, gilled mushrooms. You need a complete mushroom book for them.)

These amanitas and the little-brown-mushroom *Galerina* share one of nature's most insidious poisons. It attacks the liver within minutes, but symptoms don't appear for ten to fourteen hours (or up to four days) by which time the liver is seriously damaged. Over half of the poisonings in America by these species have been fatal, though hospitals can improve the odds if they know they're dealing with amanita cyclopeptides before symptoms are too advanced.

Autumn Galerina

Galerina autumnalis (gal-er-**eye**-na: helmeted; autumn-**nay**-lis: a somewhat misleading name for this species). Caps mostly ¾–1¾" diam [2–4 cm], slightly tacky and deep yellow-brown when wet, dull tan when dry, radially striped near the edge; gills pale, becoming brown with spores; stem thin, brown, darkening toward base, with a thin whitish ring; spores rusty brown. Typically clustered on rotting (sometimes ± buried) wood, often among mosses, in late fall or sometimes spring. Color p 518.

This unprepossessing little brown mushroom ("LBM") contains the same cyclopeptide poisons as the deadly amanitas, is just as deadly, and is more common. It is less feared simply because people don't normally bother with LBMs—unless they happen to be hunting psilocybin mushrooms. You'd damn well better know what you're doing if you hunt *Psilocybe*. Galerinas have also occasionally been mistaken for the edible honey mushroom.

Woolly Chanterelle

Gomphus floccosus (**gom**-fus: peg; flock-**oh**-sus: woolly-tufted). Also **scaly vase chanterelle**. Orange trumpet-shaped fungus; cap undifferentiated from stem; often deeply hollow down the center; inside surface roughened with big soft scales; outside surface paler and irregularly, shallowly wrinkled (no paper-thin gills); spores ochre. On ground, late summer and fall. Color p 515.

Mushroom guides, over the years, batted this species back and forth between the "Edible" and "Poisonous" lists. A recent verdict is "hard to digest"—and not so dangerous as to drag the true chanterelles down from the "Safe for Beginners" list due to possible confusion.

Waxy Caps

Hygrophorus spp. (hi-**groff**-er-us: moisture bearing). Also **waxgills**. Mushrooms 2-4" diam [5-10 cm]; gills white, clean, slightly waxy-feeling, rather thick.

H. subalpinus. All white to cream-tinged; cap sticky when wet, becoming flat or slightly concave by maturity; stem stout (often less than 2× taller than wide) with a slight ring (initially at least), the remnant of a veil from edge of cap. Spring to fall, but often near melting snow in spring. Color page 518.

H. pudorinus (pew-dor-**eye**-nus: ashamed, or blushing). Pretty, pale with a warm peachy-brown blush on all parts; cap sticky when wet, remaining shiny when dry, maturing ± flat but with down-turned edge; gills don't change color where bruised; stalk fairly slender, often curved, with minute fibers (lower) and scales (higher); no veil. Fall, under conifers, esp spruce. Color page 518.

Among the several mushrooms that often come up close to melting snow, the subalpine waxy-cap is relatively common, and may also be ecologically significant in offering food to bears at a nutritionally critical time of year, soon after they emerge from hibernation

The waxy quality is subtle, but useful in i.d. once you get to know it. Brush a fingertip across the gills, and notice a slight stickiness and moisture, together with relative strength and thickness.

Short-stemmed Russula and Lobster Mushroom

Russula brevipes (russ-you-la: red—; brev-ip-eez: short foot). Also **duff-humper**. White throughout, but may bruise brown or yellowish; cap 3–10" diam [8–25 cm]; dry, quite concave, margins usually rolled under; gills fine, crowded; spores white to cream; flesh odorless, bland to peppery; stem cylindrical, rigid, brittle: it snaps like chalk, leaving a rough, fiberless surface. Mycorrhizal with conifers; scattered, usually ± buried in forest duff; fall. Color p 515.

These two species tell a twisted sort of Frog Prince story: as the mushroom magically morphs into the object of our desire, it turns from virginal white to enflamed and pimply. Our story begins with a rather attractive mushroom which, due to its abundance and blah flavor, was voted "most boring mushroom" at one mycophagist convention. It likes to sturdily push thick duff up from underneath, and usually has many crumbs on its face. It belongs to a huge and abundant genus that David Arora dubbed JARs (for "just another Russula"); many are quite attractive, their pure white, brittle flesh and gills contrasting with a peelable cap skin that may be carmine, green, or black. There are so many Russulas, so few are tasty, and identification is so difficult, that mushroom hunters rarely identify them.

Sometimes Russula mushrooms get infected internally with a parasitic fungus, *Hypomyces lactifluorum*. Think of it as a bright orange mold. The mold prevents paper-thin gills from developing, alters the graceful form to a crude knob and the delicate, brittle flesh to spudlike firmness, and wraps the whole thing in a scurfy orange skin. *Voilá*, it's delicious, a marketable delicacy, a "lobster mushroom."

But is it safe? Once heavily parasitized, the host mushroom is no longer identifiable to species. The few high-tech identifications to date have been only to genus: *Russula* or *Lactarius*. A few members of those genera are poisonous, and yet lobster mushrooms have a safer gastrointestinal record than lobster. (I have not heard of any poisonings.) They also keep longer than any normal mushroom. Does the parasite avoid toxic species? Do you want to take the chance? Or might it neutralize toxins, the way it apparently kills or repels bugs and rot? Drug companies, are you paying attention?

I have enjoyed eating short-stemmed russula, but most reports are less favorable, and once again you should not eat any thin-gilled mushrooms without using a much more complete book than this.

Specimens with an acrid taste and a striking blue-green tinge to the gills and stalk are either a distinct variety or species or good old *R. brevipes* with a different species of mold. This needs more study.

Shoestring Root Rot/Honey Mushroom

Armillaria ostoyae (ar-mil-**air**-ia: banded; os-**toy**-ee: after Paul Ostoya) =*Armillariella mellea.* Cap yellow-brown to brown, with coarse fibrous scales radiating from the center; gills white, stained rusty in age; stalk has stringy white pith, and a substantial, up-flaring, brown-edged ring; clustered on wood or ground, caps often coated with spores where overlapped; spores white; coarse black threadlike rhizomorphs often visible around base, or netting across nearby wood, often under bark. Fall.

Mushroom-hunters know this as a popular, albeit unreliable, edible. Tree farmers know it as a pathogen deadly to trees, and have devoted much study to eradicating it. Apparently it lives saprophytically in fertile mature forests, but often becomes a deadly parasite where the trees are stressed—in highly competitive stands, and especially in logged and roaded regions. It is the most serious disease problem for foresters in the US part of our range, and in general a leading cause of white rot in wood. In ecological terms, that makes it a valuable re-cycler of nutrients and facilitator of animal habitats. White rot (as opposed to brown cubical rot, page 300) breaks down both cellulose and lignin. Quoting an unusually sensual sentence from the Forest Service tome on the disease, "the crunch of collapsing compartments of pseudosclerotial tissue when one walks on logs decayed by the fungus adds an audible dimension to its saprophytic activities."

The name "shoestring root-rot" refers to the black rhizomorphs distinctive of this genus—hyphae with tough protective black sheaths that enable them to reach across nutrient-poor stretches in search of the next nutrient-rich one, usually the roots of another stump or stressed tree. They give *Armillaria* an unusual ability to expand.

The media gave the honey mushroom its fifteen minutes of fame in 1992, calling it the World's Largest Living Thing. Michigan mycologists made headlines first with a honey mushroom spread out over 37 acres [15 ha]. Not to be outdone, researchers in Washington mapped a 1500-acre one [600 ha], and then others in Oregon's Blue Mtns came up with a 2200-acre one [900 ha]. We aren't talking about a Godzilla mushroom cap, now, but about networks of tiny hyphal tubes. The researchers matched the genes of hyphae at wide-spread spots in their forest, and found that a single spore had grown, over the course of perhaps 2400 years, into a network spread out un-der 2200 acres. However, there is every reason to doubt that all these hyphae are still interconnected. If a clone can be World's Largest Liv-ing Thing, there are likely larger mushroom clones in the world, and even they could not tip the scales against a 6,000-ton aspen clone.

Laminated Root Rot

Phellinus weirii (fel-**eye**-nus: cork—).

This is the other terrible root disease in the greater Northwest. I'm not going to bother with identification, since you aren't going to see this abundant fungus. It virtually never produces any shelves on trees, or any spores, but merely grows in tree roots, slowly, inexorably, passing from tree to tree when the roots touch each other. After many decades, the infested tree always dies, often with a bark beetle attack as the proximate cause. The easy way to see laminated root rot is from an airplane: look for a motley-colored mix of small trees and shrubs in patches breaking the continuous conifer canopy.

Laminated root rot infests at least 2% of PNW forest soils. It is so incurable and so inexorable in its growth that we can reasonably ask, "why isn't it everywhere?" For one thing, it has preferences. Douglas-fir is the chief victim. Mountain hemlock and silver fir are also susceptible; western hemlock less so, and pines still less; cedars and larches quite resistant; and hardwoods immune if not downright toxic to it. So it advances fastest where there are a lot of mature Douglas-firs, but even there it's slow. On the other hand, it is on the upswing wherever fire suppression and blister rust have tipped the scales, favoring firs over pines and larches. It's a Death Star in the constellation of ills that revolves around the mistaken fire policies of the twentieth century.

Though about as popular as Ebola virus within the timber industry, root rot is respected by forest ecologists as an agent of biodiversity. It creates refugia where species that tend to disappear from dense conifer forest—not only broadleaf trees and shrubs, and western redcedar, but also many animals—can persist and be ready to spread out again after disturbances come along. Root rot patches are ideal deer and moose habitat, richly mixing shrubs with a few tall trees, and they have plenty of snags for cavity nesters. That's good for the surrounding forests: they benefit from having lots of cavity-nesting insectivorous birds near when pest insects strike.

Red-Belt Conk

Fomitopsis pinicola (foam-i-**top**-sis: tinder lookalike; pi-**nic**-a-la: dwelling on pines). =*Fomes pinicola*. A dense, long-lasting shelf fungus on conifers; initially a ± white knob, later hoof-shaped; becoming an inverted shelf (flat bottom, sloping top), blackish brown at the base, with concentric arcs of bright, often shiny, red-browns, ocher, or white toward the edge. Color page 517.

The handsome **red-belt conk** is a serious parasite on conifers, though less disastrous than the two root rots on the previous page. It causes "brown cubical rot," since it can decompose only cellulose, and not lignin; it leaves long-lasting cubes of lignin in the soil.

Fomitopsis and laminated root rot both used to be included in a huge genus *Fomes*, but that genus was split several ways, with only the true tinder conk remaining in it. That fungus was for many centuries cut up, soaked in saltpeter, dried, and then used as matches; what made that work was its unlayered, very long internal spore tubes. The split-off genera have short tubes because they start a new layer of them every year. Yes, the fruiting bodies grow for many years, or decades, with up to seventy layers sometimes countable.

Witch's Butter

Tremella spp. (trem-**el**-a: trembling like jelly). Mass of leaflike lobes; texture earlike (gelatinous but tough) when moist, hard when dry. Spring to fall, on rotting trees

T. mesenterica (mez-en-**tair**-ic-a: intestine). Golden yellow to orange when moist, small, dull, and inconspicuous when dry; can become a shapeless blob when old and wet.

T. foliacea (fo-lee-ay-sha: leaflike). Brown; clumps up to 8" [20 cm]. Color p 517.

Tree Ear

Auricularia auricula (or-ick-you-la: little ear). Brown (drying blackish) ear-shaped or cupped shelves; texture earlike (rubbery tough) when moist, hard when dry; one side is spore-bearing and usually concave, often facing down; sterile side is silky. On dead wood; common near melting snow. Color p 517.

Tree ears are widely eaten in Chinese soups and other dishes; for Anglos their rubbery texture may be an acquired taste. Witch's butter is sometimes substituted, but its flavor is missing in action. They are saprophytes—rotters, not killers—of both conifers and hardwoods.

Orange-Peel Fungus

Aleuria aurantia (a-**loo**-ria: flour; aw-**ran**-tia: orange). Bright orange thin-fleshed cups; fertile underside paler; no stalk; brittle, not tough; in groups and/or clusters on gravelly soil, e.g. roadsides, or grass or moss. Color p 517.

Orange-peel resembles jelly fungi (the previous two entries) but its spore-bearing organs place it on the other side of the great divide in classification of macrofungi: it's an ascomycete, along with cup fungi, morels, and true truffles, whereas jelly fungi are basidiomycetes along with mushrooms and shelf fungi.

Scorched-Earth Cup

Geopyxis carbonaria (geo-**pix**-iss: earth goblet). Also **fire-following fairy cup**. Tiny (½" tall, or 12 mm) brittle brick to ochre-brown cups, usually with very short stalks; copiously abundant in the first two years after a fire; otherwise rarely seen. Color p 517.

This earth cup is one of the most ubiquitous mycorrhizal partners of the world's boreal forests. Scientists in Sweden found that it seems to be as critically needed as it is common: in the rare instances where a forest burned and *Geopyxis* did not turn up afterward, no new forest came up in its place. They speculate that *Geopyxis* sprouts cups when its host has just died, because that's when it needs its spores to go out and infect new hosts. On the other hand, post-fire studies have found fungal hyphae proliferating in charcoal in soil, so it could be that the charcoal provides some element *Geopyxis* needs in order to produce little scorched-earth cups.

Snowbank False-Morel

Gyromitra gigas (jye-ro-**my**-tra: round hat; jye-gus: giant). Also **snow morel**. Cap dull yellow-brown, convoluted, lacking gills, flesh in cross-section thin, white, brittle; stem white, often ± concealed by cap, nearly as big around as the cap and with similarly convoluted, thin, brittle flesh enclosing many irregular hollow spaces. Under high-elev conifers immediately after snowmelt. Color p 515.

This bizarre-looking fungus is an interesting member of the "snow-bank flora"—things that almost always grow in spring near melting snow. Like many others, I have happily eaten it, but will no longer do so. Countless Europeans, over centuries, happily ate the so-called edible false-morel, *G. esculenta*, yet there were occasional fatalities. The toxin was eventually isolated and found to metabolize in the body into a chemical used (coincidentally) as a rocket fuel for Apollo missions. It's a well-studied chemical—a deadly poison and suspected carcinogen. However, it is volatile enough to be removed by either drying or boiling. The unfortunate fatalities presumably ate undercooked *Gyromitra*.

Modern guides say "POISONOUS" right under the name *esculenta*, meaning "good to eat." Some buffs still eat *esculenta* after scrupulous parboilings, but that's risky: even the steam from parboiling is full of the toxin. Toxin content varies by species. Only trace quantities have been found in *G. gigas*. However, as with so many fungi, we aren't at all sure that all of our snowbank false-morels are of one species, and not many have been tested for toxicity. With so many safer mushrooms around, this one no longer seems worth the risk.

Chanterelles

Cantharellus spp. (canth-a-**rel**-us: small vase). Vase-shaped mushroom (cap undifferentiated from stem), margin often wavy or irregular when mature; spore-bearing surface of rounded ridges (not paper-thin gills) sometimes with slight cross-wrinkles to make a netlike texture; slight peppery aftertaste when raw. On ground, in fall; mycorrhizal usually with Douglas-fir.

White chanterelle, *C. subalbidus* (sub-**al**-bid-us: almost white). Cap white, bruising yellow to (eventually) rusty orange; often very stout and short; spores white. Color p 515.

Pacific golden chanterelle, *C. formosus* (for-**mo**-sus: beautiful) =*C cibarius.* Cap yellow-orange, smooth, underside paler; spores ochre.

The golden chanterelle's popularity stems not from exceptional flavor but from its rich color, easy and safe identification, profuse local

---

Cautious Mushroom-Eating

Only a tiny minority of mushrooms are seriously poisonous. A greater number may make you sick in the stomach, or uncomfortable somewhere else. Still more are considered edible by most who have tried them, but even among "good edibles," many reputations are tainted by a few reports—allergic reactions, really. Even the supermarket mushroom, *Agaricus bisporus,* upsets some tummies. Many other mushrooms go unrecommended on the grounds of flavor or texture; again, one person's "edible and choice" is another person's "Bleccch!"

All in all, the odds favor mushroom eaters, but the risks are too extreme to forgive haphazard identifications. There are old mushroom hunters, the saying goes, and there are bold mushroom hunters, but there are no old bold mushroom hunters. Actually, there was at least one old, bold mycologist: Captain Charles McIlvaine lived into his dotage despite routinely tasting mushroom species on first encounter. He claimed to have tried well over 1,000, and liked most of them.

Mushroom identification is more subtle and technical than most plant identification, often requiring chemical reagents and a microscope. There's much to be said for the rule that nontechnical guides not entirely devoted to mushrooms should forego labeling edibles. But fungal dinners have been such treasured wilderness experiences for this writer that I will share some favorable advice. For eating typical mushrooms—those with a gilled cap on a stem—I refer you to mushroom books (page 600); but I can recommend certain fleshy fungi that either lack paper-thin gills or lack a distinct stem. Each of these species can be separated from poi-

---

abundance, resistance to bugs, and the established place in French cuisine of its smaller, brighter cousin, *C. cibarius*, which grows in Europe and Eastern North America. Many mycophagists regard the white chanterelle as highly as its golden sister. The only poisonous mushroom sometimes mistaken for a chanterelle (aside from the questionable woolly chanterelle, p 296) has true paper-thin gills. Thin gills, with their higher surface-to-volume ratio, are more efficient, and evolutionarily more advanced, than chanterelle-style wrinkles.

Here's good news. Chanterelles were found to fruit slightly *more* abundantly where they're harvested year after year, at least as of thirteen years into the study. In the very long term, who knows? The fungus might suffer if it never got to reproduce from spores.

Shaggy Mane

Coprinus comatus (co-**pry**-nus: dung—, ref to a frequent habitat; co-**may**-tus: woolly). Cap taller than wide, long egg shaped becoming bell-shaped, whitish,

---

sonous species on the basis of a careful look at field characters alone. All the same, you must assume responsibility for your own results, gastronomic and gastrointestinal.

A spore print for observing spore color, used in mushroom identification, is made simply by laying a cap, without stem, flat on a piece of paper for an hour or so. If you put part of the mushroom over inked or colored paper, then white spores will show up as well as dark ones.

Nibbling by mammals or lower creatures is not evidence of safety.

Try a nibble before eating a quantity; give your stomach at least two hours to test it. Each person should test their own stomach. (Test only after identifying. Deadly amanitas and galerinas, pages 263–66, must be absolutely ruled out first, since even a nibble would be dangerous. No morels of any kind, page 282–83, should be eaten raw.)

Small children are much more susceptible to mushroom poisoning and allergies, and should not eat wild mushrooms.

Eat modest quantities, of only one species, when first trying species.

Excessive **bugginess or worminess** occasionally causes stomach upset. If the stems but not the caps show larval bore holes, leave the stems behind so they won't infect the caps.

Carry in **paper bags,** not plastic. Keep mushrooms as cool as possible.

Don't forget to take **plenty of butter,** especially on fall trips. Gentle, thorough sauteing, without a lid, is rarely a bad way to cook a fungus. Scrambled eggs, toast, or crackers rarely fail to compliment.

---

covered with scales that darken; gills fine, white, maturing pinkish; spore print black; stalk has a loose ring; with age, first the cap margins, then the gills, then the whole mushroom turn black and slimy (deliquesce), eventually becoming a black puddle. Summer and fall, usually in clusters, on mineral soil, from parking lots to subalpine meadows. Hard to mistake for anything else, good edible if picked young and cooked soon. Color p 518.

Angel Wings

Pleurocybella porrigens (ploor-oh-si-**bell**-a: a compound of two other genera; **por**-i-jenz: spreading). Pure white, thin-fleshed, fan-shaped, stemless mushrooms growing in groups from the side of fallen, dead, or wounded conifers; mildly fragrant and pleasant-tasting. Fall. Color p Color p 517.

Oyster Mushrooms

Pleurotus populinus (ploor-oh-tus: side ear; pop-you-**lie**-nus: of cottonwoods). =formerly included in *P. ostreatus*. Fan-shaped, usually stemless mushrooms growing in clusters from the side of fallen, dead, or wounded aspens, cottonwoods, or alders; cap tan, cream or oyster-gray; spore print dries pale lilac; mildly fragrant, pleasant-tasting. (Occasionally grows with a short, semihorizontal stem from one edge of the cap—never the center.) Fall.

Stemlessness makes the above pair the only gilled mushrooms I can recommend for eating without more technical identification. Several undesirable species share the stemless or offcenter-stemmed habit, but each can be excluded by at least one of these traits: **tough,** leathery, thin flesh; **saw-toothed** gills; **yellow gills** or **brown spores** or a dark, drab cap; **intense bitter** or peppery taste (take small nibbles, don't swallow). We also have an oyster mushroom, *P. elongatipes*, which usually has a distinct off-center stem, but otherwise looks a lot like *P. populinus*. You can exclude it, too, without danger of missing out on a major treat.

If you find oysters or angel wings, search the log for more; the fungus inhabits the entire log and may fruit here and there all over it. Slice them off, and they may produce another crop. Tiny beetles between the gills can be knocked loose by tapping briskly. Delicately tasty, angel-wings distinctly enhance the flavor of warm butter.

Everyone has heard of carnivorous plants, like Venus' flytrap, but carnivorous fungi are news. Tiny nematode worms have long been observed tunneling in mushrooms for dinner. Many saprophytic fungi, it now turns out, turn the tables and "eat" their nematodes. The oyster has specialized cells that splash poison onto nematodes that touch them; hyphae then seek, invade, and digest the immobilized worm. Scarcity of nitrogen in saprophytic diets has forced saprophytes to acquire ways of ingesting nitrogen-rich organisms such as animals and nitrogen-fixing soil bacteria.

Hedgehog Mushroom

Hydnum repandum (hid-num: truffle; rep-**and**-um: wavy-edged). =*Dentinum repandum*. Also **sweet tooth mushroom**. Cap yellow-orange to buff or nearly white, only vaguely differentiated from stem; underside covered with fine pale teeth of mixed lengths (average ¼", or 6 mm.) in lieu of gills; spores white. Mycorrhizal with Douglas-fir; on ground, summer through fall. Color p 516.

Eyes scouring for soft gold caps of chanterelles may jump at this one; fingers are in for a surprise when they reach underneath and find a soft, spiny texture. Don't be disappointed—this mushroom is edible, and even harder to confuse with anything poisonous. Some toothed relatives, however, are bitter. The tiniest taste-test will tell you.

Scaly Hedgehog

Sarcodon imbricatus (sar-co-don: fleshy tooth; im-brick-**ay**-tus: shingled). =*Hydnum imbricatum*. Cap large, 2–8" [5–20 cm], gray-brown, dry, with coarse dark scales in a concentric pattern; underside covered with fine teeth in lieu of gills; spores medium brown; stalk stout, light brown inside and out. Mycorrhizal with conifers, summer and fall. Color p 516.

The idea of eating this coarse dingy species disconcerts some people, and a few have reported stomach upsets or a little bitterness, mainly from overmature specimens, but I've enjoyed it. It cannot be mistaken for anything except close relatives, which are more bitter.

King Boletus

Boletus edulis (bo-lee-tus: clod; ed-you-lis: edible). Also **porcini, cepe, steinpilz**. Cap 3-12" diam [8–30 cm], skin tan to red-brown, often redder just under surface, ± bumpy but not fibrous, often sticky; flesh ± white, firm; pores white, becoming olive to tawny yellow with age or bruising, but never blue; stem often very bulbous, white with ± brown skin, upper part finely net-surfaced; spores olive-brown. Mycorrhizal with conifers. Summer to early fall. Color p 516.

Most boletes are in one of two enormous genera, *Boletus* and *Suillus*. Both words were used by the Romans for certain mushrooms; one derives from the Greek for "a lump of earth," which boletes sometimes resemble, and the other from the Latin for "pigs," who are fond of eating them. *Porcini* ("piglets") is the Italian word for them.

Boletes are generally mycorrhizal. Some serve as hosts to nongreen plants in the heath family, while also partnering with trees.

Suillus

Suillus spp. (sue-**ill**-us: piglet). Also **slippery jack** (some have slimy-caps).

S. lakei (**lake**-eye: after E. R. Lake). Cap rough with red-brown flat scales, yellow and ± sticky under the scales; flesh and tubes ± yellow, maturing orange, may bruise reddish; tubes angular and radially stretched when mature; stem has whitish ring when young; base bruises blue-green; spores brown to cinnamon. Always near Douglas-fir. Edible, tasty to some.

S. cavipes (**cav**-i-peez: hollow foot). Cap dry, with reddish to brown scales; flesh and tubes ± pale yellow, not bruising blue; tube mouths angular, strongly radial-arranged when mature; stem reddish-scaly below ring, smooth white and slightly narrower above ring, while the white-fibrous ring itself may disappear; stem becoming hollow; spores dark brown. Always near larches. Ranges from a good edible to mediocre or bitter. Color p 516.

S. tomentosus (toe-men-**toe**-sus: woolly). Cap dry, with fine fibrous scales (but may become smooth in age, and then slimy when wet; flesh pale yellow to orange-buff, bruising blue ± slowly; stem covered with brownish specks; no veil or ring; spores dark brown. Edible, ± tasty, but see below re blue stain. Color p 516.

S. granulatus (gran-you-**lay**-tus: granular, a misleading name). Cap tacky- to slimy-skinned, tan to cinnamon, faintly mottled; flesh white to cream; tubes tan to yellow, very small, "dewy" in youth, staining or speckling brown with age; no veil or ring; stem white, developing brown dots or smears with age; spores cinnamon to ochre. Under lodgepole or ponderosa pines. Good edible.

Cautious Bolete-Eating

Many of our better edible mushrooms are boletes, or members of the family Boletaceae. They look like regular gilled mushrooms from above, but when picked reveal a spore-bearing undersurface consisting of a spongy mass of vertical tubes. If you tear the cap, you will see that the tubes are distinct from the smooth-textured flesh above them, and can usually be peeled away. Most boletes range between choice and merely edible, and none are commonly deadly. The relatively few nonrecommended species can be ruled out rather simply, so the rest can be eaten without necessarily identifying them to species. Boletes begin fruiting in midsummer, earlier than most edibles, and they are often large, supplying hearty eatings from few pickings. Their main drawback, as a group, is rapid susceptibility to insects, decay and moldy growths.

Here are the cautionary rules:

Never eat a bolete with **red-orange or pinkish-tinged** tube openings; this trait characterizes all the moderately toxic species.

Try a nibble of the cap for the **bitter, burning or peppery tastes** that make some other boletes undesirable.

S. brevipes (**brev**-i-peez: short foot). Like *S. granulatus*, but cap starts deep red-brown and pales to ochre with age, and the short stem remains pure white except, rarely, for faint dots in great age; and pores don't stain. Choice edible. Color p 516.

Suillus species almost all live mycorrhizally with conifers; many require pines or larches as partners. A genus of small truffles, or underground-fruiting fungi, shares nearly all of its DNA with *Suillus*, suggesting either that some very recent ancestors split into underground and aboveground modes, or even that some of these species can produce either mushrooms or truffles. At the very least, this finding put to rest any notion of truffles as a taxonomic lineage. *Suillus*'s alter-ego, *Rhizopogon*, is of no epicurean interest, but may be critically important to western conifers, if we judge by its abundance.

No American *Suillus* is reported as poisonous aside from warnings about numerous allergic reactions often blamed on the skin, which can be peeled before cooking. However, no single field trait distinguishes *Suillus* from *Boletus*, which includes poisonous species. Traits more common in *Suillus* than in *Boletus* include a partial veil that persists for a while as a ring on the stalk; a glutinous skin on the cap (slimy when wet, tacky when dry); and glandular dots on at least the upper part of the mature stem.

Avoid boletes whose tubes **turn deep blue** (or "bruise") within a minute or two, where handled. While a few species mildly toxic to some people show this sharp reaction, as do some of the red-tubed toxics, many of the best edibles may also bruise bluish, at least slowly, at least sometimes or in some of their parts. Many mushroom eaters in this region are undeterred by the blue bruising unless it is intense and quick, or the tube-mouths are at all reddish.

If the cap has a **gelatinous or sticky skin**, remove this. It upsets some people's bowels. Most people also prefer to peel off and discard the tubes from mature specimens.

Look closely for **larval pinholes** by slicing or snapping the stem from the cap; if there are few or none, the cap is in good condition. Then slice through the stem at mid height, and look again. If you still find few or no holes or discolorations, the stem can be eaten along with the cap flesh, especially if there is a shortage of good caps. If the stem is buggy, discard it immediately rather than giving the larvae a chance to spread.

Don't expect boletes to keep longer than overnight in any case, except very clean young specimens in chilly weather or a refrigerator. Carry in paper bags, out of direct sun.

Coral Fungi

Yellow coral, *Ramaria rasilospora* (ra-**mair**-ia: branched; ra-sil-a-**spor**-a: scraped spores). Cauliflowerlike structure, but not as thick-based as the following; branches mainly erect; flesh from nearly white to ocher or light orange; ± same color throughout (exc tips brown when quite old); odor and flavor very mild.; spores pale yellow. Color p Color p 517.

Purple-tipped coral, *R. botrytis* (ra-**mair**-ia: branched; bo-**try**-tiss: bunch of grapes). Cauliflowerlike structure, the fat white bases (often clustered) much more massive than the branchings on top; the blunt branch tips brownish rose to red, dulling with age; base typically submerged in duff or moss, leaving only the tips exposed; delicately fragrant; spores ochre. Under mature conifers in early fall.

The entire group of corallike branching fungi that grow on the ground or on rotten wood is relatively harmless, but includes a few stomach-upsetting species. One of those, *R. formosa* ("beautiful"); has slim vertical branches (not thick like cauliflower), and is peachy-pink when fresh except for yellowish tips. (Actually more beautiful is the similar deep purple coral, *R. purpurea,* sometimes seen on boggy trailsides.) These and other species that show translucent, gelatinous cores in cross-section are not recommended. The remaining corals are nonpoisonous, but few are good eating. The purple-tipped has provided me with fine camp dinners (and one unpleasant night after I ate too much). It makes itself hard to spot, but once you've seen one and attuned your eyes, you may find many more. Beware of its intensely bitter look-alike, *R. botrytoides.*

Bear's Head Tooth Fungus

Hericium abietis (her-**iss**-ium: hedgehog; ay-bih-**ee**-tiss: of fir trees) =*H. coralloides.* Also **coral hydnum.** Large, 6–12" [15–30 cm] or rarely up to 30" high × 16" [75 × 40 cm] white to cream fungus consisting of many branches and sub-branches ending in fine teeth all pointing down; rounded overall, with crowded short branches from a massive, solid base; spores white. Saprophytic, on dead conifer wood or tree wounds, esp true firs; late summer, early fall. Color p 516.

Spectacular appearance puts this in both the "Safe for Beginners" and the "Scenic Resource" categories unless you find one well away from a trail; trailside specimens should be left alone as visual treasures. Though popular with small mammals, it gets mixed reviews from people: fragrance and flavor are lovely, but the texture bothers some. The larger branches can be tough and hard to digest. Cut into the mass discreetly, removing only modest quantities of such parts as are pure white and have few or no bore holes from insect larvae.

Soak them in a pot of water to float any beetles out from the crevices. Then mince and saute gently.

Nomenclature in this genus is Byzantine. *H. abietis* is in older guides as *H. coralloides*, but that species was split, with *H. coralloides* confined to hardwoods in eastern NA. Then that species was renamed *H. americanum* when *H. coralloides* was shown to be exclusively Eurasian. Western cottonwoods also have *H. ramosum.*

Puffballs

Pear puffball, *Lycoperdon pyriforme* (lie-co-**per**-don: wolf fart; pie-rif-**or**-me: pear shape). Stalkless ± pear-shaped balls, lacking any kind of gills; upper skin turning light brown; flesh initially pure white, marshmallow-textured, later turning first brown then green and soggy. In large clusters on soil.

Gemmed puffball, *L. perlatum* (per-**lay**-tum: very widespread). As above, but covered with crumb-like fine bumps. Color p Color p 516.

Warted giant puffball, *Calbovista subsculpta* (cal-bo-**vis**-ta: bald foxfart—a compound formed from bald-looking genus *Calvatia* and genus *Bovista*, an onomatopoetic German word based on the widespread puffball origin myth; sub-**sculpt**-a: somewhat sculptured). Stalkless, slightly flattened ball 3–6" diam, white patterned with brownish raised polygons. (Positive identification is technical, but similar *Calvatia* spp are also edible.) Scattered among subalpine grasses, or under conifers; in midsummer. Color p Color p 516.

Most *Lycoperdons* are as small as golf balls, but *Calbovista* is baseball-sized, and their *Calvatia* cousins can grow to basketball size or more. Puffballs are a family of fungi whose round or pear-shaped fruiting bodies have neither cap nor stem nor gills. The maturing skin either splits open or opens a small hole at the top, and spores come puffing out by the millions when the puffball is struck by feet or raindrops. Spores, like pollen, are "hydrophobic" or resistant to wetting, so their flight is undamped by rain or fog. Puffball spores, a hundred times smaller than most spores and pollen grains, are barely even subject to gravity; squeeze a ripe puffball on a breezy day, and you may truly be sending a few spores around the world.

Puffballs have been used medicinally in many cultures. Some are thought to contain anticarcinogens. No true puffballs are poisonous, but young "buttons" of deadly amanitas can be mistaken for them, so you must **slice every puffball you pick through its center vertically,** and eat only those that are pure undifferentiated white inside, from tip to toe. Amanita buttons in cross-section reveal at least a faint outline of developing stem and gills. Also discard specimens with a green-, brown-, or yellow-stained center, or a punky center distinct from a

---

smooth ⅛" [3 mm] outer rind. The former indicates a maturing puff-ball, the latter a *Scleroderma* ("hard skin") fungus; both are un-pleasant but not dangerous. Puffballs take a couple of weeks to mature, so you stand a sporting chance of catching them young enough.

If it's your first taste of puffball, just pick a small sample. You may hate it. The flavor is mild, pleasantly fungal, but the texture is slippery where sliced, marshmallowy within. Frying hot enough to brown the surface helps. My proudest trailside effort was a lunch of warted giant puffball sandwiches—half-inch slices fried in butter with garlic, on crackers thinly layered with anchovy paste and cheese.

Morels

Morchella spp. (mor-**kel**-a: from Old High German word for morel). 2–8"+ tall. Cap conical or rod-shaped to egg-shaped or round, the exterior honeycombed with strong ridges with deep pits in between; flesh brittle. Interior hollow, the single long hollow shared by cap and stalk; cap, attached very near its bottom to the stalk, has no underside and no gills. Stalk smooth or wrinkled; ± white. Odor slight or pleasant. Abundance peaks in late spring.
Black morel, *M. elata* (ee-**lay**-ta: tall) or *M.angusticeps* (ang-**goose**-ti-seps: narrow cap) or *M. conica.* Mainly in areas burned 1–3 years prior. Color p 515.
Yellow morel, *M. esculenta* (es-cue-**len**-ta: good to eat). 2–6"+ tall. Common-est at low elevs with hardwoods. Color p 515.

Black morels rise like phoenixes from the ashes of burned areas where morels have been in the soil without fruiting for many decades. It's a mystery whether these "phoenicoid" mushrooms are responding to heat-treated dirt or to a sudden plethora of food in the form of dead trees. They also fruit abundantly in forests attacked by bark beetles (not heat-treated), and in deep Mt. St. Helens tephra (heat-treated). At St. Helens they proved their value to succession, popping up on barren ash; where they rotted back into the ash, algae and mosses soon flourished. Commercial morel pickers flock to burned areas in the spring following a fire; this predictability helps make black morels the richest mushroom harvest in our region.

Yellow morels are at least as tasty, and reasonably abundant, but harder to find. They seem camouflaged among old leaves, just as black morels are camouflaged amid scorched vegetation and pine cones. Two traditional tips are to follow the sweet smell of cotton-woods in spring, or to look in old apple orchards. Though primarily saprophytic, morels occasionally form mycorrhizae.

You can eat morels safely as long as you cook them and slice them lengthwise to make sure you find the key traits: honeycombed cap attached at its bottom (i.e. it has no underside, only the full length hollow interior shared with the stem); and pleasant odor.

Morels recently succumbed to decades of efforts at cultivation, and you can order cultivated ones by mail. Though slightly inferior to wild ones and scarcely cheaper, they are available year-round.

Taxonomy within *Morchella* is in chaos. Better species concepts may be needed to resolve it. The old ideas of black and white morel species may get jettisoned: there are too many perfect in-betweens, and in the greenhouse "blacks" seem to beget "whites." Unlike most mushrooms, in which you find identical DNA in many fruiting bodies and year after year on a site, morels behave more like annual plants, or at least they don't tend to grow in extensive clones: adjacent fruiting bodies typically have different DNA.

Sulphur Shelf Fungus

Laetiporus sulphureus (lee-**tip**-or-us: bright pores; sul-**few**-rius: sulphur yellow) =*Polyporus sulphureus*. Also **chicken-of-the-woods.** Thick, fleshy shelflike growths 2-12" wide, typically in large overlapping clusters; orange above, yellow below. On conifers, summer through fall (long-lasting). Color p 517.

The shelf fungus family, Polyporaceae, is characterized by simple fruiting bodies that release spores through tiny pores on their smooth undersides. The pores are never separable from the cap flesh. Dense, rather woody flesh makes these fungi much longer-lasting than mushrooms and hence more often seen than numbers alone warrant; but it doesn't do a thing for their edibility. The one relatively tender exception is the sulphur shelf, a good edible when young. To some tastes it's just like chicken; I find it lemony.

No serious toxins have been found in the shelf fungus family. Occasional adverse reactions to this species have been blamed variously on eucalyptus as the host tree (no problem here) or on allergies, excessive consumption, or mature specimens. Take only the outer edges, and only if your knife finds them butter-tender, lemon-yellow rather than deep orange, and fat and wavy rather than thin and corrugated. New tender margins should grow in their place. Since this is both a gastronomic and a scenic resource to be shared with other hikers, limit yourself to a quantity you can easily eat, and don't even think about cutting up growths right next to a trail.

Most shelf fungi live as heart rot in either dead or living trees; in either case the cells they attack are dead cells (only the thin outer layers of a tree are alive) so they are technically saprophytes, but they can weaken trees to where the wind can break them, and they spoil the lumber, making themselves economic pests in timber country. From an ecological point of view, killing a tree here and there in the forest is beneficial: it provides habitat, lets in light, and altogether enhances plant and animal diversity. (See page 299.)

A less tasty shelf fungus called turkey-tail, with a long and nearly worldwide history as a folk remedy, has shown activity in lab tests against tumors *and* viruses *and* cholesterol levels.

Fuzzy Truffles

Geopora cooperi (geo-**por**-a: hole in the earth; coop-er-eye: after J. G. Cooper). Roundish lumps ¾-3" diam [2–8 cm]; exterior shallowly furrowed, covered with light to dark brown fuzz; interior a convoluted mass of white to cream or tan folds. Buried or in the duff layer or, if partially buried, often partly eaten; under other conifers, or possibly willow or aspen in the north. April–Oct.

Truffles live mycorrhizally just like many mushrooms, but instead of giving their spores to the wind to carry, they use distinctive aromas to entice mammals to eat them. (See page 359.) Some get by with tiny fruits that get moved around accidentally by burrowing animals.

Many truffle-like (i.e., aromatic underground-fruiting) species abound in our forests. Most are rarely seen, since they are underground, but the fuzzy, in addition to being one of our largest and tastiest, tends to reach the surface as it ages, often because it is dug up by a squirrel. If you interrupt a squirrel messing around in the duff, check what is was messing with. If you interrupt snails dining on them, expect slime. Larry Evans describes the fuzzy's aroma as

---

Mycocuisines of the World

Moira Savonius of England attributes to the sulphur shelf fungus "an unpleasant sour smell as well as a nasty taste," while American Vincent Marteka rates it the first choice in a poll of American mushroom hunters, and writes of traditional use of it by Native Americans. There are many transoceanic differences of opinion over which mushrooms are delicious, and over which are poisonous. Most flavor and toxicity differences are real, and probably trace to different soils and plant hosts. A few may be geographic races or not-yet-recognized species.

Culture also plays a role. The English have a mycophobic tradition that regards only species of *Agaricus* (like the supermarket button mushroom) as deserving either the term "mushroom" or a place on the table. In sharp contrast, Italians have a mania for amanitas and boletes; French go for truffles, morels, chanterelles and boletes; and Slavs, the most eclectic in their tastes, are intimate with species in dicey genera like

---

"fruity and morel-like at once." To retain the aroma, truffles must be cooked either sealed (e.g., in foil) or very briefly (e.g., shaved onto hot food just when it is finished cooking).

Few humans have good enough noses to locate truffles underground. Some trufflers take rakes to appropriate habitat, but raking (also practiced by some in the matsutake trade) is bad for forests. Europe's fabulously valuable truffles are harvested with the help of dogs or sow pigs that sniff them out. The dogs have to be trained, but the sows come pre-programmed, and merely have to be restrained: the French white truffle produces a fragrance chemically identical to one in a boar's pheromones, which the sows find extremely attractive.

Rhizopogon species are so ubiquitous here that you could probably find them in almost any forest. They are small, drab, and of no gastronomic interest. Their genes are so nearly identical to certain *Suillus* species that it looks like the two genera should be combined. There may even be species that fruit either above or belowground, depending on conditions. The close kinship shows us, at the very least, that gross similarities or differences in the form of the fruiting body are not good bases for classification. "True" truffles (like *Geopora*) and "false" truffles (like *Rhizopogon*) are only distantly related, being Basidiomycetes and Ascomycetes, respectively.

A certain Professor Frank, commissioned to cultivate truffles in Prussia in the 1880s, failed to grow any, but he looked at them so closely that he serendipitously made one of the great advances in mycology: he discovered and named the mycorrhiza.

Russula and *Lactarius*, some of which they render harmless by soaking and brining. Chinese and Japanese traditions are bringing stranger fungal flavors and textures to American palates—leathery "tree-ears," resiny "pine mushrooms," "straw mushrooms" grown in bottles for legginess, and "black fungus" cured in brine.

Japanese prices have exceeded $200 a pound [CDN$600 per kilo] for American matsutakes, *Tricholoma magnivelare*. Lorelei Norvell assures us we can identify matsutakes by their "delicious" fragrance, but *Mushrooms of Northeast North America* drily insinuates that the emperor has no clothes: "odor like dirty gym socks but usually described as spicy-sweet, aromatic, fruity, or fragrant." My take on this brouhaha, expressed delicately, is that there may be a chance convergence between matsutake vapors and human pheromones, analogous to the one between French truffles and pig pheromone (discussed above).

And yes, they do smell kind of like delicious dirty gym socks.

Lichens are fungi specialized to meet their carbohydrate needs from algae and/or bacteria they enclose. This symbiotic association is highly developed, producing organs, tissues and chemicals found only in lichens. Lichens differ conspicuously from other fungi in that they grow in the open and are tough, durable, and able to dry out and revive again. (Contrast this not with the mushroom but with the fungus "body," which lives all year long in soil or wood beneath the mushroom site). The lichen symbiosis seems to have evolved separately in eighteen or twenty different branches of the fungus family tree. About forty genera of "photobionts"—either algae or cyanobacteria—partner the several hundred genera of lichen fungi, comprising about one-fourth of all named fungi.

It would be misleading to single out lichens as two part combo organisms. While a few invertebrate animals also incorporate symbiotic algae, a closer analogy is everywhere staring us in the face: green plants evolved by incorporating symbiotic cyanobacteria to do their photosynthesizing. Plants have these cyanobacteria—now evolved into little cell organs called chloroplasts—within their cells.

Calling the lichen symbiosis mutually beneficial is questionable. At about seven percent of the tissue mass of a typical lichen, photobionts are in a cultivated role a bit like that of intestinal flora that live symbiotically in mammals. A farm offers a useful analogy: just as irrigation enables plants to grow in climates too dry for them, and barns and hay let cattle live in climates too snowy, lichen fungi benefit algae in allowing them to grow on sites far too severe for free-living algae. They offer both physical shelter and chemical protection; the best-known functions of special lichen chemicals are to repel herbivores, microbes, and competing plants. You might say we have here counterparts to a farmer's greenhouse, pesticides, herbicides, and deer repellent. So you could view the symbiosis as mutualistic, yet it's pretty clear who's using whom. a better description might be "controlled parasitism:" the fungi harvest their green partners, but slowly, so that the herd, or crop, can increase.

It was formerly assumed that lichen spores can't take up the farming life unless they happen to land near a free alga. It would necessarily follow that all lichen algae are species capable of living on their own. In fact, the commonest genus of lichen alga, *Trebouxia,* has never been found outside of a lichen. It turns out that lichen spores take their *Trebouxia* from other lichens. On the other hand, the second commonest alga, *Trentepohlia*, and most lichen cyanobacteria are reasonably common as free-living organisms.

Most lichens do, at least sometimes, produce spores in fruiting bodies analogous to those of other fungi. Sexual propagation via spores enables lichens to adapt to changing environments, but once they are well adapted, it is far less efficient—and far less common—than clonal reproduction from fragments that include both partners together. These may be just any old fragment that happens to break off, or they may be specially evolved propagative bundles ("propagules") in the form of powders, grains or tiny protuberances.

Lichens are loosely (not taxonomically) sorted by growth form. Three forms did the trick for over a century, but recent books tend to use several. We'll go with four:

Crust lichens are thin coatings or stains on or in rock or bark surfaces—so thin that you could not pry them up.

Leaf lichens are also thin, ranging from saladlike heaps attached to their substrate in only a few spots to closely adhering, paintlike sheets with distinct, thick, margins that can (by definition) with sufficient effort be pried intact from the substrate.

Shrub lichens are made of fine branches, either erect or pendent.

Twig lichens stand up, with moderate or no branching, often above a mat of scales.

Of all familiar, visible organisms, lichens have perhaps the most modest requirements—a little moisture once in a while, any amount of sunlight from minimal to excessive, and solid materials carried in even the cleanest air. From minimal input comes meager output; they commonly grow .02–1" [.5–25 mm] per year, but rain forest lungworts are faster and alpine crusts are much slower (see p 317).

Lichens spend much of their lives dried out, all activity suspended. In this state they can survive temperatures from 150° [65° C] (typical of soil surfaces in the summer sun) down to near absolute zero (in labs). They have to dry out and suspend respiration to get through hot days in the sun, yet at 32° [0° C] or somewhat colder they remain active and unfrozen, thanks to complex chemistry including alcohols. Our alpine lichens get some of their photosynthesizing done while buried in snow, which keeps them moist and lets sunlight in. Lichens on rocks can sustain activity as long as they are supplied with atmospheric moisture—rain, snow, dew, fog, or mere humidity. As with mosses only more so, success in lichen niches is a matter of making hay while the rain falls, and then drying up. Perhaps the best-known lichen habitats are alpine and recently deglaciated rocks. The lushest growths of lichens are in a seemingly opposite environment with moderate temperatures, low light levels and high rainfall: the bark of rain forest trees. There, too, the lichens dry out every time rain and fog stop for a few days. Most lichens will actually die if they don't get to dry out periodically.

Lichens that colonize bare rock may, after centuries of life, death and decomposition, alter the rock enough for plants to grow, initiating a succession of biotic communities. Countless naturalists from Linnaeus to our high school biology teachers have been enamored of this scenario to the point of over-selling it. Nature has faster ways of both crumbling rocks and fixing nitrogen. Many pioneer plants employ either free-living or root-nodule bacteria. Mosses loosely coated with cyanobacteria pioneer on rock, and nodulated trees and shrubs like alders pioneer in crevices that hold a bit of fine gravel or dust. On barren ash at Mt. St. Helens, nitrogen-fixing lupines and other perennials were the chief pioneers; the small lichen patches that did turn up tended more to inhibit than to nurture plant growth.

While lichens may pulverize less rock, worldwide, than frost does, their abilities are nonetheless impressive. They actually drill into rock with tiny fingers ("haustoria"), and their gelatinous gripping surfaces expand and contract as they moisten and dry out,

Air Pollution Indicators

Lichens have discriminating tastes for airborne solids and solutions which, after all, they live on. While few lichens survive in the worst urban air, different lichens tolerate different amounts and types of air pollution. They also accumulate it in their tissues. Scientists use them to monitor an airshed's pollution over the years by checking which species are present, and by taking pieces of lichen to the lab to test for particular compounds. Compared to simply testing air samples, this has the advantage of averaging pollution over a long period of time.

Archaeologists concerned about fading petroglyphs (ancient art on rocks) in Hell's Canyon asked lichenologist Linda Geiser to find out if air pollution could be the culprit even in that remote wilderness. The answer: quite possibly. This time the telltale clue came not from missing lichens but from oddly abundant ones—a belt of bright orange *Xanthoria* species (p 322), which require excess nitrogen or calcium—between the waterline and 200 feet up [60 m]. In the alpine zone, extra nitrogen comes from urine, but N in Snake River water likely comes from Idaho's feedlots, fish farms, and crop fertilizers running off and reaching riverside lichens and petroglyphs in the form of acidic spray or fog.

crumbling rock. They also secrete acids that dissolve minerals from rock. I would generalize that succession scarcely needs lichens on deglaciated terrain and volcanic ashfall, which have plenty of finely broken rock, but on solid lava lichens must be a big help.

A second appealing myth inspired by lichens' minimal needs proposes them as candidates for restarting evolution after a global ecocatastrophe. During the era of atmospheric H-bomb tests, and again after Chernobyl, arctic lichens accumulated radioactive fallout without apparent harm to themselves, while passing on carcinogenic amounts of it into the bones of lichen-eating caribou and caribou-eating Inuit and Saami ("Eskimos" and "Lapps"). But while lichens seem to tolerate radioactive pollution, most are critically sensitive to more abundant air pollutants, like sulphur dioxide

---

Fungi: crust lichens

Map Lichen

Rhizocarpon geographicum (rye-zo-**car**-pon: root fruit). Chartreuse yellow patches interrupted by black lines and black nodules, surrounded by a wider black margin. On rocks; abundant in exposed situations. Color p 519.

Lichens grow at very slow but fairly steady rates. Especially steady, and ubiquitous on arctic and alpine rocks, map lichen dominates the science of lichenometry, which estimates the number of centuries elapsed since glaciers retreated from the rocks. Radial growth rates of 3 and 3⅓ millimeters per century—after a slightly faster initial growth spurt, so to speak—were found for map lichens in Colorado and Wyoming; 3,000-year-old lichens were 4 to 4½" in diameter [10–11 cm].

Chartreuse Cobblestone Lichen

Pleopsidium chlorophanum (plee-op-**sid**-ium: full faces, ref. to a microscopic part; clor-o-**fay**-num: green appearance). =*Acarospora chlorophana*. Brilliant chartreuse (greenish-yellow) shiny, pebbly crust, without other colors; fruiting disks common but inconspicuous. Abundant on basalt, all elevs; common on other non-calcareous rocks at high elevs. Color pp 519, 540.

Alpine Bloodclot Lichen

Ophioparma ventosa (oaf-io-**par**-ma: snake shield; ven-**toe**-sa: windblown). =*Haematomma lapponica*, in part. The only crust lichen with dark red to orange fruiting disks; these are raised, pale-rimmed; the crust is thick, bumpy, pale greenish yellow to ± white. On high-elev noncalcareous rocks, uncommon. Color p 519.

Brown Tile Lichens

Lecidea atrobrunnea (les-**id**-ia: small dish; atro-**brun**-ia: black brown). Pebbly crust of black (fruiting disk) and dark brown tiles, all brown toward the margins, ± mixed near the center. Very common on (mainly igneous) rocks.

Tephromela armenaica (tef-ro-**mee**-la: ash honey, ref to the two colors; armen-**ay**-ic-a: of Armenia). Pebbly crust of black and yellow to reddish brown tiles. On high-elev rocks. There is some debate over which one of these two species appears on color p 519.

Yolk Lichens

Candelariella vitellina (can-del-airy-**ell**-a: little brilliant; vit-el-**eye**-na: egg yolk—). Bright egg-yolk yellow crust (not as green as chartreuse cobblestone lichen nor as orange as jewel lichen, p 322) in small rosettes; fruiting disks ± abundant, raised. On non-calcareous rock, esp granite. Color p 538.

C. terrigena (teh-**ridg**-en-a: earth dwelling). Bright egg-yolk yellow crust on alpine soil or moss, usually without fruiting disks.

Spraypaint Lichen

Icmadophila ericetorum (ick-ma-**doff**-ill-a: mudlover; er-iss-e-**tor**-um: among heaths). Also **pixie barf**. Pale blue-green (moist) or nearly white (dry) ± granular crust dotted with white-rimmed, slightly raised pink fruiting disks; the disks are on short stalks if you look closely enough. Growing over moist moss or rotten wood or peat—often on trailsides. Color p 519.

Bloody-Heart Lichen

Mycoblastus sanguinarius (my-co-**blas**-tus: fungus bud; sang-gwin-**air**-ius: blood red). Gray patches without sharp edges, on bark, texture grainy to warty, with clusters of ± shiny blackish fruiting disks .05-.1" diam [1–2.5 mm]; under each black disk, if it's sliced off, is a bright red spot in the lichen cortex. On bark in moist forest.

Dust Lichens

Also **imperfect lichens, powdery paint lichens**.

Lepraria spp. (lep-**rair**-ia: leprous, i.e., scurfy). Color p 519.

Chrysothrix chlorina (clor-**eye**-na: greenish yellow).

This degenerate form of lichen growth is just a granular coat of fungi and algae bundled together in little clumps called "soredia." Many lichens have soredia as their vegetative propagules. Apparently dust lichens came about when some soredia—in several unrelated lines of lichens—achieved the trick of propagating more soredia without having to propagate the rest of the lichen.

Lacking the tough cortex layer of more complete lichens, dust lichens are more vulnerable to drying out, but better able to absorb moisture from the air. Indeed, they live by absorbing humidity from the air. They are unable to absorb liquid water; they actually repel raindrops and drips. Therefore they specialize in deprived substrates like the undersides of limbs and rock overhangs. Naturally, they like foggy climates and go absolutely wild in waterfall spray zones.

"With only the slightest exaggeration," writes lichenologist Trevor Goward, "dust lichens may be said to drink without water, photosynthesize without sunshine, and reproduce, so far as we know, without sex." Early naturalists filed them under *Lichenes Imperfecti* within Deuteromycetes, two taxonomic dustbins indicating the naturalists' inability to categorize fungi that had never been seen with sexual organs. Modern molecular techniques allow transferring former members of these dustbins into their rightful places all over the great family tree. Genus *Chrysothrix* was created to hold some species formerly in *Lepraria*.

Lepraria neglecta and/or the similar *L. cacuminum* seem to fill in bare spaces in almost any sort of alpine community, frosting old dead moss turf or bare soil with white, and typically producing a nubbly texture of 2" [5 cm] mounds. *L. neglecta* also abounds on bark, specializing in twigs and in dry sides of trees. It looks simply like a powdery white coating with indistinct, fading margins and no specialized organs.

Chrysothrix chlorina forms brilliant chartreuse green coatings on rocks—typically moist overhangs or in waterfall spray zones.

Cryptobiotic Crusts

In alpine and cold steppe environments, the surface is commonly a structured mix of soil with cyanobacteria, small bits of lichens, moss, and fungi. The resulting crust, ranging from one-eighth of an inch to over an inch thick [3–25+ mm], often goes unnoticed, but is of vital benefit to plants. It stays relatively cool and moist in the sun, resists erosion, and (when it includes cyanobacteria either free-living or in lichens) fixes nitrogen.

This cryptobiotic crust (the word means "hidden life") is easy to damage and slow to repair itself. A footprint in it can last for decades. If you hike off-trail in the alpine zone, always plant your feet on bare rock or snow as much as you can; second best would be raw gravels or dense sedge turf, which are more durable than crusted soils.

In ungrazed steppe or "desert," alternatives to crust may be harder to find. In any case, staying in the trail is always best.

Dog Lichens

Peltigera spp. (pel-**tidge**-er-a: shield bearer). Also **veined lichens, pelts.** Big sheets with lobed and curled-up margins; conspicuous tan to dark red, ± tooth-shaped fruiting bodies on lobe edges; underside of some spp netted with branching veins, raised from surface, bearing coarse hairlike rhizines.Color p 521.

P. canina (ca-**nye**-na: of dogs). Gray or brownish, covered with minute hair visible with handlens; lobe edges often downcurled; rhizines tufted; forest soil.

P. rufescens (roo-**fes**-enz: reddening, a misleading name). Gray or brownish, covered with minute hair visible with handlens; lobes only 1–4⅜" wide [2.5–11 cm], upturned, often whitish; rhizines densely matted; abundant in sun, from dry forests to alpine crusts.

P. membranacea. Gray or brownish, covered (at least near edges and on underside veins) with minute hair visible with handlens; rhizines separate, long (often ⅜", or 1 cm). Moist forest floor.

P. leucophlebia (loo-co-**flee**-bia: white veins). Bright green above when wet, with many warty dark bumps; pale green to tan when dry; edges ± ruffled; white underside has thick dark veins grading to white near edges, with tufts of light or dark rhizines; if fruiting disks are present, they are smooth brown above and green-white mottled beneath.. On soil or rotten wood. Color p 521.

P. aphthosa (af-**tho**-sa: blistered). Like *leucophlebia,* exc edges not ruffled, and underside has a heavy mat of rhizines but no conspicuous veins; if fruiting disks are present on the edges, they are smooth brown above and white beneath. On mossy ground, wood, or tree bases.

"Frog's blankets," my favorite name for these lichens, is a translation of what BC's Gitxsan people called them. The European name dates from the medieval Doctrine of Signatures, which looked in nature for semblances of body parts and read them as drug prescriptions in God's own handwriting. In the dog lichen's erect fruiting bodies they saw dog teeth, so they prescribed dog lichen for dogbite disease: the decoction for rabies, right up until the last century, was ground dog lichen and black pepper in milk. The Doctrine was a serious wrong turn in the history of herbal medicine. Lichens do have medicinal value, and were used more effectively in pre-Christian Europe.

Dark gray lichens have nitrogen-fixing cyanobacteria, often of genus *Nostoc,* as their chief photosynthesizing partners. In green dog lichens like *P. leucophlebia,* which mainly employ green algae, *Nostoc* joins in here and there in dark superficial bumps cultivated where *Nostoc* colonies have fallen.

British Columbia has at least 25 gray and 4 green species of *Peltigera,* more than any other part of the world.

Green-Light Lichen

Nephroma arcticum (nef-**ro**-ma: kidney tumor). Also **green paw**. Big yellow-green sheets with lobes; undersides of lobes often bear large kidney-shaped golden-brown fruiting disks ½–1¼" [1–5 cm] or wider; underside tan grading to ± black at center, with fine hairs but without rhizines or raised veins; upper surface often has gray blotches which contain cyanobacteria. Mossy subalpine forest floor, or alpine; Canada. Color p 521.

Lungwort

Lobaria pulmonaria (lo-**bair**-ia: lobed; pull-mun-**air**-ia: lung—). Also **lettuce lichen**. Big "leaves" olive to pale brown above when dry, green when wet, with a netlike pattern of ridges sprinkled with pale "crumbs;" (on underside, these ridges are valleys between domes); underside paler, mottled with brown in the furrows; margins deeply lobed, curling; fruiting disks rare. On trees or mossy rocks—either in very old forest or near cottonwood or aspen. Color p 521.

Cyanobacteria in lichens pull nitrogen out of the air; the nitrogen moves on in the nutrient cycle when it leaches out in rainwater, or when the lichen decomposes or is eaten. To intercept nutrients before they wash away, cottonwoods and alders may extend rootlets among the lichens and mosses on their own bark. The fertilizing is mutual: Trevor Goward found that calcium leaching out of cottonwood and aspen leaves raises the pH of conifer branches to the level lungworts require. (They don't tolerate acid rain; see sidebar, page 316.) Conifers cannot offer such acid-buffering, so lungworts colonize them very slowly, but they abound in old moist cedar-hemlock forests and contribute significantly to the nitrogen cycle.

The word "lungwort" derives from the medieval Doctrine of Signatures, which prescribed this lichen for lung ailments because of its textural resemblance to lung tissue. At least seven unrelated green plants were also called lungwort for similar reasons.

Rag Lichen

Platismatia glauca (plat-iss-**may**-sha: broad—; **glaw**-ca: pale). Also **ragbag**. Fluffy wads of small sheets (up to 1" wide, or 25 mm) with strongly ruffled edges; pale greenish gray above; underside patchy with white, greenish brown, and black; surface often granular-coated. Color p 520.

Rag lichen tolerates pollution and is common on small urban trees. Native to six continents, it's a very cosmopolitan lichen. Like the puffed lichens (page 327), it grows throughout young conifer forests, but shifts into the mid-canopy as the forest ages; in ancient forests you see them mainly where they have fallen the ground.

Jewel Lichens

Xanthoria elegans (zan-**thor**-ia: yellow; **el**-eg-enz: elegant). Also **elegant orange lichen.** Bright orange patches adhering tightly to rocks, thus easily mistaken for a crustlike lichen, but with slightly raised flakes and distinct, lobed edges; fruiting discs deeper orange, small, concentrated near center of patch. Widely scattered, esp alpine; abundant and gorgeous mingled with chartreuse cobblestone lichen on basalt cliffs in sc ID and e WA. Color p 519.

X. fallax (**fal**-ax: deceptive). Deep orange clumps of lobes, often quite small, with relatively large raised orange fruiting disks. On twigs or bark of deciduous trees and shrubs, including sagebrush.

Jewel lichen often marks habitual perches of rockpile fauna like pikas and marmots, fertilized by the nitrogen in their urine. (Many lichens are killed by air pollution, but this genus thrives on at least one kind of air pollution; see page 316). More conspicuous than the pika itself, the orange splash may help us spot the source of the "eeeenk." Jewel lichen grows from seashores up to 23,000' in the Karakoram Range— possibly the greatest elevation range of any macroscopic species.

Orange Chocolate Chip Lichen

Solorina crocea (so-lor-**eye**-na: ?; **cro**-sia: crocus, i.e. saffron yellow). Upper surface bright green (wet) to dull pale green (dry) with dark brown fruiting disks; underside bright orange, showing at many upturned edges, finely woolly; with brown veins , sparse rhizines. High-elev soil. Color p 521.

This lichen specializes in late-lying snowbed sites, often alongside mosses which got their start there with the help of nitrogen-fixing cyanobacteria that grow on the moss leaves. The lichen gets its start, in turn, by incorporating some of those cyanobacteria, but isn't able to grow to conspicuous size until green algae blow in and are incorporated as its partners, perhaps many years later.

Iceland-Moss

Cetraria ericetorum (set-**rair**-ia: shield—; er-iss-e-**tor**-um: among heaths). Clumps 1–3" tall by 2–8" wide [2–8 × 5–20 cm], brown to olive when dry, consisting of narrow flattened lobes with sparsely fringed edges rolled nearly into tubes, with white specks (under 10× lens) aligned under edges. On soil, mostly alpine.

C .islandica (iss-**land**-ica: of Iceland). As above, but with white specks scattered across backsides, and lobes scarcely rolled up.

In Europe, this lichen with the misleading but time-honored common name is the best-known lichen in human consumption. It is used in herbal medicines in Sweden, in teas and throat lozenges in

Switzerland. Scandinavian sailors used to bake Iceland-moss flour into their bread to extend its shelf life at sea. The lichen had to be parboiled with soda before milling, or it would have been unspeakably bitter. In North America it was popular among the Inuit.

Snow Lichens

Flavocetraria cucullata (flay-vo-set-**rair**-ia: yellow shield; coo-cue-**lay**-ta: hooded). Like the preceding exc pale yellow with purple base; white specks beneath margins; lobes slightly ruffled, rolled nearly into tubes. Color p 522.

F. nivalis (niv-**ay**-lis: of snow). =*Cetraria nivalis*. Like the preceding, but lobes scarcely rolled up, and strongly ruffled all over; base yellow.

Yellow Ruffle Lichen

Vulpicida tilesii (vul-pih-**sigh**-da: fox killer; til-**ess**-ee-eye: after Wilhelm Tileseus). Like the preceding (*F. nivalis*) but bright yellow-orange with black specks; rhizines and fruiting bodies rare. On calcareous soil. Color p 522.

Rock Tripes

Umbilicaria spp. (um-bil-ic-**air**-ia: navel—). Dark gray to light brown leafy lichens attached to a rock by a single, central "umbilical" holdfast; tough and slippery when wet, hard and brittle when dry; ± lobed and curling at the edges; fruiting disks uncommon in first three. Abundant on non-calcareous rock.

U. decussata (de-cuss-**ay**-ta: crossed). Dark grey, crossed with delicate white ridges in an almost roselike pattern; underside smooth, black. Color p 519.

U. hyperborea (hyper-**bor**-ia: of the far north). Dark gray, pebbly and irregular all over; underside smooth, black. High elevs. Color p 519.

U. vellea (**vel**-ia: velvety). Pale or brownish gray; underside with a patchy coat of minute pale rhizines interspersed with short black rhizines. High elevs.

U. torrefacta (tor-a-**fac**-ta: roasted). Medium brown with numerous black speckles (fruiting disks) and fine perforations near edges; underside smooth.

Along the Coast, boiled rock tripe was sometimes added to herring eggs (a prized delicacy) to make them go farther. Asian people fry it up and eat it like potato chips, or relish it tender in salad or soup, always drying and boiling it first to leach out dark and bitter flavors. *Trappeurs* in nineteenth-century Canada credited *tripes-des-roches* with saving them from starvation—but never with tasting good.

Scots scraped rock-tripe from rocks for use as a dye that ended up in Harris Tweeds and litmus paper. Many lichens yield yellow, olive, or brown dyes when boiled in water; the shift to purple and red occurs when certain lichens are cured for weeks in warm ammonia. Stale human urine was the form of ammonia used for at least 2,000 years. The dyed fabric came out with a fine fragrance longer-lasting than the color. Dye-lichen gathering rarely flourishes for long in one locale, since lichens grow so slowly that they are quickly depleted.

Stipplebacks

Dermatocarpon spp. (der-mat-o-**car**-pon: leather fruit;). Also **leather lichen**. Tan leafy lichen attached to a rock by a single, central holdfast—like rock-tripe (above) but thicker and finely speckled; or unattached and balled up (see below); ± lobed; tough and slippery when wet, hard and brittle when dry.

D. miniatum (mini-**ay**-tum: scarlet, ref to a chemical test, not to what you see). Undersurface ± brown, smooth to net-patterned. On limestone or basalt.

D. reticulatum (ret-ic-you-**lay**-tum: netted). Undersurface ± black, sandpapery rough. On non-calcareous rocks.

Vagrant Lichens

Since lichens live on air, dust, sunlight, and all sorts of atmospheric moisture, it isn't necessary for them to be attached at all. In some wide-open habitats you may find perfectly healthy lichens utterly on the loose. Their closest relatives can be either crust, leaf, or shrub lichens, and they range from fully vagrant species to erratic growth forms, to mere accidents, i.e., formerly attached individuals that survived getting knocked off their holdfasts.

Several of them are enthusiastically eaten by pronghorns and sheep, though not by cattle. A Persian village was once saved from wartime starvation when a windstorm covered it with *Lecanora esculenta*, which the villagers recognized as edible and baked into a sort of bread. The same thing may have happened to Moses and company in the Sinai; that's the most plausible explanation of biblical manna.

When a specialized growth form does occur, it's branches are balled up (color page 521) a little like a tumbleweed—with the difference that tumbleweeds only tumble when they're dead. It's tempting to imagine dispersing vast distances on the wind as the main draw of vagrant life, but in fact, many vagrant lichens are restricted to small-scale habitats, like pans where rainwater persists. An always-vagrant species of rock posy, *R. haydenii*, grows only on limestone outcrops on the Beartooth Plateau. Vagrant variants of the green rock posy, sticklebacks, or footloose rock-frog are a bit more diverse. Still, they get stuck on vegetation or in hollows out of the wind, and probably don't blow nearly as far as the tiny spores and propagules of non-vagrant lichens. Roger Rosentreter, noting a geographic correlation with pronghorn range, speculates that a vagrant lichen's best hope of traveling far in the American West lies in catching on a pronghorn's fur.

Green Rock Posy

Rhizoplaca melanophthalma (rye-zo-**play**-ca: rooted plate; mel-un-off-**thal**-ma: dark eye). =*Lecanora m.* Also **rock-brights**, **rock-brooches**, **manna** (see sidebar). Small (1", or 25 cm) but sturdy round gray-green lichen largely covered with ± darker-centered, white-rimmed fruiting disks; a few small lobes showing at edges; or may take a ball-like vagrant form. Color p 521.

The white-rimmed fruiting disks in this genus almost dwarf the vegetative lobes, kind of like a bouquet of showy flowers.

Green Starburst Lichen

Parmeliopsis ambigua (par-me-lee-**op**-sis: shield lookalike). Pale yellow-green rosette of branched radiating narrow (less than ⅛") lobes; underside ± black, sparse dark rhizines; tiny mounds of pale granular soredia are scattered on top, mainly near center. On bark, esp near tree base, in full sun.

Plitt's Rock-Shield

Xanthoparmelia plittii (zan-tho-par-**meal**-ia: yellow shield—; **plit**-ee-eye: after ? Plitt). Dingy yellow-green rosette of branched radiating narrow (less than ⅛", or 6 mm) lobes; underside brown with light brown rhizines; masses of fingerlike (under 12× lens) propagules may nearly cover the top, or just the center; may have a few brown fruiting disks. On rock. Color page 521.

Footloose Rock-Frog

Xanthoparmelia wyomingica. Pale yellow-green narrow (1–3 mm) branches with rolled-down edges, forming a 3–4" [7–10 cm] rosette, or more often a messy tangle; underside variably brownish, with rhizines, few or none of them attached to substrate. Common on alpine or windswept soil, often vagrant (see sidebar).

Fungi: shrub lichens

Old-Man's-Beard

Usnea spp. (**us**-nee-a: Arabic term for some lichen). Pale greenish gray tufts on trees; our species densely bushy, 1¼–4" [3–10 cm]; when stretched gently, the thicker branches (unless very dry) reveal an elastic, pure white inner cord inside the brittle, pulpier skin—like wire in old cracked insulation. On trees. Color p 520.

Beard lichens of this genus are abundant throughout boreal regions, and have inspired schemes for industrial conversion of lichen starches into glucose for food, or alcohol for fuel or drink. But lichens grow too slowly to sustain a starch industry.

Horsehair Lichens

Bryoria spp. (bry-**or**-ia: moss—). =included in *Alectoria* until 1977. Also **tree hair, black tree lichen.** Blackish 2–18" [5–45 cm] festoons of fine, weak fibers, often with pale, powdery specks; abundant on trees, krummholz; rarely on rocks.

Edible horsehair, *B. fremontii* (fre-**mont**-ee-eye: after John C. Frémont, opposite page). Typically dark reddish brown, relatively long (to 18", or 45 cm), occasionally with big yellow specks; under 10× lens, thicker strands are grooved and twisted; most branchings are at ± right angles. Color p 520.

Dusky horsehair, *B. fuscescens* (fus-**kess**-enz: darkening). Dull brown, paler toward base, with copious white speckles; most branching is at acute angles.

Brittle horsehair, *B. lanestris* (la-**nes**-tris: woolly). Dark brown to almost black, especially fine (main branches—not the base—less than .2 mm or .008").

These fibrous festoons achieve surreal loveliness in moist western larch forests near the Idaho-Montana border, draping darkly from larch limbs with their bright green or (in the fall) bright yellow foliage. Higher up, they add drama to weather-bonsai'd timberline trees. But don't confuse them with ugly old snow mold, *Herpotrichia nigra* ("black creeping hair," color page 520), a pathogenic fungus that turns mountain hemlock and subalpine fir branches into mats of smutty needles, mainly during late-snowmelt years. Like other lichens, horsehair is neither pathogenic not parasitic. It does stand accused, though, of indirectly harming trees in interior rain forests of the Columbia Mountains by supplying egg-laying sites to hemlock looper moths, a serious pest.

Edible horsehair is certainly one of the most edible of all lichens. It lacks the chemicals that defend most lichens from herbivores. In heavily browsed areas it may show a browse line at the highest level elk can reach. Deer and elk in winter browse lichens which help them absorb nutrients from the green plants of their winter diet. For flying squirrels and for woodland caribou in winter, on the other hand, horsehair lichens are the main course, not just a digestive aid. Since these caribou need a lot of trees per animal to supply enough horsehair lichen, and young trees don't grow much of it, logging threatens their survival by shifting too much of the range into youthful forest.

Northwest tribes ate edible horsehair, especially in cold interior areas where carbohydrate foods were scarce. Reports vary as to whether it was starvation fare or delicious, soapy or sweet or bitter or bland. No doubt the lichens vary a lot, either within a species or among the several *Bryorias*, which are hard to tell apart, even for Native Americans. Some, too poor for leather footwear, bundled *Bryoria* to make padded shoes.

Witches' Hair

Alectoria sarmentosa (alec-**tor**-ia: rooster[?]; sar-men-**toe**-sa: twiggy). Pale gray-green festoons on trees; wispily pendulous, 3–30" [7–75 cm] long; when pulled, a moist strand snaps straight across. On conifers. Color p 520.

When you cross Lolo Pass or many other ridgelines that are, broadly speaking, within the marine climate influence, you see an abrupt transition from witches' hair on the wetter west side to horsehair lichen on the dryer east side.

Puffed Lichens

Hypogymnia spp. (hypo-**jim**-nia: naked underneath). Also **bone lichens**, **tube lichens**. Tufts of hollow branches, sharply two-toned, pale greenish gray above with black specks, blackish brown beneath, lighter brown at the tips.

H. imshaugii (imz-**how**-ghee-eye: after Henry Imshaug). Tufts relatively airy, erect, with tubular branches forking dichotomously; interior ceiling white; numerous yellowish brown fruiting cups on upper sides average ⅛" diam [3 mm]. Common on small limbs. Color p 520.

H. physodes (fie-**zo**-deez: bladder). Tubes flattened, ⅛ to ¼" wide [3–6 mm], yet raised from the bark; interior ceiling white, floor dark; fruiting disks rare. On bark.

H. occidentalis (ox-i-den-**tay**-lis: western). Tubes flattened, ⅛" wide [3 mm], crowded, pressed against bark; tube tips often punctured; interior surfaces dark.

Captain **John C. Frémont** explored the West throughout the 1840s. A civil engineer by training, he became enthusiastic about plant collecting, inspired by watching the diligent botanist Karl A. Geyer (page 176) in Iowa in 1841. The admiration was not mutual: Geyer wrote that Frémont didn't "understand anything about Botany" and grumped that Frémont was able to collect many new species (without knowing, of course, that they were new) because since he travelled with plenty of soldiers to protect him from attack he could go places where lone botanists dared not to tread. Well, at least Geyer dared not. One of the most exciting places Frémont went was the heart of the Wind River Range, where with Kit Carson for a guide he made a point of becoming the first white man astride the highest pinnacle (now named for him). A grandiose man, he later conquered Spanish California on his own initiative, and ran for President. Atop Frémont Peak he proclaimed another first when he captured "*bromus*, the humble bee... It is certainly the highest known flight of that insect."

Sorry, Captain: Humble bees did become bumble over time, and they still frequent Rocky Mountain tops, but they were always *Bombus*, and *Bromus* was always a grass.

Wolf Lichens

Letharia spp. (leth-**air**-ia: death—). Brilliant sulphur-yellow stiff tufts, the profuse branches cylindrical or ± flattened, often pitted, black-dotted. Drier tree-bark sites; abundant on pine and juniper.

L. columbiana (co-lum-be-**ay**-na: of the Columbia R.). With conspicuous fruiting cups with brownish disks average ¼" diam (up to ¾") [6–20 mm].

L. vulpina (vul-**pie**-na: of foxes). Fruiting cups absent or rare. Color p 520.

Somewhere there was a tradition of collecting this intense-colored lichen to make a poison for wolves and foxes; my American sources say this used to be done in Europe, while a British source writes it off as an American barbarism.

Wolf lichen imparts its chartreuse color to fabrics, as a dye. Before they had cloth, Northwest tribes used the dye on moccasins, fur, feathers, wood, porcupine quills for basketry, and their own faces.

Reindeer Lichens

Cladina spp. (cla-**dye**-na: branchlet) =included by some in *Cladonia*. Profusely fine-branched lichens 2–4" [5–10 cm] tall, in dense patches, on soil but barely attached to it.

C. mitis (**my**-tis: mild). Yellowish when moist, sometimes with bluish bloom. Commoner northward; in Yellowstone it's found only in geothermal areas. Color p 522.

C. rangiferina (ran-ji-fer-**eye**-na: of reindeer). Ash-gray; uncommon.

Though found at all elevations here, reindeer lichens are best known for covering vast areas of arctic tundra, where they are the winter staple food of caribou (known in Europe as reindeer). They aren't really very digestible or nutritious; even caribou prefer green leaves when they can get them, but for them to occupy tundra habitat entailed adapting to wintering on lichens. This requires ceaseless migration, since the slow-growing lichens are eliminated where grazed for long. The Saami people (a.k.a. Lapps) even harvest lichens for their reindeer herds. Some Inuit relish a "saladlike" delicacy of half-digested lichens from the stomachs of caribou killed in winter.

Closer to home we encounter them, dyed green and softened in glycerine, as fake trees and shrubs in architectural models. They also supply extracts for commercial uses including perfume bases and antibiotics. They are the chief source of the antibiotic "usnic acid" for German, Finnish, and Russian salves applied to ailments ranging from severe burns and plastic surgery scars to *Trichomonas* and bovine mastitis.

Froth Lichens

Stereocaulon spp. (stereo-**call**-un: solid stem). Low (1½–3" tall, or 38–75 mm) nearly white clumps of delicate ± coral-like branches. On soil, often with mosses.

S. alpinum. Often ± covered with minute wool; tiny brown fruiting bodies on tips of main branches.

S. tomentosum (toe-men-**toe**-sum: woolly). Always covered with minute wool; tiny brown fruiting bodies on ends of side branches. Color p 522.

Globe Lichen

Sphaerophorus globosus (sfee-**rah**-for-us: sphere bearer; glo-**bo**-sus: round). Robust (not hairlike), brittle, stiffly bushy tufts 1–3" diam [25–75 mm], light red-brown to gray when dry, greenish wet; fruiting bodies, if present, are tiny (.08", or 2 mm) pale globes filled with sooty black spores, on branch tips. On trees, from base well up into canopy.

Fungi: twig lichens

Rockworm

Thamnolia vermicularis (tham-**no**-lia: bushy, a misleading name; ver-mic-you-**lair**-iss: wormlike). =includes *T. subuliformis*. White tapering tubes 1-2½" tall [25–60 mm], without fruiting cups, typically in lackadaisical clumps of standing tubes with some reclining tubes and a few branched tubes. Alpine.

The rockworm is found on every continent except Africa. Since it has neither spore-bearing organs nor any sort of vegetative propagule, it must propagate from broken bits of stalk—hardly an effective or speedy mode of intercontinental travel. It probably evolved to essentially its present form hundreds of millions of years ago and spread step by step throughout suitable habitat on various land masses when plate tectonic forces brought them together; and then left it to tectonics again to split it up it among six continents.

Cladonias

Cladonia spp. (cla-**doe**-nia: branched). Clustered greenish gray fruiting stalks ½–1¼" tall [1–3 cm], from a mat of small leafy lobes. On soil
or well-rotted wood.

Pixie goblet, *C. pyxidata* (pix-ih-**day**-ta: see text). Stalks golf tee shaped,
coated with coarse scales and/or globular granules; "baby tees" may sprout from
rims of main ones. Color p 522.

Mealy pixie goblet, *C. chlorophaea* (cloro-**fee**-a: dusky green). Like the preceding, but coated with fine white granules.

Pixie trumpet, *C. fimbriata* (fim-bree-**ay**-ta: fringed). Stalks like narrower
goblets, less deeply cupped, coated with fine white meal.

Laddered pixie trumpet, *C. cervicornis* (sir-vih-**cor**-nis: deer horn). Narrow
trumpets, with tall 2nd and 3rd-generation trumpets rising from centers (not
rims) of lower ones.

Felt pixie trumpet, *C. phyllophora* (fill-a-**for**-a: leaf bearing). Variable, irregular; some small cups usually present, their rims bearing short branches and/or
brown globes; upper stalk soft, felt-like under 10× lens, often bearing leaf-like
squamules; lower stalk often blackish with white specks.

Greater pixie stick, *C. cornuta* (cor-**new**-ta: horned). Stalks fairly straight,
crowded, drawing to narrow tips without cups or decorations. Color p 522.

Sulphur cup, *C. sulphurina* (a misleading name, as these are only slightly, if at
all, yellower than other cladonias). Stalks, irregular, ± cupped at top, mealy-
coated. Color p 522.

Red-crowned sulphur cup, *C. deformis*. Stalks ± yellowish, mealy-coated,
mostly cupped at top, usually with scarlet "fruit" along some of the cup rims.
Color p 522.

Though golf tees are perhaps the most obvious resemblance, goblets
for pixies are suggested by the name *pyxidata,* which actually refers
to a *pyxis,* an ancient Greek goblet-shaped container with a lid. The
shape probably evolved because it makes raindrops splash farther, disseminating tiny propagules from the goblet.

The huge genus *Cladonia* has a two-part growth form. The
primary growth is a mat of flakes ("squamules") resembling leaf
lichens only finer. Usually, but not always, "twigs" eventually rise
from this mat.

9

Mammals

Do we even need an introduction to mammals? We are mammals. We're well schooled in the salient characteristics of mammals. Most give birth to live young; yet egg-laying platypuses are mammals and live-bearing snakes are not. We are all warm-blooded; i.e., we maintain a constant, relatively warm body temperature; and so do birds.

More definitive are the mammary glands which produce milk for the young. But only half of mammals have them. (The females). More universal, as well as unique to us, is our hair made of keratin. Whales, armadillos, and others even less hairy than humans all have at least a few hairs at some developmental stage. Mammal coats come mainly in shades of brown and gray. No fur is bright blue or green (as some feathers are) even on the few mammals, like skunks, with "showy" rather than cryptic coloring. Most mammals need to be inconspicuous. They achieve that by wearing camouflage colors, by being quiet and elusive, and by being nocturnal. This makes mammalwatching a less popular pastime than birdwatching, and makes mammal tracks, scats, and other signs the key to being woodswise to mammals. The mammals we see most often each have their reasons to be unafraid: porcupines are spiky, squirrels climb trees, marmots burrow, pikas have alarm networks and refuges, moose and bears are big, and National Park-dwelling deer, elk, and goats have adapted to their legally protected status. Beware of them!

Small mammals are especially limited to the murky corner of the spectrum. Experienced field naturalists can sometimes recognize the species they study, using color differences they have learned in a particular locale. They may report these shades as "dusky" or "buffy," "tawny" or "ochraceous"—terms somewhat less useful to nonscientists. Photos can be a big help, but their colors vary with lighting and printing. And the animals themselves vary. In a given species, there may be different shades for different seasons, for juveniles versus adults, for infraspecific varieties and color phases, for the paler underside and darker back, and between the hair tips, underfur, and guard hairs. Among closely related mammals, populations of dry regions are often paler than their wet-region relatives, each tending to match the color of the ground so as to be less visible to predators (especially owls) that hunt from above in dim light. Dry-country creatures run around on pale dry dirt, whereas moist forests have dark floors of humus and vegetation.

Positive identification of small mammals utilizes the number and shape of molar teeth and caliper measurements of skulls and penis bones (a feature of most male mammals) for which the creature must first be reduced to a skeleton. But don't worry—this chapter will not go into molar design or the meaning of "dusky," but will offer size, tail/body length ratio, form, habitat, and sometimes color, to facilitate educated guesses as to small mammal identities. Often our glimpses of shrews, mice and voles, unless we trap them or find them dead, are so fleeting and dark that we can make only a downright wild guess, based mainly on habits and habitat.

Shrews

Sorex spp. (**sor**-ex: the Roman term]. Mouselike creatures with very long, pointed, wiggly, long-whiskered snouts, red-tipped teeth, and ± naked tails. Order Insectivora (Shrews and moles). Color p 524.

Wandering shrew, *S. vagrans* (vay-grenz: wandering). 2½" + 1¾" tail [60 + 45 mm]; fur dark gray frosted brown on back, pinkish on sides, and pale on belly. Meadows. Illustrated.

Dusky shrew, *S. monticolus* (mon-tic-o-lus: mtn-dweller). =formerly included in *S. vagrans*. Also **montane shrew.** 2¾" + 1¾" tail [70 + 45 mm]; dark brown. Wet habitats.

Masked shrew, *S. cinereus* (sin-ee-rius: ashen). 2¼" + 1¾" tail [55 + 45 mm] (ratio 3:2); brown with pale gray underside.

Water shrew, *S. palustris* (pa-lus-tris: of swamps). 3" + 3" [75 mm] tail; blackish above, paler beneath; tail sharply bicolored. In or near high marshes and lakes.

Pygmy shrew, *S. hoyi* (**hoy**-eye: after Phila Romayne Hoy). 2¼" + 1⅜" tail [55 + 35 mm] (ratio 2:1); varies from gray to coppery.

Shrews, our smallest and most primitive mammals, lead hyperactive but very simple lives. As shrew expert Leslie Carraway writes, "*Sorex vagrans* exhibits some behavior that tends to indicate it does not perceive much that transpires in its microcosm." Day in and night out, from weaning, between April and July of one year, until death, generally by August of the next, shrews rush around groping with their whiskers, sniffing, and eating most everything they can find.

Shrews eat insects and other arthropods (often as larvae), earthworms, and a few conifer seeds and underground-fruiting fungi; they have been known to kill and eat other shrews, and mice. They have 24-hour cycles of greater and lesser activity based largely on when certain types of prey are easiest to get, but as a rule they can't go longer than three hours without eating, and the smaller species must eat their own weight equivalent daily. As with bats and hummingbirds, such a high caloric demand is dictated by the high rate of heat loss from small bodies: at two or three grams and up, pygmy shrews approximate the lower size limit for warm-blooded bodies. Baby shrews nurse their way up to this threshold while huddling together so that the combined mass of the litter of four to ten easily exceeds two grams. Whereas bats and hummingbirds take half of every day off for deep, torpid sleep (page 344), shrews never do. Nor do they hibernate. It's hard to imagine how our shrews meet their caloric needs during the long snowy season when insect populations are dormant, and heat loss all the more rapid. But they do—or at least enough of them do to maintain the population.

Some mortality relates to a sort of Shrew Shock Syndrome triggered, for example, by capture or a sudden loud noise. Some scientists relate it to the shrew's extreme heart rate (up to 1,200 beats per minute) and others to low blood sugar caused by even the briefest shortage of food. At any rate, the most frequent sign of our abundant shrew population is their little corpses on the ground. With poor eyesight and hearing, shrews are ill adapted to evade predators. Their only defense is simple but effective: being unappetizing. Steller's jays, owls, and trout are among the small minority of predators known to have acquired a taste for shrews.

Marsh and water shrews, the types most likely to tempt trout, spend much of their time in the water, going after tadpoles, snails, leeches, etc. They have such terrific buoyancy, thanks to fur that traps an insulating air layer next to the skin, that they can literally run across the water surface for several seconds. When they dive and swim, they must paddle frenetically to stay under; as soon as they stop, they bob to the surface. Yet marsh shrews can stay down for three minutes and more. They have stiff, hairy fringes on the side of their hind feet for more efficient paddling. Our terrestrial shrews may run on the surface or even climb trees, but most of the time they are subsurface or in the duff layer; the vagrant often tunnels *through* the duff *upon* the mineral soil.

Shrews are ferociously solitary. In order to mate, they calm their usual mutual hostility with elaborate courtship displays and pheromonal exchanges—a real-life "taming of the shrews."

Bats
Order Chiroptera (kye-**rop**-ter-a: hand wing).

As evening gets too dark for swifts and nighthawks to continue their feeding flights, bats and owls begin to come out for theirs. Though the largest bats and smallest owls overlap in size—5½" long, 16" wingspread [14 cm, 40 cm]—bats are easy to tell from owls by their fluttering, indirect flight. You're unlikely to see one well, since ours

---

Animal Sonar

You have probably heard that bats use a sort of ultrasonic radar to find their way around and to locate and catch prey. This is surprisingly recent information. In 1794 it was first observed that bats get around fine with their eyes blocked, but become helplessly "blind" with their ears blocked. The obvious deduction—that bats literally hear their way around as competently as other animals see theirs—was too strange to win acceptance for more than a century. Not until 1938 were instruments able to detect bats' high-frequency squeaks, whose echoes bats hear in a sonarlike perceptual capacity called "echolocation."

A typical bat "blip" lasts a thousandth of a second, during which it drops an octave and spreads out from a focussed sound to a nearly omnidirectional one. These precise shifts, and the very short wavelength, give the echoes such fine tuning that the bat not only locates objects but perceives their texture and their exact motion. It's strictly fast-food for a bat to nab a mosquito, for example, distinguishing it from a shower of cottonwood fluff amid an obstacle course of branches.

From a casual blip rate of several per second in the open air, the bat steps up to over fifty per second when objects of interest come within a yard or so. That's as far as a bat can echolocate, since high-pitched sounds don't carry far. (Contrast with the great carrying power of a grouse's low "booming.") To compensate for such "nearsightedness,"the bat's reactions must be extremely quick, and its blip extremely loud; the

---

never venture out in the daytime. Though I won't discuss each of our bat species, don't think they're unimportant or uninteresting. They are extremely abundant (exceeded among mammalian orders only by the rodents) and probably take a bigger slice out of the insect population than any other type of predator. Most bats, including all of ours, are insect-eaters, like their closest relatives the shrews, so calling them flying mice or flitter-mice (two colloquial names derived from the German *fledermaus*) is a near miss: these are flying shrews.

Bats catch flying prey either in the mouth or in a tuck of the small membrane stretched between the hind legs, from which the mouth then plucks it while the bat tumbles momentarily in mid-flight. Each wing is a much larger, transparently thin membrane stretched from

---

decibel level an inch from a bat's mouth is several times that of a pneumatic drill at 20 feet [6 m]. Those God-awful earsplitting nights in the country! (Well, they would be, if our hearing were sensitive to 80,000 cycles per second instead of its mere 15,000. "Concert A," the note orchestras tune by, is 440 cycles, roughly at the middle of our audible sound spectrum.) To protect the bat's own hearing from damage, its auditory canals vibrate open and shut alternately with the blips, admitting only the echoes. Bats also have lower-pitched (humanly audible) squeaks for communication.

The nocturnal aerial hunting made possible by echolocation must be a key to bats' success, since in the daytime they are at an overall competitive disadvantage to birds, whose feathered flight is much faster. Styles of echolocation in bats are highly diversified and specialized. (A few kinds of bats, though none in this part of the world, see pretty well, echolocate poorly, and shun nighttime activity.)

Aspects of echolocation are found in many unrelated animals. Some moths evade bats by emitting batlike blips to scramble the bats' radar. Some shrews echolocate, crudely. Porpoises and toothed whales echolocate as sophisticatedly as bats. Cave-dwelling birds have learned to do it. The ability may be latent in most mammals; blind humans often learn to echolocate impressively, though rarely developing special calls for the purpose. The human auditory system, according to one theory, also vibrates shut to save us from the racket of our own voices.

---

the hindleg up to the forelimb and all around the four long "fingers." Since the wing has no thickness to speak of, it is less effective than a bird or airplane wing at turning forward motion into lift. To compensate, bats generally have much greater wing area per weight than birds, and use a complex stroke resembling a human breast-stroke to pull themselves continually upward. Bats achieve only modest airspeeds, compared to birds, but they are much more maneuverable at close quarters. They actually chase flying insects rather than simply intercepting them.

Bats roost upside down, hanging from one or both feet. In this position, often in large groups, they sleep all day and hibernate all winter, except for a few winter-migrating species. Though our bats prefer to roost in caves—especially in winter, for insulation—they typically settle for tree cavities and well-shaded branches. After mating in autumn, most species females store sperm to delay fertilization, and bear a single young in spring. Except while out hunting, the mothers nurse the young almost constantly the first few weeks, hanging upside down in the roost.

Bats may carry rabies, but even rabid ones rarely bite people.

Coprophagy

An exclusive diet of vegetative parts of plants presents a severe challenge to mammalian digestive systems because of the high fiber content (and other disproportions: see page 364). As we learned in childhood, the large grazing mammals meet the challenge with cud-chewing and multiple stomachs, enabling them to take in lots of greens in a hurry, out in the open, and then retire to chew in a relatively safe hideout.

Pikas, most rabbits, packrats, and some other herbivorous rodents are able to digest food twice without having to squeeze extra stomachs into their tiny frames; they cycle their food through the whole digestive canal twice, eating their own (and sometimes others') "soft pellets" of partly digested material, and later excreting "hard pellets" of hardcore waste. Different things may be going on in different animals. In some, the food is cultured with a bacterium that requires sunlight to complete its digestive work; other animals eat their pellets immediately, before they can get a tan. Apparently, a longish spell in the caecum (a pocket between the stomach and the large intestine) releases vitamins which must go back to the stomach and small intestine to be absorbed—kind of like cud-chewing without those bulky extra stomachs.

Pika

Ochotona princeps (ock-o-**toe**-na: Mongolian word for it; **prin**-seps: chief). Also **cony**. 8" [20 cm] long if stretched out, but a thickset 5–6" [12–15 cm] long in typical postures; tailless; brown; ears round, ½" [12 mm]. On or near talus. Order Lagomorpha (Rabbits). Color p 524.

A cryptoventriloquistic nasal "eeeenk" in the vicinity of coarse talus (rockpile) identifies the pika for you. Look carefully for it on the rocks. You would think of it as a rodent, but there's something definitely rabbitlike in its posture—perhaps the sharply nose-down head angle, the neck drawn back in an S curve. Pikas are in fact more rabbit than rodent;* they comprise a family in the rabbit order.

Pikas are thought of as subalpine creatures, and most of them do live up high, but others are just as happy on talus slopes at sea level. They depend on talus crevices for refuge, making quick forays into surrounding vegetation to harvest some, and running back carrying big mouthfuls crosswise. Each year, each little haymaker stores several bushels of mixed greens for winter. Visible hay piles are often under rock overhangs, but others are deep in the rockpile. Hay piles are prone to rotting, and pikas try to include some toxic plants to inhibit rot; the toxins may degrade with age, allowing the plant to be eaten. Pikas graze on grasses in summer, but turn to broadleaved perennials and even a few shrubs for haymaking.

The young stake out their own territory (usually near the center of a rockpile, since choice sites near the meadow are taken by dominant pikas) and make their own hay their first summer, even if they're only about half grown at the time. The rockpile may appear to unite a colony, but pikas live in it solitarily except while mating.

The "eeeenk" call—amazingly loud for a tiny creature—serves as both territorial assertion and alarm. No crevice large enough to admit a pika can keep out a weasel, but the rockpile offers a maze where the pika may lose the weasel and lay low. The pika knows its rockpile, is superbly surefooted on it and, according to more than one report, may be aided by other pikas coming out from refuge to

---

*Rabbits and pikas, once considered rodents, now have their own order, Lagomorpha, having diverged early in mammal evolution. They share incisor teeth that grow lifelong as fast as they wear down. Rodents have four such incisors, lagomorphs eight—the second upper and lower pair right behind the first. Lagomorphs are also unusual in having the testes in front of the penis.

---

distract the weasel by running around like crazy. This kind of report sets some naturalists to arguing over whether it's proof of altruism (evolved traits endangering individual lives for the benefit of a genetic group) or merely foolish nervous agitation.

The name "pika" derives from the way Siberian Tungus tribespeople say "eeeenk," so it should be pronounced "peeeeka." That's the accepted pronunciation in Canada, but south of the 49th I've mostly heard "pike-a," perhaps out of confusion with "pica" or "piker." Others say "cony," a name properly used for unrelated Old-World beasts.

Mountain Cottontail

Sylvilagus nuttallii (sil-**vil**-a-gus: forest rabbit; nut-**all**-ee-eye: after Thos. Nuttall, p 222). 13" + 1½" tail [33 + 4 cm]; pale gray-brown; white under tail; ears 2½" [6 cm] (shorter than head). Sagebrush with rock outcrops; open low forest at s end of our range; not in mtns in Can; nocturnal. Order Lagomorpha (Rabbits).

The mountain cottontail ventures out to graze on grasses from its refuge under sagebrush, bitterbrush, or rabbitbrush. As steppe animals go, it is only marginally adapted to drought, and has learned to climb juniper trees at night to nibble foliage, largely for their dew—a rare ability among lagomorphs.

White-Tailed Jackrabbit

Lepus townsendii (**lep**-us: Roman word for rabbit; town-**send**-ee-eye: after J. K. Townsend, facing page). 20" + 3½" tail [50 + 9 cm]; white tail, black ear tips; otherwise graybrown in summer; in winter, most populations white with some buff around face. Nocturnal; grassland from Plains to alpine; easterly US RM and s AB. Order Lagomorpha.

Jackrabbits (genus *Lepus*) are not rabbits but hares, born fully furred and ready to run and eat green leaves within hours of birth. Rabbits, in contrast, are born naked and blind, and must be nursed for 10–12 days before leaving the nest. Physical differences between the two are quite arcane.

This is one of the biggest, fastest jackrabbits. It can sprint up to 45 mph [72 kph], and leap as high as 20 feet [6 m]. It eats grasses and some herbs; in winter it nibbles on shrubs, too. A grassland beast, it is more common on plains than in the mountains, but has been found at all elevations.

Snowshoe Hare

Lepus americanus. Also **varying hare**. 15" [37 cm] when stretched out, + 1½" [4 cm] tail; gray-brown to deep chestnut brown (incl tail) in summer; in winter, high most races turn white, with dark ear-tips; ears slightly shorter than head. Nocturnal and secretive; widespread in forest. Order Lagomorpha. Color p 325.

Thanks to their "snowshoes"—large hindfeet with dense growth of stiff hair between the toes—these hares can be just as active in the winter, on the snow, as in summer. They neither hoard nor hibernate, but molt from brown to white fur, and go from a diet of greens to one of conifer buds and shrub bark made all the more accessible by the rising platform of snow. They make the animal tracks we see most often while skiing. They also become the crucial staple in the winter diet of several predators—foxes, great horned owls, golden eagles, bobcats, and especially lynxes. Though the hares' defenses (camouflage, speed and alertness) are good, the predator pressure on them becomes ferocious when the other small

John Kirk Townsend travelled the Oregon Trail with **Nathaniel Wyeth** and **Thomas Nuttall** (page 222) in 1834, collecting and describing several new birds, mammals, and plants (Townsend's warbler, vole, chipmunk, etc.). Young (24) and enthusiastic, he wrote the most vivid naturalist's account of exploring the West. "In the morning, Mr. N. and myself were up before the dawn, strolling through the umbrageous forest ...None but a naturalist can appreciate a naturalist's feelings—his delight amounting to ecstacy—when a specimen such as he has never before seen, meets his eye, and the sorrow and grief which he feels when he is compelled to tear himself from a spot abounding with all that he has anxiously and unremittingly sought for." After portaging around the Cascades of the Columbia in heavy rain, Townsend wrote: "It was by far the most fatiguing, cheerless, and uncomfortable business in which I was ever engaged, and truly glad was I to lie down at night on the cold, wet ground, wrapped in my blankets, out of which I had just wrung the water.... I could not but recollect ... the last injunction of my dear old grandmother, not to sleep in damp beds!!!"

Occupational hazards brought him to an untimely end, as they did several other explorer-naturalists. He devised his own formula to keep pests from eating his stuffed specimens; it contained arsenic; he died at age 42 of chronic arsenic poisoning.

prey have retired beneath the ground or the snow. Hares can support their huge winter losses only with even greater summer prodigies of reproduction, the proverbial "breeding like rabbits." Several times a year, a mother hare can produce two to four young. She mates immediately after each litter, and gestates 36 to 40 days.

Drastic population swings in 8 to 11-year cycles are well known in northerly parts of snowshoe hare range, but not in the lower 48.

The other kind of "varying" the hare is named for is from summer brown to winter white pelage. The semiannual molt is triggered by changing day length. In years when autumn snowfall or spring snowmelt come abnormally early or late, the hares find themselves horribly conspicuous and have to lay low for a few weeks. Permanently brown races have evolved in lowland areas that fail, year after year, to develop a prolonged snowpack, e.g., some PNW foothills. These brown hares stand out during the occasional snows. The rest of the year they make the most of their camouflage, foraging when they can best see without being seen—by dawn and dusk, and sometimes on cloudy days in deep forest.

Snowshoe hares don't use burrows, but retire to shallow depressions called "forms," under shrubs.

Though infrequently vocal, snowshoe hares have a fairly loud aggressive/defensive growl, a powerful scream perhaps expressing pain or shock, and ways of drumming their feet as their chief mating call. A legendary courtship dance, in which they may literally somersault over each other for awhile, appears to crescendo out of an ecstatic access of foot-drumming.

Chipmunks

Tamias spp. (**tay**-me-us: storer). =*Eutamias* spp. Rich brown with four pale yellowish brown stripes and five dark stripes down the back and from nose through eyes to ears. Order Rodentia.

Yellow pine chipmunk, *T. amoenus* (a-me-nus: delightful) 4½" + 3½" tail [12 + 9 cm]; drier conifer forests up to timberline, throughout our range. Illustrated on this page and color p 325.

Red-tailed chipmunk, *T. ruficaudus* (roo-fic-aw-duss: red tail). 5" + 4" tail [12.5 + 10 cm]; tail underside rich reddish. Mainly in and near trees, ID, nw MT, Purcell Range, and southernmost Canadian Rockies.

Least chipmunk, *T. minimus.* 4¼" + 3⅜" tail [11 + 8.5 cm]; holds tail vertically while running, often flicks it up-down, but not left-right; may "chip" incessantly. Sagebrush to tundra, almost throughout our range. Illustrated.

Uinta chipmunk, *T. umbrinus* (um-**bry**-nuss: brownish) 5" + 4" tail [12.5 + 10 cm]; white patch behind ear; tail horizontal while running. Mtns of nw WY and adjacent ID and MT (and other disjunct ranges to the s).

Chipmunks are among our most conspicuous forest mammals — diurnal, noisy, and abundant. They have a diverse vocabulary of chips, chirps, and tisks easily mistaken for bird calls.

Our chipmunks forage terrestrially for seeds, berries, bulbs, flowers, buds, a few insects and, increasingly toward winter, underground fungi. To facilitate food-handling, they have an upright stance (like other squirrels and gophers) that frees the handlike forefeet. They store huge quantities of food, carrying it to their burrows in cheek pouches. They vary their winter strategies to suit the varying food supply conditions of different years, but overall they are storers of food (true to their Latin name) as opposed to fatteners. They hibernate intermittently, getting up periodically to excrete and eat from stores in the burrow. You may hear their chatter even in midwinter, and on milder days at lower elevations they may go out and forage. Even their deepest torpor is pretty shallow: if handled, they wake up, taking about an hour (far less than most squirrels) to recover fully. The young, though born naked, blind and helpless, mature fast enough to disperse and make their own nests for their first winter. Though the winter den for these species is almost always a burrow, nests in tree cavities may be used as summer homes.

These four chipmunks occupy similar ecological niches, but tend to exclude each other from particular sites. (If you have two different stripy critters in your campground, one may be a ground squirrel.) In Glacier NP, for example, three chipmunks divide the terrain vertically: Yellow Pine takes the lower forests, Red-tailed the subalpine forest, and Least the alpine tundra. Almost the reverse holds in central Idaho and eastern Oregon, where Yellow Pine is king of the mountains, leaving only lowland steppe for Least. Where they have a mountain range to themselves, either Least or Yellow Pine can occupy all elevational zones.

Ground Squirrels

Spermophilus spp. (sper-**mah**-fil-us: seed lover). Order Rodentia, Sciuridae.

Our many kinds of ground squirrels have a common pattern to their annual life cycle: they are serious hibernators. Most individuals are active for only three to four months. The colony as a whole stays in view longer—from late March, say, to early September—because they are on staggered calendars. Adult males emerge first, and go into estivation in July when the herbs and grasses begin to dry up, making it harder to put on body fat. Females are a few weeks later to do both. As soon as they emerge (or sometimes earlier, still underground) breeding begins, replete with male combat. Gestation takes 20–24 days, and the young remain in their natal burrow as many days again, not emerging until mid to late May; they're the ones you still see through August. Summer torpor is termed "estivation" as opposed to "hibernation," but ground squirrels perform the two consecutively without noting any difference, and in fact there is none.

Males, during mating season, suffer wounds and tend to severely deplete their energy. As yearlings they have to disperse, and this, too, reduces their foraging success. In consequence males have shorter lives, and colonies are preponderantly female.

Golden-mantled ground squirrel, *S. lateralis.* (lat-er-**ay**-lis: sides, referring to stripes). Also **copperhead.** 7" + 3⅜" bushy tail [18 + 9.3 cm]; medium gray-brown with 2 dark and 1 light stripe down each flank; no stripes on face, head or neck, unlike chipmunks; head and chest (the "mantle") rich yellow-brown; "milk-bottle" pose typical while looking around. Meadows, esp subalpine. Color p 525.

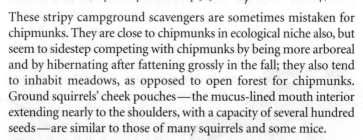

These stripy campground scavengers are sometimes mistaken for chipmunks. They are close to chipmunks in ecological niche also, but seem to sidestep competing with chipmunks by being more arboreal and by hibernating after fattening grossly in the fall; they also tend to inhabit meadows, as opposed to open forest for chipmunks. Ground squirrels' cheek pouches—the mucus-lined mouth interior extending nearly to the shoulders, with a capacity of several hundred seeds—are similar to those of many squirrels and some mice.

Richardson's ground squirrel, *S. richardsonii* (richard-**so**-nee-eye: after Sir John Richardson, p 000). Also **prairie gopher.** 8½–10" + 2¼–3½" tail [23 + 7 cm]; rather evenly gray with white flecks above, tawny beneath. Great Plains and some nearby valleys from c MT n to Banff NP. Color p 525.

Richardson's ground squirrel has a piercing alarm whistle. If it is short and descends in pitch, it signals a raptor, and the squirrels typically dive into their burrows. A long and fairly steady one signals a surface threat; responding squirrels stand and scan the horizon.

The males are furiously combative at mating time; several in the colony may die of their wounds, and few will exceed half the lifespan of an average female. The female is receptive for only a few hours, but manages to squeeze several suitors into her busy schedule. Thenceforth she is hostile to all adult males, but will associate and even sleep with her female kin. For the rest of their active year, the males focus on putting on weight for next spring's bouts.

Wyoming ground squirrel, *S. elegans* (el-eg-anz: elegant). 8½" + 2½" tail [21 + 6 cm]; distinguishable from Richardson's only by geography: extreme sw Montana, the e half of the ID RM, and disjunctly from the s end of the Winds s through CO.

Columbian ground squirrel, *S. columbianus* (co-lum-bee-ay-nus: of the Columbia R). Also **red digger.** 10" + 4" bushy tail [25 + 10 cm]; back grayish; face, throat, forelegs and tail reddish tawny. Meadows from MT and ID n. Color p 525.

This, the largest ground squirrel, is the most social and the most associated with subalpine meadows. In these ways, it approaches the marmot, for which it is sometimes mistaken, much as the small stripy ground squirrels seem to approach the chipmunk. (For i.d., remember that marmots are considerably larger, Richardson's are somewhat smaller, and neither has a reddish forehead.)

Social bonds are reinforced by "kissing"— sniffing around each other's muzzles, where scent glands are located. By scent, ground squirrels can tell close relatives from distant relatives from nonrelatives. Their protective behavior, including alarm calls, seems to favor the close relatives but not the distant ones. Big males rub their scent glands on the ground to mark territory. Females are also territorial, protecting access to food, whereas male territories guard access to the females whose territories they overlap. As with marmots, there's a lot of growly squabbling and chasing. Among youngsters it's play; between adults, it's territory; and adults of both sexes chase yearling males out of the colony, forcing them to go find new home ranges.

Thirteen-lined ground squirrel, *S. tridecemlineatus* (try-des-em-lin-ee-**ay**-tus: 13 lined). 7" + 3" tail [18 + 7.5 cm]; ears scarcely visible; 13 dark/ light stripes run length of back; each dark stripe contains light spots in a row. Lowlands e of CD. Color p 525.

These squirrels—conspicuous in High Plains towns, where they are called "gophers"—eat far more insects than most squirrels do.

Uinta Ground Squirrel, *S. armatus* (ar-**may**-tus: armed). 9" + 2–3" tail [22 + 7 cm]; head, shoulders, and underside of tail medium gray; rest of body may be gray or brown to cinnamon. W WY, e ID, and sw MT.

Uinta females are asocial and aggressively territorial. They are virtually as big as the males, and tend to dominate them after the mating season. Territoriality in this animal is believed to protect a "garden" of previously-cropped grass, whose new replacement shoots are more nutritious than uncropped grass.

Torpor and Hibernation

Most warm-blooded species have normal body temperatures about as warm as our 98.6° (37° C.), but many of them spend much of their time at sharply reduced metabolic levels, which we lump together under the word "torpor." Torpor is a state of extremely slow breathing (one per minute) and heartbeat (four to eight per minute), at body temperatures close to the ambient temperature, down to a limit near freezing. Its purpose is to conserve calories at times when they are hard to come by.

Seasonal torpor is called either hibernation (from the Latin for "winter") or aestivation (from "summer"). The animal may or may not waken occasionally to excrete, eat stored food, or go out and forage.

Daily torpor is used by bats nearly every day and by hummingbirds nearly every night. Ordinary sleep would waste too many calories through heat loss from tiny bodies like these, in temperate climates.

Opportunistic torpor is used by many, many small mammals in response to calorie shortage, or even to shock, as in "playing possum."

Animals adapt to various habitats in their use of torpor. Chipmunks commonly skip hibernation, and forage through the winter, when their food supply is ample. Chipmunk populations are more or less likely to do that depending on elevation and latitude. Many ground squirrels and lower-elevation marmots go into aestivation in the summer and don't come out until they dehibernate in early spring. Most temperate-zone bats hibernate in addition to sleeping torpidly every day of their active season.

Hibernation is costly. The animal must put on a lot of weight—33% to 67% on top of its midsummer weight. Since obesity slows it down, increasing the odds of being caught and eaten, it squeezes hyperphagia (overeating) into as short a period as possible, when the richest foods (seeds and berries) are most plentiful, and then immediately goes down. Much of the fat put on is "brown fat," which can oxidize to produce heat directly, without muscular contractions. But burning off fat draws water

Marmots

Marmota spp. (mar-**moe**-ta: the French term). Also **rockchuck**, **whistle-pig**, **whistler**. Heavy-bodied, thick-furred, large rodents of mountain meadows and talus, known for their piercing "whistles." Order Rodentia, family Sciuridae.

Yellow-bellied marmot, *M. flaviventris* [flay-vi-**ven**-tris: yellow belly). 16" long + 6½" tail [39 + 16 cm]; yellowish brown, often gray-grizzled, with ± yellow throat and belly; feet darker brown. Illustrated.

out of the bloodstream, whereas burning off muscle adds water, and dehydration is one of hibernation's worst problems; so considerable muscle tissue is also put on and burned off. Hibernation requires pituitary hormones to suppress urine formation in order to conserve water; other special chemistry converts toxic urea, which we normally get rid of in urine, into something harmless.

For roughly one day per month, some long-term hibernators raise their body temperature to normal to sleep and dream before chilling down again. During this sleep they show brainwave patterns typical of REM or "dreaming" sleep, whereas in deep torpor they show little or no brainwave activity. They probably do this to maintain brain function.

Triggers for hibernation include scarcity of food, abundance of fat, outside temperature, day length, and absolute internal calendars. As for dehibernation, a study found that Colorado marmots come out when it's warm enough, and have been coming out much earlier as the climate warmed in recent decades. But the same warming brought heavier snowfall, which kept some nearby species in hibernation later.

Many "classic" hibernators of the squirrel family are hard to rouse. To wake up, most species spend several hours shivering violently to their body temperature. Marmots hibernate in heaps, and the shivering of one will trigger the others to join in a group shiver.

Bears, in contrast, lower their temperature only a little, can rouse to full activity quickly, and commonly do rouse during winter. Therefore, some say bears are "not true hibernators." A fairer statement would be that bears are not squirrels. Bears change some bodily functions more radically than squirrels do. For example, bears, but not squirrels, go without urinating or defecating for months, and are able to maintain 100% of their muscle mass by recycling metabolic waste into protein. Perhaps bears are simply so much bigger and better-insulated that lowering their body temperature is difficult, and would serve no purpose.

Mammals

Hoary marmot, *M. caligata* (cali-**gay**-ta: booted). 20" long + 9" tail (50 + 21 cm]; grizzled gray-brown; black feet; ± white belly and bridge of nose. Alp/subalpine. Color p 324.

It's hard to feel you're really in the high country until you've been announced by a **marmot**, with a sudden shrill shriek (not a whistle, in that it's made with the vocal chords). This warning may send several other marmots lumping along to their various burrows. On the way they pause, perhaps standing up like big milk bottles, to look around and see how threatening you actually appear. A scarier predator than you, such as a red-tailed hawk, would have elicited a shorter, descending whistle conveying greater urgency. In your case, they easily become nearly oblivious to you, or even quite forward and interested in your goods. Or you may get to watch them scuffle, box, and tumble, or hear more of their vocabulary of grunts, growls and chirps.

Marmots need their early warning system because they're slower than many other prey, and count all the large predators as enemies. To protect themselves from the phenomenal digging prowess of badgers, yellow-bellied marmots locate their burrows in rockpiles. Occasionally a whole hibernating family is dug out and eaten by a bear. They are rarely hunted by people any more, though Inuit and some Rocky Mountain tribes hunted them for both fur and flavor.

As befits the largest of all squirrels, marmots take their hibernating seriously. They put on enough fat to constitute as much as half their body weight, and then bed down for more than half the year, the colony snuggling together to conserve heat. Resist the temptation to think of seven-month hibernation as a desperate response required in an extreme environment. It is one of several strategies that work here; small subalpine grazers like the pika and the water vole stay active beneath the snow at a comfortable constant 32°, while long-legged browsers forage above the snow, a few staying subalpine, most migrating downslope. Different wintering strategies go with different kinds of food, so the species rarely compete directly for one food resource. Marmots prefer perennial broadleaved herbs, and actually benefit from sharing their meadow with hooved grazers, whose selection of grasses allows more broadleaved herbs to grow, up to a point: seriously overgrazed meadows begin to have less forage to offer for either class of eater. Subalpine meadows lacking marmots may simply be too grassy.

Marmots squeeze their whole year of eating into a brief green season. A marmot mother is hard put to fatten enough for her nursing litter's hibernation as well as her own; in alternate years she is infertile, restoring her metabolic reserves while loosely tending her yearlings. A dominant hoary marmot male typically keeps two mates, impregnating the fertile one and leaving her to run a nursery burrow while he shares a burrow with the infertile one and her yearlings. The colony is like an extended family; subordinate adults are "aunts and uncles" surrounding the dominant "alpha *ménage à trois*" and this-year's and last-year's litters. As summer wears on, parents increasingly work at chasing their male yearlings away from the colony. Many marmot tussles you see are simply play between youngsters, but those that end in a one-sided chase may be adults making yearlings unwelcome. Young and yearling marmots suffer heavy casualties to both predation and winter starvation.

Yellow-bellied males don't stop at two, but tend harems as large as they can get by chasing other males out of a territory that overlaps the territory of several fertile females. The females maintain matrilineal territories, behaving amicably with their daughters and sisters, but chasing non-kin away.

Northern Flying Squirrel

Glaucomys sabrinus (**glawk**-amiss: silvery-gray mouse; sa-**bry**-nus: of the Severn River*). 7" + 5½" tail [17.5 + 14 cm]; tail broad and flat; large flap of skin stretching from foreleg to hindleg on each side; eyes large; red-brown above, pale gray beneath. Widespread in forest. Order Rodentia, family Sciuridae. Color p 325.

You aren't likely to see these pretty squirrels. They are active in the hours just after dark and before dawn. On a quiet night in the forest, you might hear a soft birdlike chirp and an occasional thump as they land low on a tree trunk. They can't really fly, but they glide far and very accurately, and land gently, by means of the lateral skin flaps which triple their undersurface. They can maneuver to dodge branches, and almost always land on a trunk and immediately run to the opposite side—a predator-evading dodge that includes a feint of the tail in the opposite direction. Owls that prey on them commonly pick off and drop the tail, so the one flying squirrel part you have a better chance of seeing is a jettisoned tail. On balance, the

---

*Sabrinus was a river nymph in Roman myth, but these squirrels did not get her name for being river nymphets. The type, or first-described specimen, of the species lived near the Severn River in Ontario, which was named after England's Severn River, to which the Romans gave the name Sabrinus.

ability to fly is probably good for energy-efficient locomotion but bad for escaping predators. (The big flaps of loose skin presumably make for slow and awkward scurrying.) Our clue is that all of the world's roughly 30 species of flying squirrels are nocturnal, and none of the world's 90+ diurnal squirrels can fly.

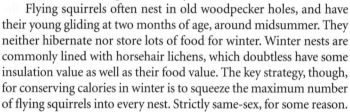

Flying squirrels often nest in old woodpecker holes, and have their young gliding at two months of age, around midsummer. They neither hibernate nor store lots of food for winter. Winter nests are commonly lined with horsehair lichens, which doubtless have some insulation value as well as their food value. The key strategy, though, for conserving calories in winter is to squeeze the maximum number of flying squirrels into every nest. Strictly same-sex, for some reason.

In the Northwest, flying squirrels mainly eat truffles (underground-fruiting fungi). Hmmnn. Truffles need eaters like these to disseminate their spores... trees need their truffles (see page 292)... It's another multidirectional mutualism demonstrating that unexpected corners of the forest community have a lot to offer.

Red Squirrel

Tamiasciurus hudsonicus (tay-me-a-sigh-**oo**-rus: chipmunk squirrel; hud-**so**-nic-us: of Hudson's Bay). Also **chickaree**, **pine squirrel**. 8" + bushy 5" tail [20 + 12 cm]; reddish brown above; white beneath, ± graying in winter; the two color areas usually separated by a black line; white eye ring. Conifer forest. Order Rodentia, family Sciuridae. Color p 325.

Noisy sputterings and scoldings from the tree canopy call our attention to this creature which, like other tree squirrels, can afford to be less shy and nocturnal than most mammals thanks to the easy escape offered by trees. A "chirr-rr-rr" that begins with a slight high-pitched "peep" lets neighborhood squirrels know there's a dangerous animal nearby. Once they know about you they don't consider you much of a threat. There *are* predators that take squirrels in trees quite easily—martens, goshawks, and large owls—but apparently they were never common enough to put a dent in the squirrel population, and are scarcer than ever today, in retreat from civilization. Unlike squirrels. A "buzz" call is used in courtship chases. Extended chatter often asserts territory near a food cache.

Sometimes in late summer and fall the sound we know red

squirrel by is the thud, thud, thud of green cones hitting the ground. Since cones are designed to open and drop their seeds while still on the tree, closed cones you see on the ground are likely a squirrel's harvest. The squirrel runs around in the branches nipping off cones, as rapidly as one every three seconds; then it runs around on the ground carrying them off to cold storage. True-fir cones are too heavy to drag or carry, so it gnaws away just enough on the outside to reduce a cone to draggable weight, leaving the seeds still well sealed in. Some day, it will carry the cones back up to a habitual feeding-limb and tear them apart, eating the seeds and dropping the cone scales and cores, which form a heap we call a "midden." Either the center of a midden or a hole dug in a streambank may be used to store cones for one to three years. The cool, dark, moist conditions keep the cone from opening and losing its seeds and also, incidentally, keep the seeds viable. A midden can be carried on for many generations, and grow to several cubic meters in size. Other species, from martens to grizzly bears, have learned to poach from middens, especially when whitebark pine nuts can be expected. (See page 375.)

Mushrooms, which must be dried to keep well, are festooned in twig crotches all over a conifer, and later moved to a dry cache such as a tree hollow. With such an ambitious food-storage industry, this squirrel has no need to hibernate. For the winter, it moves from a twig and cedar-bark nest on a limb to a better-insulated spot, usually an old woodpecker hole. This-year's young winter in their parents' nest (unlike smaller rodents such as mice and chipmunks) since they need most of a year to mature.

The proportion of all conifer seeds that are consumed by rodents, birds, and insects is huge, exceeding 99% in some poor cone-crop years. Foresters have long regarded seed eaters as enemies. But the proportion of conifer seeds that germinate and grow is infinitesimal anyway, and of those, the percentage that were able to succeed *because* they were harvested, moved, buried, and then neglected is significant. Trees coevolved with seed eaters in this relationship, and may depend on it (see page 290). Additionally, all conifers are dependent on mycorrhizal fungi, many of which depend in turn on these same rodents to disseminate their spores. Conifers limit squirrel populations by synchronizing their heavy cone crop years. A couple of poor cone crop years bring the number of squirrels way down, and then the trees produce a bumper crop, with way too many seeds for the reduced population to harvest.

Pocket Gopher

Thomomys talpoides (**tho**-mo-miss: heap mouse; tal-**poy**-deez: mole-like). 5½" + small ± naked 2½" tail [14 + 6 cm]; variable gray-brown tending to match local soil; front claws very long, eyes and ears very small, large incisors protrude. Sporadic in open areas with loose soil. Order Rodentia, family Geomyidae.

Pocket gophers spend their lives underground, and have much in common with moles—powerful front claws, heavy shoulders, small weak eyes, small hips for turning around in tight spaces, and short hair with reversible "grain" for backing up. But moles are predators of worms and grubs, and gophers are herbivores. They can suck a plant underground before your very eyes, making hardly a dent on the surface. They get enough moisture in their food that they don't even go to water to drink. In fact, only two occasions always draw them into the open air. One is mating, in spring, which takes only a few minutes and draws out only the males. Afterward they return to mutually hostile solitude, plugging up burrow openings behind them. The other is evicting young gophers from their mothers' burrows.

Though badgers and gopher snakes are well equipped to take them, the fact that gophers sustain their numbers with just one small litter per year reflects the overall safety of life underground. It also reflects enormous energy costs: burrowing ten feet takes about 1,000 times more energy than walking ten feet. Tracking that consumption on down the

---

Sex vs Survival, Underground

A pattern affects all three big genera of burrowing sciurids—marmots, ground squirrels, and prairie dogs: as you go farther north or higher into the mountains, you find species or populations with larger bodies, stronger social organization, more delayed dispersal of the young males, more delayed or intermittent fertility in females, and smaller litters. For example, young yellow-bellied marmots disperse (leave their maternal care and burrow) at the end of their first or, more often, second summer. Hoary marmots, with a shorter, colder active season, mature very slowly for rodents, dispersing only in their third summer when their mother's subsequent litter arrives, and breeding in their fourth summer. With the shorter, colder growing season, more energy must go into weight gain, and less is left over for reproduction.

Nutritional energy has to be allocated between survival (i.e., fattening up) and reproduction. Evolution selects those that reproduce the most; but those that overallocate for reproduction won't survive winter and can't reproduce the next spring. Or they may just survive, but with

food chain, we find gophers eating the most calorie-rich part of the meadow—the roots—and eating way more than their share.

In the winter, gophers can, without exactly going out, eat above-ground foods like bark and twigs by tunneling around through the snow. In spring and summer, you find "gopher eskers"—sinuous ridgelets about 3" [8 cm] wide of dirt and gravel that came to rest on the ground during snowmelt. (Color p 524; voles leave similar but smaller cores.) Shortly before snowmelt, the gopher resumed earth burrowing, and used the snow tunnels it was abandoning as dumps for newly excavated dirt. Summer "tailings" heaps are fan-shaped.

Gophers churn the soil in a big way, with big ecological effects. Churning fosters diversity in mature prairies. It sped plant recovery near Mt. St. Helens by bringing soil and seeds to the ash-buried surface. On alpine tundra, on the other hand, where high winds are nearly constant and soil development is glacially slow, it wastes a lot of soil. As soon as gophers churn a patch, the wind starts carrying soil particles off to the lowlands. Soon you have a "gopher blowout," a sharp-edged basin whose floor is rocky, with little soil or vegetation left. It may take many years for a stable meadow to return. Churning can also wipe out pine seedlings in clearcuts—but good forestry can avoid this problem by not growing the weeds that gophers like.

A pocket gopher's pocket is a cheek pouch used, like a squirrel's,

---

no fat left on their bodies to sustain mating efforts, since many populations here emerge from hibernation and/or do their mating when snow still covers the ground, and little green forage is available.

For a male in many species, such as the yellow-bellied marmot, increased reproductive effort consists of patrolling a larger territory, to include more mates. For a female it consists of bearing and nursing larger litters, and doing so without skipping years. (Hoary marmots normally skip alternate years, but may skip two years in a row if they are of low rank in the harem, and/or when food conditions are poor.) As long as they are lactating, they lose weight; they only begin fattening after weaning, which is why females return to hibernation later than males. By that time of year, vegetation is drier and less nutritious. In years with exceptionally late snowmelt, most mothers of new litters fail to fatten up enough, and will die during the winter. Nevertheless, life expectancies for males are much less than for females, mainly due to exposure to predators, both while dispersing, in youth, and while patrolling and defending in adulthood.

to carry food. Unlike a squirrel's, it opens to the outside. Fur-lined and dry, it turns inside out for emptying and cleaning. "Gopher teeth," big protruding incisors, are used (at least by gophers) for digging. The lips close behind them to keep out the dirt.

Beaver

Castor canadensis (cas-tor: the Greek term). 25–32" + 10–16" tail [75 + 28 cm]; tail flat, naked, scaly; hind feet webbed; fur dark reddish brown. In and near slow-moving streams. Order Rodentia, Castoridae (Beaver family).

The beaver is by far the largest North American rodent today, and was all the more so 10,000 years ago, when there was a giant beaver species the size of a black bear. Of all historical animals, the beaver has had the most spectacular effects on North American landforms, vegetation patterns, and Anglo-American exploration.

The sound of running water triggers a dam-building reflex in beavers. They cut down poles with their teeth and drag them into place to form, with mud, a messy but very solid structure as large as a few yards wide and several hundred yards long. A beaver colony may maintain its dam and pond for years, adding new poles and puddling fresh mud (by foot agitation) into the interstices.

Most beaver foods are on land, so pond-building is primarily for safety. The pond is a large foraging base on which few predators are nimble. Over most beaver range (though rarely here), pond ice in winter walls them off from predators. Living quarters, in streambank burrows or mid-pond lodge constructions, are above the waterline, but their entrances are all below it, as are the winter food stores — hundreds of poles cut and hauled into the pond during summer, now submerged by waterlogging. Cottonwood, willows and aspen are favorites. Beavers can chew bark off the poles underwater without drowning thanks to watertight closures right behind their incisors and at their epiglottis. They maintain breathing space just under the ice by letting a little water out through the dam. They are well insulated by a thick fat layer just under the skin, plus an air layer just above it, deadened by fine underfur and sealed in by a well-greased outer layer of guard hairs.

The typical beaver lodge or burrow houses a pair, their

young and their yearlings. Two-year-olds must disperse in search of new watersheds, where they pair up, typically for life, and found new lodges. While searching, they may be found far from suitable streams. Territories are observed with little apparent aggression.

When beavers dammed most of the small streams in a watershed, as they once did throughout much of the West, they stabilized river flow more thoroughly, subtly, and effectively than concrete dams do today. Beaver ponds also have dramatic local effects. First off, they drown a lot of trees. Eventually, if maintained by successive generations, they may fill up with silt, becoming first a marsh and later a level meadow or "park" with a stream meandering through it.

Survival of cottonwood, aspen, and willow shoots is low around colonies of these big chompers, making beaver a major factor (sometimes overlooked) in the aspen/elk equation. (See page 116.) It cannot be a coincidence that Northern Yellowstone's aspen baby boom came between 1870 and 1895, when trapping had nearly eliminated beaver. They were back in force by 1920.

Beavers were originally almost ubiquitous in the U.S. and Canada, aside from desert and tundra. Many tribes considered beavers kin to humans, and showed them respect in lore and ritual while also hunting them for fur and meat. Europeans, in contrast, originally trapped beavers just to obtain a musky glandular secretion ("castoreum") for use as a perfume base. There was a busy castoreum trade for centuries before, in the late 1700s, the beaver hat craze hit Europe, and the demand for dead beavers skyrocketed, not letting up until beavers became scarce around 1840. Beaver-pelt profits provided the impetus for early westward explorations and territorial ambitions, including the Louisiana Purchase. The Continental Divide was breached by fur trader Mackenzie in 1793, explorers Lewis and Clark in 1805, and trappers Colter and Hoback in 1810.

Changing fashions have dropped beaver pelts far below many carnivore furs in value. Populations have recovered as much as they can, but will never foreseeably regain their natural level because so much beaver habitat has been lost and an agricultural economy has little tolerance for the beaver's considerable ability to re-create it.

Beaver dams, ponds, and especially beaver-chewed trees and saplings are frequent sightings, the animals themselves far less often.

If we judge the charisma of megafauna by the number of places named after them, then in the U.S. beavers come in third, after bears and deer. (Yes, a zoology journal published a paper on geographic name counts.)

Packrat

Neotoma cinerea (nee-**ah**-ta-ma: new cutter; sin-**ee**-ria: ash gray). Properly **bushy-tailed woodrat**. 8" + 6½" [20 + 16 cm] tail covered with inch-long [25 mm] fur, hence more squirrel-than ratlike; brown to (juveniles) gray above, whitish below; whiskers very long; ears large, thin. Can either run or, if chased, hop like a rabbit. Widely but patchily distributed in non-alpine sites with rock outcrops or talus. Order Rodentia, Muridae (Mouse family).

For some strange reason, packrats love to incorporate man-made objects, shiny ones especially, into their nests. Possibly some predators are spooked by old gum wrappers or gold watches, or perhaps the packrat's craving is purely aesthetic or spiritual. She is likely to be on her way home with a mud pie or a fir cone when she comes across your Swiss Army knife, and she obviously can't carry both at once, so there may be the appearance of a trade, though hardly a fair one from your point of view. Packrats have other habits even worse than trading, often driving cabin dwellers to take up arms. They spend all night in the attic, the woodshed, or in the walls noisily dragging materials around—shreds of fiberglass insulation, for example. Or they may mark unoccupied cabins copiously with foul-smelling musk. The males mark rock surfaces with two kinds of smears, one dark and tarry, one calcareous white and crusty.

Our common species, the bushy-tailed, is an active trader, but it has evolved away from the use of stickpiles as dwellings, more often nesting in crevices of trees, talus, cliff, mine or cabin. (Other kinds of packrats build 2–8' [60- to 240-cm] stickpiles with water-shedding roofs and several rooms—storerooms, nests and latrines. In Nevada caves these last for millenia, and enable paleobotanists to calculate vegetational changes going back to the last glacial stage.) The bushy-tailed builds only modest stickpiles and uses them to cache food. If it does nest in one, it's likely to be in a tree.

Unlike its relatives, this species has a harem mating system; some reports claim the overall sex ratio is skewed, with two to three females for each male. Each female can bear several litters per year. Diet includes a great variety of plants and fungi.

Deer Mouse

Peromyscus maniculatus (per-o-**miss**-cus: boot mouse; ma-nic-you-**lay**-tus: tiny-handed). 3½" + 3–4" [9 + 9 cm] tail (length ratio near 1:1); brown to (juveniles) blue-gray above, pure white below incl white feet and bicolored, often white-tipped tail; ears large, thin, fully exposed; eyes large. Ubiquitous. Order Rodentia, Muridae. Color p 324.

The deer mouse could be called the North American Mouse; it is the most widespread and numerous mammal on the continent. Not shy of people, it makes itself at home in forest cabins, farmhouses, and many city houses. It is not as urbanized as the house mouse, which originated in Europe and is now in cities worldwide.

It builds a cute but soon putrid nest out of whatever material is handiest—kleenex, insulation, underwear, moss, or lichens—in a protected place such as a drawer or woodpecker hole. In winter it is active by night either on or beneath the snow, and spends its days huddling torpidly with other mice. It is omnivorous, with an emphasis on larvae in the spring and seeds and berries in the fall. The diverse diet adapts it well to burns and clearcuts; as a forest matures, deer mice are gradually displaced by more specialized fungus-eating voles.

Deer mice are the main carriers of hantavirus, whose flulike symptoms can turn deadly if untreated for a few days. The chief danger to humans is in dry, dusty cabins with deer mice; people can get infected by breathing mouse-contaminated dust. Avoid handling deer mice, and wash your hands promptly and thoroughly if you do handle one. If you must clean up a mousy corner, spray first with bleach solution, and wear rubber gloves, goggles, and a HEPA-filtered respirator. Deer mice can also harbor Lyme disease and pass it to humans via ticks (page 566).

Western Jumping Mouse

Zapus princeps (**zay**-pus: big foot; **prin**-seps: a chief). 4" + 5–6" tail [10 + 14 cm] (tail longer than body); back has broad stripe dark brown to black; sides ± washed with dull lemon yellow; belly buff-white; hindfeet several times longer than forefeet; ears small. Thickets and meadows near streams, May to Sept. Order Rodentia, Muridae. Color p 324.

The **jumping mouse** normally runs on all fours, or hops along in tiny hops, or swims, but if you flush one it's likely to zigzag off in great bounding leaps of 3 to 5 feet [1 to 1.5 m]. This unique gait gives you a good chance of recognizing them, even though they're mainly nocturnal and not all that common. The oversized feet are for power, and the long tail for stability: jumping mice that have lost or broken their tails tumble head-over-heels when they land from long jumps. While none of our other mice or voles hibernate at all, this one hibernates deeply for more than half the year. It eats relatively rich food—grains, berries, and tiny (¼"/6 mm or less) underground fungi that grow on maple roots.

Meadow Voles

Microtus spp. (my-**cro**-tus: small ear). Yellowish brown in summer, brownish gray in winter; eyes small; ears barely visible. Order Rodentia, Muridae.

Pennsylvania meadow vole, *M. pennsylvanicus.*
5" + 1½" tail [11 + 3.5 cm] (length ratio 3:1) Moist to marshy meadows, hay fields, sometimes forest.

Montane vole, *M. montanus.* 4¾" + 1⅝"
tail [10.5 + 3.5 cm]. In vole runways in
grass; abundant at Yellowstone; not reported from Glacier. Illustrated.

The casual term "field mouse" refers, on this side of the Atlantic, to *M. pennsylvanicus.* It inhabits all of Canada except the extreme sw and north, and the northeastern half of the US as well, and surely ranks as the most numerous North American mammal during the peaks of its population cycle. In the southern part of our range, it

Mice or Voles?

Out of the 4,000-plus species of mammals living today, almost 1,700 are rodents, and of those, almost 1,300, or 32% of all mammalian species, are myomorphs, or mouselike rodents. As with insects, songbirds, grasses, and composite flowers, such disproportionate diversification bespeaks competitive success in recent geologic times.

The three large groups within the Myomorpha are the Old World rats and mice; the New World rats and mice; and the voles or "field mice." Jumping mice are one of several smaller families. Mickey, Minnie and Mighty Mouse, with their huge ears, are based on the house mouse, *Mus musculus,* which is in the Old World group along with the black rat and Norway rat. This notorious scaly-tailed, un-American trio is adapted

yields its "most populous" title to the montane vole; the two can be told apart only by molar patterns and skull measurements.

Meadow voles are the worlds most prolific mammals. The female gestates for three weeks, and breeds again immediately after giving birth to her litter of three to ten young ones, who nurse for the first two weeks of the ensuing pregnancy. At that rate, the numbers really add up. Calling it, say, an average litter of five and a cycle of 22 days, a vole could have billions of descendants in a year. Needless to say, mortality keeps pace—this is the dietary staple of many predator species, both winged and four-legged—and prevents the numbers from actually going there, but they do go quite high, and then plummet, cyclically. Drastic population cycles three to five years long characterize many of the vole species in this large New World genus (and their relatives the arctic lemmings). Each species' cycle stays synchronized over much or all of its range. It seems to be hormonal and behavioral mechanisms, rather than either starvation or predation, that curb the population explosions somewhere short of mass starvation—though not always soon enough to prevent serious damage to seed or grain crops. Familial behavior varies along with the cycles: at low density, a montane mom abandons her litter at 15 days old, making them disperse to make way for her next brood, but at low density she lets them stay around.

Montane voles (as well as heather voles and northern bog lemmings, p 360) spend winter tunneling through the crumbly bottom layer of the snowpack, called "depth hoar." They maintain vertical tunnels to the surface here and there, perhaps for ventilation or for help in escaping weasels. Occasionally they venture to the surface, where they make short shallow tunnels to rest and warm up in.

---

to life around humans, and has spread to every urban area in the world. In the Northwest, our native mice apparently somehow confine the house mouse, true to its name, to indoor habitats.

Our native myomorphs all have more or less furred tails. Aside from the abundant deer mouse and woodrat (both New World types) most myomorphs here are voles, distinguishable to the layman by their blunter snouts and smaller tails, eyes and (often nearly invisible) ears. Voles are herbivores, whereas many rats and mice are omnivores.

Verts and Carraway rank the three big mouse groups as subfamilies (Murinae, Sigmodontinae, Arvicolinae) in one big mouse family, Muridae. The Arvicolinae (voles) were formerly named Microtinae, and "microtine" remains a common term for voles among field biologists.

Water Vole

Microtus richardsoni (richard-**so**-nigh: after Sir John
Richardson, p 155). =*Arvicola richardsoni*. Also **water rat**. 6" + 2¾" tail [15 + 8 cm] (length ratio 2:1);
fur long and coarse, ± reddish dark brown above,
paler beneath. In and near high bogs,
streams and lakes. Order Rodentia,
Muridae (Mouse family).

You might think of this
critter as a small muskrat rather than a big vole (our biggest). However, it spends time in water for refuge, rarely for forage. It dines on
our favorite lush wildflowers—lupine, valerian, glacier lilies, and
such—eschewing grasses and sedges. In winter it digs up bulbs and
root crowns of the same flowers, or eats buds and bark of willows
and heathers, while tunneling around under the snow. Look for mud
runways running straight to the water's edge from its burrow entrances, which are up to 5" [13 cm] in diameter.

Long-Tailed Vole

Microtus longicaudus (lon-ji-**caw**-dus: long tail). 4½" + 2½" tail [11 + 6 cm]
(length ratio less than 2:1); ears barely protruding; fur gray-grizzled, feet pale,
tail bicolored. Willow thickets, aspen stands, sagebrush grasslands, cattail
marshes, etc. Order Rodentia, Muridae.

Rodents and Fungi

Underground-fruiting fungi—"truffles," loosely speaking—are the mainstay of rodent diets in Western conifer forests.

Rating the nutrition in these morsels has proven tricky. Laboratory
analysis finds them very high in protein, very low in fats, moderate in carbohydrates, and very high in some vitamins and minerals. But digestibility turns out to be abysmal. After all, the principal contents are
spores, and passage of spores through the rodent's digestive tract intact
and viable is the whole point of the relationship, from the fungus' point
of view, so spores have to be pretty indigestible. After adjusting for digestibility, truffles seem barely worth eating. Two factors tip the scales in
their favor: they fruit in late fall and winter, when green foods are least
nutritious; and finding them consumes fewer calories than finding plant
foods because it's done with the nose, a small mammal's most effective
sense organ.

High moisture content dilutes the nutrition, too, but is valuable in
itself; eating it is often safer from predators and less taxing than making

---

Red-Backed Vole

Clethrionomys gapperi (cleth-ri-**ah**-no-mis: keyhole mouse; **gap**-per-eye: after Anthony Gapper). 4" + 1¾" tail [10 + 4 cm]; gray-brown with distinct rust-red band down length of back; tail ± bicolored similarly; active day or night. Common—and often seen—in mature conifer forests. Order Rodentia, Muridae. Color p 524.

Red-backed voles should be respected as gourmets. They dine largely on underground-fruiting fungi—which few of us are aware of except when, as "truffles," they are imported from France or Italy at $300 a pound. It's no accident that truffles are uniquely fragrant, delicious, and nutritious. These fungi have no way of disseminating their spores other than by attracting animals to dig them up, eat them, excrete the undigested spores elsewhere, and preferably thrive on them over countless generations. Many forest rodents evolved as avid participants in this scheme, but none are more dependent than red-backed voles. Since the fungi stop fruiting if their conifer associates die (see page 290), red-backed voles disappear after a clearcut or destructive burn. They can't switch from fungi to fibrous vegetation (though they do eat horsehair lichens) because their molars have lost the ability to keep growing throughout life to replace unlimited wear and tear. Rodent incisors, or front teeth, keep growing lifelong (see page 363); but the molars are more commonly irreplaceable, like ours. Several *Microtus* voles are exceptions, and can grind up grasses to their hearts' content. Red-backed voles are the dietary mainstay of martens in parts of our range.

the trip to a stream or puddle to drink. To put that another way, moist fungi enlarge the fungivores' habitat by freeing them from having to live near creeks. (On the other hand, some rodents like red squirrels hang fungi up to dry, preserving them for winter when, as is widely observed, moisture tends to be in good supply around here.)

Fungal spores aren't the only potent stowaways in vole and squirrel droppings. Nitrogen-fixing bacteria, which live in the truffles, also pass unharmed through the rodents' bowels, as do yeasts which contribute nutrients the bacteria need in order to fix nitrogen. Since nitrogen fertility is often a limiting factor on conifer growth, the conifers may be as dependent on the bacteria and yeasts as on their mycorrhizal partners the truffles. It adds up to a five-way symbiosis, including the rodents that disseminate all four other partners.

Heather Vole

Phenacomys intermedius (fen-**ack**-o-mis: impostor mouse). 4¼" + 1⅜" tail [10.5 + 3.5 cm] (length ratio 3:1); gray-brown above, paler beneath; tail distinctly bicolored; feet ± white, even on top. Sporadic in forests and alpine meadows. Order Rodentia, Muridae (Mouse family).

Above timberline, you may spot a heather vole's or a northern bog lemming's nest shortly after snowmelt: a 6- to 8-inch [15–20 cm] ball of shredded lichens, moss, and grass, often with a big heap of dung nearby. This winter nest was built on the earth surface within a snow tunnel; the summer nest will be two to six inches [5–15 cm] underground, its entrance perhaps an inch in diameter. Heather voles are big consumers of kinnickinnick berries and leaves.

Northern Bog Lemming

Synaptomis borealis (sin-**ap**-ta-mis: joined mouse; bor-ee-**ay**-lis: of northern forests). 4" + ⅞" tail [98 + 22 mm]; dark gray-brown above, gray below; rusty hairs at base of ears; two upper incisors have a pronounced groove, and often grind to an angular point at the outside corner. Alp/subalpine year-round, mainly near wet sedge meadows, less often bogs; fairly common in the Canadian NPs, becoming rare southward as far as nw MT. Order Rodentia, Muridae.

Bog lemmings make conpicuous runways through the sedges, often with serious latrine heaps here and there. They are not the arctic lemmings (*Lemmus* spp) famed for population irruptions and migrations that occasionally end in mass dives from sea-cliffs.

Sagebrush Vole

Lemmiscus curtatus (lem-**iss**-cus: small lemming; cur-**tay**-tus: short, referring to the tail). =*Lagurus curtatus*. 4" + ⅞" tail [10 + 2 cm] (ratio more than 4:1); pale gray with whitish buff on ears, nose, feet, belly, and underside of tail. Arid habitats at all elevs; OR, c ID, s MT, and WY. Order Rodentia, Muridae.

Like other voles, the sagebrush vole lives on greenery, but it's a rare vole in braving near-desert habitats, and in wearing sandy-colored fur to match. (Other small rodents of the arid West look to insects and seeds as the only adequate food supply.) It is active year-round, at any time of day or night, with some preference for dusk and dawn. It doesn't expose itself much, spending most time in burrows or surface runways through dense grass or brush, or under snow. Sagebrush voles cram a lot of reproduction into the spring and fall seasons, when moist greenery is relatively available. Within 24 hours of giving birth, the mother leaves her two to thirteen newborns in their nest while she steps out to look for her next mate.

Muskrat

Ondatra zibethicus (ahn-**dat**-ra: Huron tribe's term for muskrat; zi-**beth**-ic-us: civet- or musk-bearing). 9–13" + 7–12" tail [32 + 23 cm]; tail scaly, pointed, flattened vertically; fur dark glossy brown, paler on belly, nearly white on throat; eyes and ears small; toes long, clawed, slightly webbed; voice an infrequent squeak. Largely nocturnal; scattered, in or near slow-moving water up to mid elevs. Order Rodentia, Muridae.

Anatomy reveals the muskrat to be an oversized vole, but we can be forgiven for thinking of it as an undersized beaver (half as long as a beaver, rarely a tenth as heavy). Leading similar aquatic lives, beavers and muskrats grow similar fur, which was historically trapped, traded, marketed, and worn in similar ways. (The guard hairs are removed, leaving the dense, glossy underfur.) Several million muskrats are still trapped annually—more individuals and more dollar value than any other U.S. furbearer." Like beavers, muskrats build either mudbank burrows or domed lodges with multiple underwater entrances. Muskrat teeth and jaws aren't up to cutting wood, so they build no dams or ponds. Soft vegetation like cattails and water lilies makes up the bulk of their diets, their lodges, the rafts they build to picnic on, and the "pushups" they create as their pond ices over, to create season-long breathing holes. They deviate from the vegetarianism typical of voles, eating tadpoles, mussels, snails, or crayfish. Their interesting mouths remain shut to water while the incisors, out front, munch away at succulent underwater stems. They can take a big enough breath in seconds to last them 15 minutes underwater. In winter they are thought to extend their range by releasing bubbles to create an under-ice air pocket they can use on the next outing. The chilling effect of life in icewater is a greater challenge, to a mammal this small. To recoup body heat, they huddle with other muskrats, and burn off calories through "non-shivering thermogenesis."

Neatly clipped sedge and cattail stems floating at marsh edges are a sign of muskrats. Both sexes, especially when breeding, secrete musk on scent posts made of small grass cuttings.

Porcupine

Erethizon dorsatum (er-a-**thigh**-zon: angering; dor-**say**-tum: back). 28–35" [75 cm] long, incl 9" [21 cm] tapered tail; large girth; blackish with long coarse yellow-tinged guard-hairs and very long whitish quills; incisors orange. Widespread. Order Rodentia, Erethizontidae (Porcupine family).

Porcupines' bristling defenses permit them to be slow, unwary, and too blind to obtain a driver's license in any state. This is both good and bad news, for you. Though they're mainly nocturnal, you stand a good chance of seeing one some morning or evening, and perhaps of hearing its low murmuring song. And you stand a good chance of having your equipment eaten by one during the night. Porcupines crave the salts in sweat and animal fat, and don't mind eating bootleather, rubber, plywood, nylon, or for that matter brake hoses, tires, or electrical insulation, to get them. (Marmots also have been known to consume car parts.) It's a good idea to always sleep by your boots, and make your packstraps hard to get at, too. Fair warning.

   Quills and spines are modified hairs that evolved separately in many kinds of rodents, including two separate families both called Porcupines. On American porcupines they reach their most effective form: hollow, very loosely attached at the base, and minutely, multiply barbed their entire length. The barbs engage instantly with enough grab to detach the quill from the porcupine, quickly swell up with body fluids, and work their way farther in (as fast as one inch per hour) with the unavoidable twitchings of the victim's muscles.

   Though strictly a defensive weapon, quills occasionally kill, either by perforating vital organs or by starving the poor beast that gets a noseful. But if they don't happen to hit organs, they typically work their way through any amount of muscle and out the other side without causing infection, since they actually have an antibiotic greasy coating.* Just keep your dog and your

*Uldis Roze analyzed the greasy coating for antibiotic properties, and came up with this hypothesis to explain it: American porcupines are among the world's heaviest tree-climbing herbivores; they have to go out on small branches to get the buds and new twigs and leaves that have the best nutrition, and that must lead to falls when branchlets break. Antibiotic grease would prevent infections from quills self-inflicted while landing from falls.

boots away from porcupines, and maintain a modest safe distance while the porky, most likely, retreats up a tree. A white-people's myth holds that porcupines throw their quills, but in fact the thrashing tail has only a slightly greater range than you would expect.

Since they have evolved no defenses other than their quills, porcupines have to be born fully quilled and active in order to survive infancy in adequate numbers. This requires very long gestation (seven months) and small litters (one or rarely two). But still... how to get the little spikers out of the womb? Answer: the newborn's soggy quills are soft, but harden in about half an hour as they air-dry. And then again... how to get mama and papa close enough to mate? Or baby close enough to nurse? Solving these problems has given porcupines their Achilles' heel, or rather, soft underbelly. With a quill-less underside including the tail, porcupines can safely mate in the usual mammalian position, provided she draws her tail scrupulously up over her back. (They mate in late autumn, but are otherwise solitary.) The soft underbelly has to have very tough skin to hold up through being dragged firmly up and down the bark of

Gopher Teeth

The word "rodent" derives from "gnaw." Rodent incisors, or gnawing teeth, are a wonder of nature. If you find a clean rodent skull, carefully draw an incisor out: you'll find it's a long arc, sliding out from an arcuate socket the full length of the skull or the jaw. Throughout life, new material is added at the back end and hardens as it makes its way forward, continually making up for wear. In porcupines, the rate of wear approximates 100% of the length of the incisor each year. Iron oxides are added to the enamel to further harden it, incidentally coloring it orange. The front edge gets extra thick enamel, so it resists wear differentially, creating a self-sharpening chisel-like edge.

This type of tooth, neither fixed nor ever fully formed, is called "rootless." Molars also are rootless in a few rodents, but not porcupines, despite the porcupine's dependence on its molars to thoroughly pulverize bark and leaves. Like humans, porcupines replace their molars just once. The adult molars have a heavily enameled surface, but once that gets worn through at around ten or twelve years of age, tooth decay sets in and the porcupine becomes less and less able to maintain its weight. Since the porcupine's chief predator, the fisher, has been nearly extirpated from the lower forty-eight, many porcupines live until they gradually waste away due to tooth decay or parasites.

countless trees. The genitalia in both sexes are protected from abrasion, and from bark chips, by withdrawing entirely behind a closure membrane. This makes it hard to tell males from females.

If it weren't for that unarmed belly, predators would have no place to begin eating. And predators there are—mainly cougars and fishers; rarely coyotes, bobcats, and even great horned owls. The belly is protected as long as the porky is alive enough to stay rightside up. Fishers attack via the head—and so should you, with a heavy stick, if you ever find yourself lost and starving and near a porcupine. Some states protect porcupines on the grounds that they are easy prey for unarmed humans lost in the woods. They are not choice fare. They were revered, though, by several northeastern tribes for being the one prey species usually available through winter, even during famine years, when they saved many people from starvation. Native Americans made quills an elegant art medium on clothing and baskets.

Porcupines eat aspen catkins in spring, new twigs and leaves in summer, and tree cambium, preferably pine, in winter. They select cambium near the top of the tree, where it is sweetest. Bright patches of stripped bark high up in pines are a sign of porcupine use. Occasionally they kill a tree by girdling it, but more often they kill only the top. The tree responds by turning a branch upward to form a new main trunk, but this puts a permanent kink in the tree, a fate worse than death according to timber economics. Killing the tree would at least release its neighbors to grow faster, but kinking it doesn't, while greatly devaluing it at the sawmill. So foresters are alarmed at the increasing porcupine populations of this century, which resulted mainly from human persecution of predators.

Like red tree voles and blue grouse, porcupines show the nutritional stress of dining at this all-you-can-eat cafeteria. They inexorably lose weight in winter, even while keeping their grossly overdeveloped guts stuffed with bark. In summer, trees can't avoid providing more fattening fare in their new foliage, but defend themselves with toxically high levels of potassium. Keeping up with the task of eliminating potassium via its kidneys drives the porcupine to find low-acid, low-potassium sources of sodium. Your sweaty boots and packstraps fit the bill, and coolant hoses and wire insulation it finds on your car's underbelly might be even better. For similar reasons mountain goats go after human urine, and deer and elk eat mud around soda springs.

Red Fox

Vulpes vulpes (**vul**-peez: Roman for fox) = *V. fulva.* 25" + 17" [63 + 42 cm] tail; shoulder height 16" [40 cm] (terrier size); commonly red-orange with black legs and ears and white belly (red phase); other color phases are "black;" "silver" (white-tipped black fur; "frosty" (creamy pale gray, at high elevs in YS area) and "cross" (like red, but with dark brown down back and across shoulders); all typically have white-tipped tail. Widespread. Order Carnivora, Canidae (Dog family). Color p 526.

Foxes are little seen here: they're nocturnal, shy, elusive, and alert. Though they can bark and "squall," they rarely make a concert of it. Their tracks and scats are hard to tell from small coyote ones, and their dens are most often other animals' work taken over without distinctive remodeling. Rocky areas are preferred for denning, and mixed brush/grassland areas for habitat.

Native Rocky Mtn. foxes run the gamut of color phases. Red is most common at most elevations, but the unique "frosty" form is said to predominate at the very highest elevations in the Yellowstone ecosystem. Even littermates may differ, like blonde, dark, and red-headed human siblings. Foxes of the plains and open valley country probably descend partly from fur-farm escapees, inheriting a substantial genetic component from European and Eastern subspecies. But all races are considered the same species.

Red foxes mate in midwinter, bear their litters (of four to seven) in early spring, and commonly stay mated. In contrast to the cat and bear families, canids make good fathers. Foxes eat insects, earthworms, fruit and seeds, and some birds eggs in addition to the preferred mice, voles, hares, frogs, and squirrels. They hunt with devious opportunism and stealth, often culminating in a spectacular aerial pounce. The huge plumey tail can be waved in midpounce to perfect the aim of pounces of up to 15 feet [4.5 m]; it also warms the face of a curled-up fox. The large paws are good on snow.

As wolf range shrank over the last century, coyote and red fox range expanded; red foxes displaced wolves as the world's most widely distributed rural wild mammal species. Where wolves were removed and coyotes thrived especially, they tended to chase out the foxes; today, where wolves return (e.g., Yellowstone) they chase out coyotes, and foxes recover.The slender, tan, catlike swift fox, *V. velox* (**vee**-lox: swift) of the Plains may sometimes reach the eastern edge of our range. It is rare and endangered in Canada and Montana. The similar kit fox of the Great Basin and Southwest deserts barely reaches our range in Idaho. It is classified as either *V. velox* ssp. *macrotis* (**mac-roe**-tis: big ear) or *V. macrotis.*

Coyote

Canis latrans (**can**-iss: dog; **lay**-trenz: barking). 33" + bushy tail 14" [82 + 35 cm]; shoulder height 16–20"; medium sized, pointy-faced, erect-eared gray to tawny dog, grayer and thicker-furred in winter; runs with tail down or horizontal. Ubiquitous. Order Carnivora, Canidae (Dog family). Color p 526.

In pioneer days, wolves and coyotes were called "timber wolves" and "prairie wolves," respectively. Wolves ruled the forests, leaving coyotes to range over steppes, brushy mountains, and prairies. But during the nineteenth century, guns and traps tipped the scales in favor of the coyote by aiming at the bigger predators—cougar, grizzly bear, and wolf. Greater size made these animals more vulnerable than coyotes for at least three reasons: more fearless and unwary; more feared and hated by people; and fewer, because higher on the "food chain" pyramid. Where the big predators were nearly extirpated,, smaller "varmints"—coyotes, bobcats, and eagles—inherited the brunt of predator-hatred, even though they prey mainly on rodents, hares and insects.

Coyotes are America's most bountied, poisoned, and targeted predator; yet they have proven uncannily adept at surviving and even increasing. Predator control has caused a large net increase in coyotes, since they have moved in wherever the wolf disappeared. Yellowstone's reintroduced wolves are, as expected, tending to drive coyotes away as they expand their range.

Considering how abundant they are, we rarely see coyotes. You may hear them howling at night, and can guess that hair-filled scats in the middle of the trail are likely theirs, especially when placed smack dab on a stump, a footlog over a creek, in an intersection, on a ridgetop, or any combination of the above. Coyote feces and urine are not mere "waste," like yours, but more like graffiti signatures full of olfactory data which later canine passers-by, even other species, can read. Coyote consulted his dung as an oracle! The male canine habit of fiercely scratching the ground after defecating probably deposits still more scents from glands between the toes. The long noses in the dog family really are "the better to smell you with, my dear"; the large olfactory chamber is arrayed with scent receptors. Coyotes can detect the passage of other animals a mile or two away, or days earlier. No less important (in ways we puny-nosed ones have a hard time either imagining or measuring) is the ability to read "scent posts" for data on the condition and activities of fellow coyotes. "Asserting territory" doesn't well describe scent-marking by coyotes; that they are territorial at all is increasingly doubted.

As for their lovely coloratura howling at night, most people hearing it feel that it, too, conveys something above and beyond mere location—though helping a family group relocate each other is its best-understood function. Often it's hard to tell how many coyotes we are listening to; the Modoc used to say it's always just one, sounding like many. Coyote choruses intersperse long howls with numerous yips; wolves howl without yipping.

Though preferring small mammals and birds, coyotes are prepared to subsist through hard times on grasshoppers, or on fruit, on winter-killed deer and elk, or occasionally on fawns. Stalking mice, they patiently "point" like a bird-dog, then pounce like a fox. Against hares they use the fastest running speed of any American predator. To run down weakened deer, they work as a pack, like wolves, but this is rare. Usually they hunt alone or pair up cleverly, one partner either decoying or flushing prey to where the other lurks. An unwitting badger, eagle, or raven may be briefly employed as a partner.

The female tends to pick the same mate year after year, and the pair displays apparent affection as well as loyalty. To say they mate for life would be about as euphemistic as saying that Americans do. In years when coyotes are abundant and/or rodents are unusually scarce in a given area, as many as 85% of the mature females there may fail to go into heat, and those who do so will bear smaller litters than usual . On the other hand, they reproduce like crazy wherever their own populations have been depleted. Again, this helps make them impossible to get rid of—but exemplifies the population control innate in many mammal species. Currently infertile females and the corresponding unattached males often spend the year with their parents, helping to raise the new litter. This extended family displays loyalty, but for some reason isn't usually called a pack.

The ferocity of wolf packs toward outsiders (especially coyotes) may be crucial in maintaining wolves and coyotes as species. Wolves, coyotes, jackals, and domestic dogs are all interfertile and beget fertile offspring. Yet they are dramatically different even where they have long occupied overlapping ranges, so actual interbreeding must be rare. Wild "coy-dog" hybrids do occur, yet seem unable to establish reproducing populations, perhaps partly due to the dog half's maladaptation to the wilds and partly to a confused sense of a mating season: coyotes have one, domestic dogs don't.

Coyote the Trickster is a ubiquitous, complicated figure in all western tribal mythologies, possessing an unsurpassed, if devious, intelligence undermined by downright humanoid carelessness, greed, conniving lust, and vulgarity. In some myths, Coyote exemplifies the bad, greedy ways of hunting that destroyed a long-gone Edenlike abundance. In others, he brought the poor starving people rituals and techniques they needed for catching salmon. Each of those themes tells half the story that anthropologists now reconstruct: the first people that migrated into North America found an Eden-like abundance; eventually the population reached a saturation point for simple hunting and gathering, and the people had to learn to store salmon and roots. Some tribes, on learning about Jesus, saw Him as the white man's Coyote since He came to Earth to improve people's lot. And then again, in many origin myths Coyote is the Creator—which suggests the mythmakers fostered no illusions that the world always works perfectly.

Coyote and the Cedar

Coyote was traveling. He passed the mountains. He followed the trail through the deep woods. As he was traveling along, he saw an immense cedar. The inside was hollow. He could see it through a big gap which opened and closed. The gap opened and closed as the tree swayed in the wind. Coyote cried, "Open, Cedar Tree!" Then the tree opened. Coyote jumped inside. He said, "Shut, Cedar Tree!" Then the tree closed. Coyote was shut inside the tree.

Inside the tree, Coyote said, "Open, Cedar Tree!" The tree did not answer. Coyote was angry. He called to the tree. He kicked the tree. The tree did not answer. Then Coyote remembered that he was Coyote, the wisest and cunningest of all animals. Coyote began to think.

After he thought, Coyote called the birds to help him. He told them to peck a hole through Cedar Tree. The first was Wren. Wren pecked and pecked at the great cedar until her bill was blunted. But Wren could not even make a dent. Therefore Coyote called her Wren.

Then Coyote called the other birds. Sparrow came, Robin came, Finch came, but they could not even break the heavy bark. So Coyote gave each a name and sent them away. Then Owl came, and Raven, and Hawk, and Eagle. They could not make even a little hole. So Coyote gave each a name and sent them away. Then he called Downy Woodpecker. Finally Downy Woodpecker made a tiny hole. Then Pileated Woodpecker came and pecked a large hole. But the hole was too small for Coyote. So he saw there was no help from the birds.

Then Coyote remembered again that he was Coyote, the wisest and cunningest of all the animals. Then Coyote began to think.

Gray Wolf

Canis lupus (**loop**-us: the Roman term). 52" + bushy tail 20" [130 + 50 cm]; shoulder height 26–34" [75 cm]; big erect-eared gray to tan dog with massive (not pointy) muzzle, long legs; majority of pups are black, turning pale by adulthood; fur very thick in winter; runs with tail down or horizontal. Order Carnivora. Color p 526.

At night they are so fearless as to come quite within the purlieus of the camp, and there sit, a dozen together, and howl hideously for hours.

—John Kirk Townsend in Wyoming, 1834

The origins of European culture's wolf paranoia, cultivated in countless fables, are lost in the mists of time. It's strange: not only did certain prehistoric wolves so ingratiate themselves as to become our dogs, but wolves don't hurt people. I'm not saying never ever not even once, but it's so rare, we could have fun listing housepets and household objects that pose more danger. Um, pit bulls, bobby pins, …

After he thought, Coyote began to take himself apart. He took himself apart and slipped each piece through Woodpecker's hole. First he slipped a leg through, then a paw, then his tail, then his ears, and his eyes, until he was through the hole, and outside the cedar tree.

Then Coyote began to put himself together. He put his legs and paws together, then his tail, his nose, his ears, then his body. At last Coyote put himself together again except his eyes. He could not find his eyes. Raven had seen them on the ground. Raven had stolen them. So Coyote, the wisest and cunningest of all animals, was blind.

But Coyote did not want the animals to know he was blind. He smelled a wild rose. He found the bush and picked two rose leaves. He put the rose leaves in place of his eyes. Then Coyote traveled on, feeling his way along the trail.

Soon he met a squaw. Squaw began to jeer, "Oh ho, you seem to be very blind!"

"Oh no," said Coyote, "I am measuring the ground. I can see better than you can. I can see spirit rays." Squaw was greatly astonished. Coyote pretended to see wonderful things at a great distance.

Squaw said, "I wish I could see spirit rays!"

Coyote said, "Change eyes with me. Then you can see spirit rays."

So Coyote and Squaw traded eyes. Coyote took Squaw's eyes and gave her the rose leaves. Then Coyote could see as well as ever. Squaw could see nothing. Coyote said, "For your folly you must always be a snail. You must creep. You must feel your way on the ground."

Ever since that time snails have been blind. They creep.

—Cladsap tale, slightly abridged from Katherine Berry Judson

It was about 12,000 years ago that some wolves learned to live on people's leftovers, and started down the evolutionary path to domestic dogs. Wolf and dog DNA is so similar that most taxonomists now reject Linnaeus' separation of dogs as a species, *Canis familiaris*, and include them in *C. lupus* instead.

Today, the eerie howling of a wolf pack is music to the ears of urban and suburban North Americans—an amazing sea change in a very few years, matching the amazing recovery of wolf populations in the northwestern states. Wolves captured in Canada were reintroduced in 1995–96 in central Idaho and in Yellowstone, and others since 1980 had been slipping across the border on their own into Montana and Washington. These populations have thrived so far.

Few western ranchers share urbanites' love of wolves. Wolves do indeed prey on calves and lambs when those prey are the most convenient, and some packs acquire a preference for them.

Hunting as a pack enables wolves—alone, in the Americas—to take prey as large as elk and moose or (rarely) as fierce as black bears and cougars. While scientists disagree about almost every aspect of the story, it is plausible that the extinction of sabretooth tigers, short-faced bears, and other large predators by 11,000 years ago left North America ecologically skewed in that the largest herbivores faced only two significant predators—humans and wolves—greatly increasing wolves' ecological role. They affect not only prey species and the prey's food plants (page 116), but also competitors and the competitors' competitors, like foxes, which come back in when wolves chase coyotes out. So we can hope for broad benefits from their return.

Increasing numbers of wolves in British Columbia are trimming the excess of moose, who invaded southern BC between 1920 and 1950 thanks to wolf extermination, logging, and fires. Moose like shrubby habitat. Woodland caribou need mature forest habitat, so they did not increase at that time, and today the wolves are an added threat to their survival, on top of the continued logging. Wolves are far less scarce in B.C. than woodland caribou, so an argument is made for killing wolves in the name of species preservation.

Studies of wolf social life have mostly looked at captive wolves thrust together and forced to socialize, leading to an overemphasis on how they determine rank, according to David Mech, the most famous name in wolf research. He studied a pack on Ellesmere Island where wolves never had humans to fear. After a few years of habituation they let him watch from as close as one yard [meter] away. To Mech, the word "parents" is more useful than "alpha;" a typical pack is two parents and one to three years' worth of their kids; larger packs are two or three such families. As in any species, offspring are subordinate to parents. Usually everyone feeds pups preferentially; yearlings can eat side-by-side with parents when there's room enough. Certainly, social life drips with seeming expressions of submissiveness or dominance, largely connected to food-sharing. Mech's point is that he doesn't see a pecking order that is continually in play, as it is in, say, bighorn sheep. Nor does he see any wolves fated to lifelong low rank and a consequent genetic dead end: most will disperse, seek another disperser to mate with, and try to found a new pack. In the Yellowstone region, the average pack size (nine) fits this concept, but the oldest, most-watched packs have several moms and a (polygamous?) alpha male.

Black Bear

Ursus americanus. 4–6" [1.4 m] long (4"/10 cm tail inconspicuous); 3–3½" [1 m] at shoulder; typically jet black with a tan nose. (Less common phases are "cinnamon" red-brown, tannish brown, "blue" gray, and even white.) Facial profile ± straight; no shoulder hump; claws dark, 1–1½" [3 cm]. Order Carnivora, Ursidae. Color p 527.

Perhaps even more than sneaky Coyote, smart Raven, and industrious Beaver, Bear has always been seen by humans as somehow our kin. Though Bear's reflection of human nature is at once darker and grander than Coyote's or Beaver's, it's hard to pin down the essence. Mammalogists put bears among the most humanlike of animals in terms of their feet and their diet. The feet are five-toed, plantigrade (putting weight on the heel as well as the ball and toes) and about as big as ours, so that the prints—especially the hind print—look disturbingly familiar. The diet includes almost anything, and varies enormously by season, region and individual. Plant foods predominate, starting in spring with tree sapwood or cambium, horsetails, grass, bulbs, and all kinds of new shoots, and working up to enormous berry gluttony in fall, the fattening-up season. The typical prey are small mammals, and insects or larvae where they can be lapped up in quantity, as from anthills, grubby old logs, wasp nests, or bee hives—preferably dripping with honey. An adult bear can chase virtually any predator from its kill, but is less adept at hunting for itself, so large animals are most often eaten as carrion.

Many bears are skilled at snatching fish from streams. Some develop predilections for robbing woodpecker nests, grain crops, fallen orchard fruit, garbage dumps, or hiker camps.

During heavy berry-eating, bear scats become soft like cow pies, and show lots of fruit seeds, leaves (e.g., blueberry), or skins (apple). Earlier in the season, they are thick, untapered cylindrical chunks, perhaps showing animal hair, but often resembling horse manure. Fresh, they are usually as jet-black as the beast itself. Bears leave distinctive marks on trees from three activities. To eat cambium, they strip away swaths of bark, leaving irregular incisor gashes 3–6' [1–2 m] off the ground; this may kill the tree. Second, they sometimes assert territory by marking selected trees with several long, parallel, often diagonal claw-slashes 5–9" [12–23 cm] from the ground. Third, during the spring molt, bark may show lots of bear hair stuck to an abraded area 2–4' [60–120 cm] up, from bears rubbing their itchy backs against it. (Compare with cat scratch-marks, page 386).

Once the ripe fruits are all gone in the fall, there is little a bear can do to fatten up; if it isn't fat enough by then, it will likely die before spring, but that rarely happens. Activity slows down even before hibernating; bears appear listless and have no appetite while preparing their dens. This may include building a substantial nest of fluffy stuff. The bear sleeps curled up in a ball with the crown of its head down. Between the insulative nest and the superlatively thick fur, the bear loses little heat to the air of its den, and maintains a body temperature of about 88° [31° C.], in contrast to the 40° [4° C.] hibernating temperature of many squirrels. But its heart rate may reach an impressive low of just eight very weak beats per minute. And, unlike squirrels, it may go the full six or seven months without eating, urinating, defecating or, presumably, waking up. (In other instances, it may wake easily and dehibernate briefly at any time of winter.) The urea waste that would ordinarily be excreted in urine is somehow recycled into new proteins, alleviating the problem of muscle atrophy during hibernation. Fecal accumulation is so reduced that the winter's worth can be saved until spring dehibernation.

Two or three cubs are born around January. The mother wakes up to give birth, then nurses them mostly in her sleep for the next few months. A den of cubs nursing emits a hum like a beehive, only much deeper. Cubs are smaller at birth, in ratio to their adult weight, than almost any mammals short of marsupials. In nursing them to viable size for the real world, the mother may lose 40% of her weight during hibernation, as opposed to 15–30% for adult males. Rather

Hang That Food!

The Rockies have had bears that look for their dinner in campers' gear for a long time. Human injuries from black bears are extremely rare historically, but will increase if naive campers leave more and more food around. Fortunately, our bears are less technologically advanced than Yosemite's bears, which at one point were ripping doors off of two or three parked cars a night; cars are still more or less bearproof here. Away from your car, dealing with food requires constant thoughtfulness, with two objectives: to protect your body and equipment from collateral damage by bears going after your food, and to save innocent bears from becoming problem bears that will end up euthanized. Don't tempt them.

Never: **Discard** food or "leave it for the chipmunks."
Cook more than you will eat.

Always: **Pack** your food in airtight, smelltight containers.
Hang your food and garbage during day hikes and at night.
Burn out your empty cans on your stove or in your fire.
Throw fish guts into a rushing stream, or the middle of a lake.
Pack out all your empty packets, bags, and burnt cans.

Set up an eating camp and a sleeping camp 150' [45 m] apart. In the former, you cook and eat, hang your food **and** garbage in big plastic bags, wash your dishes and store them **and** the clothes you ate dinner in **and** the shorts you spilled sardine oil on, day before yesterday. In the latter, you sleep peacefully away from previous campers' food smells as well as your own. Don't use your sleeping gear stuffsacks as overnight food bags unless you want to sleep in a bear invitation.

Most campsites in parks in grizzly range provide either bearproof containers or poles with hooks for hanging your entire backpack. In other sites you must do your own hanging. Bear in mind that smart bears can learn to sever or pull a cord. Find a long, strong limb 12–15' [4 m] above ground. Put roughly equal amounts of food into two bags or groups of bags. Tie the first bag to the cord end, throw the cord over a point in the limb at least 5' [1.5 m] from the tree trunk, and pull the bag right up to the limb. At a point on your cord that's about as high as you can reach, tie on the second bag. Coil the loose cordage and tuck it into this bag. With a stick, push the second bag up until the two bags are counterbalanced equally high—and out of reach of beasts. If the trees are too small to offer suitable limbs, you'll have to climb two trees and draw your foodbags up 12' [4 m] off the ground midway between them. If you want to camp where there aren't trees for that either, you'll have to use bearproof canisters, which may put a crimp in your *haute route cuisine.*

than taking on this stress in consecutive winters, she just hibernates with her yearling cubs in alternate years.

Some speculate that the tree-climbing skills of black bears evolved for escape from the only other animals here that could prey on them—grizzly bears. The fabled ferocity of black bear mothers in the company of their cubs more likely evolved to protect cubs from grown-up males of their own species; subadult bears also may end up cannibalized if they are foolish enough to stand up to a big boar.

Bear Safety

Don't go hiking in terror of bears; go in knowledgeable wariness of them.

Consider all bears dangerous even though bears normally withdraw from contact with people. Black bears encountered by hikers often fit one of the two "abnormal" types—sows with cubs, and "problem bears" familiar with campers and camper food. Never camp in an area with torn up camp food strewn about, or with long strips of overturned sod, or recent large-mammal remains. If a bear enters your camp, distance yourself from your food.

When in grizzly country, let them know you're around. The sound that best gets their attention is the human voice. Shout, talk, laugh, and sing. (If you are brave enough, and hope to see wildlife in general, save the noise for likely grizzly habitat, such as thickets, avalanche tracks, streamsides, lily meadows, berry patches.) Bear bells are useless. Bear-bangers sound like a good idea, but grizzlies commonly ignore them. Bear pepper spray, on the other hand, is likely to save some lives. Carry it and study the instructions, then save it for in case you are charged.

If you meet one in the open, act calm; form a group; look large; avoid eye contact; retreat discreetly; never run, you cannot outrun it. (Bears being slow is an optical illusion.) Sometimes you can slowly circle widely around a black bear, if it hasn't already run off; if you are forced to try that with a grizzly, allow it at least a quarter-mile [400 m].

If a bear charges you, stand and act calm. Spray now, if you have spray. Climb a tree if you have both a strong tree and time to climb. Most charges are "bluff-charges," or are abandoned when the bear can see you're a person. (Bears are nearsighted.) If attacked, lie prone and play dead with your legs spread and your hands and your pack protecting the back of your neck. Don't move until you're sure the bear is gone.

There are additional points—and some differences of opinion—about bear safety. Your parks will make them abundantly available.

Grizzly Bear

Ursus arctos ssp. *horribilis* (**ur**-sus: Roman term for bear; **arc**-toce: Greek for bear; hor-**rib**-il-iss: horrible). 6–8" [2 m] long (3" tail invisible); shoulder height 4½" [1.3 m]; brown (rarely black) ± grizzled with light tan, but color is not reliable for distinguishing from black bear; instead, look for hump over front shoulder, concave facial profile, and very long pale claws (foreclaws typically 3" [7 cm] or longer). Canada; endangered in the lower 48, but recently increasing in Yellowstone region and nw MT, n ID. Order Carnivora, Ursidae (Bear family). Color p 527.

The grizzly is the largest terrestrial carnivore, and one of the most intimidating. It's big and fierce enough to take any hooved mammal, but isn't fast enough to hunt healthy deer regularly. So, in one of nature's twists that seem odd to humans, its omnivorous diet emphasizes things that neither run nor fight: roots, berries, insect grubs, pine nuts, spawning salmonids, small mammals, and dead large mammals. Our region's ability to support grizzly bears may decline sharply as whitebark pines decline due to blister rust (page 59); scientists are concerned about how well grizzlies will get by without them during fall. At Yellowstone, grizzly mortality correlates with poor whitebark cone crops more strongly than with any other factor. Even if pine nut shortages were merely to drive the bears down to lower elevations, increasing their contacts with people, the bottom line would be the same: more dead bears. Two other rich foods that are important to at least some Yellowstone bears are also threatened: cutthroat trout, threatened by introduced lake trout (see page 488); and army cutworm moths, which migrate seasonally to the Plains, where they are poisoned as agricultural pests.

How does a huge bear gather and eat little pine nuts? By raiding squirrel middens and trampling the heaps of cones to smash them. Its big old tongue is remarkably efficient at separating out the nuts— and, for that matter, separating grubs from rotten wood, bee honey from combs, and ladybugs, army cutworm moths, and other delicacies that bears eat a few thousand of at a sitting. Prehibernating swarms of ladybugs are an attraction high in the Mission Range.

During the long fattening-up season, when a grown grizzly needs about 35,000 calories a day, 250,000 berries would not be excessive. Flower bulbs and taproots are a mainstay. In the southern Canadian Rockies, the staple species is yellow sweetvetch, a legume; in Yellowstone it's biscuitroot, a carrot; and in between, it tends to be glacier lilies. Patches to be dug up and dined on are selected by two main criteria: proximity to a forest edge; and digability, which correlates with gravelly soil and with a history of digging. (I thank David

Mattson for coining "digability" in his research papers rather than digging up some indigestible Latinate synonym.) The bears till big patches of meadow sod in order to nip off bulbs from the sod underside. If they also turn up voles and insect larvae, so much the better. For reasons not clear to scientists nor, presumably, to grizzlies, this has the effect of increasing available nitrogen in the soil and hence the size of next year's lily bulbs (the ones the bears missed this year), as well as their nutritional content, the number of seeds they set, and the seeds' viability. The usual word for behavior that enhances one's food crop is "gardening," and scientists do use that word. Bears return to their gardens, with the big, rich bulbs and loosened soil, year after year. Meadows thick with glacier lilies are likely to have been grizzly gardens at some point, and conversely, meadows not selected by big gardeners tend to end up lily-poor.

Charlie Robbins and his students study diets of both living and long-dead bears by looking at ratios of key isotopes in hairs or bone. They can use museum specimens or hairs snagged in the woods. This technique is more accurate than either direct observation or scat analysis in several ways: it averages the bear's diet over a period of time, and it quantifies foods to the degree they were digested, whereas scats mislead by emphasizing the indigestible. The technique can't identify foods by species, but the list of things it can do keeps growing. For example, the relative quantity of mercury probably reflects the amount of freshwater fish in the diet, and isotopes of sulphur can suggest the geographic locale of plants eaten, based on soil chemistry. The studies published so far provide ratios of animal to vegetable foods, and of marine to nonmarine foods. For an inland bear, marine means salmon. Salmon contributed 60% of the diet of three 19th-century grizzlies in central Idaho. Without a recovery of Idaho's salmon runs (which probably won't happen unless several dams go) reestablishment of grizzlies there would require bears to live on a diet very different from their historical one.

Fortunately, these consummate omnivores do develop radically different diets in different locales. In Yellowstone today it's about 50% meat, but in Glacier Park it's only around 11% meat, while in Alaska it can reach 90% fish and meat. At Glacier, deer and elk (typically scavenged as carrion) are apparently less available, while fall berries are much more abundant, than at Yellowstone.

Subspecies *horribilis*, the grizzly bear of the Western states and provinces, was once considered a full species. Other *U. arctos* subspecies include the even larger Kodiak brown bear and the much smaller brown bears of Eurasia. The polar bear, *U. maritimis*, must be a close relative (captive polar bears and grizzlies have produced fertile offspring together) but it abandoned bear family traditions, becoming a marine mammal and a pure carnivore.

Life cycle and hibernation are similar to those of the black bear (pages 371, 344) except that grizzlies consistently dig very serious dens on hillsides, moving about a ton of earth. Cubs weigh about a pound (450 g) at birth, leave their mother after 1½ or 2½ years, and live 15–25 years if they're lucky. They are inexplicably fond of high places—or should I say that like us, they are fond of high places? Or perhaps I should say high places turn them on: a few times, a male has been seen using a mountaintop in the Canadian Rockies as a good place to defend a female at mating time: he would herd a female there and block her from descending, for the duration of estrus.

Grizzlies avoid contact with people, and do not normally view people as food; on the other hand, they show little fear of people in close encounters. Avoid those.

Skunks

Western spotted skunk, *Spilogale gracilis* (spil-**og**-a-lee: spot weasel; **grass**-il-iss: slender) =*S. putorius*. 11" + 5" tail [28 + 12 cm] (kitten-sized); glossy black with many ± lengthwise intermittent white stripes; tail tip a rosette of long white hairs. Lowlands W of the CD, from Missoula s. Illustrated.

Striped skunk, *Mephitis mephitis* (mef-**it**-iss: pestilential vapor). 18" + 11" tail [45 + 28 cm] (cat-sized); glossy black with two broad white stripes diverging at nape to run down sides of back, plus thin white stripe on forehead. Widespread, commoner in farmlands than in mtns, and rare at high elevs. Order Carnivora, Mephitidae (Skunk family—included in the weasel family until recently).

It's to a skunk's advantage to be conspicuous and easy to recognize, since its defenses are so good. The rare animal that fails to stay clear receives further warnings—forefoot stamping, tail raising, or a handstand with tail displayed forward like a big white pom-pom. (The handstand, rare among striped skunks but well described among spotteds, has been explained as tempting an attacker to bite the tail, doing little damage to the skunk while fixing the attacker's face in the line of fire.) Only as a last resort does the skunk curl around (with both eyes and tail facing you) and fire its notorious defensive weapon—up to six well-aimed rounds of organic volatiles in a musky vehicle secreted just above the anus. This cocktail burns the eyes, chokes the throat, and stinks like hell. It can be shot either in an atomizer-style mist or, more typically, in a water-pistol-style stream fanned across a 30–45° arc for greater coverage. Range is well over 12' [4 m]. The skunk scrupulously avoids fouling its own tail. Traditional antidotes to skunk spray include tomato juice, ammonia, bleach, gasoline, and incineration of affected clothes; fire is the most effective, juice the least unpleasant. Effectiveness of tomato juice is maximized, write Verts and Carraway, if you mix it with vodka and ingest. But never mix ammonia and bleach. The musk is extracted, chemically stripped of scent, and used commercially as a vehicle for perfumes. How's that for making a silk purse from a sow's ear?

Only great horned owls seem to prey on skunks regularly. They may sometimes hit hard and stealthily enough to forestall the spray defense, but more likely they're just thick-skinned, with their built-in protective goggles and weak sense of smell. Many big owls smell skunky and have skunk-bitten feet. As far as the odds-makers of natural selection are concerned, skunk defenses are superlative. But like porcupines, skunks seem to be as prone to little parasitic animals as they are well-defended against big predatory ones.

Of our two skunks, the spotted is slimmer, speedier, and more carnivorous, though both species eat some vegetation. Foods include insects and grubs, mice, shrews, and occasionally ground-nesting birds and their eggs. Skunk dens are most often burrows dug by other animals. Skunks fatten up for winter and sleep in their dens— not torpidly—for days at a time during the coldest spells.

Weasels

Mustela spp. (mus-**tee**-la: the Roman term). Very fast, slinky, slender, short-legged, long-necked animals; in characteristic running gait the back is arched; ears inconspicuous; rich medium brown above, white to orange-yellow beneath, incl feet and insides of legs and (long-tailed only) some of tail; most high-elev weasels turn pure white in winter, exc tip of tail always black. Ubiquitous. Order Carnivora, Mustelidae (Weasel family).

Long-tailed weasel, *M. frenata* (fren-**ay**-ta: bridled). Males: 11" + 5¾" tail [28 + 14 cm]; females: 9" + 5⅜" tail [22 + 11 cm]; deep cream to yellow underneath (in summer). Illustrated at left.

Short-tailed weasel, *M. erminea* (er-**min**-ee-a: the Roman term). Also **ermine**. Males: 8½" + 3" tail [21 + 8 cm]; females: 7" + 2⅝" tail [18 + 6.6 cm]; males about twice female weight; white to light cream underneath. Color p 526.

Narrow, linear shapes like the **weasel**'s are rare among the smaller warm-blooded animals because they are so costly to heat Small mammal prey run rotund—a shape that during sleep or torpor can be rolled up into an approximate sphere, the optimal shape for retaining heat. Weasels and their streamlined relatives roll up into, at best, a lumpy sort of disk, which takes 50–100% more calories to maintain at a given temperature than a spherical rodent of similar weight. But when it needs to eat, the weasel can chase that rodent down any hole or through any crevice; a weasel is much thinner, faster, and fiercer of tooth and claw than any animal anywhere near its own weight. Its "hunting success ratio" is among the highest of all vertebrate predators. So there's no question of the weasel's shape being worth its high price (a caloric intake requirement averaging perhaps 40% of body weight per day.)

Though mouse-sized prey are their staple, weasels can also run down squirrels in trees and hares on snow—prey several times their size. Like the smallest members of many other predatory families, they make a relatively easy living: they go after the most abundant prey, and are the surest of catching it. Perhaps the greatest wonder is that weasels aren't far more abundant than they are.

Reports of weasel "killing sprees" in which they kill far more than they can eat are numerous and confirmed. It should be allowed, though, that human observation may have inhibited or overlooked the weasel's efforts to cache the leftovers for later use. There are also clear cases of weasel cannibalism, including juveniles eating their own litter-mates, once they get carried away with the taste or smell of blood. They are undeniably among the most ferociously aggressive of predators. They may themselves fall prey to owls, foxes, bobcats, or occasionally snakes. They nest in burrows of chipmunks, ground squirrels, moles, etc., often lining these with fur plucked from the body of the former occupant.

The term "ermine" is applied by naturalists to the short-tailed weasel only, but by furriers and the general public to the fur of both species interchangeably, so long as it's in the white, winter pelage. In fact, most ermine coats are made from long-tailed weasels because there are more of them out there to catch, and it takes fewer of them to make a coat. It still takes hundreds of them, though, so a single pelt commands a surprisingly low price. It has been proposed that the black tail-tip on the otherwise white winter fur serves as a decoy; the weasel can usually escape hawk or owl talons that strike this one body part that's conspicuous against snow.

Otter

Lontra canadensis (**lon**-tra: from the Italian word for them). =*Lutra canadensis* if included in the genus of European otters. Also **river otter**. 27–29" [70 cm] + thick, tapering, muscular tail 17–19" [47 cm]; dark brown with silvery belly, pale whiskers, very small ears, webbed feet. In or near rivers, lakes. Order Carnivora, Mustelidae (Weasel family). Color p 527.

Otters are among the unlucky species for whom people are belatedly discovering fondness and admiration—only after reducing them to near rarity. (By 1920 they were extirpated from Wyoming outside of Yellowstone, but have since reestablished themselves in the Snake, Green, and Wind Rivers.) In both Europe and America they were trapped for fur or shot on sight as vermin, largely because anglers accused them of more predation on trout than they actually inflict. Ancient Chinese fishermen, in contrast, trained them to herd fish into nets; a few European hunters trained them to retrieve waterfowl.

Today, otters come up in arguments over the existence of non-human play. Many reputable observers report them running up snowy hills again and again just to body-sled down, or body-surfing in river rapids for no apparent reason. Others claim these behaviors are mere transportation. Otters would rather slide on their bellies than walk anytime, even on level ground but preferably down a steep otter slide with a big splash in the river at the bottom. They frolic and tumble in the water, often in family groups after the pups are six months old; up to that age the mother scrupulously keeps them away from the father. Oddly, the pups seem afraid of the water and have to be taught to swim. Otters have a low, mumbly "chuckle" while nuzzling or mating.

Look on riverbanks and lakeshores for otters' easily recognized slides, tracks or "spraints." The latter are fecal scent-markers placed just out of the water on rocks, mud banks or floating logs, and usually showing fish bones, scales, or crayfish shell bits under a greenish, slimy (when fresh) coating which smells distinctive but not unpleasant. Otter staples are crayfish and slow-moving fish; they rarely compete for game fish. Amphibians and voles round out their diet.

Mink

Mustela vison (vice-un: archaic French term). 13–16" + 6–8" tail [32–40 + 15–20 cm]; long, narrow and short-legged; dark glossy brown except variable white patches on chin, chest, belly; ears inconspicuous. In and near streams, marshes, and sometimes lakes. Order Carnivora, Mustelidae.

The mink is an aquatic weasel, preying on fish, frogs, crayfish, ducks, water voles, and muskrats. Some populations become fully terrestrial for a while, subsisting on hares and voles, while others line the B.C. and Alaska coast, subsisting on crabs. The muskrat, a preferred prey, is also a mink's "most dangerous game" because it is much larger; a muskrat can drown a mink by dragging it under. In deep water, muskrats even attack minks fearlessly. On the other hand, a duck that thinks it can shake a mink by taking to the air may be in for a fatal surprise: cases are on record of minks hanging on for the flight until the duck weakens and drops. But when they can, minks kill quickly with a bite into the back of the neck or skull.

The foul discharges from under the tail that we associate with skunks characterize the whole weasel family. Skunks alone developed the marksmanship and range to optimize the anal gland as a defensive weapon, but minks smell worse. They spray when angered, alarmed, or captured, when fighting each other (they are viciously antisocial) and to mark territory or repel raiders of their meat caches. The blood, gore, and stench in the pedigree of a mink coat is ironic, but anyone lucky enough to watch a mink in nature is likely to admire it. Most mink coats come from commercial mink ranches.

Marten

Martes americana (mar-teez: Roman word for them). Also **pine marten**. 14–18" + 8" tail [40 + 20 cm]; body narrow, legs short, tail fluffy, nose pointy; variably buff to cinnamon-brown to nearly black; (looks ± like a smaller red fox on shorter legs). In trees, in remote wilderness. Order Carnivora, Mustelidae. Illustrated on opposite page. Color p 526.

The marten is the one mammal that can sustain life by preying on squirrels in trees. Though martens often hang out in squirrel middens under the winter snow, they rarely ambush squirrels there, apparently being attracted more by the insulation and the conifer seeds to eat. Berries in fall, and birds' eggs and insects in summer, also play important roles in their diets, while red-backed voles and other small prey are the year-round staple.

The fact that tree squirrels and chipmunks make themselves so obvious suggests that martens have never been abundant, and in modern times they are further reduced by trapping and an aversion to civilization. They are restricted to mountain wilderness with conifers. The Bighorns and some other ranges have isolated "island" populations, since martens can't migrate across treeless steppe. Even where they live, we rarely see them. They are fast and well camouflaged up in the trees, and active mainly at dawn, dusk, or under heavy overcast. Occasional hikers strike it lucky when a weakness for human foods lures a marten right into camp.

Their musk, so mild as to be almost undetectable to us, is used mainly to mark tree branches to ward off other martens. Except of course during a brief season when about 50% of other martens find the smell not repellent but, on the contrary, quite attractive.

Fisher

Martes pennanti (pen-an-tie: after Thomas Pennant). Also **wejack, pekan**. 20–25" + 13–15" tail [55 + 36 cm]; long, thin, and short-legged; glossy black-brown, occasionally with small white throat patch; ears slightly protruding. Paw print avg 2½–3" [6–7.5 cm] wide, often showing 5 toes and claws. Rare; dense forest. Order Carnivora, Mustelidae. Color p 526.

Fishers don't fish. The name may derive from the Dutch *visse*, meaning nasty. Fishers eat mainly porcupines and snowshoe hares. In fact, they are the only predator that hunts porcupines (which outweigh them about 2 to 1) by preference. Though fishers may eat porcupines via their soft underbellies, the myth that they attack there, by means of a flip with the paw or a fast burrow under the snow, is dubious. After all, those floppy quills lie on the ground and don't really leave space to insert a paw. Darting, dodging attacks to the face, with both tooth and claw, have been observed, repeated for maybe half an hour, until the porcupine is too weak to flail. Fishers end up with quill bits scattered throughout their organs and musculature like shrapnel. Others soften in the stomach and pass safely through; scats containing pieces of quills are a sign of either fisher or cougar.

Fishers can rotate their hind feet almost 180° for running down tree trunks. They're fast enough to run down and kill martens.

The only predators tough enough to overcome fishers rarely find it worth the fight, and are too slow to chase them. The only animals that threaten the fisher are people. Fisher pelts, ringers for Siberian sable, are often the highest-priced North American pelt. Trapping virtually eliminated fishers from the lower 48 by 1940. In recent decades, foresters have been bringing them back to reduce porcupine populations that exploded in the absence of fishers.

In most weasel family females, pregnancy is extended by delayed implantation: the fertilized ovum undergoes its first few cell divisions and then goes dormant for weeks or months before increasing day length triggers implantation in the uterus and fetal growth in time for springtime birth. Fishers are an extreme case, with a total gestation of up to 370 days, around 310 of them dormant. Thus, the female often goes into heat a few days before or after giving birth, and mates before weaning her two or three helpless newborns.

Wolverine

Gulo gulo (**goo**-low: gullet or glutton). Also **skunk-bear.** 26–31" + 7–8" tail [75 + 18 cm]; somewhat like a small bear but with ± distinct gray-brown to yellowish striping across the brow and down the sides to the tail; fur thick and long. Paw print avg 4–4½" [11 cm] wide; unlike lynx or puma, many prints will show 5 small, well separated toes with claws; unlike black bear, the "heel" of the paw is small and often doesn't print, and rear edge of pad is usually very concave. Near timberline; rare. Order Carnivora, Mustelidae. Color p 526.

Wolverines' reputation as our scrappiest predators should come as no surprise, as they're the biggest in the weasel family. Biologists in the Selkirks found a 300-pound caribou brought down by a 25-pound wolverine, which must be close to the extreme size ratio a lone mammal predator can tackle. Despite their awesome predatory ability, wolverines more often scavenge carrion. Some specialize in cruising avalanche basins, sniffing and digging out goat and deer carcasses deep in the packed avalanche snow. Extra-strong jaws enable them to pulverize frozen meat and bone. They sometimes raid trappers' cabins and caches, trashing them and spraying them up with truly execrable musk. The powerful scent repels other carnivores from the wolverine's caches, and is crucial, along with a summer-long mating season, when wolverines seek compatible wolverines. ("SWF, attractive, into winter sports, for nonconfining relationship...")

Wolverines have always been ceaseless solitary roamers over vast home ranges, making it relatively difficult to keep track of their presence. Since 1965 they seem to be coming back within the lower 48 states, even raiding a few campgrounds, after reaching the verge of extinction a little earlier.

Badger

Taxidea taxus (tax-**eye**-dee-a **tax**-us: both from the Roman term). 25" + 5" tail [60 + 13 cm]; very broad, low, flat animal with thick fur grizzled gray-brown, while ± yellowish, esp the tail; white stripe down face; forefeet heavily clawed for digging. Grasslands and sagelands; rarer northward in Canada. Order Carnivora, Mustelidae (Weasel family). Color p 526.

This animale burrows in the ground & feeds on Bugs and flesh…. his head Mouth &c is like a Dog with its ears cut off, his hair and tale like that of a Ground hog…

So runs the first written description of an American badger, by Captain Clark. This squat, ungainly, but fantastically powerful burrowing creature lives mainly by digging ground squirrels, gophers, mice, and snakes out of their holes. It often digs itself a temporary den for resting through the heat of the day. It spends winter mostly torpid, in 29-hour cycles with brief active periods, rather than prolonged hibernation. Badgers are solitary except for the mother and her young. Burrow entrances are large (1' diam, or 30 cm) and may have a latrine nearby—a heap of mixed bones, fur, and scat. Badger hair brushes are made from the very different European badger, genus *Meles*, and "badgering" is not something badgers do, but to what is done to them by European hunting dogs, who wisely avoid fang-to-fang combat.

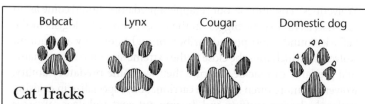

Bobcat   Lynx   Cougar   Domestic dog

Cat Tracks

Claws: cat claws are normally retracted while walking, and hardly ever print. In contrast, claws show up clearly in *full* footprints of dogs and wild canids, not to mention otter, wolverine, badger, and bear prints which all have five clawed toes rather than four.

Pad: the wide main sole of a cougar or bobcat print is indented or scalloped once in front and twice in back; dog pads are not indented in front, nor are lynx pads though lynx fur often obscures this feature.

Proportion: the two outside toes on a cat print are more nearly alongside the two central toes; on a dog print they're farther behind.

Size: cougar's are 3-3.5" long and wide, bobcat's are 1.75-2" [7-9 versus 4 cm]. Otherwise the two are much alike.

Look near the tracks for feline scratchings and scats.

Lynx

Lynx canadensis (links: Greek word for it). =*Lynx lynx, Felis lynx** 31" long + 4"
tail [80 + 10 cm]; gray cat ± tawny-tinged, not clearly spotted or barred exc the
black tip of stubby tail; long hairs tuft the ears and ruff the cheeks. To confirm a
lynx sighting, you must measure several footprints well over 2" [5 cm] long, or see
that tail-tip is black both above and below. Wilderness with deep winter snowpack, mainly Can and n MT. Order Carnivora, Felidae (Cat family). Color p 527.

Often thought of as a larger version of the bobcat, the lynx actually
averages a bit lighter, but looks larger with its much longer fur and
legs and bigger feet—all adaptations to deep snow and cold. It preys
almost single-mindedly on the snowshoe hare. Lynx numbers rise
and plummet roughly in tandem with hare population cycles, peak-
ing typically one two three years after the hares do. When hares are
scarce, most lynx females become infertile, and individuals migrate
as far as 700 miles [1100 km]in search of happier hunting. Lynxes of
the lower 48 states are listed as threatened, but probably have always
been marginal dispersers from population irruptions up north.
That's especially true in Colorado and Oregon, where many people
are understandably enamored of their desultory lynx populations.
Lynxes maintain an evanescent but more or less full-time presence
in the northern tiers of Montana, Idaho, Wyoming, and Washington.
In Canada they are declining but still numerous—and still lucrative
for fur trappers. They are genuinely shy of people, staying far away,
unlike the bobcats that infiltrate developed country unseen.

Bobcat

Lynx rufus* (**roo**-fus: red). =*Felis rufus*. Also **wildcat**. 28" long + 6" tail [72 +
16 cm]; tawny to gray cat, generally with visible darker spots, and bars on outside of legs and top (only) of tail; ears may show tufts, and cheeks ruffs, but
these tend to be shorter than on lynx. Widespread, esp in brushy, broken, or
logged terrain. Order Carnivora, Felidae. Color p 527.

The bobcat is a lovely creature we see all too rarely even though it
lives throughout our range, probably as abundantly as it ever did.

---

* Some texts lump this lynx with Eurasian ones, and/or the genus as a whole
with the mewing cats, making our lynx *Lynx lynx* or *Felis lynx*, and our bobcat *Felis rufus*. (Note the use of "lynx Lynx lynx" in a sentence. But what links
lynx, *Lynx lynx*, to…) "Lynxes" and "lynx" are both accepted plurals. Geist
(1998) and Wilson and Ruff (1999) say "lynxes." Given a choice, I always favor
an 's.' Almost any animal can be heard in the plural without 's' sometimes, as in
"We saw three sow bear." To my ear, the 's'-less plural serves to distance us from
animals, or to put them on a more abstract plane.

You just might surprise one if you travel quietly, but generally they keep out of sight.

Wild cats all like to work out their claws and clawing muscles on tree trunks, just like house cats scratching furniture. Bobcat or lynx scratchings will be 2' to 5' [1–1½ m] up the trunk, cougar scratchings 5' to 8' up [1½–3 m]. These gashes may be deep, but rarely take off much bark; tree-clawing that strips big patches of bark is more likely bear work. Wild cats also often scratch dirt or leaves to cover their scats, at least partly. These scratchings may be accurately aimed at the scats, unlike the random pawings of male dogs next to their fecal markers. Bobcat and cougar scats also tend to me more segmented than coyote scats.

To preserve their sharpness for slashing or gripping prey, cat claws are kept retracted most of the time, and rarely show in cat tracks. One toe (the first, or "thumb") has been lost from the hind foot, but on the forefoot has only moved a short way up the paw, enlarging the grip. The hind legs are powerful, for long leaping pounces, but cats other than the cheetah aren't especially fast runners. The cat jaw is shorter and "lower-geared" than most carnivore jaws, and has fewer teeth. (Since mammals evolved from reptiles with many teeth, having fewer teeth is a sign of further evolution; typically they're also more efficiently specialized. Humans are evolving toward fewer teeth by losing the four wisdom teeth.) Cats have relatively small and unimportant incisors, huge canines for gripping and tearing, and a quartet of enlarged, pointed molars called carnassials which, rather than meeting, shear past each other like scissor blades for cutting up meat. Cat tongues are raspy with tiny recurved horny papillae, which can clean meat from a bone or hair from a hide. The cat nose is short, suggesting less reliance on smell than in the dog family. As in owls, the eyes are large, far apart, and aimed strictly forward to maximize three-dimensionality. Their eyes, like an owl's, reflect fire or flashlight beams in the dark. A reflective layer right behind the receptor cells on the retina redoubles light intensity at night. Except in cougars, which have round pupils, cat pupils narrow to vertical slits for maximum differentiation between night and day openness.

Hares and rodents predominate in bobcat diets. In winter they turn to deer a little more, hunting fawns occasionally but more often finding carrion.

Cougar

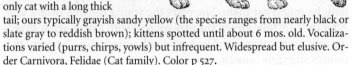

Puma concolor * (**poo**-ma: name for it in the Quechua language of Peru; **con**-color: all one color). Also **mountain lion, puma**. 4-5' long + 2½' tail (130 + 75 cm]; our only cat with a long thick tail; ours typically grayish sandy yellow (the species ranges from nearly black or slate gray to reddish brown); kittens spotted until about 6 mos. old. Vocalizations varied (purrs, chirps, yowls) but infrequent. Widespread but elusive. Order Carnivora, Felidae (Cat family). Color p 527.

Cougars take many kinds of prey from grasshoppers and mice on up through porcupines and coyotes to elk—but their staple is deer. A male (the larger sex) can eat about one deer every 10–14 days, up to 20 pounds [9 kg] at a time, burying the remains to come back to later. Buried meat, which may assault your nose, is a sign of cougar. He (or she) locates deer by smell or sound, stalks it slowly, crouching, freezing for periods, then pounces the last ten meters or so in a few bounding leaps. He bites the prey in the nape, and may either bite through the spinal cord or snap it by twisting the head back. Failing that, he tries to hang on until the prey suffocates. Our cougars are lighter than our deer, on average, and much lighter than elk, so their hunt is risky. They are sometimes trampled or thrown hard enough to kill them, and one was found pinned until it starved under an elk it had killed.

Most game managers agree on the value of cougars as the main remaining predator of deer. Their chief benefit to deer and elk may lie in keeping them moving on their winter range, which helps avoid overgrazing of particular areas. Cougars select young, old, or diseased herd members—the easiest and safest to attack—minimizing their impact on total deer and elk numbers.

Cougars are solitary, with large home ranges, the males' overlapping those of females. Males respect established home areas,

---

* Many texts include this and most cats in genus *Felis*, but it's now *Puma* in both major American checklists (Wilson and Reeder, 1993; Jones et al., 1997). The number of genera in the cat family is a notoriously long-running taxonomic tempest. The current checklist of the American Society of Mammalogists divides Felidae into eighteen genera, where the previous version saw only four. The new checklist as a whole doesn't seem given to radical splitting, so the case for splitting up the cats must be pretty strong.

---

rarely fighting over them. They mark their presence by scraping piles of dirt together with their urine or scats. After seeing a cougar, I found scats on the trail in several piles a few feet apart, and each had claw marks in the dirt radiating out from it. The same scent markers help the sexes find each other when a female is in heat, which may be at any time of year. A male roams with and sleeps near the female for about two weeks, and no longer: if she let him approach the kittens, he might eat them. She rears the young for well over a year. After they are fully grown she may consort with a male again, breeding only every other year. She has a loud, eerie mating "scream" that sounds strangely human.

Cougars sometimes follow solitary hikers, even for several days. They rarely let hikers catch a glimpse of them, and you can consider yourself lucky if you even see a clear set of cougar tracks. Most following apparently is not predatory (is it simple curiosity?) but recent decades have seen a "trend" toward preying on humans, mainly children and solitary small adults. But the deaths—13, in 73 cougar attacks in North America between 1970 and 2000—are still very, very few compared to human deaths from either lightning, hunting, domestic dogs, or car-deer collisions. Cougars have been know to snatch dogs and cats, even from large campgrounds. As development shrinks cougar habitat, subdominant and dispersing cougars are pushed into more marginal habitat, closer to more humans and with a poorer supply of prey; these individuals are hungrier more of the time, forcing them to get more daring in their choice of prey. The idea that more hunting of cougars would keep them in line is intuitively appealing, but scientifically doubtful. British Columbia, where they are still heavily hunted, has had at least its share of human fatalities.

Caution in Cougar Country

Never leave small children unattended, even in campgrounds. If you see a cougar, pick up any children immediately, stand tall and confident, and maintain eye contact. Move your arms and backpack in any way that will make you look bigger. Act unlike prey: do not run or turn your back. Retreat slowly. If the cougar still seems aggressive, throw sticks or rocks at it if you can do so without having to crouch first. If attacked, fight back aggressively with any weapon you can grab, and stay on your feet. Make the cougar give up in favor of easier prey.

Woodland Caribou

Rangifer tarandus (**ran**-jif-er: from "reindeer" in Old Norse; ta-**ran**-dus: Greek word for them). 6¼' long + 6" tail [190 + 7.5 cm]; 3½' [110 cm] high at shoulder; females smaller; dark brown with narrow white stripe down from underside of tail; males have grayish pale neck; male antlers very large, flattened in places; one antler (rarely both) has a "brow tine" directly in front of, and close to, the muzzle. Tracks 4" [10 cm] long, rounder and wider than elk. Alpine tundra in summer, forests during snow seasons; Canada, n ID. Order Artiodactyla, Cervidae. Color p 523.

A secretive herd of two or three dozen woodland caribou roams the northern Idaho Selkirks. They've been called the rarest, most endangered mammal in the lower 48, but that's partly a matter of political geography. Across the border in the Columbia Mtns. and Rockies, the mountain population numbers fewer than 3,000, which still rates as Vulnerable; the *species* still numbers in the hundreds of thousands in northern Canada, Alaska, and Eurasia. *Rangifer tarandus* includes North American subspecies ("caribou") and Eurasian ones called reindeer. Some reindeer are domesticated.

Caribou have the largest of all antlers relative to body size. They compensate with lower density, making the racks worse for fighting; they were presumably selected for display. Caribou does are the only females that commonly grow antlers. On tundra caribou, doe antlers are much like yearling male antlers, but in the woodland race antlers grow on few does, and are thin, weak, and asymmetrical. Woodland bucks have heavier but narrower antlers than tundra bucks, since broad racks are a hazard among branches. In fact, woodland caribou share very few of the best-known characteristics of tundra caribou— huge herds, long-distance migrations, fawns that run with the herd from day one (literally) rather than hiding, etc. But what exactly is true of woodland caribou? It's something of a mystery.

Caribou eat more lichens than any other animal, subsisting on lichens through winter. Reindeer lichen, *Cladina rangiferina,* is their staple on arctic tundra, but in forest they turn to edible horsehair lichen (p 326), and drop shiny black scats. Moose and deer also eat this lichen, but can't move around on penetrable snowpack deeper than about 32 and 16 inches [80 and 40 cm], respectively. Caribou have the advantage of bigger feet for their weight, so they can walk on softer snow. All three move upslope onto deeper snowpacks after the snow packs down into something they can walk on. Caribou require mature forest: more horsehair lichen is found there, and snow falls from the canopy in big clumps that do a better job of packing. Logging of older forests is the chief reason they are getting scarce.

White-Tailed Deer

Odocoileus leucuris (oh-doe-co-**ill**-ee-us: hollow teeth; loo-**cure**-iss: white tail). 4¾' long + 12" tail [145 + 30 cm]; medium tawny brown or in winter grayish, with white patches on throat, inside of legs, and rump just under the tail; upper side of tail is brown with white fringe and tip, but tail is raised in flight, the pure white underside "flashing" and waving; antlers branch from one main tine (see p 398); fawns are white-spotted; ears smaller (4–7", 10–18 cm) than mule deer's. Mainly lowland and riparian areas. Order Artiodactyla, Cervidae (Deer family).

America has a lot more deer than it did two hundred years ago. Especially white-tails. Anglo civilization has been good to them, thanks more to its war on forests than to its war on predators: deep forest supports relatively few deer, but brushy clearcuts are deer heaven. At the other extreme, the wide-open Great Plains once supported very few deer, but farmers opened that vast area to white-tails by planting trees for windbreaks. Though the clear pattern has been westward expansion, early explorers did report a few white-tails in the Rockies; we don't know exactly what their "natural" range was.

Our two deer tend to separate ecologically, white-tails preferring riparian areas and muleys the montane slopes. White-tails are rare in Yellowstone, all of which is high. In the Canadian Rockies they have been reported summering in alpine meadows after passing quickly through the intervening slope areas. The two species are pretty similar in size, color, teeth, and other adaptable body parts. They are easy to tell when fleeing, because of the flashing, erected white tail. White-tails can bound or simply run very fast—a good strategy on prairies and in deciduous woods.

Mule Deer

Odocoileus hemionus (hem-ee-**oh**-nus: half ass, i.e. mule). 4½' long + 6–8" tail [140 + 15–20 cm]; medium tawny brown or in winter grayish, with white patches on throat, inside of legs, and rump just under the tail; belly paler; first branch of antlers (males only) may itself fork (see page 398); fawns are white-spotted; ears mulishly large [8–9", 20–22 cm], rotate independently. Widespread. Order Artiodactyla, Cervidae. Color p 523.

Browsing is a sophisticated, serious business. Spend a while sitting quietly and watching deer eat. Notice their odd way of clipping their browse, almost gumming it with lower incisors against an upper pad; they lack upper incisors. They may show an intense preference for an individual plant that has either less tannin or more of some nutrient. They lap up springwater (no matter how muddy it has become from trampling hooves) containing mineral salts they crave. They chomp mushrooms, "nature's salt licks," for other hard-to-find minerals. They strip horsehair lichen from tree limbs; it has modest nutritive value on its own, but offers minerals that enhance utilization of the austere winter diet of twigs and evergreen needles. In recent burns they find the particular species of grass that exhibits the sharpest post-burn spike in protein content. Like other cud chewers that can live on a high-roughage diet thanks to cellulose-digesting bacteria in their first stomach, deer have to browse for the nutritional demands of their bacteria. Insufficient protein can kill the bacteria, leaving the browser dangerously malnourished with its belly full.

In the absence of wolves, deer tend to increase beyond the carrying capacity of their habitat; then, during severe winters, they are malnourished, and fall prey to parasites and/or coyotes. (That's the conventional wisdom, anyway; some biologists challenge it.) Degraded deer habitat isn't stripped bare; it's just short on the particular species

Pheromones of Deer

Deer are outstanding subjects for the study of pheromones—chemical messages, usually between conspecifics. Mule deer are rather antisocial: they use several pheromones apparently to repel each other (a function akin to territoriality, though mule deer are not territorial). Tarsal glands, for example, are buried in patches of dark hair on the inside of the ankle joints, midway up the rear legs; to activate tarsal pheromones, deer of any age and sex urinate on these patches and rub them together. While most pheromones are secreted in sweat or sebum (skin oil), deer urine is itself pheromonal—its chemistry reveals the animal's health and strength. A subordinate deer will sniff the tarsal patches of a dominant deer and then retreat to a respectful distance, showing that it got the message. Glands on the forehead are rubbed on shrub twigs to advertise the presence and condition of a dominant buck, or to mark possession of a sleeping bed. Interdigitate glands, between the two toes of the hoof, secrete a more attractive pheromone, marking a deer's trail for other deer to follow. Metatarsal glands, on the outside of the lower hind leg, secrete a garlicky odor to signal fear or alarm.

Actively detecting pheromones looks like sniffing; since we're barely able to do it we call it "smelling," but it is truly a sixth sense, and uses its own organ, the vomeronasal organ. (Actually, it can look pretty different from mere sniffing: e.g., lip-curling as performed by a bull elk, p 523.) Whereas the nose detects complex chemical recipes made up of a few basic odors, each vomeronasal nerve ending—which is 1,000 to 10,000 times more sensitive than typical olfactory (smell) nerve endings—is lit up by only one pheromone. "Bingo! This female will be receptive within six hours."

that supply adequate fats, proteins, and trace minerals. Wolves and cougars used to be the chief nonhuman predators of American deer, but since we've decimated them they rank behind domestic dogs, hunters, cars, and trains as deer killers. Even dogs that wouldn't know what to do with a deer if they caught up with one can often run it to death via barbed wire entanglement or a broken leg. Deer are transfixed by a strong beam of light at night, making them frequent victims of cars and trains. Coyotes, bears and bobcats are infrequent predators of deer, taking mainly fawns or critically weakened adults.

When fleeing, mule deer break into a bouncy high-bounding gait called "stotting." Though slower than a flat-out run, it allows them to react to rough terrain with abrupt, unpredictable changes of direction—a hard act to follow for any predator giving chase, who has to respond at once both to the obstacles under its own feet and to the deer's changing course.

Steep south slopes just above river-bottoms are ideal winter range. The low elevation and insulating tree canopy offer warmer temperature and shallower snow, while the south aspect lets in a little of the low-angle sunlight, and tends to have more shrubs to nibble. In summer, our deer move upslope to meadows, clearcuts, and open woods, where they fatten up on herbaceous plants.

The only close social tie among deer is between a doe and her fawns and yearlings. Males are solitary or form loose small groups, except during rutting when the sufficiently dominant ones follow single does in heat for a few days each. A doe seeks seclusion even from her yearlings before and after giving birth; it's up to the yearlings to reunite with her afterward. For their first few weeks she hides the new fawns—separately, if there are two or three—in nestlike depressions under brush. She browses in the vicinity, strives to repel other does, and comes back to nurse mainly at night. If a threatening large animal like you approaches, she nonchalantly ignores the fawns. (She will meet a fox or bobcat, however, with a bold counterattack.) Occasionally people come across a hidden fawn and not its foraging mom, and make the cruel mistake of "rescuing" the "abandoned" fawn. Unless you actually find the mother dead, assume a fawn is being properly cared for, and leave it in peace, untainted by human scent.

Elk

Cervus elaphus (**sir**-vus: the Roman term for deer; **el**-a-fus: the Greek term for deer). Also **wapiti**. 7–8' long + 4–6" tail [225 + 14 cm]; tan with a large, well-defined creamy pale patch on rump; extensive brown tinges on neck, face, legs and belly; males have antlers; fawns are white-spotted. Widespread. Order Artiodactyla, Cervidae (Deer family). Color p 523.

Today, elk inhabit coniferous forests and high mountains of the West. Before white settlement they were common all the way to Vermont and South Carolina. Great herds of them on the Plains were second only to buffalo in sheer biomass and as a food and material resource for humans. Like bison, they were shot in huge numbers. They were able to hold on in the mountains and deep forests until an alarmed public, rallying around a famous hunter named Teddy Roosevelt, got refuges and hunting restrictions enacted to allow their population to recover. The very idea of conserving species was essentially new to (white) America at the end of the last century. Even then, the point, as popularly understood, was to conserve them for future generations of people to hunt.

Politicized controversies rage over the "natural" population levels of elk in many areas. The best data show they are native to most parts of the U.S. and Canada that supported either forest or grassland. They may have been reduced a few thousand years ago by aboriginal hunting, and rebounded a few hundred years ago when the natives were decimated by introduced diseases. They were high (would that be "naturally" or "unnaturally" high?) when white settlement began, and plummeted due to market hunting in the late 19th century. They've done well in the 20th with regulated sport hunting, and become very abundant in some National Parks with no hunting, no wolves, and reduced cougar numbers.

The battle cry "Too many elk!," has been heard around Yellowstone for a century. Park scientists looked hard for clear evidence of harm, and found little. They decided to let elk find their own level, which elk seem to be doing, or at least fluctuating within a broad range. Postfire plant regrowth fed a dramatic rebound after a huge winterkill in the harsh winter of 1988–89. While beliefs that elk at this level harm vegetation, streambanks, or competing grazers may be unfounded, elk browsing is clearly preventing aspen and willow shoots from reaching tree stature over large areas. (See page 116.) The Park predicts a modest decrease in elk as the reintroduced wolves multiply, but a substantial decrease wouldn't surprise me. (A new interest group has already formed around the battle cry, "Not enough elk!")

Most of the year, elk travel in segregated herds, the mature bulls in bands of ten or fifteen, and the females and young males in larger herds. In late summer, the bulls become mutually hostile, and the largest, most aggressive of them ("primary bulls") divide out harems from the cow herds. They tolerate yearlings, but drive away two- and three-year-old males. The harem's movements, like those of the cow herd in winter, are subtly directed by a matriarch apparently respected for her maturity rather than her size or strength. The bull seems to tag along rather than to lead, and he may lose part or all of his harem if he lets himself be distracted. Other bulls will surely be distracting him, hoping to take over the harem by overcoming him in a clash of antlers staged at dusk or dawn. It's the rutting season.

Bulls have evolved many curious behaviors for challenging each other and working up their sexual or combative frenzies:

Bugling. This call includes a deep bellow and a farther-carrying whistle. Elk cows also bugle, less commonly, when calving in spring.

Antler-thrashing. These attacks on small trees and brush (common also among deer bucks) were formerly described as "polishing the antlers" or "rubbing off the itchy velvet" but they are now interpreted as making visual challenges or markers, as warm-up or practice for sparring, or as autoerotic stimulation.

Pit-wallowing. Shallow wallowing pits are dug and trampled out and lined with urine and feces. Bulls also use their antlers to toss urine-soaked sod onto their backs. Water may collect in a wallow the next winter, turning it into a pool lasting several years.

The reek of urine advertises the bull's physical condition, helping him avoid injuries by intimidating a challenger before combat begins. Elk can smell the degree to which a bull has been metabolizing fat as opposed to fresh food or, worse yet, muscle. A bull metabolizing only fat is one so well fed that he can devote all of his energy to the rut without being weakened by hunger.

Keeping track of a harem, defending it from other bulls, and reaping the sexual rewards is not only hard work, but so time-consuming that this once well-fed bull can no longer eat or rest.

Almost inevitably, primary bulls succumb in the same season to lesser but better-rested rivals, and often these "secondary bulls" yield in turn to "tertiary bulls." After defeat, they wander off alone, catch up on sleep, and show no further interest in sex that year. They may so weakened as to reduce their chance of surviving winter. Large, sexually successful bulls have several years shorter life expectancy than bulls who never grow large enough to compete. The latter "opportunistic bulls" spend the rutting season alone, but stand at least a chance of mating with a stray cow. All in all, it's quite an extravagant courtship system.

Rocky-Mountain elk cows may bear young every year, starting at age two. Browsing techniques and care of the young among elk are much like those described for deer (page 390) except that to an elk cow, humans are puny meddlers to be chased from the nursery. Biologists who tag elk calves learn to be quick tree-climbers.

In Europe, a smaller, darker subspecies (*C. elaphus elaphus*) is the red deer or stag that Robin Hood hunted. (Most market venison in the U.S. is red deer from farms in New Zealand.) If you're thinking that the species known to the English as a "deer" ought, in English, to be a deer, you're right. A different genus exists which Europeans had called "elk" for centuries before Americans ever dubbed it a "moose." American races of both *Cervus* and *Alces* are much larger than their European relatives, and the confusion must have begun when English colonists first met the American whitetail, about the size of a European red deer, and called it a deer. When they met a race of *C. elaphus* about twice as big, they thought it must be an "elk"—the larger European cervid whose flattened antlers and

Diseases of Elk, Deer, and Humans

The bacterium *E. coli* 0157:H7, which has proven deadly in undercooked hamburgers, is common in North American deer. Hunter-bagged venison, including jerky, should be cooked to 165° (74° C.). (Venison sold commercially is imported, and has not been implicated.) Windfall apples are suspect since they may have contacted deer scats.

It's hard to write much in 2003 about "chronic wasting disease" of elk, because it is so poorly understood. As a prion disease, it is related to "mad cow disease" and to new-variant Creuzfeldt-Jakob Disease in humans. Those are acquired by eating infected meat. CWD is transmitted among herbivorous elk, perhaps when they gnaw bones to get calcium for new antlers. There is no evidence that humans can get it, but a few scientists ask, "How do we know we can't?" If we can, cooking the meat won't help. It is suspected to be 100% fatal like its relatives, but again, research has yet to demonstrate that.

huge loose-fleshed muzzle they had doubtless never seen. The misnomer stuck, even through generations of texts trying to replace it with the Shawnee name "wapiti." American elk and American moose were each formerly recognized at the species level (*Cervus canadensis* and *Alces americana*), but today taxonomists insist that our moose is merely a subspecies of European elk, our elk a subspecies of European red deer, and our deer something else again.

Moose

Alces alces (al-sees: Latinized Norse name which, in English, became "elk"). 8½' long, 7' high at shoulder [2.5 m, 2 m]; females smaller; tail negligible; dark gray-brown; long horselike head with loose overhanging upper lip; antlers have broad flat blades and many points; long dewlap ("bell," of no known function) hangs from throat; pronounced shoulder hump. Tracks 5–6" [14 cm] long, more pointed than elk; winter scats oval, 1½–1⅞" [4–5 cm] long; summer scats often loose like cow pies; willow thickets with numerous broken, chewed, and bent-over tops are a sign of moose. Order Artiodactyla, Cervidae (Deer family). Color p 523.

The 20th century saw a continent-wide moose population explosion caused mainly by logging converting old forests to brushy second-growth. Willow twigs are a moose's winter staple. The greatest range expansion was in the southern half of BC and adjacent WA and ID. Almost unknown there before 1920, moose were common by 1950. In the great boreal forests, forest fires are infrequent and vast, producing moose heavens that last a decade or two. Moose are well adapted to that pattern: they migrate into burns and then double their birth rate. Logging in the coniferous West gives them similar habitat bonanzas. The postfire increase in moose browse takes a season or two to grow, so many of Yellowstone's moose died of malnutrition in the winter of 1988, after the fires. Moose abound today in the Yellowstone ecosystem, but the earliest report of them there dates from 1870; not even archeological digs have found earlier evidence. It's possible they really hadn't been there since before the last Ice Age.

Moose were hardly ever preyed upon during their 130 years of coexistence with grizzlies at Yellowstone. However, as wolves moved into Jackson Hole recently, they soon killed ten adult moose that, presumably, had not learned to be wary of them. Mothers who lost offspring to wolves learned fast, soon responding hyperdefensively to wolf howls. (Joel Berger, analyzing data on these and other "naive moose," concluded that they support the "blitzkrieg hypothesis"— that the earliest humans in North America might have wiped out the Ice Age megafauna because even the largest species are easy to kill when they have been without predators for generations. If the hunters had the habit of killing offspring and their mothers at once, prey species might not have learned to be wary.)

For most of the year, bull moose are solitary and cows are accompanied only by their yearlings. They form loose groups in fall, for mating, and become more vocal, with a sort of tremolo moan.

With massive bodies, and stomachs hard at work fermenting cellulose, moose run hot. Heat limits their range southward, and when they retreat into water in summer, it's to cool off as well as to dine on succulent pond vegetation. They don't act as if they mind the biting flies and mosquitoes that swarm them. On the other hand, heavy infestation with winter ticks (40,000 ticks per moose are common during bad tick seasons) can cause severe blood loss, hair loss, heat loss, and winter mortality. Dramatically pale, fuzzy "ghost moose" are individuals who have lost most of their long "guard" hairs, leaving the paler underhair. Infested moose have been observed paying little attention to magpies pecking at their backs, leading some scientists to infer that a symbiotic "cleaner" relationship is in effect. Others, however, claim that the magpies aren't gleaning ticks but eating scabs (and keeping wounds open) and that, in fact, most of the world's fabled "cleaner" symbioses are just that—fables.

A third odd mortality factor (after heat and ticks) is gum disease and molar wear. Moose reach peak foraging efficiency around age five to seven. Males therefore grow the biggest racks then, and win the most mates of any period in their lives. Wear and tear from the sheer volume of woody stuff chewed takes its toll on teeth, and as browsing efficiency dwindles, the adults become wolf bait—or parasite bait and then wolf bait. Moose in their prime are hardly ever preyed on, and calves are well defended by their mothers. Moose fleeing from wolves are amazingly fleet—almost as fast as a whitetail deer. They "glide" over logs and brush, taking advantage of their long legs to hold their center of gravity at constant height over a course that looks like high hurdles to a wolf. (In the minus column, long legs require moose to kneel, awkwardly, in order to reach food near ground level.) Gliding over soft snow, moose easily outrun wolves, which flounder; but if the snow gets well crusted the wolves can run fast on top of it and catch the moose, which break through. Deer and elk also flounder when the snow gets deep. For winter habitat, Yellowstone moose tend to seek snow deep enough to inhibit elk, which can otherwise outcompete them for browse.

Moose tolerate humans, up to a point. They're often described as docile, but "self-confident and relaxed" would be more accurate. A skittish, unpredictable streak combines with sheer mass to produce the surprising statistic that more people are killed by moose than by grizzly bears. While some deaths are in car crashes—moose are the one common species of roadkill weighty enough to assure mutual destruction in high-speed collisions—many others are from aggressive behavior. Lowered ears and raised hair on the neck and shoulders are a serious warning. **Do not try to "shoo" a moose.** Since cleared hard ground or snow is the most advantageous platform for moose defending themselves in nature, a spot on a road or a groomed ski trail may be fiercely defended. Their heavy hooves are deadly weapons against wolves and humans, and effective deterrents even against grizzlies. They can put a serious dent in a car.

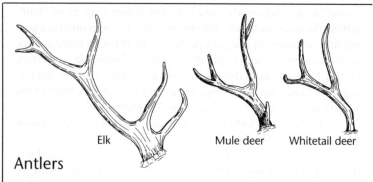

Elk   Mule deer   Whitetail deer

Antlers

True horns are sheaths of keratin, like fingernails; they form from epidermal tissue at their bases, and slowly slide outward over small bone cores, growing throughout life; they never branch. They are found, generally on both sexes, in the cattle family, including sheep, goats, and antelope. Antlers, on the other hand, made of solid bone and usually branched, are a defining characteristic of the deer family. (The deer and cattle families are the two largest families of ruminants, or cud-chewers; ruminants plus the pig family make up the cloven-hooved order.) Antlers form inside living skin—complete with hair and blood vessels—and stretch the skin outward as they grow. This skin, or "velvet," must die and slough off before the antlers come into use in the fall. In late winter the antlers weaken at their bases and are soon knocked off. On the forest floor, tiny incisors set to work converting them to mouse bones. A new pair will begin to grow by early summer.

Cumbersome and easily entangled in brush, antlers probably affect survival negatively. Not they, but hooves, are a deer's defensive weapon. (Caribou, or reindeer, are a partial exception: most females have small

Bighorn Sheep

Ovis canadensis (oh-vis: Roman for sheep). Also **mountain sheep**. 5–6' + 6" tail [170 + 15 cm]; 3⅓' [1 m] to shoulder; females smaller; brown with white rump patch; very ragged and (ewes) cream-colored during May or June molt; rams have massive curled horns, often broken-tipped; ewe horns smaller, merely curved; horns brown and ± blunt, as opp to black and very sharp in mtn goats. Open habitats. Order Artiodactyla, Bovidae. Color p 523.

Bighorn sheep habitat has three characteristics: wide open, making approaching predators conspicuous; near cliffy terrain to escape to; and with high quality grasses or sedges to eat. In winter, both the forage and the escape terrain have to be kept nearly snow-free, by wind and/or steepness. Some herds

---

antlers and use them defensively.) Antlers exist to help establish dominance among males during the rut. Big antlers, like bright plumages on small male birds, are an example of "fitness" evolved through sexual selection: the survival of the fittest is as a genetic line, not as long-lived individuals. In other words, highly competitive large-antlered elk bulls tend to die younger than weaker ones who rarely fight over cows, but the latter, leaving few offspring, are unfit. Some scholars think antlers' primary value is visual—to attract females and/or to intimidate rival males, decreasing risk to life and limb. Much sparring goes on for practice or to release rutting energy; much goes on in the absence of females. Antlers are clearly not the deadliest possible headgear; like boxing gloves, they may regulate and extend combat. But don't think antlers don't really mean it. Closer study has failed to prove a major role for antlers in either erotic stimulation or intimidation, while it *has* traced a large share of male mortality to combat injuries.

Each antler on elk and whitetail deer has one main beam from which all the other points branch. On mule deer, both branches off the first Y may be again branched. The number tends to increase year by year, but also responds to nutrition, and thus serves to advertise physical condition. Rich feeding in captivity has produced five-point antlers on yearlings, while meager range can limit dominant bucks to forks. Average sexually mature elk have five-pointed antlers; older bulls may grow six, seven, or rarely more. British Columbia has recorded freakishly high numbers of antler points—48 on a mule deer, 25 on a white-tail.

---

have winter and summer habitat a few hundred yards apart, whereas others migrate ten miles [16 km] or more. Bighorns are spottily distributed, in part because of the exacting habitat needs. Habitat is reduced when forest expands due to fire suppression and/or warming climate.

Highly social, bighorns are usually seen in herds of five to a hundred. Outside of the November-December rutting season, adult males herd together, often far from the herd of females and juveniles. The latter has to find range with few predators. Males, being bigger and more heavily armed, are less vulnerable to cougars and wolves, and not at all vulnerable to coyotes and bobcats, freeing them to focus on forage quality, which for them is the name of the game. It determines horn size, and thus social rank—the year-round obsession of rams. Usually it's settled by displaying the horns, with perhaps a bit of kicking. Only when two rams' horns are equal do they butt heads, facing off at several paces, rearing on hind legs, charging forward with forelegs flailing. Slam. Stagger, reel. Repeat. Repeat. Repeat. Repeat until one gives up, as much as 24 hours later. Ram necks and skulls are massive, with spongy bone mass around the horn base to absorb impacts, which may be audible a mile off. The victor is able to "tend" estrous ewes. Subordinate rams do manage to sire about half the lambs. They have two techniques: dashing past the tending dominant ram; or blocking a ewe, beginning early, so that when she goes into estrous she isn't anywhere near a dominant male.

Bighorns today are heavily affected by humans. They are mortally vulnerable to several diseases brought by domestic sheep. Historically, many local populations have died out due to disease, hunting, or both, and many of today's herds (including all of Oregon's) descend from individuals brought from elsewhere by wildlife agencies. Introduced herds tend to fluctuate—multiplying for a while, then plummeting during an epidemic, then either recovering or not. Failure often follows contact with domestic sheep, or sometimes high cougar populations. When herds are doing well, agencies often open them to limited trophy hunting, which seems to pose no threat to numbers or health of the herd. Herds that are hunted become very shy and elusive, while those that live in National Parks are brazenly bold. Roadkill takes over as the chief human-related mortality in Canada's Parks, which have major highways that get salted in winter. Sheep loiter on the roads, licking salt. **Drive slowly, and never take advantage of their boldness by attempting to touch or feed them.** As with other mammals, that could be hazardous to your health.

Bison

Bison bison (bye-sun: from an old Germanic term for the Eurasian bison). Also **buffalo**—a misnomer that scientists avoid. 10–12' long [3–3.8 m], 5–6' [1.5–1.8 m] to shoulder; shaggy, dark brown cattle-like beast with upcurved horns; woolly mane and goatee, esp on older males; calves are red-brown. Low-elev prairies, grassy openings. Order Artiodactyla, Bovidae (Cattle family). Color p 523.

Saw large herds of buffalo on the plains of the Sandy river, grazing in every direction on the short and dry grass. Domestic cattle would certainly starve here, and yet the bison exists and even becomes fat...

John Kirk Townsend in Wyoming, 1834

Townsend's comment hits the nail on the head, and offers the kernel of a modern view that reconverting large areas of the High Plains into bison range (a "Buffalo Commons") would be the most economically efficient as well as ecologically harmless way to produce food there. Grazing by bison benefits the shortgrasses which coevolved there with the bison. (See page 168.) The Great Plains as they were first described in writing were an ecosystem unusual in supporting grazing animals of awesome total biomass, but oddly few species: mainly elk, pronghorns, bighorn sheep in a few locales, and millions upon millions of this one kind of cattle.

Some scientists believe early Americans wiped out most large mammal species here between 16,000 and 10,000 years ago; bison may have survived because their huge herds could lose themselves in the vastness of the Plains. The herds were so far apart, and moved so far and so fast, that hunters without horses couldn't keep up with them, and couldn't feed themselves year-round in many parts of the High Plains. People probably never lived there in significant numbers until the late 1600s, when they acquired horses in trade from southwestern tribes. At that point, in flight from white men and their diseases in the east, tribes which had been farming—and occasionally hunting bison—from permanent villages on the eastern plains moved west and created the famous nomadic Plains culture.

So the downward spiral of the bison began in the 1600s from several causes. They were pushed out of eastern North America by the destruction of prairie habitat there, including the destruction of native cultures whose fires had produced and maintained prairies. In the West it was more the arrival of horses. Wild horses competed directly for grass, and domesticated ones enabled tribes to move onto the Plains and make a good living hunting bison.

The idea that Native Americans used every part of the bison has become almost a nursery fable. An amazing array of non-meat parts was utilized, but that isn't the same thing as using all of the meat. Accounts tell of many hunts where only the most prized parts, the tongue and the hump, were cut out, leaving mountains of meat to the wolves. This was almost unavoidable: a diet consisting of all parts of a bison has too much lean protein and too little fat to sustain humans. Consider also that driving a herd over a cliff ("buffalo jump") was the only effective way to hunt bison in the pre-horse days, leaving the hunters little choice as to how many they would kill. How could a small band possibly dry that huge volume of meat before it spoiled?

But the bison waste of those days was nothing compared to the years 1868–1882. Plains warriors were frustrating the U.S. Army's efforts to make the West safe for white settlers, so the Army decided that exterminating the bison would starve the tribes into submission. It worked. (General Sherman, whose notorious March to the Sea had recently proven the effectiveness of scorched earth, commanded the Army in Sioux country.) Army-subsidized hunters with long-range rifles littered the plains with carcasses after shipping the hides east to be made into robes or factory drive belts. Later, picking up the bleached bones became a cottage industry for struggling settlers; these also went to factories in the East. In Canada, market hunting proved equally effective without military backing.

Today's bison descend from fewer than 400 individuals that were spared. The majority descend from about 100 in six private breeding operations, and the rest were in three wild herds that were protected just in time: a herd in Wood Buffalo N.P. in far northern Alberta; a tiny herd in Texas; and the Yellowstone herd. The latter was reduced to 23 animals by poachers when the new park had no law enforcement and little local support. Ironically, some Army units that oversaw bison extermination in the 1870s were reassigned to protecting the remnant herd. Again, it worked.

Wood buffalo are a dark type with a taller, shaggier hump, sometimes called *B. bison athabascae*. It is probably not a subspecies but an ecotype; i.e., Plains buffalo if moved to the boreal forests would develop those features. If true, it may not matter much that the bison in Jasper and Banff today are Plains transplants instead of native "wood buffalo." Still, lack of genetic diversity in the whole population is a serious problem. It is implicated in the persistent problems with brucellosis and tuberculosis, which led to the notorious slaughter of Yellowstone bison as they leave the Park.

All that extra wool around a bison's head has at least two benefits. It pads male heads when they butt, in rutting competition (and is progressively shorn by scissoring between opposing horns over the course of the butting season). To gore each other, they have to lower their heads extremely, since the horns point almost backward. Second, it insulates while they clear snow for winter browsing by swinging their huge heads back and forth, rather than by kicking with puny little hooves like deer and sheep. Females have the "goatee" but not the forehead bush. Bison can clear depths of up to about 30" [75 cm]. The frequency of greater depths west of the Continental Divide was probably the chief factor that kept their numbers low there. Cold temperatures in themselves are no problem; bison coats are densely haired and warm (hence the popularity of buffalo robes). In summer they pant, which cools them by rapidly evaporating water from the lungs. Wallowing in dust may help cool them and discourage parasites, as well as serving the rut-related purposes described on page 394. As with elk, a few dominant bulls sire almost all the calves. Even while seemingly "lost in the herd," a strong bull can tend a few dozen cows serially, after identifying each as she goes into estrus.

Mountain Goat

Oreamnos americanus (or-ee-**am**-nos: mountain lamb). 5' long + 5" tail [150 + 12 cm], 3' high [90 cm] at shoulder; all white, with "beard," shoulder "hump," and "pantaloons" formed of longer hair; black hooves; sharp, curved black horns. Alp/subalpine; Canada, n ID, nw Mt; and introduced in the Tetons and Absarokas. Order Artiodactyla, Bovidae (Cattle family). Color p 523.

Cold wind may not penetrate their insulation, but floundering through wet snow all day and night is a problem. Goats in the Rockies seek bare windswept ridges in winter. They eat enough huckleberry twigs, lichens, and fir needles to keep their stomachs busy, but extract so little nutrition from this winter fare that they live mainly on stored fat. They eat snow rather than seeking running water.

Apparently, mountain goats are nowhere limited primarily by predation. Eagles have been known to take kids and yearlings, dive-bombing to knock them off ledges, and cougars occasionally take even adults, but overall goats are fairly predator-proof with their proverbial evasive skills on precipitous terrain, as well as hooves and horns as defensive weapons. The hooves have strong, sharp outer edges and a hard, rubbery corrugated sole for superlative grip. Forage and climate seem to be the limiting factors on goat populations. Winter starvation and disease are ranking causes of death, along with the inevitable attrition from falling. They have been decimated

---

wherever they were freely hunted, but they lose their fear of people after a few generations in a national park. Be careful to suspend your stashed gear and bestow your urine only on the rocks.*

Mountain goats are probably not native to Wyoming, and the two National Parks there are watching closely to see if their introduced populations may threaten alpine vegetation, as introduced goats do in Olympic National Park.

The ridgecrest paths they beat are an unreliable aid on hikers' high-routes: they may betray you by leading you out onto rock faces that require climbing technique or hardware. Tufts of white floss on branch tips remind us these are not paths for mere Vibram.

Mountain goats are classified in a tribe with chamois, which lead a similar life in the Alps. Both differ from true goats and sheep in several respects, though all are in the cattle family. Mountain goat horns and skulls are not massive enough to sustain bouts of butting. Male mountain goats are thickened at the other end instead; the skin of their rumps, where they are likely to be gored in their flank-to-flank style of fighting, has been known to reach $7/8$" thick [22 mm], and was used by Alaskan tribes for chest armor. More important, the males evolved a powerful inhibition against any real fighting or sparring at all; the occasional pair who get carried away and actually fight are usually both retired from further rutting competition, with broken horns if not severe wounds. The effective breeding males are those who manage to intimidate the others with visual and olfactory displays, without ever coming to blows. Pit wallowing is indulged in, as among elk, and males often spend the winter in filthy coats, looking rattier still in spring while these molt in big sheets, revealing immaculate new white.

Males are commonly chased around by the females and immature males, who aren't as inhibited from using their horns. Females may viciously charge males who come too close, except during a brief sexually receptive period in fall when they allow the male a creeping, submissive-looking courtship. A single kid is normally born in May or June. Mothers are legendarily protective, walking, for example, against a kid's downslope flank to prevent a fall in steep terrain.

---

* Mountain goats get too little sodium in their diets, so they crave the sodium in our urine, as well as in mineral springs. Many are brazen enough to enter camps to eat urine-soaked earth. In the process they demolish precious alpine turf, which is slow to heal. To prevent this, try to urinate always on bare rock or gravel—especially in goat country, but deer sometimes do the same thing.

Pronghorn

Antilocapra americana (an-til-o-**cap**-ra: antelope goat). Also **pronghorn antelope**—a misleading term that most scientists avoid. 4' long + 5" tail [122 + 13 cm]; tan with a white rump patch that can "flash" in alarm, tan tail, white lower jaw, white blazes on neck, white belly and inside of legs; adults of both sexes have black horns; male horns up to 20" [50 cm], with one forward prong and a sharp rearward curve at tip, or tip frequently broken off from combat; female horns 4" [10 cm], prongless; the slight mane (tan) is erectile. Open plains, s AB to Mexico, W to ne CA. Order Artiodactyla, Antilocapridae.Color p 523.

Pronghorns are evolutionary orphans. They have no living relatives—no other species in their family, not just their genus. Scientists are divided as to whether they are closer to the cattle family (or even belong in it, like the antelopes) or to the deer family. Their horns are shed annually, like antlers, but are made of keratin, like horns, and are unique in growing around a permanent bony core.

Their great speed—sustainable at better than 45 mph [72 kph]—is as curious as their horns. Other than pronghorns, you just don't find animals a lot faster than their predators: evolution seems to always come up with a predator fast enough to catch each prey species at least some of the time. The likely explanation is that pronghorns evolved their speed at a time when North America held a far greater variety of large mammals. Not one, but thirteen species of pronghorn lived during those glory eras.* Predators included a cheetah, a hyena, and a bear each longer-limbed and faster than their modern relatives. The African cheetah is the only living predator much faster than a pronghorn, but a pronghorn could easily outpace a cheetah over any distance greater than a couple of hundred yards. It may have been packs of long-legged hyenas that drove pronghorn evolution to produce unequaled endurance at high speed.

We would have to look to migratory birds to find anatomical adaptations for endurance that parallel those of the pronghorn: a heart three times larger than that of a similar-sized goat, and lungs with five times the oxygen diffusion rate. To maximize breath intake, pronghorns run with mouth open.

The chief surviving predator is the coyote, which any adult pronghorn can not only outrun but also chase away. It's the fawns up to 45

---

*The last wave of large-mammal extinctions that ended those days in NA came as the last Ice Age ended, 15,000 to 10,000 years ago. Debate rages on as to whether invading human hunters caused it. Obviously, climate changed sharply then, but the humans-didn't-do-it school of thought has yet to come up with a convincing hypothesis of exactly how warming caused all those extinctions.

---

days old that are vulnerable, and suffer predation rates of forty to eighty percent in most herds. Coevolution of pronghorns and coyotes has produced a fascinating shell game of hiding and searching strategies. After a bout of nursing, fawns trot off alone to pick featureless hiding spots in the grass, where they lie motionless, chin down, for several hours. The mother's interdigitate glands leave a scent trail a coyote can follow, but the fawn is odorless except for its urine and feces, which it holds in until the mother is there to stimulate and then eat them. During hiding, the mother's job is to remember the fawns' exact locations without ever conspicuously looking at them, while grazing far enough away to not lead a coyote to them, but close enough to chase away any coyote that happens to approach them. To reduce the coyote's chance of searching successfully based on her location or her reactions, she varies her distance from the fawns and her sensitivity threshold for giving chase, and sometimes chases deceptively in a fawnless area. She varies the length of time between nursing reunions, so it won't be worth the coyote's time to come back and follow her every four hours or so. After five days of age, the fawn's instinct to lie perfectly still when approached begins to switch to an instinct to hop up and run, emitting the bleat that any mother will respond to with a chase. At that age they can outrun you or me, but not a coyote. As they grow more rewarding to eat and easier to spot, their mortality rate rises. In Montana on the fenced-in National Bison Refuge, ninety percent of fawns die, suggesting that the hiding strategy works better where there are vast plains to spread out over.

The greatest single evolutionary response to the fawn predation problem is the sheer quantity of calories pronghorn mothers invest in their young, to minimize the vulnerable period. Compared to mammals of similar size, the total weight of the litter at birth, and its rate of growth while nursing, are extreme. The young are almost always twins, giving each mother two chances at success.

Pronghorns adapt poorly, so far, to fences and paved roads. They hardly ever jump fences, even though perfectly capable of it, and they cross roads or step through wire fences reluctantly. This is perhaps their greatest human-related problem today. Populations are fairly stable at around half a million, compared with perhaps 35 million in 1820, and only 20,000 in 1920. (Before 1920, Westerners slaughtered pronghorns, fearing competition with livestock.) Most are out on the Wyoming basins where people are few, but pronghorns are easily seen at Yellowstone, Grand Teton, and the Bison Refuge. They rank among the more avid consumers of sagebrush.

10

Birds

Birds are winged, warm-blooded vertebrates with feathers. Wings first developed in some dinosaurs; whether or not birds are direct descendents of dinosaurs is debated. Fossils found recently appear to show primitive feathers on a winged dinosaur, and some scientists in this field think dinosaurs generally were feathered. DNA evidence shows that birds and crocodilians are each other's closest living relatives—closer than crocodiles to lizards or birds to mammals.

In one conspicuous way, birds and mammals (which diverged from reptiles earlier) evolved in parallel: both bird and mammal lines produced keratinous skin growths to serve as insulation and make warm-bloodedness possible. While mammals made hair, birds made feathers, whose extreme light weight is well-suited for flying. As you know from the sales pitch on down sleeping bags, bird plumage is still unequaled among resilient, deformable, durable substances, in its insulation value per weight.

In addition to insulating, feathers do much for the bird's shape, size, and color: plucked, a duck, a crow, a hawk, and a gull would look surprisingly alike in form, as well as pathetically small. A calliope hummingbird or a golden-crowned kinglet would be no bigger than a large grasshopper. Body plumage may double a bird's girth, or more. The "fat" gray jays you see while skiing aren't fat; they're puffing out their plumage to maximize its insulation value, like what you are trying to do, unwittingly and ineffectually, when you raise goosebumps. Less fluffed out in flight (an intense activity that supplies heat in excess) body plumage serves the equally crucial function of streamlining. The long outer feathers of wings and tail, meanwhile, provide most of the bird's airfoil surface at very little cost in weight. They constitute typically 35% to 60% of a bird's wing-spread and 10% to 40% of its length. Feathers make the bird.

Color in most plumages—nearly all female and juvenile plumages and a great many fall and winter male plumages—emphasizes camouflage. Since pale colors make good camouflage against the sky, and darker colors against foliage or earth, most birds are paler underneath than on top. A mother and young in the nest need to be especially well camouflaged, since they can do little but sit tight when predators pass overhead. (The mother could fly, of course, but she stays to protect the flightless young.) Males are freer from the need for camouflage than females, and much freer than earthbound mammals. In them (and in the females of a very few species) sexual selection has been free to evolve gaudy plumage.

A showy plumage doesn't look equally good to all female birds; it looks best to females of the same species. For efficient pairing up, conspecifics need to recognize each other quickly and accurately; but no efficiency is lost if only females can do so. The same goes for songs, the main courtship display of many species. Some females sing, but far less commonly than males. ("Songs" are distinguished from "calls" as being longer and more complex, and characteristic of Order Passeriformes, often called "songbirds." Experienced birders can identify many species by song alone; but some females and juveniles are nearly impossible to identify with no male nearby.)

Birds molt, or replace all of their feathers, at least once a year even if they don't have different seasonal plumages. The latter are mostly a matter of making the male alternately showy for courtship and camouflaged for the nonbreeding seasons. Ptarmigan, however, simply alter their camouflages to suit the season; they may go through two or three seasonal plumages (to match snow, no snow, or patchy snow) and the females and juveniles go through them along with the males. With a few exceptions like the mallard and the dipper, the large feathers of the wings and tail molt just a few at a time, making the bird look tattered but still permitting flight.

Another feather maintenance procedure is preening with the toes or beak, aided in most birds by oil from a preen gland. Much time is devoted to this crucial task of aligning and oiling plumage to keep it intact as an airfoil, as insulation and as waterproofing.

Along with wings and feathers, the evolution of bird flight entailed radically larger and more efficient respiratory systems. The stamina needed for a single day of flying, let alone for migrating across oceans, would be inconceivable in a mammal. It demands a lavish supply of oxygen to the blood, and of blood to the muscles. Cooling—direly needed during flight—is also done through the breath. Breathing capacity is augmented by several air sacs and, in many birds, by hollow interiors of the large upper leg and wing bones, all interconnected with little air tubes. Each breath passing through the lungs to the sacs and bones and back out through the lungs is efficiently scoured of its oxygen.

Hollow bones, their interiors crisscrossed with tiny strutlike bone fibers in accord with the best engineering principles, doubtless evolved to save weight, yet some birds lack them. Loons, for example, have solid bones—perfectly serviceable in a bird that dives for a living and doesn't fly much. But some diving birds have hollow bones, and a few soaring birds manage with solid bones.

The other large bone in a bird is the sternum, or breastbone, projecting keel-like in front of the rib cage to provide a mechanically advantaged point of attachment for the flight muscles. These muscles, known on the dinner table as "breast meat," are the largest organs in flying birds. They power the flapping wings, and also guide flight by controlling the orientation of each and every feather along the wing edge through a system of tendons like ropes and pulleys. There is scant muscle in the wing and none in the foot, which is moved via tendons from muscles along the upper leg bone, held against the body. A flying animal ideally concentrates all its weight in a single aerodynamic "fuselage" close to its center of gravity.

The wing is analogous at once to both wing and propeller of an airplane. This is no accident; pioneers of mechanical flight studied and tried to copy bird flight for centuries before Wilbur and Orville finally, albeit crudely, got it right, using a design that separated the propelling and lifting functions of the bird wing. Like a propeller, wings provide forward thrust by slicing vertically through the air while held at a diagonal—the rear edge angled upward on the downstroke and vice versa.

Once there is enough forward motion and/or headwind to provide strong airflow across the wings (bird or airplane), their shape provides vertical lift by creating a low-pressure pocket in the air curving over their convex upper surface, while the lower surface is effectively flat. This upperside-convex principle applies in all flying birds except perhaps hummingbirds; but wing outlines are specialized. See water wings (loon, page 411, and dipper, page 449), soaring wings (page 414), speed wings (page 422), little-used wings (grouse, page 425), and hovering wings (hummingbirds, page 436).

Highly mobile and often migratory, birds wander from their usual ranges more than plants or mammals do. The 103 species described in this book are fewer than half of those reported for our range. I have mainly tried to include the birds most characteristic of our mountains, conspicuous or not, but I admit making exceptions for some large and striking species even if they are not common, or even if they characterize lowlands at least as much as mountains.

Names of species follow the American Ornithologists' Union *Checklist*. Birds are the only group for which decisions on names, both scientific and common, are made by a committee and then accepted as "official" by just about everyone on the continent. In this chapter, common names that used to be official are annotated as "formerly," and vernacular names that were never official as "also."

The size figure that begins each description is the length from tip of bill to tip of tail of an average adult male; females are the same or more often a little smaller, except among raptors, where they are considerably bigger. The *Golden Guide's* figures are used—measurements of "live birds hand-held in natural positions." These run about 10% shorter than those in many bird manuals which, following taxonomic tradition, are measurements of long-dead specimens or skins, forcibly hand-stretched. Novice birders would do well to fix in their minds images of sparrow size (4–6"/10–15 cm), robin size (8–10"/20–25 cm), jay size (9–12"/23–30 cm), crow size (17"/43 cm), and raven size (21"/53 cm) as a mental yardstick. Unfortunately, size is hard to judge against the open sky.

Habitat and behavior are good clues, especially if you're content with a smart guess as opposed to positive i.d. Many small birds are faithful to plant communities they have adapted to for forage and/or cover. For example, some birds of deciduous streamside thickets are rarely seen in the adjacent conifer forest, and vice versa. In a forest, one species may prefer the canopy, another the tall shrubs, and another the low shrub layer. After the nesting season, birds that don't migrate away may shift to different habitats for forage and cover, as their caloric needs, the weather, and the available foods all change.

As this book goes to press, there is great concern, but little firm information, about how West Nile virus will affect birds. Individuals killed by the virus have been found for 42 species in this chapter; high mortality rates have been reported for red-tailed hawks, great horned owls, black-capped chickadees, and American crows.

However, susceptibility and mortality both seem to vary a lot by region; no one knows why. An educated guess would be that many species will suffer sharp drops in numbers, but for species that start out with high numbers these should be temporary and often local. There are likely to be at least a few extinctions of already-rare species.

Probably most birds can grow high levels of the virus, and can then pass it on via mosquitoes. Humans (especially young, healthy ones) are not very susceptible: your odds of getting the disease from any one mosquito bite, even if it carries the virus, are quite small. But some scientists are concerned that long-term effects may turn up in "recovered" individuals, making the disease worse than it seems now.

In the lab, magpies can transmit the disease without mosquito intermediaries. Avoid handling dead birds, and if you must do so, use gloves or at least wash thoroughly and immediately.

Common Loon

Gavia immer (gay-via: Roman name for them; im-er: sooty). 24" [60 cm], ws 58" [147 cm] (variable size, but generally larger than ducks); bill heavy, tapered, ± ravenlike; breeding-season adults (both sexes) with iridescent green/black head, white collar, black/white checked back, white belly; winter plumage dark gray-brown above, white below; in flight, head is held lower than body, and feet trail behind tail. Lakes; uncommon. Gaviidae (Loon family). Color p 528.

The varied nocturnal and crepuscular "laughs" and "yodels" of loons have been called beautiful, horrible, hair-raising, bloodcurdling, magical, and maniacal. Unequivocally they are loud, and if they don't make a deep impression on you, you aren't very impressionable.

Loons resemble diving ducks in their feeding and locomotion skills. They eat mainly fish, plus some frogs, reptiles, leeches, insects, and aquatic plants. Like ducks they use both wings and webbed feet to swim underwater. Diving either headfirst or submerging submarinewise, they can go deeper than any other birds (250 feet down, or 75 meters) thanks largely to their heavier bodies—only slightly less dense than water. Their heavy bones are a primitive trait that doubtless remains advantageous for diving. It is disadvantageous for flying; though loons can fly fast and far, they land gracelessly, with a big plop, and take off by beating their wings hard while skimming along a considerable length of watery "runway." They can become trapped for days or weeks on forest-lined lakes too small for their low-angle takeoff pattern—waiting to take off into a gale, if one arises. A few have apparently mistaken highways for water, stranding themselves there. (They are one kind of wild animal that can and should be rescued.) On their feet they're still more inept and cumbersome; the extreme rear placement of their legs is great for swimming but awful for walking. They go ashore (on an island) only to breed, and nest in soggy plant debris at the water's edge. She and he take turns on the eggs, and both carry the chicks on their backs (swimming, not flying) after they hatch.

After wintering near the coast, some loons move to mountain lakes, arriving soon after the ice breaks up. Please do not approach loons closely during the breeding season; they are very sensitive.

Grebes

Order Podicipediformes, family Podicipedidae.

Western grebe, *Aechmophorus occidentalis* (eek-mof-or-us: spear bearer). 18" (45 cm); black and white bird with red eyes; needle-like yellow bill; long graceful neck, held nearly straight, is white in front, black in back; head white from eyes down, black above; in flight, head and feet are lower than body. Color p 528.

Pied-billed grebe, *Podilymbus podiceps* (pod-i-lim-bus: from the Greek term; **pod**-i-seps: rump feet). 9" [23 cm]; stocky; bill high, stout, with downcurved ridge, pale with a black band across it (on summer adults); both sexes drab brown mottled white, white under tail; summer adults marked with black on face and throat; in flight (rarely seen), head is slightly lower than body, and feet trail behind the very short tail. Lakes, marshes.

Like loons, grebes are a primitive order of birds poorly adapted for flying and worse for walking, but superlatively built for diving. Grebe toes—fat scaly lobes—paddle even more efficiently than webbed feet; they use a side by side stroke resembling the human butterfly stroke but without any help from the forelimbs. (Diving ducks, in contrast, paddle their feet alternately, and also use their wings.) By exhaling deeply to decrease their buoyancy, grebes can quietly submerge and skulk with only head or nostrils above water. Grebe hatchlings take up submersible life before they can even swim, clinging to a diving parent's back. Because grebes can only take off from open water, they can become trapped on the shrinking ice-free centers of lakes in fall. Ben Gadd reports this happening each year in Jasper N.P.

The remarkable vocalizations of the widespread but shy pied-billed grebe have been compared to a braying donkey or a squealing pig. Crayfish are a favorite food.

Courting western grebes skitter across lakes together, necks arched in parallel, rising out of the water purely on foot power.

Great Blue Heron

Ardea herodias (**ar**-dia her-**oh**-dias: Roman and Greek words for heron). 38" [95 cm], ws 70" [175 cm]; gray (± bluish) with some white, black, and dark red markings; bill, neck, and legs extremely long; neck held "gooosenecked" in flight; huge birds seen in slow-flapping low flight over rivers and lakes are generally this species. Various loud, guttural croaks. Order Ciconiiformes, Ardeidae (Heron family). Color p 528.

The heron's way of life is to stand perfectly still in shallow water until some oblivious frog or small fish happens by, and then pluck or spear it with a quick thrust of the beak. Prey see little of the heron but its legs and shadow, and perhaps mistake it for an odd reed or cattail. A heron can nail prey even at night, as members of this order have excellent night vision.

bird of rebirth
buzzard
meat is rotten meat made
sweet again and
lean.

—Lew Welch

Turkey Vulture

Cathartes aura (cath-**ar**-teez: purifier; aura: breeze). Also **turkey buzzard**. 25" [63 cm]; ws 72" [180 cm]; plumage black exc whitish rear half of wing underside; head naked, wrinkled, pink (exc black when young); soars with wings in a shallow V, often tipping left or right, rarely flapping. Open country. Migratory: here late Feb through Oct. Order Ciconiiformes, Cathartidae (New World vulture family).

Linnaeus was wise to name this creature "Purifier" to counter its unsavory reputation. Its bald head and neck are virtually self-cleaning (no feathers to foul) after mucking around in carrion. Its digestive tract is immune to disturbance by the meat-rotting organisms that would do in the rest of us. Its beak and talons are too weak to tear up freshly dead mammals, let alone kill live ones. Predatory birds, in contrast, are equally ready to either kill or eat carrion. Vultures go long periods without food, and when they find it they gorge themselves, perhaps accounting for their apparent lethargy on foot and difficulty in taking flight. (If hungry enough, they'll fill their stomachs with plant foods.) Once on the wing, they are the best soarers of all land birds, rarely needing to flap.

A congregation of vultures wheeling usually means carrion below, and other vultures seem able to read this sign, slowly gathering from miles around. Vultures locate their food by both sight and smell. Birds generally have little sense of smell, but vultures have a sharp sense at least for certain carrion smells. Natural gas pipeline companies found that by perfuming their gas with ethyl mercaptan they could get vultures to lead them to pipeline leaks.

Several turkey vultures may gather around a carcass, but they eat one at a time, in order of dominance yielding occasionally to desperation. Dominant individuals have redder heads, and seem to flush redder still, as a dominance display.

"Buzzard," an old word tracing from the Roman *buteo*, is used in Britain to include hawks (genus *Buteo*) as well as Old World vultures, which are in the hawk family. American vultures and condors resemble Old World vultures due to convergent evolution, but are not closely related. (Since 1873, some scientists have argued that they are closer to storks than hawks; the Seventh *Checklist* made that view official. DNA evidence has not resolved the issue.)

Soaring Wings

Vultures share with the large Falconiformes—eagles, vultures, ospreys, and buteo hawks—a broad, spread-tipped wing and tail design specialized for soaring over land. These contrast with the short wings of accipiter hawks, the narrow wings of falcons, and the clean, linear wings of gulls and albatrosses which also soar superlatively, but on entirely different air currents, over the ocean.

Falconiform soarers stay aloft largely by seeking out "thermals," or upwellings of warm air—the daytime convection pattern of low, warm air rising in bubble-like masses to trade places with higher, cooler air. They don't try to cross large lakes, or travel at night or in the early morning, since thermal air is warmed by land absorbing and reradiating sunlight. Dry, sparsely vegetated land does it best, so steppes and prairies are especially popular with soaring birds. To travel, they may climb one thermal spirally, then glide obliquely downward to the next thermal, and climb again. To migrate, they often wait for a low-pressure weather trough, or follow long north-south mountain ridges that produce wavelike updrafts by deflecting westerly winds. Tightly packed mountain topography, like ours, produces oblique thermals along creek headwaters. Soarers can use these just as well.

Swans

Cygnus spp. (**sig**-nus: Greek for swan). Huge white waterfowl with very long neck; black bill and skin reaching up from the bill to a point at each eye (see species distinctions); immatures light gray. Anatidae (Waterfowl family).

Trumpeter swan, *C. buccinator* (buc-sin-**ay**-tor: trumpeter). 45" [112 cm], ws 8' [2.4 m]; black all the way from bill to eye. Call is one or two deep, resonant honks. Lakes of nw WY and nearby MT and ID; rare and few.

Tundra swan, *C. columbianus.* NA ssp is the **whistling swan.** 39" [98 cm], ws 7' [205 cm]; most adults have yellow spot in front of eye. Calls include high yelps, long reedy whoops. Flocks migrate very high (often 1,000– 5,000' up, or 300–1500 m) in V formation, stop over at RM marshes and lakes; spring and fall.

Once widespread in the U.S. and Canada, the second largest North American bird—the trumpeter swan—was brought to the brink of extinction by market hunting. Red Rocks Lake National Wildlife Refuge, MT, nurtured its subsequent recovery. We have breeding populations there and at Yellowstone and Grand Teton. If you see them, maintain a quiet and respectful distance, as they need undisturbed habitat for nesting.

The tundra swan, breeding only in the remote Arctic, has kept its numbers above 100,000. City parks have Mute Swans, *Cygnus olor,* introduced from Europe.

Canada Goose

Branta canadensis (**bran**-ta: origin moot, perhaps from Anglo-Saxon 'burnt'). 25" [63 cm]; ws 68" [170 cm]; head and long neck (held straight forward in flight) are black exc for a white chin strap; body brown, massive; tail black/white; wings brown; belly white. Deep "honk;" migrating flocks form a V or skein, and honk continuously. On and near water. Anatidae (Waterfowl family).

Though geese are famous for their migrations, those that breed in our region mostly stay put through winter unless their lake freezes over, forcing them into a modest trip to one that doesn't. In spring and fall we also see migrators; these tend to be much smaller arctic tundra subspecies, some with a white ring around the neck. The best-established explanation of their V formation in flight is that all but the leader save considerable energy (71% in one scientist's calculation, 3.5% in another's) by flying in the draft of the bird ahead. Different birds, usually females, trade off in the leader position, maximizing the range of the group as a whole. Males are socially dominant. Geese mate for life.

This fowl feeds sometimes by dabbling, more often by grazing on land. It is a serious crop pest in a few locales.

Common Merganser

Mergus merganser (**mer**-gus: diver; mer-**gan**-ser: diving goose). 18" [45 cm]; breeding males mostly white beneath with black back and head, and red bill, the head showing greenish iridescence in strong light, and becoming brown in non-breeding season; females with red-brown head sometimes showing slight crest on nape, and red bill, otherwise grayish, with darker back and ± white throat and breast. Lakes and streams. Anatidae.

Mergansers are carnivorous "diving ducks" as opposed to "dabbling ducks" who don't dive, but merely dip, for their mostly vegetable foods. Instead of a Donald Duck-type broad bill, mergansers have a long, narrow bill with a hooked tip and serrated edges for gripping their slippery aquatic prey—amphibians, insects and other invertebrates, and fish. Of our three merganser species, the common is the largest, most montane, and certainly the commonest. Those who don't fly north to breed generally move up to mountain lakes, finding woodpecker holes or other cavities to nest in.

Mallard

Anas platyrhynchos (**ay**-nus: the Roman term; plat-i-**rink**-os: broad nose). 16" [40 cm]; males (Sept-June) have iridescent dark green head separated from red-brown breast and brown back by white neckband; bill yellow on males, black/orange on females; both sexes have a band of bright blue with black/white trim on upper rear edge of wing, and much white under wings; females, juveniles, and summer males speckled drab. Loud quack. Marshy lakes. Anatidae (Waterfowl family).

The mallard is a good example of the many surface-feeding, or "dabbling" or "puddle" ducks. It is conspicuous over much of the Northern Hemisphere—except during duck hunting season, when it makes itself perplexingly scarce. Tasty flesh contributes to its renown. Domestic ducks were bred largely from mallards, centuries ago, and breed with them when given the chance; city park ducks often include mallards and hybrids together.

Dabbling ducks feed by upending themselves in shallow water and plucking vegetation from the bottom. They eat a few molluscs and insects and a very few small fish. They take flight abruptly and steeply, unlike diving ducks which splash along the surface.

Mallards are among the birds that molt their flight feathers all at once, rendering them flightless; to escape predators they hide out for the duration in large groups in marshes. You may then see mallard mothers with chicks trailing behind, but no fathers. After the young are independent, it's the mothers' turn to molt. While flightless, they are "sitting ducks," but the rest of the time they can practice "sleeping with one eye open." If four mallards are asleep in a row, the two in the middle close both eyes while the two on the ends tend to keep the end-of-the-line eye open for predators. A scientist ran brain scans on mallards in this condition, and found that the brain hemisphere connected to the open eye remained semi-wakeful and capable of rousing the bird upon sighting a predator, while the other hemisphere experienced normal sleep.

Harlequin Duck

Histrionicus histrionicus (hiss-tree-ah-**nic**-us: actor or jester, ref. to clownlike facial markings). 12" [30 cm]; breeding males plumed in a clownlike patchwork of slaty blue-gray, rich brown on the flanks, and white splotches with black trim—but may appear merely dark from a distance; others dark brown with several small white patches on head, and whitish belly. Rough water; mainly YNP, GNP(MT) and Canada. Anatidae (Waterfowl family). Color p 528.

Whether in whitewater rivers or heavy surf, harlequins display phenomenal pluck and strength as swimmers. Many live on rocky seashores, where they dive for shellfish, and migrate inland to build their grass-lined nest among brush or boulders along mountain streams, where they feed largely on insects. But Wyoming's few harlequins may be full-year residents. Unlike most ducks, harlequins rarely mix with other species.

Wags have compared harlequin plumage to unfinished paint-by-number art. The feathers were once used to adorn ladies' hats.

Bufflehead

Bucephala albeola (bew-**sef**-a-la: buffalo head, referring to oversized head; al-be-oh-la: small white). 10" [25 cm]; males white with black back, black head with big erectile white patch crossing crown behind eye; females brown with elongated white patch behind eye; short, thick bill. Anatidae (Waterfowl family).

Buffleheads are the only ducks small enough to move right into a flicker's old nest without alteration, and seem quite dependent on that convenience. Though excellent divers, they catch relatively few fish, relying mainly on crustaceans, molluscs, and insect nymphs. Courting males fly over the target female and make a splashy sort of ski-landing, with white crest erect, just past her.

Goldeneyes

Bucephala spp. Also **whistlers**. 13" [33 cm]; male has black head with green or purple iridescence, white spot below bright yellow eye, white belly, row of white spots on black wings; female brown with dark brown head, pale yellow eye. Wings whistle distinctively in flight. Lakes, beaver ponds, slow rivers. Anatidae (Waterfowl family).

Barrow's goldeneye, *B. islandica* (iss-**land**-ic-a: of Iceland). Male has white crescent below eye; female bill usually yellow.

Common goldeneye, *B. clangula* (**clang**-you-la: small racket). Male has round white spot; female bill usually black with small yellow tip. Color p 528.

Cold-loving ducks, goldeneyes stay on their boreal forest nesting grounds as long as the progress of fall freeze-up allows. Some individuals (especially the Common) treat our range as the balmy south, merely wintering here. Barrow's, nonetheless, is the commonest breeding duck in Greater Yellowstone. All three *Bucephala* species commonly breed at Glacier, but both north and south of there we mainly see spring/fall migrants or wintering birds. Goldeneye males have striking courtship displays, including a "head-throw-kick": first thrusting his head forward, then pressing it way back into his rump, bill pointing skyward, then forward again while kicking up a splash.

Osprey

Pandion haliaetus (pan-**die**-un: a mythic king; hal-ee-**ay**-et-us: sea eagle, the Greek term for osprey). Also **fish hawk**. Males 22" [55 cm], ws 54" [135 cm], females larger; blackish above, exc white crown; white beneath, with black markings most concentrated at wing tips and "elbows"; the "elbow" break is sharper both rearward and downward than on similar birds, suggesting a shallow M while soaring. Frequent calls include loud whistles and squeals. Near rivers and lakes. Order Falconiformes, Pandionidae (Osprey family). Color p 529.

In a hunting technique that wins respect if not utter astonishment, the osprey dives into water from fifty to a hundred feet up, plucks a fish from a depth of one to three feet, and bursts immediately back into flight, gripping a squirming fish sometimes as heavy as itself. The soles of its feet are toughened with minute barbules that help grasp wet fish. The osprey is a nearly worldwide species comprising a genus and subfamily by itself.

Ospreys are among several birds of prey that suffered heavy losses in some areas from toxic chemicals like DDT. Toxins from prey concentrate in the tissues of predators; birds are especially sensitive to them. But in the Northwest, so far, ospreys coexist with civilization. Dams have created a lot of new osprey habitat.

Bald Eagle

Haliaeetus leucocephalus (hal-ee-**ee**-et-us: sea eagle; lew-co-**sef**-a-lus: white head). Males 32" [80 cm], ws 80" [2 m], females larger; adults blackish with entire head and tail white; immatures (1–3+ years) brown; wings held flat while soaring. Near large lakes and rivers; year-round, but with sharp peaks (migrating) in spring and late fall. Calls: various weak chips and squawks, or louder ± gull-like shrieks. Order Falconiformes, Accipitridae (Hawk family). Color p 529.

The U.S. national symbol, bald eagles were considered vermin to be shot on sight for most of America's history. Shooting them was even rewarded with bounties in Alaska until 1952, twelve years after becoming a crime in the lower 48 states. Some Westerners still fear and hate eagles enough to break the law.

Despite a public image as a fearsome predator, the bald eagle far more often scavenges carrion or robs other birds—ospreys, gulls, kingfishers, and smaller bald eagles—of their prey. Most salmon it eats are spawned-out carcasses. At lambing time on sheep ranches, bald eagles eat afterbirths and stillborn lambs. Grossly exaggerated fears of lamb and salmon predation fueled America's animosity toward eagles for the last two centuries.

Our bald eagles breed in spring. Grand Teton and Yellowstone have a few dozen nests, and others are scattered northward at least as far as Banff. Fondness for fish and waterfowl tends to keep bald eagles near water. They gather in large numbers at spawning runs, including those of freshwater species like kokanee. The best-known case of that was along the North Fork Flathead, but those kokanee runs collapsed after non-native opossum shrimp invaded the watershed, and bald eagle numbers dwindled in turn.

A spectacular courtship "dance" of bald eagles is well known: the male dive-bombs the female in midair, she rolls over to meet him, they lock talons and plummet earthward, breaking out of their death-taunting embrace at the last possible instant. Juvenile bald eagles engage in every kind of courtship behavior short of mating, which waits for the fifth or sixth winter.

North American tribes associated the bald eagle with sickness, death, and healing, and hence as an ally or guardian of shamans. Eagle feathers were used in healing rituals, and it was variously said that an eagle would fly over a sick person, would eat a dead person, or would scream to a person soon to be killed by an arrow.

Northern Harrier

Circus cyaneus (circus: Greek term for a circling hawk; sigh-**ay**-nee-us: blue). Formerly **marsh hawk**. Males 16¼" [41 cm], ws 42" [105 cm], females much larger; conspicuous white rump patch on both sexes; males ash gray above, whitish underneath with black wing tips and tail bars; females speckled reddish brown, paler beneath; tail long and narrow; wings held well above horizontal while gliding. Grasslands and marshes. Accipitridae (Hawk family). Color p 529.

The harrier cruises dry grasslands and wet meadows alike. It nests among tall grass, and spends several hours a day cruising just inches above the tops of the reeds, grasses, or low shrubs. When a vole takes off running underneath it, the agile hawk may harry it through many dashes and turns before dropping on it. It is an unusual hawk in hunting primarily by sound; in experiments, harriers precisely locate and attack tiny tape players concealed in meadow grass peeping and rustling like voles. In this respect harriers evolved convergently with owls, developing an owl-like facial ruff of feathers, which enhances hearing.

Unlike most hawks, harriers mate polygamously. Some males manage to feed two or even three nests of about five young each. The mothers often leave the nest momentarily to take midair delivery of morsels from their harried breadwinners. A female, having paired and begun a nest, may dump that mate if he is turning out to be a poor provider, and join the harem of a better one. A male courts by means of a "sky dance" in a grand **U** pattern, culminating by landing on the nest site he proposes. More vigorous dancers get more mates.

Accipiters

Accipiter spp. (ak-**sip**-it-er: Roman term meaning a fast flier). Tell these from other hawks by behavior, and by proportionately short, broad wings and long tails; the tail is often narrow (not fanned out), is broadly barred (± black/ white) its full length, and has a pure white tuft under its base; three species hard to tell from one another — size ranges overlap, females being about as big as next bigger species' males; both sexes slaty gray above, or ± brownish; yearlings brown above, pale beneath with red-brown streaking. Calls cackling, infrequent. Order Falconiformes, Accipitridae (Hawk family).

Sharp-shinned hawk, *A. striatus* (stry-**ay**-tus: striped). Males 10½" [26 cm], ws 21" [43 cm] (jay-sized); tail square-cornered, dark-tipped; underside pale with fine brownish barring. Often at forest/clearing edges, or alpine. Illustrated.

Cooper's hawk, *A. cooperii* (coo-**per**-ee-eye: after William Cooper). Males 15½" [39 cm], ws 28" [70 cm] (crow-sized); tail rounded, with slight white tip; underside pale with red-brown barring. Forest under-story or edges; streamside brush.

Goshawk, *A. gentilis* (jen-**tie**-lis: aristocratic). Males 21" [53 cm], ws 42" [105 cm] (red-tailed hawk size) tail rounded, with slight white tip; underside pale with fine blue-gray barring. Deep wilderness forests.

These hawks evolved in the forests. Their long tails lend maneuverability while the short wings avoid branches. Cooper's typically bursts out from a concealed perch; the sharp-shinned flies around more or less constantly and randomly, and chases the birds it happens to surprise; the goshawk also cruises, flushing grouse and ptarmigan, its chief prey, and also taking some squirrels and hares.

Each day while young are in the nest, a sharp-shinned father brings home about two sparrow-sized birds apiece for his family of seven or so. That's a lot of hunting. He seems to stay in shape with playful harassment of larger birds, even ravens. Accipiter males select a limb not far from the nest and take prey there to pluck it before eating it or delivering it to the nest. An indiscriminate scattering of thousands of small feathers may be a sign of one such pluckery in the branches above. Either parent may make a nasty fuss over an animal, such as yourself, happening to approach the nest.

Accipiters are often described as nonsoarers, with a flight rhythm of five flaps and a short glide—sometimes a useful identifying trait. But in the strong, sustained updrafts of rugged mountains they appear perfectly capable of soaring till hell freezes over.

Red-Tailed Hawk

Buteo jamaicensis (**bew**-tee-o: the Roman term; ja-**may**-ik-**en**-sis: of Jamaica). Males 18" [45 cm], ws 48" [120 cm], females larger; tail (adults) red-brown above, pink below, broadly fanned out; brown above, highly variable beneath, from dark brown to (most often) white with delicate red-brown patterning. Usually seen soaring. Call a short, hoarse descending scream. Order Falconiformes, Accipitridae (Hawk family). Color p 529.

The red-tail is easily America's oftenest-seen large bird of prey. It is comfortable around freeways, often perching on roadside fenceposts. Its preferred natural habitat is grassland mixed with some trees. On a continental scale it has increased as forest and tallgrass prairie have been converted to more transparent habitats.

Adaptability, opportunism, and economy are the keys to the red-tail's success. Lacking the speed that makes falcons and accipiters perfect specialists, it adopts a variety of hunting ploys based on acute

---

Birds

vision and effortless soaring. Hares and ground squirrels, the preferred prey, may get an aerial swoop after a patient, stealthy approach. Or the hawk may brazenly land between a rodent and its
refuge, forcing the rodent into an end run; the hawk tries to snatch
it. Birds may be swooped upon while feeding in brush. Lizards,
snakes, and slugs are easy, and form a large part of the diet in some
seasons. Red-tails are also pirates, robbing hawks and even eagles or
great horned owls of their kills. In winter, individuals that remain in
the snowy North show a remarkable ability to conserve calories and
subsist on a skimpy, irregular diet.

Swainson's Hawk

Buteo swainsoni (**swain**-son-eye: after Wm. Swainson). Males 18" [45 cm], ws
49" [125 cm], females larger; tail broadly fanned out, pale grayish beneath with
black outer band; brown above, highly variable beneath: leading edge may be
white or dark, but feathers are never white; wings more pointed than other big
soarers. Call a shrill descending scream. Prairies and sparse woodland; March
to Nov; less common to n. Order Falconiformes, Accipitridae (Hawk family).

This large hawk snatches a lot of large insects—dragonflies in
midair, grasshoppers in the fields, hunted with low, teetering cruises
like a harrier's. In late fall it gathers in large flocks and migrates all
the way to Argentina, making much use of thermals. It is in a severe
decline probably due to pesticides or habitat loss in South America.

Speed Wings

Tell falcons from other hawks by their pointed, swept-back wings (and
by their straight, or even slightly tapering, tails in flapping flight; but soaring they fan their tails out like other hawks). This must be the optimal
wing design for sustained speed, since most of the fastest flyers—falcons,
swifts, swallows, and nighthawks—evolved it independently.

The fastest of all falcons in level flight is said to be the largest falcon,
the gyrfalcon, *Falco rusticolus*, of the Arctic (rarely reported seen here). In
ancient falconry, only kings were entitled to fly gyrfalcons.

The slightly smaller peregrine may edge out the gyrfalcon as world's
fastest animal, when it "stoops"—not exactly flying, but plummeting
toward an airborne target. The wings are held close to the sides to provide control while minimizing drag. Most hawks and eagles will stoop
occasionally, when presented with an irresistible target, but only the
peregrine nearly limits itself to midair prey, and has perfected the stoop.
Ornithologist Vance Tucker watched peregrines spotting small birds
nearly a mile [1500 m] off, and then flying in a logarithmic curve to

Peregrine Falcon

Falco peregrinus (**fahl**-co: the Roman term; pair-eg-**rye**-nus: wandering). Also **duck hawk.** Males 15" [38 cm], ws 40" [1 m], females larger; wings pointed, tail narrow. Color variable, ours mostly slate blue to (immatures) dark brown above; white beneath with dark mottling and ± reddish wash except white throat and upper breast; face has high-contrast rounded dark bar descending across and below eye. Thinly scattered in US, esp near rivers with cliffs, incl the Yellowstone R in YS Park; on prairies in AB, but few, if any, up in the mtns. Order Falconiformes, Falconidae (Falcon family).

In decline worldwide, peregrines were very nearly extirpated from our range in the 1970s, leading to U.S. and Canadian bans on the pesticide DDT and on capture of peregrines for falconry. Scientists figured out that DDT contamination is a primary culprit, causing thin eggshells that break under the mothers' weight. Captive breeding and release programs completed this famous success story, but it came slowly, hindered by poaching and perhaps by other insecticides still in use. Now peregrines have moved into Calgary, Edmonton, and other cities where two of their favorite things abound: high ledges to perch and nest on, and pigeons to eat. They hunt birds almost exclusively, often by stooping and striking the prey a stunning blow to the neck, with outstretched fist. (See sidebar.)

---

approach them. Their sharpest long-distance vision is to the side, not straight ahead, but if they stooped with head turned to the side it would slow them down a lot. The curving approach fits Tucker's calculation that they should reach prey soonest by keeping their heads straight and the target at a 40° angle relative to straight ahead.

The figure 180 miles per hour [290 kph] was heard ever since a small plane pilot in 1930 reported a stooping peregrine passing him while he was diving at 175 mph. He was disbelieved by some who maintained that the race belongs to the swifts. Tucker retorts that swifts are probably no swifter than pigeons. His instruments optically tracked a peregrine at 157 mph [253 kph], but he thinks, based on aerodynamics, that they can do over 220 [360]: "Searching for the top speed is something like trying to measure the top speed of a Porsche by watching cars on a freeway. The longer you watch, the higher the record, but you are unlikely to measure the top speed that the car is capable of, because that speed is seldom practical on a freeway."

Close tracking of a gyrfalcon found it accelerating quickly to 130 mph [210 kph], then spreading its wings slightly to check its speed. Ken Franklin sky-dives with a trained peregrine; it kept up with him on dives whose free-fall portion he calculated as faster than 200 mph [325 kph].

American Kestrel

Falco sparverius (spar-**ver**-ius: sparrow). Formerly **sparrow hawk**. Males 9" [23 cm], ws 21" [53 cm], females slightly larger; red-brown above, exc wings blue-gray on adult males only, and tail tipped with heavy black band and slight white fringe; brown-flecked white beneath (exc dark tail). Call a sharp, fast "killy-killy-killy." ± open country. Falconidae. Color p 529.

The kestrel is one of the smallest, most successful, least shy, and most often seen raptors. When not perched on a limb or telephone wire, it often hovers in place, wings fluttering, body tipped about 45°, facing upwind, 10-20' [3-6 m] above a field or roadside. From this vantage it can drop and strike prey quickly, as a larger, broader-winged hawk might do from a low soar. Grasshoppers and other big insects are staples; mice are also taken. If all these are scarce, the kestrel may fly down sparrow-sized birds.

Prairie Falcon

Falco mexicanus. Males 16" [40 cm], ws 40" [1 m], females larger; wings pointed, tail narrow. Dusty to (less often) slaty brown above, strongly mottled cream white beneath, with blackish wingpit (as in "armpit") patches; may have a vertical streak below eye, but narrower and less distinct than on peregrine. In steppe canyons year-round, wandering in summer to timberline meadows; uncommon n of WY. Color p 529.

This is one falcon that specializes in prey on the ground. In our region, ground squirrels are a staple, along with ground-dwelling meadowlarks and horned larks. It rarely stoops, but often overtakes small birds in level flight. A grassland bird that nests in steppe canyons, it may visit subalpine meadows to hunt ground squirrels after its nesting season is over. A parent may defend its nest by means of dive-bombing attacks at the heads of intruders, veering away at the last instant, and provide a lucky hiker with one of the great adrenalin-stimulating wildlife encounters.

Golden Eagle

Aquila chrysaetos (ak-**will**-a: Roman term for eagle; cris-**ay**-et-os: gold eagle). Males 32" [80 cm], ws 78" [195 cm], females larger (up to twice as heavy); adults dark brown all over; juveniles have white bases to their main wing and tail feathers (but never an all-white tail, as in bald eagle, nor a white rear edge of wing, as in turkey vulture); wings held flat while soaring. Call (rarely used) is rapid chipping. Open country. Accipitridae (Hawk family). Color p 529.

Golden eagles inhabit any North American terrain that has lots of vertical relief, few trees, and populations of hares and large diurnal rodents like marmots or ground squirrels. The hares provide winter fare while the rodents hibernate. Winter may impel an eagle to attempt larger prey such as a fox, or rarely a coyote or deer, by means of a plummeting, falconlike dive. Momentum multiplies the eagle's ten pounds [4½ kg] into enough force to overpower heavier prey.

Normally, golden eagles hunt from a low, fast-soaring cruise, using angular topography both for visual cover and for updrafts. They often rob hawks and falcons of their kills; hawks rarely venture, let alone nest, within half a mile of an eagle's aerie. The latter is a stick structure 4' to 6' [120–180 cm] in diameter, and growing from 1' deep to as much as 5' [30 cm to 150 cm] with many years of reuse—yet somehow hard to spot against its cliff.

White-tailed Ptarmigan

Lagopus leucurus (la-**go**-pus: hare foot; loo-**cue**-rus: white tail). Also **snow grouse**. 10" [25 cm]; underparts white; upper parts white in winter, mottled brown in summer, patchwork of brown and white in spring and fall; feet feathered; bright red eyebrow-comb on males in spring. Soft clucks and hoots. Alp/subalpine, sometimes lower in heavy snow seasons; from Flathead R n, and disjunct in YS, Bitterroots, and Wallowas (where introduced). Order Galliformes, Phasianidae (Pheasant family). Color p 530.

Ptarmigan are the largest creatures that make our alpine zone their exclusive home. Dwarf willows are their staple in winter, crowberries in fall. Ptarmigan moms have been seen dropping a tidbit of one of these relatively nutritious foods in front of their young, pointing at it and at the plant, and uttering a food call. Such clear teaching behavior has mainly been described in chimpanzees and a few other mammals. Like other grouse, ptarmigan rely on camouflage to protect them from predators. Considering the visual acuity of hawks, this seems an especially risky strategy above tree line. In winter they switch to pure white plumage and stay on pure white snow as much as possible, digging into it for shelter and to reach willow buds. Once their summer plumage grows in, they stay off the snowfields.

The "p" in ptarmigan is not only silent but silly. It must have found its way into print long ago in the work of some pedant who imagined "ptarmigan" to be Greek. It's Gaelic.

Birds

Blue Grouse

Dendragapus obscurus (den-**drag**-a-pus: tree lover; ob-**skew**-rus: dark). Also **hooter;** our variety the **sooty grouse.** 17" [42 cm]; adult males ± mottled dark gray above, pale gray beneath, with yellow eyebrow-comb; others mottled gray-brown; both sexes have blackish tail. Male's courtship call a series of 5 or 6 low hoots; hen with chicks clucks. Fairly common and frequently seen; all elevs in montane forest. Order Galliformes, Phasianidae (Pheasant family). Color p 530.

Blue grouse spend the breeding season in relatively open habitats, enriching their diets with caterpillars, plant shoots, berries, and even mushrooms. For winter they move into dense conifers, which offer thermal cover, visual cover, and plenty of needles, which are all they'll find to eat in winter anyway. In some populations this pattern means they actually migrate upslope for winter. They prefer Douglas-fir needles, and in experiments have been able to maintain their body weight on 100% Douglas-fir needles, but not on needles of other species. (See spruce grouse, facing page; digestibility rates and adaptations are probably pretty similar.)

Both the courting "hoot" and the males' chief visual display—exposing bare yellow patches on the neck—are performed by inflating a pair of air sacs in the throat.

Spruce Grouse

Falcipennis canadensis (fahl-sih-**pen**-iss: sickleshaped feather; can-a-**den**-sis: of Canada) =*Dendragapus canadensis.* Our variety the **Franklin's grouse,** also **fool-hen.** 13" [32 cm]; males slaty to brownish black above, with red-orange eyebrow-comb, black beneath with white bars or flecks; others mottled red-brown (darker than ruffed grouse, redder than sooty grouse); tail black, with a row of white flecks on male. Very quiet vocally; courting males drum, in a series of low thumps, and can produce a pair of sharp "wing-claps" to assert territory. Mossy subalpine forest. Order Galliformes, Phasianidae. Color p 530.

The spruce grouse earns its nickname "fool hen" by being preposterously fearless around humans—vulnerable even to sticks and stones. Combine that unfortunate naiveté with tender, juicy, tasty flesh (at least in summer when the bird hasn't been eating conifer needles) and you get severely reduced numbers of spruce grouse.

Birds of the chickenlike order, Galliformes, feed and nest on the ground, and fly only in infrequent short bursts. They have under-sized wings and pale breast meat, indicating mostly fast-twitch muscles suited for brief, intense use. After the fowl has been flushed a few times in quick succession, these muscles are too oxygen-short to fly again until they are rested. Tirelessness in flight is more the norm among other kinds of birds which, being infrequent walkers, have dark (iron-rich) breast meat and pale and scanty leg meat. Even in winter, when the spruce grouse spends most of its time in trees, it mainly walks along the branches, getting added grip from special comblike tissue that grows along its feet in fall and falls off in spring.

In winter, spruce and blue grouse subsist entirely on conifer needles, a very poor diet but a plentiful one. To adapt, their intestine lengthens by about 40% each fall; they pack their digestive tracts full each evening and spend all night digesting, and still some 75% of the fibrous matter passes through undigested, creating a thick buildup under roost trees. They lose muscle mass inexorably on this diet, but are able to make it up on insects and berries in summer.

Ruffed Grouse

Bonasa umbellus (bo-**nay**-sa: bull; um-**bel**-us: umbrella). Also **drummer**. 14" [35 cm]; mottled gray-buff; tail red-brown or gray (two color phases) with heavy black band at tip and faint ones above; males have slight crest; black neck "ruff" is erected only in courtship display. No vocal mating call; distinctive "drumming" is common in late spring, occasional at other seasons; also an owl-like hoot is sometimes heard. Lower coniferous forests, usually near broadleaf trees. Order Galliformes, Phasianidae.

With sharp downstrokes of his wings while perched on a log, the male ruffed grouse makes a mysterious noise—an accelerating series of muffled thumps, known as drumming or booming. You can't tell what direction or distance it's coming from. Very low-pitched sounds carry farthest in forests, but sound nondirectional. An attracted female must have a tantalizing search in store for her.

At the end of it, she can watch his fantailed, ruff-necked dance, and then mate with him, but that's all he has to offer her; she will incubate and raise the young by herself. She nests on the ground, like other grouse, and trusts her excellent camouflage up until the last second, when you're about to step on her unaware. Then she flushes explosively, right under your nose. She may actually try to scare you away, if there are young to protect, or to draw you away from them with her famous broken wing routine. You are touched. She knows a thing or two about psychology.

Sandhill Crane

Grus canadensis (groose: the Roman term). 37" [93 cm]; ws 80" [2 m]; gray (sometimes rusty) with red forehead; long black bill; long legs; long neck held straight out front in flight; when standing, tailfeather "bustle" droops over rump. Very loud guttural "kraaaak" esp when flying in flock or dancing. Lake shores, beaver ponds, willow thickets in US. (In Canada: common on prairies but not mtns.) Order Gruiformes (Cranes). Color p 528.

The song and dance of this huge bird are impressive, albeit indelicate. In the dance, pairs bounce like balls several feet into the air, with wings half-spread, legs dangling, and voices full-throated. This is associated with courtship and nesting, but also performed at other times of year. For fun?

Sandhill cranes eat all kinds of small animals and mass quantities of roots and tubers, from submerged to dry.

Spotted Sandpiper

Actitis macularia (ak-**tie**-tiss: shore dweller; mac-you-**lair**-ia: spotted). Also **teeter-tail**. 6¼" [16 cm]; light brown above with white eye stripe and wing bars, white below; summer adults dark-spotted white below, with ± yellowish legs and bill; dips and teeters constantly when on the ground; flies with wings stiffly down-curved. Call a high clear "peep-peep," usually in flight or when landing. Single or in pairs, along streams and lakes, esp subalpine. Order Charadriiformes, Scolapacidae (Sandpiper family).

Like the dipper, which also feeds in frothy streams, the spotted sandpiper dips from the knees; it distinguishes itself in tipping forward and back, hence its nickname "teeter-tail." When threatened by a hawk it can dive like a dipper as well. In feeding it doesn't dive, but plucks prey from shallow water or the bank nearby, or sometimes from midair. Prey range in size up to trout fry, though insects predominate. No plant foods are eaten. Spotted sandpipers are widespread, breeding in almost any mountains north of Mexico and then wintering on seacoasts with reliably mild weather.

Sex roles are reversed in this and a few other sandpipers. The females are larger, more aggressive, and more dominant; they migrate to the breeding grounds first; establish and defend territories; court the males; initiate sex; do less than their share of sitting on the eggs; and do very little raising of the young brood aside from serving as a sentinel. They have less prolactin than the males, prolactin being a hormone that promotes parental caregiving. Many females are monogamous, but the fittest are serially polyandrous: a pair courts, bonds, builds a nest, and provisions it with four fertile eggs, and then she leaves that family and goes off to do it all over again with a second, a third, and even a fourth male in one season. It's different, but it makes sense. But......why sandpipers?

Killdeer

Charadrius vociferus (ka-**rad**-ree-us: the Greek term). 8" [25 cm]; brown back, rusty rump; white belly, breast. and neck with a heavy black neck ring and a second black ring across breast; another black band from black bill across eye and nape; red eye ring; tan legs. "Kil-dee," "kil-dee-dee," and other sharp calls; often heard at night. Low to mid-elev shores and fields, esp where gravelly. Order Charadriiformes (Shorebirds).

A gleaner of insects, the killdeer feeds and nests on the ground. To distract predators from the nest, a parent does the "broken wing" display; also chases trampling cattle by flying at their faces.

Wilson's Snipe

Gallinago delicata (gal-in-**ay**-go: chickenlike). =*G. gallinago,* **Common snipe** (our snipes were, until recently, included with Eurasian ones in this species). 9" [23 cm]; females larger; plump bird with 2½" [6 cm] long straight bill, brown, longitudinally striped on head and streaked on back; belly ± white. Grating "ski-ape" call when flushed; rarely seen until flushed. Marshy ground. Order Charadriiformes, Scolapacidae (Sandpiper family). Color p 528.

Male snipes (and sometimes females) have a flight display called "winnowing" or "whinnying," for its sound. The wind vibrates the spread tail feathers as the snipe plummets from 100' up [30 m], making a unique hollow, quavering "whoooo." This may go on all night during courtship (late May) but is also heard at other seasons and times of day. The slender, somewhat pliable bill probes for larvae, earthworms, and crustaceans in mud or shallow water.

Sora

Porzana carolina (por-**zah**-na: Italian word for crake, a relative). Also **sora rail.** 6¾" [17 cm]; thick stubby yellow bill, short upturned tail; looks plump from the side but is laterally compressed; gray-brown with white flecks lengthwise on back, crosswise on belly; black face, gray throat. Calls: a squeaky chirp; a rising "sor-UH;" a haunting nocturnal whinny—a rapid, then slowing, descent of notes more musical than the snipe's whinny. Widespread; rarely seen until flushed. Marshy ground; nests among cattails. Order Charadriiformes. Color p 528.

Despite clumsy-looking flight, soras migrate as far as South America.

California Gull and Ring-Billed Gull

Larus californicus and *L. delawarensis* (**lair**-us: the Roman term). 17" [43 cm], ws 52" [132 cm] (Ring-billed is slightly smaller); white exc top of wings, where black at tip and otherwise gray; yellow bill; California has greenish legs; immatures are speckly brownish with black tails. April to Nov. Mtn. lakes, town dumps, croplands. Order Laridae (Gulls and Terns).

The **California Gull** is the Utah State Bird, revered for consuming a plague of locusts that threatened the pioneer Mormons' crops. Wintering at the Coast but coming inland to breed colonially on islands in intermountain lakes and reservoirs, it owes much of its increase in numbers to the Bureau of Reclamation, which has multiplied the number of large lakes. From these, individuals make long foraging day-trips, and are often seen around alpine lakes. Gull species are mixed in the large colonies, and these shockingly opportunistic feeders commit a fair amount of nest predation upon their neighbors. Even the smaller **Ring-bill** can eat amazingly large prey, such as young ground squirrels. Canny gulls commonly live into their twenties.

Owls

Order Strigiformes, Strigidae (Typical owl family).

Great horned owl, *Bubo virginianus* (**bew**-bo: the Roman term; vir-jin-ee-**ay**-nus: of Virginia). Males 20" [50 cm], ws 55" [140 cm], females larger; large "ear" tufts or "horns," yellow eyes, and reddish tan facial ruff; white throat patch, otherwise finely barred and mottled gray-brown. Identifiable by long, low hoots (four to eight in series) heard year-round, but oftenest in Jan–Feb breeding season. Nocturnal; widespread and common in forests. Illustrated.

Great gray owl, *Strix nebulosa* (strix: as in "strident," Greek term imitating screech owl;.neb-you-**low**-sa: cloudy). 22" [55 cm], ws 60" [150 cm]; gray with vertically streaked breast; large facial ruff of many concentric rings; yellow eyes; no tufts. 4 to 6 low hoots evenly spaced. Nocturnal, rarely seen; in conifers.

Barred owl, *Strix varia* (vair-ia: variegated). Males 17" [43 cm], ws 44" [112 cm], females larger; dull brown, white-barred above and vertically flecked beneath; no "ear" tufts; dark eyes, yellow bill. 6 to 9 strident, reedy hoots, like a deep-voiced rooster. Nocturnal; in forest.

Boreal owl, *Aegolius funereus* (ee-**jo**-lius: Greek for some owl; few-**near**-ius: associated with death). 10" [25 cm], ws 24" [60 cm]; females 70% heavier; brown with white-spotted wings, white-streaked breast; obvious facial disk whitish-centered, blackish-rimmed; yellow bill and eyes. 8 to 15 rapid staccato hoots on one note. Nocturnal; mature spruce-fir forests.

Northern pygmy owl, *Glaucidium gnoma* (glaw-**sid**-ium: small owl, from "gleaming"; **no**-ma: gnome). Males 6" [15 cm]; ws 15" [38 cm]; females larger (owl-shaped but barely robin-sized); brown with slight pale barring, dark eye-like pair of spots on nape; eyes yellow; longish tail often held cocked; flight swift, darting, audible, with rapid beats—qualities atypical of owl flight. Steady hoots like whistling, a bit faster than 1 per sec. Primarily diurnal; ±open forest. Color p 531.

Owls have universally evoked human dread, superstition, and tall tales with their ghostly voices and silent, nocturnal predatory flight. Various parts of their anatomies found their way into talismans and potions medical and magical. Owl pellets seem almost ready-made talismans, while they provide naturalists with clear information on owl diets and distribution. Pellets are strikingly neat oblong bundles coughed up by owls to rid them of indigestible parts of small prey (and anything else) they swallow. Hard, angular parts are smoothly coated with fur. A spot with many pellets suggests an owl's roost on a limb above. (Hawks make similar, but smaller and fewer, pellets, eating their prey in smaller pieces and digesting it more completely.)

While all owls are formidable hunters, evolution has specialized them for a broad spectrum of habitats and roles, roughly paralleling the specializations of hawks and eagles. The ferocious little pygmy owl darts about catching insects and also birds up to and greater than its own size. Like some 40% of owl species, it hunts mainly by day. The nocturnal great horned owl can hunt mammals much heavier than itself, such as porcupines and large skunks, as well as almost any sort of creature down to beetles and worms. Where common, cottontails are its chief prey.

Owls' sensory adaptations are the stuff of legends. They have the broadest skulls of any birds, separating their eyes and their ears as widely as possible to maximize three-dimensionality of vision and directionality of hearing. Their ears pinpoint prey along the vertical axis as well as the horizontal, thanks to asymmetrical skulls. Great gray owls nab mice under many inches of snow, locating them by hearing alone, and barn owls can locate and catch them in absolute darkness. The facial ruff of feathers, plus ear flaps hidden under its outer rim, funnel sound to the highly developed inner ears. (The "ear tufts" or "horns" on top of some species' heads are unconnected with hearing, but serve expressive and decorative functions.) Owls' eyes are the most frontally directed of any bird's; this narrows the field of vision but makes nearly all of it three-dimensional. The squashed-down bill also expands the 3-D area. (Force your eyes far left, then right, to see the translucent profile of your nose on either side; only that portion—about a third—of your field of view lying between the "two noses" is seen in 3-D, by both eyes.) The owl's adaptive tradeoff—narrower field of view, but all of it three-dimensional—favors zeroing in on prey, not watching out for predators. To look around, an owl can twist its neck in a split second to anywhere within a 270° arc. The eyeballs, which don't rotate in their sockets (the neck does it all), have the optimal light-gathering shape: somewhat conical, like a deep television tube, with a thick powerful lens. The retina has a reflective backing (the kind that makes nocturnal mammals' eyes gleam in your headlights) behind the photoreceptor cells. These are almost all rods (high-sensitivity vision) and few cones (color vision). Owls' light perception threshold is between a thirty-fifth and a hundredth of ours. They have much sharper acuity for detail than we do, even by day, and a modicum of color perception as well.

Most owls practice utterly silent flight, a magical thing to witness. Their feathers are literally muffled, or damped, with a velvety surface and soft-fringed edges, incurring a tradeoff in efficiency and speed. Their flapping is slow and easy, thanks to low body weight per wing area. (With extra fluffy body plumage, owls are far slimmer and lighter than they look.) Silent flight enables owls in flight to hear the movements of small rodents, while in turn it keeps the sharp-eared prey in the dark over someone coming for dinner. This tempts one to fancy that mice live in utter ignorance of owls except as invisible agents of disappearances from the family.

Great horned owlets seem to attempt flight from the nest before

Raptors

Once long ago, the hawks, eagles, owls, and vultures comprised a single order, Raptores, from the Latin for "snatcher." When scientists learned that hawks and owls are not related, but merely resemble each other due to convergent evolution, they put owls in their own order, but "raptor" persevered as a casual term. Recently, New World vultures were moved to the stork order because they, too, seem to be unrelated birds with convergent similarities. Today the word "raptor" isn't very useful: some people include owls as raptors, and some don't, and who knows about vultures if they are neither predators nor hawk relatives?

It does still highlight a classic case of convergent evolution. Shared traits include heavy, hooked bills; large, muscular feet; and females larger than males. The value of the first two in predatory life is clear, but the third is puzzling. The female-to-male weight ratio averages as high as 3:2 in northern harriers and can reach 2:1 in golden eagles. The fact that hawks and owls separately evolved larger females, while equal or larger males are almost universal in the other bird orders, argues that the trait must offer a significant advantage to birds of prey. (But: see Sandpiper, p 428. As for the rest of the animal kingdom, groups with larger females predominate regardless of predatory status, but mammals—excepting hyenas—make an obvious case of larger males.)

Traits that Old World and New World vultures share include featherless heads, weak talons, hooked beaks, and soaring wings.

they are ready; landing on the forest floor, there they must reside until fully fledged. The parents continue to feed and guard them—aggressively in the case of the great horned. If you find an adorable, fluffy owlet on the ground, **back off**.

Barred owls were unknown in our range until 1912, and in the U.S. Rockies until the 1980s. They are spreading remarkably fast. It may have been global warming that enabled them to expand their range northward into the boreal forests, enabling a Saskatchewan end-run around the Great Plains by 1912.

The small, cryptically colored boreal owl is hard to spot while roosting, but if you do spot one it will let you approach quite close. Scientists who look for them find them, and think they probably live in most mature spruce-fir forests in our range, even though some range maps show none south of the 49th parallel. Further study may show boreal owls to be as dependent on old-growth in the Northern Rockies as spotted owls are in the coastal forest. Only old forests provide abundant voles combined with enough maneuvering room for owls to hunt voles.

Common Nighthawk

Chordeiles minor (cor-**die**-leez: evening dance; minor: lesser, a false name since this is now the larger species of nighthawk). 9" [23 cm], ws 23" [58 cm]; wings long, bent backward, pointed, falconlike; mottled brown/ black, with white wing-bar; males also have white throat and a narrow white bar across tail. Marshes and ± open areas; June–Sept. Caprimulgidae (Nightjar family). Color p 502.

No self-respecting nighthawk would be on the ground at dusk, when so many insects are on the wing. Like swifts and swallows, nighthawks prey on insects by flying around with their mouths open. Their flight is wild and erratic like a bat's, but swift like a falcon's—though they aren't really any kind of hawk at all. Males may interrupt their erratic feeding flights with long steep dives that bottom out abruptly with a terrific raspy, farting noise of air rushing through the wing feathers. This is their courtship. The vocal call is a softer, nasal beep repeated while feeding. Nighthawks nest on gravelly ground with very little construction work, and they have an odd style of perching, lying lengthwise along a branch. A population decline related to the general use of insecticides is suspected.

Birds

Swifts

Order Apodiformes, Apodidae (Swift family).

Vaux's swift, *Chaetura vauxi* (key-**too**-ra: hair-thin tail; **vawks**-eye: after Wm. S. Vaux, below). 4½" [12 cm]; slaty to brownish gray, somewhat paler beneath; wings long, pointed, gently curved; tail short, rounded. Staccato chipping. ID and MT from Bitterroots n; se BC. Color p 531.

White-throated swift, *Aeronautes saxatilis* (arrow naughties: flyer; sax-**at**-il-iss: rock dweller). 6½" [17 cm]; black with black/white underside; wings long, pointed, gently curved; tail long and forked. Rapid twittering. Around cliffs; ID, WY, and sw MT (rare at GNP).

Black swift, *Cypseloides niger* (sip-sel-**oy**-deez: like *Cypselus*, the Old World swift; **nye**-jer: black). 7" [18 cm]; black all over; wings long, pointed, gently curved; tail slightly forked. Call rarely heard. Subalpine; uncommon (best known from Banff and Jasper, and ranging s to Bitterroots). Illustrated.

Swifts may not be the swiftest after all, but they sure are impressive flyers, doing all their hunting, eating, and drinking aloft. They even mate in free-fall, disengaging after several seconds to resume flying. They often fly 600 miles [1,000 km] in a day—and make it look playful, interspersing short glides between spurts of flapping, and creating their famous optical illusion of flapping left and right wings alternately. Too bad most of this goes on too high up for us to see in detail.

"Strainers of aerial plankton," as Evelyn Bull so felicitously puts it, swifts can only maintain their high metabolisms on a steady supply of flying insects. Few insects fly during cold weather, so when it's cold and gray, swifts go cold and torpid (see page 344) or else fly off for a few days, as far as they need to to find sun. Nestlings remain torpid while Mom and Dad cavort in the sun. People have picked up

---

William Sansom Vaux, curator of the Philadelphia Museum of Natural History, never saw the Rockies, but his niece and nephews **Mary, George and William Vaux**, Jr. turned their vacations here into the first annual study of glacial retreat in North America. The idea began when Mary, on her second trip to B.C., was shocked by the visible retreat of the Illecillewaet Glacier. They photographed it every year from 1897 to 1913, developing their big glass plates in the Glacier House wine cellar, and contributed to the growing understanding of glaciated landscapes and glacial cycles. They were avid peak-baggers; B.C. has a Mt. Mary Vaux today. When the Smithsonian published her wildflower paintings in five volumes in 1925, reviews called her "the Audubon of American wild flowers."

torpid swifts and nighthawks, mistaking them for dead, and been startled when they fly off in perfect health as soon as they warm up.

Swifts' stiff, spine-tipped tail-feathers help them perch on sheer surfaces. Black swifts nest on cliffs, often behind waterfalls. Vaux's swifts glue their nests to the insides of hollow trees or chimneys. Southeast Asian "birdsnest soup" features filmy masses like boiled egg whites—the special saliva swifts work up for gluing nests.

Groups of Vaux's swifts numbering in the thousands congregate at a hollow tree or chimney over a period of a few weeks in fall, building up for massed migration. After sundown, they create a tornado-like vortex as they all fly into the roost. Their numbers are in a severe decline, as fewer and fewer big trees are allowed to remain standing in the forests as rot hollows them out.

Belted Kingfisher

Ceryle alcyon (**ser**-i-lee **al**-see-on: two Greek terms for kingfishers). 12" [30 cm]; head looks oversized because of large bill and extensive crest of feathers; blue-gray with white neck and underparts and (females only) reddish breast band. Call a long, peculiar rattle. Along streams, year-round. Alcedinidae (Kingfisher family). Color p 530.

The Greeks had a myth that the Halcyon, a kind of bird we presume was a kingfisher, floated its nest on the waves of the sea while incubating and hatching the young. Hence "halcyon days" are a fortuitous respite from the storms of life.

Our kingfishers, in real life, raise their young amid a heap of re-gurgitated fish bones at the end of a hole in a mud bank. Is "nest" too sweet a term for such debris? They look for their prey—fish, cray-fish, waterbugs and larvae—from a perch over a stream or occa-sionally a lake. (They can also hunt from a hover where branches are in short supply, as is rarely the case on our streams.) After diving and catching a fish, they often return to thrash it to death against their branch before swallowing it headfirst. Fishermen have long resented kingfishers' success rate, but statistically the birds are unlikely to re-duce trout numbers significantly. The kingfisher population has plummeted during the advance of civilization; there was once a pair of kingfishers for virtually every creek in the U.S.

Hummingbirds

Order Apodiformes, Trochilidae
(Hummingbird family).

Calliope hummingbird, *Stellula calliope* (stell-you-la:
starlet; ca-**lie**-o-pee: a Muse). 2¾" [7 cm]; bronze-green
above, white below with reddish tinges; throat has long deep purple streaks on
adult males, small dark speckles on others.
Meadows, low shrublands, alpine in
Aug; summer. Color p 530.

Rufous hummingbird, *Selasphorus rufus* (se-
lass-for-us: lightbearer; **roo**-fus: red). 3½" [9 cm];
males red-brown with iridescent red throat patch,
and some white on belly and green on wings and
crown; females and juveniles mostly green with some
reddish tinge near base of tail. Flight produces a deep
dragonflylike hum. Nesting Jasper to GNP (MT) in summer; migrate through WY mainly Aug–Sept.

Attractiveness to hummingbirds is the redeeming virtue of bright
red and yellow colors on hiking gear. My red bootlaces alone draw
several hummers a day in the alpine country in July; they pause only
an instant to discover my boots are no bed of columbine. I can only
hope the pleasure they bring me doesn't cost them much.

Most bright red flowers that bear nectar at the base of tubes 1–2"
long [2–5 cm] are adapted to pollination by hummingbirds. Columbine and skyrocket are stereotypical, and are certainly beloved of
hummers, but various pinkish to red flowers are also important nectar sources: currants, fireweed, paintbrush, lilies, fool's-huckleberry.
Rufous males often jump the gun in migrating north, and have to
make up for the lack of nectar by gleaning aphids, hawking midges,
and sucking sap from sapsucker wells.

The Rufous ranges farther north than any other hummer—
Valdez, Alaska—and the Calliope migrates farther per gram of flesh
than any other warm-blooded creature. At one tenth of an ounce [3
g], it is the smallest U.S. bird. Both of these species tend to migrate
in a counterclockwise loop, north along the Pacific, then inland in
summer, and south along the Rockies to central Mexico.

The age-old mystery of how birds navigate on long migrations
is finally beginning to yield. By day, they orient themselves by the polarity of sunlight (which they see, somehow) and use that to recali-
brate their sense of the earth's magnetic field. (See p 458.) By night,
which is when small birds tend to migrate, they use both the stars

and the magnetic field. Hummingbird individuals seem to adhere rigidly to their route maps, which must reside solely in their genes.

The smallest of all birds, hummers have frantic metabolisms in common with shrews, the smallest mammals. Ounce for ounce, a hummingbird flying has ten times the caloric requirement of a person running—and we don't have to spend all day running, while hummingbirds do spend most of their waking hours flying around in search of nectar for those calories. Daily, they consume up to half their body weight in sugar. Before migrating, they need lots of extra carbohydrates to convert into fats. Their whirring flight, suggestive of a huge dragonfly, does in fact work more like insect flight than like that of other birds, and allows stationary and backward hovering, but no gliding. The wings beat many times faster than other birds' thanks to an extremely shortened wing with long feathers; there's very little mass to flap. Hummers' hyperkinetic days are complemented by torpid nights (no, not torrid nights), with temperature and metabolism sharply lowered (see page 344).

Hummingbirds are belligerent toward their own and larger species: calliopes have been seen dive-bombing red-tailed hawks. Harassment of large birds by small ones is called "mobbing." There are records of predators actually being killed by mobs of smaller birds, but single hummingbirds don't seem like a threat. Still, studies have shown that small birds that mob—even when it's two or three little birds harassing a predator twenty times their size—are preyed upon less than those that don't. Possibly the predator conserves energy by saving its killer moves for unwary prey.

Rufous hummingbirds' territoriality seems to concern food rather than sex. (Hummers don't pair up anyway, but mate freely.) Both sexes stake out their patch of the nectar resource even during two-week refueling stops during migration, and defend it with the same tall elliptical flights they use for courtship: a courting rufous male swoops around and around in an ellipse hundreds of feet high, at the lowest point passing at high speed only inches from the demure object of his attentions, simultaneously eliciting a shrieking noise from his wings. Males flash their "gorgets" (iridescent, erectile throat patches) both in courtship and in aggression.

---

*The smaller the warm-blooded body, the more energy is required to keep it warm. Heat is produced in proportion to size (i.e., volume) but is dissipated into the air in proportion to surface area. Reducing the length and width of a body by half, for example, divides its surface area by four (2×2) and its volume by eight ($2 \times 2 \times 2$), thus doubling the rate of heat loss.

Woodpeckers

Order Piciformes, family Picidae. Color p 531.

Hairy woodpecker, *Picoides villosus* (pic-**oy**-deez: like *Pica*—a Roman term for both magpies and woodpeckers; vil-**oh**-sus: woolly). 7½" [17.5 cm]; black and white exc (males only) a small red patch on peak of head; wings barred. Widespread in ± wooded habitats, esp with aspens.

Downy woodpecker, *P. pubescens* (pew-**bes**-enz: fuzzy). 5¾" [14 cm]; like Hairy only smaller. Common in ± wooded habitats; less so in Can.

Northern flicker, *Colaptes auratus* (co-**lap**-teez: pecker; aw-**ray**-tus: golden). 11" [27 cm]; gray-brown with black-spotted paler belly, black-barred back, black "bib," and red to orange crown, underside of wings and tail, and sometimes moustache (males only). Varied calls: one a flat-pitched rattle. Semiopen habitats. Illustrated at left.

Three-toed woodpecker, *P. tridactylus.* 8" [20 cm]; black/white barred back and sides, black wings; white belly, face black with white streaks from eye and from bill; male has yellowish crown. Conifer forests with bark beetles; moves in *en masse* a few weeks after forest fire (nipping at the heels of bark beetles).

Pileated woodpecker, *Dryocopus pileatus* (dry-**oc**-o-pus: tree sword; pie-lee-ay-tus: crested). 15" [38 cm]; all black exc bright red, large, pointed crest, black/white-streaked head with (males only) red moustache, and white under-wing markings visible only in flight; drumming very loud, slow, irregular; call a loud rattling shriek with a slight initial rise in pitch. Deep forest with many standing dead trees or snags; from Bitterroots n and w. Illustrated opposite.

Woodpeckers are the one kind of non-songbird that often flocks with songbirds. Woodpeckers resemble songbirds (pages 442–62) but differ in several specializations. Most have two front and two rear toes, though the three-toed is missing one rear toe. Strong sharp claws on 2-and-2-toed feet, plus short stiff tail feathers, give them the grip and the bracing they need for hammering the full force of their bodies into a tree. Naturally, they also have adamantine chisel-like beaks, and thick shock-absorbing skulls to prevent boxers' dementia. Before diving into work on a tree, they listen for the minute rustlings of their insect prey boring around under the bark. Insect larvae and adults provide the bulk of their diets, seeds and berries the rest. Females are smaller and thinner-billed than males. They excavate less than males, foraging often by prying bark up, and so exploit a slightly different resource than their mates. For snatching grubs out of their tunnels, the woodpecker has a barb-tipped tongue much longer than its head. The tongue shoots out and then pulls back into a tiny tubular cavity looping around the circumference of the skull.

Though jackhammering for food is the woodpecker norm, and

was likely the first task woodpecking evolved for, not all woodpeckers forage that way. Flickers peck for insects in the soil or catch them in midair, three-toed woodpeckers pry the bark up, and sapsuckers (below) wound trees to lure surface bugs. But all woodpeckers (or at least these woodpeckers) peck wood for two other vital tasks. First, they chop large squarish holes for their nests, padding them with a few of the chips. Such nests are dry and easy to defend, allowing prolonged rearing—advantages that have led several other species to depend on abandoned woodpecker holes for their nests. Second, they drum—the classic woodpecker drumroll—on resonant trees to assert territory or to point out a nest site to a prospective mate. (When you hear slower, irregular tapping on trees, that's either foraging or spousal communication.) Not that either sex lacks a voice. Flickers vocalize diversely and often; white-headeds and downies rarely.

The pileated, our largest woodpecker, has an especially strident and impressive call like a harsh, maniacal laugh, which it seems to use when disturbed—such as whenever you or I come around. Once you know the pileated's "laugh" you'll know, when you hear it, to pause and look for a glimpse of one of our flashiest birds.

Pileateds eat ants almost exclusively, and often chop many inches deep into rotten wood to dig out carpenter ant nests. Each bird requires lots of dead trees, so the species dwindled as old-growth forests vanished from most of the continent. It was also hunted. More recently it has recovered, and is quite willing to brave urban woods if they have enough snags. A few pileateds have become pests, chopping away at house and phone-pole timbers.

Red-Naped Sapsucker

*Sphyrapicus nuchalis** (sfie-ra-**pie**-cus: hammer woodpecker; noo-**kay**-liss: nape—). 7¾" [18 cm]; sexes alike; head has three red patches—forehead, throat, and back of crown—and is otherwise black/white-striped; back and wings black with white bars and rump; belly pale, dull yellowish. Taps in a syncopated rhythm, but does not jackhammer, on trees. Calls are catlike mews and "cherrrrs." Forest, esp with aspens. Picidae (Woodpecker family). Color p 531.

---

*Recently separated from the Yellow-bellied Sapsucker, *S. varius*, of the Plains (and Canadian Rockies) and the Red-breasted Sapsucker, *S. ruber*, of the Pacific Coast. The three hybridize where ranges overlap.

Neat horizontal rings of ¼" [6 mm] holes drilled through tree bark are the work of **sapsuckers**, which drill these "wells," leave, and come back another day. Time allows sap not only to flow, but also sometimes to ferment, and certainly to go to work as bait for adult insects, which figure even more than sap in the sapsucker's diet. Butterflies and moths in experiments prefer their foods fermented, and inebriated behavior has been observed in butterflies and sapsuckers alike.

Damage to the bark is insufficient to kill the tree by girdling it, but any breaching of the bark increases the odds for fungal diseases to invade. On balance, though, sapsuckers are good for trees, because they're leading predators of spruce budworm moths, which are major pests. They can nab insects in midair, glean ants from bark crevices, and vary their diets with berries.

Other birds also dine at these sap wells, which are especially critical to the rufous hummingbird when it finds itself too early, during northward migration, for adequate nectar supplies.

Extra-Pair Goings-On

> "Birds don't do it,
> bees don't do it,
> WE are the only ones
> that fall in love."

Sly and Robbie and Bootsy showed a better grasp of bird behavior in 1987 than Cole Porter in 1928. The DNA police have been looking into avian paternity, and they've demolished the faithful chirping couples stereotype which inspired centuries of bad verse. In many bird species a male may help build the nest, sit on the eggs, defend the territory, and/or bring food to the young, but that species' "social monogamy" rating bears little correlation with that male's likelihood of being the sire of all the young in that nest. There's a whole lot going on on the sly.

Even more interesting than the rate of EPCs (extra-pair copulations) is the diversity of patterns among closely related species, or even between populations of the same species. For example, the extant study of cliff swallows found that 2% of fertilizations were extra-pair, whereas the study of tree swallows found 44%. The EPC picture in swallow colonies is further complicated by a great deal of "intraspecific brood parasitism," in which a female waits for a neighboring nest to be momentarily unattended, and then slips in and lays an egg. Her victims will feed her young along with their own. This gets worse: a male slips into an unattended nest and rolls an egg out, to its doom, perhaps to make

Swallows

Order Passeriformes, family Hirundinidae.

Violet-green swallow, *Tachycineta thalassina* (tacky-sin-ee-ta: fast moving; tha-**lass**-in-a: sea green). 4¾" [12 cm]; dark with green/violet iridescence above; white below, extending around eyes and up sides of rump to show as two white spots when seen from above; wings backswept and pointed, tail shallowly forked. Various high tweets. Open areas; in flocks; spring and summer.

Tree swallow, *T. bicolor* (by-color: 2-colored). 5" [13 cm]; iridescent blue-black above, white below (not extending above eye or rump); otherwise like violet-green swallow. Open areas at lower elevs. Color p 531.

Cliff swallow, *Petrochelidon pyrrhonota* (pet-ro-kel-id-on: rock swallow; per-o-**no**-ta: red back). =*Hirundo pyrrhonota*. 5" [13 cm]; blackish wings and tail, whitish below, with cinnamon red cheeks and paler rust-red rump and forehead; wings backswept and pointed, tail square to barely notched.

A swallow's flight is graceful, slick, and fast (though less swift than a swift's). A swallow's swallow, or rather its gape, is striking. The wide, weak jaws are held open almost 180° while the swallow knifes back and forth through the air intercepting insects. Lightning-quick visual and neck muscle reflexes, and ultraviolet vision that may make insect wings glitter, aid in gathering up to fifty live insects, which they can hold in a single mouthful. One expert swears he has seen them jerking their heads this way and that, intercepting raindrops.

Swallows generally nest in large colonies. Cliff swallows build striking gourd-shaped mud nests on cliffs or under bridges or eaves. *Tachycineta* swallows use ready-made crevices and tree holes.

---

room for his mate to lay an egg there, or perhaps to keep his female neighbor receptive to his seductions. Either way, it's his genes.

Diverse strategies are being pursued here, and there are ongoing academic imbroglios—replete with anthropomorphic terms like "harem," "divorce," and "cuckold"—over how to interpret them. There are male strategies and female strategies; the latter are more likely the key, since females apparently control the fertilization success of copulations. One scientist who watched black-capped chickadees in a small area over a 20-year period witnessed thirteen extra-pair trysts; in each case the female actively sought out a male of higher social rank than her own mate. A later study using DNA fingerprinting corroborated his observations. A study in one warbler species found that males with larger song repertoires were able to seduce more females, and that the females were getting what they were looking for: fitter genes, as measured by the likelihood of offspring returning to breed a year later.

Olive-sided Flycatcher

Contopus cooperi (**cont**-o-pus: short foot; **coo**-per-eye: after Jas. or Wm. Cooper). 6¼" [16 cm]; olive-gray with pearly white smear down throat and breast; white downy tufts on lower back visible esp in flight. Order Passeriformes, Tyrannidae (Tyrant flycatcher family).

The olive-sided's song, usually sung from some conifer pinnacle, is a treat. Its been transcribed as "THREE cheers," "Quick!...FREE beer," or "Tuck...THREE bears." These flycatchers summer throughout our forests, clear-cuts, and timberlines. They eat winged insects, spotting individuals from their perch and darting out to snatch them. In contrast to the continual seining method of swifts and swallows, which nets small insects, flycatchers eat medium-sized insects, including bees.

Willow Flycatcher

Empidonax traillii (em-**pid**-o-nax: gnat king; **trail**-ee-eye: after Thomas Traill, a friend of J. J. Audubon). 4¾" [12 cm]; olive brown above with 2 dull wing-bars; pale yellowish olive beneath; two-toned bill; no conspicuous eye-ring. Summer; streamside and wetland brush; common but inconspicuous. Tyrannidae.

It's next to impossible to identify *Empidonax* birds in the bush. They are hard to see, staying camouflaged among foliage. This one has a fairly recognizable song, though: a sneezelike "fitz-bew." An identical bird (though with a less sneezy song) in the Canadian parks might be an alder flycatcher, *E. alnorum.*

Horned Lark

Eremophila alpestris (air-em-**ah**-fill-a: loving lonely places; al-**pes**-tris: alpine). 6½" [16 cm]; pinkish brown back; ± white underparts; sharp black breastband and cheek smear; tiny "horns" (feather tufts) above eyes may be visible; white outer tail feathers show in flight. Nests and forages on ground, walking (not hopping); grassland, steppe, overgrazed rangeland, tundra; summer; also year-round on lowlands. Song a long, tinkling twitter prefaced by a few ascending notes, mainly before sunrise. Alaudidae (Lark family).Color p 532.

This male's courtship display is famous. He spirals steeply to several hundred feet [30 m] up, then circles round and round singing his faint tinkle, then plummets with wings held to his sides. One song type, the "recitative," lasts several minutes.

Warbling Vireo

Vireo gilvus (veer-ee-oh: green; jil-vus: pale yellow). 4¾" [12 cm]; greenish gray above; heavy white eyebrow, no eye-ring; solid gray wings; white belly, ± yellowish flanks; generally slow-moving. Song a 2–4-second twitter with final upbeat accented. Forest, esp riparian; May-Sept. Vireonidae (Vireo family).

Female and male vireos take turns warming the eggs. The nest is a small cup of grasses lined with lichens, moss, or feathers, often decorated outside with bark, petals or catkins held on with spider webbing. It dangles from a fork in branches high up in a tree.

Steller's Jay

Cyanocitta stelleri (sigh-an-o-sit-a: blue jay; stell-er-eye: after Georg Steller, below). 11" [28 cm]; deep ultramarine blue with ± black shoulders and dramatically crested head. Widespread near conifers. Corvidae (Crow family).

Birds of North America describes the following repertoire of vocalizations documented by students of the Steller's jay: creak; squawk; growl; rattle; song; Ut; Ow; Wah; Wek; Aap; Tjar; Tee-ar; guttural notes; and mimicry. Mimicry includes an uncanny imitation of a red-tailed hawk's scream. This presumably deceives other birds into clearing out while the jay feeds, but perhaps it sometimes warns of an actual hawk. Jays and crows are the birds most often seen harassing or "mobbing" birds of prey—a defense of smaller birds against larger ones (see page 437). This jay is omnivorous, smart, and aggressive—traits that run in the crow family. It often robs the caches of its cousin, Clark's nutcracker.

"Blue jay" in Rocky Mountain parlance refers to Steller's, the Provincial Bird of British Columbia. The smaller, paler Blue Jay proper, *C. cristata*, is a rare visitor here from the East.

Georg Steller was the first European naturalist-explorer on northeast Pacific shores. A German, he crossed Siberia to accompany Danish Captain Vitus Bering on a Russian ship built and launched from Kamchatka in 1741. They were just east of present-day Cordova, Alaska when they turned around late that year, and they didn't quite make it back to Kamchatka. Marooned for a terrible scurvy-ridden winter on small, rocky Bering Island, the Captain and many of the crew died. Steller survived, but took to drink and died in Siberia without ever reaching Europe again.

Common Raven

Corvus corax (**cor**-vus: the Roman term, from **cor**-ax: the Greek term, imitating raven's voice). 21" [53 cm], ws 48" [120 cm]; black with purple-green iridescence, and shaggy grayish ruff at throat; bill heavy; tail long, flared then tapered; alternates periods of flapping and flat-winged soaring. Calls include a throaty croak and a deep "tock" like a big wood block. Forest and alpine. Corvidae (Crow family).

You can tell Raven from little sibling Crow by Raven's greater size, heavier bill, ruffed throat, more prolonged soaring, and by its voice, an outrageously hoarse guttural croak rather than a nasal "caw." At timberline you are more likely to see ravens. Their courtship flights in spring are a sight to remember: they do barrel rolls or chaotic tumbles while plummeting, then swoop, then hang motionless, all the while exercising their vocabularies. The ensuing family group—four or five young are flying by June, typically—may stay together through the young ones' first winter, and may flock with other families. The nest is high, solid, and cozy, perhaps lined with deer hair, but filthy, smelly, and often flea-ridden. Ravens can eat anything crows can, and then some. Groups of them can take live prey up to the size of hares.

Ravens were once abundant throughout the West, flocking around bison herds to eat carrion. The bison resource was deleted, countless ravens were killed with poisoned bait left out for wolves and coyotes, and many were shot on purpose. Perceived threats to agriculture, though mostly imaginary, were deeply ingrained in European culture. No dummies, ravens became shy, retreating to remote deserts and mountains.

Ravens were valued members of Native American villages. Their thievery of food was tolerated; killing them was taboo. Raven was at once a trickster and a powerful, aggressive, chiefly figure—much as Coyote was in other tribes. He was a Creator in origin myths. His croaks were prophetic; a person who could interpret them would become a great seer. To inculcate prophetic powers in a chosen newborn, the Kwakiutl fed its afterbirth to the ravens. On other continents, a mythic view of ravens and crows as powerful, knowing, and usually a bit sinister is almost universal. French peasants once thought that bad priests became ravens, and bad nuns, crows.

The raven is the largest of all Perching birds* (Order Passeriformes). This is the most recently evolved avian order, with by far the greatest number of species, which indicates success and rapid evolution. The evolution of seed plants was accompanied by the specialization of seed eaters—perching birds and rodents, mainly—and a wave of predators specializing in eating seed-eaters. The raven rides the crest of both waves: it eats rodents, nestlings, and eggs, as well as seeds. By some accounts it is the most advanced bird.

Bernd Heinrich, who wrote a whole book on raven intelligence, casts doubt on one tale often repeated as proof of it—their teaming up to heist meat from coyotes—but he believes (as many native tribes do) that ravens will lead a wolf or a human hunter to prey, on the odds that they will end up with the scraps. They certainly follow wolf packs. Heinrich devises ingenious tests of raven intelligence. For example, he learned that they relocate their cached seeds under snow purely by strength of memory, not smell. Moreover, they keep a corner of their eye open for where other ravens are caching seeds, and try to rob those caches first. To avoid being robbed in turn, they fly much farther before caching when other ravens are within view.

His book *Ravens in Winter* recounts his studies of why ravens frequently bring ravenous crowds to share in a feast of carrion. He concluded that pairs of adult ravens that find carrion will naturally try to keep it to themselves, and can defend it against one or a few ravens. Younger ravens, in order to stay fed through winter, need to collect gangs of their peers, forcing the older dominants to share. Secondarily, the gangs offer the subadults opportunities to attract mates by demonstrating dominance and food-providing ability. Choosing a husband is serious business, he points out, since ravens mate for life, live so long, and depend utterly on the male to provision the nest for a critical month in the life of each brood.

A 1911 paper on animal longevity reported a captive raven living 69 years, which if true would easily be the record for a bird. A raven in the wild would be lucky to reach twenty.

---

* Perching birds are also known as "songbirds." Both perching and singing are characteristic of this order but are also done, depending on how you define them, by many other birds. "Perching" becomes definitive by virtue of one feature—the foot with one long rear toe opposing three front toes.

American Crow

Corvus brachyrhynchos (**cor**-vus: raven; brak-i-**rink**-os: short beak). 17" [43 cm]; black with blue-purple-green iridescence; tail squared-off; rarely glides more than 2–3 seconds at a time. Mainly lowlands. Corvidae (Crow family).

Crows are fond of farmlands, and are most often seen here along lowland streams and meadows, or in partly deciduous forest. In our mountain wilderness they are less common than ravens, and seem to avoid potential habitat, such as Jackson Hole, when it has lots of ravens. Crows scavenge carrion, garbage, fruit, snails, grubs, insects, frogs, and eggs and nestlings from birds' nests. Species as large as ducks, gulls, and falcons may be victims, and some songbirds count crows among their major enemies.

Clark's Nutcracker

Nucifraga columbiana (new-**sif**-ra-ga: nut breaker; co-lum-be-**ay**-na: of the Columbia R.). 11" [28 cm]; pale gray (incl crown and back) with white-marked black wings and tail (white outer tail-feathers and rear wing-patch); long thin grayish bill. Call a harsh "kraaa, kraaa." Subalpine habitats with whitebark, limber, or lodgepole pines. Order Passeriformes, Corvidae. Color p 532.

Flashy black/white wings and tail distinguish Clark's nutcracker from the more numerous gray jay. Like the jay, the nutcracker has been known as the "camp robber," but mainly in California where there are none of the nervy jays that better deserve the name.

Clark's nutcrackers and whitebark pines (page 54) are one of the niftiest examples of mutualism. (And four similar Eurasian pines coevolved similarly with several species of corvids; several other pines, including our limber pine, also depend on corvids but are less specialized.) Whitebark pine cones do not open by themselves. They are 100% dependent on animals to pick them open, and they attract animals to do so with big, high-fat, high-protein seeds, or "nuts." Clark's nutcrackers oblige, collecting the nuts compulsively, selecting the best ones (most nutritious and most viable), eating some on the spot and burying the rest to eat later.

A nutcracker can pinpoint most of its cache locations—thousands of them each year—as much as nine months later. Often these are in the middle of expanses of snow. The bird locates them by triangulating (probably using its built-in magnetic compass, page 458) from landmarks like crags and lone trees. Still, some seeds are misplaced, and some never needed. They are thus planted, often many miles from their source—a great advantage to the pines, especially in recolonizing large severe burns or recovering range given up during the Ice Age. The strong-flying nutcrackers have a foraging range of 15 miles [24 km] from their caches, and can carry 150 whitebark pine seeds in sublingual pouches that bulge conspicuously at the throat. Lodgepole pine seeds are eaten, too. Poor pine seed crop years cause irruptions of nutcrackers into far-flung lowlands in search of substitute fare, and the decline in whitebark pines due to white pine blister rust has caused a great decline in the number of nutcrackers.

Gray Jay

Perisoreus canadensis (pair-i-**sor**-ee-us: "I-heap-up"). Also **Canada jay, camp robber, whiskey-jack.** 10" [25 cm]; fluffy pale gray with dark brownish gray wings, tail, rump and (variably) nape and crown; short, ± black bill; juveniles all dark gray exc pale cheek-streak. Calls a whistled "Whee-oh," and various others; flight exceptionally silent. Deep forest and timberline, often with spruces. Order Passeriformes, Corvidae.

Like their close relatives the crows, jays seem coarse and vulgar but are intelligent, versatile and successful. Their voices are harsh and noisy, but capable of extreme variety and accurate mimicry of other birds. Equally versatile in feeding, ours eat mainly conifer seeds, berries and insects, but also relish meat when they can scrounge some up or kill a small bird or rodent. Gray jays, or "camp robbers," were known for thronging around logging-camp mess halls; a trapper would sometimes find them nipping at a carcass while he was still skinning it. You will find them just as interested in your lunch, and bold enough to snatch proffered food from your fingertips. Their nonchalance reminds skiers that winter here is perfectly livable for the well-adapted. Gray jays and Clark's nutcrackers are so comfortable in the cold that they nest and incubate their young with plenty of snow still on the ground—or even on their heads. Gray jays are food storers with a unique adaptation to snowy habitats—saliva that coagulates in contact with air. This enables them to glue little seed bundles in bark crevices or foliage, up where they won't get buried in snow. Food storing as a winter strategy is common in the crow and chickadee families, but apparently in no other birds. It entails phenomenal ability to remember exact locations—feats of memory that humans could not match. The gray jay at least avoids the added difficulty of finding items buried in snow.

Black-Billed Magpie

Pica pica (**pie**-ca: Roman word for magpie). 16" [40 cm]; black with white belly, wingbars, and wing undersides that flash in flight; very long tail glitters with green iridescence, esp in males. Harsh calls include a whining "mack," a chattering babble directed at larger beasts, and a soft song during pair activities. Deciduous or open woods; streamsides; farmland; ± year-round, but migrates to coastal lowlands from some BC mtns. Corvidae (Crow family).Color p 531.

More beautiful than its jay and crow cousins, the magpie, like them, is omnivorous, adaptable, smart, aggressive, noisy, and unloved by farmers. In days of old, magpies flocked around bison herds, picking parasites from woolly backs. To Lewis and Clark they were relentless camp robbers, but after decades of bison genocide and magpie genocide, magpies became relatively few and wary.

As for picking parasites from big beasts, ecologists no longer assume that these "cleaner symbioses" are always mutually beneficial. Magpies pick maggots from sores on livestock, but also pick at the sores. They follow moose and pick winter ticks from them, but also cache many live ticks on soil, where they lay eggs and multiply. Moose carrion is as important as ticks as a winter food for magpies, so it's in their interest for ticks to kill more moose, not fewer.

Mobbing behavior (page 437) reaches a peak of audacity in the magpie. One magpie pecks at the tail of an eagle with prey, while others stand by to snatch the prey when the distracted eagle drops it; or the eagle may end the harassment by flying off with just part of his meal. Young male magpies form gangs, and are socially dominant over adult males (able to chase them from carrion) probably due to strength in numbers. Then there are the mysterious magpie "funerals." A magpie finds a magpie corpse, calls loudly, and within minutes dozens of raucous magpies congregate, perching in trees and flying down two or three at a time to walk around the corpse, vocalizing. Sometimes they even do this around a few magpie feathers.

The males are family men, building a huge stick nest in riparian brush or trees, and bringing home much of the bacon; but they aren't particularly faithful, and are generally "randy" (the word used by Craig Birkhead, who wrote the book on magpies.) They have a good ability to bury food and remember the location; but other magpies (especially females) often rob caches, utilizing their sense of smell—a sense that is poor to lacking in most birds.

Birds of North America asserts that our magpies, *P. pica hudsonia*, are less closely related to Eurasian magpies, *P. pica*, than to the yellow-billed magpie of California, and should be a species all their own.

American Dipper

Cinclus mexicanus (**sink**-lus: Greek word for it). Also **water ouzel**. 5¾" [14.5 cm]; slate gray all over, scarcely paler beneath, often with white eye-ring; tail short; feet yellow. In or very close to cold mtn streams. Order Passeriformes, Cinclidae (Dipper family). Color p 532.

It's no wonder that dippers make a strong impression on campers throughout the West, considering how much trouble campers have keeping warm. Winter and summer, snow, rain, or shine, dippers spend most of their time plunging in and out of frigid, frothing torrents, plucking out invisible objects—actually aquatic insects such as dragonfly and caddis fly larvae, and sometimes tiny fish. Somehow they walk on the bottom, gripping with their big feet. They can also swim with their wings, quickly reverting to flight if they get swept out of control downstream. They can dive to considerable depths in mountain lakes, and occasionally they forage on snowfields. They show little interest in drying off. Even in flight they are usually in the spray zone over a stream, and they often nest behind waterfalls. In August they have a flightless molt period when swimming becomes their only escape from predators. They never really get soaked to the skin, thanks to extremely dense body plumage and extra glands to keep it well oiled.

No, "dipper" doesn't imply shyness toward water, not in these birds. The name refers to their odd, jerky genuflections repeated as often as once a second while standing, and accompanied by blinking of their flashy white eyelids. Their call, "dipit dipit," is forceful enough to carry over the din of the creek. Even in midwinter they occasionally break into song. Both sexes are virtuosi, with long, loud, lyrical, bell-like, and extremely varied songs.

Winter Wren

Troglodytes troglodytes (tra-**glod**-i-teez: cave dweller, a misleading name). 3¼" [8 cm]; finely barred reddish-brown all over; tail rounded, very short, often (as in all wrens) held upturned at 90° to line of back. Near the ground in forest with dense herb layer, from c MT n; year-round. Order Passeriformes, Troglodytidae (Wren family).

The **winter wren** is conspicuous mainly by its song, a prolonged, varied, often-repeated, virtuoso sequence of high trills and chatters. It moves in a darting, mouselike manner, eats insects, maintains a low profile among the brush, and goes to great lengths to keep its nest a secret. Several extra nests are often built just as decoys, and the real occupied nest has a decoy entrance, much larger than the real entrance but strictly dead-end. Real and decoy nests are camouflaged to boot.

In Europe, this species (the only native wren) has long been familiar around cities and towns, whereas on this continent it favors undisturbed habitat. Apparently, adaptation to civilization is possible even for a species that has resisted it for dozens of generations.

Rock Wren

Salpinctes obsoletus (sal-**pink**-tease: trumpeter; ob-so-**lee**-tus: dull). 4¾" [12 cm]; gray-brown, sparsely speckled with pale; ocher-tinged rump; white breast with fine streaking; white belly white with yellow flanks; tail much longer than winter wren; dips body frequently. Announces song with a few strong notes, follows with varied buzzes and trills. April to Oct; rocky canyons. Order Passeriformes, Troglodytidae (Wren family).

Brown Creeper

Certhia americana (**serth**-ia: the Greek term). 4¾" [12 cm]; mottled brown above, white beneath; long down-curved bill. Call a single very high, soft sibilant note. On tree trunks in older forest, year-round, widespread but inconspicuous. Order Passeriformes, Certhiidae (Creeper family).

You probably won't see a brown creeper unless you happen to catch its faint, high call, and then patiently let your eyes scour nearby bark. (Many of us are literally deaf to its call, if our hearing is high-frequency-challenged—a defect associated with males and with rock and roll.) This well camouflaged full-time bark dweller gleans its insect prey from bark crevices, and nests behind loose bark. In contrast to nuthatches, which usually walk down tree trunks, the creeper spirals up them, propping itself with stiff tail feathers like a woodpecker's. Crevices approached from above and below would reveal different types of prey, putting creepers and nuthatches in different ecological niches.

Nuthatches

Sitta spp. (sit-a: the Roman term). Order Passeriformes, Sittidae (Nuthatch family).

Red-breasted nuthatch, *S. canadensis*. 4" [10 cm]; blue-gray above, pale reddish below, with white throat and eyebrow, black (males) or dark gray crown and eye-streak. Conifer forest. Illustrated at left, and color p 532.

White-breasted nuthatch, *S. carolinensis* (carol-in-en-sis: of the Carolinas). 5" [12.5 cm]; blue-gray above, white below (may have a little red under tail), with black (males) or gray crown, but all-white face. Deciduous or pine woodland.

Nuthatches are known for walking head first down tree trunks, apparently finding that way just as rightside up as the other. They glean insects from the bark, and eat seeds in fall through spring. They nest in dead snags, quite inconspicuous but identifiable by their odd habit of smearing pitch around the nest hole. Even in deep wilderness they aren't shy, and draw our attention with their penetrating little call, a tinny "ank" or "nyank." They are year-round residents, but may move to different elevations or subregions when cone crops or other conditions are poor.

Chickadees

Poecile spp. (pee-sil-ee: many-colored). =*Parus* spp. Order Passeriformes, Paridae (Chickadee family).

Mountain chickadee, *P. gambeli* (gam-bel-eye: after William Gambel). 4¼" [11 cm]; black crown, eye-streak and throat; white eyebrow and cheeks, grayish belly, gray-brown upperparts. Mid-elev forest. Illustrated this page and color p 533..

Black-capped chickadee, *P. atricapilla* (ay-tri-ca-pill-a: black-haired). 4½" [11.5 cm]; black crown and throat, white cheeks; grayish belly, gray-brown upper parts. Lower thickets, streamsides.

Boreal chickadee, *P. hudsonica* (hud-so-nic-a: of Hudson's Bay). 4¼" [11 cm]; brown crown, black throat, white cheeks, white belly, rusty flanks, gray-brown back. Conifer forest, from Glacier (MT) n.

Chickadees seem to epitomize the chipper dispositions people want to see in songbirds, and they let us see it, being tamer than most. "Chick-a dee-dee-dee" transcribes a characteristic call; black-cap and mountain sing a laid-back song of two to four notes descending, but boreal cannot whistle, and has only wheezy calls. The various chickadees, gleaners of caterpillars and other insects from the branches, reside here year-round, nesting in fur-lined holes dug rather low in tree trunks either by woodpeckers or by themselves, in soft punky

---

wood. For winter they store both insects and seeds in thousands of bark crevices (see below), speedily wedging them into place or gluing them with saliva, and often hiding them with lichens or bark bits. Pilferage is a very serious problem, and they also seem to remember which hiding places have been robbed before, and avoid reusing them. They form flocks in winter, except for boreals, which pair full-time and for life. Some mountain chickadees move upslope and winter near timberline, while others move down to the plains.

Recycling for Bird Brains

To the long list of amazing weight-saving adaptations in birds, recent studies of chickadees add the ability to grow new brain cells. You may have heard that you lose brain cells throughout adulthood (especially when you overindulge) and never grow new ones. Not true. The discovery of newly-formed neurons in chickadees foreshadowed a similar find in humans. In both species, the new cells are in the hippocampus, a part of the brain involved with learning and memory.

Chickadees were found to grow new neurons in the hippocampus in a big burst each fall, when they store seeds in thousands of crevices they will have to find again through winter. An even bigger hippocampal growth spurt hits juveniles when they disperse from their natal territory, and have to learn the ins and outs of the environs they will inhabit for the rest of their lives. But their number of hippocampal cells does not grow through life, as it does in small mammals. One hypothesis is that each hippocampal neuron can store only one memory, and birds resorb and replace neurons whose memories are no longer needed. In a tiny flying animal, a brain big enough for a lifetime of memories might never get off the ground.

Very small birds actually have far more of their body mass in the form of brains, as a percentage, than we do. The fact that natural selection produced big brains here demonstrates that brainpower is critical to survival and reproduction in tiny food-storing birds, as it carries a Nieman-Marcus price tag in energetic terms. Brains burn energy far more intensively than other types of tissue. Phenomenal ability to remember exact locations evolved convergently in several unrelated species, all of which lead lives that put those powers to good use. Some of them have nonmigratory close relatives whose memory doesn't amount to diddly squat.

Some kinds of memories are apparently worth holding onto: male warblers recognize the song of each neighbor male. As long as each singer is known to the other, and stays on his own territory, both are spared a fight. They remember each other's songs from year to year, as they return from Central America and reclaim their old haunts.

Kinglets

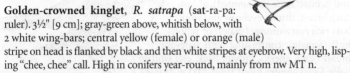

Regulus spp. (**reg**-you-lus: small king).
Regulidae.

Golden-crowned kinglet, *R. satrapa* (**sat**-ra-pa:
ruler). 3½" [9 cm]; gray-green above, whitish below, with
2 white wing-bars; central yellow (female) or orange (male)
stripe on head is flanked by black and then white stripes at eyebrow. Very high, lisping "chee, chee" call. High in conifers year-round, mainly from nw MT n.

Ruby-crowned kinglet, *R. calendula* (ca-**lend**-you-la: larklet). 3¾" [9.5 cm];
gray-green above, whitish below, with white eye-ring and two white wing-bars;
rarely-visible scarlet spot on crown is displayed only by excited males, leaving
kinglet very hard to tell from Cassin's vireo. Scolding "jit-it" calls, and long, variable song of chatters, warbles, and rising triplets. Conifer forest; May–Oct.

Constant movement—wings twitching even when perched—characterizes kinglets. They catch insects, sometimes in flight but mostly on
bark and foliage, where their tiny size enables them to specialize in
inhabitants of twig-tips too weak to support other gleaning birds.
Gleaning is a full-time job; insects are a more diluted energy source
than seeds, and occur less predictably. Traveling in flocks seems to help
gleaners locate insect populations. Mixed flocks of golden-crowned
kinglets, chickadees and woodpeckers are often seen in winter.

A kinglet weighs about as much as two pennies. Among birds
and mammals, only a few species of hummingbirds and of shrews
are smaller, and not by much. But kinglets expose themselves for
months at a time to much colder air than hummingbirds or shrews.
They fly in the face of Bergmann's rule, which generalizes that northerly birds or mammals will likely be larger than their southerly
relatives, because small bodies lose heat faster. (See p 437 footnote.)
In winter they spend nearly every waking minute foraging, raising
their body fat content each day from around 5% to around 11%,
enough to keep them alive through the night if they are lucky. When
it gets too dark for foraging to pay off, they plunge into the first insulative spot they see, such as a soft bit of snow in thick brush, twist
their necks to wedge their eyes and bills in among their back feathers, and go to sleep. In other cases they probably stay warm at night
by huddling together. It's a harsh life. Mortality in northerly kinglets
is estimated to be 87% per year. They compensate by producing a
phenomenal 18 to 20 eggs per pair, nesting twice in one summer.

DNA study suggests the kinglets are too distantly related to belong
in the same genus; look for a genus split soon, and/or for the golden-crowned to be reclassified as a Eurasian goldcrest, *R. regulus*.

Varied Thrush

Ixoreus naevius (ix-**or**-ius: mistletoe mountain, ref to food and habitat; **neev**-ius: spotted). 8" [20 cm]; breast, throat, eyebrow and wing-bars rich rusty-orange (males) or yellow-buff (female), contrasting with slate-gray breast band, cheeks, crown, back, etc; whitish belly. Deep conifer forest from c ID n; Mar–Oct. Turdidae (Thrush family).

The varied thrush is an early-arriving migrant, and leaves only when the snow gets too deep for it to keep foraging on the ground for insects and berries. It sings a single note with odd, rough overtones, like two slightly dissonant notes whistled at once; after several seconds' rest, it sings a similar tone, higher or lower by some irrational interval. Prolonged early or late in the day, in deep forest or fog, this minimal music acquires powers of enchantment over people.

American Robin

Turdus migratorius. 8½" [21 cm]; like varied thrush (above) but no breast band, eye streak, or orange on wings, and belly is brighter red, posture more steeply angled. Song brash, overly cheerful, exacerbates crepuscular insomnia. Anywhere with partial cover; Apr–Oct. Eats worms. Turdidae (Thrush family).

Swainson's Thrush and Hermit Thrush

Catharus spp. (**cath**-a-rus: pure). 6¼" [16 cm]; gray-brown above; pale eye-ring; belly white, breast spotted. Turdidae (Thrush family).

Hermit thrush, *C. guttatus* (ga-**tay**-tus: spotted). Tail, but not back, is rusty red; tail is "nervously" raised and lowered every few seconds, while wings may twitch. Shady forest; Apr–Nov.

Swainson's thrush, *C. ustulatus* (ust-you-**lay**-tus: singed). Back and head ± reddish; tail less so. Nests in riparian thickets or aspens, wanders in forest, northerly subregions; May–Oct; winters in Central America. Illustrated.

Catharus thrushes sing lyrically, virtuosically. Hermit prefaces a fast phrase with a single long clear note, then performs variations at different pitches. Swainson's begins with a slow phrase of a few notes, then spirals upward, flutelike, and often repeats at different pitches.

Both forage on the ground for earthworms, insects, and berries.

I don't know if it's something about Mr. Swainson, but both the thrush and the hawk bearing his name migrate as far south as Argentina, putting each near the top of the distance charts for its genus. Swainson's and hermit thrushes illustrate the principal that a long-distance migrator is likely to have longer primaries (the longest main wing feathers) than its short-distance relatives.

Townsend's Solitaire

Myadestes townsendi (my-a-**des**-teez: fly eater; **town**-send-eye: after J. K. Townsend, p 339). 6¾" [17 cm]; gray with white eye-ring; dark tail has white feathers on sides (like the more abundant junco, p 459; solitaire is longer, slenderer, more upright, more arboreal); dark wings have buff patches, visible underneath in flight. Call a high, ringing "eep"; song a long melodious warble heard at any season. Forest; year round, wintering lower; uncommon. Order Passeriformes, Turdidae (Thrush family).

The solitaire returns to high elevations early, searching the first snow-free areas for a nesting cavity in a stump or rotting log. After the breeding season it may gather in large flocks, belying its name. Most populations seek out juniper woodlands for winter, subsisting on juniper berries. They defend their berry territories with fierce attacks on intruders. In summer they mainly eat insects.

Mountain Bluebird

Sialia currucoides (sigh-**ay**-lia: the Greek term; cue-roo-**coy**-deez: warbler-like). 6" [10 cm]; summer males turquoise above, shading through pale blue beneath to whitish on throat; females and winter males gray-brown with varying amounts of blue on tail, rump, and wings. Soft warbling song at dawn; "phew" call. Semiopen vegetation; Mar-Oct, or longer in WY. Turdidae. Color p 532.

Bluebirds drop on insect prey from a low hover or perch. In fall they fatten up on berries. They nest in woodpecker holes; the related western bluebird, *S. mexicana*, is in severe decline, partly due to competition for these holes from introduced sparrows, starlings, etc. But the mountain bluebird has prospered from clearcutting, ranching, and nestbox construction.

American Pipit

Anthus rubescens (**anth**-us: a Greek name for some bird; roo-**bes**-enz: reddish). Formerly **water pipit**, *A spinoletta* . 5½" [14 cm]; sexes alike: gray-brown above, buff below, with white outer tail feathers and dark legs; bill slenderer than sparrows.
Alpine/subalpine in summer. Order Passeriformes, Motacillidae (Pipit family).

Distinguish the **pipit** from our other common species with white outer tail feathers (junco and solitaire) by its habit of regularly jerking its tail down as it walks along foraging for invertebrate prey, sometimes in shallow water or on snow. To attract a mate and, once he has one, to assert territory, the male flies straight up and then drifts down on spread wings, singing a thin, high "cheee" or "che-wee" all the while. Often the song or the call can identify the bird while it flies too high to be spotted. The call note suggests "pipit."

Warblers

Townsend's warbler, *Dendroica townsendi* (den-**droy**-ca: tree house; **town**-send-eye: after J. K. Townsend, p 339). 4¼" [11 cm]; whitish beneath, greenish gray above, with two white wingbars; crown black ; sides of face (exc dark cheek patch) and breast bright yellow. Song a series of wheezes rising to 1–2 clear notes. Mid-elev to high forest, all exc driest parts of our range. Parulidae (Wood Warbler family).

Yellow-rumped warbler, *D. coronata* (cor-o-**nay**-ta: crowned). Includes **Audubon's** and **myrtle warblers**. 4¾" [12 cm]; yellow in 5 small patches (mere tinges on females): crown, rump, throat, sides; mostly gray/black (breeding males) to soft gray-brown (others), with white eye-ring and one ± vague wing bar. Song a long trill. Widespread. Color p 533.

Yellow warbler, *D. petechia* (pet-**eek**-ia: red-dotted). 4" [10 cm]; yellow ± overall; wings and tail gray with some yellow; male breast red-streaked. Brush, forest edges; May–Sept.

Wilson's warbler, *Wilsonia pusilla* (wil-**so**-nia: after Alexander Wilson; pew-**sil**-a: very small). 4¼" [11 cm]; yellow beneath, olive above; male has shiny black crown; tail entirely dark. Willow or alder thickets; May–Oct.

Common yellowthroat, *Geothlypis trichas* (gee-**oth**-lip-iss: ground finch; **try**-cus: thrush—for a bird that's not a finch and not a thrush). 4¼" [11 cm]; olive-brown with yellow throat and breast, male has black mask; duller female has gray cheeks. Song "witchity-witchity." Wetland brush; Apr–Oct.

MacGillivray's warbler, *Oporornis tolmiei* (op-or-**or**-nis: autumn bird; **tole**-me-eye: after Wm. Tolmie). 4½" [11.5 cm]; yellow beneath, grayish olive above; solid gray "hood" (head and throat) with incomplete white eye-ring. Short song of about 3 rising and 2 falling notes. Shrubs in forest gaps; May–Sept.

Most sparrow-sized birds around here with some yellow on them are some kind of warbler. This large family is known for long winter migrations to the tropics and for distinctive (but not always warbling) songs. Most also have "chip chip" calls which often serve as alarms, or to warn another male that aggressive defense of territory will come next. Birders concentrate on learning the songs, since there are so many kinds of warblers and they all tend to keep themselves inconspicuous among foliage. Most are gleaners of insects; many also hawk at larger insects; some vary their diets with fruits and seeds. Wilson's warbler is a "leapfrog" migrator: individual that breed farther north winter farther south, in Central America. (Data based on a ratio of hydrogen ions in feathers, which varies with latitude.)

Waxwings

Bombycilla spp. (bom-bi-**sil**-a: silky tail). Sexes alike; largely gray; yellow/black tail tip; swept-back crest on rusty brown head with black mask, throat, and beak; in flocks, making constant high hisses. Forest and woodland. Order Passeriformes, Bombycillidae (Waxwing family).

Bohemian waxwing, *B. garrulus* (garrulus: referring to the European jay). 6¼" [16 cm]; rusty under tail; wings have yellow and red bits. Year-round from Glacier n; mainly Nov–Apr farther s.

Cedar waxwing, *B. cedrorum.* 5¾" [14 cm]; white under tail; yellowish belly; wings have yellow bits. Mainly May– Oct,but a few overwinter at Grand Teton. Illustrated this page, and color p 532.

Though they like insects (Bohemian is big and fast enough to hawk dragonflies) these avian sugar freaks mainly seek out sweet berries. Staples in the Rockies would be mountain-ash, chokecherry, and junipers—called cedars in the East, hence "cedar waxwing." They like their berries fermented, and don't seem to know their limits: mass deaths from fermented fruit are on record. In following the ripened fruits they come and go like gypsies. (Hence "Bohemian waxwing.") The need for abundant ripe fruit makes them unfaithful to any particular locale for either wintering or nesting, and leads Cedar to delay laying til full summer, later than any other North American bird.

Western Tanager

Piranga ludoviciana (pir-**ang**-ga: Tupi word for it, in Brazil; loo-do-vis-i-**ay**-na: of "Louisiana"). 6¼" [16 cm]; summer males have bright red to orange head, yellow breast, belly and rump, black backband, tail and wings, and white wingbars; others yellowish to greenish gray above, yellow beneath. Lower woodlands; May–Sept. Order Passeriformes, Thraupidae (Tanager family). Color p 532.

Lewis and Clark described many new plant species, but only four new birds: Lewis' woodpecker, Clark's nutcracker, the tundra swan, and the western tanager, whose scientific name refers to the

Louisiana Purchase, the tract they explored. "Tanager" and "Piranga" are native words from deep in the Amazon rain forest, where some tanagers winter. This particular species travels only as far as Central America. Its breeding plumage here rivals that of gaudy jungle birds, but when in the jungle it wears dull winter plumage.

Tanager beaks are intermediate between the insect-picking thin beaks of the preceding birds and the heavy, seed-crushing beaks of birds to follow; tanagers switch from an insectivorous diet to one of ripe berries in late summer.

Sparrows

Order Passeriformes, Emberizidae
(New World sparrow family).

White-crowned sparrow, *Zonotrichia leucophrys* (zo-no-**trick**-ia: striped head; loo-**koff**-riss: white brow). 5¾" [14 cm]; striking black/white-striped crown; mostly brown above, gray beneath; golden bill. April to Oct; habitats with brush and usually some grass; abundant, esp in WY. (Similar **White-throated** has gray bill, white throat; mainly in AB or in winter).

Chipping sparrow, *Spizella passerina* (spy-**zel**-a: finchlet; passer-**eye**-na: sparrow—). 4¾" [12 cm]; brown back with dark streaking, gray nape and underside; red-brown crown, whitish eyebrow streak above black eye streak. March to Oct; edge habitats (see text); abundant. Color p 533.

Song sparrow, *Melospiza melodia* (mel-o-**spy**-za: song finch). 5½" [13.5 cm]; brown with blackish streaking above, white below with brown streaking convergent at throat, above a mid-breast brown spot; pumps its tail in flight. Year-round in US, summer in Canada; edge habitats. Illustrated.

"Sparrow" is a catchall term for a lot of common, drab brown birds which few beginners care to identify. They aren't really a taxonomic group—less so with each new revision of bird taxonomy. These three are all very widespread across the continent. Chipping sparrows exemplify the need of a great many animals for "edge habitats." They nest in conifers, forage in brush, and consequently spend their time where open forest meets brush. They multiplied in number in the nineteenth century, as farmers clearing forests created millions of new edges. In the twentieth they declined, partly due to competition from introduced house sparrows and nest parasitism by brown-headed cowbirds. (Cowbirds lay their eggs in nests of smaller birds; when the host parents try to feed all the ensuing chicks, the bigger cowbirds get most of the food and are soon strong enough to push the proper offspring out of the nest.)

Bits of magnetite (iron ore) are embedded in white-crowned

sparrow cheeks, enabling them to orient to magnetic north. Different kinds of birds navigate by similar internal compasses, or by the stars, the polarity of sunlight, or memory of landmarks, in varying combinations. We may yet learn of more ways they navigate.

Song sparrow's typical song—heard on spring and early summer mornings—is a few clear piping notes, then a lower, raspy buzz or series, ending with around three quick, clear but unemphatic notes.

Dark-Eyed Junco

Junco hyemalis (**junk**-oh: rush, the plant, for no clear reason; hi-em-**ay**-lis: of winter). =formerly 3 spp: **slate-colored**, **white-winged**, and **Oregon juncos**. 5¼" [13 cm]; tail dark gray-brown exc for white feathers at sides; belly white with ± reddish flanks; back chestnut brown (gray in c AB); head and neck gray; in the "Oregon" race of most of n RM (exc WY and AB) the gray contrasts sharply, like an executioner's hood. Simple, hard trill. Nests and forages on ground. Emberizidae (New World sparrow family). Color p 533.

Juncos are primarily seed-eaters, turning to insects in summer and feeding insects and larvae to their young. After the young leave the nest, juncos travel in loose flocks until the next summer. Ours mostly migrate short distances downslope for winter.

Western Meadowlark

Sturnella neglecta (stir-**nel**-a: little starling; neg-**lec**-ta: overlooked). 8½" [21 cm]; streaky light brown back; yellow belly and throat separated by heavy black chest V; long pointed bill. Striking song: pure flute notes, then a watery burble. On ground or low perches; grasslands up to alpine meadows, though more abundant on Plains. Icteridae (Blackbird family.) Color p 532.

Eastern and western meadowlarks look alike, and were not officially separated as species until 1908. In the extensive areas where they overlap, the males don't notice the difference, but defend territory against both their own species and the other. They sing quite differently, though, and the females notice that, and thus the genetic lines are kept separate. Males have an average repertoire of seven songs, and can learn new ones in adulthood. A male with a large song repertoire usually gets two mates, and guards them successfully against paramours. Females build the nests in and of the grass, with variable elaboration ranging up to extensive arched runways with 2–3" [5–8 cm] entrances.

Humans, equally captivated by the western meadowlark's singing, named it the State Bird of which state: Kansas? Oregon? Wyoming? North Dakota? Montana? or Nebraska?

All of the above.

Red-Winged Blackbird

Agelaius phoeniceus (adgel-**ay**-us: flocking: fee-**niss**-ius: reddish purple). 7¼" [18 cm]; male all black exc for erectile red shoulder patches with yellow edge; female gray-brown with a touch of red on shoulder. Song "BONK-ra-leee." Nest in wet habitat; at other times wander widely, e.g. in grain fields; often in large flocks. Icteridae (Blackbird family.)

Red-wing males sing their gurgling-brook songs and flash their red epaulets to defend territory. (Conversely, trespassing or submissive males cover their epaulets, and experimental subjects with shoulders blackened have no chutzpah whatsoever.) While males pay attention to epaulets in divying prime territory, females pay attention mainly to territory. The male with the best territory will find that a harem of ten or fifteen has moved in with him. The very best marshy habitat with cattails or bulrushes may acquire blackbird densities high enough to describe as a colony.

Rosy Finches

Leucosticte spp. (lew-co-**stick**-tee: white patch). =both of these spp. were formerly (but briefly) included in **Rosy finch**, *L. arctoa.* 6¼" [11 cm]; brown with blackish face, gray crown or entire head, and (males esp) reddish tinges on rump, shoulders, belly. Either hoarse or high chips and chipping chatters. Arctic fellfields, snow, etc. Fringillidae (Finch family).

Gray-crowned rosy finch, *L. tephrocotis* (tef-**roc**-o-tiss: ashen head). From Bitterroots n and w. Color p 533.

Black rosy finch, *L. atrata* (a-**tray**-ta: black). Darker. Nw WY, sw MT, c ID.

The finch family name, Fringillidae, comes from the same Latin root as "frigid." Rosy finches are the most alpine birds of the West, at least in summer. They nest in high rock crevices, reportedly even in ice crevasses, and often forage on glaciers, utilizing a resource all climbers have noticed—insects that collapse on the snow, numbed by cold after being carried astray by diurnal upvalley winds. The bulk of their diet is vegetable, including seeds, white heather flowers, and succulent alpine saxifrage leaves. In winter they form flocks in valleys or on the Plains, proving congenial with such conveniences as window feeding-boxes, grain elevator yards, and spilled grain on railroad beds. Some entire flocks are males; for unknown reasons there are six times more male than female rosy finches.

Cassin's Finch

Carpodacus cassinii (car-**pod**-a-cus: fruit eater; cas-**in**-ee-eye: after John Cassin). 6" [10 cm]; older males have crimson crown, pale red breast; females (and males up to breeding yearlings) sparrowlike gray-brown with streaked white breast and belly; undertail feathers dark-streaked white. Song (May–June) a varied warble full of breaks and squeaks, often with a series of good imitations of other birds; call "tidilit." Drier forests, esp OR and c ID; rare n of Waterton. Order Passeriformes, Fringillidae (Finch family). Color p 533.

Flocks of these mountain-loving birds subsist through winter eating conifer buds, then switch to emerging male catkins of aspen in time to fuel their nesting efforts. They nest in the conifer canopy, often in colonies of several hundred. Locally abundant some years and scarce others, they're also erratic about migration. Some stay near their nests in our mountains, while greater numbers move downslope a bit, or migrate to the Southern Rockies.

Red Crossbill

Loxia curvirostra (**lox**-ia: oblique; cur-vi-**ros**-tra: curve bill). 5½" [14 cm]; older males red; females yellowish beneath, greenish gray above; young mature males often orange while grading from yellowish to red; wings (all) solid dark gray. "Chip, chip" call; warbling song. In flocks, in the coniferous canopy. Order Passeriformes, Fringillidae (Finch family).

A small shower of conifer seed coats and seed wings often means a crossbill flock is above. You have to be close to see the crossed bill: the lower mandible hooks upward almost as much as the upper one hooks downward. These odd bills can move sideways to efficiently pry cone scales apart. Evolution has specialized crossbills to clean up conifer seed crops when the remaining seeds are too sparse for larger seed-eaters like squirrels and woodpeckers, and too tightly encased in the cone for siskins and finches. They can keep cleaning up the leftovers from the fall crop well through winter and usually spring, depending on tree species; then in summer their jaws open wide to glean insects.

The catch to crossbill specialization is that one size and style of crossed bill can only be really efficient at one size of cone, which in any given region means one species of conifer—a species that retains many of its seeds through winter and keeps many of them out of the tiny bills of siskins. To pass their bill size on to their offspring, the birds must find mates of similar bill size. They do so with slight differences in their call notes, which enable different-billed populations to share range without interbreeding. And not interbreeding means—you guessed it!—the red crossbill is really eight different species, distinguishable by bill size and call note but not by plumage. (They aren't named yet, let alone officially recognized. One scientist wants to compromise and call them "cryptospecies." Most birders aren't happy with the idea of species that can't be distinguished by plumage, but others are already trying to learn the different calls.) The Douglas-fir or ponderosa pine eaters migrate sweepingly, because these trees produce a good cone crop in one area one year, then somewhere else next year. Specialists in western hemlock and lodgepole pine, which are consistent producers, get to stay put.

Pine Siskin

Carduelis pinus (card-you-**ee**-lis: thistle—; **pie**-nus: pine). 4¼" [11 cm]; gray-brown with subtle lengthwise streaking; yellow in wings and tail may show in flight. Various distinctive scratchy twitters and sucking wheezes. In large flocks in treetops; year-round exc in AB, where summer/fall. Order Passeriformes, Fringillidae (Finch family).

Siskins' narrow, sharp bills (in contrast to the heavy conical ones typical of their family) limit them to lighter seeds—thistle, foxglove, and birch seeds, for example—along with insects and buds. Siskins hang upside down from catkins while extracting the seeds. The populations move around sweepingly, tending to be locally abundant in alternate years.

Pine siskins look nondescript, but call and fly quite distinctively. A flock's twitterings seem to match its breathtaking undulations and pulselike contractions and expansions in flight. I once saw one of these aerial ballets on the same day as a performance by the Blue Angel fighter jets, and thought, "Why do people bother to watch those clutzes?"

11

Reptiles

We may habitually say "reptiles and amphibians" in one breath, or even lump them together as "herptiles," but they are quite different. Amphibians evolved from fish. They pioneered on land with the use of two key innovations: air-breathing organs (lungs or skin) and legs. Certain lunged amphibians eventually developed thicker skin and eggshells—moisture barriers that facilitated truly terrestrial life, even on dry terrain. That step led to birds, mammals, and reptiles. In desert habitats with relatively infertile food chains, cold-bloodedness gives reptiles a big advantage over mammals because it demands far less caloric intake than warm-blooded thermoregulation. Reptiles can lie in wait for a long, long time, expending next to no energy, between meals. They can wait two years or more for an auspicious season to produce a brood of young. Their whole life story tends to be slower—and longer—than those of similar-sized mammals on the same habitat.

The term "reptiles" has to be considered provisional, at this point. While exact relationships among the four longstanding reptilian orders (tortoises, crocodilians, tuataras, and snakes/lizards) are debated, most parties to the debate have long agreed, on both skeletal and molecular grounds, that the closest kin of the crocodilians are the birds. Unless we reclassify birds as a kind of reptile, this seems to call for separating the lizards from the crocodilians and from the turtles, all at the class level; i.e., no such thing as a Class Reptilia. The Center for North American Herpetology has endorsed this change. To what degree the snakes and lizards belong together is also questioned.

Reptilian evolution turned egg layers into live bearers in dozens of separate lineages, apparently starting long ago; the boas, a relatively primitive family of snakes, all bear live young. Eggs predominate in the tropics, and births in cooler climates, suggesting that carrying the embryos around in her body makes it easier for a mother to keep them warm enough to incubate. Genus *Sceloporus*, with about 75 species, and genus *Elgaria*, with two, are each evenly divided between egg layers and live bearers, with their more northerly species—including those on this page—giving birth.

Sagebrush Lizard

Sceloporus graciosus (skel-**op**-or-us: leg pores; gray-see-**oh**-sus: agreeable). 5–6¼" long [13–16 cm]; belly relatively wide, legs big; very long toes on hindlegs; scales abrasive to the touch; back gray-brown, striped lengthwise; belly pale; males develop large pale blue patches on lower flanks and mottling on throat; females in Apr–May may develop bits of grayish blue and some red-orange on flanks. Diurnal; warm sunny habitats. OR, WY, s ID, sc MT. Iguanidae (Iguana family).

For courtship, territory assertion, and other communication, Iguanid species each have a precise gestural language including pushups, headbobbing, teeth-baring, throat-puffing, and side-flattening. Contact with you may alarm one enough to provoke these gestures, or a quick scurry under a bush. Sagebrush lizards can also climb shrubs or rocks as an escape. They seek out crevices or rodent burrows for keeping cool. At Yellowstone they seek out hydrothermally heated areas, apparently occupying higher-elevation habitat than they would be able to without the heat.

The similar western fence lizard, *S. occidentalis*, reaches our range in the Wallowas and western Idaho. It is distinguished by one or two blue patches, rather than mottling, on throat, and by longer-pointed scales that make the back quite prickly.

Northern Alligator Lizard

Elgaria coeruleus (el-**gar**-ia: no known meaning, and its author was notorious for inventing such names; see-**rue**-lius: blue). =*Gerrhonotus coeruleus*. 8½–10" [21–25 cm] long; body thick, legs and toes slender; scales heavy, rough; dark olive back with light stripe; belly gray to bluish. Diurnal; extreme nw MT, n ID, WA, and Kootenays. Anguidae (Anguid lizard family).

Scaly skin distinguishes lizards from salamanders. The scales on

alligator lizards are heavy
enough to serve as armor,
but at considerable cost
to flexibility; they walk
stiffly, somewhat snakewise,
on legs too weak to get their
bellies off the ground. A pair of
large pleats along the lizard's sides facilitate breathing. If you pick up
an alligator lizard, it can bite quickly and hard, defecate all over your
hand, or snap off its tail. (See Skink, below.) This species preys on
millipedes, snails, and other crawling things

Western Skink

Eumeces skiltonianus (you-**me**-sees: long; skil-tony-ay-nus: after Avery J. Skilton). 7½" [19 cm]; scales smooth, shiny, with rounded outline; tail very long and tapered, bright blue in youth, gradually fading to match the body coloring, which is lengthwise stripes of brown, black, and yellow to cream. Diurnal. Up to around 6800' [2070 m] in WA, OR, ID, extreme w MT and s Columbia Mtns. Scincidae (Skink Family).

Skinks are slick, fast, bright lizards. They can nip you fiercely if you pick them up. They are among the lizards most given to autotomizing, or breaking their tails off in a defensive ploy which lets the lizard escape while a predator holds and likely consumes the still-writhing tail. The lizard grows a new tail within weeks, but this is not quite the perfect miracle you might imagine. Vertebrae do not regenerate, so the new tail section has only a cartilaginous rod to stiffen it. The muscles and scales, too, are inferior to the originals, and the whole endeavor is very costly in terms of long term survival and reproductive success. Still, it must be at least somewhat advantageous overall, or evolution would not have selected it so widely. In many areas the majority of adult skinks have rebuilt tails.

Painted Turtle

Chrysemys picta (**cris**-em-iss: golden turtle; **pic**-ta: painted). 4–10" [10–25 cm]; head, neck, and legs dark green with bright yellow stripes; underside, side flesh (between shell halves) and rim of upper shell marked with bright red, sometimes fading to orange. Our only native turtle. Slow-moving water at lower elevs (usually below 3500', or 1070 m); BC, WA, OR, MT, and extreme n ID. Order Emydidae Family .

The herpetologist of the Hayden Expedition of 1871 reported collecting a painted turtle at Yellowstone Lake, but there may have been

---

a cataloguing error. In all the years since, no breeding populations of turtles have been found anywhere near that high, anywhere in our range. (Abandoned pets of this and other species are reported from time to time.)

Garter Snakes

Thamnophis spp. (**tham**-no-fis: shrub snake). 16–43" long [45–110 cm]; variable in color, but generally with 3 yellow-buff stripes down back, and ± distinctly spotted between the stripes. Often in or near marshes; also meadows, forest, throughout n Rockies. Family Colubridae.

Western terrestrial garter snake, *T. elegans.* Background color most often gray-brown or (esp in nw) black; spots ± dull, often indistinct.

Common garter snake, *T. sirtalis* (sir-**tay**-lis:). Flanks above the lateral yellow stripes regularly spotted or checkered with red. Below 8,000' [2450 m].

Garter snakes like to bask in the sun, sometimes intertwined in groups. Despite the name, they are partially aquatic; *T. sirtalis* preys largely on amphibians, to whose skin toxins it is nearly immune. They give birth in summer to three to fifteen live, worm-sized snakelets. In our region they generally hibernate.

As a defense they exude musk and feces. If you pick up a garter snake, your hands will be very very stinky.

Northern Rubber Boa

Charina bottae (care-eye-na: graceful; **bot**-ee: after Paolo Botta). =*Lichanura bottae.* 18–27' [45–70 cm]; unpatterned dark greenish brown above, grading to dull ± yellowish belly; scales small, smooth, shiny, skin rather loose; tail does not taper to a point, but is almost as broadly rounded as the head. Forests; east of the CD from Helena s; west of the CD from near Golden, BC s.

This smaller cousin of the tropical boa constrictors is quite an odd fish in a northern Rockies context. Our other reptiles prefer sunny habitats where they can bask, get good and hot, and then be active. The boa avoids hot sun like a plague. It lives only where there's ample shade along with a little sun, and even tends to be active at dawn, dusk, night, and on cloudy days. It tolerates higher elevations—up to 8600' [2620 m] at Yellowstone. But calling it "active" is a stretch. This is one sluggish snake. Somehow it manages to catch small mammals, mainly the young in their nests. Perhaps some adults don't notice it's alive, and scamper right into its coils. Its only defenses are a foul smell and the use of its blunt tail as a fake head decoy, or as a club to fend off a mother mouse while devouring her young. You can pick it up and handle it safely—just expect to wash assiduously afterward.

Racer

Coluber constrictor mormon (**col**-ub-er: Roman term for some snake). Our subspecies the **western yellowbellied racer**. 20–48" long [21–25 cm]; grayish olive above, yellowish beneath; adults plain, but juveniles patterned with brown for all or part of their length. ID, sw MT, dry parts of se BC. Family Colubridae.

This agile, slender snake is true to its name "racer," but not to its name *constrictor* since it kills its prey—mostly insects and some small rodents and reptiles—with its mouth, not with its coils. Though nonvenomous, it may bite and thrash when captured.

Gopher Snake and Bullsnake

Pituophis catenifer (pih-**too**-o-fis: pine snake; ca-**ten**-if-er: chain-bearer, referring to the pattern). =*P. melanoleucus*. 3–6' long [80–180 cm], heavy-bodied, relatively small-headed; tan with blackish blotches in a checkerlike pattern, largest ones along the back. Family Colubridae.

Great Basin gopher snake, *P. catenifer deserticola* (dez-er-**tic**-a-la: desert dweller). Along the w and s edges of our range, from Shuswap Lake to near Jackson WY.

Bullsnake, *P. catenifer sayi* (**say**-eye: after Thomas Say). Nose looks ± upturned and pointed due to a single enlarged scale; the tan background color may be tinged reddish to yellowish. MT.

The only snake you would likely mistake for a rattler around here is the gopher snake. The resemblance may be a case of adaptive mimicry for fright value; it even includes a threatening vibration of the tail which, when it rustles dry leaves, can sound much like a rattler. This snake is nonvenomous, killing its prey, including gophers, by constriction. It can also climb trees and prey on nestling birds. Constricting characterizes one small branch of the huge family Colubridae, which contains some 68% of all snakes. The young are already many inches long when they hatch from eggs in moist, often communal, burrows.

Western Rattlesnake

Crotalus viridis (crot-a-lus: rattle; **veer**-id-iss: green, a somewhat misleading name for this species, which ranges at most to a greenish yellow background shade.). Adults usually 16–36" long [40–90 cm], or rarely up to 5' [1.5 m], heavily built, with large triangular head; tail terminates in rattle segments; variable brown, black, gray, and tan colors in a pattern of regularly spaced large ± geometric dark blotches against paler crossbars. Dry rocky lower elevs, from Flathead Lake s. Viperidae (Pit viper family).

Rattlesnakes hunt at dusk, dawn, and night. A brisk, dry buzz of the tail rattles, a little like a cicada, is the typical warning to large intruders. Far from being aggressive toward humans, they will usually flee if given the chance. This species can inject a dose of venom lethal to small children and many mammals, though almost always merely painful to adult humans. (A solitary victim might possibly be incapacitated long enough to die of hypothermia if warm clothes and food are far away.) The strike itself is at least as fast as you ever imagined it to be: starting from any of a variety of positions, (i.e., not necessarily "coiled") striking and pulling back, together, take half a second, and are very accurate. The main advantage to this speed is that rodents are hardly ever quick enough to bite the snake's head. The disadvantage is that it limits the amount of venom delivered, sometimes allowing prey to get away. There is also of risk of damaging the jaw or fangs if they hit too hard. High-speed films of strikes show the snake taking care to have its head and near-head parts already decelerating before impact, while its parts a little farther back are still accelerating, all within that quarter-second time frame.

A recent paper proposes elevating the seven subspecies of western rattler to full species rank. The type in Montana is the Prairie Rattlesnake (and would still be *C. viridis*) but the western edge of our range has two other subspecies. There is considerable intergradation where the ranges meet, so this change may not win broad acceptance without a lot more supporting data.

12

Amphibians

Though classed among the terrestrial vertebrates, amphibians are only marginally terrestrial; they lack an effective moisture barrier in either their skins or their eggs, so to avoid deadly drying they must return to water frequently, venturing from it mainly at night or in the shade, and never far. Most of them hatch in water as gilled, water-breathing, legless, swimming larvae (e.g., tadpoles), later metamorphose into terrestrial adults, and return to water to breed. Hence the word "amphibious," from "life on both sides." A few amphibians manage to be completely terrestrial in moist habitats; some others have resumed fully aquatic lives. The moistest rocky Mountain forest habitats support ungodly numbers of unnoticed (quiet, nocturnal, largely subterranean) amphibians.

Today, amphibians are in decline worldwide. The causes are poorly understood. Permeable skin makes amphibians vulnerable to environmental contaminants, which are certainly one of the leading causes of decline, along with draining of wetlands and deforestation. One study implicates ozone depletion. (See page 473.) Another finds tiny parasitic worms causing treefrogs to grow extra legs, but offers no data on either trends or ultimate cause.

Among vertebrate animals, mammals and birds are "warm-blooded," whereas reptiles, amphibians and fish are "cold-blooded." This doesn't mean they're self-refrigerating, but they're never a lot warmer than their environment. Herps warm themselves by basking, with careful placement and positioning of their bodies. They need some ambient heat to help them be active, yet they can sustain activity in astonishing cold—long-toed salamanders in our high country typically breed in sub-40° [4° C] water with winter's ice still on it. Nevertheless they hibernate through most of the freezing season. At the other extreme, amphibians rarely survive heat over 100° [38° C]. Ironically, their intolerance of heat won salamanders and newts a superstitious reputation as fireproof; they know how to survive a ground fire, taking refuge in a familiar wet crevice or burrow, just as they do from the midday sun. At Mt. St. Helens, amphibian species likely to be swimming in mid-May (when the eruption came) survived well in the blast zone, but those more likely to be in shallow burrows died.

Tiger Salamander

Ambystoma tigrinum
(am-**bis**-ta-ma: blunt mouth, or to cram into the mouth; tie-**gry**-num: tiger). Ours are ssp *melanostictum*, the **blotched tiger salamander.** 9–12" long [23–30 cm] (the largest RM amphibian); very wide, blunt head; dirty yellow to olive, marbled (or ± tiger-striped) with black. WY, e ID, s MT and north along CD, just entering AB RM; also disjunct in Okanogan Mtns. Ambystomatidae (Mole salamander family).

Adults occur in four morphs: any combination of gilled versus terrestrial and "typical" versus "cannibalistic." The latter have broader heads and an extra row of teeth and, sure enough, they count tiger salamander larvae as a major part of their diet. Individuals can eat larvae nearly their own size.

Artificially stocked trout displaced tiger and long-toed salamanders from the top of the food chain in many high mountain lakes. Finding themselves prey for the first time in untold generations, the salamanders became scarce and very secretive, but generally survived. They multiply quickly if the fish are removed.

Long-Toed Salamander

Ambystoma macrodactylum (macro-**dac**-til-um: big toes). 4–6" long [20–25 cm]; wide, blunt head; long legs; dark gray-brown with an irregular, often blotchy full-length back stripe bright yellow to tan. Ambystomatidae. ID, w MT, and Canada. Color p 534.

Like other amphibians, this one stays close to water, especially in arid terrain. In the high country it breeds even before the ice is gone, to make the most of its brief, frigid active season, and still the larvae need two summers before metamorphosing. Laying eggs in shallow water makes it vulnerable to UV-B (see page 473).

Lungless and mole salamanders have elaborate mating rituals ending, in many species, with a procession: he walks along dropping gelatinous sperm cases and she follows, picking them up with her cloacal lips for internal fertilization. A long-toed male may literally interlope: he slips in between the romantic duo, mimics a female walk to escape notice, and places his sperm cases on top of each of the first male's, assuring himself of paternity.

Idaho Giant Salamander

Dicamptodon aterrimus (die-**camp**-ta-don: twice-curved teeth; a-**tair**-im-us: blackest). =*D. ensatus*. 7–10" long [18–25 cm], stocky; back blackish, finely mottled with dark brown; belly light brown; ribs indistinct. Nc ID, MT Bitterroots. Family Dicamptodontidae.

While many salamanders are limited to insects and other small invertebrates as food, this one can catch and eat mice, garter snakes, and small salamanders. In some small mountain streams it is the dominant predator, outweighing salmon and trout put together.

Salamanders of this genus are unique in having a real voice, variously described as a "yelp" and a "rattle." Salamanders have no eardrums or external openings to receive communications, but they do have inner ear organs sensitive to vibrations transmitted up through the legs. Where we might expect ears, the larvae have intricate plumelike red (blood-filled) structures. These are external gills that "breathe" or absorb oxygen suspended in water. Some Idaho giant larvae metamorphose into terrestrial adults; others never do metamorphose, but instead mature sexually while still gilled and fully aquatic. In the mole salamanders and this family it is common to find both gilled and terrestrial adults.

Coeur d'Alene Salamander

Plethodon idahoensis (**pleth**-o-don: full of teeth). =*P. vandykei*. 3–4½" long [8–12 cm], slender; blackish exc for a nearly full-length narrow back stripe that may be yellow, red, orange or green. N ID, Cabinet Mtns of MT; Kootenay Lake, BC. Rare and little studied. Plethodontidae (Lungless salamander family).

Salamanders of this family have neither lungs nor gills, and breathe through their skins exclusively. Most hatch as miniature "adults," having breezed through the larval stage within the egg; they are completely terrestrial. This species spends much time underground—

e.g., under logs or stones in wet talus—venturing out mainly at night and when rain or a creek splash zone assure it of staying wet. It gleans insect larvae from wet rocks.

Chorus Frogs

Pseudacris spp. (sue-**day**-cris: false cricket-frog). Hylidae (Treefrog family).

Pacific treefrog, *P. regilla* (ra-**jil**-a: queenlet). =*Hyla regilla*. 1–2¾" long [2.5–7 cm]; skin bumpy; toes bulbous-tipped; color extremely variable, and may include green or red; in N RM usually gray-brown with large irregular black splotches; males' throats gray. N ID, w MT.

Boreal chorus frog, *P. maculata* (mac-you-**lay**-ta: spotted). =*P. triseriata, Hyla triseriata*. ¾–1½" long [2–4 cm]; gray-brown to green, with generally 3 dark stripes down back, though these may be broken or reduced to spots; pale lip line; toes scarcely bulbous. Mainly near and e of CD.

Voiced frogs employ a variety of calls, including alarm, warning, territorial, and male and female release calls. Pond frog choruses are likely to be mating-call duets and trios of males. The male treefrog amplifies his rather musical, high-pitched call, heard both day and night, with a resonating throat sac he blows up to three times the size of his head. Tree frogs are distinguished by their bulbous toe pads, which offer amazing grip on vertical surfaces such as trees. Our species probably spends more time in water and on the ground than on shrubs and trees. It has a sticky tongue for catching insects.

The more easterly boreal chorus frog calls nocturnally in a raspy, toneless voice, beginning in early spring.

Columbia Spotted Frog

Rana luteiventris (**ray**-na: the Roman term; loo-tee-ih-**ven**-tris: yellow belly). =formerly included in *R. pretiosa*. 2½–3½" long [6–9 cm]; brown with poorly defined blackish spots above; ridges on back ± same color; belly yellow to salmon (or red in som outlying populations); toes fully webbed. Diurnal near, or most often in, cold lakes or streams; n and w from Tetons. Ranidae.

Spotted frogs range higher in the Rockies than other frogs, but are considerably slowed down (compared to conspecifics at sea level) when the do so, taking four to six years to mature, and then laying eggs only at two-to-three-year intervals. The male's deep croaks, in a series of six to nine, are modest in volume.

Western Toad

Bufo boreas boreas (**bew**-foe: the Greek term; **bor**-ius: northern). Also (our ssp) **boreal toad.** 2–5" long [5–13 cm]; thick; sluggish; skin has large bumps, the largest being two oval glands behind the eyes; olive to grayish, with a narrow pale stripe down back, and blotches on belly. Widespread. Bufonidae. Color p 534.

Toads are distinguished from frogs by their warty skin, toothless upper jaw, sluggish movement (generally walking rather than hopping), and parotoid glands behind the eyes. These bulbous protrusions exude a thick, white, nauseating, burning poison related to digitalin, effectively deterring predators. (It does not cause warts.) Toads' slow pace limits them to slow, creeping invertebrate prey.

Toads resist drying better than most frogs and salamanders. Our only toad, the western, inhabits animal burrows and rock crevices, and is often seen in mountain meadows and woodlands well away from watercourses. It is less strictly nocturnal than most toads, especially at elevations where nights are too cold for much toad activity. Lacking the inflatable vocal sac many of its relatives boast, it has a weak, peeping voice.

In 1995, a team of Oregon zoologists made headlines worldwide with an investigation of western toads' disappearance from seemingly pristine Cascade lakes. They found most eggs in some high ponds killed by a fungal disease common among hatchery trout. If they shielded the eggs with mylar that blocked ultraviolet-B rays, a healthy number of eggs resisted infection, and hatched. The problem, in other words, was a combination of two human interventions: stocking high lakes with trout, and depleting atmospheric ozone, with resultant dramatic increases in UV-B. This was the first demonstrated case of ozone depletion threatening a species. The team also found long-toed salamanders hatching with debilitating deformities unless they were shielded from UV-B. In contrast, the Pacific treefrog was able to repair UV-B damage.

While these findings showed that even remote or protected wilderness is vulnerable to global change, subsequent studies suggest that they explain only a small fraction of the worldwide amphibian decline. Most amphibians lay eggs in shady pools or deeper water and may not be much affected by ozone depletion.

Amphibians

Northern Leopard Frog

Rana pipiens (**ray**-na: the Roman term; **pip**-ee-enz: peeping). 2¼–4" long [6–10 cm]; green or brown with light-haloed dark spots; back has conspicous pale ridge from each eye to groin, and also along jawline; toes fully webbed. Lowlands. Ranidae (True frog family).

Leopard frogs hunt with a quick dart of the tongue. Their croak is feeble, rough, and prolonged. Some call it a "snore" followed by "clucking" or "moaning." Gravid females become huge, and lay several thousand eggs.

They are in serious decline. Predation by introduced bullfrogs (*R. catesbeiana*) is a big problem for them, along with stream pollution and habitat alteration.

Tailed Frog

Ascaphus truei (**ask**-a-fus: lacking a spade—a body part; **true**-eye: after F. W. True). 1–2" long [2.5–5 cm]; skin has sparse small warts; olive to dark brown with large irregular black splotches and black eye-stripe. Voiceless. Nocturnal; in undisturbed mtn streams. Ascaphidae (a family of just this one species).

Tailed frogs spend most of their time in fast, cold creeks, where their little-seen but sizable populations are perfectly able to withstand trout, but not logging. They attach their eggs like strings of beads to the downstream side of rocks. The tadpoles suck firmly onto rocks, or perhaps to your leg or boot when you wade a creek, but don't worry, they aren't bloodsuckers. The adults don't have real tails; those soft protuberances are male cloacas, and they fertilize the females internally. You might think a penis prototype to be an advanced item on an amphibian, but sorry, guys: it's a primitive trait that most amphibians have long abandoned. Tailed frogs may have kept it to enable mating in fast streams without the semen washing away. Another evolutionary oddity about tailed frogs is that their closest relatives are in New Zealand.

13
Fishes

When Euroamericans arrived and began throwing new fish species into watersheds, the existing species distribution was still in flux from the last Ice Age. Where glaciers advanced, aquatic life retreated; when glaciers retreated, fish returned only as far as they could swim. Salmon may be phenomenal waterfall leapers, but still, there are limits. Most streams would, in nature, be fishless above a certain impassable waterfall. There are the odd exceptions. At Two Ocean Pass in the Absarokas, a stream splits: two branches flow down opposite sides of the Continental Divide. Atlantic Creek has no high waterfalls, so fish were able to ascend it all the way to the pass, where cutthroat trout and dace—but not sculpins, for some reason—swam over the Divide into Pacific Creek and occupied Yellowstone Lake and its drainage, which until then was fishless above Yellowstone Falls.

Above the critical waterfall live healthy aquatic communities whose animal members got there overland or airborne—invertebrates, small mammals, and amphibians. Salamanders would rule many lake food chains, if things were still as they were when Euroamericans first came to the Rockies. But they are not. A high proportion of these aquatic communities were joined, and much altered, by fish that arrived in saddlebags or buckets, or skydived from airplanes. Fish populations today are largely a product of human efforts favoring the most popular game species. Amphibians almost disappear from high lakes when fish are added, and countless effects cascade down through the food chain. Sometimes escaped baitfish have multiplied to where they threatened to outcompete trout; managers have poisoned entire lakes to prepare them for restocking.

Another fish-limiting factor in some high lakes, strange as it may sound, is high temperature. Trout may suffer or die of heat in water that could chill and "freeze" a person in short order. Since they are "cold-blooded," their body temperatures drop with that of the water, but their health isn't at risk; only their activity and growth rates are reduced. Under ice for nine months, high country trout spend a very slow winter without danger or discomfort, but also without growing. In the smallest and/or highest bodies of water that support trout, they never grow very big, maturing and spawning at three to six years of age while only 3–5" [8–12 cm] long and still displaying the parr marks typical of juvenile trout elsewhere.

Some lakes are too clean to make good fish habitat. The aquatic food pyramid rests upon algae, which in turn depend on minerals not present in rain or snow; water has to pick these up in its passage over or through the earth. Small drainage basins, high snowfall, barren or impermeable terrain, and rapid turnover of lake water sometimes combine to severely limit nutrients. Stocked trout grow poorly in such lakes, and may not reproduce.

Check a lakeshore near an inlet or outlet stream, and follow the stream to its first waterfall; if you find a shallow gravelly spot in early summer, you may see a spawner busy swimming back and forth over it. A logjam at the outlet stream, or slabby shallows nearby, may be good places to spot fish at any time of year. Polarizing sunglasses (or a camera polarizer) can help you see fish. Trout don't feed all day—only when the insects are most active. When the lake is first ice-free, feeding may go on from midmorning to midday. By October they may feed all afternoon. If luck brings you a calm feeding period after an extended blow, look for frenzied feeding where floating insects are concentrated against the downwind shore.

Most fishes in this chapter are omnivores, generally taking the biggest foods luck brings them that will fit down their throats. They eat plankton throughout life, straining it with their gill rakers. That's all they can handle as tiny "fry," but later they move up to insects and larvae, snails, worms, isopods, freshwater shrimp, amphibian larvae, fish eggs and fry, and finally adult fish or even birds. Any fish species is fair game, even their own. Lake trout thrive in a few lakes where most of the fish are lakers; implying that the main food of big lake trout there is small lake trout. The small ones eat plant matter and tiny animals... Not an unusual food chain, but for that one detail.

Cutthroat Trout

Oncorhynchus clarki (clark-ee: after William Clark, p 257) =formerly *Salmo clarki*. Lower jaw bears a long heavy red line (occasionally pink or orange); jaw longer than other trout, opening to well behind the eye; throat just behind the tongue has tiny teeth, usually palpable; dorsal fin has 9–11 rays, pelvic rays usually 9, anal rays 9 (range 8–12); adults dark-speckled, esp above middle, and near tail; various amounts of pink and red on sides and belly; juveniles develop the jaw streaks quite early, and have many small spots above and between the lateral parr marks but none or few (1–5) in a median line ahead of the dorsal fin. Family Salmonidae. Illustrated below, and color page 535.

The cutthroat is the archetypal Rocky Mountain fish, the naturally-occurring "top dog" of more crystal-clear, icy-cold bodies of water in our range than any other fish. Its populations are greatly diminished from what they once were. The first eighty years or so of white men's management here intentionally favored all kinds of introduced fish over the less popular cutthroat, mainly because it was too easy to catch, and considered not much of a fighter. It also doesn't take to hatcheries the way rainbows do. But few ever complained about its beauty, its flavor, or its size—it can get larger than rainbows, browns, goldens, or brookies—and of course for the less-experienced majority of anglers, being easy to catch is a plus. So lots of people are glad to add their recreational motives to the ecological ones that now drive fishery managers to want to hold on to all the wild cutthroat stocks that we possibly can.

Though they may be easy prey, and poor competitors against challenges they didn't evolve with, cutthroats are formidable predators, with their big mouths and extra teeth. Fish use teeth for gripping prey prior to swallowing it, not for chewing. (Teeth can be a useful i.d. character, but only for fish on their way to the frypan. Groping around in a fish's mouth is life-threatening, so never do it to catch-and-release fish.)

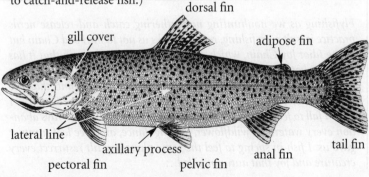

dorsal fin

gill cover

adipose fin

lateral line

axillary process

pectoral fin

pelvic fin

anal fin

tail fin

For spawning (and here I describe a generalized salmon-family behavior) the female chooses a gravelly spot, usually in a riffle, and begins digging a trough, or "redd," by turning on her side and beating with her tail. A dominant male moves in to attend her, and becomes aggressive to outsiders, attacking any who come too close. He may nudge her repeatedly. When she signals her readiness by lowering a fin into the redd, he swims up alongside her, they open their jaws, arch their backs, quiver, and simultaneously drop her eggs and his milt. Other males hitherto kept at bay now dash in and try to eject some of their own milt onto the eggs. Hundreds to thousands of orange-red eggs (1,000, on average, from a 14-inch, or 35-cm cutthroat) come out tiny, then quickly swell, absorbing water along with the fertilizing milt. The female's last maternal act is to cover them with gravel as she extends her redd, digging the next trench immediately upstream from the last. Different males may attend her subsequent efforts. Pacific salmon die soon after spawning, as do a majority of steelhead.

The eggs take several weeks to hatch; the colder the water, the longer they take. The newly hatched "alevin" remains in the gravel a few weeks more, still nutritionally dependent on the yolk-sac suspended from its belly. As it depletes the yolk, it adapts to a diet of zooplankton and emerges from the gravel as a "fry." In a year or two they grow to "parr" size, displaying the "parr marks" that make them easier to identify.

On the coast there are anadromous runs of cutthroats, but none swim far enough upstream to reach our range.

The redd "cuts" on a cutthroat's throat serve to emphasize gestures and displays. Coloring varies a lot among the several cutthroat subspecies. Notably, the Yellowstone cutthroat has a yellow-brown

---

Flyfishing as we nonhunting nongathering catch-and-release nerds practice it isn't even fishing, really. It links us not to the Food Chain but to the Idiot Joy Chain, which differs from a Food Chain in that it has no top or bottom. Rod in hand on the Idiot Joy Chain, I find myself no more worthy or wise or deserving or in touch with I.Q. points than the stone-, water-, insect-, fish-, and sunlight-links in the same Chain... I fish in fall to feel the slow tilt of planet and weakening solar rays abandon every waterbug, wildflower, mating dance, and tree leaf summer gave us. I fish in spring to feel the same planetary tilt resurrect every creature and joy that autumn killed...

---

cast overall; red shades are strongest on the gill cover and of course the lower lip; dark spots are relatively large, round, and become quite sparse toward the head and the belly. The Snake River cutt has finer dark spots, and more of them, more broadly distributed. The West-slope cutt (which has the broadest native range) rarely reaches impressive size, and may retain faint parr marks through adulthood; it is heavily dark-spotted even in the front half, and the spots may be roughly ×- or comma-shaped as well as round; the belly may be crimson. The rainbow/cutthroat hybrid (which has occurred widely where rainbows were stocked in cutthroat range) is difficult to distinguish. It may look pretty much like either parent species, but if it has one key character of the other it's a hybrid—namely, tongue teeth or a red jawline on a "rainbow," or white-bordered or dark-spotted anal and pelvic fins, or a dark-spotted head, on a "cutthroat."

One reason for the wide variability in color is that trout, like chameleons only much slower, alter their camouflage in response to colors they see. Experimentally blinded trout eventually contrasted sharply with their associates.

Rainbow Trout

Oncorhyncus mykiss (me-kiss: a Kamchatkan tribal word for it) =formerly *Salmo gairdneri*. Also **redband trout**. Coloring extremely variable; flesh bright red to white; spawning adults usually have a red to pink streak (the "rainbow") full length on each side, much deeper on males; returning sea-run fish (steelhead) are silvery all over with guanine (a protein coating on all salmonids fresh from the sea) which obscures any coloring underneath; dorsal fin rays typically 11–12, pelvic fin rays 10, anal fin rays 10 (range 8–12); juveniles have a distinct row of 5–10 small dark spots along the back straight in front of the dorsal fin, plus 8–13 oval parr marks along the lateral line. Rainbows common in high lakes and streams. Salmonidae. Illustrated next page, and color page 535.

It leaps again…and I suddenly know a litany of things I can't possibly know: that the souls of trout too leap, becoming birds; that trout take a fly made of plumage out of yearning as well as hunger; that an immaterial thread carries a trout's yearning through death and into a bird's egg; that the olive-sided flycatcher, using this thread, is as much trout as bird as it rises to snatch the mayfly from its chosen pool of air;… that the flycatcher that was the trout was the mayfly that was the river that was the creeks that were last year's snowpack that was last year's skies…

—David James Duncan

The West's best-known sport fish is native up and down the Pacific Slope from Mexico to the Alaska Peninsula and inland through most of the Columbia River system, though apparently not on the Snake above Hell's Canyon. Today the **rainbow trout** lives almost anywhere in the world with a temperate climate, both in fish farms and stocked in streams. Anglers love its leaping ability. In hatcheries it grows faster and suffers less mortality than other trout, and in streams it survives in a wide variety of conditions.

Yellowstone provides an extreme example of the latter: stocked rainbows in the Firehole River tolerate water temperatures up to the high eighties [over 30° C.] for brief periods, and this hot-spring water heavily laden with minerals. Under these conditions, trout that can survive actually grow much faster than normal, but have shorter life expectancies, and some of them fail to mature sexually.

After a century of stocking, much of it ungoverned and unrecorded, the genetics of rainbow trout in the West are irretrievably muddled. Not only are the different stocks of rainbow interblended, but rainbow-cutthroat hybrids are abundant and widespread. The long trend toward the ascendancy of rainbow genes in our rivers may have started to reverse due to whirling disease which, so far, affects other trout species less than rainbows. (See page 486.)

The sea-run form of this species, known as steelhead, reaches our region in the Wallowas and central Idaho. These are summer-run steelhead; they typically spend all fall and winter in the streams, waiting to spawn in early spring. Most swim to sea when two years old, and feed for one to four "salt years" before their first spawning run. At sea, steelhead grow faster and reach larger sizes than their freshwater cousins. Steelhead eat more than salmon do while running upstream, so they're somewhat more inclined to bite, and their flesh is in good condition. Some individuals, unlike salmon, return to sea and spawn again the following year. Big and strong, steelhead are notoriously hard to land and hard to locate. A favorite riffle for steelhead is a fiercely guarded secret.

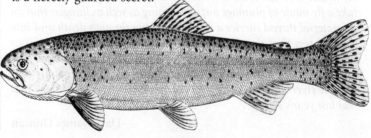

Kokanee and Pacific Salmon

Kokanee and sockeye salmon, *Oncorhyncus nerka* (ner-ka: Kamchatkan native word for it). No dark spots on back or tailfin; 28–40 long thin rough gill-rakers in first gill arch; 13+ rays in the anal fin; silvery overall, finely black-spotted bluegreenish above lateral line; spawning adult has greenish dark head, crimson body; male is slightly humpbacked; 4" [10 cm] juveniles have small, oval parr marks almost entirely above lateral line. Non-anadromous kokanee are widespread in bigger lakes and their tributaries; anadromous sockeye runs survive in our range in the Fraser, Grande Ronde and Salmon River systems.

Sockeye
(spawning male)

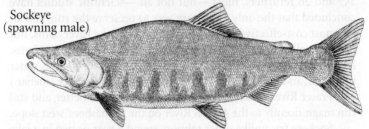

Chinook salmon, *0. tshawytscha* (cha-**witch**-a: Kamchatkan native word for it). Also **tyee, king salmon.** Black spots on back and both lobes of tail fin; black gums on lower jaw; spawning adults dark, rarely red; juveniles at 4" [10 cm] have tall parr marks bisected by the lateral line, and a dark-margined but clear-centered adipose fin; 13+ rays in the anal fin. Lower Snake River and its tributaries.

Pacific salmon range the Pacific from California to Korea, the Arctic from the Mackenzie to the Lena. First described to science by Steller (p 443) in Siberia, they got species names in Russian and Kamchatkan languages. They're named salmon after the Atlantic fish, *Salmo salar*.

Most salmon are anadromous (a-**nad**-ra-mus: up-running) fishes; they migrate up from the sea to spawn. They require clear, cold, well-aerated gravelly creeks to nurse them in infancy, and larger bodies of water richer in animal life to rear them to maturity. It may be no surprise that the ocean is ideal for the latter phase; what's amazing is that they're perfectly adapted, as water-breathing creatures, to handle the chemical shock between salt and fresh water.

The ability to home back to their natal stream is a wonder of animal navigation. Once they get close to the right river, they zero in on the mineral "recipe" of the precise tributary of their birth by means of smell, a sense located in fish in two shallow nostrils unconnected to their mouths. Some go only a few miles upriver, but some chinooks used to go 2,000 miles [3,200 km] up the Columbia to its source, Columbia Lake, B.C. Today, dams stop them from reaching our region except for the few that make it to the Grande Ronde, Clearwater, and Salmon drainages, and the Fraser near Mt. Robson.

Fishes

Sockeyes can swim nearly as far, and to higher elevations. Ascending almost 7,000' [2100 m] to the foot of the Sawtooths, Idaho's Redfish Lake sockeyes hold the record. The lake was named for them when they were abundant. They became a *cause celebre* when their numbers dwindled to four, one, and zero in some years in the 1990s. Those few survivors were captured and bred in hatcheries in an effort to show that with enough dollars, we can sustain even a stock that migrates through eight huge dams. Though 2000 and 2001 saw 257 and 26 returners, most—but not all—scientific studies have concluded that the only long-term way to preserve the run, and/or the most cost-effective way, is to breach four Snake River dams. But no one really knows the relative importance of overfishing, dams, hatcheries, non-native introductions, global climate change, water pollution, and habitat issues in the decline of salmon. (See sidebar.)

Fraser River sockeye have been managed much better, and still run magnificently to the Adams River on the Monashees' west slope.

Sockeye fry, unlike other salmon, spend a year or two in a lake before migrating to sea. Sockeyes that were landlocked in several lakes when the glaciers retreated (and in more lakes when dams were built) became a distinct freshwater form. Called kokanee, they stay pretty small on a diet of micro-animals including the crustaceans that turn their flesh pink. Salmon that get big in fresh water can eat waterfowl chicks, adult amphibians, and water shrews.

On returning to freshwater to spawn, chinooks eat little or nothing, but metabolize stored fat and muscle tissue. Sockeyes will feed en route to spawning during a last summer vacation in a lake. They typically turn deep red both inside and out. By spawning time, salmon are at death's door, and look like it. With pale, fungus-ravaged flesh, they make poor eating (but bears and eagles don't complain).

The decomposition of spawners is far more than a spooky detail. It's a central glory of salmon, one whose loss, with their decline, is an ecocatastrophe in progress. It evolved because the parents' dead bodies become the major food source for their offspring. Salmon used to move about 8,000,000 tons of nutrients per year from the sea far into the interior of the greater PNW. Bears that ate them spread the nutrients around, dropping them in urine and feces. This has been confirmed and measured in Alaska: the isotopic signature of marine based nitrogen is found in plant leaves up to a mile from salmon streams, but not in similar leaves near streams that lack salmon. Since nitrogen is a main limiting factor on plant growth in the Northwest, the decimation of salmon literally stunts tree growth in much of the region—as well as populations of bears, of course, and bald eagles, mink, and salmon themselves, which shrank in both size and number.

We always knew dead fish are good fertilizer; we knew the rivers used to shimmer crimson with spawners; the people who lived here told us in many ways. It was always staring us in the face, but no one got it, no one ran the numbers on salmon as fertilizer until the 1990s. Few people in the public policy sphere get it, even now. It was a simple scientific breakthrough, but it will make ripples for years to come.

Fish Habitat Destruction

In the tragedy of salmon decline, a century of overfishing on a horrendous, mindless scale plays a big role, but not the only role worth paying attention to. Far from it. Almost everything people have done that makes the West less natural seems to make life harder for fish.

Siltation ruins the clean gravel salmonids need for spawning. Streambed gravel gets muddy where livestock tromp, for example, or where slopes erode after logging, roadbuilding, or any other construction.

Loss of shade makes some small streams too warm for salmon after either logging or livestock remove streamside plants.

Snags and logs used to have huge effects on streamflow, slowing it down and creating pools and meanders—essential fish habitat. Logs were taken out of streams for lumber or to enable navigation. As recently as 1980, some logs were still being removed in the mistaken belief that it would help fish get upstream.

Draining of marshes and beaver ponds has eliminated habitat.

Seasonal fluctuation is aggravated when a watershed's forest is either burned or clearcut. Rain and snowmelt runs off much faster because less is absorbed by soil and plants, and snow melts sooner. Then summer water levels are lower—and warmer—for longer.

Irrigation of farms diverts water out of streams, reducing many of them to warm, muddy trickles in summer.

Pollution comes from mines, farms, feedlots, fish farms, sewage, and lawn and pavement runoff.

Dams are the problem that gets the most press. We keep learning of more ways that dams kill fish. Some dams are too high to have fish ladders; even on moderate ones many fish get lost or exhausted at fish ladders. Electric turbines cut up smolts on the way down. Smolts die of bubbles that form in their blood due to pressure changes during the drop. Big reservoirs warm the water up in the sun; harbor non-native warmwater predators; lack the current that orients smolts so they can swim downstream fast enough; and dilute the chemistry of small tributaries, making it hard for adults to locate their natal stream.

Golden Trout

Oncorhyncus mykiss ssp *agua-bonita* (ah-gwa-bo-**nee**-ta: pretty water, name of creek where first collected). =*O. aguabonita.* Yellow overall, exc bright red along lateral line, greenish on top, ± orange on belly; black spots on rear half, but few or none on front half; dorsal, anal, and pelvic fins white-tipped; fewer than thirteen rays in anal fin; no teeth on back of tongue; 11 parr marks persist into maturity; rarely over 10". Selected alpine lakes. Salmonidae.

Golden trout are native only to a small area in the southern Sierra Nevada, in California. Though they're small and slow-growing, some anglers go to great lengths to fish for them because they are exceptionally beautiful, different, and hard to get to. Fish agencies generally stock them only in very remote high lakes, usually where there are no competing fish. The Wind Rivers   are a prime destination.

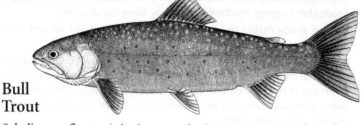

Bull Trout

Salvelinus confluentus (sal-vel-**eye**-nus: the German term Latinized; con-flu-en-tus: of rivers) =formerly included in *S. malma*, **Dolly Varden** trout. Adults broadly built, the head and midsection typically as wide as they are tall. Olive-greenish back and sides regularly pink- to yellow-dotted; juvenile parr marks wider than the light spaces between; dorsal fin unmarked, with 10 or 11 rays, anal fin usually with 9. Cold, clean, lakes and streams; all exc WY. Salmonidae.

Commonly called trout, fish of this genus are more properly char, or charr, or charrr (in the American, English, and quasi-Scottish spellings). Mature char generally have light spots against a darker background; whereas trout have the reverse. Char are praised as crafty in Washington F&W literature: "Log jams, cascades and falls that are barriers to the chinook's brute strength and the steelhead's acrobatic abilities may be only minor obstacles to the cunning and guile of [char]…Some go as far as to stick their heads out of the water to peek and find the easiest route." But when it comes to fishhooks they are seen as more naive and less feisty, making them less popular with anglers out for sport, and more popular with ones out for meat.

The bull trout, once an abundant Western trout with huge catch limits and even bounties (because it eats salmon fry) is now in dicey condition, extinct in many watersheds and endangered in others. It requires even colder, cleaner streams for spawning than other salmonids. When logging in a watershed muddies the gravel and warms the water by reducing shade, it may take decades before the stream is again good enough for a bull. That's one reason why many scientists think a streamside buffer should be at least 300 feet [90 m]. Looking ahead, global warming could make even a pristine stream too warm.

Two introduced char species (page 486–89) also threaten bulls. Brook trout have crossbred with bull trout and produced sterile hybrids, reducing bull trout reproduction. (Brookies were, after rainbows, the second most commonly stocked trout; they are no longer stocked in watersheds with bull trout.) A third char species, lake trout, seems to occupy pretty much the same ecological niche as bull trout when they're in the same lake, and almost always wins out competitively, regardless of elevation. Bull trout tend to be found in higher, colder lakes, presumably owing their existence there to rapid migration into headwater areas as the ice age glaciers receded. By the time lake trout were making their way upstream toward these lakes, the rapid deposition of big rocks from the glaciers, or other landform changes, may have created obstacles to the lakers, leaving bulls the sole trout of may upper reaches. One exception is Flathead Lake, where the two species are both native, and coexist. Scientists have not figured out what's different there to enable the bulls to persist.

While our native char all spawn in mountain stream headwaters, populations vary in how far they migrate: they may live the bulk of their lives in small streams (nonmigrating) or bigger ones, or in lakes or the ocean (anadromous). They migrate far for trout. In the Rockies they reached a record 32 pounds [14.5 kg].

The Lateral Line

Fish hear with their skins. Sensory cells called neuromasts are scattered over their bodies near the surface and also (of a different type) imbedded in a visible full-length canal, the lateral line, on each flank. Surface neuromasts are so sensitive that rushing water overwhelms them with noise. Slow-water fish have lots of those, and hear with them, whereas fast-water species like sculpins and trout have just a few, with a different function: detecting the current to orient the fish to it. These fish have highly developed lateral lines with buried neuromasts that screen out the white noise, and yet remain finely sensitive to nonconstant splashes and ripples—such as a dry fly hitting the riffled water.

Brook Trout

Salvelinus fontinalis (fon-tin-**ay**-lis: of springs). Dark green back and sides with "wormy" patterns and red spots encircled by blue haloes; dorsal fin dark-spotted, with 8–10 rays, anal fin with 7–9; juveniles' parr marks dotted with lighter red and yellow; tail hardly forked. Introduced. Salmonidae. Color p 535.

This Eastern North American native was the most popular trout for stocking in the early years of Western sport fishing, and became very widespread. Some consider it the tastiest and most beautiful trout. It is gullible and not especially feisty, making it more popular with less experienced anglers. It requires cold water, and has succeeded in some small alpine lakes where rainbows did not, apparently because brookies can spawn on a beach, whereas rainbows require an inlet

Whirling Disease

A mysterious introduced parasite of trout is a grave concern to anglers and other nature-lovers in Montana and Idaho. How far it will go, and why, are among its mysteries. For a couple of years it seemed to deci-mate the famous rainbow trout fishery of the Madison River, and it has been equally deadly in several Colorado rivers. In laboratory tests, all of our trout species can be infected. However, many rivers that have had the parasite for several years still haven't seen any severe mortality, and even the rivers that have suffered most show wide variations in severity from year to year, season to season, species to species, and even from one spawning area to the next.

And what is this beast? *Myxobolus cerebralis* (mix-**ob**-o-lus sarah-**bra**-liss: slimy lump on the brain) is a myxozoan ("slimy animal"), a one-celled protist with a complex multi-stage two-host life cycle. In trout, it infects cartilage and compresses spinal nerves, causing sluggishness, blackened tails and heads, and eventually brain damage that induces tail-chasing, or "whirling." Many fish die before they reach that point, as reduced function disables them from evading predators or competing effectively for food.

The decomposing victim releases myriad parasites in a resting "spore" form that can survive for decades in the mud. These come back to life if eaten by a small primitive worm named *Tubifex*. After growing in the worm's gut, they take form as larger triactinomyxons ("TAMs" for short). These actively swim, attach to trout fry like grap-pling hooks, and fire shotgun-shell loads of 64 small spores each, into their victims' bodies.

The worms are far more abundant in more fertile, sediment-laden stream. They sometimes thrive until they both crowd out other species and stunt their own growth through overcrowding. In Yellowstone they are exceptionally tolerant of acid and alkaline water. In fact they like high-calcium (limestone-terrain) alkaline water so much that they can grow both large and abundant in it, escaping the curse of stunting.

streams. In our region that often means the ones with streambank damage or agricultural runoff. Temperature is another reason that different streams vary. Fry that hatch in our coldest streams rarely get severe cases. After they grow up and their cartilage turns to bone, they can safely migrate and live anywhere. Apparently the Madison was hit hard because most of its native rainbows, for unknown reasons, spawn in relatively few areas, all on the river's main stem. Non-native brook trout on the Madison have not suffered much, and non-native rainbows on the east slope in Montana mostly spawn in small tributaries, and are doing okay so far.

In all likelihood whirling disease is going to kill off the fish stocks most susceptible to it, over large areas, thus selecting for the more resistant stocks, which will eventually reoccupy most trout range. It is not at all clear that any trout are genetically resistant in the sense of being able to either survive or fight off a severe infection. However, genes program trout as to where and when they will spawn. Stocks that spawn at colder times of year and/or in cleaner, higher-elevation tributaries should be among the trout of the future, and if we're lucky, enough will migrate, when they mature, to populate most of the less favorable waters.

Whether or not we should use hatcheries, and even gene-splicing, to try to hasten this Darwinian selection process is an issue. Doing so would reduce the naturally huge genetic diversity of trout that gives trout populations some hope of evolving past disease threats in the first place. A much narrower gene pool might defeat this disease only to be completely killed off by another disease that comes along later. Far wiser to be patient, and let selection happen on its own. But (as with so many other problems) it will also help if we can cut back on pollution, water diversion, and other human alteration of streams.

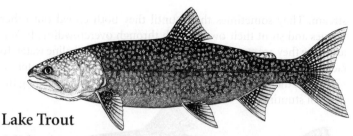

Lake Trout

Salvelinus namaycush (**nam**-ee-kush: the Cree name for it). Also **mackinaw**, **gray trout**. Bluish or greenish gray to brown, with pale spots, and whitish belly; proportionately narrower, as seen from the side, than our other salmonids; tail deeply forked. Introduced in deep cold lakes. Salmonidae.

Widespread in northeastern North America, lake trout are native here only in two little lakes high in Montana's Jefferson River drainage, in Alberta, and in B.C.'s Fraser drainage. They probably crossed the Continental Divide in an end-of-the-ice-age lake that temporarily filled a portion of the Rocky Mountain Trench, and later split between Fraser (Pacific) and Peace River (Atlantic) drainages.

Until rather recently, anglers and fisheries managers alike assumed that the object of management is to provide the most desirable catches possible wherever they can be induced to live. If anyone made a generous little donation of a few live fish into waters that lacked that species, they did so freely, without fear that anyone might object. Today, while brown and brook trout are a *fait accompli* (and much appreciated by many) in most of our waters, there is a new breed of anglers who go out of their way to fish where they can expect to catch only wild fish—a category that excludes hatchery stocks of native species, as well as non-natives.

For decades it has been illegal to introduce non-natives, but there probably are still a few scofflaws who think that doing so is among the inalienable rights mentioned in the Declaration of Independence. The illegal introduction, in the 1980s, of lake trout into Yellowstone Lake provides a textbook case of a highly esteemed gamefish becoming a catastrophe.

The sole native trout in the Lake—its natural top predator—is the smaller Yellowstone cutthroat. Its size disadvantage is accentuated by the pattern of lake trout spending their mature years in deep waters, where cutthroats spend their juvenile years. Lake trout both prey on cutthroats and outcompete them for smaller prey. In most western lakes where they have been introduced they have either almost or entirely eliminated the native trout, especially bull trout. They will do the same to Yellowstone Lakes cutthroats, if allowed to.

But the loss of a sport fishery worth $36 million a year isn't the worst of it. (That value includes Yellowstone River trout that winter in the Lake.) The worst is that grizzly bears, ospreys, otters, mink, pelicans, dippers, and kingfishers all prey on these cutthroats. Lake trout, because they live and can even spawn in deep water, offer very little food to predators. If the Lake loses its cutthroats it will have no ospreys, and the entire Park will support considerably fewer grizzlies.

There is no way to get rid of the lake trout, but Park scientists calculate that for about $300,000 a year they can gillnet enough of them to maintain a strong cutthroat population. With careful study of the right mesh sizes, locations, and times they think they can avoid the cutthroats. Needless to say, all fishers who prefer to catch-and-not-release are welcomed with open arms if they reserve that treatment for lake trout. The program won't work without them.

Ironically, lake trout were themselves decimated in the Great Lakes by overfishing and introduced species.

Some record lakers were 42 pounds in Yellowstone, well over 60 in B.C., and 102 in Lake Athabasca [19, 27, and 46 kg]. In the Park's Lewis and Shoshone Lakes, where they were introduced in 1890, lake trout will probably continue to provide some of the West's biggest catches. Those lakes had no native fish, so the lakers' impact seems less dire from our point of view, but of course their ecological impact via salamanders and other prey was devastating. Lakers reach their great sizes slowly, and are more likely to reach age 20 than any of our mammals.

The mentality that wants lake trout everywhere also salivates for walleye and northern pike, the most sought-after gamefish of eastern North America. Both are already in the mid-Columbia system, and walleyes are in the Bitterroot. Idaho's Lake Coeur d'Alene has been producing some of the biggest pike in the West, but before long we can expect it to have a big population of runty little pike, hardly any trout, and God knows what other ill effects on lake ecology. Do-it-yourself introductions like this are smarmy, selfish, foolish crimes against nature as well as against the law.

Brown Trout

Salmo trutta. The only trout with both black and (fewer) red spots; the red spots are near and below the lateral line, and have pale (cream to pink or bluish) haloes; yellowish to olive brown background; dorsal and anal fins each 10–11-rayed. Widely introduced, though barely into BC. Salmonidae. Color p 535.

Angling as a sport was nurtured in Scotland more than anywhere else, and browns are the favored objective there, so Americans were always eager to have them. They were first introduced in the East in 1882, and in Yellowstone just eight years later, but not in interior B.C. until 1957. They are warier of fishhooks than any other trout, probably because only the wariest genetic lines were able to survive a thousand years of angling in Europe. Scottish "Loch Leven" and German "Von Behr" brown trout were considered distinct species in the nineteenth century, when they were   first introduced; by now they're thoroughly blended in most   streams.

Whitefish

Prosopium
and *Coregonus* spp.
(pro-**soap**-ium: mask;
cor-eg-**oh**-nus: angle eye). Pale silver fish without spots; mouths small, without teeth; scales relatively large, bumpy. Salmonidae.

Mountain whitefish, *P. williamsoni* (after Lt. R. S. Williamson, p 242). Trout-shaped, avg 12" [30 cm] fully grown; 10–13 rays in anal fin. Widespread.

Pygmy whitefish, *P. coulteri* (after botanist J. M. Coulter). Cigar-shaped, with very blunt head, average 5" [12 cm] fully grown; 8–10 branched rays in anal fin. Mountain streams and lakes in Canada and n edge of US.

Lake whitefish, *C. clupeaformis* (clue-pia-**for**-mis: herring-shaped). Laterally flattened, with high arched back and concave forehead profile; avg 14+" [30+ cm] fully grown; 10–12 rays in anal fin. Introduced in bigger lakes and reservoirs; native just n of our range, and in the East. The whitefish of Jewish deli glory.

Whitefish mostly use their little mouths to search the bottom for insect larvae, but occasionally they will rise to a surface hatch. They spawn in late fall and winter, in water as cold as 35° (2° C). The eggs have a sticky coating that sticks them to rocks, so no redd needs to be dug. Some heavily fished streams lost all their wild salmonid stocks except whitefish, so I suspect they're pretty wily.

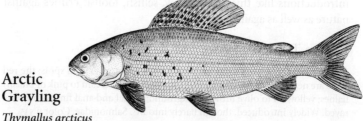

Arctic Grayling

Thymallus arcticus
(thigh-**mal**-us: Roman word for it, ref to aroma of thyme). Body shape simple, streamlined, laterally compressed; generally silver-gray, but in various lights and

seasons this gray can flash an gorgeous range of tints and hues; a few small black spots near front end and on the often turquoise-colored dorsal fin, which is large, with 16–21 rays, and can extend and look sail-like. A few high lakes and streams. Any grayling caught must be released immediately. Salmonidae.

Arctic grayling range encircles the Arctic Ocean. The Ice Ages evicted grayling from the Canadian part of our range and pushed them down into the lower 48. The retreating ice left two small disjunct populations, but the one in Michigan died out in the 1930s. Montana grayling thrive where introduced into small high lakes, but efforts to restock them in their former river habitats have failed. In the nineteenth century they shared rivers with cutthroats and whitefish (an unusual instance of resource partitioning by three salmonid species) and they share some lakes today with cutthroats and rainbows. Introduced brown trout seem to make life impossible for grayling. Since we can't get browns out of any major stretch of river, we probably won't have grayling in rivers again.

Longnose Sucker

Catastomus catastomus (cat-a-**sto**-mus: mouth underneath). Mouth set back on underside of head, with fleshy lips; no adipose fin; anal fin as long or longer than pelvic and pectoral fins; generally dark greenish gray, with pale belly, but breeding fish (esp males) develop reddish streaks and tinges; some subspecies occasionally reach 24" [60 cm] at ages up to the upper twenties. Widespread. Catastomidae.

Suckers move around slowly, using their underside mouths to scrape algae, bacteria, and some tiny animals off the rocks.

Minnows

Cyprinidae (Minnow family). These species rarely more than 6" [15 cm].

Redside shiner, *Richardonius balteatus* (richard-**so**-nius: after Sir John Richardson, p 155; bal-tee-**ay**-tus: girdled). Mouth at tip of snout; flanks pink to red; dorsal fin entirely behind midlength point; no adipose fin; 8 rays in anal fin. Widespread. Color p 535.

Dace, *Rhinichthys* spp (rye-**nick**-thiss: snout fish). Mouth just behind (and below) tip of snout; generally drab and dark above, grading paler toward belly; breeding males may get reddish lips, gills, belly, etc.; no adipose fin. Widespread.

Dace seem equally at home in either slow and very fast water. They even live at the "cool" 90° bottom of one hotspring creek, just inches below its 147° surface [32° C. versus 64°].

Fishes

Sculpins

Cottus spp. (**cot**-us: Greek term for some river fish). Also **muddler minnows, bullheads, blobs.** Scaleless, sometimes ± prickly, minnow-sized fishes with wide mouths, thick lips, depressed foreheads, very large pectoral fins, a ¾-length dorsal fin in 2 parts, and a rounded unforked tail fin. Widespread in streams, much of the time under rocks, logs, etc. Cottidae (Sculpin family).

Torrent sculpin, *C. rhotheus* (**roe**-thius: of noisy waters).
Slimy sculpin, *C. cognatus* (cog-**nay**-tus: related, ref to European *C. gobio*).
Mottled sculpin, *C. bairdi* (**bear**-dye: after biologist Spencer F. Baird).
Shorthead sculpin, *C. confusus* (con-**few**-sus: clouded).

These funny-looking little fish are adapted to life on the bottom: wide, depressed mouths for bottom-feeding; motley drab colors for camouflage against the bottom; eyes directed upward (the only direction one can look, from the bottom); and huge pectoral fins to reduce the energy cost of anchoring them in strong current. They actually swim with those fins, in a darting motion, rather than by wiggling their whole bodies like most fish. The eggs, laid in spring, adhere to the underside of stones, and are guarded by the father.

Sculpins eat some trout eggs and fry, and compete with young trout for aquatic insect prey, their main food. Larger salmon and trout, in return, are fond of sculpins. (They have inspired a trout fly pattern, the "muddler minnow.") In all likelihood, most trout eggs that end up in sculpin bellies were ones not adequately buried in gravel by their mothers, and would have perished anyway.

Sculpins are found above impassable waterfalls on some rivers, presumably getting there via periglacial lakes that crossed present-day drainage divides briefly while the ice sheet was retreating. Ancestors of today's mottled sculpins in the Flathead River drainage must have crossed the Continental Divide from the Maries River.

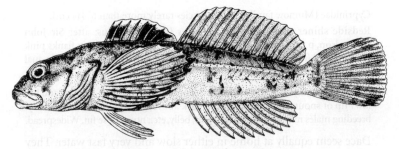

We are all in the gutter, but some of us are looking at the stars.

— Oscar Wilde

14

Insects

Insects — six-legged animals with jointed external skeletons made of chitin — are far and away the most diverse and successful kind of animals on earth. Almost a million species have been named, and many millions remain to be discovered and described. Only a tiny sampling of our insects can be discussed in this space: mostly butterfly and dragonfly beauties, the invaluable pollinators — bumble bees and hover flies — and a rogues' gallery of unloved insects.

A majority of insect life cycles entail metamorphosis from a wingless larva, which does most or all of the eating and growing, to a pupa or resting stage, and finally to a winged, sexual adult. Minority life cycles, called "gradual metamorphosis," are seen in grasshoppers, water striders, and dragonflies (pages 508, 513, 510).

Mosquitoes

Order Diptera (Flies), family **Culicidae**.

A female mosquito has a most elaborate mouth. What we see as a mere proboscis is a tiny set of surgical tools — six "stylets" wrapped in the groove of a heavier "labium" flanked by two "palps." The operation begins with the two palps exploring your skin for a weakness or pore. There the labium sets down. Delicately and precisely, two pairs of stylets — one for piercing, one for slicing — set to work. They quickly locate and pierce a capillary, then bend and travel a short way within it. The remaining two stylets are tubes; one sucks blood out while the other pumps saliva in, stimulating bloodflow to the vicinity and inhibiting coagulation. Up to the point of blood stimulation, to which you may be allergic, you probably feel nothing.

Unlike bee stings, whose function is to inflict pain or injury, a mosquito bite raises its itchy bump—an allergic reaction to mosquito saliva—only incidentally. The sensitivity is acquired. The first few times a given species of mosquito bites you, there's no pain or welt. As you develop sensitivity to that species, your response speeds up from a day or so, at first, to one or two minutes. Eventually you may become again desensitized to that species. We may fail to notice this cycle because we rarely distinguish among the species.

The females need at least one big blood meal (greater than their own weight) for nourishment to lay eggs. It takes human-feeding species about two minutes to draw enough. Aside from that meal, they eat pollen and nectar; some plants may depend on them as - pollinators. Male mosquitoes eat nectar only, but contribute to our discomfort all the same: they hover around warm bodies in the reasonable expectation that that's where the girls are. If we wanted, we could get males to fly down our throats by singing the pitch that female wings hum. Male antennae have evolved into plumes that vibrate sympathetically with conspecific female wing beats, and the males home in toward any steady source of this pitch.

Each mosquito species has its own wing beat frequencies, one for the males and a slightly lower one for the females; wing beats speed up as an individual reaches sexual maturity. They range up to 600 per second in mosquitoes, and peak at over 1,000 in their relatives, the midges. Anything over 50 beats per second is too fast to be triggered by individual nerve impulses. Instead, the thoracic muscles are in two groups: each is stretched by the contraction of the other, then contracts in a twitchlike reflex. The thorax shell snaps back and forth between two stable shapes, like the lid of a shoe polish tin, one shape holding the wings up and the other down. The nervous system need supply only a slow, unsteady pulse of signals to keep this vibration going. (Flies, bees and many other insects fly similarly.)

Most mosquitoes are active only a short period each day, with the typical peaks coming around sunset and just before dawn. They need an air temperature of at least 40° [4° C.] to fly, and their bodies are too small to retain a temperature much above that of the air.

Some varieties of the familiar urban species *Culex pipiens* never bite people, but others rank among the peskiest. A common species here is *Aedes vexans* (ay-**ee**-deez: repugnant; **vex**-anz: vexing). Instead of floating its eggs on bodies of still water, *A. vexans* lays them in fall on bare soil; the larvae hatch and thrive after heavy rains. Successive rainy spells can hatch generation after generation. Hatching is triggered by water whose oxygen is depleted—proof that microorganisms are present and active. Mosquito larvae, called "wigglers," feed by filtering algae and bacteria out of water.

Some boreal *Aedes* overwinter as fertilized females and lay eggs on the melting snowpack in spring. Gruesome concentrations of mosquitoes typify the Far North, where musk-oxen and nesting ducks make ideal hosts. One stoical researcher counted 189 bites on a forearm exposed for one minute in Manitoba. From that he extrapolated 9,000 bites per minute for one entire naked person, who could lose one-fourth of his blood in an hour. That estimate may be on the high side, since mosquitoes like arms better than other human body parts, and like some humans better than others.

The females zero in on the carbon dioxide we exhale, together with various trace chemicals that emanate from skin. Studies are under way (studies of forearms, naturally) to pin down the exact chemistry that attracts. Someday we may repel mosquitoes by taking pills to alter our natural aromas, either reducing or masking key attractants. But what might that do to interhuman attractions? IBI-246, a natural repellent in tomatoes, recently tested out as more repellent twelve hours after application than DEET. Stay tuned.

In the meantime we have DEET, which effectively reduces the biting, but not the vexing, since it is a contact repellent; i.e., the mosquito has to land on you before it is repelled. DEET is somewhat toxic, and should be avoided by small children and pregnant women. Herbal repellents with citronella oil have some effectiveness if reapplied frequently. Ultrasonic repellents don't pass scientific muster..

Mosquitoes are the best studied of all insect families because, as vectors of malaria and yellow fever, they wrought sweeping effects on human economics and warfare. In 1803, yellow fever in the tropics changed history in the Northern Rockies by killing nine-tenths of a French army sent to conquer Haiti and New Orleans, leaving Napoleon in a mood to sell "Louisiana" to President Jefferson at a price Congress couldn't refuse. The purchase led to Lewis and Clark's Expedition, and ultimately to the PNW south of the 49th parallel being part of the U.S. rather than of Mexico, Canada, or Russia.

Malaria has come back as, by some measures, the world's worst disease problem today. With a few decades of global warming, it could become a serious problem here. The mosquito-borne disease on the immediate horizon here is West Nile virus: see page 410.

No-see-ums

Culicoides spp. (cue-lic-**oy**-deez: gnat-like). Also **punkies**, **biting midges**. Order Diptera.

"No-see-ums" suffices to identify these pests. Less than ⅛" [2 mm] long, they are just big enough to see, but small enough to invade screened cabins. They are hard to make out in the waning light of dusk, when they do most of their biting. To most people they cause more exasperation than pain, but some people do get serious welts. No-see-ums are so localized around their breeding grounds—puddles, intertidal sands, humus, etc.—that we can usually escape by walking thirty steps. The chief victims of this bloodsucking family are other insects ranging from their own size on up to dragonflies. In some species the females prey on the males, and one "pirate" species sucks mammal blood from mosquito abdomens.

Deer Flies

Chrysops spp. (**cry**-sops: appearing golden). Order Diptera (Flies).

Ranging from dull gray-brown to nearly black, with pale brown blotch patterns crossing their clear wings and zigzag stripes crossing their eyes, deer flies sometimes turn up as the most hellish local pest. Swatting them, though easy, is futile: you're just too outnumbered.

Black Flies

Simulium spp. (sim-**you**-lium: simulator). Order Diptera. Also **buffalo gnats**.

These vicious biters raise a welt way out of proportion to their size, sometimes drawing blood, and reportedly causing bovine and human deaths when biting *en masse*. They render many boreal North American vacationlands uninhabitable for the month of June. Fortunately they tend to dissipate by midsummer.

"Black" flies are medium to dark gray, and stocky for their length (⅛", or 3 mm). They look humpbacked, and tilt steeply forward while biting. Only the females bite. Once fed, they dive in and out of cold, fast streams attaching eggs singly to submerged stones. The larvae stay underwater, straining plankton, moving around and then reanchoring themselves with a suction disk. After emerging from pupation, the adults burst up through the water in a bubble.

Horse Flies

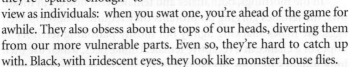

Order Diptera, family Tabanidae.

Horse flies are our biggest, fastest, strongest biting flies, so we're lucky they're sparse enough to view as individuals: when you swat one, you're ahead of the game for awhile. They also obsess about the tops of our heads, diverting them from our more vulnerable parts. Even so, they're hard to catch up with. Black, with iridescent eyes, they look like monster house flies.

With larvae that overwinter twice, horse flies are long-lived, for flies. They frequent large-mammal habitat. We see the nectar- and pollen-eating males less often than the bloodsucking females. While many of our species are in genus *Tabanus*, our most common may be *Hybomitra lasiophthalma*, with a half-inch [12 mm], grayish body and nearly horizontal iridescent purple and green stripes across its eyes. It likes wet human skin, and habitats near water.

Hover Flies

Order Diptera, family **Syrphidae**. Also **flower flies**.* Color p 104.

Hummingbirds, kestrels, and many insects achieve midair stasis, but only certain hover flies adopt it as their normal stance. They are much better hoverers than bees or other insects, which inevitably bob and weave. A pair of built-in gyroscopes may be the key. All true flies, unlike bees, have their hindwings reduced to a pair of stubby "halteres." These vibrate in flight as if they were wings, and gyroscopy is the leading hypothesis of their function.

---

*Chris Thompson, a leading syrphidologist, implores me to praise his beloved specialty under the name "flower flies" rather than "hover flies". With all due respect (I love them too, and implore you, dear reader, to look kindly on them) I find their hovering far more distinctive than their interest in flowers, as well as being better established in our language.

Hover flies in the woods, seemingly transfixed by an afternoon shaft of sunlight, are males maintaining territory near a good spot (such as a rotting tree hole) for a female to lay eggs. The female's last mating before laying eggs confers the best odds of prolific fatherhood. The sunbeam heats the fly, reducing the number of his own calories he needs to burn to maintain flight temperature, and thus extending the time he can hold his post without feeding. Watch a stationary male, and you may see him abruptly chase an approaching male or an unreceptive female, then reclaim his post.

In the mornings, both males and females visit flowers in meadows, the females gorging on proteins they require to develop their eggs, the males snacking lightly but mostly patrolling territory in hopes of a chance at a receptive female. Unlike bees, which use their long tongues to draw nectar out of deep flowers, flies have short tongues, visit shallower flowers, and primarily eat pollen. Pollen grains are encased in extremely durable, acid-resistant shells. (That's what makes 50,000-year-old pollen deposits so useful for studying prehistory.) But they release their protein-rich contents after soaking in the plants' own nectar; so the fly takes a sip of nectar after stuffing its gut with pollen.

Only bees are more valuable than hover flies as pollinators worldwide, and in high mountain meadows, where bumblebees are the only common bees, flies do more pollinating than bees. They also carry pollen farther (an advantage in terms of plant genetic diversity) but are less faithful to a plant species on any given day.

As the leading predators of aphids, the maggotlike larvae of many hover flies perform another huge service to plants. Frightful though the larva must look to an aphid, hover flies are perfectly charming to us, once we outsmart the adults' mimicry of black-and-yellow-banded bees and wasps. Hover flies even sound like the bees or wasps they mimic, by using the same buzz frequencies. Mimicry of sting-bearers protects the flies from predators. The simplest way for us to tell hover flies from bees and wasps ought to be counting the wings. Flies (Order Diptera, "two wings") have two, other flying insects have four. Unfortunately, the very narrow hindwings of bees and wasps (Order Hymenoptera, "membrane wings") are translucent and hard to see on a live insect. Yellowjackets (*Vespula* spp) at rest fold their wings straight down their backs; hover flies and bees make a V shape. Long antennae, especially if clubshaped, warn you of a wasp; most hover flies have tiny antennae, less conspicuous than their thick tongue which, if you let it, will probe around on your skin sponging up dried sweat. If it looks like a yellowjacket, slender, not furry, and seems to like you and flowers, trust it.

Cooley Spruce Gall Aphid

Adelges cooleyi (a-**del**-jeez: unseen; **coo**-lee-eye: after R. A. Cooley). Soft hemispherical bodies .04" [1 mm] long, covered at most stages with waxy, cottony white fluff; wings (if present) folded rooflike over body; on Douglas-fir needles (related spp also on true firs, pines); more conspicuous are their conelike galls (illustrated) on branch tips. Widespread on and near spruces. Order Homoptera. Color p 541.

Many spruces seem to have an odd, spiky sort of cone in addition to their larger papery-scaled ones. Looking closer, we see these aren't cones because they are at branchtips rather than a few inches back, and because they are fused wholes, not made of wiggleable scales. The "spikes" are simply spruce needles with a hard brownish skin drawn tight like shrinkwrap that shrunk. This is a "gall," material secreted by the tree in response to chemical stimulation by an insect. Other examples of galls include bright red marginal swellings on shrub leaves (color p 541), or lightweight tan orbs on oak limbs.

Though each spruce gall ends one branchlet's growth, galls themselves are hardly ever a serious drain on their host plants. Living aphids sometimes are. They suck plant juices through minute piercing tubes nearly as long as their own bodies. They suck in far more plant sugar than they can utilize, so they pass copious sticky "honeydew" excretions. Some aphids are "herded" by ants or other insects that feed on aphid honeydew, but on our fir trees honeydew is more likely to end up consumed by a dreadful-looking black smut fungus. All the same, neither the feeding nor the housing activities of this aphid make it a major economic pest.

Spruce gall aphids actually feed mostly on Douglas-fir trees. Their life cycle includes no larvae, pupae, or males as those terms are normally understood. Instead it is divided into five forms or castes, each egg-laying. One wingless form overwinters on spruce, then lays the eggs of the gall-making form, which emerges from the gall in late summer and flies to a fir to lay eggs. These eggs produce the fir-over-wintering form which in turn engenders two forms, one wingless and firbound, the other flying to spruce to beget either the spruce-overwintering form or a short-lived intermediary sexual generation. But sexuals are unknown, or at least very rare, in our region. The various female forms are perfectly able to perpetuate their clone "parthenogenetically," or without fertilization.

Insects   499

Balsam Woolly Aphid

Adelges piceae (pie-**see**-ee: of spruces). Soft hemispherical bodies ½–5" [1.2–12 cm] long, covered at most stages with waxy white wool; rarely found in winged stage. Sporadically epidemic on true firs. Order Homoptera (Aphids etc.).

The balsam woolly aphid coevolved in an unthreatening relationship with the fir species of Europe, but when accidentally introduced into North America, where it has no natural enemies, it proved deadly to several American firs. Subalpine firs have been devastated by it in many areas. The tree's leader may droop and break off early in an attack, then all the foliage may turn red-brown from the top downward and the trunk hemorrhage with resin.

This aphid resembles the innocuous Cooley spruce gall aphid (p499) but feeds on true fir stems or twigs, which swell up in "gouty" knobs. Dispersing mainly on wind currents, this species rarely grows wings and never migrates to spruces or makes galls. Reproduction is asexual; males have never been seen.

Bumble Bees

Bombus spp. (**bom**-bus: "buzz"). Large, rotund, furry, yellow-and-black bees; queens in most species are ⅝–⅞" long [16–22 mm], and fly in the spring; workers ⅜–⅝" long [10–16 mm], appearing late spring to fall. Ubiquitous. Order Hymenoptera (Ants, wasps, bees). Color p 98.

Bumble bees, our commonest bees, are in the honey bee family, and have a strong social order though their colonies are relatively small and short-lived. A bumble bee colony begins with a queen coming out from hibernating among dead leaves, having mated with several males the previous fall. Typically choosing a mouse or vole burrow for her nest, she secretes beeswax to make "pots." In some she lays eggs on a liner of pollen and nectar, sealing them over with more wax. Others she fills with honey (nectar concentrated within her body by evaporation) which she sips for energy while working her muscles and pressing her abdomen onto her eggs— incubating them with body heat. The first brood is all workers, or small, non-mating females. Maturing in three or four weeks, they take over the nectar and pollen gathering chores while the queen retires to the nest to incubate eggs and feed larvae. The simple fact that the adults work like crazy, gathering food for both themselves and their bedridden brood, is the most anomalous thing about social bees and ants. In most insect orders it's the larvae that do the grunt work, crawling after their own food and eating for the entire life cycle, and the adults have little to do but mate and lay eggs.

Much "common knowledge" about bees is about honey bees, natives of Eurasia. A honey bee worker stings only once, losing her stinger and often her life, but other bees have repeat-use stingers. Honey bees have an elaborate social order and communication rituals, but most native bee species, aside from bumble bees, are "solitary": they may live gregariously, but have no division of labor. First introduced in Virginia in 1620, the honey bee, *Apis mellifera*, was numerous in Nebraska by 1811—feeling the Westward imperative more urgently, it would seem, than the white man. In the 1990s, wild honey bees in America were decimated by an introduced mite. Scientists are watching to see how well native bees reclaim the pollinator roles that honey bees displaced them from long ago.

Protein-rich pollen nourishes the growing larvae, while pure carbohydrate nectar and honey are all that the energetic adults need. Bumble bee honey is as delicious as honey bee honey but can't be exploited by large omnivores like people and bears because bumble bees don't store much of it; the queen keeps producing as many broods of larvae as the growing colony of workers can feed. As the food supply allows, late broods will include increasing numbers of sexuals—male drones from unfertilized eggs, and new queens produced by more generous and prolonged feeding of female larvae. Only queens eat well enough to survive the onset of winter. The rest die in the fall, after the drones and queens have mated. By feeding only a small minority for hibernation, bumble bees conserve nectar and pollen resources which are scarce in cool climates.

Other key adaptations include the use of ready-made insulated nests; the relatively large, furry bodies; and the skill of employing different body temperatures for different activities and conditions. For example, a bee can conserve energy by walking, visibly sluggish, from blossom to blossom, with body temperature low enough to qualify as torpor. It does this only on cold days when large numbers of good nectar flowers are available within walking distance of each other, i.e., in big inflorescences on one plant. Bernd Heinrich catalogued the many techniques of thermoregulation in insects, and makes a strong case for thinking of many insects as "hot-blooded." Arctic bumble bees have been seen in flight in a snowstorm at 6° below freezing [−3.3° C]. Together with hover flies, bumble bees are the most valuable plant pollinators at high latitudes and altitudes.

Some queens visually identical to the proper ones are false bumble bees, genus *Psithyrus* (**sith**-ir-us: whisper). These nest parasites murder queen bees and usurp their colonies. *Bombus* queens may also usurp each other's colonies if they can, but *Psithyrus* queens are genetically committed to it; they produce no *Psithyrus* workers, and their legs carry no pollen. Worker bees on guard duty sometimes get enough stingers through an invader's armor to kill her, but once a false queen has established herself, the workers keep bringing home the bacon obliviously. It is not unusual to find several dead queens in a nest, or to find colonies of mixed species.

Golden Buprestid

Cypryacis aurulenta (sip-**pry**-a-sis: love barb; or-you-**len**-ta: golden) =*Buprestis aurulenta.* ½–¾" [13–20 mm] beetle; metallic emerald green, coppery iridescent down center, edges, and underneath; back ridged lengthwise. Widespread but shy, adults may be found feeding on foliage, esp Douglas-fir. The green rose chafer, *Dichelonyx backi*, is also bright metal-green, but rarely reaches ½" [13 mm] long. Order Coleoptera (Beetles).

This beetle beauty rivals our most glamorous butterflies. Foresters count it among our pests. Because it attacks trees in relatively small numbers it rarely does more than cosmetic damage, but that can add up to a lot of dollars. The larvae bore deep into seasoned heartwood, and may continue to do so as long as fifty years after the wood is milled and built into houses. Such records make the buprestid a contender for the title of longest-lived insect, though the larvae mature in less than a decade in natural habitats.

Fire Beetles

Melanophila spp. (mel-a-**nof**-il-a: black-loving). ½" [13 mm] beetle; metallic bronzy black; often with a pattern of six yellow dots on back. Order Coleoptera.

Some *Melanophila* species chase forest fires so efficiently that they get there in time to bite the firefighters, earning notoriety as plagues of "firebugs." While it may not surprise you to read that they can detect smoke, we now know that they also detect the *heat* of fires at distances up to fifty miles [80 km], using tiny infrared sensors on the thorax. Laying eggs under the bark of dying trees, still smoldering, they accelerate the recycling process by providing entry points for decomposers. The larvae etch whorls resembling those of a rotary buffer, barely scoring the wood surface.

Ten-Lined June Beetle

Polyphylla decemlineata (poly-fil-a: many leaves; des-em-lin-ee-ay-ta: ten lined). ⅞–1¼" [22–30 mm] long, brown, with broad white stripes lengthwise on back; hairy underneath; males have large, thick, twisting antennae; adults feed conifer foliage, fly into lights at night. Order Coleoptera.

The white, usually C-curved larvae (typical of this family, the Scarabs) feed on plant roots, becoming occasional pests in conifer nurseries. The handsome adults huff and puff audibly through their breathing holes when disturbed.

Ponderous Borer

Ergates spiculatus (er-ga-teez: worker; spic-you-lay-tus: with little spikes). Also **pine sawyer, spiny longhorn beetle**. Large 1¾–2½" [45–7 mm] beetles; back minutely pebbled, dark reddish brown to black; thorax ("neck" area) may bear many small spines; antennae long, jointed, curved outward. Order Coleoptera.

Attracted to light, these clumsy nocturnal giants startle us when they come crashing into camp. The equally ponderous larvae take several years to grow to a mature size of up to 3" [75 mm], chewing 1" to 2" [25–50 mm] diameter holes through pine or Douglas-fir heartwood. Loggers call the larvae "timber worms." One logger was inspired by their mandibles in inventing the modern saw chain design.

The Beetle order's name, Coleoptera, means "sheath wings." The forewings are modified into a hard sheath that encloses and protects the hindwings when they're folded, enabling beetles to bore into hard materials without damaging their flight wings. The ability to both fly and bore in adulthood may be a key to beetles' success. They are the largest and most diverse order, not only among insects but among all living things: one out of every four animal species is a beetle.

Pine Beetles

Dendroctonus spp. (den-**droc**-ton-us: tree murder). Small (⅛–¼") [3–6 mm] black to pale brown or red beetles with tiny, elbowed, club-tipped antennae; adults and larvae both live in inner bark layer, hence are little seen, but their excavation patterns in the bark and cortex are distinctive. Ubiquitous. Order Coleoptera (Beetles). Color p 541.

Western pine beetle, *D. brevicomis* (brev-ic-**oh**-mis: short hair). On ponderosa pines.

Mountain pine beetle, *D. ponderosae* (ponder-**oh**-see: of ponderosa pine, misleadingly). On most pines, but especially lodgepole and whitebark.

Douglas-fir beetle, *D. pseudotsugae* (soo-doe-**tsoo**-ghee: of Doug-fir). On Doug-fir and larch. Illustrated.

Spruce beetle, *D. rufipennis* (roo-fip-**en**-iss: red wing). On spruce.

Pine beetles are among the most devastating insect killers of western trees, especially pines. The first signs of their attack are small round entrance holes exuding pitch and/or boring-dust. The pitch is the tree's counterattack, an attempt to incapacitate the beetles. The many exit holes, a generation later, look as if they were made by a blast of buckshot. (Color p 541.)

After the bark falls away you can see distinctive branched engravings underneath. The beetles, though less than ⅛" [3 mm] wide, chew much wider egg galleries through the tender inner bark layer, just barely cutting into the sapwood. The hatched larvae set off at right angles to the gallery—often in neat, closely spaced left/right alternation—growing as they proceed, and then pupating at the ends of their tunnels. From there they bore straight out through the bark upon emerging as adults. The tunnels are left packed with "frass" of excreted wood dust. In most species, the egg gallery runs from several inches to a yard [meter], straight up and down the wood grain, and the tunnels of the larvae run straight to the sides or fan out slightly. Engraver beetles' patterns (page 506) express further variations on that theme. Western pine beetle galleries, in contrast, curl and crisscross all over the place like spaghetti, and the larvae leave little impression on the inner bark, preferring the outer bark.

These are native beetles. In their normal "endemic" mode they cull damaged, diseased, and suppressed trees. Vigorous trees are un-palatable; the beetles must overpower the tree's health or it will over-power them. They do so by attacking *en masse* and by infecting trees

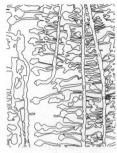
Mtn. Pine Beetle

Western Pine Beetle

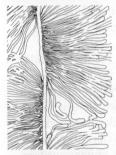
Douglas-Fir Beetle

Spruce Beetle

with fungal diseases. Single females scout, and then release scented pheromones to attract others to a vulnerable tree. A male follows a female into an entrance hole, and they work as a pair.

And then there's the epidemic mode. The beetle population explodes, their economic equation shifts, and they go for the biggest, healthiest trees. They devastate entire stands. Apparently this happens when forests are stressed. The mountain pine beetle has been in near-epidemic mode chronically for the past century, suggesting that our forests have been chronically stressed for as long as we've been putting fires out. On the other hand, predation is what brings outbreaks to an end. Chronic epidemism may result from loss of some other habitat needed by the predators, leaving them unable to multiply in response to beetle outbreaks.

Conventional wisdom holds that beetle outbreaks create so much dry fuel as to make conflagrations inevitable. At Yellowstone, though, Don Despain sees the opposite: less fuel, and smaller fires, in areas with the most beetle-killed trees.

The best preventive seems to be thinning the forest. This may work by invigorating the remaining trees; or by putting each tree out of range of beetle pheromonal communication—about 20 feet [6 m]—from the next tree; or by making the stand hotter and breezier. Unfortunately, the stumps left after thinning often incubate serious fungal diseases. Nature used to keep ponderosa pine stands thin with frequent fires, and pine beetle outbreaks were less common. But as foresters seek ways to heal the "sick forests" left by decades of fire suppression and high-grade logging, they meet frustration after frustration, as a fix for one problem often exacerbates another. "Once the straw has broken the camel's back, simply removing the straw does not allow the camel to rise again."

Engraver Beetles

Scolytus spp. (sco-**lie**-tus: truncated) ⅛" [3 mm] long, shiny blackish beetles; abdomen appearing "sawed off" a bit shorter than the end of the wing covers; known mainly by their egg galleries in the inner bark of dead and dying trees. Ubiquitous. Order Coleoptera (Beetles).

Douglas-fir engraver, *S. unispinosus* (you-ni-spy-**no**-sus: one-spined).

Fir branch engraver, *S. subscaber* (sub-**scay**-ber: somewhat rough).

Fir engraver, *S. ventralis* (ven-**tray**-lis: on the belly).

Doug-firs that fall in full or partial sunlight are likely to bear the signature of the Douglas-fir engraver—a deep but short (4–6", or 10–15 cm) egg gallery carved in line with the grain of the inner bark and sapwood, from which issues an array of larval tunnels that start out perpendicular but soon curve up or down, finally running with the grain (illustrated upper left). The fir engraver's signature on true firs (illustrated below) is 90° different: the main gallery runs across the grain, the larval tunnels run with the grain. Even more distinctive is the mark of the fir branch engraver, which looks like a rounded E branded into the inner bark of dead lower (or fallen) branches of true firs. This species rarely attacks the main trunk.

Dozens of species in the family Scolytidae have different specializations within the field of woody waste recycling. Many have special organs ("mycangia") for holding and disseminating spores of fungi which, along with bacteria, are partners in this great symbiosis. Most, like the Douglas-fir engraver, rarely attack trees or branches that aren't already done for. Then again, some are killers. Dutch elm disease is a fungus inadvertently introduced to America on its *Scolytus* beetle host, with disastrous results; the disease never threatened European elms, which are genetically resistant to it. When it comes to native pests like the western pine beetle and the fir engraver, we aren't sure how "natural" the occasional disastrous infestations are. Even the killer species are, in normal years, cullers of infirm individuals, benefitting the health of their victim population like wolves culling an elk herd.

If not for its attackers, a tree would be virtually immortal—as long as it could keep growing—since trees do not age in the sense that animals do. Without beetles and fungi, would the forest stop growing short of impenetrability? Can you even imagine such a world?

Striped Ambrosia Beetle

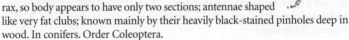

Trypodendron lineatum
(try-po-**den**-dron: bore tree; lin-ee-**ay**-tum: lined). ⅛" [3 mm] long,
shiny black to brown beetles with
faint paler stripes lengthwise on wing
covers; head hidden from above by tho-
rax, so body appears to have only two sections; antennae shaped
like very fat clubs; known mainly by their heavily black-stained pinholes deep in
wood. In conifers. Order Coleoptera.

Ambrosia beetles feed mainly on "ambrosia" fungi which they cultivate, inoculating them into holes they bore in downed or dying trees.
If conditions are perfect, the fungi will grow just fast enough to feed
the beetles and their larval brood without smothering them.

Though bark beetles (above) also bring fungal allies to their attacks on trees, their food is the tree cambium itself. Only ambrosia
beetles live directly off of the fungus, which feeds on the tree. Since
the fungus can break down the hardest of heartwood, ambrosia beetles are not confined to the tender layers under the bark, but burrow
into the sapwood and sometimes even the heartwood. The fungus
stains the wood around each bore hole black, wreaking economic
havoc on lumber felled in autumn and left out through winter.

Big logs take centuries to decompose, and would take longer still
without borers to make a rapid initial penetration of the protective
bark, opening the way for decomposers (fungi and bacteria). The
forest needs its logs to decompose to make both space and nutrients
available for new plants.

Snakefly

Agulla adnixa (ag-**you**-la:
big throat?; ad-**nix**-a: attached).
Reddish ½" [13 mm] fly with
striking long, flexible neck; dark
head; clear wings with obvious
veins, folded rooflike over back; female has long upcurved tail-like ovipositor.
Order Raphidioptera (formerly included in Neuroptera with the Lacewings).

Western orchardists value snakeflies for preying fiercely on pest insects. If we knew their diets better, lumbermen might also. We do
know that they're common on Rocky Mtn. conifers, and that their
close relatives eat close relatives of the western spruce budworm, one
of the worst pests of our conifers.

Insects

Grasshoppers

Order Orthoptera (Grasshoppers and Crickets).

Alpine grasshopper, *Melanoplus alpinus* (melon-**op**-lus: black tool).

Boreal grasshopper, *M. borealis* (bor-ee-**ay**-lis: of northern forests).

Bruner's spur-throated grasshopper, *M bruneri* (**brew**-ner-eye: after Lawrence Bruner). Illustrated.

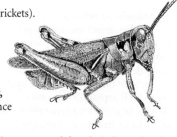

The Orthoptera ("straight wings") are named for their long, leathery protective forewings. These protect the thin, collapsible hindwings, which fly effectively with only slight help. The order also includes many flightless crickets and katydids, with reduced wings. But nearly all Orthoptera have huge hindlegs, and can hop like crazy.

Meadows have shifting assemblages of several kinds of grasshoppers which occupy different seasonal and spatial niches. Some crawl up plants and chew leaves off. These three *Melanoplus* species walk on the ground and eat vegetation harvested by other grasshoppers, along with seeds and small carrion. They take flight, low and silent, only when flushed out, or when they need to disperse.

Grasshoppers are notorious for population irruptions that devastate crops. "Locusts" are simply hoppers in flocks numbering in the multimillions. Though not qualifying as locusts, Bruner's and boreal hoppers do irrupt, and sometimes overgraze mountain meadows, leaving little for the hooved grazers. But since they would far rather eat lupine, locoweed, dandelions, field chickweed, and other broadleaved herbs than grasses, they more often benefit grasses and grazers alike. The alpine grasshopper maintains a fairly stable presence in mountain meadows. A short-hop flier, it rarely gets blown onto glaciers. There are three Grasshopper Glaciers and one Hopper Glacier in Wyoming and Montana, all named for their copious debris of frozen hoppers. Hundreds of specimens are *M. spretus*, the locust that plagued pioneers on the Plains but was last seen alive in 1902—"the only documented extinction of a pest insect." (Jeff Lockwood.)

Grasshoppers of our cold montane climate have a long "diapause" (period of dormancy) in the egg stage: they don't hatch until they've been in the soil for two or three years. After that they develop fast, requiring just four to six weeks before taking wing as adults in June. The eggs hatch into "nymphs" that resemble adults except that they lack wings. A series of five nymphal "instars" (growth stages separated by molting) precedes adulthood. This life cycle is called "gradual metamorphosis." Nymphs of *alpinus* are green in the first instar and tan in the fifth; individuals shift at different points along the way.

A grasshopper's daily cycle in the Rockies begins with crawling out from a crevice and basking for two hours, with body held sideways to the sun and the sunny-side leg lowered to better warm the abdomen. A few hours of midday activity are followed by a late afternoon bask before wedging down for the night.

Grasshoppers and crickets "stridulate," or make loud raspy noises by rubbing the toothed edges of specialized body parts together. In crickets it's two forewings rubbing together. Grasshoppers make a deeper pitch with big hindlegs rubbing sections of the forewing. (Some species also flash their hindlegs in visual signals.) Sections of the abdominal flanks are the hearing organs. In some genera (e.g., *Trimerotropis*, with bright yellow hindwings) the hindwings rattle loudly by snapping rapidly in flight. These songs cover the usual set of essential communications—alarm, asserting territory, locating conspecific mates, jilting unwanted suitors. They are disproportionately loud for a small creature for the same reason that antlers are disproportionately bulky: sexual selection. Females go for the loudest guys, forcing guys to blow their wads on racket in order for their genes to carry on.

Northern Rock Crawler

Grylloblatta campodeiformis
(grill-o-**blat**-a: cricket/cockroach; cam-po-dee-if-**or**-miss: shaped like a bristletail). Wingless, ⅜–1¼" [1–3 cm] long; amber yellow, cricketlike, with long rearward-arcing antennae and two conspicuous tails. Nocturnal on glaciers, snowfields, and nearby rocks. Order Grylloblattodea (formerly included in Orthoptera).

This remarkable creature should be called an ice crawler. It prefers temperatures near freezing and is active down to 28° [–2° C], foraging for carrion at night and burrowing into a crevice to stay cool by day. If you pick one up and hold it for long, your body heat could roast it to death. You're less likely to pick up the living beast than a hollow replica of one; that would be a molted exoskeleton, left behind. Eight quite similar instars, none of them winged, complete the life cycle over a period of several years. The northern rock crawler was first described in 1914, from Banff. Rock crawlers are so primitive and so unlike other insects that they stand as an Order unto themselves, consisting of just one genus of exactly ten species.

Mountain Emerald

Somatochlora semicircularis (so-mat-o-**clor**-a: body green). Body 2" [5 cm] long; eyes and thorax metallic green; abdomen ± black; wings clear. Sedge marshes and pond edges. Order Odonata (Dragonflies). Color p 546.

Dragonfly and damselfly nymphs, as fiercely predacious as the adults, rank among the chief predators of mosquito larvae. The largest, at 2" [5 cm], are big enough to take small tadpoles and fish. Dragonflies do without a pupal stage; instead, they metamorphose gradually through ten to fifteen molts (instars) as larvae (a.k.a. nymphs or "naiads"). Late instars may show the beginnings of wings, but still don't look much like the adults. Most don't swim, but either burrow and wait for prey or crawl sluggishly on their six sturdy legs. Some use a kind of rectal jet propulsion for a burst of speed to escape predators.

They will crawl up out of the water, usually on an emergent sedge or other plant, when ready to molt and release their inner adult. It takes the new adult about one very vulnerable hour or longer to straighten out its wings (by pumping blood in through the veins) and dry them for flight. The larval skin, split down the back, is left behind grasping the sedge stem.

Both larvae and adults hunt by eyesight, using big compound eyes. (Burrowing larvae hunt by touch.) Adults use their legs to grasp prey, not to walk. They have four similar but independently working wings, enabling hovering as well as fast, buzzing flight. Males typically hover territorially while watching for females, or while guarding an already-mated one until she lays eggs.

Many damselflies and some dragonflies become dull and dark when they cool off, helping them absorb heat more efficiently when the sun comes out again. Their brilliant colors recharge when body temperature exceeds 68° [20° C]. Also, in many species some females look like males and others are more dull. This is puzzling. Different scientists hypothesize advantages in attracting either more or fewer males by looking just like one; but to most observers the males appear eager to mate with anything that moves on four long clear wings, regardless of either gender or species.

Hudsonian Whiteface

Leucorrhinia hudsonica (loo-co-**rye**-nia: white nose; hud-**so**-nic-a: of Hudson's Bay). Body 1⅜" [35 mm] long; black with a row of bright red dots along abdomen, many red dots on thorax; white face; black dot near tip of clear wings; perches with wings below horizontal. Ponds, often with pond lilies. Order Odonata. Color p 546.

Darners

Aeshna spp. (**eesh**-na: possibly a misspelling of *aechma*, Greek for spear). Body 2¾" [7 cm] long; background color is dark brown; each flank of thorax has 2 diagonal pale stripes. Order Odonata (Dragonflies).

Paddle-tailed darner, *A. palmata* (pahl-**may**-ta: fanned out). Thorax stripes and face yellow; dots on abdomen blue or (on some females) yellow. Forest lakes, ponds, and fens, often with sedges. Color p 546.

Sedge darner, *A. juncea* (jun-see-a: rush). Stripes and dots whitish; tip of abdomen bluish. Forest lakes, ponds, and fens, often with sedges.

Blue-eyed darner, *A. multicolor*. Bright blue eyes; stripes and dots all sky blue or (on some females) all yellow. Near ponds, often with pond lilies; sometimes seen well away from water. Mainly in US, at lower elevs.

Some scientists think dragonflies react instantly to prey's flight paths so as to camouflage themselves by remaining in the same spot in the prey's peripheral vision. Darners are among the biggest, fastest dragonflies, reaching 33 mph in pursuit of prey such as mosquitoes.

Both large size and icy waters tend to prolong development; our darners spend between two and five years as naiads.

Before seeking mates, a male curls his abdomen down and attaches a sperm packet just behind his waist. To mate, he uses his tail-tip claspers to grasp a female by the head; she then curls her abdomen way down, forward, and up, to retrieve the packet. It's called the "wheel" position. Female darners typically lay their eggs surreptitiously to escape the harassment of repeated attempts to mate, since the males don't guard their mates as some dragonfly males do.

In the wheel position they can both fly perfectly well, facing forward. That's one advantage of long skinny abdomens. Another is the long counterweight for flight stability, and a third is thermoregulation: elongation gives the abdomen a high surface-to-volume ratio, making it a good radiator for excess flying-muscle heat pumped out of the thorax. Giant dragonflies with 28-inch [70-cm] wingspans, back in the Permian epoch, may have been among the first thermoregulators. (Insect gigantism was rife 270 million years ago thanks to a much richer atmosphere. Plants had recently evolved the ability to grow huge, but animals hadn't yet, with dinosaurs still 50 million years off, so a lot of oxygen was being produced and not much consumed.) The abdomen also absorbs radiant heat, either basking or in flight. As long as the sun is out it gets positioned—east-west, north-south, down or straight up—to either maximize or minimize heat absorption, as needed. Perching with the abdomen pointed toward the sun, to keep cool, is called the "obelisk position."

Emerald Spreadwing

Lestes dryas (**les**-tease: robber; **dry**-us: wood nymph). Also **stocky lestes**. Body 1⅜" long [35 mm]; metallic green with bluish iridescence, blue eyes, blue tip, yellowish flanks and underside; wings clear with black spot near tips; held at angles at rest. Sedge marshes, fens. Order Odonata (Dragonflies).

The species on this page are damselflies. Tell them from dragonflies by their eyes, which bulge out left and right like iridescent earmuffs, rather than all across the face. Dragonflies also have thicker bodies, and rest with their wings out flat, whereas damselflies either hold them swept back at an angle (spreadwings) or pressed together over the body (other damselflies). With a range circling the northern hemisphere, this species may be the world's best known damselfly.

Vivid Dancer

Argia vivida (**ar**-gee-a: leisure). Body 1⅜" long [35 mm]; abdomen brilliant blue with black bands; black stripe on side of thorax ± ends at midlength; some females purplish brown; wings as above, but folded together at rest; bobs and weaves ("dances") in flight ± close to ground. Streamsides and springs in US, and disjunct at a few hot springs in Canada. Order Odonata (Dragonflies).

This species probably spread into Canada during the 5,000-year warm period that followed the last Ice Age, and then retreated south of the 49th when things cooled. Geothermal warmth enabled just a few to hang on near several Canadian hot springs.

Males of many damselflies have developed an organ that, as they commence mating, can pluck out and discard a sperm packet left by a previous male, and replace it with this male's own sperm packet. (See Darners, above, for dragonfly sex basics.) In response, dancer males have come up with what must be the surest way to guard a mate: keep her in tow. The pair fly around attached "in tandem" for several hours beginning with mating and ending with egg-laying. Using a pair of claspers at his abdomen tip to grasp her neck, he lifts her out of the water when she's done dipping her ovipositor to insert eggs into a submerged leaf.

Bluets

Enallagma cyathigerum and *E. boreale*. (en-a-**lag**-ma: crosswise—; sigh-ath-**idge**-er-um: cup bearer; bor-ee-**ay**-lee: of northern forests). Body 1¼" long [31 mm]; male abdomen brilliant blue with black bands; thorax has blue/black stripes running its full length; female body tan. Marshes and lake edges, often with sedges; *E. boreale* abounds at alkaline dry-country lakes. Order Odonata (Dragonflies). Color p 546.

Water Strider

Gerris comatus (**jair**-iss: shield; co-**may**-tus: hairy). Also **Jesus bug**. Body ⅜" [1 cm] long; head and thorax have fine gold hairs; forewings gold-flecked; skates rapidly on tips of four very long legs, on still water; forelegs short. Order Hemiptera (True Bugs).

BUG WALKS ON WATER—
SCAVENGES FLOATING CORPSELETS.

Its tarsi (feet) have greasy hairs and end in a claw that retracts into a hollow; somehow this arrangement rests on the surface tension of still water. Each foot dimples the surface tension; the dimple acts like a lens, making round shadows on the bottom if it's shallow. Tiny insects falling on the water make rippling shadows on the bottom too, and these are what the strider watches for, and chases. Once striders could "read" those shadows, it was a short step for them to learn to read the shadows of other striders, and then to use their ripples as a mode of communication. Their metamorphosis is gradual, with around five nymphal stages. Some adults grow full-size wings, and migrate; others have useless reduced wings. Genetics, day length, and ample food supply all help to determine who will get wings that fly.

Aspen Leaf Miner

Phyllocnistis populiella (fill-oc-**nis**-tiss: leaf rasp; pop-you-lee-**el**-a: poplar—). Larva inside aspen leaf, carving a pale, mazelike, gradually enlarging path, consuming a green epidermal layer one cell thick; adult a small drab moth. Order Lepidoptera, Gracillariidae (Leaf Blotch Miner Family). Color p 541.

Leaf-mining larvae evolved convergently in moths, beetles, flies, and wasps, but moths are most common. In each case the larva is flattened to fit between the leaf's two cuticles. This one infests aspens throughout our region, occasionally reaching pest levels. From an egg laid near a leaf tip in May, a new larva makes a beeline for the leaf base, right alongside the midvein, but is so small that this part of its path is hard to see. Growing, it mows back and forth on one side of the midvein—an obstacle it will cross only where small, near the leaf tip. It may consume much of the second half of the leaf before spinning its silken cocoon and rolling the leaf edge around itself. If two mothers lay eggs on the same leaf, each larva typically settles for one side of the midvein; it looks like nice resource partitioning, but it may stunt each larva's growth. Densities of more than two per leaf often lead to cannibalism: the larva overtaken from behind gets eaten.

Insects 513

Tent Caterpillar Moths

Malacosoma spp. (ma-la-co-**so**-ma: soft body). Moths ws ¼–1½"[6–38 mm], variably brown, forewing divided in thirds by two parallel fine lines; full-grown caterpillars 2" [5 cm], bristling with tufted long hairs, dark brown with blue, orange and reddish markings; egg masses on small twigs, esp at crotches, covered with a gray to dark brown foam that hardens to a ± waterproof coating. Irruptively abundant on aspen, alder, or chokecherry; sporadic on conifers. Order Lepidoptera (Moths and butterflies), Lasiocampidae (Lappet moth family).

Forest tent caterpillar moth, *M. disstria* (dis-**try**-a: variously striped). Egg masses evenly encircle twigs; no tents; colony may spin a rudimentary web.

Western tent caterpillar moth, *M. californicum.* Egg masses plastered against twigs; makes conspicuous tents over parts of branches. Color p 541.

Occasionally a region gets hit with an outbreak of tent caterpillars. Many trees are defoliated and achieve little growth for a year or two, but few are killed. After a season or two, pathogens and predator populations rise to the occasion, sometimes with help from harsh weather, and reduce the tent caterpillar moths to almost invisibly low levels, where they remain for many years.

The "tent" is a big web of silk that affords caterpillar groups protection and insulation during resting periods between feeding sprees. Tent caterpillars are related to silkworms; they pupate within silken cocoons, coated with a skin-irritating dust, under curled leaves. The adults lack working mouthparts; they get by on what they ate as caterpillars, for the few days it takes them to mate and lay eggs. (It can be said of insects generally, to varying degrees, that adults are ephemeral bridges from one larval generation to the next.) Tent caterpillars do most of the traveling as well as all the eating and growing. Their long bristles help the wind carry them. Lacking wind, they crawl *en masse*. Tent-building, mass migration, group basking, and other collective skills make them the most social of all caterpillars.

Trees are far from defenseless against leaf eaters. They need only slow caterpillars' growth by a few percent to double the number taken by predators and parasites. They can do this by loading their leaves with tannin or cyanide. But producing tannin takes an energy investment that the trees do well to minimize, so they may load only some of their leaves with tannin, forcing caterpillars to expose themselves to flying predators while they search for the more digestible leaves. Or trees may wait until attacked, and only then step up tannin production. They may increase their tannin in response to an attack on a nearby tree of the same species, sensing chemicals cast upon the breeze by the attacked tree. Some scientists

Black morel, p 311. Calypso orchid, p 187.

White chanterelle, p 302.   Snowbank false morel, p 301.   Yellow morel, p 311.

Woolly chanterelle, p 296.   Lobster mushroom, p 297.

Fungi: with wrinkles but no gills   515

King boletus, p 305.

Suillus, *S. tomentosus*, p 306.

Suillus, *S. brevipes*, p 306.

Bear's-head tooth fungus, p 309.

Suillus, *S. cavipes*, p 306.

Hedgehog mushroom, p 305.

Scaly hedgehog mushroom, p 305.

Red-belt conk, p 299.

Sulphur shelf fungus, p 312.

Witches' butter, p 300.

Yellow coral fungus, p 308.   Tree ear, p 300.   Angel wings, p 304.

Orange-peel fungus, p 300.

Scorched-earth cup, p 301.

Fungi: shelf-, cup-, or coral-shaped, with little or no stalk   **517**

Shaggy mane, p 304.   Fly amanita and panther amanita, p 293.

Waxy caps, p 296: *Hygrophorus pudorinus, Hygrophorus subalpinus*

Autumn galerina, p 295.   Destroying angel, p 294.

Gemmed puffball, p 309.   Warted giant puffball, p 309.

Jewel lichen (deep orange), p 322.
Map lichen and chartreuse cobblestone lichen, p 317.

Spraypaint lichen, p 318.

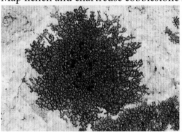
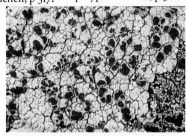

Brown tile lichen, p 317.

Alpine bloodclot lichen, p 318.

Peat moss, p 282.

Rock tripe, *Umbilicaria decussata*, p 323.

Dust lichen, *Lepraria neglecta*, p 318.

Rock tripe, *U. hyperborea*, p 323.

Moss; and Fungi: crust, dust, and leaf lichens on rock or soil   *519*

Horsehair lichen, p 326. Wolf lichen, *L. vulpina*, p 328.   Snow mold, p 69.

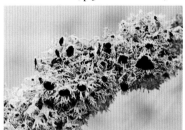
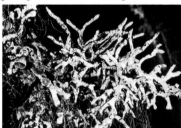

Wolf lichen, *Letharia columbiana*, p 328.   Puffed lichen, p 327.

Rag lichen, p 321.   Witches' hair, p 327.   Old-man's-beard, p 325.

Algae; and Fungi: lichens on trees

Plitt's rock-shield, p 325.
Green rock-posy (lower right), p 325.

Orange chocolate-chip lichen, p 322.

Green rock-posy (vagrant form), p 324.

Green-light lichen, p 321.

Lungwort, p 321.
on Western yew, p 78.

Dog lichens, *P. leucophlebia* and *P. canina*, p 320.

Rockworm, p 329.   Greater pixie stick, p 330.   Sulphur cup, p 330.

Froth lichen, p 329.   Pixie goblets, p 330.

Reindeer lichen, p 328.   Red-crowned sulphur cup, p 330.

Yellow ruffle lichen, p 323.   Snow lichen, p 323.

Mountain goat, p 403. Rocky Mountain bighorn sheep, p 399.

Bison, p 401. Pronghorn, p 405.

Elk (bull, lip-curling), p 393. Mule deer, p 390.

Caribou, p 389. Moose, p 396.

Deer mouse, p 355.

Jumping mouse, p 355.

Red-backed vole, p 359.

Wandering shrew, p 332.

Muskrat, p 361.

Gopher cores, p 350.

Pika, p 337.

Snowshoe hare, p 339.

Yellow pine chipmunk, p 340.

Hoary marmot, p 345.

Golden-mantled ground squirrel, p 342.

Porcupine, p 362.

Richardson's and Columbian ground squirrels, p 342.

Red squirrel, p 347.

Thirteen-lined ground squirrel, p 343.

Wolf, p 369.

Coyote, p 366.

Red fox, p 365. Paper birch, p 122.

Fisher, p 382.

Marten, p 381.

Badger, p 384.

Short-tailed weasel (ermine), p 378.

Wolverine, p 383.

Mammals: carnivores: Dog and Weasel families

Grizzly bear, p 375.

Black bear, p 371, alerted and looking around.

Cougar, p 387.

Otter, p 380.

Bobcat, p 385.

Lynx, p 385.

Sandhill crane, p 427. Common loon, p 411.

Harlequin duck, p 417. Common goldeneye, p 418.

Great blue heron, p 412. Western grebe, p 412.

Wilson's snipe, p 429. Sora, p 429.

Birds: water birds, shore birds, and crane

Osprey, p 418.

American kestrel, p 424.

Harrier, p 420.

Bald eagle, p 419.

Red-tailed hawk, p 420.

Prairie falcon, p 424.

Golden eagle, p 425.

White-tailed ptarmigan, p 425.

Blue grouse, p 426.

Spruce grouse (female), p 426.

Belted kingfisher, p 435.

Northern pygmy-owl, p 430.

Nighthawk, p 433.

Rufous hummingbird (female), p 436.

Birds

Vaux's swift, p 434.

Pileated woodpecker, p 434.

Tree swallow, p 441.

Red-naped sapsucker, p 439.

Northern flicker, p 438.

Black-billed magpie, p 448.

Downy woodpecker, p 438.

Horned lark, p 442.

Western meadowlark, p 459.

Dipper, p 449.

Mountain bluebird, p 455.

Clark's nutcracker, p 446.

Cedar waxwing, p 457.

Red-winged blackbird, p 460.

Western tanager, p 457.

Birds: songbirds

Yellow-rumped
warbler, p 456.

Cassin's finch, p 461.

Rosy finch, p 460.

Mountain
chickadee, p 451.

Common
yellowthroat, p 456.

White-breasted
nuthatch, p 451.

Dark-eyed junco, p 459.

Chipping sparrow, p 458.

Painted turtle, p 465.

Western skink (juvenile), p 465.

Common garter snake, p 466.

Bullsnake, p 467.

Racer, p 467.

Western rattlesnake, p 468.

Northern leopard frog, p 474.

Long-toed salamander, p 470.

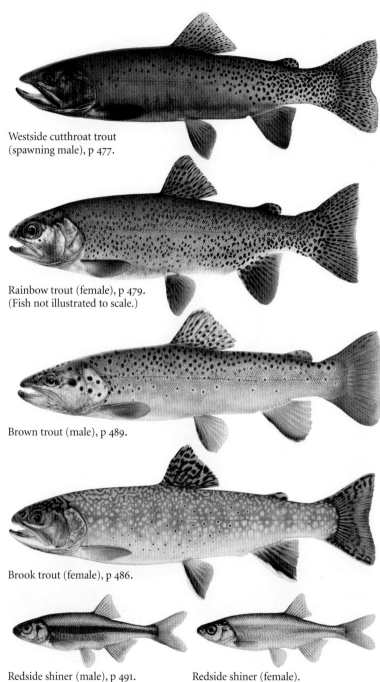

Westside cutthroat trout
(spawning male), p 477.

Rainbow trout (female), p 479.
(Fish not illustrated to scale.)

Brown trout (male), p 489.

Brook trout (female), p 486.

Redside shiner (male), p 491.   Redside shiner (female).

Fishes

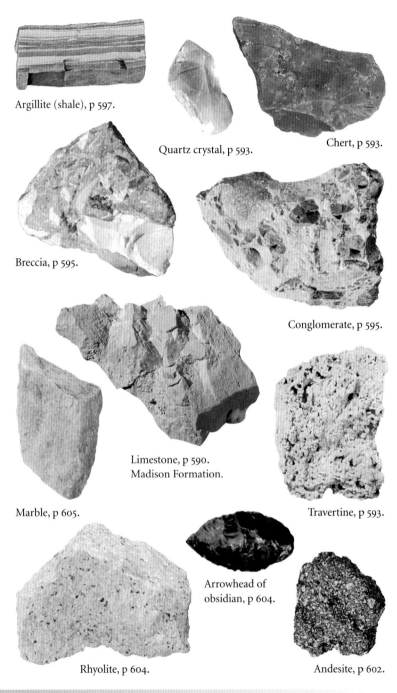

Argillite (shale), p 597.

Quartz crystal, p 593.

Chert, p 593.

Breccia, p 595.

Conglomerate, p 595.

Limestone, p 590.
Madison Formation.

Travertine, p 593.

Marble, p 605.

Arrowhead of
obsidian, p 604.

Rhyolite, p 604.

Andesite, p 602.

Granite, p 599.
Lolo batholith.

Granite (pink), p 599.

Diabase, p 601.

Granodiorite, p 599.

Quartzite, p 606.

Schist, p 606.

Phyllite, p 605.

Gneiss, p 607.

Amphibolite, p 607.

Gneiss (p 607) sheared down to the right; scale ~2' [60 cm]; Bitterroot Fault Zone.

Bitterroot Batholith Granite (p 599); scale ~2½" [6 cm]. Yolk lichen, p 318.

Gabbro (p 601); with a quartz vein, in a dike in Archaean migmatite; ~14" [35 cm].

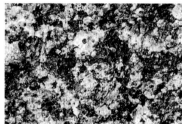

Gneiss (p 607), 3-billion-year-old Wind River granite/gneiss basement; ~3" [7.5 cm].

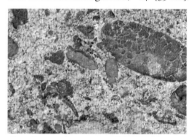

Conglomerate, p 595; ~6" [15 cm].

Paleozoic Madison limestone, p 590, with nodules of chert; scale ~14" [35 cm].

Purcell Lava flow metamorphosed to greenstone, p 607; scale ~16' [5 m].

Geology: igneous, metamorphic, and sedimentary textures

Microlaminated mudstone and siltstone, p 596; scale ~3" [7.5 cm]. Belt Supergroup.

Grinnell (Belt) argillite, p 597; ~7' [2 m]. Different layers variously wave-rippled.

Fossil rugose coral in Paleozoic limestone, p 590; scale ~6" [15 cm].

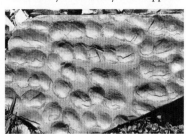

Argillite, p 597; ~30" [75 cm]. "Ladder-back" criss-crossed wave ripples. Belt.

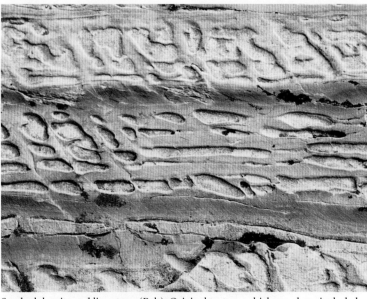

Sandy dolomite and limestone (Belt). Original texture, which may have included thin layers, ripples, and a filled earthquake crack, is now accentuated by the limestone layers weathering away faster than the dolomite. Scale ~14" [35 cm].

Geology: sedimentary textures

Sill (dark horizontal layer) and dike (vertical) cutting Archaean basement, Wind Rivers.

Pinker Belt strata were more oxidized while forming. Siltstone (foreground) broke into blocks along stress joints initiated during Lewis Thrust fault motion.

Columns in basalt, p 603, Idaho. Chartreuse cobblestone lichen, p 317.

A cliff of 2-billion-year-old migmatite, p 608; Idaho Pioneers. Dead whitebark pine.

Bark beetle larval galleries, p 504.

Bark beetle adult exit holes p 504; on Douglas-fir.

Aspen leafminer, p 513, mining aspen leaf, p 115.

Galls on Rocky Mtn. maple, p 123.

Galls on Big sagebrush, p 138.

Cooley aphid galls, p 499, on Engelmann spruce.

Galls on Rock willow, p 119.

Tent caterpillars, p 514, in tent, on chokecherry.

"Brooms" caused by dwarf-mistletoe, p 209.

Insect and mistletoe effects on plants

Western tiger swallowtail, p 516.

Pale tiger swallowtail, p 516.

Anise swallowtails (mating), p 516.

Clodius parnassian, p 517;
female, with sphragus.

Pine white, p 518.

Smintheus parnassian, p 517.

Becker's white, p 518.

Western white, p 518, on
Douglasia, p 227.

Western spangled fritillary (female).

Western spangled fritillary (male, lower and upper sides), p 524.

Common ringlet, p 519.

Orange sulphur, p 519.

Sara orange-tip, p 519.

Queen Alexandra sulphur, p 519.

Chryxus arctic, p 520.

Common alpine, p 521.

Insects: butterflies

Checkerspot, p 524, on
woolly mullein, p 214.

Lorquin's admiral, p 522.

Anglewings, *Polygonia
satyrus*, p 523.

Milbert's tortoiseshell,
p 523, on rabbitbrush, p 139.

Painted lady, p 522.

Anglewings, *Polygonia
oreas*, p 523.

Mourning cloak, p 523.

Insects: butterflies, Brush-footed family

Sheridan's hairstreak,
p 527, on buttercup, p 244.

Rocky Mountain dotted blue, p 526,
on a buckwheat.

Purplish copper, p 525; male upperside and underside, and female upperside.

Northern blue, p 525, on
spotted knapweed, p 201.

Moss's elfin, p 528.

Boisduval's blue, p 528.

Insects: butterflies, Copper family

Bluets, p 512, male clasping female.

Bluebell tiger moth, p 515.

Black-veined forester, p 515.

Mountain emerald, p 510.

Eyed sphinx
moth, p 516.

Paddle-tailed
darner, p 511.

Hudsonian.
whiteface, p 510.

Insects: moths; dragonflies

think these trees are communicating. In the words of one, "plants, after all, are really just very slow animals." (But see p 139 for a contrary interpretation.)

Diurnal Moths

Bluebell tiger moth, *Gnophaela vermiculata* (noff-**ee**-la: darkness—; ver-mic-you-**lay**-ta: wormy-patterned). Also **police-car moth** (per Calgary's Weaselhead Park website) after the old black-and-whites "complete with orange lights." Ws 2" [5 cm]; wide black margins surround white patches divided by black veins; yellow-orange fur on "cheeks;" antennae plumelike; flight tends to be very erratic. Larvae eat bluebells; adults often near goldenrod. Order Lepidoptera, Arctiidae (Tiger moth family). Color p 546.

Black-veined forester, *Androloma maccullochii* (an-dro-**lo**-ma: man fringe?). Ws 1⅝"[4 cm]; wide black margins surround cream patches divided by black veins; white fringe on trailing edge of wings; deep orange fur on upper legs; antennae threadlike, with black/white alternating on the inner half. Larvae eat fireweed. Order Lepidoptera, family Noctuidae. Color p 546.

A few day-flying moths rival butterflies in beauty. Similar wing patterns hint these two might be related, but the antennae show they aren't.

White-Lined Sphinx Moth

Hyles lineata (**hi**-leez: of woods; lin-ee-**ay**-ta: lined). Ws 2½–3½" [65–90 mm]; large heavy-bodied moths with rapid, buzzing wingbeats suggestive of hummingbirds; forewings dark olive brown with a broad pale stripe to the tip, and white-lined veins; hindwings pink and black, much smaller; thorax white-lined; abdomen cross-banded. Most often seen seeking nectar at dusk. A very similar species without fine parallel white lines on wings or thorax would be a bedstraw sphinx, *H. gallii*. Order Lepidoptera, Sphingidae (Hawk moth family).

Various species in this nectar-feeding moth family may be active by day, night, or dawn and dusk. Their deep-pitched buzzing flight enables them to hover, and they seem on first acquaintance to resemble other nectar feeders—bumble bees or, in the case of this genus, hummingbirds—rather than other moths. The bee-like species have hairy bodies and mostly clear wings. Some plant species depend on particular hawk moths as pollinators. (See page 246).

Eyed Sphinx Moth

Smerinthus cerisyi (smer-**inth**-us: cord—; sair-**iss**-ee-eye: after ??? Cerisy). Ws 2⅜–3⅜" [60–85 mm]; mostly a gray to sepia camouflage pattern, exc each hindwing has a dramatic black/blue/black eyespot in a pink/golden triangle. Streamsides; feeds on willow, aspen, cottonwood. Sphingidae. Color p 546.

Swallowtails

Papilio spp (pa-**pil**-ee-o: butterfly). =includes *Pterourus* spp. Large butterflies with "tail" lobe trailing each hindwing (four tails on these species, but none on some others), dramatically black-patterned, often with blue or orange spots near tail. May–Aug. Lepidoptera, Papilionidae (Swallowtail family).

Anise swallowtail, *P. zelicaon* (zel-ic-**ay**-on: a name from *The Iliad*). Ws 2¼–3" [58–75 mm], yellow with black markings; yellow area of hindwing has fine black veins. Widespread near larval host parsley-family plants, esp desert-parsley, cow-parsnip. Color p 542.

Western tiger swallowtail, *P. rutulus* (**root**-you-lus: shining, red-orange, or gilded). Ws 2⅝–3⅝" [60–88 mm]; like the preceding, but the forwardmost marginal spot on hindwing is yellow. US, and near Arrow Lake, BC. Color p 542.

Canadian tiger swallowtail, *P. canadensis.* Ws 2⅜–3½" [6–9 cm]; yellow area of hindwing crossed by black stripe that extends the first of several "tiger" stripes on forewing; forwardmost marginal spot on hindwing is orange. From Missoula n; often abundant, usually near water; eats willow and cottonwood.

Pale tiger swallowtail, *P. eurymedon* (you-**rim**-e-don: Agamemnon's charioteer in *The Iliad*). Ws 2¾–3¾" [67–95 mm], cream (females) to ± white (males) with heavy black "tiger" stripes. Often near snowbrush. Color p 542.

Anise and pale swallowtails are often seen "hilltopping." That's the use of tall landmarks (trees, buildings and even TV towers where hills are lacking) to help locate mates. The males arrive first, staking out sections of ridgeline and defending them against conspecific males while waiting for females. Similarly, western tiger swallowtails use riverbanks, canyons, or other lineations of trees as singles bars.

The larvae (caterpillars) flourish by late summer, and pupate over winter. Caterpillars of the anise swallowtail have striking black/yellow back bands against green, and are found on parsley-

Moths vs. Butterflies

Moths and butterflies together comprise the order Lepidoptera ("scaly wings"). Some generalizations can be made about differences between the two, though there are exceptions to all except antenna shape.

Moths...

are mostly nocturnal;
have slender-tipped, or else fernlike, antennae;
have bigger bodies for their wing size;
may pupate in a chrysalis with an outer "cocoon" of silk;
raise their body temperatures before flying by vibrating their wings;
perch with wings spread to the sides, either flat or angled rooflike, forewings covering hindwings.

family plants such as garden fennel or anise. Caterpillars of both tigers have eyespots; these mock eyes function defensively, as do the antlerlike scent glands (on all swallowtail caterpillars) which they stick out when disturbed.

Linnaeus named many butterflies, putting them all in one genus, *Papilio*, which more attentive lepidopterists have progressively divided, decade after decade. However, a rash of genus splits that were published conspicuously in the 1970s, like *Pterourus* for *rutulus* and *eurymedon*, were by the 1990s dropped for being *too* rash. Since neither their genus names nor their common names enjoy unanimity, we're lucky that butterflies' spriteliness has inspired a tradition of naming them after mythical figures: few species names are used in more than one genus, so butterfly buffs can usually understand each other by using the species name alone, without its genus.

Parnassians

Parnassius spp. (par-**nas**-ius: of Mt Parnassus, referring to montane habitat). White butterflies with gray to black markings and small red, often black-rimmed eyespots. Lepidoptera, Papilionidae (Swallowtail family).

P. smintheus (**sminth**-ius: Mouse God, a name of Apollo). =*P. phoebus*. Ws 1⅝–2⅜" [4–6 cm]; fore- and hindwings usually with several red spots; antennae ringed black/white. WA, above timberline, typically on or near stonecrop, the larval food. June–Aug. Color p 542.

P. clodius (**cloh**-dius: a Roman politician). Ws 2–2¾" [5–7 cm]; eyespots (usually four) on hindwings only, antennae black. Pupates in a cocoon. Widespread near forest edges; larvae feed on bleeding-heart. May–Aug. Color p 542.

The gray patches on parnassian wings actually just lack the minute scales that otherwise cover butterfly wings, leaving them translucent like the wings of bees or flies. Scales give butterfly and moth wings their opacity, color, and softness. Scales by the hundreds will dust your fingertips if you attempt to grasp a butterfly or a moth.

Female parnassians are usually seen with a waxy object on the

---

Butterflies...

are diurnal;
have club-tipped antennae;
have smaller bodies relative to wings;
pupate in a naked, more or less rigid shell, or "chrysalis;"
warm their muscles before flying by basking;
perch with left and right wings pressed together vertically, except when basking in sunlight.

---

rear end, as in the photo. Hardening from a liquid extruded by her last mate, this blocks other males from mating with her. It is largest on *clodius*, whose mating style some scientists describe as rape. In butterflies with consensual courtship behavior, already-mated females can and often do decline. Parnassians use this chastity belt instead.

Pine White

Neophasia menapia (neo-**fay**-zia: shines like new; men-**ah**-pia: moon bee?). 1¾–2" [42–50 mm]. White with darker veins, blackish blotch patterns near forewing tip, and (uniquely) a blackish bar along front edge of forewing from base to a little more than halfway out; on males, the vein lines under hindwing are fine, not broad. Larvae eat conifer needles; adults spend most of their time up among the tree limbs. Order Lepidoptera, Pieridae (Sulphur family). Color p 542.

Pine white caterpillars irrupted in parts of central Idaho in 1922 and 1953, killing many ponderosa pines. Bark beetles are drawn to the weakened pines, and finish them off, while wasps that parasitize pine white pupae multiply, and reduce the butterflies to normal numbers. The eggs are attached to pine needles in very neat rows.

Margined White

Pieris marginalis (**pie**-er-iss: a Greek Muse). =*P. napi, Artogeia marginalis*. Ws 1⅜–1¾" [35–45 mm], white with veins ± broadly shaded gray-green, esp beneath; dark-stained near body. Forest, often near streams; larvae and adults feed on mustard family. April–Aug. Order Lepidoptera, Pieridae.

Western Whites

Pontia spp. (**pon**-sha: a name of Aphrodite). =*Pieris* spp. Ws 1⅜–1¾" [33–45 mm]; white with broad gray-green vein lines, esp beneath hindwing, and variable gray pattern near margins of fore- or all wings; black-stained near body. Larvae feed on mustard family. April–Sept. Order Lepidoptera, Pieridae. Color p 542.

Western white, *P. occidentalis* (ox-i-den-**tay**-lis: western) =*P. callidice*. Underside has only two colors—white and gray-green. Alp/subalpine; occasionally lower.

Becker's white, *P. beckerii* (beck-**er**-ee-eye). = P. *chloridice*. More green than white under hindwing; black spot on leading forewing edge. Sagebrush.

Pairs of butterflies are often seen following each other upward in tall spirals. It may please us to think of these spiral flights as prenuptial stairways to heaven, but they may actually be countererotic—competition between males, or an impregnated female's last-ditch effort to escape an unwanted suitor by wearing him out in flight.

Sulphurs

Colias spp. (**coh**-lius: a name of Aphrodite). Ws 1½–2⅜" [38–60 mm]; yellow to light orange above, often with a heavy black border or corner; light green to yellow under hindwing; (or some females white overall); usually with a dark dot in center of forewing and a pale dot on hindwing. Larvae feed on legumes (lupine, sweet-vetch, milkvetch, sweet-clover, clover, etc). Order Lepidoptera, Pieridae.

Clouded sulphur, *C. philodice* (fil-**odd**-iss-ee: a nymph?). No orange tint; a close look usually reveals minute pink fringes, and not one but two small, pale, pink-rimmed spots on hindwing. Abundant, e.g. on roadsides; May–Oct.

Orange sulphur, *C. eurytheme* (you-**rith**-im-ee: a nymph?). Also **alfalfa butterfly**. Like clouded, but orange-blushed above; often shows a row of faint brown spots parallel to margin. Abundant. July–Oct. Color p 543.

Queen Alexandra sulphur, *C. alexandra*. Wings fringes greenish to pale yellow; pale spot on hindwing is ± rimless. Meadows, prairies, tundra. May–Sept.

Christina sulphur, *C. christina.* =included in *alexandra* by some. Wing fringes pink; red-rimmed spot under hindwing; uppersides usually quite orange. Roadsides, open forest; absent or rare in ID and in Columbia Mtns. May–Sept.

Alexandra and *christina* both were mere subspecies of *C. occidentalis* until their wings were studied under ultraviolet light. Special scales reflect UV in patterns butterflies see, and recognize conspecifics by. Females get better at it with experience; newly emerged ones are often fooled by arduous suitors from the wrong species. Dark scales that stain part of the wings absorb extra heat close to the body, making basking more efficient. The caterpillars overwinter even in arctic climates, except *eurytheme* which migrates here each summer.

Sara Orange-Tip

Anthocharis sara (an-**thoc**-a-ris: flower grace; **sar**-a: the female first name). =*A. stella.* Ws 1⅛–1⅝" [28–40 mm], white to (females only) ± yellow with deep orange forewing tips, gray-green marbling under hindwing. Widespread in sunny habitats; larvae feed on mustard family plants. An early butterfly: April (at low elevs) to July (high). Order Lepidoptera, Pieridae. Color p 543.

Common Ringlet

Coenonympha tullia (see-no-**nim**-fa: common nymph; **too**-lia: a daughter of Cicero). =includes *C. ampelos*, *C. california (BC).* Ws 1⅛–1½" [27–40 mm], variable: ours usually creamy to bright yellow-orange exc under hindwing, where ± gray; underside usually has median white bands, and may have black eyespots near margins. Around grasses, the larval food. Late May–Aug. Order Lepidoptera, Nymphalidae (Brush-footed butterfly family) Color p 543.

Wood Nymphs

Cercyonis spp. (ser-**sigh**-o-nis: a legendary thief?). Drab black-brown above, barklike brown beneath; 2 black eyespots on each forewing; spots ± yellow-rimmed beneath and sometimes above; up to 6 tiny eyespots (often indistinct) on hindwings. Larvae eat grasses, adults sip various nectars. Order Lepidoptera, Nymphalidae (Brush-footed butterfly family).

Common wood nymph, *C. pegala* (**peg**-a-la: a mythic name). Ws 1¾–2¾" [48–68 mm], much paler beneath (esp females). Roadsides, meadows; June–Sept.

Dark wood nymph, *C. oetus* (**ee**-tus: doom, i.e., blackness). Also **small wood nymph.** Ws 1½" [38 mm], almost as dark beneath as above; second forewing eyespot small and often inconspicuous. Dry grasslands, brush, open forest. June–Sept.

Arctics

Oeneis spp. (ee-**nee**-iss: a mythic king). Orange- or gray-brown exc silvery gray-brown under hindwing (for camouflage against bark or soil); 1 to 3 smallish black eyespots; forewing long and angular. Nymphalidae.

Macoun's arctic, *0. macounii* (ma-**cow**-nee-eye: after John Macoun, below). Ws 2–2½" [46–65 mm]; rich yellow-brown wings have dark margins like burnt edges; Canada, June–Aug of odd-numbered years only.

Chryxus arctic, *0. chryxus* (**crix**-us: gold, misspelled?). Ws 1¾–2" [40–52 mm]. June– Aug. Color p 543.

Arctics, like anise swallowtails (page 516) are "hilltoppers" with a powerful drive to travel uphill. Ridgelines acquire dense, evenly spaced populations of hilltopping males, with scattered cameo appearances by eligible maidens foraying up from the more benign meadow environment. The male (lacking sharp eyesight) will rush out from his perch to greet any lepidopteran, and if it's a conspecific he engages it in a spiral duet flight. Somehow while spiralling upward he learns the visitor's gender, and the spiral ritual becomes either a courtship flight or a duel to defend his territory. On each forewing's front edge a *chryxus* male has a dark stainlike patch of

---

John Macoun came to Ontario at nineteen, a penniless immigrant from famine-blighted Ireland. The native flora so captivated him that he taught himself botany, and eventually was appointed the first Dominion Botanist of Canada. On foot, in the 1870s, he made three prodigiously productive trips in western Canada, collecting plants, lichens, insects, and birds. He changed history by convincing Canadians that crops would grow in southern Alberta and Saskatchewan. Until then the region was seen as a "desert" that could support, at best, a few cattle.

"scent scales" which emit attractant pheromones.

Arctics spend two years as caterpillars. Adults of *macounii* fly only in odd-numbered years in the Rockies, but their conspecifics in eastern Canada fly mainly in even-numbered years. Odd- and even-year populations of *chryxus* also exist, but are more local, and may overlap; the species is seen every year in our range. Caterpillars of arctics and alpines feed on grasses and sedges.

Arctics are among the minority of basking butterflies that bask with their wings folded and tipped aside. A butterfly basking in the morning is generally a butterfly trying to raise its temperature to the minimum required for flight. In the meantime it is sluggish, offering you a good chance at a close view or a photo.

Common Alpine

Erebia epipsodea (er-ee-bia: underworld, i.e., darkness; ep-ip-**so**-dia: resembling *Erebia psodea*). Ws 1½–1⅞" [35–47 mm], dark brown with marginal rows of orange-haloed, yellow-pupilled black eyespots on all four wings; the forewing haloes coalesce into an orange band. Meadows or prairies; alpine in WY, but mostly low-elev grasslands in Canada; May–Aug. Nymphalidae.

Eyespots

The dots framed in concentric rings that decorate many butterfly wings offer valuable protection from predators. Sometimes birds are fooled into pecking at fake eyes, thinking them vital targets, but butterflies have little trouble flying with tattered hindwings—where most eyespots and all "tails" (similar diversionary ornaments) are located.

At other times the eyespot can frighten a bird away. A butterfly may respond to an exploratory first peck by abruptly opening its folded wings; between the two "eyes" suddenly revealed, the bird imagines a larger face than it had meant to take on. Since moths more often rest with wings spread, many of them (e.g. the sphinxes, p 547) sport camouflage patterns all over their uppersides except for big eyes at the rear corners of the hindwings. Basking on bark (or whatever their camouflage resembles) they hide the eyes with their forewings until disturbed, then shift the forewing to reveal eyespots and startle the bird.

Newly emerged butterflies go through a few hours when their wings are soft and useless. Wings first take form wadded up inside the pupal shell, or "chrysalis," and as soon as the adult emerges it pumps fluids in through the veins to extend the wings to their proper shape. They take several hours to dry into rigidity. During that vulnerable time the eyespot ruse is especially critical, and saves many lives.

Painted Lady

Vanessa cardui (va-**nes**-a: a name for a lady, no?; **car**-dew-eye: of thistles). Ws 2–2¼", salmon to orange above with short white bar and black mottling near forewing tip, row of 4–5 tiny eyespots near hindwing margin; larvae are spiny, lilac with yellow lines and black dots, and typically spin nets around thistle tops. Occasionally ubiquitous. April–Sept. Similar West Coast Lady, *V. annabella*, has a row of 4 small blue-filled spots above each hindwing. Order Lepidoptera, Nymphalidae (Brush-footed butterfly family). Color p 544.

The painted lady normally resides in climates warmer than ours. Occasionally the population irrupts thousands of miles in all directions, making painted ladies the most nearly worldwide of all insects. (The irruption requires several generations, with individuals migrating "only" a few hundred miles.) They don't survive winter here, and few make the trip up from Mexico in non-outbreak years, so they have been rare here except (most recently) in 1966, 1973, 1983, 1992, and 2001. In recent years they have been bred for commercial butterfly releases, which are not as benign as they seem. Preferred foods are thistles and other composites, but when irrupting the adaptable larvae become omnivorous.

In the large and colorful family Nymphalidae, the front two legs are short, brushlike appendages useless for walking or perching.

Admirals

Limenitis spp. (lim-en-**eye**-tiss: harbor goddess). =*Basilarchia spp.* Ws 2–3" [50–75 mm]; mainly black and white above, the white in a heavy band (broken by black veins) across both wings parallel to margin; underside dramatically striped, the same white band flanked by orangey shades; sexes alike, but males smaller; in flight, twitchlike beats alternate with gliding. Larvae feed on willow, aspen, and cottonwood. Order Lepidoptera, Nymphalidae.

Lorquin's admiral, *L. lorquini* (lor-kwin-eye: after Pierre J. M. Lorquin, who took his butterfly net with him on the California Gold Rush). Red-orange forewing tips; underside primarily white and orange, with minor black. Widespread, notably on streamsides. Columbia Mtns., and RM from Crowsnest Pass to Bitterroots. May–Sept, thanks to two generations per summer. Color p 544.

Weidemeyer's admiral, *L. weidemeyerii* (wide-**my**-er-ee-eye: after J. W. Weidemeyer). No orange above; white, orange, black, and bluish gray beneath. Streamsides, aspen groves, tundra. From Bitterroots and Swan Range s and e. June–July.

The handsome admirals are scavengers of dung and dead things, as well as nectar feeders. These two species hybridize where they meet in the Bitterroots and central Idaho.

Anglewings

Polygonia spp. (poly-**go**-nia: many angles). Also **commas**. Ws 1¾–2¼" [45-55 mm], wing margins lobed fancifully, as if tattered; burnt orange above with dark margins and scattered black blotches; silvery gray-brown beneath, with a "comma" (see text). Ubiquitous; larvae eat currants and nettles; adults may eat sap, carrion, or scats. Mainly March–Sept. Nymphalidae. Color p 544.

Anglewings are amazingly well camouflaged against bark: one moment they flit about almost too fast to follow, and in the next they disappear by abruptly alighting with wings folded. A tiny but distinct pale mark centered beneath the hindwing is variously C-, V-, boomerang-, or comma-shaped on different species.

Mourning Cloak

Nymphalis antiopa (an-**tie**-o-pa: a leader of Amazons). Ws 2–3¼" [5–8 cm]; ± iridescent deep red-brown above with full-length cream yellow border lined with bright blue spots; drab beneath, barklike gray-brown with dirty white border; margins ragged. Streamsides with willows; throughout N Hemisphere. Mainly March–Oct. Order Lepidoptera, Nymphalidae. Color p 544.

Mourning cloak adults hibernate in tree holes, occasionally coming out to fly on sunny winter days, and sometimes aestivate in late summer. They exploit some unusual foods, such as sap sipped from sapsucker licks. They breed during both spring and fall active seasons.

Tortoiseshells

Milbert's tortoiseshell, *Nymphalis milberti* (nim-**fay**-lis: nymph—; **mil**-bert-eye: after Milbert, a friend of the namer). Ws 1½–2" [37-50 mm], dark brown above exc for a huge sunsetlike (to white) band parallel to margin, plus two small, less distinct orange blotches on each leading edge; gray-brown beneath with a broad paler band parallel to margin. Widespread, common in high meadows; larvae eat nettles, adults often visit daisies. April–Oct. Color p 544.

California tortoiseshell, *N. californica*. Ws 1¾–2¼" [45-55 mm]; blotchy yellow-orange above; several large dark blotches on leading edge, and a continuous dark margin; barklike mottled gray-brown beneath—much like a big comma but less ragged in outline, and *not* much like its *Nymphalis* kin. Open forest or brush; larvae eat *Ceanothus*. Feb–Nov. Nymphalidae.

Tortoiseshell and comma adults hibernate, often in tree hollows. Emerging in spring, they look very different—worn, and usually paler than fresh adults. After the early start, California tortoiseshells may breed two or even three generations a year. Their populations are volatile, with wild boom-and-bust cycles. During boom years thousands smash into cars as they stream through mountain passes.

Meanwhile, the larvae defoliate snowbrush far and wide.

Pale green egg clusters—or bristly small black web-spinning caterpillars—on nettles are often those of Milbert's Tortoiseshell.

Checkerspots

Euphydryas (you-fid-rius: shapely nymph) and *Chlosyne* spp. (clo-sigh-nee: a nymph?). =*Charidryas, Occidryas, Microtia.* Ws 1⅛–2" [28–52 mm], upperside black in fine checkered patterns with red-orange, pale yellow, and/or cream; underside red-orange with yellow to white checks, black veins. Sunny, dry habitats; *Euphydryas* larvae eat figwort family, esp penstemon, *Chlosyne* eat composites. April–Aug. Nymphalidae (Brush-footed butterfly family). Color p 544.

Gillett's checkerspot, *E. gillettii* (jil-et-ee-eye: after Charlotte Gillett). Also **Yellowstone checkerspot.** Broad red-orange band across both wings near rear edge; otherwise mostly dark above, cream beneath. Larvae eat twinberry.

Just enjoy checkerspots; don't even think about identifying them to species (aside from the single easily-recognized species named above). Not only does that require examining genitalia under a microscope, but the genus and species names are moving targets. It may be years before the specialists have the relationships worked out.

Field Crescent

Phyciodes pulchellus (fis-eye-o-deez: seaweed-red; pool-kel-us: beautiful). =*P. campestris, P. pratensis.*Ws 1¼" [32 mm], largely black above with rows of red-orange and yellow-orange spots, the outermost spots crescent-shaped; patterns similar beneath but much paler, orange and yellow-brown with little or no dark brown. Common in sun at mid to high elevs; larvae eat asters. May–Sept. Nymphalidae.

Fritillaries

Greater fritillaries, *Speyeria* spp. (spy-ee-ria: after Adolph Speyer). Ws 1½–3½" [33–87 mm]; orange with ± checkerlike black markings above; hindwing gray to golden tan beneath, with many round silvery-white to cream spots; forewing pale ochre to golden brown beneath, with blackish checks sometimes giving way to small marginal silver spots. Ubiquitous; larvae eat violets, adults suck nectar from composites, penstemons, dogbane, stonecrop, etc. May–Sept. Nymphalidae. Color p 543.

Lesser fritillaries, *Boloria* spp. (bo-lor-ia: 000). Ws 1⅓–2" [33–49 mm]; orange with ± checkerlike black markings above; undersides variously orange and dark brown, with white pattern elements either smeary chevrons (not round nor checkery nor in rows) or lacking. Larvae eat violets, willows, mtn. avens; adults sip nectar. Higher elevs, often where wet. Late April– Aug. Order Lepidoptera, Nymphalidae (Brush-footed butterfly family).

Fritillaries are as difficult as they are spectacular, with many similar species overlapping in range and each of them variable. The western spangled fritillary, *S. leto (=cybele)*, is sexually dimorphic: females are black with pale yellow to almost white margins, quite unlike the males, and unlike most other fritillaries—more like a flashier mourning cloak. The name fritillary (for both lilies and butterflies) refers to a Roman dice-box with checkered markings.

Coppers

Lycaena spp. (lie-**see**-na: she-wolf). =includes *Epidemia* spp. Ws 1" [25 mm], males dark brown above with purplish iridescence catching light; females yellow-orange above with brown speckles and borders. Order Lepidoptera, Lycaenidae (Copper family).

Purplish copper, *L. helloides* (hel-**oy**-deez: like species *helle*, the violet copper of Europe). Both sexes have prominent orange zigzag along hindwing margin; forewing ochre beneath with spots, hindwing ± pinkish ochre, with orange zigzag. Abundant; roadsides, wet meadows, streamsides; larvae eat buckwheat family. May–Sept. Color p 545.

Lilac-bordered copper, *L. nivalis* (niv-**ay**-lis: of snow). Upperside like the preceding; hindwing underside partly pale lilac, partly yellow; forewing underside yellow with dark spots; gorgeously colorful fresh, soon dulling. U.S. meadows, canyons, sage steppe; larvae eat *Polygonum*. May–Aug.

Mariposa copper, *L. mariposa* (mar-ip-**oh**-sa: butterfly in Spanish). Little or no orange marginal zigzag; hindwing underside ashy gray with barklike pattern, white chevrons; forewings dull orange with spots. Mid- to high-elev meadows, bogs; larvae eat low blueberry species. July–Sept.

Iridescence is common among tropical butterflies; here we find it in coppers, a large group of small, mostly orange-brown butterflies. Iridescent butterfly scales may have microscopic ridges that reflect light prismatically, or they may be of two types on one butterfly, regularly interspersed on the wing surface and held at different angles—not unlike the way fabric designers combine contrasting warp and weft threads to make an iridescent satin weave.

Northern Blue

Lycaeides idas (lie-see-id-eez: like genus *Lycaena;* **eye**-duss: a hero, one of Jason's Argonauts). =*L. argyrognomon*. Ws ¾–1" [18–28 mm]; undersides of bright blue males and both sides of brown females usually show a bit of a line of orange crescents. Higher elevs; larvae eat heathers and legumes. June– Sept. Order Lepidoptera, Lycaenidae (Copper family). Color p 545.

Blues

Icaricia spp (ic-a-**ree**-sha: after Icarus and genus *Aricia*). =*Plebejus* spp. Lycaenidae (Copper family).

Boisduval's Blue, *I. icarioides* (ic-a-**ree**-sha: after Icarus and genus *Aricia;* ic-airy-oy-deez: like Icarus, who flew too near the sun). Ws ⅞-1¼" [21-32 mm]—large for a blue; white spots underneath with or (on hindwing) often without dark centers. Locally abundant near lupine, the larval food. May–Aug. Color p 545.

Acmon Blue, *I. acmon* (**ak**-mon: a gnome who stole Hercules' weapons). =*I. lupini.* Ws ¾-1" [18-28 mm]; males deep or greenish blue; orange crescents (often fused into a line) on hindwing only are conspicuous above and below. Dry open slopes; larvae eat buckwheats or sometimes legumes. June–Aug.

Rocky Mountain Dotted Blue

Euphilotes ancilla (you-fill-**oh**-teez: after genus *Philotes;* an-**sill**-a: maid). =*E. enoptes, Philotes enoptes.* Ws ⅝-1" [17-24 mm], males blue above; females brown, usually with an orange flare near hindwing margin; fringes white, ± checkered with black; bluish white beneath, with scattered dark spots and orange hindwing flare. All exc BC; near sulphur (or rarely other) buckwheats, the larval food. May–Aug. Order Lepidoptera, Lycaenidae. Color p 545.

Caterpillars of many species of blues are attended by ants who eat "honeydew" secreted by the caterpillars. In this mutualistic symbiosis, the "stock-herding" ants sometimes attack and repulse beetles that parasitize caterpillars.

A Guy Worth His Salt

We often see butterflies congregating on patches of mud, a behavior called "puddling." They are sucking water out of the mud, but not because they're thirsty. They are siphoning dozens of gut-fulls per hour in one end and jetting it out the other, quickly extracting dissolved salt and excreting potassium. The salt ends up as a nutritional supplement for the next generation. Butterfly eggs will be far more numerous and more likely to succeed if the parents have plenty of sodium to give them.

Plant leaves evolved potassium/sodium imbalances as a defense. Just like herbivorous mammals (which seek salt licks, sweaty boots, etc; page 364, 404) caterpillars face a problem of too much potassium and too little sodium in their diets. Getting enough protein for the eggs is a similar problem. Many butterfly females solve it by breaking down their own flight muscles. Day by day or hour by hour as they lay eggs, their abdomens—their heaviest body part—get lighter, so less and less muscle is needed for flying. Nitrogen, the critical element for proteins, is probably the key nutrient acquired by puddling, in some species.

Arctic Blue

Agriades glandon (a-**gry**-a-deez: wild—?; **glan**-don: a pass in the Alps). =*A. aquilo, A. franklinii, A. rusticus.* Ws ⅞" [22 mm], males silvery blue above, females rusty gray-brown with white-haloed dark spots; both sexes ± white-fringed; light gray-brown beneath with white-haloed spots. Alp/subalpine; larvae eat saxifrage, shooting stars, etc. Late June–Aug. Lycaenidae.

Scarce and drab, this doughty blue is nonetheless conspicuous from time to time as the only butterfly flying in gray weather on high windswept ridges. It ranges around the Arctic Circle in the lowlands, and ventures southward along the Cordilleran summits.

Colleen Sculley, working in the Colorado Rockies, found that male arctic blues puddle for nuptial gifts of salt, as do male common alpines, margined whites, and mormon fritillaries. See below.

Sheridan's Hairstreak

Callophrys sheridanii (cal-o-fris: beautiful eyebrows; **share**-id-en-eye: after Lt. Gen. Phil Sheridan). Ws ⅞" [19 mm]; unmistakable: both sexes apple green beneath with (at least in the RMs) a white band crossing both wings; gray above. Open slopes; more common southward; larvae eat sulphur-flower and other buckwheats. March–July. Lycaenidae (Copper family). Color p 545.

Here comes the twister: in most butterfly species, nearly all puddlers are males. They are going to transfer the salt to a female together with their sperm. One shot of ejaculate commonly comprises 15 percent of male body weight, and takes an hour to deliver. Zoologists call this a "nuptial gift," something nutritious conveyed from male to female at mating, which will then nourish the progeny. For a bird, the appropriate gift might be a berry, or a bug, but for a butterfly it's a big, salty spermatophore. Then the female doesn't need to spend her own time puddling, leaving her with more time to search for ideal spots to lay eggs— a big advantage to both parents.

Repeated salt supplements are especially valuable in species whose females mate more than once. That raises the issue, for the male, of assuring that his salt goes mainly to his own offspring. In general, the larger his gift, the longer she will go before hungering for another mate. But *Pieris napi* males (and some others) go beyond crude quantity. They synthesize aromatic methyl salicylate to transfer to the females, who then exude it as long as it lasts. The smell is a turn-off to other males, who turn away in search of a less aromatic female.

Sooty Hairstreak

Satyrium fuliginosum (sa-**tee**-rium: satyr —; foo-li-jin-**oh**-sum: sooty). Also **sooty gossamer wing**. Ws 1" (25 mm]; uniformly dark gray above, ashy gray beneath with faintly lighter and darker speckles. Wy, c ID, s MT; locally abundant in high meadows with lupine, the larval food plant. June–Aug. Lycaenidae (Copper family).

This species lacks the "hair" that hairstreaks are named for—a pair or quartet of hair-thin wing "tails"—but it sure has the "streak." Notoriously hard to keep track of when streaking around, it can sometimes be seen when flowers hold its attention. Both sooty sexes resemble females of the large group known as blues. While male blues are indeed usually blue, the unblue female blues tend to be a bit browner than the sooty hairstreak on top, a bit whiter and more strongly speckled underneath.

Elfins

Western pine elfin, *Callophrys eryphon* (er-if-un: ?). =*Incisalia eryphon.* Ws 1" [22–27 mm], light brown above with black/white-dashed marginal fringe usually visible; sharp zigzag patterns beneath, light and dark reddish brown with black; older larvae pine green, with paired whitish lengthwise stripes. Often abundant near pines, the larval food; adults visit willows, spiraea, buckwheats, etc. April–July. Color p 000. Lycaenidae (Copper family).

Moss's elfin, *C. mossii* (**cal**-o-fris: beautiful eyebrows). =*C. fotis, Incisalia eryphon, I. fotis.* Ws ⅞" [22 mm], all brown (females ± reddish) with black/white-dashed marginal fringe ± visible; two-toned beneath, the paler gray-brown outer sections sharply, irregularly divided from the darker inner sections. Sporadic in ± low rocky, sunny habitats with stonecrop, the larval food plant. Unlikely in Canada. March– early May. Color p 545.

Brown elfin, *C. augustinus* (august-eye-nus: after a helpful Inuit man nicknamed Augustus by Sir John Richardson, p 000). =*Incisalia augustinus.* Ws ¾–1" [20–25 mm], plain brown above; no white fringe; reddish brown beneath with vaguely-defined dark inner portion of hindwings. Larvae eat buds and flowers of shrubs, esp heath family, sagebrush. Abundant in Canada, uncommon in WY. March–June.

Butterflies of this genus overwinter as pupae, enabling them to emerge early, sometimes while snow still covers much of the ground. Any other butterflies flying then (anglewings or tortoiseshells, most likely) have almost surely hibernated as adults. Most butterflies of the Rockies overwinter as eggs, and emerge later.

15

Other Creatures

Extremophiles

Yellowstone's hot springs get their stunning "grand prismatic" hues mainly from "biofilm" organisms that tolerate—no, *require*—hot water. These thermophiles ("heat-lovers") differ radically from familiar life forms in the elements they use in their metabolisms, and, inevitably, in the chemistry they produce in the process. That makes them a gold mine for both basic and applied (read "pharmaceutical") research. Yellowstone provided science with its first big window into this world, which was barely known to exist before 1965.

Thermophiles excite scientists for several reasons. First that old favorite, profits. The bacterium *Thermus aquaticus*, discovered in Yellowstone, produces a heat-stable enzyme that enables polymerase chain reactions, a pivotal and ubiquitous technique in molecular biology. Hoffmann-Laroche takes in around $100 million a year selling the *T. aquaticus* enzyme; the U.S. government gets nada. Subsequent legal efforts established that the Park can sell research contracts requiring royalties on profits from future finds.

Second, shear numbers. The heat limit for life on earth is now placed at 250° [121° C] or hotter—still below the water-boiling point in high-pressure habitats in the deep sea and in deep rocks. Lithotrophic ("rock eating") organisms live in pore spaces in rock way below the surface, gleaning their energy by stripping electrons from minerals; their metabolisms require neither sunlight nor air, even indirectly.

Clearly, the land surface cannot offer nearly as much habitat as the two or three miles of rock beneath it, nor as much as the oceans, so we may well be outweighed by both of those dark biospheres.

Third, antiquity. Visits to "black smoker" hot springs at deep sea-floor spreading centers led to great advances in our knowledge of "extremophiles," a broader category joining thermophiles with organisms that live in acids or alkaline brines. (Yellowstone has both acidic and alkaline springs with suitable extremophiles.) Most are provisionally classed in the domain Archaea (ar-**kee**-a: ancients), formerly considered a type of bacteria but now seen as at least as closely related to complex cells as to bacteria. (See page 613.)

Both archaea and bacteria lack cell nuclei. Both are traditionally considered one-celled, but many bacteria form slimy gelatinous biofilms in which they communicate, aggregate in thick structures, and collectively defend themselves against antibiotics—in short, they behave almost like primitive multicelled organisms. The free single cell phase of these bacteria produces different chemistry, and may be little more than a dispersal phase in between biofilms. Yellowstone is a hotbed for biofilm research, too.

From about 3.8 to 2.5 billion years ago (the Archean Eon, but not named after archaea, nor vice versa) the metabolic alchemy of primitive archaea and bacteria created the biosphere on earth, sorting the elements, giving us our beneficent atmosphere, fixing nitrogen in usable form, even concentrating gold into usable deposits.

Life on earth most likely originated as extremophiles, either at deep sea hot springs, or in deep rocks, or in rocks crashing to earth from space. Jack Farmer studies bacteria in Mammoth Hot Springs for clues to where NASA should look for life on Mars and Europa, a moon of Jupiter. He thinks many extraterrestrial bodies have geothermal water systems which "could have provided cradles for the emergence of life in other planetary systems within our galaxy, and beyond."

If primitive life forms are naturally, even commonly, synthesized in sulfide-rich, pitch-dark 300° [148° C] water, as many scientists believe, then we who have adapted to life on the frigid skin of the world, frying in all kinds of damaging radiation, are the true extremophiles.

Snow Worms

Mesenchytraeus spp. (mez-en-kih-**tree**-us: after genus *Enchytraeus*). Also **glacier worms**. Slender worms, average 1" [25 mm]; body segmented or ringed by fine constricted bands. In late-lying snowfields or glacier surfaces, spring and summer; of doubtful occurrence in U.S. part of our range.

Snow worms are segmented worms (oligochaete annelids) related to earthworms and, more closely, to the enchytrae cultured and sold as aquarium food. They eat snow algae including watermelon snow (below), and may be eaten by birds like dippers and rosy finches. Some kinds of spiders, insects, and nematodes (more primitive worms) are also adapted for life in snow. All are active at temperatures near freezing, and able to survive even colder temperatures either by dehydrating to prevent tissue freezing, or by restricting freezing to their intercellular spaces. Both strategies require special proteins that lower the protoplasmic freezing point to well below 32° [0° C].

Watermelon Snow

Chlamydomonas nivalis (clamid-o-**mo**-nus: mantled unit; ni-**vay**-lis: of snow).

Pinkness in late-lying snowfields consists of pigments in living algae. These algae are the producers in an entire food cycle that operates in snow. Snow worms, protozoans, spiders and insects are grazers on the algae, and are eaten in turn by predators like the rosy finch. Droppings from the predators, bodies of producers and grazers, and pollen and spiders blown from downslope provide food for decomposers (bacteria and fungi) that complete the cycle. The algae live on decomposition products and on minerals that fall on the snow.

Most of the pinkness is in energy-storing oils within "resting spores" that sit out the winter wherever they happen to end up in the fall. In spring, under many feet of new snow, they respond to increasing light and moisture by releasing four "daughter cells" that swim up to the surface. The year's crop becomes visibly pink where concentrated by melting, or where it gravitates into depressions in the surface, or where your footstep compresses it to a thin film.

Some say watermelon snow smells or tastes like watermelon;

Sun Cups

Depressions in snowfields amplify themselves by reflecting light to their centers, enhancing melting there—but only if they are the right size. Eventually the snowfield is regularly patterned with "sun cups" all over. Notice how footprints get incorporated into the pattern. Thin dirt that gravitates to the bottom absorbs heat, contributing to the process; but thick dirt (or a conifer branch) insulates the snow, prevents melting, and ends up as a cap on a cone of snow. With the right weather and dirt, high points between sun cups can grow into slender towers, "penitentes." In the Andes and Himalayas these may reach 20' [6 m] high.

others warn of diarrhea. Of the more than 100 species of snow algae, *C. nivalis* is our most abundant by far. Yellow, green, and purple snow algae are also known. The snow algae cover a significant portion of the earth surface, and are probably a serious beneficial part of the greenhouse gas equation. *Chlamydomonas* was long called a "green alga" due to its chlorophyll and celluloselike cell, but its swimming ability and well-developed eyespot are animal-like, and many protozoologists claim it as theirs. Let's say it's in a non-plant, non-animal Kingdom to be announced.

Giardia

Giardia intestinalis* (**jar**-dia: after Alfred Giard). =*G. lamblia*, *G. duodenalis.*

One single-celled critter of intense interest to hikers is this intestinal parasite. Much remains unknown about giardia, but two points seem clear: one, it can cause very unpleasant symptoms, colorfully described by the Oregon State Health Division as "sudden onset of explosive, watery, foulsmelling diarrhea with nausea and anorexia and marked abdominal distention with flatulence" perhaps accompanied by "chills and low-grade fever, vomiting, headache and malaise"; two, those who wish not to risk picking it up in the mountains must treat all drinking and toothbrushing water.

An Australian parasitologist couple rhapsodized over Giardia—"the only microorganism we know to smile"—in a paper titled, "My Favorite Cell: *Giardia*." Their affection is inspired less by the smile than by Giardia's unusual biochemical and metabolic traits bridging the realms of protists and bacteria. (Being one-celled and motile, Giardia were protozoan animals in the days when plant and animal kingdoms sufficed, but not in modern multi-kingdom systems.)

Of the many mysteries of giardia, the burning issue for nonscientists is how to avoid it. There are ways, but all sacrifice the immediacy, flavor, and spiritual fulfillment of prostrating ourselves to the mountain stream goddess and drinking deeply. (If there is a safe place to do that still, it might be at a glacier's foot. Springwater isn't necessarily safe, since neither passage through earth nor freezing are

---

*Most popular sources say *G. lamblia*, but scientists in this field have mainly used the other two names for decades. Species-level taxonomy of *Giardia* is a moot point awaiting resolution of species concepts. (The biological species concept defines a species as a group of interbreeding populations, but that doesn't work for one-celled organisms that reproduce asexually.)

any problem for giardia cysts, a communicable dormant phase of the creature.) Bringing water to a full boil, even for an instant, is 100% effective at any elevation in our range, and also adequate for *Cryptosporidium*, another water-borne intestinal pathogen. Disinfectant tablets of tetraglycine hydroperiodide are effective, but only if given enough time to work; the colder the water, the more time they need. A good filter pump yields the best-tasting safe water, by far.

Symptoms appear one to three weeks after exposure. They last a few days at a time, but may recur *ad nauseam*. If you think you've got them, see a doctor. If your stool sample comes back negative, try again, since cysts pass out of your system only at intervals. The three medications currently used here for giardiasis each have nasty side effects and many contraindications, including pregnancy; some are carcinogen suspects. Atabrine is the most effective, Flagyl the close second and a bit less nasty. A cure may require more than one week-long course. Some people (pregnant ones especially) may prefer giving their own systems time to bring the giardia into balance.

We develop tolerance of particular strains of giardia. Human populations *not* reporting giardiasis turn up many giardia carriers in random samples. Ten to twenty percent of North Americans host giardia asymptomatically. I'll bet I do, for one, along with most of you who drank from as many mountain streams as I did in years past. (Children are more susceptible than adults. However, infants seem to be protected by a giardicidal toxin in normal human milk.)

Giardia lives in both industrialized and developing nations worldwide; it abounds within feces of dogs, cats, cows, coyotes, horses, moose, beaver, muskrats, water voles, and birds. Some strains appear highly host-specific, while others are thought to be transmissible between species, including humans. Beavers are the wild species most likely to share them with us, hence the nickname, "beaver fever." Water voles have been named as suspects, but in fact *G. muris*, the species in small rodents, does not infect humans.

It is still possible that we rarely catch giardia from other mammals, and mainly have human slobs to blame. If this proves true, we can at least feel a bit safer in remote areas, and earlier in the season, since the cysts are not thought to live more than a few months outside of hosts. In the meantime, don't count on it. Since we do know that humans transmit the parasites to other humans, always defecate well away from any body of water, and cover up with 6" [15 cm] of dirt.

Why was Giardia unheard-of sixty years ago? It could have come to the back country in the modern hordes of hikers and their dogs (both species often careless about burying their scats). On the other hand, journals of early explorers are rife with bowel complaints. The mix of sheepherders, loggers, hunters, and fishers of fifty years ago probably included a much higher percentage of long-term area residents than today's backpackers, as well as a higher proportion of rugged types unlikely to report or seek treatment for giardiasis.

Rocky Mountain Wood Tick

Dermacentor andersoni (derma-**sen**-ter: skin pricker). Adults about ⅛"; reddish brown with darker shield on back, behind head; a pair of pale zigzags down the shield; females become much larger and paler, resembling dried beans, when engorged with victim's blood. Dog tick, *D. variabilis*, is very similar, but is found ± everywhere in the U.S. and s Canada *except* our range. Class Arachnida (Spiders), Order Acarina (Mites and ticks).

Ticks, mites, and spiders differ from insects in having eight legs and two main body sections, rather than six and three. Ticks live on blood they suck from warm-blooded animals. They climb to the tips of grasses or shrubs and drop off when the stem shakes following a jump in carbon dioxide levels—a telltale of mammalian breath.

Ticks carry some serious diseases, but this is one of the best areas on the continent for not catching them. That's ironic: Rocky Mountain spotted fever got its name when it was a big problem in Montana a hundred years ago. It's rare here now. It can be fatal, so it must be recognized and treated with antibiotics. It starts 2 to 12 days after tick bite, with high fever, severe headaches, and variable other flu-like symptoms. Many victims get a distinctive rash that starts on or near the hands and feet, and spreads. Colorado tick fever is fairly rare outside of Colorado. It is neither life-threatening nor treatable. Very high fever and other flu-like symptoms typically occur in two bouts of two or three days each, separated by two or three days' respite. Lyme disease is still almost unknown here.

If you find a tick on you and can brush it off easily, do so at once; you haven't been bitten yet, so don't worry. If it has taken hold, pluck it carefully: using tweezers, grab the tick by the head, not the abdomen, and tug gently and repeatedly until it releases its grasp. Avoid either crushing it or leaving its mouthparts imbedded in your skin; both juices and mouthparts can convey infection. Immediately wash and sterilize the site (with alcohol, for example). If you can't get to a proper pair of tweezers, pull it with your fingers (technique as above) after dousing it with insect repellent to encourage it to back out. Ticks are a good reason to use insect repellent. (See p 493.)

16

Geology

Our part of the Rockies offers as gorgeous and varied an assortment of rocks as you could ask for. That's no surprise, since our ranges are diverse in terms of age, cause, composition, shape, and history. (For an overview of their geography, see Chapter 1.) Before describing the kinds of rocks, this chapter will offer a history of the Rocky Mountains as a sequence of processes and their driving forces. Be warned: it's a saga, not a short story. And it has more loose ends than a bad murder mystery. In other words, geologists disagree, often and loudly.

A hundred years ago, ancient strata in dramatic varicolored bands earned the Rockies (and Glacier National Park in particular) high rank as a geologists' playground. The strata beautifully illustrated the geosynclinal theory of mountain-building, which one eminent geologist complained was "a theory for the origin of mountains with the origin of mountains left out." After Plate Tectonics took over as the prevailing theory, geologists tried anew to explain *why* mountains rise. Yet after decades of debate, the Rockies stubbornly resist plate tectonic theory. No geologist I've read doubts that plates exist and subduct, but all agree that plate tectonics can't explain continents as neatly as they do oceans. Phil England writes about our area, "The continent of North America must be much weaker than the stiff oceanic plates, so weak in fact that it makes no sense to treat it as a plate at all." Don Anderson puts a positive spin on this by suggesting that plate tectonic theory becomes more powerful if you leave out adjectives like "rigid." About 15% of the earth's surface is taken up by mountainous regions soft enough to deform under tectonic forces.

Plate Tectonics

The Earth's surface is divided into large plates, which move. They grind along at speeds of a few inches per year. Seven huge plates and several small ones underlie today's crust.

"Oceanic crust," a sheet of basalt rock four miles [6.5 km] thick, is generated at mid-ocean ridges, where plates move apart. Under an ocean for millions of years, the sheet accumulates thick beds of marine sediments on top that gradually become sedimentary rocks. All plates carry some oceanic crust; many also carry some "continental crust"—thicker but less dense (i.e., lighter) crust of many kinds of rock, but predominantly granite as opposed to basalt.

You can think of crust as floating. Due to its thickness and low density, continental crust rides high upon its semifluid underpinnings; not much of it is covered with sea water, at least in this day and age. Conversely, most oceanic crust does lie under an ocean.

The crust is only the upper layer of the plate. The lower layer, "lithosphere," moves as part of the plate but, in terms of its mineral composition, is part of the underlying "mantle" rather than part of the crust. The longer this material is part of a plate, the cooler it gets; and the cooler, the heavier. So the plate is inherently conflicted as to whether it should float or not. Crust alone is light enough to float, but not lithosphere, which eventually gets heavy enough to drag the plate down into the mantle, in a process called "subduction."

Temperature differences cause the movement. When the earth first coalesced into a solid mass, it was hot and it also contained elements whose radioactive decay produces heat. Because the solid-rock mantle conducts heat poorly, a lot—thousands of kilocalories—of heat accumulated. That would put most of earth well above melting, but for the fact that being buried under miles of other rock creates intense pressure which jacks the melting point sky-high. Therefore the earth's interior, though it gets hotter and hotter toward the center, is mostly solid. Only in the outer core, just beneath the mantle, does heat overcome pressure and melt an entire thick layer.

Nevertheless, given a sufficient force, the solid mantle can flow, albeit very, very slowly, like toffee, just as the solid ice of a glacier can flow. The temperature difference between the earth's interior and its surface provides a sufficiently powerful force. "Slabs" of cold lithosphere sink into the hotter mantle. Hot mantle is displaced and forced up elsewhere, including melted rock ("magma") that fills the cracks left at the plate's trailing edge. In this manner Earth gives up a substantial part of its inner heat.

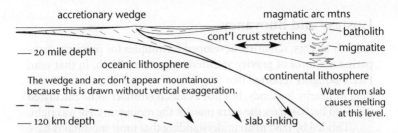

accretionary wedge   magmatic arc mtns

cont'l crust stretching

batholith

— 20 mile depth

migmatite

oceanic lithosphere

The wedge and arc don't appear mountainous
because this is drawn without vertical exaggeration.

continental lithosphere

Water from slab
causes melting
at this level.

— 120 km depth   slab sinking

The main driving force is the cold slabs peeling off of the surface and sinking, sucking the overriding plate forward and pushing mantle out of the way down below. Some geologists believe that rising convection columns of hot mantle add significant oomph.

Subduction grows continents and mountains in several ways:

Accretionary wedge: Ocean sediments scraped onto the overriding edge rise isostatically (next page) as a coast range like California's.

Arc volcanism: Some mantle material above the descending slab melts, about 37 miles [60 km] down, and rises. Magma that reaches the surface erupts there as a chain of volcanoes parallel to the line of subduction, either offshore (creating islands) or up to 200 miles [325 km] inland. Both island and inland chains are called arcs; many take an arc shape, like the Aleutian Islands. The mantle material melts when its melting point is lowered by increasing water content coming from the seafloor slab, which gets wrung out like a sponge.

Intrusion: About 90% of magma fails to reach the surface and erupt. It crystallizes slowly into a deep mass of intrusive rock. This can be either an entire magma body that never got there, or a portion of a magma body that got left behind. (See p 599). A mountain range may result from the thickening or deepening of continental crust along the line of magma formation, as described on the next page.

Collision: When a continent or island arc carried on the subducting crust plate reaches a subduction zone at another continent's edge, both plates are usually too light and too rigid to dive. The two land masses "suture" together, and sooner or later the zone of subduction jumps to a new line behind the accreted land. In a great slow-motion scrunch, the edges of both pieces are compressed, causing folding, faulting (up, down, and/or sideways movement on two sides of a break) and thickening of the crust. Continent-to-continent collisions are raising three of the world's highest mountain ranges: the Himalayas, Alps, and Caucasus. The Rockies when they were young seem to have resembled those great ranges, but if a continent hit North America, it remains something of a mystery guest.

Geology

Isostasy and Buoyancy

As early as 1745, scientists developed techniques for precisely comparing the force of gravity at different spots on Earth. In that year, Pierre Bouguer reported that gravity was stronger high in the Andes than in nearby lowlands, but not as much stronger as he calculated it should be, based on the extra mass of the mountains. He was right.

This led by 1889 to an understanding that most mountains have "roots" of "lightweight" rock. Continental crust floats on the denser mantle, and mountains, if they are to project higher into the air, must necessarily also project deeper into the mantle, just as a bigger block of wood floating next to a smaller block must extend deeper into the water as well standing taller above the water. This early view of a crust on a fluid mantle was a giant step toward plate tectonics.

Continental crust floats higher than ocean crust because it is both thicker and less dense. The continental surfaces that float highest—mountain ranges and plateaus—usually have beneath them either the thickest crust of all, or the least dense. Thickness is the greater influence, but density also contributes, since granite and most volcanic rocks are lighter than the crustal average.

Since crust is somewhat rigid, isostasy (eye-**soss**-ta-see) works regionally, and slowly. Skyscrapers sink only imperceptibly. When tectonic forces compress a region sideways, much of its rock gets squeezed up or down, mainly by means of folding in the deep, viscous fluid part of the crust, and by both folding and thrust faulting in the brittle upper crust. Volcanoes may contribute a little bit. Segregation of granite from denser magma also helps to reduce density. The result will be mountains, and roots. The initial cause may be horizontal forces, but most of the immediate cause is isostasy—the tendency for all points on the earth to counterbalance, or "compensate isostatically."

Thanks to ongoing erosion, isostatic compensation may continue for tens of millions of years. Erosion may actually make mountaintops higher. Let me explain with an analogy. As you may have heard, 90% of an iceberg is hidden below the waterline. That's because the ice is only slightly lighter than water: it's density is about 90% of water's. (The crust/mantle density ratio is about 5:6.) Think of an imaginary iceberg in a perfect cylindrical hockey puck shape, 100 feet tall, 10 feet above water and 90 feet below. If you hack off the top ten feet, you get a 90-foot cylinder which will float with 90%, or 81 feet, below the waterline: the iceberg isostatically compensates, or rises, 9 feet in the water, so that your net elevation loss is only one foot, not ten. Now suppose instead you carve the top ten feet into a perfect cone, leaving the top center point intact. The iceberg rises 6 feet, because you removed two-thirds as much weight as in the previous case, which caused a 9-foot rise. But since you didn't reduce the iceberg's total height at all this time, its top center point (the mountaintop) rises to 16 feet above water.

Similarly, in the real world: a broad, flat plateau could sit at isostatic equilibrium for millions of years, and then the climate could change from arid to wet and stormy, carving canyons and then broad valleys until the original plateau surface remains only as a few ridgetops. Erosion has now removed a huge weight of rock, carrying it off to distant lowlands and seas. Isostatic compensation will raise the ridges to new elevations, higher than before.

Because glaciers carve more vigorously than streams do, the Ice Ages sped up the rate of erosion and of isostatic uplift. But the size of this effect is controversial, at least for small alpine glaciers, which do move rock, but not very far. If the rock they moved still sits in moraines at the margins of a mountain range, it still weighs the region down, and isostasy won't be able to lift it much.

The continental ice sheets themselves weighed northern North America down by 400 feet [122 m]. After they melted, the land rose 400 feet in "isostatic rebound"—a twelve-thousand year bounce.

Typically, erosion and isostatic uplift proceed hand in hand, and the average elevation of a mountain region changes very slowly: while the continental crust is thickening, the region rises; after thickening has ceased, the range crest falls very slowly, for a long time. But even while the average surface elevation is slowly falling, some mountain ridges here and there may be rising, perhaps due to valley erosion, but especially due to extensional faulting (see p 581.)

That said, our Cordillera, again, doesn't entirely fit. The Columbia Mtns, the Sierra Nevada, and the ranges of the Basin and Range are rootless. They sit on very thin crust, yet they sit high—and hot. Geologists increasingly attribute the rise of many areas of the globe to a third force that they know far less about than either isostasy or plate tectonics: hot, buoyant mantle underneath.

An Archean Craton Joins a Proterozoic Continent

From 4 to 1.6 billion years ago

When oceanic plate plunges beneath continental plate, much of the accumulated marine sediments scrape off onto the continental edge and become a part of it. For billions of years the continents have grown in this fashion, starting from quite smallish "cratons" of ancient, stable crust.Barely a third of the way through earth's history, granites of the Wind River and Beartooth Ranges were part of one of the earliest cratons, the Wyoming. Some of their crust formed as early as 3.96 billion years ago, in the era of intense asteroid bombardment. Rocks of that age rank close to the oldest rocks in the world. Outcrops of the craton reach from Montana's Ruby Range to the Black Hills, and south to near Cheyenne. Wind River gneisses metamorphosed in one of the earliest known subduction events, 2.7 billion years ago.

Subduction was different back then, in the Archean eon. Earth was not far along in the process of sorting elements—raising lighter ones to the surface, sinking heavy ones to the core. Life consisted of bacteria and archaea. One type got its energy from sulfates and produced methane, giving us the first climatic greenhouse. Without that the water would have all been ice, and photosynthetic life would have been impossible. Photosynthetic bacteria gave us breathable oxygen. They were at work for several hundred million years before there was enough oxygen for oxygen-respirating life to come into being. Free oxygen was all nabbed

Lost Supercontinents

A mere 200 million years ago, the seven continents were all stuck together on one side of the earth, forming the supercontinent Pangea. But what of the preceding three billion–plus years of drifting continents?

Today's sea floors provide a diagram of Post-Pangea plate movements, which created them. Pre–Pangean movements are much harder to map, requiring indirect evidence, which gets harder to find the farther back you go. Geologists argue for many conflicting models. Most recognize one earlier all-earth continent, Rodinia, but disagree about its configuration and dates. Some describe a previous all-earth continent, Columbia.

Some geophysicists hypothesize a cycle of supercontinents assembling, breaking up, and reassembling. The life of a supercontinent might be limited to about 100 million years by the way it would trap mantle heat. Hot, buoyant mantle would first dome and then crack the supercontinent. The opening cracks would spew lava and eventually become sea floor spreading centers. Around the time the oldest edge of the new sea-floor plate reaches 200 million years old it has cooled and densified too much to remain at the surface; its weight rips it away from the continental plate and it sinks into the mantle, creating a subduction zone. Subduction would reel the continents back in (though not to exactly the same places as before). If they moved back at the same speed, that would take another 200 million years, and complete a cycle.

by oxygen-hungry compounds in volcanic gases until a critical balance was tipped about 2.3 billion years ago. We don't know why. It may have been the gradual escape of hydrogen into space from the top of the atmosphere. In any case, plate tectonics were part and parcel of the development of life on earth. Elements erupted into the atmosphere and the ocean, where microbes recombined them, then subduction returned them to the crust and mantle, metamorphism resorted them, volcanism again ejected just some of them, and so on in a great sorting cycle until there was an atmosphere, a climate, and an ocean that could nurture complex life. Chemical shifts in the biosphere continued as complex life evolved, so that we had one main era that produced coal, and others that produced petroleum, iron ore, red rocks, giant insects, etc.

In the middle Proterozoic Eon, Wyoming, a few other cratons, and several island arcs smashed together, forming Laurentia (a term for all early versions of North America).

Ancient Sediments Pile Up

From 1.6 billion to 400 million years ago

For a long, lonely, lonely, lonely, lonely time (the late Proterozoic Eon and the early Paleozoic Era) our present-day Continental Divide was under fairly shallow water. There were probably at least three rifting episodes, and also mountain-building episodes. The crust sank in basins, twice accumulating sedimentary piles more than 5 miles thick—the Belt and Windermere Supergroups. Over long periods, these enormous piles accumulated and slowly turned into rock.

The Belt forms most of Glacier/Waterton and much of western Montana, northern Idaho, and the Purcells and southern Selkirks. (Canadian geologists call it the Purcell Supergroup; I use its U.S. name since most of it is in the U.S.) It's the eastern half of a basin whose sediments derived mostly from land to its west—that is, from land that must have drifted away. Where is that land today? Antarctica or Australia. In some reconstructions, the East Antarctica craton attached to western Laurentia by 1.7 billion years ago, the Central Australia craton somewhat later, and the two rifted and drifted away together around 1.1 billion years ago. The collision when these continents arrived presumably thrust up great mountains overlooking a wide basin that sank more than ten vertical miles [16 km] while receiving the eroding sediments. These became the Belt Supergroup. The rate of sedimentation was phenomenal, though some argue that the offshore sediment fans of the Indus and Ganges Rivers today are in the same league. There was no life on land to hold the soil in place, but on the other hand there was no life on land to help crumble the bedrock. It's hard to picture. Why did the basin sink so fast, and then lie almost undisturbed for the next 1.1 billion years? Belt rocks are as exceptional in their mystery as in their beauty. (Color pages 538–40.)

Sediments of the thinner but lengthier Windermere Supergroup settled much later, on a sloping continental shelf—like the one off Atlantic shores today—created by the rift of 500 million years ago. They contain detritus from volcanism and at least one vast, more or less global ("Snowball Earth") glaciation.

Belt and Windermere rocks can be called either Precambrian (an old term for all rocks too old to have fossils of macroscopic animals) or Proterozoic. The subsequent Paleozoic Era, from 600 to 200 million years ago, left lots of fossils, but still preceded dinosaurs. Our region remained at Laurentia's western edge, generally quiescent and low, and getting lower and lower, eventually lying hundreds of miles out from the beach. Our abundant Paleozoic sedimentary rocks originated variously on continental shelves, lake bottoms, as mudflats, and as beaches of sand or wave-rippled mud.

Pangea

From 400 to 200 million years ago

The long era of relative peace ended early in the Paleozoic. The West Coast became a subduction zone, and has been one most of the time since. Island arcs rose. The undersea shelf where sediments accumulated was now a broad back-arc basin—like the modern Sea of Japan. The island arc collided with the continent; the resulting Antler Orogeny (mountain-building episode) is seen clearly in northern Nevada, but probably extends to the Idaho Pioneers and perhaps well into B.C. During the Antler, Laurentia's westerly sea floor subducted beneath the island arc; i.e., the polarity of subduction was the reverse of what it now.

Meanwhile, the continents were joining, one after another, into the supercontinent Pangea (pan-**gee**-a: all the earth). South America drove northward into lands now in the Southwest, raising mountains called the Ancestral Rockies about as far north as Casper, Wyoming.

Pangea's breakup began with the North Atlantic cracking open. Oceanic crust ripped and subducted under the NW Coast, which at that time ran down easternmost B.C. and the Washington/Idaho line.

Terranes Collide

From 200 to 50 million years ago

In three or four hundred million years of subduction, the West Coast must have overridden an area of ocean floor equal to today's Pacific. The vast vanished floor carried island chains on the scale of Indonesia, the Philippines and Japan together—or a small continent. Nearly all of Alaska, British Columbia, Washington, Oregon, California, Mexico, and half of Nevada and the Yukon are a vast mosaic of fragments (illustrated) slammed onto the continent's edge and sutured to it after breaking, sliding, rolling, and/or smearing out northward.

Each piece can been called a "terrane," or an "exotic" or "allochthonous" or "suspect terrane." A terrane is an area interpreted as having a different geologic history from the areas now next to it. Most of the exotic terranes lie west of our region. Their impact on us derives from, well, their impact.

Arc or Collision?

Problem: Why did huge ranges rise so far from the subduction zone? Why is the Cordillera so broad, especially at Colorado's latitude? For decades, geologists have tweaked the subduction-caused mountain arc model trying to produce a broad range. These efforts coalesced around the idea of a shallowly subducting slab (a subducted plate). This slab was the broken-off final edge of the Farallon Plate, about as young and warm (hence light) as oceanic plate can be; the crust was also thickened by an oceanic plateau. Something like that made it too buoyant to plunge steeply, so instead it slid in right under North America as far as Colorado. The slab's buoyancy and the seawater it released into the overlying continental plate might explain the remarkably diverse mountains now spread across 900 miles [1400 km].

Other geologists couldn't stop thinking about the Cordillera's resemblance to mountains pushed up by collisions. The breadth

from the Sierra Nevada to Pike's Peak is similar to that
from the Himalayas north to the Kunlunshan, or from
Crete to the Carpathians. And America's western terranes,
when you see them all on a map, plainly add up to a small
continent's worth of land. Could three dozen islands
have the same impact as a continent? Or could almost
all of them have been joined before the collision?

Since 1996, these geologists have exercised their
imaginations tweaking the island arc-to-continent collisional model to leave the Cordillera broadest and most
diverse in the lower 48 while the colliding objects are
strung out across Canada and Alaska. Julie Maxson
and Basil Tikoff describe a "hit and run collision;"
Eldridge Moores envisions a lost plate, "Americord,"
including ocean basins and island masses on the scale
of Indonesia and the Philippines; and Stephen Johnston reconstructs a "ribbon continent" breaking up in "the great
Alaskan terrane wreck." Like a northbound train, this strip hit Asia; the
engine stuck, becoming the tip of Siberia; the next four cars buckled
into a Z shape forming Alaska; and the final cars came to rest in B.C.
(Illustrated with his drawings, modified, with Canadian parts of our
area shaded.) He envisions the ribbon continent barely 300 miles wide
but 5,000 miles long [500 by 8,000 km]—much longer than the closest modern analog, Japan. Since Japan is an island arc, Johnston's
model is essentially a kind of island arc-to-continent collision.

Regardless of whether it was a sliver continent that hit and broke,
or island chains that joined into superterranes before hitting, there's
a case for the Rockies as a collisional range centered on the Columbia
Mtns, the Idaho Batholith, and eastern Nevada—not far inland from
North America's edge at the time. Many geologists still explain the
U.S. Rockies by subduction alone, which certainly could have melted
and intruded the magmas of Idaho and B.C. It's harder to get subduction to account for the fan of splayed faults in the Selkirks (illustrated in the next sidebar) let alone for this complex compressive
cordillera a thousand miles wide [1600 km]. (I suspect national in-
sularity at work: flat-slab proponents tend to simply ignore Canada,
as if the 49th Parallel separates two Cordilleras.) Looking around the
world, even where slabs are subducting shallowly, we don't see mountain belts this wide without collisions. The Andes have been used as
an example about half as wide, but terranologists have recently found
all the signs of another magnificent arc wreck there.

The Big Squeeze

180 to 59 million years ago

The Columbia Mountains were the first impact zone. Picture a large precipitous offshore island at the edge of the continental shelf, like New Guinea at the edge of Australia's shelf. Shards of island terrane are mixed today with shattered continental margin material and granites and gneisses created at great depth before, during and after the collision. These deep rocks now lie above 9,000' [2,750 m]. As they rose they eroded, yielding copious sediments that piled up and turned to rock, often right on top of old Belt and Windermere rocks. They piled up under seawater—since the terrane hit not shoreline but continental shelf, which was not forced up out of the sea until later.

The resulting superthick stack of sediments was destined to become the Canadian Rockies, an almost purely sedimentary mountain range. Their huge, long, parallel ridges formed as "thrust faults." Under the pressure of terrane collisions, long parallel cracks broke the layered crust into strips. If you ever slid a shovel under a few inches of fresh wet snow, you have seen a tiny model of multiple thrust faults. The east edge of each strip tilted up and slid onto the next, eventually totalling about 150 miles [240 km] of "crustal shortening." The overlaps thickened the crust, raising elevations through isostasy (as usual). All of that deformation was in the sedimentary veneer on top of the ancient continental core, or craton, which was was too strong to crumple or fracture: farther west, islands seem to have "beached," forming a huge, fractured and crumpled overthrust on top of the continental edge (which later rose and broke through to the surface in one area—the Monashee Dome, west of Revelstoke).

Geology

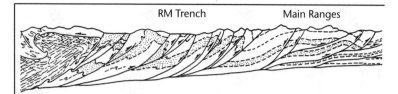

Compressional Faults

Tilted thrust faults: cross-section of Canadian Rockies (top of pages)

Mt. Yamnuska, Alberta, just north of the Highway 1/Kananaskis Hwy junction, is the most conspicuous piece of a thrust block of 535 million-year-old carbonates which moved 25 miles [40 km] east (left to right in your view.) Underlying (but much younger) shales form the dark talus. Some 125 miles [200 km] of the Front Ranges consist largely of this one thrust.

The many parallel ridges in the Rocky Mtn. Front area (both Montana and Alberta) relate to thrust faults. The strata most resistant to erosion become ridges. In the Sun River Canyon, MT, those are Madison limestone, which you meet three times as you drive upriver, because thrusting stacked the same sequences on top of themselves several times over.

Hoback Canyon, Wyoming, on the road between Jackson and Pinedale, is a cross-section exposing many thrusts, and later normal faults.

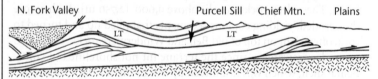

N. Fork Valley   Purcell Sill   Chief Mtn.   Plains

Thrust sheet: the Lewis Thrust in Glacier National Park

Chief Mtn. is the easternmost remaining part of the sheet, isolated by erosion.

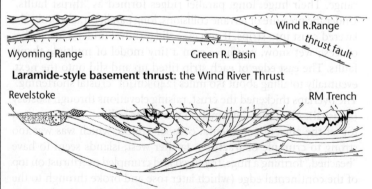

Wind R.Range

thrust fault

Wyoming Range   Green R. Basin

Laramide-style basement thrust: the Wind River Thrust

Revelstoke   RM Trench

Splayed faults: the Selkirk Fan (terrane collision)

Front Ranges   Foothills   Plains

Problem: When did the Canadian Rockies rise? Many geologists envision two terrane collisions raising B.C.'s mountains. The first hit the continental shelf 180 million years ago, and there has been little respite from deformation since. The Columbias began crumpling up at once, but the Rockies thrust belt waited another 25 million years for the impact to reach it; and most faulting, folding, and elevation gain in the main ranges may have waited until the second collision, 100 million years ago.* That one hit the west side of the earlier terrane, which absorbed some of its force (with more scrunching) and transmitted some on east to the Rockies. Compression rippled eastward at a crawl, bending the continent down in front of it to form a narrow sea trough that collected sediments from the rising range. Those turned to stone in time to be crumpled up as part of more easterly ranges. The Alberta foothills rose last, 60 million years ago.

Seismic profiles show the tilted blocks as upturned tips of vast nearly-horizontal moving sheets beneath. In segments dominated by flat strata such as the Belt Supergroup, some thrust sheets remained horizontal throughout. The largest of these, the Lewis Thrust, includes almost all of Glacier/Waterton, plus narrower strips an additional 90 miles [145 km] north and south. (Total length, 290 mi/ 470 km; maximum eastward movement, 60–85 mi/100–140 km.) Its horizontal strata across rugged modern topography are striking.

Problem: Sheet thrusting has been compared to trying to push a blanket off the far side of a bed by pushing on its near edge. Geologists struggle to explain the physics of this trick. Apparently a certain shape of wedge is required, with a slope of about 4°. "Slide" surfaces are usually slippery layers of soft shale, dolomite, or evaporites (gypsum, salt, etc.). Some geologists think movement may be facilitated by seismic vibration and/or by volcanic gas or water pressure

---

*The 180-million-year newcomer was Stikinia, or the Intermontane Superterrane; the 100-million-year one Wrangellia, or the Insular Superterrane. Many terranes in these groups clearly spent some time as far south as today's Baja California. The "Baja B.C. controversy" concerns whether Wrangellia moved north and collided here by 100 million years ago, or much later—late enough for its "hit-and-run collision" to have caused the Laramide orogeny. The Columbias mostly fall within Quesnellia, once mapped as an exotic terrane but now seen as old continental crust partly covered by thin sheets of exotic skin.

in a porous underlying layer, at least in some cases.

The Canadian Rockies are part of a fold-and-thrust belt which continues south through central Montana, western Wyoming, and on to southeastern California. The timing may be similar, beginning in eastern Idaho and western Wyoming by 89 million years ago, and ending on Montana's Front around 56 million years ago. Terrane interpretation gets more difficult southward. Much of the evidence got covered up later by volcanic rocks all over eastern Oregon, Idaho, and Nevada. Could there have been a single fold-and-thrust orogeny all the way to Mexico? Just possibly. A large terrane seems to have hit Nevada 180 million years ago on the outboard edge of two earlier accretionary belts; and at least one small one hit western Idaho 100 million years ago. That one—the Wallowa/Seven Devils Terrane—was a small island-arc group, differing from its huge contemporary in coastal B.C. in that it accreted directly to the old North American craton. It was sliding north as it ground to a halt. The suture, along the Salmon River valley near Riggins, has a massive mylonite zone—a fault plane of rocks smeared out in one direction.

The Laramide Orogeny

(or-**ah**-jen-ee) 89 to 51 million years ago

After raising parallel mountains in the fold-and-thrust belt for tens of millions of years, the compressive forces expanded their repertoire. Sharp folds overextended and snapped; angular thrust faults cut all the way through the cratonic crust, almost to the mantle, raising discrete, abrupt mountain ranges separated by basins. These run in almost every compass direction, especially in Wyoming. Total vertical displacement on the Wind River Fault was around eight miles, raising Archean basement rocks to the sky. At last we had the ranges many think of first and foremost as The Rockies, including the Beartooths, the Wind Rivers, and all Colorado and New Mexico ranges.

What caused the deep thrusts? The long reach of the flat slab (page 575) dominates the hypotheses, but collisionists find similar structures in other collisional orogenies. And why are they at crazy angles? They may have reactivated ancient Wyoming Craton faults; or they may result from northeastward pressure from a rigid block, the Colorado Plateau, hitting from the southwest.

So the big Wyoming and Colorado ranges, like the Canadian Rockies, were born in the shadow of mighty ranges to their west. Now they're the highest things standing. They were raised a bit, and the main axis was sharply lowered, by the processes described next.

Extension

The past 59 million years

As the Laramide was reaching its climax, the region began getting stretched (extended) east/west, even before it stopped being squeezed (compressed). The huge Rocky Mountain Trench fell open, almost literally. The Trench probably already existed as a line of weakness following a huge fault which slid land on its west side northward. But extension took that weakened line and widened it into the huge trough that, much later, collected Ice Age glaciers that carved it wider still. Some old thrust faults, including the Lewis, were reactivated in reverse, sliding westward now instead of east.

Extension began in the north and worked its way south. It covered a large area of Idaho and southern Montana with volcanoes for 15 million years. After a hiatus about 20 million years ago, it resumed with renewed vigor in an area from eastern California northeast to Montana's Mission Range and Wyoming's Tetons. Across this vast area (the Basin and Range province) parallel fault-block ranges alternate with flat valleys. The faults are "normal faults:" they accommodate stretching. Many remain active, especially near the northeast and western edges of the province. The Teton, Madison, Lemhi, and Lost River Ranges have the most active faults in our range, and produced two of the three strongest earthquakes south of Alaska and north of Mexico since 1906: Hebgen Lake in 1959 and Borah Peak in 1983. The Mission Range had a comparable one 7700 years ago.

Extension means that the crust thins and the region loses average elevation—a fact in no way contradicted by fault-block mountains and/or volcanoes rising at the same time. "Normal faults" raise ranges while dropping the intervening valleys about four time as far. Extensional normal faults are usually "listric:" the faultlines arc belowground, tilting the raised blocks so that they resemble fallen dominoes in cross-section (page 582). The mid-crust widens along a long ramplike fault while the lowest crust layer stretches like taffy.

Taffy-like swirls can be seen in metamorphic rocks that rose from the mid-crust. (We have metamorphic core zones in the Columbia Mtns., the Bitterroots, and Idaho's Pioneers.) Geologists know the temperature and pressure that produce each metamorphic mineral, and can calculate the depth where a rock metamorphosed.

Some geologists explain Basin and Range extension as incipient rifting, i.e. North America starting to split into two continents along a line west of the main Rockies. Others say a mantle plume (page

---

585) pushes the crust upward, stretching it. But it's hard to explain a plume extending the vast area of the Cordillera.

A breathtakingly simple alternative is "collapse:" mountain ranges spread out under their own weight, beginning while they're still rising, and continuing for 50 or 100 million years. They may have deep roots that raise them isostatically at first, but the roots are soft and weak (partly because they're hot) and can only support

Extensional Faults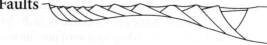

Listric normal faults on shallow ramp shear (Basin and Range style)

The Tetons and Idaho's Lemhi and Lost River Ranges are three of the most spectacular Basin and Range fault blocks. The latter two have their fault scarps facing west. On the base of the Lost River Range you can see the fresh scarp from the 1983 earthquake snaking along. Up Doublespring Pass Road you can put your hand right on it.

Idaho's Sawtooth Range is an east-facing fault block dating from the earliest post-Laramide extension, long before the Basin and Range.

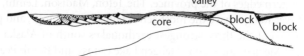

Deep-seated detachment, with metamorphic core complex

The west side of the Bitterroot Valley is a huge fault scarp where a ten-mile-deep block (now the Sapphire Range, opposite side of the valley) slid down and east off of the Bitterroot Metamorphic Core Complex.

Thin-skinned detachment

The Heart Mountain detachment sheet, everywhere to the southwest of Hwy 296 and the Beartooth Highway in Wyoming. The base of the sheet that slid is somewhat above the long white cliff of Cambrian limestone that snakes down the Clark's Fork valley. Half a mile [800 m] due south of Silver Gate you can see the east-facing "breakaway fault," the part that stayed put while several blocks (also visible) slid a short distance eastward, almost horizontally. A breakaway fault shows that the block wasn't pushed; the driving force could only have been gravity. The detachment area spreads southeastward over tens of square miles.

them as long as strong compression buttresses them from two sides.

Both the flat slab model and the hit-and-run collision models employ changes in the speed, direction, and/or boundaries between plates to weaken compression at the right time to let the range collapse. The flat slab eventually took a nosedive, leaving a slab gap to be filled by upwelling hot mantle, which heated, weakened, thinned, and still uplifts the crust throughout the interior Cordillera.

Analogies are drawn to the youthful Himalayas, which show the first signs of collapse, and the somewhat older Andes, still near their full height but with parts of their western flanks slipping. The much older Rockies have a collapsed core on their western side, and once-smaller but now more intact ranges to the east.

Conventional wisdom long held that the Rockies eroded down to lowish elevations by about 30 million years ago, then rose again in the last 12 million years. Tundra "summit flats," a common feature from the Beartooths south, were thought to have taken shape as low plains. Though you still read this on some interpretive signs, it's implausible on its face. The world is full of mountain ranges 50, 100, 200 million years old that are still mountains. It takes a l-o-n-g t-i-m-e to get rid of a mountain range; you carve away 30 feet, you've only lowered it by one. (See p 571.) Newer studies refute the lines of reasoning based on fossil vegetation and on summit flat formation requiring flat lowlands. So the timing of uplift is again an open question. In one scenario, plate tectonics finished raising mountains here by 45 million years ago, and gradual collapse (including local uplift through extensional faults and isostatic compensation) has dominated the story ever since. A new one puts most of the uplift between 45 and 20 million years ago—after the Laramide faults. And others find new evidence of reinvigorated uplift since 12 million years ago.

Recent uplift in our range likely consists of two local events—the Yellowstone swell and the Wallowa fault block—plus areas of mysterious broad upwarp originating in the mantle.

The Mile-High Warp

The last 40 million years?

Problem: Why are the western Great Plains high, even where they've had scarcely a fold or a fault for a few hundred million years? Why are the Great Basin and the Sierra Nevada as high as they are despite having very thin crust under them, as seismic tomography shows?

Something (or some things) may be pushing the Great Basin, the Rockies, *and* the High Plains up, but few explanations match this uplift in terms of age, location, and structure. The Rockies and Basin are hot, and stretching; the Plains are cold, and being squeezed.

Several possible answers probably combine in different proportions in different areas. In the Basin, hot mantle may well up into a slab gap following the trailing edge of the Farallon plate. The Yellowstone hotspot swell is a factor, but only 150 miles [240 km] wide. The Rio Grande Rift, in New Mexico and southern Colorado, may produce substantial uplift there, tapering off to slight uplift in southeast Wyoming. But the Plains tilt (though less sharply) even in Alberta, too far northeast to be affected by any of the above. Accelerated erosion during the Ice Ages produced substantial isostatic uplift, even on the Plains, but that also pencils out as insufficient to explain all of the upwarp.

So how could the mantle lift the Plains without being hot? In Jerry Mitrovica's hypothesis, broad regions where big slabs subduct are sucked down by the slabs' density, making long-lasting depressions. (Picture dropping a lead weight into a tub of honey: the surface remains depressed where the weight sank.) The Plains and adjacent Rockies were tugged down by the Farallon slab sinking under them, flooding them with shallow Cretaceous seas where dinosaurs splashed, and letting sediments more than two miles thick accumulate on the sinking sea floor. After subduction shifted far westward, the area slowly rebounded to its original level, just fast enough to counter the erosional demolition of the eastern Rockies. The location is a good fit, if the slab subducted shallowly about as far east as the Rocky Mtn. Front before plunging. The timing is on the early side, though, for any uplift that may continue today; it would require a very long-lasting isostatic feedback loop, as rivers haul mountain rocks off to eastward.

The Yellowstone Volcanic Track

At least the past 16 million years

Can you name the biggest non-extinct volcano in the Americas?

Try Yellowstone. The Yellowstone volcano consists of three overlapping calderas almost as big as the Park, on top of a broad swell. The calderas are basins where the volcano collapsed into its own emptied magma chamber at the end of an eruptive sequence. Each of the eruptions was much bigger (i.e, more powerful and producing more lava) than any volcanic eruption in written history. They happened 2, 1.3, and .6 million years ago, respectively. At that rate we should be due for another one in 100,000 years, and there is no reason to doubt that that will happen. The heat is obviously still there,

Hotspots, Mantle Plumes, CAT Scans

According to a dominant hypothesis of recent decades, the earth's mantle convects its heat away via plate tectonics; the core, in contrast, shoots its heat—but not its matter—up through the mantle via "plumes." Think of the liquid outer core as a hot plate under the hyperviscous mantle. Blobs of superheated mantle form on the mantle floor (like at the base of a lava lamp) then rise 1700 [2750 km] miles to the mantle ceiling. There they melt some lower crust into magma, which erupts as a megavolcano. Meanwhile, the crustal plate drifts across the plume, which melts a new hole through the crust, producing a second volcano, and eventually a long string of them. The textbook case is the Hawaiian Islands chain. Early hot spot lists were all oceanic, but starting with Yellowstone, varying lists of continental hot spots have been proposed.

The sharp bend in the Hawaii hotspot track was long seen as the mark of a sharp shift in plate motions 43 million years ago; hotspots were assumed to remain fixed in place, offering a frame of reference for maps of ancient plate movements. But as more data came in, it looked more and more like the shift 43 million years ago didn't happen. Today, few geophysicists maintain that plumes are fixed or, for that matter, that hotspots necessarily originate at the core-mantle boundary.

We now have a way to "see" the mantle, a sort of geophysical CAT scan based on precisely timing earthquake shock waves as they reach seismic sensors all over the earth. If a wave takes slightly longer to reach a given point than simple distance predicts, then it must have passed through a "low velocity zone" (presumed to be hotter rock) on its way through the earth. Seismic images under Yellowstone seem to show heat only 125 miles [200 km] deep. Gene Humphreys suggests that Yellowstone may be a "self-organizing volcano" on one of two mirror-image tracks. The opposite track leads to Newberry Caldera, the west end of a row of younger-westward rhyolitic calderas that parted from the Yellowstone row 12 million years ago in southwest Idaho. A pair of tracks moving opposite directions on the same plate cannot be hotspots.

The American Geophysical Union's 2002 and 2003 meetings featured rip-roaring debate between plume and nonplume explanations for Yellowstone and between plumes believers and detractors in general. Warren Hamilton, a highly respected senior theorist of tectonics of the West, methodically argued that "Plumes do not exist." It's hard to guess which parts, if any, of the plume hypothesis will still be taught twenty years from now. The trend has been toward viewing mantle convective forces more in terms of cold slabs sinking than hot stuff rising. In terms of how plates are driven, that would suggest more a pull than a push.

as are some interesting up and down motions of the caldera floor in the last 30 years. (These motions, and ground tremors, are monitored, and should give us plenty of warning if a magma body rises to the surface.) Yellowstone may be the earth's hottest large caldera.

Yellowstone's eruptions could be called explosions. Rather than piling their lava up to make a mountain, they blasted it into the sky. (This is typical of rhyolite volcanoes; see page 604.) The finer particles darkened skies and chilled weather for years, if not decades, while the coarser ash blanketed two thirds of the U.S. Geologists use the three three big ash layers for dating sediments far and wide.

Yellowstone's swell raises the entire area by about 1200 feet [365 m]. (The swell is not a volcano: it's caused by upward pressure on the underside of the earth's crust, not by lava piling up.) Even after caldera collapse gave up two-thirds of that rise, the swell was high enough to give Yellowstone a huge ice cap during the Ice Ages.

Yellowstone volcanism aligns with a series of progressively older volcanic areas across Idaho's Snake River Plain. This linear series is usually considered a "hotspot track"—the surface expression of a plume that stays at one spot in the mantle while the crust drifts over it, so that it appears to move in a straight line. (See previous sidebar.)

Problem: How/where/when did the Hot Spot begin? Some answers:

As rhyolitic calderas 17 million years old near McDermitt, Oregon, if we simply trace the straight and narrow track of known calderas.

As basalt floods—the Steens and Columbia River Basalts—just south of the Wallowas. Many geologists think hot spots as a rule start out as basalt floods—vast provinces of flat basalt flows like the ones that erupted through fissures in eastern Oregon 16.6 million years ago. Chemical analysis of the Steens and Columbia basalts supports a tie between them and Yellowstone.

As an asteroid impact instigating the basalt floods. Some geologists correlate flood basalts with impacts *and* with major extinctions, which could have been caused by the one-two punch of extraterrestrial impact and a million years of intense volcanism. They draw up a mechanism for instantaneous removal of a craterful of rock to provoke floods of basalt. Alt and Hyndman say that this can't have not happened here, but their view is iconoclastic, not mainstream.

As Basin and Range extension commenced, 40 million years ago. A hotspot could have caused extension, or vice versa: if mantle heat and pressure get trapped under continents, they would likely break through where the crust is stretched thin, as it is in the Basin and

Range. A straight line would put the hotspot near the California/ Nevada state line at that time, but evidence there is slim.

Offshore, 70 million years ago. The Oregon-Washington Coast Range terrane looks like a string of hotspot seamounts smeared northward as they accreted to the continent's edge. Certain 70 million-year-old basalts in the Yukon also could be far-travelled early Yellowstones. An emerging hypothesis combines these with the Columbia basalts.

Geysers, Hot Springs, Mudpots

Yellowstone has dozens of hot springs and mudpots, and a majority of the world's geysers—an increasing percentage, as geothermal drilling has killed off much of the competition. This must not be allowed here.

Almost anywhere, temperature increases with depth in the earth. No volcanoes or near-surface magma are required. At two miles down, for example, seeping groundwater commonly heats to 200° [94°]. Hot, it tends to rise. For it to flow (or blast) out at the earth's surface as hot water or steam, it needs broken or porous rock to flow up through all the way to the surface fast, before it cools down or dilutes completely. The Rockies abound in hot springs near deep faults—seams of broken rocks.

Yellowstone, a huge collapsed caldera of thoroughly fractured rock inviting water to rise, takes "geothermal" to a higher level. Molten rock (interlaced in solid rock) is just three miles down; 460° [240°C] rock is just 1500 feet down [460 m]; and 400° [215° C] water is very close to the surface. Under a geyser, pressure keeps even 400° water from boiling, as long as the slender vent is plugged with mineral crusts. Pressure builds until it bursts the plug, reducing the pressure, instantly boiling the super-heated water, shooting more water and steam out, and so on in a chain reaction that perpetuates itself for the several seconds it takes to shoot out thousands of gallons of water. Old Faithful takes about 80 minutes to rebuild its pressure, but most geysers take far longer. While the pressure is down, minerals precipitate in the neck of the vent, making a new, but weak, plug. Sooner or later they will plug the vent permanently, unless earthquakes come along to keep cracking them. The Yellowstone area obliges with frequent small local tremors, and less frequent large Basin and Range quakes, like the 1959 Hebgen Lake quake, which reactivated 160 geysers and turned a few of them full on, as steady spouters.

Mudpots occur where sulphuric steam seeps up without water. The sulphuric acidity breaks down the rock, and steam saturates the resulting silt and keeps it bubbling.

Mineral-rich hot water provides habitat for colorful, highly specialized organisms that hold as much magic for scientists and pharmaceutical companies as they do for sightseers. (See page 561.)

Geologic Time

4.7 billion years ago, Earth formed.

4 billion	Oldest rocks solidified from magma. Oceans formed.
3.96 billion	Oldest crystals in the Rockies solidified from magma.
3.85 billion	Possible origin of life in the form of primitive bacteria.
3+ billion	Cyanobacteria began making free oxygen.
2.3 billion	Oxygen abundant enough to oxidize most elements.
1.9 billion	Wyoming and other cratons formed continent Laurentia.
1.4 billion	Sediments settled which would become Belt/Purcell rocks.
1.2 billion	Complex (eukaryotic) single-celled life originated.
580 million	Oldest large multicelled animal fossils.
530 million	Burgess Shale sediments laid down, with strange fossils.
440 million	Fungi and algae moved onto land; first plants soon after.
245 million	Permian Extinction, the most severe ever.
225 million	Dinosaurs became dominant on land. Pangea rifted.
180 million	First superterrane collision initiated the Columbia Mtns. Most of our Rockies still flat and shallowly submerged.
100 million	Flowering plants came to predominate over spore plants.
140 million	Thrust faulting began raising the Canadian Rockies.
89 million	Laramide/Sevier Orogeny began raising U.S. Rockies.
65 million	Cretaceous Extinction deleted dinosaurs.
59 million	Extensional faulting began in the Canadian Rockies.
50 million	Laramide orogeny ceased here, but continued farther south. Challis/Absaroka volcanoes were active.
40 million	Extension took over the Basin and Range.
16.6 million	Columbia Basalt floods began. =Yellowstone Hotspot?
3.5 million	Wells Gray volcanism began.
2.5 million	A long cooling trend climaxed in the Pleistocene Ice Ages.
2 million	Huckleberry Ridge eruption, Yellowstone's largest.
1.8 million	Ancestral hominids shaped stone tools.
1,293,000	Mesa Falls eruption at Yellowstone.
630,000	Lava Creek eruption at Yellowstone.
130,000	Earliest anatomically modern humans.
115,000	Most recent Ice Age began.

<Hadean Eon> < Archean Eon > < Proterozoic Eon > Paleozoic Age Mesozoic Age Cenozoic Age

Earth formed | asteroids let up / first life? | first free oxygen | enough oxygen / Laurentia | Belt Formation / complex cells | complex animals / land plants | dinosaurs / Rockies | Ice Age & recent

Human Time

30,000 BCE	Possible first human migration from Asia to NA.
16–14,500	Last major advance of most alpine glaciers here.
15–13,000	Purcell and Flathead Lobes of Cordilleran Ice Sheet at their maximum. Missoula (or Bretz) floods.
11,500	Ice Cap almost completely gone from Yellowstone.
11–9,500	Alpine glaciers readvanced at Banff and Wind Rivers, simultaneous with a 1,500-year cold snap in Europe.
11,200	Hunters with Clovis spear points and spear throwers—the first human migration? Many large mammals died out—possibly the first broad human effect on NA ecology.
9,000	Pyramid Mtn eruption at Wells Gray.
7,000	"Hypsithermal interval" began: warmer than 20th century.
5,700	Mt. Mazama (OR) erupted, shot pale gray ash far and wide, leaving a conspicuous marker of that date in soils.
2,000	Warm interval over.
0	Latest basalt flow at Craters of the Moon, Idaho.
730 ce	Oldest living whitebark pine germinated in Idaho.
1500	Latest Kostal Cone eruptions at Wells Gray.
1600s	Invasive species: Plains tribes learned to use and trade horses, initiating (?) the decline of bison populations; first wave of European epidemics depopulated Native Americans; European honeybees reached the Plains.
1785	Fur trade began between NW Coast, China and Europe.
1792	A Hudson's Bay Co. trader reached Canadian Rockies.
1805	Lewis and Clark crossed the U.S. Rockies.
1820	Greatest post–Ice Age extent of glaciers ("Little Ice Age"). Fur trade active in most of our region.
1887±	Plains bison population reached its low, 541 animals.
1959	Hebgen Lake earthquake, our largest recorded (7.5).
1983	Borah Peak (Idaho) earthquake, magnitude 7.3.
today	Glaciers retreating. Human-caused extinctions accelerating.

This entire timeline fits within the "Ice Ages" tick on the geologic timeline.

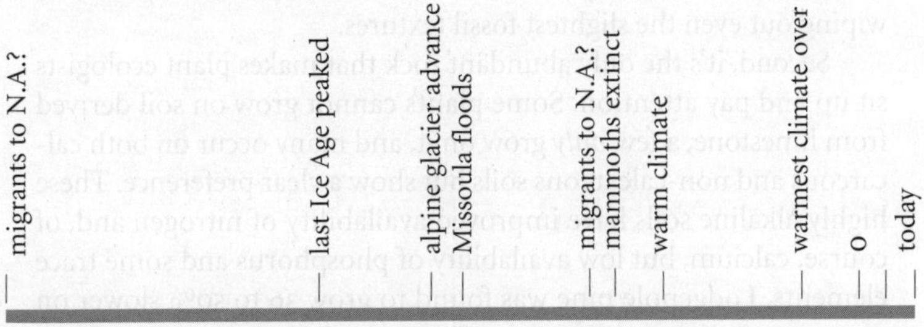

Timeline labels (left to right):
migrants to N.A.? | last Ice Age peaked | alpine glacier advance, Missoula floods | migrants to N.A.?, mammoths extinct | warm climate | warmest climate over | 0 | today

Classification of the earth's materials begins with the three ways in which a rock became the kind of rock it is today:

Igneous rocks solidified from lava, or molten rock.

Sedimentary rocks settled as fragmentary material (such as mud) and were then compacted and/or chemically cemented.

Metamorphic rocks recrystallized (but did not melt) from other rocks under intense heat and pressure.

Geology: sedimentary rocks (color pages 536, 538, 539)

Limestone and Dolomite

Limestone's abundance belies what an exceptional rock it is.

It's the most abundant rock that typically originates through the work of living organisms. (Coal is a distant second). Various kinds of plants, animals, and bacteria separate the mineral calcite ($CaCO_3$, a.k.a. lime) out from solution in sea water. Animals typically use it to make protective shells. You see a lot of those shells—trilobites, crinoid segments, weird tubes, etc.—in some Paleozoic limestones. In others, and in all Proterozoic (older) limestones, there are no macroscopic fossils. Their calcite was produced by those amazing creatures to whom we owe everything we are today: cyanobacteria. (It was they that freed oxygen, making animal life possible, and fixed nitrogen, allowing plants to evolve.) Some calcite is made by free-floating cyanobacteria and settles to the sea floor after they die; some is made *in situ* on the sea floor by cyanobacterial mats and stromatolites. As the lime mud turns into limestone, the microscopic needles that the cyanobacteria made—as well as the much larger forms that animals made—mostly break down, and the calcite recrystallizes, wiping out even the slightest fossil textures.

Second, it's the only abundant rock that makes plant ecologists sit up and pay attention. Some plants cannot grow on soil derived from limestone, a few *only* grow on it, and many occur on both calcareous and non-calcareous soils but show a clear preference. These highly alkaline soils have improved availability of nitrogen and, of course, calcium, but low availability of phosphorus and some trace elements. Lodgepole pine was found to grow 36 to 50% slower on calcareous than on acidic soils. Rocky Mountain alpine plants widely turn to mycorrhizal fungi as the only way to find usable phosphorus in calcareous soils. Even sedges commonly form mycorrhizae in this situation, unlike most others. Lime's effect is patchy: rain leaches lime downward, creating lime horizons six to twenty inches [15–50 cm] down depending on water flow patterns. Shallow-rooted lime-hating plants can find happiness where this horizon is relatively deep. On alpine tundra, limestone inflicts physical hardships more critical than the chemical ones: it breaks down into fine chips that are more subject to both drought and frost heaving than other soils.

Third, it's the easiest abundant rock to dissolve. It engenders an entire vocabulary of "karst" landforms produced by the dissolution of rock: long, labyrinthine caves, subterranean waterfalls, stalagmites and stalactites, sinkholes, clusters of springs, and even the tower-shaped hills of southeast Asia. The main stem of the Canadian Rockies is a karst region, with many caves and underground rivers. Castlegard Cave is the longest in Canada. The Maligne River drains out of Medicine Lake through a network of limestone caves that emerge as springs many miles downvalley. The icefields offer a laboratory for studying the ways that even ice can take advantage of lime's solubility.

Actually, lime is not very soluble in pure water, but water easily picks up enough carbon dioxide to make a weak carbonic acid solution which dissolves the alkaline stone.

By definition, limestone is a sedimentary rock with more than 50% calcite content. If the two chief minerals in a rock are calcite and dolomite—$CaMg(CO_3)_2$—but dolomite predominates, you have dolomite, the rock. (There was an attempt to rename the rock dolostone, reserving "dolomite" for the mineral, but "dolomite" is still widely used for both.) The test is a drop of hydrochloric acid, which effervesces in reaction with the alkaline calcite. On dolomite it effervesces only weakly. Many sedimentary geologists carry a squirt bottle of HCl; others, not wanting to be seen wearing shreddy shirts, avoid the acid test by calling both rocks just "carbonate rock."

Limestones get dolomitized by magnesium-rich brine percolating through them, replacing some of the calcium atoms with magnesium. One plausible scenario would be shallow Proterozoic seas where cyanobacteria thrived for centuries, creating a limestone sea floor; then some climate or drainage shift reduced the influx of fresh water; evaporation concentrated the salts while cyanobacteria kept on consuming the calcium, turning the sea to high-magnesium, low-calcium brine. Dolomitization deletes most fossils and yields a porous, "vuggy" rock. (Macroscopic holes are called "vugs.") Much of Alberta's natural gas is found in the vugs of lower Paleozoic dolomites.

Limestone formations commonly have a bad case of the stripes. Dark gray limestone bands alternate with brown shale bands, or with pinkish-buff dolomite bands. The stripes may originate from cyclic changes in sea level. Limestone formed as "carbonate platforms" in vast shallow seas—rapidly when the seas were shallow, then slowing and getting overwhelmed with mud (→shale) when they were a little deeper. What could have caused slow, regular sea level cycles? During the Carboniferous Epoch, a huge ice cap waxed and waned in Gondwanaland in long cycles which may have caused sea level cycles here, as well as cyclic coal formation almost worldwide. Carbon dioxide levels in the air may have been involved with climate cycles and/or limestone cycles, since CO_2 controls the rate at which calcite forms and dissolves. The challenge is to figure out a great cyclical mechanism among climate, carbon dioxide, sea level, possibly tectonic movements, and the flourishing of different forms of life.

Though one kind of very pure limestone is chalk, most limestone in the Rockies is hard, hard enough to be an overhang on a cliff. Calcite is white, chalk is white, but limestone strata in the Rockies look like dark gray bands because old limestone surfaces weather to gray. A typical mountain in Alberta's Front Ranges would consist of gray Paleozoic limestone cliffs above an eroded (perhaps vegetated) layer of younger shale. In Glacier, the massive lower cliffs of most mountains are dark gray Altyn carbonates. The Altyn Formation forms the base of the Lewis Thrust sheet, and is the oldest rock (at ~1.5 billion years) in the park. In central Montana, the very pale gray mid-Paleozoic Madison limestone provides an erosion-resistant backbone for several ranges. Southward, it crops out in Hoback Canyon and all along the east flank of the Wind River Range.

In Proterozoic limestones of Glacier/Waterton, look for patches of whorls about 6–20" [15–50 cm] across. Since these "stromatolites" are far older than other fossils (up to 3.5 billion years old) geologists long assumed they had nonbiological origins, and came up with many competing hypotheses. However, they turn out to be a kind of cyanobacterial colony that still lives today in a few small, saline, tropical bays. They were the dominant life form for billions of years (much longer than dinosaurs) but became uncommon after creatures evolved to eat them. They thrive today only in water too salty or too hot for those creatures.

Travertine

Rocks of calcium carbonate can also form without biological help. If the mineral precipitates to the the sea floor it still becomes limestone, but if it precipitates from the dripping water of a cave (as a stalactite, etc.) or the gushing water of a hot spring, it takes a denser, more colorful form called travertine. The drip in the cave becomes supersaturated with dissolved carbonate, precipitating some carbonate as the drip evaporates. In a hot spring, water becomes supersaturated when it reaches the outside world and cools, reducing the amount of minerals it can hold in solution. The amazing terraces of Yellowstone's Mammoth Hot Springs are all travertine. The water cools abruptly at the exact moment when it becomes a thin film going over the "dam" of the terrace, so new travertine forms right there and builds the dam higher. Algae sometimes get in the way of precipitating a dense travertine, yielding porous **tufa**. (But some texts use "tufa" and "travertine" interchangeably.) Similar but long-defunct springs produced travertine that's quarried near Gardiner, Montana, and sliced into facing stone with lacy-patterned holes.

Quartz and Chert

The most familiar kind of "rock crystal" is quartz—transparent (though sometimes tinted) with six generally unequal sides and a six-faceted point. It's the only stone in this chapter that forms single crystals; it's the only one that's a mineral rather than a rock. In geologists' terms, a rock is a mixture of minerals whose proportions to each other vary only within limits that define that kind of rock; the respective mineral crystals, whether visible or microscopic, are discrete. A mineral, on the other hand, is a single chemical compound or continuum of compounds with one characteristic crystal shape. Quartz is silicon dioxide (SiO_2, usually simply called silica) adulterated with too few impurities to break up its proper crystal form. It is harder than steel (ergo, too hard to scratch with a knife) lightweight and light-colored, and very abundant as a rock ingredient; it is a significant component of nearly every light- to medium-colored rock you see, except limestone. Its abundance at the earth's surface probably results from its light weight: it has risen among heavier materials while powerful forces stirred the earth around for some four billion years. (Meanwhile, the heavy metals nickel and iron accumulated toward the Earth's core. They are the most abundant elements in the Earth, but not at the surface.)

Large, free-sided quartz crystals are uncommon, but they do catch the eye. They form in cavities in rocks that spend a long time with groundwater rich in dissolved silica seeping through them. Silica precipitated out as "rock crystals" on the cavity lining, like sugar crystallizing on a string as "rock candy" (named after quartz.) Quartz veins in intrusive and metamorphic areas reflected as a gleam in a prospector's eye, since precious metals occur in or near them; silica and minerals are dissolved in the same deep hot groundwater.

Virtually pure quartz may also occur as the opaque rock **chert**, a cryptocrystalline or microcrystalline (i.e., not visibly crystalline) form. Chert resembles porcelain while crystalline quartz is transparent like glass, and that's no coincidence: ground-up silica rock is the main ingredient in both glass and porcelain. Either porcelain or hard chert (e.g., Arkansas novaculite) can be used to whet a fine edge on a knife. Like glass and obsidian, chert chips with an even, shallowly concave fracture; chert's dark form, flint, was second only to obsidian as a material for arrowheads and blades.

The deep ocean floor accumulates massive chert beds of silica that precipitates out from solution in sea water. These may or may not include crumbled shells. (While most seashells are made of calcite, the main mineral in limestone, there are also organisms— diatoms, radiolaria, and sponges—that make a sort of shell of silica.) Oceanic plate subduction tends to destroy massive chert beds rather than to toss them up onto continents, and sure enough few are found here. One thin, dark chert streak runs through the Alberta Front Ranges. More common are small nodules of chert formed within carbonate formations (color p 538).

Don't infer that silica dissolves easily in water, just because quartz and chert have histories as silica solutions. The silica in the percolating water dissolved under enormous pressure, deep in the earth. At surface pressures, the insolubility, hardness, and chemical stability of silica are what make quartz more durable than most rocks in a stream, ultimately yielding the high quartz content of beaches, sandstones, and quartzite. Pressurized superheated water in the Yellowstone caldera picks up silica as it flows through high-silica rhyolite, then precipitates it around geysers as a porcelain-like glaze called sinter, or geyserite. This too has a lime counterpart, travertine, which forms at hot springs that flow through carbonate strata, e.g., Yellowstone's own Mammoth, just outside the caldera. (Page 593).

Sandstones

Sandstone is a broad term for sedimentary rock made up of compacted sand-size (.06-2 mm) particles cemented together with water-soluble minerals like silica or calcite. The sand grains may almost all be quartz. It's amazing that beds or beaches of nearly pure quartz sand ever collect, since the waters that bring them are eroding all the diverse rocks of a watershed. The reason is that quartz is both hard and chemically stable, tending to break down to sand-size particles and then stop breaking down. In contrast, feldspars and other abundant minerals weather chemically, and end up as silt and clay mud. Ocean waves collect the sand into beaches, while washing the finer silt and mud particles out to sea. Rivers can sometimes do the same.

When sand-sized particles are in a shale-like matrix of finer particles, the rock can truly be called wacky. Actually it's spelled wacke. Wackes probably formed in deep ocean trenches. Avalanchelike bursts of mud-and-sand slurry course down the slopes of these trenches at intervals of several hundred years, dropping many inches or feet of sediment at a time. These "turbidity currents" are the only well-accepted mechanism for laying down unsorted sediments (i.e., a range of particle sizes in each bed). Though unsorted, "turbidite" beds are more or less "graded": each single bed (deposited by one turbidity avalanche) starts at its bottom with coarse sediments that settled quickly, and grades upward to fine sediments which took days or weeks to settle; those adjoin coarse sediments of the next bed.

Conglomerate

Conglomerate is sedimentary rock made up of at least 50% erosion-rounded stones over 2 mm in diameter. It typically forms when pebble beaches and river bars turn to stone. It has to include both smaller rock particles to fill in the spaces and soluble minerals for glue. Well-cemented conglomerates will break straight through pebbles and interstices alike—a fine sight. Weaker ones break through the glue ("matrix") only, leaving pebbles sticking out just like from a gravel bank. Some"metaconglomerates" were compressed during metamorphism, ovalizing the pebbles all in parallel directions. See examples in the Beaverhead and Madison Ranges—around the Sphinx.

Breccia

Breccia ("bretch-ia") consists of a fine-grained matrix full of unrounded rock pieces. This difference from conglomerate (with

---

erosion-rounded pieces) is puzzling, since only eroded rocks commonly form sediment beds. Breccia derives from breakage.

Sedimentary breccia is often a turbidite, sort of a coarse graywacke containing shaley shards ripped from deep-sea sediments by a turbidity current, and redeposited. Alternatively, ordinary landslides in shaley, slaty, or limestone terrain can get compacted into breccia.

Volcanic breccia can be the skin of a slow lava flow that shatters and then slips back into the flow. It can be the edge of a magma body that incorporates broken chunks of surrounding rock; the magma must have been cool enough to leave sharp unmelted edges on the chunks.

Tectonic breccia is a mix of coarse and fine rock fragments broken by shearing forces within a fault, and then compacted; sometimes you can visually match the broken edges of nearby fragments.

There is a lot of breccia out there, but much of it looks like an obscure mess. It takes rock saws and polishers to reveal the splendid breccia sections we see in books and as architectural facings.

Shale, Mudstone, Argillite

Throughout the fold-and-thrust belt, layers of soft, weak shale provided surfaces where the earth could break into thrust blocks and sheets (page 578). While playing this important role, shale also tended to disappear, crumbling or eroding away where exposed.

Shale was clayey river mud carried out to sea and piled up to such depths that through thousands or millions of years under the weight of subsequent layers it was compacted into more or less solid rock. Most sediments need water-soluble minerals to cement them into sedimentary rocks, but clay particles are so minute and flaky that they become shale through compaction alone, or with minor amounts of cement. You can break shale in your hands, or breathe on it and smell clay, or scrape it with your knife and spit on the scrapings to mix up some clay mud. Shale is generally gray, and breaks into flattish leaves along its bedding planes. **Mudstone** is similar, but doesn't break in thin leaves due to different mineral content. Where we find shales and mudstones, we may find less- and more-processed beds nearby—dense clays that lay on the ocean floor too briefly and shallowly to get compacted into rock, and others that got buried long and deeply, metamorphosing into slate or phyllite.

Proterozoic Belt mudstones break on their original bedding planes, which often show mudcracks or perfect ripples, as if small waves had rippled a shallow pond floor just last week. Many of these patterns are enigmatic. "Ladderback" criss-crossed ripples, for example, may have been imposed in one direction by occasional storms strong enough to stir fairly deep water, then stabilized by algae, then imposed in the second direction by a tsunami from a major earthquake. Squiggly-crackle-textured pavements may owe their striking texture to the shock of earthquakes themselves. Mudcracked surfaces may be just what they look like—billion-year-old mudflats—but some dried out due to pressure while they were deeply submerged.

The Proterozoic was the eon of few or no animals. Younger mudstones don't often show good ripple marks, even if they formed in shallow seas, because worms, mollusks, and other animals burrowed through those muds before they fossilized, messing up any ripple marks. All kinds of fine sedimentary details, like the thin alternating layers in the siltstone on page 539, are common in Belt rocks but rare, thanks to burrowers, in younger ones.

Slightly metamorphosed shale may be called **argillite**. Grinnell Formation rocks are the most colorful in Glacier/Waterton (e.g., Red Rock Canyon) thanks to their iron-rich argillite, either green or red

The Burgess Shale

A lost kingdom buried in ancient mud lies beneath a scenic high slope in Yoho National Park. The Burgess Shale offers a rare large set of finely preserved fossils of soft shapes from the Cambrian Explosion, an unequalled rapid diversification of multicelled marine animals, soon after an extinction event. Burgess fauna—many distantly related to crabs—were just starting to have exoskeletons, but not very hard ones, so most of their kind disintegrated and left no fossil. Geologists debate what could have made this continental shelf mudflow so gentle to soft bodies. A search of Yoho turned up several smaller, and not identical, sets of similar fossils. Some Burgess shells are so well preserved that they show diffraction gratings which may have glimmered in the water, as a visual cue for predators to associate with defensive spines. Both the first eyes and the first predators may be key factors in the Cambrian Explosion.

Stephen Jay Gould drew from the Burgess fauna a lesson that evolution is random on a grand scale. This one mudbed shows a wider disparity of body plans than exists today. Almost all of the body plans disappeared soon after, yet Gould saw no evidence that we can call the few forms that went on to engender today's animals "stronger" or "better" body plans. If we could rerun the evolutionary program two or three times, starting from Burgess time, he thought we would come up with two or three entirely different worlds of animals.

depending on whether there was much oxygen around to rust the iron during deposition. That formation is 1.5 billion years old. Vast red shales were again laid down—probably on arid coastal plains at the downwind edge of Pangea—between 270 and 210 million years ago in Montana and Wyoming. Apparently the oxygen-rich epochs that made giant insects (page 511) also made redbeds.

Geology: igneous rocks

Igneous rocks are divided into two textural classes—fine-grained and coarse-grained—and graded by chemical (or mineral) composition. High-silica rocks tend to be "light," low-silica rocks "dark." Each "darkness" grade on the compositional scale can occur with either fine or coarse texture. The two textures tend to correlate with two origins; for our purposes we will assume they always correlate:

volcanic, from magma that erupted upon the continental surface or the ocean floor, congealing quickly to produce fine crystals; or

intrusive, from magma that solidified into rock somewhere beneath the surface, and cooled slowly, producing coarse texture.

Igneous rocks in our Rockies fall into eight groups:

Archean basement granites in the Tetons, Wind Rivers, Beartooths, and other ranges of extreme southern Montana.

Proterozoic and Paleozoic volcanic rocks in scattered remnants (e.g., Purcell lavas at Glacier). Northern Montana and the Canadian Rockies have seen hardly any igneous activity since the Paleozoic.

Exotic basalts that arrived as part of terranes in the Columbia Mtns.

Laramide intrusions and volcanism 89 to 55 million years ago in the Idaho Batholiths and Montana's Elkhorn Mtns.

Extension-related volcanism and intrusions 53 to 46 million years ago—notably the Absarokas and central Idaho. Erosion removed the individual volcanoes and carved today's peaks out of their pedestals.

Columbia River flood basalts of 16.6 to 7 million years ago, in the Wallowas and westernmost Idaho. These may be the oldest of the...

Hotspot volcanics of the last 17 million years, reaching our area at Yellowstone and alongside the Snake River Plain.

Wells Gray volcanism of the past 3.5 million years. The scale is modest, the cause obscure; it may relate to the terrane's northward slip.

Diorite and Granite

Granite has high name recognition, partly for its role as the heavy in rock-climbing thrillers, partly for its countless appearances in cemeteries and kitchen counters. From the polished surfaces we know the texture of granitic intrusive rocks—interlocked coarse crystals of varicolored minerals. Quartz is the white to buff, translucent component; feldspars are salmon to pale gray; glittering black flakes are biotite, or "black mica"; hornblende and pyroxene are duller blacks.

The word *gran*itic derives from these *gran*ular crystals, and the word intrusive describes their typical origin. While some magma (molten rock) rises and *extrudes* onto the earth's surface through a volcano, other magma merely *intrudes* among subsurface rocks and solidifies there, at depth. This may be an entire magmatic pulse that fails to ever reach the surface, or it may be a remnant left behind in the "roots" or "plumbing" of a volcano. In either case, if it cools in a large mass, it changes from liquid to solid state very slowly, allowing its atoms plenty of time to precipitate out in an organized manner, forming larger and larger mineral crystals. Large (coarse) crystal size characterizes the granitic class of igneous rocks.

Large intrusions are "plutons." The very largest (over 100 km², or 38 square miles, at the surface) are "batholiths" (deep rocks). Places like central Idaho and the Sierra Nevada were long thought of as single humongous batholiths, but on close examination they turn out to be dozens of separate plutons. In fact, not much of what was once common knowledge about batholiths goes unquestioned any more. Most textbooks have illustrated them as bottomless capital-dome-shaped cross-sections. These were said to take millions of years to rise and to crystallize, but no one could figure out how they made so much room for themselves, even over millions of years. A new (still hotly contested) picture of them resembles instead a big cluster of honey mushrooms, each individual intrusion vanilla-wafer-shaped and fed by a slender dike, over a short time frame, like several centuries. These flat layers are said to eventually add up to "batholiths."

Rock climbers and kitchen designers speak of any sort of coarse-grained igneous rock as granite, but geologists do not. Hedging with the word "granitic" is vague but correct. ("Granitoid" embraces true granite and all intrusive rocks with at least a 1:5 quartz/feldspar ratio.) **Diorite** is a common salt-and-pepper speckled rock with less than 20% quartz. Geologists say diorite is darker than granite, with granodiorite (the most abundant granitic rock in Idaho) in between, but by "darker," they really mean "containing less quartz." A diorite can look paler than a granite if it has a higher percentage of quartz and feldspar together (both being pale) while the granite has more quartz but a lot less feldspar, and more of the blackish minerals instead. Granite is pinkish or yellowish white with darker speckles.

Diorite is the coarse-grained equivalent of fine-grained andesite: lava of the right chemical proportions could crystallize coarsely as diorite, or finely as andesite. So diorite is often found in the roots of andesitic volcanoes. A diorite pluton related to Challis/Absaroka volcanism forms the core of the Crazy Mountains. Granite is equivalent to rhyolite; these magmas are so viscous that 90% of them freeze in their own plumbing to become plutons but not volcanoes.

Let's see if we can cram just two more "-ites" into your brain. **Pegmatite:** granitic rocks with extra large crystals (1 cm plus) of any mineral content; most often found as pale dikes, or swirls in migmatite (p 608); beloved of designers (though some take it for granite).

Syenite: pinkish all-pale granitoid rock, made up almost purely of feldspars; rare; found in the northern Crazies, Skalkaho Peak in the Sapphires, around Arrow Lake, and near the Ice River in Yoho; it's a "foiditoid" (I'm not making this up!) like its cousin, nepheline syenite.

Countless peaks attest to granite's durability, yet huge heaps of coarse sharp sand show it can "rot" and crumble. Plutons are massive, without any kind of internal layering, yet heat expansion and contraction cause them to split in patterns: they may "exfoliate" in sheets parallel to the surface. In the Wind Rivers—which get my vote for finest granite mountain range on the continent—the trail disappears on an enormous exfoliation sheet below Deep Lake.

Peridotite

Peridotite ("per-**id**-o-tight") rocks are apparently pieces brought up from the mantle. They are largely restricted to environs of deep faulting within mountain ranges, because they're too heavy to reach the surface without exceptionally deep and fast rock movement. The shear zone in western Idaho—where the Wallowa terrane slid north along the old continental edge before suturing—is such an environment. Look for patches of blackish green peridotite, flecked with black crystals, in the roadcut just north of the bridge two miles [3.2 km] north of Riggins.

Peridotite is defined by a 40%+ proportion of the yellow-green mineral olivine, thought to be the predominant mineral in the mantle—and thus in the earth as a whole. It has no fine-grained (volcanic) equivalent because volcanoes aren't hot enough to melt it. Solid peridotite rocks carried in molten lava occasionally shoot out of volcanoes. Find peridotite inclusions in the Kostal Flow at Wells Gray, or chunks of it in mine dumps in the Stillwater Complex, an oddly segregated very old pluton on the north edge of the Beartooths. Gem-quality large crystals of olivine are known as peridot.

Peridotite and its relatives weather into reddish "serpentine" soils very difficult for most plants to grow in.

Gabbro and Diabase

Magma of the same mineral composition as basalt that crystallizes slowly underground without reaching the surface and erupting becomes gabbro, a dark rock with a coarse texture like granite.

While basalt is the most abundant volcanic rock, gabbro is a rather rare intrusive rock. Basalt is very fluid, and doesn't tend to plug up plumbing. So it's rare for basaltic magma to form large plutons, but common for it to crack rock formations in forcing its way up, filling the crack and then solidifying in it. If the magma took advantage of a weak plane between sedimentary beds, it's a "sill." If it cut across bedding planes (or if there are no bedding planes) it's a "dike". Both are lines or stripes across a rocky landscape (color page 540):

The Purcell Sill runs horizontally between two beds of Siyeh limestone through much of Glacier National Park. The magma's heat vaporized the organic impurities that make Siyeh limestone gray, leaving dramatic white outlines above and below the sill. The magma cooled fast enough to make a fine-grained black rock which you can call either basalt or **diabase**, a name reserved for basalt when it's in a sill or dike so that we know it's intrusive rather than volcanic. Dikes branch off from the Sill in several places. For that matter, thick sills and dikes are widespread throughout the Belt (Purcell) Formation.

The Black Dike—the stripe up the middle of Mt. Moran's face—is the most photogenic of several 1.2 billion-year-old dikes in the Tetons. Dikes perforate the ancient Wyoming craton in the Winds and Beartooths as well—clues of a likely rift zone. Basalt commonly explores many cracks on its way to erupting as a new spreading center.

The Chief Joseph Dike Swarm is a batch of some 1800 dikes that supplied much of the lava of the Columbia Flood Basalts. About 40% of them are in the Wallowas. Look for dark stripes through pale granite—for example, on Craig Mtn., as you look southwest from the south end of Wallowa Lake. If you get to see one up close, note how its heat altered the granite, partially melting it and mixing with it a bit. Unmelted crystals drift a few inches into the basalt.

Many of these dikes are several yards wide, and miles long. But the word "dike" applies to crack fillings even two inches wide and swirly, so long as they are an igneous-type mixture of minerals, which shows that they solidified from magma. Many white crack fillings, on the other hand, are veins, which form by precipitating from solution in a water-based fluid that flows through a crack. Most white veins are quartz. Gold and silver commonly occur in veins within metamorphosed intrusions.

Geology: volcanic igneous rocks (color pages 536, 538)

Andesite

Andesite is named after the world's highest volcanoes, the Andes. It is better than other lavas at building up tall, layered stratovolcanoes. Picture the andesitic volcanoes that erupted in Idaho and Montana 80 to 40 million years ago as magnificent, Andean-scale mountains.

Andesite lavas make rough gray, greenish, or sometimes reddish brown rocks. Often they are speckled with crystals up to ¾" [2 cm] across, scattered throughout a fine matrix otherwise lacking crystals of visible size. These were already crystallized in the molten magma when it erupted. With close examination and a little practice, you can easily tell them from the shards of noncrystalline whole rock jumbled up in tuff. It can be hard, though, to tell andesite from lavas like basalt and dacite.* Color descriptions are unavoidably vague; andesite is "medium-dark," between dark basalt and light dacite and rhyolite, but actual tints overlap: green and reddish hues are not diagnostic.

---

*The technical definitions are ranges on a graph of bulk chemistry, so positive identifications often require specimens to be pulverized and analyzed by a lab. Light color correlates with silica (SiO_2) content—around 50% in basalt, 60% in andesite, 70%+ in rhyolite. Most SiO_2 in magma forms silicate (SiO_4) tetrahedrons that bind to other elements as feldspar and other minerals; only the SiO_2 excess over about 55% stays more or less pure, as quartz crystals. Thus andesite has just a little quartz, and basalt has none.

Basalt

The most abundant rock in the Earth's crust as a whole, basalt is dark lava. Typically black, it ranges down to light gray and is often altered to greenish or reddish. Its surface is drab and massive, usually without conspicuous crystals or other features except, frequently, bubbles, or "vesicles." These show that the lava rose from the depths full of dissolved gases. Just as uncapping a bottle of soda releases bubbles of carbon dioxide which, under pressure, had been dissolved invisibly in the liquid, so lavas often foam up as they near the surface. Vesicles abound near the original top surface of a lava flow. In old basalts they have often turned into solid polka-dots, having filled with water-soluble minerals such as calcite. Polygonal (6-, 5-, or 4-sided) basalt columns, often neatly vertical at one level and splayed-out at another, result from shrinkage during cooling of large flows.

Basalt lava erupts in several styles. One of them, the basalt flood, isn't a mountain; floods are so liquid that they flow out flat. The Columbia River Basalt is a vast series of floods that covered much of eastern Oregon and Washington between 17 and 12 million years ago. See it on Hell's Canyon walls, or raised high in the western part of the Wallowas. Much younger, less voluminous Snake River Basalts (color page 540) cover the Snake River Plain in Idaho, at the edge of our range. The youngest flow at the Craters of the Moon is about 2,000 years old.

Sea-floor basalt is far and away the most voluminous lava in the Earth's crust. When basalt erupts underwater it chills and solidifies quickly, in small batches that we see as glassy-rinded, blob-shaped "pillow" basalt forms, about one to four feet across [30-120 cm]. A blob squeezes out of the sea floor, freezes; then another blob squeezes out next to it; and so on. You can see pillow and other oozy flow shapes in Glacier Park's Purcell Lava formation. It crops out at Boulder Pass and Granite Park (a misnomer referring to its basalt). Having been around the block a few times in its 1.4 billion years, Purcell Lava has metamorphosed to sea-green in places. You can call that greenstone. (See color page 538)

In Wells Gray Provincial Park, entire small volcanoes ("tuyas") erupted within the Ice Sheet during the last Ice Age, chilling so fast that they became glassy-rinded blob-shaped basalt mountainlets.

Basalt flows are common in the large Challis, Absaroka, and lesser volcanic fields of similar age in east-central Idaho and southern Montana, though these are primarily andesite.

Rhyolite, Tuff, Obsidian

Rhyolite lavas typically become pale pinkish tan rocks, usually easy to tell from other lavas but sometimes confused with tuff, which is often made of rhyolite magma that exploded rather than flowing as lava. Though named for the Greek word for flow, rhyolite is actually among the least fluid lavas. Lava viscosity increases dramatically with silica content, and flowing rhyolite may reach a thousand times the viscosity of basalt, squeezing out of the ground more like dried-up peanut butter. It so resists flowing that it may plug up a vent forever, marking the final phase of activity for some volcanoes.

Rhyolite magma is often rich in gases and water vapor that it can contain only as long as it remains under pressure. On nearing the surface the magma literally explodes, as the Yellowstone volcano did three times in the last two billion years, each time blasting mountains of pumice, ash, rocks, and gases into the air with hundreds of times the explosive force St. Helens released in 1980. Ashfall from Yellowstone's second biggest eruption is seen in soil profiles from Los Angeles to Galveston. As the Yellowstone Hotspot marched across southern Idaho over the last 15 million years, it demolished the mountains that had crossed the area, and left an immense trough, the Snake River Plain. Basalt flows that cover most of the Plain are just a thin skin over piles of rhyolite tuff thousands of feet thick.

Lava blasted into fine smithereens is called ash. Amalgamated into solid rock, it becomes **tuff**. If ash settles back to earth at modest temperatures, decades pass before enough groundwater full of dissolved silica percolates through to cement it into an **ashfall tuff**. If, on the other hand, ash is carried by hot whirling volcanic gas—a "glowing avalanche" or *nuee ardente*—its own heat quickly cements it into a **welded tuff**. Ashfall tuff is often crumbly, and vulnerable to erosion; it resembles sandstone. Welded tuff resembles lava. Tuff and lava are easiest to tell apart if there are inclusions; in lava these are crystals, often of a contrasting color. In tuff they're irregular fragments about the same color as the rest of the tuff stuff.

A few rhyolite lavas have hardly any gas or water. These erupt quietly as flows of **obsidian**, or volcanic glass. Like other glass it makes concentric arc patterns where it breaks. It was so prized for chipping into sharp arrowheads and other tools that Yellowstone obsidian was traded all the way to the East Coast, even in pre-horse times. Use of it near Yellowstone began more than 10,200 years ago.

Metamorphic provinces are areas of rock altered by intense heat and pressure while deeply buried. The metamorphic rocks are described below in order of their "metamorphic grade," from less heat and less pressure to more. The Wind Rivers, Beartooths, Tetons, and Madison and nearby Ranges are granite/gneiss outcrops of the ancient Wyoming Craton. Any rock that makes it to the ripe old age of two or three billion is likely to suffer some high-grade metamorphism during that time, and these are no exception. High-grade metamorphism also runs through the tectonic core of our range—the Columbia Mtns., parts of the Bitterroots and the Idaho Pioneers.

Milder metamorphism is rife in our Proterozoic and early Paleozoic sediments, turning limestone to **marble**, shale to argillite or slate, sandstone to quartzite, and occasionally reaching schist grade.

Slate and Phyllite

Slate looks like what it is: metamorphosed shale. Even the names look alike. They share platy textures that break into flat pieces, and dark gray colors (varying to reds and greens in slates and argillites). But the flat cleavage of slate was never the flat bedding plane of its parent rock, the shale. Bedding planes started out horizontal, as layers of sediment settling out from water. Slate cleavage planes, in contrast, are perpendicular to the direction of pressure that metamorphosed the rock. There may have been two or more such directions at different times, yielding slate that fractures into slender "pencils." Some slates metamorphosed from mudstone, and never had distinct bedding planes; in others the bedding has faded. Commonly, though, the parent shale's bedding planes are visible as streaks or bands in slate, either happening to align with the new cleavage planes or crossing them, but no longer causing a plane of weakness.

Slate gets a satiny luster from microscopic crystals of mica and other minerals. Metamorphism aligned these all parallel, creating the cleavage plane and the shine. Higher-pressure metamorphism of the same rock produces larger crystals (barely visible without a lens), a stronger, glittery but often wavy gloss, and a weaker tendency to split. This rock is **phyllite**, properly, though it is sold as roofing "slate." Slate is shatter-prone and weak in landforms, and phyllite only slightly less so. (Unless it gets cooked; see Hornfels, page 000.)

Quartzite

The mineral quartz resists not only physical and chemical break-down, but also metamorphism: a 99%-quartz sandstone will come out of metamorphism denser and harder than before, but still 99% quartz. The crystals are rearranged and compacted, binding together so tightly that you can no longer scrape sand off of the surface with a knife, and you can scarcely see sand with the naked eye, but under any magnification at all a sugary texture catches the light.

Gog Formation quartzite, 550 million years old, is the hardest abundant rock in the Canadian Rockies. Hardest, not strongest—prone to splitting, and slippery when wet, it's deceptively dangerous. Pale on the inside, it more often looks blackish *en masse* because it hosts lots of rock tripe and crust lichens—as on Mt. Edith Cavell's entire face. But while lichens like quartzite substrates, plants hate them.

Schist

Metamorphic layering changes with increasing heat and pressure; the parallel layers may get crimped, crumpled or curved, while the rock's strength increases. At the same time, the flaky crystals (mainly mica) first grow larger as "slaty cleavage" converts to "schistose foliation," and then are replaced altogether by coarser crystals that may show "gneissose banding." Though "schist" derives from the Greek for "split" (as in schizophrenia) schists aren't nearly as easy to split as slates. Schistose texture is often dulled and obscured by weathering or rust, but in unweathered specimens the parallel mica flakes glimmer in the sun. Black mica gives many schists a charcoal gray hue overall, often streaked with white quartz layers. Some schists have scattered reddish, smeared garnet crystals ¼" [6 mm] or larger, often with foliation circling around them in almond shapes.

Metamorphism makes new minerals by recombining atoms into new molecules. Migration of atoms between molecules is extremely slow unless there is water flowing between the rock particles—but there usually is. Geologists call it "fluid"rather than water, since it carries so many dissolved minerals that it's a strong hot brine. And it's often so hot that it's a brine vapor. Each mineral product requires not only the right "grade" of heat and pressure but also the right elements. Mica forms in the middle of the grade range for schists, garnet near the high-grade end. They both need aluminum, and typically get it from the clay minerals that comprise shale.

Low-grade metamorphism (greenschist grade, with characteristic green minerals) turns basalt to **greenstone** (color p 538). Very high-pressure, rather low-temperature metamorphism yields **blueschist**. Terranes colliding under modern-day Revelstoke produced both.

In blueschist terrain (much of the Selkirks) you may find glittery pure-black **amphibolite** rocks (color p 537) with aligned fine crystals almost purely of one mineral in the "amphibole" group. Very similar-looking rocks entirely made of pyroxene-group minerals are **pyroxenites**. They usually have igneous origins; for example, they may occur with peridotite (page 600) as mantle rocks brought up from great depths during intense mountain-building.

Gneiss

Gneiss ("nice") excels as mountain material: not only is it hard, but it has few microfractures to admit water and invite frost splitting. Most gneiss in our range is part of the ancient basement, but the Columbia Mtns. have some exposures of youngish gneiss. It falls in between schist and granitic rocks in appearance, in grade, and often in location. Some gneiss started out as shale or sandstone and was metamorphosed by heat and pressure past the phyllite and schist stages, nearly to the point of melting. Other gneiss was granitic before metamorphism. Gneisses of sedimentary and igneous parentage look similar in the field. Coarse gneiss may overlap fine-grained granitics in crystal size, but the grains are at least slightly flattened and aligned parallel in gneiss, never in granite. The plane of flattening may also show lighter and darker bands, often contorted. Gneiss fragments may break along planes of glittery mica flakes—planes that appear to be little bands of schist. For the rock to be gneiss rather than schist (which also has minerals segregated in bands) flaky minerals must be outweighed by fatter grains overall. If heat and pressure go beyond gneiss grade, the rock begins to melt in places, producing gneiss/magma mixtures called migmatites (next page) or in some locales just subtle shifts between aligned and non-aligned crystals.

Gneiss and granite make up the bulk of continental crust, the ancient "basement." To illustrate the scale with a metaphor borrowed from Alt and Hyndman, if the earth were a house, the basement would the clapboard siding, and the world's sedimentary rocks would be the paint. The basement is exposed in the Wind Rivers, Beartooths, and Tetons.

Hornfels

If you ever notice that you have just left an area of granitic rocks, you may be in the vicinity of hornfels. It's a "contact metamorphic" rock, baked by close contact with hot intrusive magma. That gives it a high metamorphic grade in terms of heat, but low in terms of pressure. It was also altered by the addition of volatile chemicals suffusing out from the magma. Where hornfels occurs in shale, it may grade into spotted slate and then shale as you walk a few yards farther from the granite. Hornfels is a fine-grained, often dark gray to black crystalline rock resembling basalt; the easiest way to tell it from basalt is by its location near granitics. The word means "horn rock" in German; I'm not sure whether the reference is directly to animal horns or to "horn"-shaped Alps, but in either case the idea is that this is one tough rock. In the heart of the Crazy Mountains, magma intruded very soft, weak mudstones, and baked them granite-hard.

Migmatite

View magnificent migmatites (from the Greek for "mix") on cirque walls above Kane Lake, Idaho, or in most parts of the Wind Rivers, Beartooths, and the Columbia Mountains, especially west of Glacier National Park, BC. Migmatites make our very most luscious rock slabs, and certainly our best aid for visualizing continental tectonics. It's one thing to say that when terranes "scrunch" together, the rock deep down in the thickening crust can flow, like a glacier only much slower. It's another to look at a massive chunk of too, too, solid rock that obviously flowed like swirly cake batter full of nuts, marshmallows, and fudge—yet largely without melting.

This—this migmatite—is what was going on deep in the heart of an orogeny. Even right before our eyes it retains its mystery; between granitic swirls are darker, older gneiss and schist. Edges between the two are sharp, so we know the mass as a whole didn't melt. Nearby magma bodies injected dikes, or the dikes filled with magma that oozed out of the solid rock like melting fat oozing from a steak in a pan; crumples were superimposed on earlier folds; crosscutting cracks filled up with silica, making quartz veins—

At least that's how I think it happened.

> *All these have never yet been seen—*
> *But Scientists, who ought to know,*
> *Assure us that they must be so…*
>
> —*Hilaire Belloc*

Appendixes

Scientific Latin

For centuries, we writers of field guides have preached that you readers should learn the Latin names because they are used consistently—from one region, or nation, or book, or decade, to another—unlike common names.

Not so. That argument has come unglued.

For example, most writers agree on the common names red elderberry and blue elderberry, but we find three different scientific names for the blue and five for the red, and that's just in recent, respected floras. Many biologists acknowledge that common names will be the more stable names in the foreseeable future, and call for committees to arbitrate "official" common names.

Nomenclature is in a state of ferment. One reason is decentralization: regional botanists rebel against the taxonomic tradition in which judgments were made by a few senior taxonomists examining animal skeletons or pressed, dried herbarium specimens. They point out that the real thing—the live organism in its native habitat—can look quite different.

Another is a conflict between two of taxonomy's roles: a stable, internationally agreed-upon set of names, versus a "family tree" of evolutionary descent. High-tech molecular biology offers a level of accuracy in drawing the family tree that Linnaeus and Darwin never dreamed of. Taxonomists have leapt to the task of overhauling old hierarchies, but with limited funding and personnel, this very noncommercial field will make the current overhaul take decades, if not forever. Many recent name changes result from new takes on family tree relations; others are skirmishes in the age-old war between "splitters and lumpers," who argue over the proper size of genera and families.

Taxonomists are aware of their "customers'" discomfort. Some, like

Robert Dorn, defend instability: "This is a necessary but temporary phenomenon that is needed to correct our unnatural classifications." That's optimistic.

Some others would change the entire name book all at once in an attempt (the Phylocode) to reconcile stability with the family tree. For example, a "uninomial" name, as opposed to the "binomial" of genus and species, would name just the species. It wouldn't need to change to reflect any family-tree rearrangements at the genus level or higher. That might eliminate many of the name changes we see currently. Higher levels would fall into disuse among these taxonomists; many already publish their findings as family-tree diagrams ("cladograms") without trying to force those branchings onto the artificial and arbitrary hierarchy of kingdom, phylum, class, order, etc.

A countermovement wants a divorce from the family tree. If you want to know about genetic lineage, they say, study a cladogram; if you want to compare organisms, the practical, logical system is the frankly artificial hierarchy based on whole organisms rather than molecules. A crocodile can truly be more like a lizard than like a bird, even if its genes show a closer relationship to birds. Seeking a perfect "natural" system through molecular analysis, they say, will never bring stability—and is already a musty old conventional wisdom.

In the meantime, the path of least resistance is to be conformist, to insist that new ideas be debated among specialists until more or less of a consensus is reached, and only then look for adoption by non-taxonomists.

Conformist caution, to varying degrees, guides many western floras published since 1980: those of Alberta, British Columbia, Montana, Glacier National Park, the *Intermountain*, the *Alpine: Middle Rockies*, and California. And it guides the two works-in-progress that I turn to first on nomenclatural issues: *Flora of North America North of Mexico*, and the Oregon Flora Project. These are far from completion, but I got advice directly from OFP leaders, and from some FNA authors, regarding treatments currently in progress.

The U.S. government proffers a basis for unanimity in the form of its PLANTS database. Unfortunately, it tends to change too hastily and carelessly for the sensibilities of botanists involved in the regional floras listed above.

And then there's Colorado. Dozens, if not hundreds of plant names used in *Colorado Flora* and *Plants of Rocky Mtn. National Park* are little known on this continent, outside of Colorado. That's because Dr. William A. Weber, after five editions of *RM Flora*, threw off the blinders of conformist lumping to become an unrepentant splitter: "It has taken forty years for me to gain enough experience with the flora of the world to see that lumping is not a virtue." Neither is caution, apparently. An example: rather than keeping several species in *Senecio* where most books still have them but where he is sure they won't remain forever, he commits them in his *Flora* to the Asiatic genus *Ligularia*, while admitting that where they belong is "still a question." I lack the competence to argue with Dr. Weber's experience or with his points of view on the size of genera; I can only sympathize with his readers, most of whom, I suspect, care less about fine degrees of relationship than about having names they can use in common with the larger community of plant name users on this continent.

My earlier *Cascade-Olympic Natural History* (farther from Dr. Weber's region) placed alternate scientific synonyms in footnotes indicating the nature of the disagreement. *Rocky Mountain Natural History* doesn't have that luxury; the plethora of synonyms would clutter up half the pages with two or three footnotes apiece. Instead, synonyms found in recent works follow an = sign, coming right before the species description. (You should read the = sign as "other names include," not "is exactly the same as." In many cases the issue is whether to include one species in the other, as a variety, or raise it to full species rank.) Databases or books using the names are abbreviated as follows:

FNA: *Flora of North America North of Mexico*. (Not completed.)

OFP: the Oregon Flora Project. (Not completed.)

WY: Robert Dorn's 3rd Edition of *Vascular Flora of Wyoming*.

BC: Douglas, Meidinger, and Pojar's *Illustrated Flora of BC*.

INT: Holmgren et al, *Intermountain Flora*. (Not completed.)

CO: Weber's *Colorado Flora* and Beidleman's *Plants of Rocky Mtn. NP*.

USDA: the PLANTS database of the Dept. of Agriculture. (The Lone Pine guides generally follow earlier editions of PLANTS.)

AB: Packer's 2nd Edition of Moss's *Flora of Alberta*.

You'll find analogous battle lines in recent butterfly guides. Jeffrey Glassberg resists most recent splits, while the others endorse many of them.

I still like Latin names, regardless of whether they're more stable than common names. At least they're more international. Scientists generally have to use them, because the code regulating them anchors them to particular specimens — something common names can never offer.

I also like real common names — the ones that are a rich folklore. I hate to see common names coined purely for the sake of avoiding italics. (Come on, Latin names aren't *that* hard: five-year-olds eat *Velociraptor* for breakfast.) If a name has to be coined, how can you call it "common"?

Many commonly used names apply at the genus level, so I leave them there and stick to Latin for the species. This is especially true among lichens, where we're lucky when we have any traditional name at all to turn to. I believe any English name that's been in use for centuries, if one exists, is the common name, even if transferred from Eastern or European members of the same genus — lungwort, corkir, rock tripe, British soldiers, Iceland-moss, etc. I don't mind calling one lichen a moss any more than I mind calling another one a soldier or a tripe. A lot of scientists bridle at the misleading common names within their own discipline, but don't think twice about using flagrant misnomers, like red cedar and western hemlock, in someone else's. When I have to pick among lichen neologisms I try to balance what makes subjective sense with what has a toehold in regional speech or in other guide books.

Suggested pronunciations of genus and species names are in this book only to keep the names from being too intimidating to use at all. If you want to pronounce them some other way, feel free. Biologists themselves are far from uniform in their pronunciations. There is a schism between American and Continental styles. Dr. Weber argues that Americans should adopt the Continental style so that taxonomic Latin can be more of an international language.

Unfortunately, the two styles are different enough that Americans who adopt Continental pronunciation will find themselves frequently misunderstood during the 99% of their discussions that are with other Americans.

In brief, in Continental style the five vowels are always "ah, eh (or ay), ee, oh, oo," the *ae* diphthong is "eye," *c* is always "k," and *t* has a crisp sound even in *-atius* (ah-tee-oos). American style thoroughly Americanizes vowel sounds, both long and short, but sticks to Greek or Latin rules on most consonants and syllable stressing. An initial consonant *x* is phonetically a "z," final *es* is "eez," *ch* is "k," *j* is "y," and *th* is always soft as in "thin," never hard as in "then."

Syllable stressing causes difficulty and variation within the American style. The Latin rule says the second-to-last syllable is stressed if its vowel is long, is a diphthong (vowel pair), or is followed by two consonants before the next vowel; otherwise the third-to-last syllable gets the stress; *-ophila* is **ah**-fill-a, but *-ophylla* is o-**fill**-a. When uncertain of the length of the vowel, I refer to *Webster's Third New International Dictionary*, *Gray's Manual of Botany*, or Jepson's 1925 *Manual of the Flowering Plants of California*.

I depart from the rule for a few names that have entered the English language. For example, we stress the third-to-last syllables in *Anemone* and *Penstemon*, though ancient Romans stressed the second-to-last.

In the many cases of proper names with Latin endings tacked on, I try, up to a point, to respect the way the person whose name it was would have pronounced it. For example, *jeffreyi* obviously starts with a "j" sound rather than a "y" sound as in Latin. Similarly, the *ch* in *Marchantia* is like English *sh*, not *k*, since Marchant was French. But for species that end in double *-ii*, few scientists go so far as to violate Latin rules with, for example, "**Doug**las-eee" rather than "Da-**glass**-ee-eye." (Weber does argue for "**Doug**las-eee," on both Continental-style and honoring-Douglas grounds.) Parochial though it may be, we Anglicize when the honored person's language is too tricky for Anglo tongues. For example, *Castilleja*, named after a Spanish botanist, is "cas-ti-**lay**-a" here, while in Spain it would be "cah-stee-**yeh**-ha."

For the *-oides* ending I say "-**oy**-deez," which I hear more often from scientists today than the "oh-**eye**-deez" I once learned from Dr. Hitchcock.

I devised no airtight phonetic system; my attempt was simply to break each name into units that, as English, are hard to mispronounce.

If I omit the pronunciation and translation of a genus or species, it's either the same name as the preceding entry, or obviously similar to its English translation (e.g., *americanus, densa*). A family name with no English equivalent given is either the same as in the preceding entry, or visibly similar in English (e.g., Orchidaceae), or so obscure that the only way to come up with an English equivalent would be to anglicize the Latin name.

For pronouncing names of families and orders, a few rules will suffice. Plant families end in *-aceae* with the "a" stressed: Pinaceae is "pie-**nay**-see." (I'm streamlining again. Dr. Hitchcock said "pie-**nay**-seh-ee.") Bird orders end in *-formes*, "**for**-meez." Insect orders end in *-ptera*, with the *p* pronounced and stressed, as in "**Dip**-ter-a." Animal families end in *-idae*, with the third-to-last syllable stressed: Felidae is "**fee**-lid-ee."

The Tree of Life

Molecular biology has dealt a series of sharp blows to humankind's preference for seeing itself as the center of life on earth, or if not the center, then at least *able to see* most of life on earth. Much of humankind, of course, is blissfully unaware of receiving these blows. On these two pages I will do my humble best to reduce the number of those so unafflicted.

The traditional division of life into Animal and Plant Kingdoms fell by the wayside in several steps. First it was conceded that animals and plants were obviously more like each other than like the simple microorganisms without cell nuclei (bacteria, etc.), so a third kingdom, Prokaryota, was recognized to hold the latter. (All organisms with cell nuclei are "eukaryotes.") Further study showed that the fungi have basically nothing in common with plants (with whom they had been included) except that neither of them cares to go for an evening stroll. In fact, they have more in common with animals, but we certainly aren't going to admit them to Our kingdom. Kingdom Fungi was recognized, and soon a kingdom of simple eukaryotes ranging from "algae" to "protozoans." This kingdom, which Lynn Margulis calls Protoctista, includes the organisms that cause pink snow, page 563, whirling disease, page 486, Rocky Mtn. spotted fever, page 566, and giardiasis, page 564.

Most biologists were content with four or five kingdoms for decades, until an iconoclast named Carl Woese studied the RNA of bacteria and a group called archaebacteria. These primitive cells had only become known to science within the past century (partly through discoveries in hot spring water at Yellowstone). They include many "extremophiles"—organisms that live at extremely high temperatures or pressures, or with noncarbon-based metabolisms. Woese found that although they look like bacteria, on the genetic family tree they are no closer to bacteria than to you and your mama. He renamed them the "domain" Archaea, alongside the domains Bacteria and Eukaryota. He placed plants, animals, fungi, algae, and several other hard-to-classify groups as Kingdoms within the domain Eukaryota. (A list of eukaryote kingdoms would be anyone's guess at this point.) The scientific community put up major resistance to Woese, but no one put forward a cogent argument that the divergence between prokaryotes and eukaryotes was further back in evolution than the divergence of bacteria from archaea.

Lynn Margulis does still argue for five kingdoms. She points out that bacteria and archaea are profoundly similar, in being prokaryotes, regardless of how deep in the evolutionary tree their split may have been, so it is realistic to combine them as just one of the five kingdoms. (And she is herself a microbiologist who describes Earth as a "bacteriocentric world.") This is part of a movement to liberate taxonomy from slavish adherence to the family tree of organisms.

There is also a challenge to Woese's three-trunked tree on strictly cladistic grounds. The archaea/bacteria split cannot be represented simply as tree branches, because bacteria and archaea traded genetic material at many points in their evolution. In other words, the base of the tree should look more like a mass of roots that separate and then rejoin, more than once.

Some biologists argue that prokaryotes also exchange genetic material with eukaryotes. While that particular behavior may be rare, it is universally true that eukaryotic cells have several organelles (e.g., mitochondria and chloroplasts) that are, in essence, entire prokaryotic organisms living as internal symbionts. How would you depict this relationship—fundamental to the entire eukaryote domain—as tree branches? The latest hypothesis holds that eukaryotes came about by a process of certain archaea more or less swallowing bacteria whole.

Branch-tip twigs can also grow back together after separating, when two distinct but related species hybridize, giving rise to a third species. One example of this "reticulate" (netted) evolution is our wood fern, *Gymnocarpium dryopteris*, the hybrid offspring of Appalachian and Pacific NW wood ferns, which probably diverged from a common ancestor millions of years ago.

Meanwhile, there is a question of where life on earth lives. Life on and above the land surface is probably outweighed by life below it, in the soil. Life in the oceans outweighs both of those together—no surprise, when you consider the relative volume of available habitat. And more than half of all marine life, by weight, is bacterial. Now we learn that extremophilic archaea are common in rocks as far as a few miles down. Thomas Gold's calculations from the amount of available habitat suggest that this no-air, no-sunlight biomass may also outweigh the biomass of our entire sunlit biosphere.

Wait, I still have one more assault on anthropocentrism to report. You know that insects are more numerous than mammals, and more diverse, more ubiquitous, more tolerant of extremes, and often more complex in their social structures—in a word, more successful. Well, the same goes for bacteria, plus a greater speed at adapting to changing environments than any other genetic lineage. We could quibble with the part about social organization, but then, bacterial "biofilms" are seen as a kind of social organization by scientists who study them. Now a few scientists are finding clues that at least some bacteria evolved from eukaryotes—an evolutionary step toward simplicity, stripping away inefficient complexity, like mammals improving on reptiles by cutting back on the number and replaceability of teeth. In a sense, an evolutionary step "forward."

In the face of all these ongoing developments, this book will make no attempt to present a "consensus" tree of the relationships among the kingdoms or their higher divisions.

Chronology of Naturalist Explorers

1741	Georg Steller, sailing from Kamchatka under Captain Vitus Bering, explored islands now in Alaska. Page 443.
1787	Archibald Menzies visited Vancouver Island briefly. Page 67.
1793	Fur trader Alexander Mackenzie (not a naturalist) crossed the Canadian Rockies at Peace River Pass and reached the Pacific.
1792	Menzies returned to the Northwest under Captain Vancouver.
1805–06	Lewis and Clark crossed and recrossed the Rockies. Page 257.
1815–18	Chamisso and Eschscholtz studied Alaska and California under Russian captain Kotzebue. Page 186.
1820	Edwin James and Thomas Say (traveling with Major Long) made the earliest collections of RM alpine flora, on James' (Pike's) Peak, Colorado. Pages 230.
1825–27	David Douglas explored the PNW and the Columbia Basin for the Royal Horticultural Society, returning via the upper Columbia and the Athabasca. Page 66.
1825–27	Drummond and Richardson collected in western Canada on Franklin's second expedition. Page 155.
1826–29	Karl H. Mertens sailed around the world; his stop at Sitka yielded many new plant species. Page 152.
1830–33	David Douglas, on his 2nd journey to NA, worked in the Blue Mtns and in Interior BC as far n as Ft. St. James. Page 66.
1833	Maximilian Alexander Philipp, Prince of Wied and Neuwied, having decided to devote the latter part of his life to science, investigated the Missouri almost to Great Falls, Montana.
1834	Thomas Nuttall and John Kirk Townsend travelled the Oregon Trail with Nathaniel Wyeth. Pages 222 and 193.
1838	Plant hunter Robert Wallace fell in love with, married, and soon died with a mixed-race daughter of Sir George Simpson, in a rapids on the Columbia above Revelstoke.
1842	Lieutenant John C. Frémont, with Kit Carson his guide, explored, climbed, and collected in the Wind Rivers. Page 327.
1843–44	Karl A. Geyer and Alexander Gordon explored from the Wind Rivers to Spokane. Page 176.
1843–46	Joseph Burke botanized throughout our region, but none of his collections survived. Pages 176, 246.
1853–67	U.S. Army expeditions surveyed the western states for their economic potential. They often carried scientists. Page 242.
1857–62	David Lyall studied plants while surveying the 49th Parallel for the Boundary Commissions. Page 63.
1871	The first of Ferdinand V. Hayden's famous scientific expeditions, the "Hayden Surveys." Page 242.
1872–85	John Macoun collected in the Canadian Rockies. Page 552.

Abbreviations and Symbols

', "	feet, inches
+	or more
±	more or less
×	by (as in length by width); also: lens magnification power
n, s, e, w	north(ern), south(ern), east(ern), west(ern)
AB	Alberta; also *Flora of Alberta*; see pages 574, 597
avg	average
BC	British Columbia
c	central
Can	Canada
CD	Continental Divide
CO	Colorado; also *Colorado Flora*; see pages 574, 597
diam	diameter (at breast height: 4'6", or 135 cm, above ground)
elev(s)	elevation(s)
esp	especially
FNA	*Flora of North America*; see pages 574, 597
Glacier	Glacier NP, Montana (Glacier NP, BC, is spelled out or included in "Selkirks")
exc	except
ID	Idaho
incl	including
MT	Montana
mtn(s)	mountain(s)
NA	North America
NP	National Park
OFP	Oregon Flora Project; see pages 574, 597
OR	Oregon
USDA	the plant list of the US Dept. of Agriculture; see pages 574, 609
PNW	the Pacific Northwest: our range in the Rockies and everything west of it, to the coast.
spp.	species plural: any and all of the species of a genus
ssp.	subspecies
var.	variety (a taxonomic level slightly less distinct than subspecies)
WA	Washington
WY	Wyoming; also *Vascular Plants of Wyoming*; see pages 574, 597
ws	wingspread: the measurement across outspread wings
YS	Yellowstone Plateau

Glossary

Abundant: present in great numbers—even more numerous, at least within some habitats, than what is implied by "common."

Alevin: a hatchling fish, especially a salmon or trout in the stage when it is still attached to and nourished by an egg yolk sac.

Allelopathy: the addition to the soil, by a species of plant, of chemicals hostile to the growth of other species of plants.

Alpine: of or in the elevational zone above where tree species are found growing numerously in upright tree form. (Some texts define "alpine" as above the growth of tree species in any form, even **krummholz**.)

Alternate: arranged with only one leaf at any given distance along a stem. Contrast with **opposite** or **whorled**.

Anadromous: participating in a life cycle of birth and breeding in streams or lakes separated by an extended period of growth at sea.

Angle of repose: the steepest slope angle that a given loose sediment can hold.

Ascending: held well above perpendicular to the stem or axis, but not nearly parallel or aligned with it; intermediate between **spreading** and **erect**.

Ash: fine particles of volcanic rock (usually glassy in structure) formed when **magma** is blasted out of a volcano in a fine spray.

Archaea: (ar-kee-a) primitive one-celled organisms resembling bacteria.

Archean Eon: early geologic time, about 3.8 to 2.5 billion years ago, following the utterly hostile Hadean Eon, and preceding the Proterozoic Eon during which the atmosphere acquired substantial oxygen. (also **Archaean**.)

Aspect: the compass direction a slope faces.

Awn: a stiff, hairlike extension of the tip of a **bract** in the **floret** of a grass.

Axil: the crotch between a stem and a leaf.

Basal: (leaves) attached to a plant at its root crown, not higher on the stem.

Batholith: an **igneous intrusion** exposed at the surface over a large area—technically at least 100 square km at or near the surface.

Biomass: total [quantity of] living matter.

Bisexual: with functioning stamens and pistils in the same flower.

Bloom: a pale, powdery coating on a surface.

Boreal: of the Northern Hemisphere-wide belt dominated by coniferous forests and transitional between Arctic and **Temperate** climate.

Bract: a modified leaf or leaflike appendage, often **subtending** a flower or inflorescence, and generally smaller and/or more specialized than a leaf.

Broadleaf: common term for all trees and shrubs other than **conifers.**

Calcareous soil: alkaline soil derived from **carbonate** bedrock.

Calciphile: a plant species that prefers calcareous soil.

Call: any vocal communication common to birds of a species. Compare **song.**

Calyx: a flower's **sepals** spoken of collectively, or a ring of sepallike lobes that would be sepals if they were separate all the way to their bases; i.e., the outermost **whorl** or circle of parts of most flowers. Plural: "calyces." Compare **corolla.**

Canopy: in forest structure, the uppermost layer of tree branches and foliage.

Cap: the spreading top portion of a typical mushroom, supported by a stem and supporting **gills**, tubes, or spines on its lower surface only.

Capsule: a seed pod, technically a nonfleshy **fruit** that splits to release seeds; in mosses, the spore-containing organ.

Carbonate rocks: limestone and dolomite. Paleozoic and older limestones tended to alter into dolomite, so the two commonly intergrade or alternate in thin layers.

Catkin: the form of **inflorescence** of certain trees and shrubs, consisting of a dense **spike** of minute, dry, petal-less flowers.

Chrysalis: a ± hard case in which a butterfly encloses itself for its pupal stage.

Cirque: a head of a mountain valley, given a characteristic amphitheater shape by glacial erosion.

Class: a **taxonomic** group broader than an **order** or **family** and narrower than a (plant) division or (animal) phylum. Examples: mammals, fishes, spiders.

Climax: a hypothetical condition of stability in which all **successional** changes resulting from plant community growth have taken place, so that further changes can only follow destructive disturbances.

Cloaca: an anal orifice (in birds, reptiles, fishes, etc.) through which the urinary, reproductive, and gastrointestinal tracts all discharge.

Clone: a group of genetically identical progeny produced by vegetative or other asexual reproduction from a single progenitor. (In nonscientific use, **clone** often refers to the seeming individual, rather than the aggregate.)

Clone: to reproduce asexually.

Composite: a member of the plant family Asteraceae, with composite flower heads—well-organized inflorescences of tiny flowers. E.g., daisies, thistles.

Compound leaf: a structure of three or more leaflets on stalklike ribs. Distinguished from three or more leaves on a branchlet by (1) terminating in a leaflet rather than a flower, a bud, or a growing shoot, and (2) growing from a node on a stem, while its leaflets do not each grow from a node.

Congener: a member of a species in the same genus.

Conifer: a tree or shrub of a large group characterized by needlelike or scale-like leaves and by seeds borne naked between the woody scales of a "cone," or (in the yew family) borne naked but cupped within a berrylike "aril."

Conspecific: (an individual) of the same species.

Convect: to move upward and downward due to temperature contrasting with that of other fluids in the same system—hot air rises, cold air sinks.

Cordillera: "Mountain range" in Spanish, derived from "string;" specifically, the entire mountain system of the western half of North America.

Corolla: the whorl or circle of a typical flower's parts lying second from the out-side; i.e., the **petals** spoken of collectively, or else a ring of lobes that would be petals if they were separate all the way to their bases. **Compare calyx**.

Cosymbiont: a "partner" in a **symbiotic** relationship with a given organism.

Cotyledon: a seed leaf—the specialized leaf first produced by a plant after ger-minating from a seed' the most consistent distinction between **dicots** and **monocots** is whether two simultaneous seed leaves are produced, or just one.

Crevasse: a large crack in a glacier, expressing flow stresses.

Crown: the leafy (top) part of a tree.

Crust: the surface layer of the earth, mostly between 3 and 25 miles thick [5–40 km], defined primarily by lower-density (lighter) rock than what's underneath.

Crystal: the specific structure of many chemical compounds (including all **minerals**) in which the atoms position themselves in a particular geometry that repeats indefinitely; usually visible in broken surfaces of the material.

Deciduous: (a tree or shrub) shedding its leaves annually; i.e., not **evergreen**. (Can also refer to any part, e.g., sepals or bark, that sheds anomalously early.)

Dicot: any member of one of the two traditional groups of flowering plants; in-cludes all of our **broadleaf** trees and shrubs and virtually all of our terrestrial **herbs** except lilies, orchids, and grasslike plants (the **monocots**). Short for "dicotyledon." Taxonomic status of the dicots is questionable: they now appear to have arisen on several different branches of the family tree.

Dike: a body of one kind of rock much longer and deeper than it is thick: usu-ally an **igneous** rock body from fluid **magma** intruded into a **fault** or crack. Spelled "dyke" by British and some Canadian geologists.

Disk flower: one of the tiny, often dry and drab flowers making up a dense cir-cle either in the center of a **composite** flower head (the "eye" of a daisy) or com-prising an entire composite flower head such as a pearly-everlasting.

Disturbance: an external force which causes abrupt changes in a plant com-munity. E.g., logging, extraordinary floods, fires, but not "normal" weather.

Disjunct: separated (said of a population separated from other populations of the same species by a wide area lacking that species).

DNA: (deoxyribosenucleic acid) a key molecule in genes, which largely control the form taken by each living cell. Analysis of genetic make-up to infer the lin-eage or relative kinship of organisms is loosely called DNA study.

Dominant: plant species with the greatest cover percentage within a community.

Duff: matted, partly decayed litter on the forest floor.

Erect: aligned nearly parallel with the stem, if describing a leaf, a flower-stalk, etc.; or more or less vertical, if describing a main stem.

Evergreen: bearing relatively heavy leaves which normally keep their form, color, and function on the plant through at least two years' growing seasons. Opposite of **deciduous**, with **persistent** describing an in-between leaf type.

Family: a **taxonomic** group broader than a genus or species and narrower than an **order** or **class**. Latin name ends in -*aceae* for plants or -*idae* for animals.

Fascicle: a bundle, especially the characteristic cluster of one to five pine needles sheathed at their base in tiny dry, membranous **bracts**.

Fault: a fracture in rock or earth (or a zone of several parallel fractures) where relative earth movement on the two sides has taken place; may be of any size.

Floret: a small, inconspicuous flower within a compact inflorescence such as the **head** of a **composite** or the **spikelet** of a grass.

Fruit: among the seed plants, an **ovary** wall matured into a seed-bearing structure; also, more broadly, any seed-bearing or **spore-bearing** structure.

Fry: young fish (both singular and plural). In salmon and trout, the fry stage follows the **alevin** stage and precedes the **parr**; some species enter the sea as fry.

Fused: unseparated; fused **petals** (or **sepals**) form a single **corolla** (**calyx**) ring or tube, usually with lobes that can be counted for identification purposes.

Gelifluction: Slow downslope movement of frozen soil or rock rubble. (The term "solifluction" was used more in the past, but gelifluction is now preferred, for referring explicitly to flow of frozen stuff. *Sol* is soil, *gel* is ice.)

Gills: (1) in aquatic animals, respiratory organs where oxygen from the water passes into the animal; (2) on some mushrooms, radial paper-thin or sometimes wrinklelike **spore**-bearing organs on the underside of the **cap**.

Gland: an organ that secretes a fluid; on plants surfaces, these can be detected as dots or short hairs that give the surface a sticky or greasy feel. "Sticky-hairy" plants have short hairs tipped with microscopic bulb-shaped glands.

Granitic rocks: coarse-grained **igneous** rocks; see **intrusive** rocks.

Head: a tight, compact **inflorescence**.

Herbaceous: not **woody**; aboveground parts normally dying or withering at the end of the growing season.

Herb layer: all the **herbaceous** plants and low shrubs, as a group comprising a structural element of a plant community.

Here: in our range. See page 14, or back cover.

Hybrid: offspring of parents of different species.

Hyphae: the countless, minute filaments that carry on all the normal nutritive and growth functions of a fungus. (Singular: "hypha.")

Igneous rocks: rocks that reached their present **mineral** composition and texture while cooling from a liquid into a solid state; may be either volcanic or, if they solidified underground without ever erupting, **intrusive**.

Inflorescence: a cluster of flowers from one stem, or the cluster's pattern.

Instar: a stage in life lasting from one molt to the next, in insects with incomplete metamorphosis (i.e. several instars instead of larva/pupa/adult stages).

Intergrade: to vary along a continuum between two well-defined types.

Introduced: not thought to have lived in a given area (**the Rockies**, in this book) before the arrival of white people; opposed to **native**.

Intrusive rocks: **igneous** rocks that did not surface as fluid **lava** in a volcanic eruption, but solidified underground; generally coarser-grained than volcanic rocks.

Inuit: Eskimo(s).

Involucre: a whorl of small leaves circling a stem immediately beneath an **inflorescence** (most often a flower **head** in the **composite** family).

Irregular flower: one made of **petals** (or of **sepals**) that are conspicuously not all alike in size and/or shape; usually they make a bilateral symmetry.

Irruption: a population explosion within a species, often one that seems to be a case of ecological imbalance, but also perhaps apparently cyclical.

Juvenile plumage: feathers (and their color pattern) of birds old enough to fly, but not yet in their first breeding season; usually similar to adult female plumage.

Krummholz: dwarfed, ground-hugging shrubby growth, near **alpine timberline**, of **conifer** species that would grow as upright trees under more moderate conditions; from the German for "crooked wood." (Ben Gadd chides "people who should know better" for "improperly applying" *krummholz* rather than *kruppelholz*—"crippled wood"—to environmentally stunted growth; but I'd say that an alpine-ecology word means exactly what most alpine ecologists think it means.)

Landlocked: (said of fish) completing their life cycle in fresh water, where some barrier (usually a dam, but sometimes natural) prevents the **anadromous** (seagoing) life cycle the species is capable of.

Larva: an insect, amphibian, or other animal when in a youthful form that differs strongly from the adult form; e.g., caterpillars, maggots. Also "grub."

Lava: rock that is flowing, or once flowed, in a more or less liquid state across the earth in a volcanic eruption; see **magma**.

Leader: the topmost central shoot of a plant.

Leafstalk: a narrowed stalk portion of a leaf, distinguished from the "blade."

Lithosphere: the surficial layer of the earth that moves as plates. It consists of crust bonded to (but chemically different from) a thin layer of mantle.

Low-grade: (rocks) metamorphosed by relatively mild heat and pressure.

Lumpers: scientists inclined to adopt relatively broad species and genus concepts, thus reducing the number of species, genera, etc. Opposed to **splitters**.

Magma: subsurface rock in a melted, liquid state.

Mantle: the major portion of earth's interior, below the **crust** and above the core.

Margin: outer edge, as of a leaf.

Matrix: in some rocks, the fine-grained material in which much larger grains, crystals, or contrasting pieces of rock are embedded.

-merous: a suffix derived from "numerous." Example: a 5-merous plant species is one whose **petals**, **sepals**, and **stamens** each number 5, 10, 15, or 20.

Metamorphic rocks: rocks whose **mineral** composition and texture was set when they were "cooked" at great heat and/or pressure within the earth.

Metamorphism: the heat/pressure process that makes **metamorphic** rocks.

Metamorphosis: the process by which **larval** animals transform into adults.

Milt: fish semen.

Mineral: any natural ingredient of the earth having a well-defined chemical formula and a characteristic crystalline structure. (The formula may express a range of compositions.) Rocks and soils are largely mixtures of minerals.

Monocot: member of group of flowering plants (opposed to **dicots**) most of which have parallel-veined leaves and flower parts in 3s or 6s. Most monocots here are lilies, orchids, aquatic or grasslike plants. Short for "monocotyledon."

Moraine: a usually elongate heap or hill of mixed rock debris lying where it was deposited by a glacier when the glacier retreated from that point.

Mycology: the branch of biology dealing with fungi.

Mycophagy: the eating of fungi; the collecting of wild fungi for food.

Mycorrhiza: a tiny organ formed jointly by plant roots and fungi for passing nutritive substances between plant and fungus. Plural: "mycorrhizae" is preferred in the U.S., "mycorrhizas" in Britain.

Native: thought to have been living in an area (the **Rockies**, for our purposes) before travel there by people—in practice, white people, since hardly anything is known of pre-Columbian introductions. Opposed to **introduced**.

Nature: the universe as it was preceding or is outside of human civilization.

Nectar: a sugary liquid secreted in some flowers to attract pollinating animals.

Niche: the role of a species within an ecological community, especially in terms of food, habitat, and other community members.

Nurse log: a rotting tree serving as a seedbed for tree reproduction.

Old-growth: late-successional natural forest. Everyone talks about old-growth, but it's hard to define precisely. In practice, most users define the term with some number of years since the last clearing **disturbance**.

Opposite: arranged in pairs (of leaves) along a stem. The stem terminates in a bud, flower(s), or growing shoot; if it appears to terminate in a leaf or **tendril**, these are not opposite leaves, but leaflets of **compound** leaves.

Order: a **taxonomic** group broader than a **family**, **genus** or **species**, and narrower than a **class**. Plant orders have a very low profile (or are largely disregarded by some) but bird and mammal orders are very familiar, important groups. Examples: Rodents, carnivores, owls, woodpeckers, perching birds.

Ovary: the egg-producing organ; in flowers, this is generally the enlarged basal portion of the **pistil**, at the base of the flower.

Overstory: in plant community structure, whatever layer is highest; e.g., **canopy**.

Our: of or in the range explicitly covered by this book. See map on page 14–15.

Outwash: fragmental rock debris deposited by a glacier and subsequently carried and more or less sorted by a stream. Distinct from **till**, which is still lying, unsorted, where the glacier melted away from it.

Pacific Northwest (PNW): Our range plus everything between it and the Pacific. "Greater PNW" adds all coastal drainages from Alaska to NW California.

Palmately lobed: shaped (like a maple leaf) with three or more main veins branching from the leaf base, and the leaf outline indented between these veins.

Panicle: an **inflorescence** around a main stem or axis with at least some of the side branches again branched to bear several flowers. Compare **raceme**, **spike**.

Parasite: an organism that draws sustenance for at least part of its life cycle out of an organism of another kind, more or less detrimentally to the latter (the "host") but without ingesting the host or any whole part of it.

Parr marks: vertical blotches that appear on the sides of **anadromous** fish at the "parr" stage—of actively feeding in fresh water, before migrating to sea.

Pendent: attached by a downward stem from a larger stalk.

Persistent: (leaves) tending to stay on the stem through fall and winter even though dead, and lacking the heavy weight and gloss of true **evergreen** leaves.

Petal: a modified leaf, typically non-green and showy, in the inner of two or more concentric **whorls** of floral leaves. If there is only one whorl, no matter how showy, its members are considered **sepals**.

Pheromone: a chemical produced by an animal that serves to stimulate some behavior in others of the same species.

Photosynthesis: the synthesis of carbohydrates out of simpler molecules as a means of converting or storing sunlight energy—the main function of chlorophyll.

Pinna: a segment of a fern or a **compound** leaf, branching directly off of the main fern stalk or leaf axis; may be divided further. Plural: "pinnae."

Pinnately compound: (a leaf) composed of an odd number of leaflets attached (all but the last one) in opposite pairs to a central leaf axis. If attached to mini-axes paired along a central axis, the leaf is pinnately twice-compound.

Pioneer: a species growing on freshly disturbed (e.g., burned, clearcut, deglaciated or volcanically deposited) terrain.

Pistil: the female organ of a flower, including the **ovary** and ovules and any styles or stigmas that catch pollen.

Plate tectonics: the dynamics of the Earth's **crust**; the major unifying theory of geophysics since the 1960's, when it was expanded from "Continental Drift".

Pollen: dustlike male reproductive cells (pollen "grains") borne on the **stamen** tips of a flower, capable, if carried by wind, animal "pollinators" or other agents to the **pistil** of a **conspecific** flower, of fertilizing a female reproductive cell.

Pore: a minute hole; especially, one allowing passage of substances between an organism and its environment.

Propagate: to reproduce, either sexually or not.

Propagule: (in lichens and mosses) any multicelled structure that breaks off and can grow into an organism independent of (but genetically identical to) the one it grew on; a means of asexual reproduction or cloning.

Prostrate: growing more or less flat upon the **substrate**.

Pupa: an insect in a generally quiescent life stage transitional from a **larva** to an adult. Plural: "pupae." Verb: "pupate."

R**aceme**: a slender **inflorescence** with each flower borne on an unbranched **petiole** from the central axis. (Compare **panicle**, **spike**.)

Radial symmetry: an arrangement of several more or less identical elongate members (e.g., **petals**) from a central point.

Raptor: a bird of the Hawk and Owl orders. Not the same as "bird of prey"; see p 432.

Ray flower: in a **composite** flower **head**, a **petallike** part strap-shaped for most of its length but tubular at its base, often enclosing a **pistil** or, in dandelion-type composites, both pistil and **stamens**. (Technically, the ones with stamens are "ligulate," but they look much like rays and are considered "rays" in this book.)

Red belt: a phenomenon of conifer needle death in landscape-scale patches, resulting from abrupt temperature changes on the Rocky Mountain Front.

Regular: with all of its **sepals** and with all of its **petals** (if any) essentially alike in size, shape, and spatial relationship to the others.

Relief: the vertical component of distance between high and low points.

Resin blisters: horizontally elongate blisters conspicuous on the bark of younger true fir trees, initially full of liquid pitch.

Rhizine: a tough, threadlike appendage on the underside of some lichens, serving not as a vessel but as a holdfast to the **substrate**.

Rhizome: a rootstock, or horizontal stem just under the soil surface connecting several aboveground stems; sometimes thickened for storage of starches.

Rhizosphere: the layer of soil permeated and affected by roots and **hyphae**.

Rut: an annual period of sexual excitement and activity in certain mammals.

S**aprophyte**: a fungus or bacterium that absorbs its carbohydrate nutrition from dead organisms. Non-green plants, p 188, were once mistakenly thought to do that, and were called saprophytes, but they get their carbohydrates from living plants, via living **mycorrhizae**. ("Sapro phyte" means "rot plant;" since the organisms that do rot things are no longer considered to be plants, many scientists have dropped "saprophyte" in favor of "saprotroph" or "saprobe.")

Scats: feces. (Wildlife biologists' slang, by back-formation from "scatology.")

Scree: loose rock debris lying at or near its **angle of repose** upon or at the foot of a steeper rock face from which it broke off. Used by some as synonymous with **talus**, but gravel-sized debris in gullies is usually "scree," and boulder-sized debris at the bottom is usually "talus."

Sedimentary rocks: rocks formed by slow compaction and/or cementation of particles deposited by wind or water or by chemical precipitation in water.

Sepal: a modified leaf within the outermost **whorl** (the **calyx**) of a flower's parts. Typically, sepals are green and leaflike and enclose a concentric whorl of **petals**, but in many cases they are quite showy and petallike. (Sepallike leaves enclosing a **composite** flower **head** are **involucral** bracts.)

Smolt: an **anadromous** fish in its first year, migrating to sea.

Softwood: any **conifer**, in industry jargon.

Song: a relatively long and variegated form of bird **call**, usually particular to a species and used for i.d. both by conspecifics and by humans; practiced mostly by males in the Perching Bird order (Passeriformes).

Songbirds: a popular term for the bird order Passeriformes, comprising over half of all bird species. Also known as "perching birds."

Soredia: lichen granules containing both fungus and green partner, capable of growing into a new lichen after being dislodged from the parent lichen.

Sorus: a small clump of **spore**-bearing organs visible as a raised dot line, crescent, etc. on a fern or other leaf. Plural: "sori."

Spawn: to breed (said of fish and other aquatic animals).

Spike: an **inflorescence** of flowers attached directly (i.e., without conspicuous stems of their own) to a central stalk. Compare **raceme, panicle**.

Spikelet: in the **inflorescence** of a grass, a compact group of one to several **florets** and some scalelike **bracts**, on a single axis branching off of the central stem.

Splitters: scientists inclined to adopt relatively narrow genus (etc.) concepts, thus increasing the numbers of species, genera, etc. Opposed to **lumpers**.

Sporadic: irregularly distributed over a range, perhaps common in some locales but not reliably so for any zone or major community type.

Spore: (in the lower plants and fungi) a single cell specialized for differentiating into a new multicelled individual; corresponds functionally to a seed, since it travels; but in ferns and mosses it is comparable genetically to a **pollen** grain, since it is not the sexually produced stage in the life cycle of the species.

Spreading: (leaves, branches, etc.) tending to grow in a horizontal to slightly raised position. Compare **erect, ascending, pendent**.

Steppe: arid plant communities dominated by sparse bunchgrasses and/or shrubs. Ecologists call our dry flats "sagebrush steppe," reserving "desert" for sites so barren that no real plant community exists. In the U.S. and Canada, true deserts persist only on active dunes or saline or alkaline dry lakebeds.

Stamen: a male organ of a flower; typically, several of them surround a central **pistil**, and each consist of a **pollen-covered** tip on a delicate stalk.

Stigma: the **pollen**-receptive tip of the **pistil** of a flower.

Stolon: a stem that trails along the ground, producing several upright stems and thus enabling the plant to spread vegetatively.

Stomata: minute **pores** in leaf surfaces for the **transpiration** of gases. Singular: "stoma." Plural sometimes anglicized to "stomates."

Style: the stalklike part of a flower's **pistil**, supporting the **stigma** and conveying male sexual cells from it to the **ovary**.

Subalpine: of or in the elevational zone lying below the **alpine** zone where tree species are absent, dwarfed, or **prostrate**, and above the continuous forest.

Subduction: the process in which the edge of a "plate" of the Earth's **lithosphere** sinks under the edge of another plate.

Subshrub: a perennial plant with a persistent, somewhat **woody** base; intermediate between clearly an "herb" and clearly a "shrub."

Substrate: the "underlayer" an organism lives on. Examples: soil, rock, bark.

Subtend: to be immediately below and next to.

Succession: change in the species composition of a plant community that results from soil/biotic interactions internal to the community.

Symbiosis: intimate association of unlike organisms for the benefit of at least one of them. Symbioses include **mutualism**, where both or all partners benefit; **parasitism** (one benefits, one suffers); and **commensalism** (no material is transferred, and neither partner suffers substantially).

Talus: rock debris lying at the foot of a rock face from which it broke off. Sometimes implies cobble- to boulder-sized rocks, in contrast to finer **scree**.

Taxon: a species, genus, or other unit of classification. Plural: "taxa."

Taxonomy: the scientific naming and classifying of organisms.

Tectonic: related to geologic deformation (folding, **faulting**, volcanism, **metamorphism**) considered on a regional to global scale.

Temperate: of the zone between the Tropics and the Arctic.

Tendril: a slender organ that supports a climbing plant by coiling or twining.

Tepal: a **petal** or **sepal** on a flower whose petals and sepals are ± identical.

Terminal: at an end, such as a growing tip of a plant or the foot of a glacier.

Terrane: any geologically mapped area interpreted as having a history substantially different from the histories of neighboring terranes.

Till: rock debris of mixed sizes, once transported by a glacier and still lying where the glacier deposited it while melting back. Compare **outwash**.

Tolerance: the relative ability of various plant species to thrive under a given stressful condition.

Transpiration: emission of water vapor into the air through plant surfaces.

Turf: an upper layer of soil permeated by a dense, cohesive mat of roots, especially of grasses and/or sedges.

Ubiquitous: found ± everywhere (in **our range** or a given part of it) with the possible exception of the **alpine** zone.

Umbel: an **inflorescence** in which several flower **pedicels** diverge from a single point atop the main stem. Example: carrot tops or "Queen Anne's Lace."

Understory: in plant community structure, any community layer except the highest one, or all such layers collectively.

Veil: a membrane extending from the edge of the **cap** to the stem, in certain mushrooms when immature, soon rupturing and often persisting as a ring around the stem; also (the "universal veil") in *Amanita* mushrooms, an additional, outer membrane extending in the button stage from the edge of the cap to the underground base of the mushroom, soon rupturing and often visibly persisting as a more or less cup-shaped enlargement of the mushroom's base.

Whorl: arrangement of 3+ leaves (or other parts) around one point on a stem.

Widespread: widely distributed, but not quite **ubiquitous** or **abundant**.

Woody: reinforced with fibrous tissue, remaining rigid and functional from one year to the next. Woody plants are trees or shrubs. Opposed to **herbaceous**.

Zooplankton: nonplant aquatic organisms that drift in water, lacking powers of either locomotion or attachment. E.g., one-celled organisms, jellyfish, insect **larvae**. Pronounced "zoh-oh-**plank**-ton." Singular: "zooplankter."

Selected References

Cross-Disciplinary

Arno, Stephen F., and R. Hammerly. 1984. *Timberline*. Seattle: Mountaineers.

Arno, Stephen F. and Steven Allison-Bunnell. 2002. *Flames in Our Forests: Disaster or Renewal?* Washington, DC: Island.

Borror, Donald J. 1960. *Dictionary of Word Roots and Combining Forms*. Mtn. View, CA: Mayfield.

Cantino, P. D. 1998. Binomials, hyphenated uninomials... *Taxon* 47: 425–49.

Clark, Tim W., et al. 1999. *Carnivores in Ecosytems*. New Haven: Yale U Pr.

Cox, Geo. W. 1999. *Alien Species in NA and Hawaii*. Washington, DC: Island.

Dale, V., et al. 2001. Climate change and forest disturbance. *BioSci* 51(9): 723–34.

Douglas, David. 1980. *Douglas of the Forests: the North American Journals of David Douglas*. Edited by John Davies. Seattle: U of WA Pr.

Dukes, Jeffrey S., and Harold A. Mooney. 1999. Does global change increase the success of biological invaders? *Trends in Ecol. and Evol.* 14(4): 135–39.

Ewan, Joseph. 1950. *Rocky Mountain Naturalists*. Denver: U of Denver Pr.

Gadd, Ben. 1995. *Handbook of the Canadian Rockies*. 2nd Ed. Jasper: Corax Pr.

Geiser, Samuel Wood. 1948. *Naturalists of the Frontier*. Dallas: SMU Pr.

Goetzmann, William H. 1966. *Exploration and Empire: the Explorer and the Scientist in the Winning of the American West*. NY: Knopf.

Goward, Trevor, and C. Hickson. 1995. *Nature Wells Gray*. Edmonton: Lone Pine.

Hansen, Andrew W., et al. 2002. Ecological causes and consequnces of demographic change in the New West. *BioScience* 52 (2): 151–62.

Hardy, W. G., Ed. 1967. *Alberta: a Natural History*. Edmonton: M. G. Hurtig.

Heinrich, Bernd. 2003. *Winter World*. NY: HarperCollins.

Knight, Dennis H. 1994. *Mountains and Plains: the Ecology of Wyoming Landscapes*. New Haven, CT: Yale U Pr.

Kohm, Kathryn A., and Jerry F. Franklin, eds. 1997. *Creating a Forestry for the 21st Century*. Washington, DC: Island.

Laundré, J. W., L. Hernández, and K. B. Altendorf. 2001. Wolves, elk, and bison: reestablishing the "landscape of fear" in Yellowstone NP. *Can. J. Zool.* 79: 1401–09.

Lewis, Meriwether, and William Clark. *The Journals of Lewis and Clark*. Edited by Bernard DeVoto. 1953. Boston: Houghton.

Meagher, Mary, and Douglas B. Houston. 1998. *Yellowstone and the Biology of Time: Photographs Across a Century*. Norman, OK: U of Oklahoma.

Millspaugh, S. H., C. Whitlock, and P. J. Bartlein. 2000. Variations in fire frequency and climate over the past 17,000 yrs in YS NP. *Geology*. 28 (3):211–214.

Perry, David A. 1994. *Forest Ecosystems*. Baltimore: Johns Hopkins.

Ripple, Wm. J., and Eric J. Larsen. 2000. Historic aspen recruitment, elk, and wolves in N Yellowstone NP, USA. *Biological Conservation* 95: 361–70.

Romme, W. H., et al. 1995. Aspen, elk, and fire in N YNP. *Ecology* 76(7): 2097–2106.

Schullery, Paul. 1997. *Searching for Yellowstone*. Boston: Houghton Mifflin.

Townsend, John Kirk. 1839. *Narrative of a Journey across the Rocky Mountains to the Columbia River*. (Reprinted 1999. Corvallis, OR: OSU Pr.)

Whitlock, Cathy. 1993. Postglacial vegetation and climate of Grand Teton and southern Yellowstone National Parks. *Ecological Monographs* 63(2): 173–98.

Wolfe, David W. 2001. *Tales from the Underground: a Natural History of Subterranean Life*. Cambridge, MA: Perseus.

Yellowstone N.P. 1997. *Yellowstone's Northern Range: Complexity and Change in a Wildland Ecosystem*. Mammoth Hot Springs, WY: NPS.

Climate (Chapter 2)

Broecker, W. S. 1999. What if the conveyor were to shut down? Reflections on a possible outcome of the great global experiment. *GSA Today* 9(1): 1–7.

Dale, Virginia, et al. 2001. Climate change and forest disturbances. *BioScience* 51(9): 723–34.

Geiger, Rudolf, et al. 2003. *Climate Near the Ground*. 6th Ed. Lanham, MD: Rowman & Littlefield.

Graedel, Thomas E., and Paul. J. Crutzen. 1995. *Atmosphere, Climate, and Change*. NY: Scientific American Library.

Paillard, Didier. 2001. Glacial cycles. *Reviews of Geophysics* 39(3): 325–46.

Perry, D. A., et al. 1991. Biological feedbacks to climate change: terrestrial ecosystems as sinks and sources of C and N. *NW Env J* 7: 203–232.

Whiteman, C. David. 2000. *Mountain Meteorology*. NY: Oxford U Pr.

Plants (Chapters 3-7)

Beidleman, R. G., L. H. Beidleman, and B. E. Willard. 2000. *Plants of Rocky Mtn. N.P.* Helena, MT: Falcon. A revision of Ruth Ashton Nelson's 1934 book.

Brayshaw, T. C. 1996. *Trees and Shrubs of BC.* Victoria: Royal BC Museum.

Chambers, Kenton L., and Scott Sundberg. 1998—. *Oregon Vascular Plant Checklist.* Corvallis: Oregon Flora Project (OSU).

Cronquist, Arthur, et al. 1972—. *Intermountain Flora.* 000 volumes to date. NY: NY Botanical Garden Press. The Great Basin plus the rest of Utah.

Despain, Don G. 1990. *Yellowstone Vegetation.* Boulder: Roberts Rinehart.

Dorn, Robert D. 1984. *Vascular Plants of Montana.* Cheyenne: Mtn West.

——. 2001. *Vascular Plants of Wyoming,* 3rd Ed. Cheyenne: Mtn West.

Douglas, George W., et al. 1998–2001. *Illustrated Flora of BC.* 7 vols. Victoria: BC Ministry of Environment, Lands, and Parks.

Farrar, John L. 1995. *Trees in Canada.* Markham, Ontario: Fitzhenry & Whiteside. Publ. in US as *Trees of the N US and Can.* Ames, IA: Iowa St. U. Pr.

Flora of N. A. Editorial Committee. 1993—. *Flora of North America N of Mexico.* 6 volumes to date, of 30 planned. NY: Oxford U Pr.

Flowers, Seville. 1973. *Mosses: Utah and the West.* Provo, UT: B. Young U. Pr.

Grescoe, Audrey. 1997. *Giants: the Colossal Trees of Pacific NA.* Vancouver, BC: Raincoast; and Boulder, CO: Roberts Rinehart.

Hallworth, Beryl, and C. C. Chinnappa. 1997. *Plants of Kananaskis Country.* Edmonton: U of Alberta Pr.

Harrington, H. D. 1967. *Edible Native Plants of the RM.* Albuquerque: UNM Pr.

Hart, Jeff. 1976. *Montana Native Plants and Early Peoples.* Helena: MT Hist Soc.

Hayes, Doris W., and George A. Garrison. 1960. *Key to Important Woody Plants of Eastern Oregon and Washington.* USDA Agr. Handbook No. 148.

Hickman, J. C., ed. 1993. *Jepson Manual of Higher Plants of CA.* Berkeley: UC Pr.

Hitchcock, C. Leo, and Arthur Cronquist. 1976. *Flora of the Pacific Northwest.* 3rd Printing. Seattle: U of WA Pr. Compressed version of the following.

Hitchcock, C. Leo, A. Cronquist, M. Ownbey, and J. W. Thompson. 1955–69. *Vascular Plants of the PNW.* 5 volumes. Seattle: U of WA Pr. More complete for our range than *Intermountain Flora* (if and when finished)—it covers from coast to CD in MT, s BC, and nw WY—but many scientific names are out of date. Jeanne R. Janish's botanical illustrations are gorgeous at full size. They are reproduced in many other books, including the one in your hands.

Hurd, Emeranciana, et al. 1997. *Field Guide to Intermountain Rushes.* USDA For. Serv. INT-GTR-306.

——. 1998. *FG to Intermountain Sedges.* USDA For. Serv. RMRS-GTR-10.

Johnson, Frederic D. 1995. *Wild Trees of Idaho.* Moscow: U of Idaho Pr.

Lesica, Peter. 2002. *Flora of Glacier NP.* Corvallis, OR: OSU Pr.

King, J. 1997. *Reaching for the Sun: How Plants Work.* Cambridge: Cambridge U.

Mason, Georgia. 1975. *Guide to the Plants of the Wallowa Mtns of NE Oregon.* Reprinted 2001. Eugene: U of OR.

McKelvey, Susan Delano. 1955. *Botanical Exploration of the Trans-Mississippi West, 1790–1850.* (Reprinted 1991. Corvallis, OR: OSU Pr.)

McQueen, Cyrus B. 1990. *Field Guide to the Peat Mosses of Boreal NA.* Hanover, NH: Univ Pr of New England.

Moerman, Daniel E. 1998. *Native American Ethnobotany.* Portland: Timber.

Moore, M. 1993. *Medicinal Plants of the Pacific West.* Santa Fe: Red Crane.

Moss, E. H. 1983. *Flora of Alberta.* 2nd Ed, rev J. G. Packer. Toronto: U of T Pr.

Nelson, Ruth A. 1992. *A Guide to RM Plants.* 5th Ed revised by Roger L. Williams. Boulder: Roberts Rinehart.

Parish, Roberta, Ray Coupé, and Dennis Lloyd, eds. 1996. *Plants of Southern Interior BC.* Edmonton: Lone Pine.

Phillips, H. Wayne. 1999. *Central RM Wildflowers.* Helena, MT: Falcon.
———. 2001. *Northern RM Wildflowers.* Helena, MT: Falcon.

Scott, Richard W. 1995. *Alpine Flora of the RM: Vol. 1, the Middle Rockies.* Salt Lake City: U. of Utah Pr.

Scotter, George W., and Hälle Flygare. 1986. *Wildflowers of the Canadian Rockies.* Toronto: Hurtig.

Sudworth, George B. 1908. *Forest Trees of the Pacific Slope.* USDA Forest Service.

Sumner, Judith. 2000. *The Natural History of Medicinal Plants.* Portland: Timber.

Schofield, W. B. 1992. *Some Common Mosses of BC.* 2nd Ed. Victoria: BC Prov. Mus.
———. 2002. *Field Guide to Liverwort Genera of Pacific NA.* Seattle: U of WA.

Smith, Jane K., and Wm. C. Fischer. 1997. *Fire Ecology of Forest Habitat Types of Northern ID.* USDA Forest Service INT-GTR-363.

Strickler, Dee. 1997. *Northwest Penstemons.* Columbia Falls, MT: Flower Pr.

Tilford, G. L. 1997. *Edible and Medicinal Plants of the West.* Missoula: Mtn Pr.

Tomback, Diana F., Stephen F. Arno, and Robert E. Keane. 2001. *Whitebark Pine Communities: Ecology and Restoration.* Washington, DC: Island.

Turner, Nancy J. 1995. *Food Plants of Coastal First Peoples.* Vancouver: UBC Pr.
———. 1997. *Food Plants of Interior First Peoples.* Vancouver: UBC Pr.
———. 1998. *Plant Technologyof First Peoples of BC.* Vancouver: UBC Pr. Nancy

Turner, Nancy J., and Adam F. Szczawinski. 1991. *Common Poisonous Plants and Mushrooms of NA.* Portland: Timber.

Van Pelt, Robert. 2001. *Forest Giants of the Pacific Coast.* Seattle: U of WA Pr.

Weber, William A., and Ronald C. Wittmann. 2001. *Colorado Flora.* Two Vols.; 3rd. Ed. Boulder: Univ Press of Colorado.

Wilkinson, Kathleen. 1999. *Wildflowers of AB.* Edmonton: U of AB Pr.

Plant Articles

American Forestry Assoc. 1998. National register of big trees. *Am. Forests.*

Arno, Stephen F., and J. R. Habeck. 1972. Ecology of alpine larch in the PNW. *Ecological Monographs* 42: 417-50.

Anderson, L. E., H. A. Crum, and W. R. Buck. 1990. List of the mosses of NA N of Mexico. *Bryologist* 93: 448-71. **Our authority** on scientific names of mosses.

Bidartondo, Martin I., and T. D. Bruns. 2001. Extreme specificity in epiparasitic Monotropoideae (Ericaceae). *Molecular Ecology* 10: 2285-94.

Cooper, S. V., K. E. Neiman, and D. W. Roberts. 1991. *Forest habitat types of N ID.* USDA For. Serv. INT-GTR-236. 2nd Ed.

Cooper, S. V., P. Lesica, and D. Page-Dumroese. 1997. *Plant community classification for alpine vegetation on the Beaverhead N.F.* USDA For. Serv. INT-GTR-362.

Crowe, Eliz., and R. R. Clausnitzer. 1997. *Mid-montane wetland plant associations of the… Wallowa-Whitman N.F.* USDA For. Serv. R6-NR-ECOL-TP-22-97.

Cullings, K. W., T. M. Szaro and T. D. Bruns. 1996. Evolution of extreme specialization within a lineage of ectomycorrhizal epiparasites. *Nature* 379: 63-5.

Fertig, Walter. 1992. A floristic survey of the west slope of the Wind River Range, WY. Unpublished MS thesis, Univ of WY, Laramie.

Galen, Candace, and M. L. Stanton. 2003. Sunny-side up: flower heliotropism… effects on pollen quality… in the snow buttercup… *Am J Botany* 90: 724-29.

Johnson, E. A., and G. I. Fryer. 1989. Population dynamics in lodgepole pine– Engelmann spruce forests. *Ecology* 70(3): 1335-45.

Johnson, P. L., and W. D. Billings. 1962. Alpine vegetation of the Beartooth Plateau in relation to cryopedogenic processes… *Ecol Monographs* 32(3): 105-34.

Kay, Charles E. 1997. Is aspen doomed? *J of Forestry* (May, 1977): 4-11.

Klironomos, John N. 2002. Feedback with soil biota contributes to plant rarity and invasiveness in communities. *Nature* 417: 67-70.

La Roi, George H., and Roger J. Hnatiuk. 1980. *Pinus contorta* forests of Banff and Jasper NPs. *Ecological Monographs* 50: 1-29.

Lynch, Elizabeth A. 1998. Origin of a park-forest vegetation mosaic in the Wind River Range, WY. *Ecology* 79(4): 1320-38.

McCune, Bruce, and T. F. H. Allen. 1984. Will similar forests develop on similar sites? *and* Forest dynamics of the Bitterroot Canyons, MT. *Can J Bot* 63: 367-83.

Perkins, Dana L., and T. W. Swetnam. 1996. A dendroecological assessment of whitebark pine in the Sawtooth … region, ID. *Can J Forest Res.* 26: 2123-33.

Steele, R., et al. 1981. *Forest Habitat Types of C ID.* USDA For. Serv. GTR-INT-114.

Stevens, G. C., and J. F. Fox. 1991. The causes of treeline. *Annu Rev Ecol Sys* 22:177-91.

Walker, D. A., et al. 1993. Long-term studies of snow-vegetation interactions. *BioScience* 43: 287-301.

Wied, Anna, and Candace Galen. 1998. Plant parental care: conspecific nurse effects in *Frasera speciosa….* *Ecology* 79: 1657-68.

Fungi (Chapter 8)

Arora, David. 1986. *Mushrooms Demystified.* 2nd Edition. Berkeley: Ten Speed Press. My first choice in mushroom guides. 960 pages for your knapsack.

Bessette, Alan E., Arleen R. Bessette, and David W. Fischer. 1997. *Mushrooms of Northeastern NA.* Syracuse, NY: Syracuse U. Pr.

Brodo, Irwin M., Sylvia Duran Sharnoff, and Stephen Sharnoff. 2001. *Lichens of NA.* New Haven: Yale U Pr. A (heavily subsidized) bargain at $70. If you love lichens, you've gotta have it.

Evenson, Vera S. 1997. *Mushrooms of Colorado.* Englewood, CO: Westcliffe.

Goward, Trevor, Jim Pojar, and Andy MacKinnon. In press. *Ways of Enlichenment: macrolichens of NW NA.* Edmonton: Lone Pine.

McCune, B., and Linda Geiser. 1997. *Macrolichens of the PNW.* Corvallis, OR: OSU Press. Well illustrated with color photos by Stephen and Sylvia Sharnoff.

Miller, Orson K., Jr. 1972. *Mushrooms of North America.* NY: Dutton.

Purvis, William. 2000. *Lichens.* Washington, DC: Smithsonian.

Pyrozynski, K. A., and D. L. Hawksworth, eds. 1988. *Coevolution of Fungi with Plants and Animals.* London: Academic Pr.

Schalkwijk-Barendson, Helene M. E. 1991. *Mushrooms of W Canada.* Edmonton: Lone Pine.

St. Clair, L. L. 1999. *A Color Guideb ook to the Common RM Lichens.* Provo, UT: Bean Life Sci Mus of Brigham Young Univ.

Weber, W. A., and J. N. Corbridge. 1998. *A RM Lichen Primer.* Niwot: U Pr of CO.

Fungi Articles

Barron, George. 1992. Jekyll-Hyde mushrooms. *Natural Hist.* 101(3): 47–52.

Helgason, T., et al. 1998. Ploughing up the wood-wide web? *Nature* 394: 431.

Hosford, David, et al. 1997. Ecology and management of the commercially harvested American matsutake. USDA Forest Service PNW-GTR-412.

Jongmans, A. G., et al. 1997. Rock-eating fungi. *Nature.* 389: 682–83.

Klironomos, John N. and Miranda M. Hart. 2001. Animal nitrogen swap for plant carbon. *Nature* 410: 651–52.

Lesica, Peter, et al. 1991. Differences in lichen and bryophyte communities … in the Swan Valley, MT. *Can J Botany* 69: 1745–55.

Lesica, Peter, and R. K. Antibus. 1986. Mycorrhizae of alpine fell-fields on… crystalline and calcareous parent materials. *Can J Botany* 64: 1691–97.

Molina, Randy, et al. 1993. Biology, ecology and social aspects of wild edible mushrooms in the forests of the PNW. USDA For. Service PNW-GTR-309.

Näsholm, Torgny, et al. 1998. Boreal forest plants take up organic nitrogen. *Nature* 392: 914–16.

Selosse, M-A., and F. le Tacon. 1998. The land flora: a phototroph-fungus partnership? *Trends in Ecology and Evolution* 13(1): 15-20.

Rosentreter, Roger. 1993. Vagrant lichens in NA. *Bryologist* 96(3): 333–38.

Simard, Suzanne W., et al. 1997. Net transfer of carbon between ectomycorrhizal tree species in the field. *Nature* 388: 579–82.

Thies, Walter G., and Rona N. Sturrock. 1995. *Laminated root rot in western NA.* USDA Forest Service Gen. Tech. Report PNW-GTR-349.

Trappe, J. M., and D. L. Luoma. 1992. The ties that bind. In *The Fungal Community*, 2nd Ed., ed. G. C. Carroll and D. T. Wicklow. NY: Marcell-Decker.

Mammals (Chapter 9)

Barash, David P. 1989. *Marmots.* Stanford, CA: Stanford U Pr.

Byers, John A. 1997. *American Pronghorn.* Chicago: U of Chicago Pr.

Craighead, John J., Jay S. Sumner, and John A. Mitchell. 1995. *The Grizzly Bears of Yellowstone.* Washington, DC: Island.

Foresman, Kerry r. 2001. *Wild Mammals of Montana.* Am Soc of Mammalogists Spec Pubn No 12. Lawrence, KS.

Geist, Valerius. 1998. *Deer of the World.* Mechanicsburg, PA: Stackpole.

———. 1999. *Moose: Behavior, Ecology, Conservation.* Stillwater, MN: Voyageur.

Isenberg, Andrew C. 2000. *The Destruction of the Bison.* NY: Cambridge U Pr.

Lott, Dale F. 2002. *American Buffalo: a Natural History.* Berkeley: U of CA Pr.

McKenna, Malcolm C., and Susan K. Bell. 1997. *Classification of Mammals Above the Species Level.* NY: Columbia U Pr.

Murie, Olaus J. 1975. *A Field Guide to Animal Tracks.* Boston: Houghton.

Roze, Uldis. 1989. *The N American Porcupine.* Washington, DC: Smithsonian.

Searfoss, Glenn. 1995. *Skulls and Bones.* Mechanicsburg, PA: Stackpole.A book on the "whys" of comparative skeletal anatomy in mammals of NA.

Shackleton, David. 1999. *Hoofed Mammals of BC.* Vancouver: UBC Press.

Ulrich, Tom J. 1990. *Mammals of the N Rockies.* Missoula: Mtn Pr.

Valdez, Raul, and Paul R. Krausman, eds. 1999. *Mountain Sheep of NA.* Tucson: U of AZ Pr.

Verts, B. J., and L. N. Carraway. 1998. *Land Mammals of Oregon.* Berkeley: U of CA Pr.

Whitaker, John O., Jr. 1998. *The Audubon Society Field Guide to North American Mammals.* Rev. Ed. NY: Knopf.

Wilson, D. E., and D. M. Reeder. 1993. *Mammal Species of the World.* 2nd Ed. Washington, DC: Smithsonian. The 3rd Edition is forthcoming.

Wilson, D. E., and Sue Ruff, eds. 1999. *The Smithsonian Book of NA Mammals.* Washington, DC: Smithsonian.

Zeveloff, S. I. 1988. *Mammals of the Intermtn. West.* Salt Lake City: U. of Utah.

Mammal Articles

American Society of Mammalogists. *Mammalian Species*. Series.

Armitage, Kenneth B. 1998. Reproductive strategies of yellow-bellied marmots. *J Mammalogy* 79(2): 385–93.

Berger, Joel, J. E. Swenson, and I-L. Persson. 2001. Recolonizing carnivores and naïve prey: conservation lessons from… extinctions. *Science* 291: 1036–39.

Clutton-Brock, T. H. 1982. The functions of antlers. *Behavior* 79: 108–23.

Jones, J. K., et al. 1997. Revised Checklist of North American Mammals N of Mexico. Occasional Papers, The Museum, Texas Tech. U., No. 173: 1–19.

Hayward, G. D., and P. H. Hayward. 1995. Relative abundance and habitat associations of small mammals in… Central ID. *NW Sci.* 69(2): 114–25.

Hilderbrand, Grant V., et al. 1996. Use of stable isotopes to determine diets of living and extinct bears. *Canadian J Zoology* 74: 2080–88.

Lyman, R. Lee, and Steve Wolverton. 2002. The late prehistoric–early historic game sink in the NW US. *Conservation Biol* 16(1): 73–85.

Mech, L. David. 1999. Alpha status, dominance, and division of labor in wolf packs. *Canadian J Zoology* 77: 1196–1203.

Pease, Craig M., and David J. Mattson. 1999. Demography of the Yellowstone grizzly bears. *Ecology* 80(3): 957-75.

Ruggiero, L. F., ed. 1994. American marten, fisher, lynx, and wolverine in the Western US. USDA For. Serv. GTR RM-254.

Schwartz, Michael K., et al. 2002. DNA reveals high dispersal synchronizing the population dynamics of Canada lynx. *Nature* 415: 520–22.

Smith, Andrew. 1997. The art of making hay. *National Wildlife* 35(3): 31–35.

Tardiff, Sandra A., and Jack A. Stanford. 1998. Grizzly bear digging: effects on subalpine meadow plants… *Ecology* 79(7): 2219-28.

Birds (Chapter 10)

American Ornithologists Union. 1998. *Check-list of North American Birds.* 7th Edition. Lawrence: Allen Press. **Our authority** on names of birds.

Beebe, F. L. 1974. *Field Studies of the Falconiformes of BC.* Victoria: BC Prov. Mus.

Heinrich, Bernd. 1989. *Ravens in Winter.* NY: Summit Books.

Johnsgard, Paul A. 1986. *Birds of the RM.* Lincoln, NE: U. of Nebraska Pr.

Kaufmann, Kenn. 1996. *Lives of North American Birds.* Boston: Houghton.

McEneaney, Terry. 1988. *Birds of Yellowstone.* Boulder, CO: Roberts Rinehart.

Natl Geog. Soc. 2002. *FG to the Birds of NA.* 4th Ed. Washington, DC: Natl. Geog.

Robbins, C. S., et al. 2001. *Birds of NA.* Revised and updated. NY: St. Martins.

Sibley, David Allen. 2000. *The Sibley Guide to Birds.* NY: Knopf. [[[[]]]]

Stokes, D. and L. 1996. *Stokes Field Guide to Birds: W Region.* Boston: Little, Brown.

Terres, J. K. 1980. *The Audubon Soc. Encyclopedia of NA Birds.* NY: Knopf.

Wauer, Roland H. 1993. *Visitor's Guide to the Birds of the RM National Parks, US and Canada.* Santa Fe: John Muir.

Bird Articles

Barnea, A., and F. Nottebohm. 1996. Recruitment and replacement of hippocampal neurons in... chickadees. *Proc Natl Acad Sci USA* 93: 714–18.

Benkman, Craig W. 1993. Adaptation to single resources and the evolution of crossbill (*Loxia*) diversity. *Ecological Monographs* 63(3): 305–25.

Birds of NA. Phila: Acad. of Nat. Sci.; and Washington DC: Am. Ornith. Union. Huge series will summarize published data on all species N of Mexico.

Brown, C. R. and M. B. 1990. The great egg scramble. *Nat. Hist.* 99(2): 34–40.

Griffiths, C. S. 1994. Monophyly of the Falconiformes... *Auk* 111(4): 787–805.

Hutto, Richard L., and Jock S. Young. 1999. Habitat relationships of landbirds in the Northern Region... USDA For. Serv. RMRS-GTR-32.

Otter, Ken, et al. 1998. Do female black-capped chickadees prefer high-ranking males as extra-pair partners? *Behav. Ecol. and Sociobiol.* 43: 25–36.

Rattenborg, N. C., et al. 1999. Half-awake to the risk of predation. *Nature* 397: 397–98.

Reptiles and Amphibians (Chapters 11–12)

Bartlett, R. D., and A. Tennant. 2000. *Snakes of NA: W Region.* Houston: Gulf.

Collins, J. T. 1990. *Standard common and current scientific names for NA amphibians and reptiles.* 3rd ed. Soc. for Study of Amph. and Rep.: Herp. Circ. No. 19. **Our authority** on scientific names of herps.

Corkran, Charlotte C., and Chris Thoms. 1996. *Amphibians of Oregon, Washington and British Columbia.* Edmonton: Lone Pine.

Greene, Harry W. 1997. *Snakes.* Berkeley: U of Calif Pr.

Hedges, S. B., and L. L. Poling. 1999. A molecular phylogeny of reptiles. *Science* 283: 998–1001.

Kiesecker, J. M., A. R. Blaustein, and L. K. Belden. 2001. Complex causes of amphibian population declines. *Nature* 410: 681–83.

Koch, Edward D., and Charles R. Peterson. 1995. *Amphibians and Reptiles of Yellowstone and Grand Teton National Parks.* Salt Lake City: U of Utah Pr.

Leonard, W. P., et al. 1993. *Amphibians of WA and OR.* Seattle: Sea. Aud. Soc.

Leonard, W. P., and R. M. Storm, eds. 1995. *Reptiles of WA and OR.* Seattle: Seattle Aud. Soc.

Petranka, J. W. 1998. *Salamanders of the US and Can.* Wash., DC: Smithsonian.

St. John, Alan. 2002. *Reptiles of the NW.* Edmonton: Lone Pine.

Stebbins, Robert C. and Nathan W. Cohen. 1995. *A Natural History of Amphibians.* Princeton, NJ: Princeton Univ Pr.

Fishes (Chapter 13)

Behnke, Robert J. 2002. *Trout and Salmon of NA.* NY: Free Press.

Gresh, T., J. Lichatowich, and P. Schoonmaker. 2000. An estimation of historic and current levels of salmon... evidence of a nutrient deficit. *Fisheries* 25(1): 15–21.

Lichatowich, Jim. 1999. *Salmon Without Rivers.* Washington, DC: Island Press.

Troffe, Peter M. 1999. *Freshwater Fishes of the Columbia Basin in BC.* (PDF computer file). Victoria: Royal B.C. Museum. (http://rbcm1.rbcm.gov.bc.ca)

Varley, John D., and Paul Schullery. 1998. *Yellowstone Fishes.* Mechanicsburg, PA: Stackpole.

Insects (Chapter 14)

Arnett, Ross H. 2000. *American Insects.* 2nd. Ed. Boca Raton, FL: CRC Pr. **Our authority** on scientific names of insects exc Lepidoptera and Orthoptera.

Clements, A. N. 1992. *Biology of Mosquitos.* 2 vols. London: Chapman & Hall.

Cole, Frank R. 1969. *The Flies of Western NA.* Berkeley: U of CA Pr.

Corbet, P. S. 1999. *Dragonflies: Behavior and Ecology.* Ithaca, NY: Cornell U Pr.

Dunkle, Sidney W. 2000. *Dragonflies Through Binoculars.* NY: Oxford U Pr.

Furniss, R. L., and V. M. Carolin. 1977. *Western Forest Insects.* USDA Forest Service Misc. Publ. No. 1339. Mainly on insects destructive to trees.

Gillett, J. D. 1971. *Mosquitoes.* London: Weidenfeld and Nicolson.

Glassberg, Jeffrey. 2001. *Butterflies through Binoculars: the West.* NY: Oxford.

Guppy, Crispin S., and J. H. Shepard. 2001. *Butterflies of BC.* Vancouver: UBC Pr.

Heinrich, Bernd. 1979. *Bumblebee Economics.* Cambridge: Harvard U Pr.
———. 1993. *The Hot-Blooded Insects.* Cambridge: Harvard U Pr.
———. 1996. *The Thermal Warriors.* Cambridge: Harvard U Pr.

Layberry, Ross A., P. W. Hall, and J. D. Lafontaine. 1998. *The Butterflies of Canada.* Toronto: U of Toronto Pr.

Lockwood, Jeffrey. 2002. *Grasshopper Dreaming.* Boston: Skinner House.

Milne, Lorus, and Margery Milne. 1980. *The Audubon Society Field Guide to North American Insects and Spiders.* NY: Knopf.

Opler, Paul A., and Amy B. Wright. 1999. *Western Butterflies.* 2nd Ed. Boston: Houghton.

Paulson, Dennis. 1999. *Dragonflies of Washington.* Seattle: Seattle Aud. Soc. This slim volume is more complete and useful for our species of Odonata than Dunkle's "complete" tome, which excludes damselflies.

Pettinger, L. F., and D. W. Johnson. 1972. *A Field Guide to Important Forest Insects and Diseases of OR and WA.* USDA Forest Service PNW Region.

Pyle, Robert Michael. 2002. *Butterflies of Cascadia.* Seattle: Seattle Aud Soc.

Swan, L. A., and C. S Papp. 1972. *The Common Insects of NA.* NY: Harper.

Thornhill, Randy, and John Alcock. 1983. *Evolution of Insect Mating Systems.* Cambridge: Harvard U Pr.

Waldbauer, Gilbert. 1996. *Insects Through the Seasons.* Cambridge: Harvard.
——. 1998. *The Birder's Bug Book.* Cambridge: Harvard U. Pr.

Insect Articles

Andersson, J., A. Borg-Karlson, and C. Wiklund. 2000. Sexual cooperation and conflict in butterflies... *Proceedings Royal Soc London B* 267: 1271–75.

Cannings, Robert A. 1996. The blue darners. (Computer file) Victoria: Royal B.C. Museum. http://www.rbcm.gov.bc.ca/nh_papers/aeshna

——. 1999. Dragonflies of the Columbia Basin. (Computer file) Victoria: Royal B.C. Museum. http://livinglandscapes.bc.ca/www_dragon

Condrashoff, S. F. 1964. Bionomics of aspen leaf miner. *Can Entomol* 96: 857–74.

Deyrup, Mark. 1981. Deadwood decomposers. *Natural History* 90(3): 84–91.

Hubbell, Sue. 1997. Trouble with honeybees. *Natural History* 106(5): 32–43.

Karlsson, Bengt. 1998. Nuptial gifts, resource budgets, and reproductive output in a polyandrous butterfly. *Ecology* 79(8): 2931–40.

Lockwood, Jeffrey.2003. Death of the super hopper. *High Country News* 35(2): 1–11.

Miller, Jeffrey C., and Paul C. Hammond. 2000. *Macromoths of NW Forests and Woodlands.* USDA Forest Service publication FHTET-98-18.

Pfadt, Robert E. 1994. Field Guide to Common W Grasshoppers. 2nd Ed. WY Ag. Exp. Sta. Bulletin 912. (http://www.sdvc.uwyo.edu/grasshopper/fieldgde).

Sculley, Colleen E., and Carol L. Boggs. 1996. Mating systems and sexual division of foraging effort affect puddling behavior.... *Ecol Entomol* 21: 193–97.

Weiss, Martha R., and Byron B. Lamont. 1997. Floral color change and insect pollination. *Israel J of Plant Sci.* 45: 185–99.

Wu, Corinna. 2000. Mosquito magnets. *Science News* 157: 268–70.

Other Creatures (Chapter 15)

Farmer, Jack D. 2000. Hydrothermal systems: doorways to early biosphere evolution. *GSA Today* 10(7): 1–8.

Madigan, Michael T., and B. L. Marrs. 1997. Extremophiles. *Sci Am* 277(4): 82–87.

Margulis, Lynn, and Karlene V Schwartz. 1998. *Five Kingdoms.* 3rd Ed. NY: W. H. Freeman.

Meyer, Ernest A. 1985. Epidemiology of giardiasis. *Parasitology Today* 1(4): 101–5.

Netting, Jessa. 2001. Sticky situations. *Science News* 160(2): 28–30. On biofilms.

Shain, Daniel H., et al. 2001. Distribution and behavior of ice worms... *Can J Zool* 79: 1813–21.

Upcroft, J., and P. Upcroft. 1998. My favorite cell: Giardia. *BioEssays* 20(3): 256–63.

Williams, Wm. E., et al. 2003. Surface gas-exchange processes of snow algae. *Proceedings of Nat'l Assoc Sci* 100(2): 562–66.

Geology (Chapters 1 and 16)

Alt, David D. 2001. *Glacial Lake Missoula.* Missoula: Mountain Press.

Alt, David D., and Donald W. Hyndman. 1986. *Roadside Geology of Montana.*
——. 1989. *Roadside Geology of Idaho.*
——. 1995. *Northwest Exposures.* (All three titles) Missoula: Mountain Press.

Burchfiel, B. C., P. W. Lipman, and M. L. Zoback, eds. 1992. *The Cordilleran Orogen: conterminous US. (Geol of NA: v G-3)* Boulder, CO: Geol Soc of Am.

Davies, G. F. 2000. *Dynamic Earth: Plates, Plumes...* NY: Cambridge U Pr.

Ferguson, Sue A. 1992. *Glaciers of NA: a Field Guide.* Golden, CO: Fulcrum.

Good, John M., and K. L. Pierce. 1998. *Interpreting the Landscapes of Grand Teton and Yellowstone NP.* Rev. Moose, WY: Grand Teton Nat. Hist. Assoc.

Gould, S. J. 1989. *Wonderful Life: the Story of the Burgess Shale.* NY: Norton.

Lageson, David R. and Darwin R. Spearing. 1991. *Roadside Geology of Wyoming.* 2nd Ed. Missoula: Mountain Pr.

McPhee, John. 1998. *Annals of the Former World.* NY: Farrar, Straus. A great essayist blends plate tectonics with a life of WY geologist J. David Love.

Moores, Eldridge, and R. J. Twiss. 1995. *Tectonics.* NY: W. H. Freeman.

Smith, Robert B., and Lee J. Siegel. 2000. *Windows into the Earth: the Geologic Story of Yellowstone and Grand Teton NPs.* NY: Oxford U Pr.

Snoke, Arthur W. 1993. *Geology of WY.* Memoir #5. Cheyenne: Geol Soc WY.

Vallier, Tracy. 1998. *Islands and Rapids: ...Hells Canyon.* Lewiston: Confluence.

Vernon, Ron. 2000. *Beneath Our Feet.* NY: Cambridge U. Photography + info.

Yorath, C. J. 1997. *How Old is That Mountain? a Visitor's Guide to the Geology of Banff and Yoho National Parks.* Victoria: Orca.

Geology Articles

Anderson, Don L. 2002. How many plates? *Geology* 30(5): 411–14.

Abbott, Dallas H., and Ann E. Isley. 2002. Extraterrestrial influences on mantle plume activity. *Earth & Planetary Sci Letters* 205: 53–62.

Benito, Gerardo, and Jim E. O'Connor. 2003. Number and size of last-glacial Missoula floods in the Columbia River... *GSA Bull* 115: 624–38.

Dettman, David L., and K. C. Lohmann. 2000. Oxygen isotope evidence for high-altitude snow in the Laramide RM during the ...Paleogene. *Geology* 28: 243–46.

Dewey, J. F. 1988. Extensional collapse of orogens. *Tectonics* 7(6): 1123–39.

Fischer, Karen M. 2002. Waning buoyancy in the crustal roots of old mountains. *Nature* 417: 933–36.

Frost, B. Ronald., et al. 2000. Late Archaean structural and metamorphic history of the Wind R Range, WY. *GSA Bull.* 112: 564–78.

Geist, D., and M. A. Richards. 1993. Origin of the Columbia Plateau and the Snake R Plain: deflection of the Yellowstone plume. *Geology* 21: 789–92.

Glen, Jonathan M. G., and David Ponce. 2002. Large-scale fractures related to inception of the Yellowstone hotspot. *Geology* 30 (7): 647–50.

Gregory, Kathryn M., and Clement G. Chase. 1992. Tectonic significance of paleobotanically estimated climate and altitude… *Geology* 20: 581–85.

——. 1994. Tectonic and climatic significance of a late Eocene low-relief, high-level geomorphic surface, CO. *J of Geophysical Res.* 99(B10): 20,141–60.

Gurnis, Michael. 2001. Sculpting the earth from inside out. *Sci Am* 284(3): 40–47.

Hamilton, Warren B. 2002. The closed upper-mantle circulation of plate tectonics. *In* Stein and Freymuller, eds., *Plate Boundary Zones*. AGU Geodynamics Series, v. 30. An argument against mantle plume hypothesis (e.g., Davies 2000).

Hooper, P. R., G. B. Binger, and K. R. Lees. 2002. Age of the Steens and Columbia R flood basalts and their relationship to extension… *GSA Bull* 114: 43–50.

Humphreys, Eugene D., et al. 2000. Beneath Yellowstone: Evaluating plume and nonplume models… *GSA Today* 10(12): 1–7. And personal communication.

Hyndman, R. D., and T. J. Lewis. 1999. Geophysical consequences of the Cordillera-Craton thermal transition in sw Canada. *Tectonophysics* 306: 397-422.

Johnston, Stephen T. 2001. The great Alaskan terrane wreck: reconciliation of paleomagnetic and geological data… *Earth & Planetary Sci Letters* 193: 259–72.

Jones, C. H., J. R. Unruh and L. J. Sonder. 1996. The role of gravitational potential energy in…the sw US. *Nature* 381: 37–41. (Comment by P. England, p 23–24.)

Kessler, M. A., and B. T. Werner. 2003. Self-organization of sorted patterned ground. *Science* 299: 380–83. (Comment by D. Mann, p 354–55.)

Konrad, S. K., et al. 1999. Rock glacier dynamics… *Geology* 27 (2): 1131–34.

Licciardi, Joseph M., et al. 2001. Cosmogenic ^{3}He and ^{10}Be chronologies of the late Pinedale northern Yellowstone ice cap… *Geology* 29(12): 1095–98.

Livaccari, Richard F. 1991. Role of crustal thickening and extensional collapse in the tectonic evolution of the Sevier-Laramide orogeny… *Geology* 19: 1104–07.

Lowry, A. R., N. M. Ribe, and R. B. Smith. 2000. Dynamic elevation of the Cordillera, western US. *J of Geophysical Res.* 105(B10): 23,371–90.

Maxson, Julie, and Basil Tikoff. 1996. Hit-and-run collision model for the Laramide orogeny, western US. *Geology* 24(11): 968–72.

McMillan, Margaret E., C. L. Angevine, and P. L. Heller. 2002. Postdepositional tilt: …evidence of late Cenozoic uplift of the RM. *Geology* 30 (1): 63–66.

Mitrovica, J. X., C. Beaumont, and G. T. Jarvis. 1989. Tilting of continental interiors by the dynamical effects of subduction. *Tectonics* 8(5): 1079–94.

Molnar, Peter, and Philip England. 1990. Late Cenozoic uplift of mountain ranges and global climate change: chicken or egg? *Nature* 346: 29–34. Comments and replies on this and a related article, 1991. *Geology* 19: 1051–54.

Moores, Eldridge M., J. Wakabayashi, and J. R. Unruh. 2002. Crustal-scale cross-section of the U.S. Cordillera…. *International Geol Rev* 44: 479–500.

Murphy, J. Brendan, et al. 1998. Plume-modified orogeny. *Geology* 26: 731–34.

Selected References

Parker, A. R. 1998. Colour in Burgess Shale animals... *Proc R Soc London* 265: 967–72.

Petford, N., and J. D. Clemens. 2000. Granites are not diapiric! *Geol Today* 16: 180–84.

Pratt, Brian R. 2001a. Oceanography, bathymetry,... sediments, storms, earthquakes and tsunamis in the Belt Supergroup... *Sedim Geol* 141–142: 371–94.

———. 2001b. Calcification of cyanobacterial filaments. *Geology* 29: 763–66.

———. 2002. Storms versus tsunamis. *Geology* 30(5): 423–26.

Saleeby, Jason. 2003. Segmentation of the Laramide Slab... *GSA Bull* 115: 655–68.

Shaw, John, et al. 1999. The Channeled Scabland: Back to Bretz? *Geology* 27(7): 605–08. Comments and reply on this article, 2000. *Geology* 28(6): 573–76.

Small, Eric E., et al. 1997. Erosion rates of alpine bedrock summit surfaces deduced from *in situ* [10]Be and [26]Al. *Earth & Planetary Sci Letters* 150: 413–25.

Small, Eric E., and R. S. Anderson. 1998. Pleistocene relief production in Laramide mountain ranges, western U.S. *Geology* 26: 123–26.

Sonder, Leslie J., and Craig H. Jones. 1999. Western US Extension: how the West was widened. *Ann. Rev. Earth & Planetary Sci.* 27: 417–62.

Snyder, D. B., et al. 2002. Proterozoic prism arrests suspect terranes. *GSA Today* 12(10): 4–10. Revision of terrane/continent relations in BC.

Vanderhaeghe, Olivier, and Christian Teyssier. 2001. Crustal-scale rheological transitions during late-orogenic collapse. [In BC]. *Tectonophysics* 335: 211–228.

Wolfe, Jack A., Chris E. Forest, and Peter Molnar. 1998. Paleobotanical evidence of... paleoaltitudes in midlatitude western NA. *GSA Bulletin* 110(5): 664–78.

Zhao, Guochun, et al. 2002. Review of global 2.1–1.8 [billion-year-old] orogens: implications for a pre-Rodinia supercontinent. *Earth-Sci Reviews* 59: 1125–162.

Web Sites

Search engines offer the best way to find the Web's vast resources on both science and recreation. Most of the scientific journals cited above have Web sites; some give abstracts or summaries of articles; some offer complete articles. Here are a few good web with a reasonable chance of lasting a few years:

http://plants.usda.gov (The PLANTS database of names)
http://hua.huh.harvard.edu/FNA/ (*Flora of North America*)
www.rmh.uwyo.edu (The Rocky Mtn Herbarium.)
www.orst.edu/dept/botany/herbarium/ (OFP, soon to be an interactive atlas)
www.mgd.nacse.org/hyperSQL/lichenland (a key to lichens, and much else)
http://nmnhgoph.si.edu/msw/ (Wilson and Reeder mammal list)
http://rbcm1.rbcm.gov.bc.ca (The Royal British Columbia Museum)
www.birdsofna.org/ (*Birds of North America*)
www.mbr-pwrc.usgs.gov/bbs/bbs.html (population numbers for all NA birds)
www.nature-discovery.com (wildlife information and artistic products)
www.wildrockiesalliance.org (environmentalist umbrella organization)

Index

Numbers in boldface are color photograph pages.

Index